SIGNALMAN'S TRILOGY

Adrian Vaughan

AMBERLEY

First published individually as *Signalman's Morning* by John Murray in 1981, *Signalman's Twilight* by John Murray in 1983 and *Signalman's Nightmare* by John Murray in 1989. This edition published by Amberley Publishing, 2016

Amberley Publishing
The Hill, Stroud
Gloucestershire, GL5 4EP

www.amberley-books.com

British Library Cataloguing in Publication Data.
A catalogue record for this book is available from the British Library.

ISBN 978 1 4456 5622 9
Ebook ISBN 978 1 4456 5623 6

Typesetting and Origination by Amberley Publishing.
Printed in the UK.

SIGNALMAN'S MORNING

To my parents,
who loved Old England
and her Greatest Railway

Contents

Come, fill the Cup, and in the Fire of Spring
The Winter Garment of repentance fling:
The Bird of Time has but a little way
To fly – and Lo! the Bird is on the Wing.

The Rubáiyát by Omar Khayyám, trans. Edward FitzGerald, I, vii

Prologue

I am sitting in my car in the market place at Wantage in early summer 1978. It is midday. The morning started cool and clear under the chestnut trees, progressing to harsh heat, sun hot on black paint, dazzling on the white statue of King Alfred. Close by me the market stalls are full of fruit – curved, long, round, shining, yellow and orange, bright. Assistants shadowy under an awning, customers waiting patiently, unaccustomed eyes in winter-pale faces screwed up against the strong light. Opposite, a red Thames Valley diesel rattles unrhythmically. Mill Street roofs, ochre tiles and sideways chimneys drop crookedly downhill; a fringe of green trees on the ridge behind.

My mind sees beyond the willows on the hill to the railway line three miles away and I recall days more distant than any mileage when 'Castles' ran on steel rails not mirage-like in the hot sun of Now. Stopping trains stopped at sunny silent stations deep in the elm tree fields. But now – no elms, no trains, no stations – only the hot Today sun to remind me of those halcyon days.

I knew the steam-hauled railway for twenty years. I loved its beautiful engines whose rhythms were so innately musical that you can hear a 'Castle' skimming down the Vale of the White Horse in at least three great symphonies; I loved it for its handsome signals and signal boxes, for the homely, farming countryside it ran through, but most of all for its men – patient and understanding, the salt of the earth. Through them I learned the technicalities of railway work and absorbed the intangible spirit of 120 years of tradition. For that I will always be grateful.

For the help I received in writing this book, my thanks are due to the following railwaymen and women: Mrs E. Halford and Mrs H. Strong, David Castle, Sam Loder, Elwyn Richards, Albert Stanley, Sid ('Brush') Tyler, Basil Titchener and H. R. Hayden, Area Administration Officer at Swindon. During the Christmas holidays 1979 my family and I were practically homeless, and the hospitality of several kind friends helped me to finish this book: my parents, Martin and Joy Brown, Paul and Sue Dye,

Ken and Pat Fuller, Frances and Camillus Travers, Jane and Jim White – and thanks to my wife, Susan, who suffered all hardships cheerfully. I would like to thank my friend Ivo Peters for his helpful criticism of the book; thanks, too, to my publishers, and in particular to my friend Simon Young for his unstinted help in revising the manuscript.

Finally, I would like to thank all the old-hand railway gentlemen for so generously taking me into their world, teaching me the meaning of railway work, and making work a pleasure.

Adrian Vaughan

Acknowledgements for the Edition of 2011

Grateful thanks to Mr Philip Shepherd of Aston Cantlow, who was inspired to paint a magnificent picture of Uffington station after reading *Signalman's Morning*. He very generously donated the 30 x 15-inch painting to me, and I am delighted to be able to use the central section of it as the cover of the book that gave him so much pleasure.

And finally, I must thank my editor and friend, Nicola Gale at Amberley Publishing, for her kindness for working so hard to make the book a success.

Adrian Vaughan
Barney
North Norfolk
2011

Acknowledgements for the Edition of 2016

I must thank Claire Hopkins at Amberley Publishing for her hard work on this edition of the book.

CHAPTER ONE

First Love

At the age of five I ran away from home. I left my bed late one evening not to go to sea but to a signal box. It was two miles from our house in Earley, Reading, separated by the dark trees of Palmer Park, the London road, Sutton's seed ground and two gasometers. I ran hard all the way, arriving at the foot of the signal box stairs to be greeted by a fox terrier barking furiously. The signalman came to the door of his box and called, 'Who's about?'

'Only me, mister.'

He peered down at me standing dim in the faint light from his windows. 'You'd better come up into the box, sonny, and we'll see what this is all about.' He was very kind, gave me some tea and one of his sandwiches while he asked me where I came from. I explained my great desire to go into a signal box, so he delayed telephoning for the police until he had shown me round his box. Significantly, I cannot remember how I got home but I do remember feeling very pleased with myself and looking forward to another visit.

I had been bewitched by the atmosphere of the railway since the age of three. On Wednesday afternoons my father closed his radio repair shop and took the family for a drive in his Austin Seven, and because of a long-standing family connection with the Great Western Railway, the usual destination was Sonning Cutting. We went to a place where the quiet, unfrequented lane and the railway were level with each other and separated only by a wide, grassy verge. It was the perfect site for a picnic with wild flowers to gather and grass snakes to hunt – and, above all, Great Western trains to watch.

The Southern Railway branch line from Reading to Redhill and Waterloo climbed steeply in a cutting within earshot of our house; the ancient engines labouring heavily up the grade, throwing half-burnt coal and soot out of their chimneys so high that it rose above the roofs of the houses that lined the south side of the cutting's rim and fell smuttily on my aunt's washing. The incline passed by 'Solly Joel's' playing field before levelling out and reaching Earley station. Here a thick forest of beech and oak, extending over hundreds of acres, came up to the railway line and fringed it eastwards for a mile.

My elder sister used often to walk me along a gravelly lane through the woods to the station, passing a favourite, red-brick house with tall gables decorated with ornate barge-boards which stood close to the line. Gates across the lane, protecting the rails, were opened by the signalman, who came down from his signal box to swing them open by hand. His signal box was tall and narrow with small windows and a skimpy roof. It was made of horizontal, overlapping planks, once bright yellow, now faded and muddy, and on its front wall a green enamel sign with white letters read: EARLEY. When I was five, I thought this was the signalman's name and always called him 'Mr Earley' when asking to go into his box.

There were two platforms connected by a concrete footbridge. The Up platform – for London – was nearest the woods; behind it lay a couple of sidings with accommodation for emptying railway petrol tank wagons. The Down platform – for Reading – carried the station office: a substantial, two-storey building with lower walls of brick and upperworks clad in horizontal planking under a hip gable roof.

The station was only 200 yards from a busy main road yet it was smothered in silence and had a magical air of remoteness from the twentieth century. Facing Reading, my back to the footbridge, I would see a tall signal cantilevered out over the tracks, the narrow old signal box and the tracks curving sharply to the right out of sight. From the chimney of the red-brick house woodsmoke, rising blue against the silent, dark green trees, was the only movement. Then the clear 'ting-ting' of a signal box bell would bring the signalman to his levers, his body shadowy within the box. He heaved against the levers, wires squealed over pulleys, the Up line signal arms were raised. Soon an engine of the most antique kind would come into view, leaning to the curve, its tall, thin chimney snorting like a winded horse as it accelerated from the summit of the climb, its exhaust beat uneven – 'dot and carry one' I used to call it – and towing a train of equally ancient green coaches with windowed lookouts for the guard raised above coach roof level. Gasping a rapid staccato, missing every fourth beat, the Victorian engine took its drumming coaches past in a cloud of steam at 30 mph and, followed by my hungry eyes, accelerated up a long straight to a mysterious curve and vanished.

That long, tapering distance and the curve which blotted out the rest of the line was one of the great romances of my five-year-old life – what was it like, just around the corner? Those disappearing rails created in me a lasting curiosity for things just out of sight.

Starting school at St Anne's in Caversham, I rode by bus past the Southern engine shed. The pavement and the tracks were separated only by a railing fence so that engines standing against the buffers were only a few feet from the road. This magnetic attraction was countered each morning by the obligation to go to school – I do not remember ever playing truant, not even for the railway – but on the return home it drew me irresistibly. Each evening, those of us who went home by bus were formed into a crocodile and marched to the bus stop; it did not take me long to find a technique for deserting, missing the bus and thus becoming free to visit the engine shed.

A gate gave access from the pavement to a dozen locomotives; those closest to the road were 'dead', that is, not in steam; those nearest the shed building were being serviced for duty. The men always seemed friendly. I could walk round an engine with its driver while he oiled it, sit in the cab while the fireman stoked his fire up to running condition or play drivers on the dead engines by the road. I was taken to see an engine that had been standing so long that it had two birds' nests, one in the V of two spokes of a driving wheel and another in the cab and the men had postponed bringing the engine into service until the birds had flown.

After the engine shed my way home took me thirty feet above the Southern shunting yard, which was in a cutting between the road and the Great Western embankment. It was fun to watch ancient tank engines shunting wagons, rolling them along, changing tracks, free-wheeling, till they came up with a crash against a line of stationary trucks. Then, one memorable evening, I saw a Great Western 'King' class engine come onto the embankment beyond the sidings. I had a wonderful, broadside view of his side-rods swinging easily as he braked for the station, his massive boiler polished green, his copper and brass gleaming, the last word in elegance and strength. I was converted into a 'Western' man immediately.

The Great Western station then became my second home; indeed, in 1947 it was 'home' to a regular crowd of boys who spent all day, in their holidays, watching the working. At the east end of the station, outside a wire fence, on top of an embankment scuffed bare of grass by our shoes, a dead tree gave comfortable seating for several boys and the rest stood or sat by the fence. We were warned of the approach of trains by a tall, wooden signal carrying four arms on three posts, branching like an angular candelabra; and we waited for each express in company with the station's stand-by engine, a 'Saint' or a 'Bulldog' which, between bouts of shunting, rested on a siding almost within arm's reach.

Up express trains, London bound, which were booked to call at Reading, stood for at least five minutes at the platform opposite our perch, giving us broadside views of 'Kings' and 'Castles' at rest and starting away under the cloud of their hugely exciting, noisy exhausts. They began with a crashing beat, four explosions for each turn of their driving wheels —NOW—HERE—WE—GO— a rhythm and a volume suggesting indomitable courage and irresistible power quite unlike any sound that even the best Southern engines made.

Between the Western and Southern stations, below our vantage, was a large timber shack which served as a canteen for Thames Valley bus crews. As soon as an Up train stopped, the fireman would go onto the tender to put the water hose in and fill up the tank while he shovelled coal forward and the driver came through the fence to fill his tea can at the canteen. He did so under the admiring gaze of a dozen boys hoping for a friendly nod and a short 'Hello lad'. Some men responded, others were, I think, disconcerted at this concentration of hero worship. I recall my thrill at seeing close-up his faded blue, soot-smudged overalls – even being *brushed* by them – as he bent and climbed through the strands of wire – this man who drove 'Kings' from Plymouth to Paddington.

One lunchtime the driver of a 'King' which had stopped at Reading on an Up express had gone into the Thames Valley canteen and had not emerged by the time the train's guard had given 'Right Away'. The fireman on the engine was blowing the whistle and us boys were watching the canteen with interest, wondering what had gone wrong.

The canteen door burst open, out came the engine driver – backwards – dragging by the lapels of his jacket a bus man. Both men were rather red in the face. 'Right then, we're outside now,' shouted the engine driver, 'now tell me my "King" isn't as good as the *Mallard*.'* His fireman blew an agonised screech on the whistle – 'Come on, *Come on*' – the driver broke away, up the bank, through the fence past an astonished crowd of boys and, for the benefit of the bus man, made the fastest exit from Reading that I saw for many years. On the Down main platform at Reading, aged seven, pennies warm and sticky in my hand, I would go to the stand-by engine and ask its driver

---

* The *Mallard* was an LNER engine that holds the world record for steam speed — 126 ½ mph.

'Want a cup of tea, mister?' The driver, good-natured and understanding, would say, 'That's very kind of you, sonny. Yes please.' When I returned with the tea, I had to climb onto the footplate to give the driver the cup and did not dismount until I was told to do so. When the engine went shunting, to remove a horsebox, milk tank or parcels van from the rear of a passenger train, I went too and learned about footplate work from the age of seven on *Saint David*, last of her class, and on *Seagull* and *Skylark*, last of the 'Bulldogs'.

Drivers appreciated people – even small boys – who took an interest in their engine and would explain the working with great patience. It was a fascinating experience. To look through the firehole at the furnace seven or ten feet long; to see the driver pulling up or winding round the big, steel handles to make the engine move; to feel that great mass of metal move smoothly; to hear the long, breathless 'haaah' of the ejector steam from the chimney to release the brakes and the burping, gurgling sound which happened when the brakes were fully released and the ejector was allowed to continue; the juicy 'ffutt' when the throttle, or regulator, was opened before the first barking exhaust beat; the 'spit-spit-spit' of the mechanical vacuum pump, which could be heard when the engine was free-wheeling; and the hissing, sucking 'sheeesh' of inrushing air through the valve when the brakes were applied. When the fireman turned on the water from the tender and then the steam jet to force water through the injector into the boiler, there was first a loud, gurgling roar, subsiding when the jet was adjusted to a sweet, modulating whistle, like birdsong – indeed, I heard some men say that the injectors were 'whistling like a linnet'.

These pleasant, varied sounds with which the engine responded to her driver's commands made her seem like a living creature, warm and breathing. Like the footplatemen, I grew fond of them when they ran well and hated them when they misbehaved.

When the engine left the platform I felt I was leaving a quay, putting out onto a silver river of rails. We would pass through the shadow of the East signal box and stop, a wheeled boat isolated in midstream, waiting for the points to change. From the oiled steel and copper strength of the cab with its core of fire, I looked out over the narrow Southern river that flowed between wide banks of sidings lined with coaches and wagons, dotted with Victorian and Edwardian locomotives, and saw the silent green serpents of the 'Southern Electric' go gliding up and down the stream.

In between rides on engines, I joined a group of boys and spent hours – a large part of my life in fact – sitting at the west end of the Up main platform.

We prided ourselves on being able to recognise any class of engine at a mile in clear weather, each of us wanting to be the first to shout correctly the type that was approaching. 'Elbow steam pipes,' we would yell, 'a Star!' and then jump about and cheer as 4021 *British Monarch* came racing through the station at 70 mph.

At one o'clock each lunchtime any boys on the station would gather on the Up platform, about thirty yards from its western end and wait for the passing of the 8.30 a.m. Plymouth to Paddington express. They chose their stand carefully so as to see the exact moment when the rear coach separated from the main train; they might even see the guard pull the special lever in the coach – for the 'Plymouth' was a slip coach train.

At about 1.5 p.m. the signal on the gantry routing the train to the Up platform was lowered, and if the road was clear right through the station, the special 'slipping distant' signal below the main arm was also lowered; if it remained at 'Caution', the train had to stop to uncouple the coach. The train came free-wheeling around the side of the West box, 'King'-hauled, snaking over the junctions, swerving into the platform line at 20 mph. As soon as the slip coach separated from the main train – the driver always seemed to know exactly when – the big engine erupted into life and went storming away, leaving the slipped coach to run gently by the platform – accompanied by some boys running alongside – and to come to a stand at the head of the subway stairs.

The slip guard stepped down from his compartment in the leading end of the coach as his passengers hurried past and, looking through the guard's open door, we could see the slipping lever pulled to drop the coupling off the hook and the brake handle he used to bring the coach to a stand. As we looked, a tank engine came sneaking up to the coach, the buffers meeting with a 'clonk'. The coupling-up process was always fun to watch and made a fitting end to the show. The engine pushed against the coach, fascinating me with the terrible ease with which it compressed the hidden springs inside the buffers till the circular heads were hard against their stocks. A shunter, crouching between the rails, slung the locomotive's heavy coupling link over the coach draw-hook and shortened its length with a few turns of the screw. Grasping the coaches and the locomotive's vacuum brake pipes, one in each hand, he locked them together with a dextrous twist of his wrists and secured them with a cotter pin.

He scrambled onto the platform, raised an oily hand to the driver. 'Righto, Harry!' The engine then withdrew to its siding to wait for an Up stopping train to which it could attach the coach so that it could return to Paddington for the Down working next day.

By the time I was ten, I was tall enough to ride my mother's bicycle standing up and I began to explore the area around Reading. I discovered a little signal box in Sonning Cutting, close to a bridge which crossed over the line and gave the box its name: Woodley Bridge. After several hours spent sitting on the parapet staring down at the box, I willed the signalman to ask me in.

Harold Summerfield's box had eight levers, two for each track through the cutting, and provided me with a perfect school to learn the basic principles of semaphore signalling. Harold was patient even when I turned up day after day, explaining everything and allowing me to ring the bells and pull the levers.

It was hard work for him, anyway, because traffic was heavy, bells had to be answered quickly and levers pulled over snappily, yet he found time to teach me the art of signalling. Not for twenty years did I realise how much more difficult he made his work for my benefit.

Harold and the various engine drivers were good friends to me; Reading station and its complicated working was perfectly familiar; the whole range of railway operations was my hobby and filled all my out-of-school life.

Then, in 1953, my father became so ill that he was obliged to sell his small shop and go into the country. He had always wanted to live on the Berkshire Downs and managed to buy a run-down cottage in Childrey, four miles from White Horse Hill, which pleased him mightily but appalled me. I felt that no railway station in the world could be as busy and exciting as Reading, least of all some sleepy little place far out in the Berkshire vale.

In recognition of my devotion to railways, I was allowed to travel by myself, by train, to the village station, Challow, while the rest of the family led the removal van in the Austin Seven. I caught the 2.40 p.m. Down stopper from my magnificent Reading station, convinced that my life was ruined, and headed westwards with a sinking heart.

CHAPTER TWO

A Station in the Vale

'Challer! Challer!' a Berkshire voice called as the 2.40 from Reading squealed to a halt for the eighth time since starting its journey. A tall porter in a dark-blue uniform and peaked cap, his red tie blowing in the wind, passed the narrow window of my compartment, calling 'Challer' energetically as if he enjoyed mispronouncing the station's name. I lowered the window by its leather strap, turned the outside handle and stepped down onto the platform.

The porter was collecting tickets and turned back for mine, took it and closed my door firmly. 'All right?' shouted the guard from five coaches back. 'Right you be,' replied the porter. The guard blew his pea-whistle and waved his green flag above his head at the same time. There was an answering 'toot' from the 'Hall' at the head of the train before she went snuffing gently away from the station.

I watched it pass a fair-sized signal box and turn across points from Down Relief to Down Main line. The driver then put on steam and with an accelerating rhythm the train drove west for Swindon, the continuous, snorting exhaust beat growing faint and broken as the breeze took the noise where it pleased till a curve in the track shut off sight and sound. A signal at the platform's end thudded up to 'Danger' and I turned to go, getting a look of friendly curiosity and a nodded Berkshire 'Mornin'' from the porter as I did so.

I walked up a wide, gravel slope to the main road, which crossed the railway on a bridge, and looked around. The railway came from the Reading direction four tracks wide in a shallow cutting through gently undulating fields, under the bridge, between the platforms, merging into double track just beyond the signal box. The box was on the down-side of the line, the cutting not quite reaching the level of its window sills. The station office was on the up-side and looked modern; a plain red-brick building, long and low. Beyond it was an open space taken up by a car park and some allotments, on the far side of which was a row of terraced, slate-fronted cottages for station staff. At the left-hand end of the row was a detached house that looked as if it belonged to the station master and at the other end was a public house, the Prince of Wales. The road ran north and fell downhill, out of sight between the pub and a fine old farmhouse. Beyond the terrace there was only the grey sky and, very faint, the horizon of a line of hills upon which stood a very prominent clump of trees.

Looking south, the road dropped off the bridge, past the junction with a lane lined on both sides with tall elm trees, rose and disappeared over swelling ground, the ridge lined with evenly spaced trees. A solitary, black car came over the brow and ran down the slope towards me. Two or three houses showed and in the far distance I could see the long, clean, clear outline of the Berkshire Downs. My town-dull ears began to register country sounds – I heard the wind hissing in the roadside grass and high overhead a bird I guessed to be a skylark sang as if it had some serious obligation to do so. 'This is a queer place for a railway station,' I thought, as the wind began to feel chill, and, following the instructions I had been given before I left Reading, went down to the lane. 'Childrey 2 ½' said the signpost and, hoping I would get a lift, I set off.

The lane made a series of S-bends before straightening past a mock-Tudor farmhouse, on, between tall, ragged hedges past a derelict brickworks, mysterious and interesting and over the marshy remains of a canal. I stopped to rest and a moorhen dashed for cover. Beyond the canal the road ran through clean fields bordered by well-kept hedges, rose past an expensive-looking stable and came to a T-junction where a sign pointed left for Childrey.

I walked past an old orchard screening an ancient manor house and, rounding a sharp bend, found myself in the main street of the village. 'Go to the far end of the street, we're next to the Crown,' my father had said. I passed an ivy-grown farm by a pond, a row of thatched cottages, between two rows of brick cottages and saw the road rising steeply out of the village in a deep cutting arched in by tall beeches – there was the Crown and on a high bank above the road was a long, thatched cottage – my new home.

The sound of express trains as they whistled through Challow came up clearly to the village – especially in the quiet of Sunday. Each time I heard that faint, clear note and the drumming rhythm of the wheels, sounding curiously hollow with distance, I longed to be at the lineside. As soon as we had settled in and my services as a general assistant were no longer required, I took myself off to the station.

After a couple of long days spent sitting on a four-wheel barrow, being nodded at by the station master and ignored by a very stern-looking porter,

I met the tall man who had taken my ticket the day I had arrived from Reading.

'Hi-up then,' he said, 'I shall want that barrow,' and sat down on it with me. 'D'you live around here then? I haven't seen you before.'

'You saw me a couple of weeks ago when I got off the train here from Reading. We've just moved to Childrey.'

'They told me you liked trains, because you've been here a lot in the last couple of days.'

'I love the engines. I used to ride on the Pilot at Reading and there was a signal box in Sonning Cutting I used to visit almost every evening after school – do you think I could get into the signal box here?'

'Well, of course. Ken Rowlands is on now. Haven't you met him? He lives in Childrey. Come on, I'll take you up. What's your name, mine's Sam – Sam Loder.'

Sam went before me up the stairs of the box and I heard him saying, 'Hi-up, Ken. I've got a young lad here from Childrey wants to see the box.'

'From Childrey?' said a puzzled voice. 'Who can that be?' I stepped from the stairs below Sam to the operating room floor. Ken Rowlands was a slim, fair-haired man with blue eyes and a quiet, gentle manner. I introduced myself, 'We've just moved in,' I finished, realising I would be saying those words quite a lot in the next few weeks. He smiled, extended his hand and said, 'I've heard about the new arrivals. Pleased to meet you.'

Practically, my only experience of signal boxes up to that moment had been of the tiny, cramped Woodley Bridge box. Challow was quite the opposite and quite superb. It must have been 40 feet long and 10 feet wide,* its polished linoleum floor reflecting any of the fifty-one levers that happened to be pulled over. I recognised the yellow lever at each end of the row as operating the distant signals, the red levers as working stop signals and the black/white levers that placed an audible danger signal – a 'shot' or detonator – on the rail for emergencies. There were also black levers, blue levers, blue/brown and red/yellow levers that I had not seen before; all of them had polished brass plates giving details of their function. There were a lot of instruments and telephones and, though the box handled only half the traffic that passed Woodley Bridge, its work was much more interesting and important.

The signalman spent a lot of his time sending and receiving information over the telephones concerning train running, making and answering

---

* The actual dimensions were 25 feet by 11 feet.

enquiries to and from other boxes, which resulted in goods trains leaving Challow's Down Relief line for the Down Main or switching from the Up Main to the Up Relief line just as he thought would be best for the free running of the express trains. I felt completely overwhelmed by the complexity of it all and went home at teatime, my head full of bell codes, trying to understand it all. I remember telling my mother that the man who could operate Challow box must be a species of genius.

Challow box became an irresistible attraction and the following afternoon I was knocking on the box door asking to be let in. Ken never refused, though I am sure there were times when he would have liked to be on his own. I saw from the lever brasses that the black levers worked points, the blue levers operated bolts to hold certain points firmly in position while a train was passing over them, the blue/brown levers were for electrically operated points and the red/yellow levers worked simultaneously the distant and home signals of something called 'Circourt IBS'.

Ken explained that the points from the Up platform to Up Main and from the Down Main to Down platform line were considered to be too far away to be worked by a lever and rodding so they were 'motor worked' instead. The relevant lever was pulled over two thirds of its travel and then the handle of the hand-generator, which he called the 'hurdy-gurdy', was turned to make a current to turn the motor at the points. An indicator showed when the points had been correctly set and then the lever could be dropped to its final position and the necessary signals lowered for the route. The IBS – Intermediate Block Section – had been installed only a few weeks before I arrived and replaced a signal box similar to Woodley Bridge, called 'Circourt' after a nearby farm. Instead of a signalman lowering semaphore signals from a 'break-section' box, colour light distant and stop signals had been installed, those on the Up Main and Up Relief lines being worked from Challow by levers 6 and 10 respectively, while Wantage Road, the next box eastwards, worked those on the Down lines. Because the blue/brown and red/yellow levers were no more than switches in an electric circuit, they had only short, steel handles so that the signalman would not forget himself and pull them over with a mighty swing.

There were three 'block bells' in the box paired to three 'block indicators'. One pair signalled trains over the Up and Down Main lines to Uffington, the next box westwards, the others were for the Up and Down Relief and Up and Down Main lines to Wantage Road. No train could come towards Challow from either Uffington or Wantage Road until the signalman at Challow had given his permission by acknowledging a bell code and by turning the block indicator to 'Line Clear'. No train could pass Challow in either direction until the signalman at Uffington or Wantage Road had given his permission; the action of turning the block indicator to 'Line Clear' actually released an electric lock on the stop signal, giving access to the next man's section of line.

Trains were signalled along the track by a series of bell codes – asking permission for the train to proceed, warning of its imminent approach and saying when it had passed and the section was clear for the next train. It was just a routine and simple enough once you got the hang of it; with my experience at Woodley Bridge to draw upon, I was able to grasp Challow's *routine* quickly but the *regulation* of goods and passenger traffic required a far wider experience, a full knowledge of the train service throughout the twenty-four hours of a day, an understanding of the layouts at other signal boxes and the running times of all the various types of trains between point A and point B. This would take months to pick up.

I worked the bells and levers under Ken's directions all week. There was a special pleasure in setting the route from Up Main to Up Relief line and seeing a goods or stopping passenger train turning into the slow line at my direction. There was an even greater pleasure to be gained in lowering the signals on the Down Relief line, hearing the engine of a goods train whistle acknowledgement and actually start up in response to my signal. But there was one train each afternoon that Ken would not let me signal, the Up Bristolian; when the bell rang for it at about five past five, he would say, 'Let me see to that.'

This train was 'King'-hauled and, with seven coaches, had to cover the 117 ½ miles from Bristol to Paddington in 105 minutes, an average start to stop speed of 67 ½ mph. It was the fastest train in Britain – possibly in the world. The service had been introduced by the Great Western Railway in 1935 to mark the centenary of the company, had been withdrawn in 1939 and now, in June 1954, had been reintroduced. With a massive 'King' hauling a piffling load, some very fast running had been achieved with times well within the official schedule, the train had taken on the prestige of the pre-war Cheltenham Flyer and become utterly sacred. Hence Ken's concern that it should not be accidentally delayed at Challow by a schoolboy.

Imagine my delight when, on Friday evening, after five afternoons of practice, he trusted me sufficiently to 'pull off' for this Train of Trains! I cannot remember enjoying any train so much as that one. I had not only signalled the finest train in the country, I had been recognised as trustworthy by the signalman who had to 'take the can back' if I did anything stupid.

My confidence soared as I leant professionally from the window to observe the train as it thundered past at 90 mph behind 6015 *King Richard III*. I actually left the box early that night and tore home, bursting indoors to tell my parents, 'Ken let me pull off for the Bristolian this evening!'

Before I left that evening, Ken had said, 'I'm on nights next week but Bill Mattingley will be here on late turn, I've had a word with him and it'll be all right for you to come up when he's on. I dare say he'd be glad of some help with the box – he does barbering here on Thursdays.'

The following Monday I went along to the box at teatime and met Bill. He already had an assistant and was lying in his armchair, his legs stretched out along a low bench, enjoying a conversation with a colleague called 'Wally' or 'Wal', whom I gathered worked at Wantage Road box. Bill got out of his chair as I came in, roared 'Here he is!', crushed my hand, fell back into his chair and roared again, 'Well – how's the boy doing?' Bill was a big man with a strong voice, a loud laugh and a presence that filled the box.

Lying in a chair, holding a telephone, Bill waved his free arm in the direction of his assistant. 'That there's Basil, my mate. He lives over in the station houses; his Dad's the lampy (lampman), and he comes over most evenings to help with the frame – especially Thursday nights. Eh, Bas?' Basil, with fully two years more than my thirteen, grinned at Bill and agreed but did little more than nod at me – we were immediately jealous of each other, I think – but Bill did not appear to notice, only returned to his interrupted conversation with Wally at Wantage. 'Yes then, Wal ...' A bell rang and Basil moved confidently to answer it, one of the several telephones rang, Basil knew which one and handed it to the recumbent Bill – he even switched goods trains in and out of the Relief lines without asking! There was nothing for me to do and I felt thoroughly squashed but stuck it out until 'going home time' at ten.

The following evening Bill had two chess wallets on the table, one for a game he was playing with his mate Alec at Steventon, the other for 'Chalky' White, the local policeman, who would come into the box most evenings when Bill was on duty to make his move and have a cup of tea before reporting by public phone to his sergeant at Wantage. Basil and his young brother Robin and I arrived at seven o'clock, 'Chalky' turned up at eight, Bill had tea, milk and sugar for all of us, and we had an interesting party for an hour as Bill, Basil and 'Chalky' argued about chess, Robin tried to do his homework and I had the fifty-one levers all to myself.

I missed only Thursday and Friday evening that week and on Saturday had the box to myself.

'Come in! How's the boy?' boomed Bill. 'Need your help; ol' Basil's gone to the cricket over Frilford. I missed you on Thursday, had to manage the box and do the barbering too. I expected one of you and neither turned up. I'll tell you what, you promise to be here, for certain sure, Thursday evenings and I can guarantee you the box to work. There's only two or three customers, so I shan't keep you long.'

I replied that it did not matter if he kept me all night and we sealed the bargain over a cup of his tea.

A few minutes later Sam Loder came to the box carrying a shotgun and a wireless. Bill poured him the dregs of the pot, Sam took a cushion and sat in comfort on the back window sill, looking over the fields and a line of trees, shotgun at the ready, tea within reach, and John Arlott droning out a cricket commentary – a comforting accompaniment to a quiet afternoon.

'What do you think of our new station master then, Sam?' asked Bill.

'Fred Halford? Not a bad sort of chap, bit quiet. He comes from somewhere up Worcester way, don't he – the Bromyard branch, Basil said.'

'Suckley, Mr Halford told me, p'r'aps that is the Bromyard line. He was a station master there for a few years but he's been a signalman since before the war. Did you know that him and his wife worked the same box together, turn and turn about, during the war?'

'Get away!' exclaimed Sam. 'That must have been awkward for getting meals; they'd hardly have seen each other. I wonder if they had to do a night shift.'

'He never said, but that's just the sort of thing you would think of, Loder,' Bill said with mock severity.

'How's your strapper getting on then?' said Sam, changing the subject.

'Oh, he'll do, he might come to work here one day and then he'll find a difference – no coming and going as he pleases, just eight hours a day seven days a week.'

'Oh-ho!' cheered Sam. 'You don't do so bad, sitting on your backside with plenty of help.'

'Depends what else you want to do,' said Bill. 'I've got my bees to see to – I lost a swarm back in May because I was here on early turn, now that hive'll be producing nothing for me this summer.'

I had never heard anything as near a complaint as this before, neither had it occurred to me that railwaymen might have some other interests besides their work, probably because I only spoke to them about railways. I wondered if I *would* be so keen if I came to work in the box day after day.

'Don't you like your job here, then, Bill?' I asked.

'Yes, o'course I do,' he replied, 'I'm my own boss more'n if I worked in a shop or a factory, but it gets in the way sometimes.'

'Go on!' Sam said, exasperated. 'If you was in a shop all day, you'd never get a chance to see to your bees, shift work's ideal for you if you're bee-keeping on the side.'

'Yes, I know, you're right. Challow's a good steady old number wi' some railway work to do –'

Sam broke in, 'And plenty of people to help you do it – hey up! Here comes Mr Halford.'

My heart leaped and sank like a stone – the Station Master!

'Do you think he'll mind?' I asked. Bill looked at Sam, Sam looked back at him and hid his shotgun behind a locker.

'I dunno. What's he coming over for anyway on his day off?'

The door opened and Mr Halford came up the stairs. Bill got up, Sam was already standing by the wall, I was trying to hide behind the row of levers.

'Afternoon, sir,' said Bill nervously, 'very fine day, everything all right?'

'Yes thanks, I was just out for a stroll – who's this?' he pointed towards me.

'That's Adrian, Bill's strapper,' said Sam, quickly, while Bill was groping for words, cheerfully aggressive, 'he's teaching him the job against the day when he comes to work here.'

Bill shot Sam an appealing glance – ('Shut your great mouth!') – and grinned more nervously than ever at the station master.

'Are you learning anything?' he asked me.

'Um ... well ...'

'When can you give "Line Clear" for a train?'

'When the line is clear for a quarter of a mile ahead of the home signal and all points within that distance are set for the safety of the approaching train.'

'Oh ho! This isn't your first visit. You've done a good job, Bill,' he said with a smile, 'well done.'

Mr Halford was about fifty years old, slightly less than average height, of slim, even slight build with dark hair, going silver, and blue eyes; beside the broad Bill Mattingley and tall Sam Loder, he looked almost frail. He was obviously disposed to be friendly. 'Er ... um, we were wondering where Suckley was,' said Bill.

'On the Bromyard branch. It turned off the Worcester to Hereford line near Worcester at Bransford Road Junction and went twenty-seven miles across to Leominster on the Newport to Shrewsbury line. It was a quiet little place, a single track with the boxes open from seven in the morning to half past eight at night – quite a contrast to this place.'

'Did you always work on that line?'

'No, I started at Long Marston in 1928 and worked at various places after that between Blockley and Pershore till I got a class six signalman's job at Fencote on the Bromyard in 1937. Promotion was waiting for dead men's shoes in those days.'

'I went in the RAF before the war,' volunteered Bill, 'and did all right. I'm the strapper round here. I didn't start till 1947. Would you like some tea, Mr Halford?'

'If there's one going.'

'Things were bad in the '30s,' continued Sam, 'I went on the farm when I left school in 1927. Joined the Guards to get away from cowshit and landed up to my neck in bullshit!'

We all laughed, though I thought Mr Halford did so with a slight wince.

'What regiment, Sam?' he asked.

'The Grenadiers,' he said with hint of pride showing through his casual tone. I saw him better then – no wonder he walked so straight and tall. 'I came out in 1933, after three years, went on the Reserve and worked with the branch gang at Faringdon. When the war came I went back to the Colours and my wife joined up too – she came on here as a porter.'

'Ha! That's good,' said Mr Halford, 'my wife worked on the railway too, during the war. We worked Fencote together.' He finished off his tea and put down the cup. 'Ah! That's better, thanks for the tea, Bill. I'll love you and leave you now – keep on with the rules young man.' And he went down the stairs.

When the door had been closed, Sam settled himself back onto the window sill. 'There you are, he's a good bloke – I told you so.'

'Yes, he's all right,' agreed Bill, 'he's been through the mill.'

CHAPTER THREE

On the Fly

After the station master had given his unspoken approval to my presence in the box, I felt secure and visited Ken and Bill frequently. I had to divide my spare time between the box and a part-time job looking after two horses, but I fitted it all in – particularly my promise to Bill – and became quite a good horseman as I learned more about signal box work.

On Thursdays I rushed to get to the signal box so as to have as long as possible 'in charge' without fear of having to share it with Basil. Bill would be loud and hearty in his greetings. 'Well done, young man. Here's the duster, pull off on the Down Main for the 4.55.' I would heave over levers 62, 61, 60, 54 and 63, in that order, and feel very confident and proud. Almost all passenger trains on the Down line at Challow originated from Paddington so that signalmen referred to them simply as 'the 8.45' or '4.55' (from Paddington) while Up line expresses were known by their place of origin – the 'Kingswear' or the 'Pembroke' as they were trains *from* those places to Paddington.

In 1954 the 4.55 was followed by the 5.5 and the 2.28 (6.4 Didcot) stopper, which came along the Down Relief to Challow at 6.27. This was followed by the 5.14 Paddington express, which turned turned into the platform through power points 45 from the Down Main with signals 62 and 59 lowered. It arrived at 6.47 and left at 6.49, rejoining the Down Main through points 30, bolted by lever 31, signalled by 56, 55 and 54. The levers at Challow were numbered 1 to 63 from left to right – there were eleven spaces. The box faced north so lever 1 was at the west end operating the Up distant signal and lever 63 was at the east end for the Down distant, the levers' position in the frame corresponding with their signals' and points' sequence over the ground.

I asked Bill if No. 1 was always the Up distant.

'No, it could be the Down distant but it is always at the left-hand end of the frame. You want to pop up to Wally's place at Wantage Road, then you'd understand.'

After the 5.55 – the Red Dragon – had passed at about 7 p.m., Bill's customers started to arrive. I walked about the bells and levers, seeing Bill with his spectacles on, poring over some grizzled old neck busy with his clippers – then I felt I was 'on my own'. It was a wonderful feeling.

The express trains and stoppers I knew how to handle, but I had to ask him what to do with the freights.

'There's a 3-2 off Uffington, Bill.'*

'What time is it?' he mumbled, with a comb in his mouth.

'7.28.'

'Let it run!' and I pulled off up the Main – 2, 3, 5, 6 and 1 in that order.

The following Monday I was standing with my mother on the green at Childrey, outside Bradbrook's thatched shop, waiting for some people to come out to give us space to get in, when Ken Rowlands came out of a lane by the shop. I introduced him to my mother.

'I do hope he isn't a nuisance to you, Mr Rowlands,' she said, 'he spends a lot of time at the signal box.'

'Oh, not at all,' said Ken, with what might have been a wan smile, 'he's very keen – I don't think you've seen the Fly yet, have you Adrian?'

'The Fly? What's that?'

'The local goods. It comes quite early in the morning to shunt the yard. There's two or three boys from here that go down to ride round the station on it, you've missed it today but if you get down to the station for eight on Wednesday you'll be in time.'

On Wednesday I cycled down to the station with two boys, Peter and Mike. They told me they went down only for the ride on the engine. 'Watching trains all day is silly,' they said. As we cycled along the final stretch of lane before the main road, we could see the steam and hear the noise of a shunting engine at work. We pedalled as fast as we could, up the slope of the bridge, down the station approach, threw our bikes roughly on the ground and dashed onto the platform. 'Who's driving?' panted one boy to the other. 'Can't see ... it's Wilf! Come on, we'll be all right with him,' and they dashed over the footbridge to the upside where the train was shunting.

The engine was one I had never seen before, except in photographs – an 0-6-2 tank No. 5639. According to books, they were confined to South Wales, so I was pleased to see such a rarity. It came into the platform, preparing for a shunt, and Mike asked, 'Can we come up, Wilf, please?'

'You can if you like,' he said, moving his bulk to clear the gangway. Three boys were onto the footplate in three jumps, cramming themselves in till the cab bulged with boys; the fireman was only sixteen.

---

* See Appendices 1 and 2.

Sam Loder was in charge of shunting, and it occurred to me that I could go up to Wantage Road to see Wally and his signal box on the Fly if Sam would ask the driver on my behalf, so I waited for an opportunity to speak to him. The engine stopped sharply to shunt a wagon off, placing Sam – leaning on his pole watching the truck bowling along the siding – just below the gangway. I climbed down to the track.

'Hello Sam.'

'Well, I'm blowed! Where have you sprung from?'

'I've been on the engine. Sam, would you ask the driver if he'd take me to Wantage Road?'

'Wilf's all right. You can ask him yourself, but make sure the others don't hear or he'll say no.' I got back onto the engine feeling nervous about asking the driver a favour when I did not know him.

Wilf brought his tank engine gently into the platform with the whole train in tow. Shunting was over for the day. 'Right then, boys,' said he briskly, 'that's all for now. See you again on Friday.' We shuffled off the engine onto the platform. I felt uneasy at the thought of asking and ashamed of feeling scared. Peter and Mike were heading for the footbridge steps so as to be directly over the engine's funnel when it started off and I was about to follow when Sam, standing a little way off, caught my eye, urging me to ask.

'Er, um ... thank you for the ride, er, Mister,' I said desperately.

'That's all right, son,' replied Wilf, wiping his hands on some cotton waste as he leant over the cab side and grinned down at me.

'Um, I often go into the signal box here and the signalman said I ought to go to see the box at Wantage – er, do you think I could ride up with you?'

Wilf was grinning again, but not down at me. I turned to find Sam standing right behind me, nodding his head vigorously at the driver!

'All right then, jump on at the top end of the platform.'

The tank engine, which was running bunker first, pulled gently through the station toward the Up Relief line starting signal – No. 8 lever in the box – which was at 'Danger'. Wilf blew his whistle and I jumped aboard as No. 8 lowered. Half a mile up the line I saw No. 9 arm drop, the IBS colour light distant signal below the arm remaining at amber 'Caution' for a few seconds before changing to green in response to lever 10 being thrown over in the signal box. Wilf looked back along his train until it was safely under way, waved acknowledgement to his guard's 'All Right' wave and then turned to watch the road ahead.

'I'm Wilf and that's my son Steve. What's your name?'

I told him.

'Been on an engine before?'

'Only round Reading station on the Pilot, never on a long journey.'

'Ha! I wouldn't call it long – only three miles.'

'Well, it's all through fields. It looks different when you see it from the engine instead of from a coach.'

'When do you leave school, Adrian?'

'In three years.'

'Steve's been left a year now. You could be doing his job in four years' time – that's not long.' It seemed like a lifetime to me, and I looked admiringly at Steve who could ride around on a steam engine with his dad. A loud bell rang out from above a green box fixed to the side of the cab.

'The Pilot at Reading had one of those. What is it for?'

'That's the ATC. It's a Great Western idea and all our engines are fitted with them. None of the other lines has anything like it. We've just passed Circourt's distant signal at 'All Right' and got the bell but if the signal had been at 'Caution' we'd have got a siren and the brakes would have gone on. You'll see what I mean in a few minutes.'

We rattled merrily through the fields, our white exhaust swirling round twenty assorted wagons which bobbed up and down over the rail joints. 'Look here now,' commanded Wilf. I moved to his side of the cab. 'Look – between the rails ahead – there's a long, thin ramp and a bit further on is the distant signal. We're going over the ramp now.' *Veeeeee* – a siren sounded in the green box. 'Look at the vacuum gauge.' One of the needles was dropping and I could feel the brakes going on. Wilf flicked a switch on the side of the box, the wailing stopped and the needle rose.

'If I hadn't turned it off the brakes would have gone on harder and harder until the train was stopped – even if the regulator was fully open. The ATC tells you when you are approaching a distant signal, it gives you the correct "All Right" or "Caution" signal and would bring you to a stand if you ignored the siren. Once you've acknowledged the "Caution" by turning the thing off, it's up to you to take over the braking and be ready to stop at the first stop signal. It makes life safer when the fog is thick.'

'But what if you turned off the siren and then didn't do any braking yourself?' I asked.

'You'd be a bloody fool,' he said.

He began to brake the train and we ran quietly into the platform at Wantage Road. I got off the engine and thanked Wilf for a lovely ride and an interesting talk. 'You're very welcome,' he said. 'It's nice to see you enjoying yourself.' I turned away as a porter, the image of the stern man I had seen at Challow on several occasions, came across the 'barrow crossing' and up the platform ramp, his shunting pole in his hand. I was so busy wondering whether it was the same man or his identical twin that his slight nod of recognition did not register with me at first – then it sank in and I realised that, somehow, he must work at both stations.

The train drew away preparatory to reversing into the goods yard and I saw, standing on the opposite platform, under an awning, an odd little tank engine, painted bright green with a very tall, thin, black chimney, a small dome of unusual and elaborate shape, a huge, square cab and four tiny driving wheels. I was gripped with excitement – an engine I had never heard of or seen in a picture. I stared in amazement across the tracks and saw that she carried a name – *Shannon* – and on her cab were yellow letters – W.T. Co. No.5.

Wantage Road box was, from the outside, the twin of Challow. I went in and was greeted by Wally Randall, who had obviously been briefed by Bill to expect me. The box interior also looked exactly like Challow, controlling the same layout with levers numbered 1 to 63.

'So you're Bill's strapper. Pleased to meet you,' he said with a wide smile and a Londonish accent, unusual in our part of the world. He was short and inclined to be stocky, his grey hair brushed straight back from his forehead, his face pale, tending to be fleshy and round and just beginning to become lined. He wore his uniform, blue serge trousers and an open-necked white shirt.

'Everyone says I'm a strapper – what does it mean?'

'Well, I'd have thought that was obvious – a learner.'

'I suppose what I mean is what does a strapper have to do with being a learner – what's the connection?'

'Goodness only knows. It's the word we've used for as long as I've been around. I was a strapper thirty years ago.'

'The engine on the platform is lovely – where does *that* come from?'

'Well, I'd have thought you'd have known that too – answer that bell, it'll be the Weston – that's *Shannon* that used to work the tramway that ran from here to the town. I only knew it when they were hauling goods. We used to get old *Shannon* out on the Main line to do shunting now and then, but back in the '20s the tram took passengers too. They say that all the station staff here were allowed free travel and the landlord and his wife at the Rifle Volunteer just up the road, too. If you come to the window – look, see that siding curving down the middle of the station yard, you can see it's heading out to the main road; that was the start of the line to Wantage till they put the blocks up in 1945. It went right past the pub's front door. I s'pose that's why they had free travel, to make up for the inconvenience.'

'The engine looks very old.'

'Didn't you see the plaque? It tells you there that she was built in 1857. When the line was closed, the Great Western did her up and put her on show – very nice of them really. You wouldn't get no modern firm thinking of a thing like that. Answer that "Approach", get the road from Lockinge and pull off up the Main.'

I looked at the instruments and rang the bell marked 'Lockinge' – four beats. Back came the code as the indicator needle swung to 'Line Clear'. I walked to the end of the box to pull off 2, 3, 5, 6 and 1.

'What are you doing?' asked Wally.

'Pulling off up the Main.'

'Aha! You're not at Challow now. Up the Main is 62, 61, 60, 54 and 63,' Wally beamed triumphantly. I pulled the levers over feeling decidedly awkward – these were the Down Main levers at Challow! 'You see,' said Wal, 'the box here faces south, opposite to Challow, so when the levers are numbered from left to right, 1 to 63, 1 is at the opposite end of the box to Challow's 1.' I saw the point and felt sheepish about it, but it was still awkward to be pulling Down line levers for an Up line train!

'There's another thing you could explain, Wally. The porter on the station this morning, I've seen him at Challow a lot, how does he work here too?'

'That's Harry Strong. He's a reliefman and covers all over the Swindon district though they keep him up this end – Challow to Steventon.'

'As far away as that!' I exclaimed.

'Huh! He considers himself lucky. They could send him to Ludgershall every day.'

I didn't know where that was, but it sounded like a long way away. 'He doesn't say much,' I ventured.

'Harry's all right, the very best. Him and Albert Stanley are about the oldest hands on this patch; they've both been on since about 1920. Harry was a signalman at Circourt and went portering on the Relief when they took the box away – there's not much he can't do. He made 'em all sit up and take notice a few years back when he was at Circourt. It was all over the slip coach on the Up Weston in the morning. Slip coaches were taken off in 1939 as an economy measure for the war and were reintroduced in 1946 so the blokes had got rusty about recognising the different tail lamps – I wouldn't be so bold as to say I wouldn't have made the same mistake. You've seen the Weston going up with the slip tail lamp on red and white side by side – haven't you? When that coach comes off at Didcot the Main train goes on with the special tail lamp – red over red – to show the slip's gone, so if you ever see that train showing that lamp at Challow you'll know he's lost his slip coach somewhere.

'Well, on this occasion, the slip guard pulled his lever just after Knighton Crossing – no one ever heard how he came to do it – and then, instead of letting the coach roll to Uffington, he put the brakes on there and then and stopped out in the section. The chap at Uffington saw the double tail lamps, thought it was the slip lamp, gave "Train out of Section" to Knighton and the "Line Clear" for the Up stopper. The guard was slow in getting down onto the track and didn't go back to protect the coach with "shots". Luckily for him the "packers" were working a bit towards Knighton, saw the coach stopped, heard the stopper coming fast, put two and two together and got some detonators down on the rail. The stopper pulled up about a hundred yards from the slip.

'In the meantime, the train had passed Challow and the bloke *there* didn't notice anything wrong and sent the "Train out" to Uffington. It was Harry at Circourt who spotted that the slip was missing and sent me the 5-5, "Train Divided". Thanks to the gang, there was no harm done, except to several blokes' pride – they all had to go to Bristol for it.'

I soaked all this up, trying to grasp the casual mention of the operation of so many rules – the gang's actions, Harry's, what the guard ought to have done – Wally spoke with such familiarity about things which seemed so complicated and even mysterious. I burned to know more.

'But what if a train slips a carriage at Swindon according to schedule? It will come up through here with the "slip gone" signal showing. How would you know whether it was *meant* to be showing or whether it was a mistake like the one you've just told me about?'

'Ah! You must know your service, you see. You must *know* what each train does and the stations and the sequence they run in. That's why box to box messages are so important – to let people know if there's any "out of course" running. Not just for slips, either. All expresses are "four bells" to us, as you know, and at a place like Didcot the sequence might be the Taunton first and then the Swansea. Say the Taunton is booked to go up the Relief line at Foxhall and stop at Didcot while the Swansea goes straight up the Main. Then the sequence is reversed down at Wootton Bassett and the signalman there lets the Swansea off the South Wales road in front of the Taunton. The Taunton may be late – well, if he don't tell anyone then Foxhall gets a four bells about the time he's expecting the Taunton, sets the road for the Up Relief and the Swansea comes to a grinding halt and has to wait while the signalman swears and finally finds out it's not his Taunton but the Swansea! Whenever you get a boxer message, make sure you pass it on.'

'All right, I will, but what about the slip coaches, how would you go on in a case like that?'

'Like I say, you'd just have to *know*. At the moment there are no slip coaches on the Down line for Didcot or Swindon, and on the Up the only train with slips is the seven o'clock Weston with a coach for Didcot in the mornings and the 1.50 Bristol and 4.35 Weston with coaches for Reading in the afternoon, so it's straightforward – when you are dealing with those trains you expect to see the red/white side-by-side lamp.'

'I used to stand on the platform at Reading and watch the coach separate from the train. I think I'll go and watch it at Didcot.'

'Huh! You won't see much. They slip them at anything up to eighty miles an hour. It's a straight run into the platform, not like on the Up line at Reading, so the guard slips a mile before the station to give himself braking distance. The Main train has gone through before the slip arrives.'

'Um, it seems a bit odd, to me, letting a coach go whizzing about all on its own especially over all those junctions near Didcot,' I said hesitantly, rather expecting to be told off for criticising a Great Western speciality.

'It is odd,' agreed Wally warmly, 'and it breaks the basic safety rule – one train at a time on one section of line – when the coach is slipped it makes a second train within one section. It's very good for the passengers because they get an express service to a big junction with connecting service laid on and the railway doesn't have to stop the express, but it is risky, even the rule book recognises that – hold on,' he rummaged in his desk, brought out a thick, blue-covered book and thumbed through it. 'Ah! Here it is, listen. "Where there is a public level-crossing between the place where the slip is made and the station, the crossing must not be fouled until the slip has passed." It makes me smile when I read that but it could be a disaster – the crossing keeper opening the gates after the train has gone by, forgetting about the slip trailing somewhere behind, till Wham! – it goes piling into something on the crossing. You've got to be on your toes when them things are about. By the way, the Down stopper's just off Steventon. Are you going to go home on it?'

'Yes, I think I'd better, so's to be home for dinner.'

'Well, just get the road from Challow for it and pull off down the Relief.'

I rang the bell code and then walked towards 58 signal lever. Wally laughed. 'Don't forget we're arse about face here, compared to Challow.' Feeling foolish for forgetting, I went to the opposite end of the frame and pulled point and bolt, 17 and 18 and signals 7, 8, 9, 10. These would have been the Up Relief signals at Challow. It did feel odd.

I thanked Wally very much for his long talk and went out, over the tracks, onto the Down platform to buy a ticket. The stern porter was standing in the doorway of the ticket office. I did not see him until I was walking along the platform but realised then that he had seen me walk across the tracks. He might have been a policeman, standing in his clean, blue uniform and he looked at me very steadily, as a policeman would. Large butterflies fluttered in my stomach.

'Trespassing, young man?' he asked quietly.

'I've been to see Wally, Mr Strong,' hoping to show how well in I was, 'and now I've come to buy a ticket to Challow.'

'And making enquiries about me,' he said shrewdly. 'I could have told you who I was if you'd asked. I hope you didn't talk about me for the whole two hours you were up there?' His upper lip was rather long and he seemed to hold it in such a way – as if he was preventing it from curling into a smile. I regained some confidence.

'Wally was telling me about slip coaches and things that go wrong,' I said, hoping to draw him out on the subject of his work at Circourt.

'I see,' he replied, very solemnly, 'and did he tell you' – I thought he was about to tell me his story; I looked at him expectantly and it showed in my face – 'did he tell you', he said again, 'that there was a slip coach here every day but Sunday off a Paddington express from 1874 to 1914 and that the shunting horse and sometimes the tram engine took it back into the siding?'

'No, he didn't. But he did say that all the station staff and the landlord of the Rifle Volunteer were given free travel on the tram.'

'Yes, they were, the old Company were a fair crowd – mind yourself now, here comes the stopper, I must get on but when I see you again I'll expect you to tell me what train carried twenty tail lamps. I'll give you a clue, I saw it every day when I was a strapper.'

He walked away to a four-wheel barrow with a box on it as the train rumbled towards us and called over his shoulder, 'There's no one in the booking office, you'd best jump on the train.'

Back at Challow, Sam said, 'Hi-up then, Ady. Had a good morning?' He did not seem to be worried about my lack of a ticket. 'Yes thanks, Sam. Thanks for getting me on the engine.'

'Nothing to do with me. That was between you and your driver mate. See you again soon.'

'Righto. Tomorrow, I expect.'

CHAPTER FOUR

Taking Serge

For nearly three years I went back, riding on the engines and working in the signal box, and because the railwaymen had made their work the focus of their lives, I was not considered eccentric by them but, rather, accepted as an honorary member of the station staff. I left school in December 1955, a month before my fifteenth birthday and after Christmas started looking for a job. The natural course would have been to join the railway but my grandmother sent a pamphlet extolling the benefits of a boys' infantry training unit at Plymouth. My father flatly refused to allow me to join and a fierce battle developed.

I was determined to do as I pleased; I felt sure that the Army must be something pleasant if my father did not want me to join and, if that was not inducement enough, I looked forward to frequent 200-mile-long journeys behind or even upon 'King' class engines and to hearing them working flat out as they climbed over the slopes of Dartmoor. All that and a bright new shilling too.

Mr Halford and Sam were at the station when I arrived with my mother and father to catch the Up stopper for the first part of the Plymouth journey. The train arrived behind 1005 *County of Devon* and we talked at length about the possibilities of the omen. The guard's whistle blew and my father squeezed my hand hard as we parted. 'Good luck, lad,' he said quietly looking straight into my eyes. The short train drew quickly away and I waved back at the little group on the platform, Mum and Dad waving, Sam and Fred Halford standing behind and waving too. I turned to look at the engine, got smuts promptly into both eyes and brought my head inside the compartment, tears pouring down my face. The other people in the compartment stared furtively; I felt terrible but there was no escape in a non-corridor train.

After two years at the Junior Leaders' regiment I became an instructor and realised that, whilst I was technically expert, I was utterly incapable of leading. I took some of the last National Service conscripts through their basic training – the youngest was five years older than me – and muddled along to my own and everyone else's embarrassment for two years. Then, sitting in the barrack room one evening with my latest squad, 'fraternising with the men', I heard someone talking about steam engines. He was a fireman from somewhere in Norfolk and his description of footplate life, told with sincere affection, made me realise my true vocation. I had kept up my connection with Challow station when I was on leave and now, on a weekend off, I went to see Fred Halford. He was as friendly as ever.

'Do you think I could get a job on the railway?' I asked him.

'Bless me, yes!' he replied.

'We could give you a job here straight away but surely you've got to give the Queen a few more years yet?'

'Well yes, officially. But I'm going to see if I can get out sooner.' His face clouded over. 'Look here now, young Adrian, don't go doing anything silly. The Army don't take things like that lightly; you'd get into a miserable fix, you'd upset your parents and don't forget that the railway'll want a good reference before they'd take you on.'

'It's all right, Mr Halford, I've seen some of the glasshouses, you won't find me in one. I'll get an honourable discharge if you're sure I can get a job on the railway.'

'Yes, you can come here. David Castle's just gone up to Wantage as a van driver. I don't suppose anyone else will be after his job here.'

Mr Halford was so keen to help that I did not like to tell him I had no intention of coming to Challow but rather to work on locomotives. The problem now was how to get out of the Army. I spoke to the medical officer about it and he suggested that I developed asthma. During my time as an amateur stable lad in Childrey I had developed an allergic asthma induced by close contact with horses, and as there was a cavalry barracks down the road from our depot, it was easy to bring on crippling attacks of the wheezes; in due course I received my discharge as medically unfit. As I drove away from the barracks, a glorious feeling of freedom surged through me, something, I thought, that no true regular soldier would ever feel.

I underwent an examination by the railway doctor at Park House, Swindon, where a million Great Western men had received similar examinations for a hundred years. After a thorough check the doctor said, 'Well, you appear to be fit, yet your Army discharge was for asthma. What do you want to do on the railway?'

'I'd like to work on the engines.'

'Oh! I can't let you do that. The fumes in the shed and in the Severn tunnel would be very bad for you.' My heart sank under the disappointment. For a few moments the shock made me forget that there were other sorts of railway work and I felt well and truly hoist with mine own petard. Then I remembered Mr Halford's kind offer of a job and Challow box.

'Can I go into a signal box?'

'Certainly, with your asthma that would be the best place,' adding with a smile, 'and I expect you will get a few footplate rides once you get to know the drivers.'

So I went as a Lad Porter to Challow station in September 1960, aged nineteen, till I was old enough to go as a signalman. But even if I had been twenty-one (the preferred minimum age), I do not think that the District Inspector would have let me – or anyone – go into a box 'straight off the street' as the saying was. Some sort of probationary period was then considered essential.

I had been told to report to the station at ten o'clock on a Friday morning and drove down the lane full of excitement to be going to work at the place where I had completed a long, childhood association with kind people and fine machines. I mentally compared the friendly familiarity of 'Challer' with the first, bleak night at Plymouth when I was shown into a Victorian barrack room filled with thirty beds and twenty-nine staring strangers – and wondered if Sam Loder would be on duty at the station.

Parking in the yard I entered the station by the parcels office. Mr Halford came out from his inner sanctum and shook my hand. 'I suppose I could say "Welcome back",' he said, with a smile. 'Sam! Come in here a minute – our trained assassin has arrived to protect us.' The door from the platform opened and in came Sam with an ear-to-ear grin, his hand outstretched. 'Hi-up, kid. How's-yer-bum?' He finished very quickly and I was not sure if I had heard him correctly.

'What was that, Sam?'

'Nice bit o' sun.'

'Oh – er – yes,' said I, uncertainly. Mr Halford was keen to get me into uniform. 'Fetch him the spare hat, Sam.' Sam rummaged in a cupboard and came out with a derelict, peaked cap which he jammed on my head. 'Now the passengers will know you're in charge,' he said. 'Right then,' continued Mr Halford, 'we'd better get him measured for his uniform. Let's go into my office where there's more light.'

Straight ahead of me as I came through the door, against the furthest wall, was a row of cupboards extending the width of the room under a single bench top. In the centre was a small, glass window with an oval hole for passing tickets; to the right was a cast-iron date-stamping machine, a tall, wide, pigeonholed rack full of pasteboard tickets; and, leaning back against the cupboards facing me, his elbows resting on the bench top, was Basil, grinning like a Cheshire cat. 'Hello, Adrian. Decided to combine work with pleasure, eh?'

'Of course, you know Basil, don't you,' Mr Halford said to me, 'he's our booking clerk.' Sam turned Quartermaster and spread some forms on the station master's leather-topped desk while Mr Halford picked up an eighteen-inch boxwood ruler marked GWR ready to take my measurements according to Sam's instructions. 'Half arm' and 'half back' was fairly simple, he had some difficulty with 'shoulder to wrist, arm bent' but succeeded in the end by using his finger to keep the place while he moved the ruler. 'Inside leg' was uncomfortable and accompanied by a hoary joke.

'Overcoat or mac?' asked Sam.

'Have the waterproof,' said Mr Halford with a solicitous look.

'No, take the overcoat,' said Sam, 'it's warmer. Those macs are stiff and cold and the collar sticks into your neck when you turn it up in a wind.' I ordered an overcoat. Sam looked down the list of measurements, smiled to himself, glanced up at me and said, 'Well, I suppose they'll be all right. I'll get them on the next Down stopper for Swindon.'

He put the forms in an envelope, took it to the parcels office letter rack, opened the door and went out. I heard him say 'Hi-up, Harry' and saw him pass the windows, apparently going home.

'Isn't Sam on duty then?' I asked.

'Ah – no. He just happened to be around when you arrived,' said Mr Halford. 'Harry, come in here and meet your learner.' Harry came in looking exactly the same as he looked four years before. 'Do you know Adrian?'

'Yes, Mr Halford. We have met.' He said, looking across at me and nodding in a friendly way. 'He's come to work here then, has he?'

'Yes, he'll be with you until you've shown him the ropes and he can manage on his own.'

'That'll be all right. I must get on now, there's some stuff for the Up stopper to see to.'

There was a knock on the oak slide in front of the ticket window and Basil lifted it, bending slightly. On the other side a face appeared as if its owner was lying on his side as he looked through the glass. A passenger was bowing from the waist – a supplicatory posture that the Great Western would have considered no more than correct – asking for a ticket. 'Cheap day to Reading, please.' Basil took his money, flicked a ticket from the rack, got change and slid the money and pasteboard through the little, oval hole with a cheerful, 'Thanks very much.' The passenger grunted something, taken aback perhaps by Basil's manner, and moved away. 'Cheerful cove,' said Basil. 'Haven't seen him before. I wonder what he's on.'

A telephone on the wall rang the stopping train code – 3-1. 'That's the Up stopper just leaving Uffington; the signalman rings the telephone to warn us. Come on, we'll go out to the platform.'

The train arrived behind a shiny 'County' class engine, just out of the factory. Harry put some boxes in with the guard, took a parcel off, made sure the passengers' door was shut and waved to the guard. The guard gave 'Right Away' and within a minute of its arrival the train was on its way again. Harry went immediately to his office, Basil slipped off to the signal box for his coffee and Mr Halford led me along the platform. 'You know your way around the station. I'll take you out to the power points and show you what to do if they go wrong.'

We strolled along the platform on a warm, comfortable September day while he told me about the station. 'In spite of those four tracks up there making the place look like the outer suburbs of London, Challow is a country station and depends on the villages for its support. There's no big centre of population to help us. The atmosphere is like on a branch line; we have a stopping service connecting with the junction at Didcot and Swindon and one express to London in the morning and another back at night. Those express trains going through the middle roads are really nothing to do with us and you soon learn to take no notice of them.' I did not believe I would ever come to ignore them but said nothing. 'We have a good following of regular passengers – we know them all by sight, some by name and *they* know us. Some of them come to Challow in preference to a station closer to their home because they appreciate the service we give them. The passengers are our bread and butter and the first rule in the book, as far as I am concerned, says to be "prompt, civil and obliging". I hope you will remember that and not let the station down.'

Although he said all this with the utmost seriousness, he seemed glad to change the subject. 'The lines through here were quadrupled during 1932 and '33; before that, it was ordinary double track – the present Up Relief and Up Main lines used to be the Up and Down Mains – there was an old Up goods loop but that came out in 1933. You can see the space it occupied on the left of the Up Relief all covered in bushes. Albert Stanley has his chicken run on it. Have you met Albert yet?' I said I had not. 'You must have seen him. He lives in the station terrace and goes out every evening to feed his chickens – he's a well-built man with quite a ruddy face and close-cropped grey hair.'

'I know who you mean. He always walks with a collie at his heels.'

'That's the man. Come down the platform ramp. There's the 63 ¾ mile post from Paddington – Albert and Harry are the best men I've ever worked with; they're both old hands. Harry started at Woodborough in 1916 and Albert started at Dauntsey about 1920, I think.

'Now, here are the power points and there is one of the motors you turn with the hurdy-gurdy; the other motor is at the other end of the turn-out. If the signalman can't get the points over on the motor, he'll call you. Go to the box for the hand crank. It's like a wheel nut spanner for a motor car and it's padlocked into a contact box on the instrument shelf of the signal box. Once you take the hand crank out, you lock all point and signal levers relevant to the set of points you're working on, so get it back to the signal box and into the contact box as soon as you can when you've finished with it. Don't forget to take a red and green flag and a point clip, padlock and key as well. When you get to the points, have a look between the movable blade of the points and the rail at both ends to see if there is anything preventing the blades from closing, a stone or bit of grit, but if you can't see anything, you'll have to wind the points over by hand till the lineman can come to put them right.

'Take the cover off here. There, you see that squared end? You put the crank mouth over it and turn till the points are reversed. Don't forget to wind both ends of the turn-out, facing and trailing. Then you must put a clamp on the blade at the facing end and screw it up tight against the rail and padlock the handle so that the vibration of the train cannot unscrew it. Do you know what I mean by "facing" end?'

'The end where the train first meets the points.'

'Right. That's the dangerous end. If the blades are not closed up tight against the rail the train will come off the road. If the trailing end is wrong, the train will smash the rodding and the motor but at least it won't derail.'

Railway work immediately took on a more serious aspect for me – I felt nervous at the very thought of moving points by hand and at all this talk of derailments and resolved to be very wary. I could imagine myself being so careful in making the facing end safe that I would forget about moving the trailing end and thus be responsible for smashing up hundreds of pounds' worth of equipment.

'When you've got the points turned and clamped,' Mr Halford continued, 'go over to that telephone by the Down Relief inner home and tell the signalman and then work under his instructions. When he wants you to let a train pass over the points, you will stand at the facing end and hold out your green flag.'

We stepped back onto the path just as a man I took to be Albert Stanley emerged from the bushes, a bucket over his arm, a dog at his heels.

'Good morning, Mr Halford, nice day,' he said in a gentle Wiltshire voice.

'Hello, Albert. Have you met Adrian?'

'No, I can't say I have. Is he starting on the railway?'

'Yes, he'll be on with Harry first thing Monday at seven o'clock.'

'Well, I hope you enjoy the job. It's a quiet little number and you couldn't have a better teacher than Harry.'

I liked Albert immediately. Somehow his voice sounded cheerful and optimistic and he looked like the classic countryman, straightforward and honest with blue eyes and broad shoulders, standing solidly on the path in his wellingtons, his dog to heel, tongue lolling, smiling at the world.

An Up express came into earshot and then into sight. It was 'Castle'-hauled and travelling unusually fast, the thrilling, thudding, rapid tiff-tiff-tiff-tiff of a locomotive 'notched up and flying', growing louder by the second till it was suddenly drowned by a crescendo of rail noise as the wheels thundered past our little group, shaking the very ground we stood on. I had watched trains for years and loved them – now that I was going to have some very small part to play in controlling them, I was a little bit afraid.

'My goodness, they were going well,' Albert said appreciatively, staring after the train.

'A good eighty, I should think,' said Mr Halford. 'Shall we go back to the station?' We moved towards the platform. 'When I was a young porter I had a very fast ride down Honeybourne bank – over four miles downhill at one in a hundred – I reckon we touched a hundred at the bottom. I was on early turn at Blockley sometime in 1932 and travelled home to Evesham each day by train with my bike in the van. Well, on this occasion the train ran into Blockley; I knew the driver by sight and he waved me up to the engine. "Do you want to ride with us, Fred?" he says. Of course I was all for it, put my bike in the van and then hopped up on the engine. "How fast shall we go down the bank?" this driver says and like a fool I said, "I bet you can't manage a hundred." "I wouldn't want to take advantage of your youth," he says and turns to his fireman. "Hey mate, Fred here doesn't reckon we can do a hundred down Honeybourne." Well, the fireman just laughed, the guard gave "Right" and off we went.

'They had a "Saint" and they opened her up so hard that I fell back against the tender – she had only six coaches – and I then I realised they weren't joking. They were building up as high a speed as possible before the start of the downhill run. I looked at my watch as we passed Chipping Campden – it said 2.38. We were going great guns there; it's uphill but you wouldn't have thought so and I began to worry about the long bank ahead – it wasn't even a straight run downhill but curved this way and that.

'We tipped over the summit, I'm not exaggerating, I felt the engine go, the trees at the lineside just became a blur and I travelled down wedged tight in the front corner of the cab, looking along the boiler and watching it heeling to the canted curves like a ship on a stormy sea. At the foot of the bank was Honeybourne station with facing junction, crossovers and all sorts of point work. I just about bit my tongue as we hit them, the engine seemed to jump into the air and come crashing down, the noise was deafening and we were swaying still from that enormous crash as we came up to the station or rather the station came out to meet us. I thought we'd hit the platforms but we'd steadied by that time and we went straight in, whistle wide open. The footbridge just didn't look high enough – I ducked instinctively as we went under it. There was one more crash as we passed over some more junctions at the far end of the station and we were clear.

'My goodness, they frightened me! And even then the cranky old devil didn't slow up. I barely saw Littleton & Badsey and I'd just begun to think he'd gone out of his mind as Aldington Sidings distant signal came tearing up to us along the track when he slammed the brakes on and almost before I knew it we were grinding to a halt in Evesham station.

'When I got down off the engine, my knees were like jelly and I couldn't walk straight. My ears were ringing too but I heard him laughing, saying, "Hey, young Fred, what's the time?" I'd forgotten that and looked at my watch – 2.46 – and told him. "How fast is that then?" says he, with a stupid great grin. I told him I'd work it out and tell him next day and went off to get my bike from the van. I never bothered to go home on the engine again. Well, not on that bit of line. We'd taken just less than eight minutes from passing Campden to stopping in Evesham, which was an average speed of just over eighty so we may have touched a hundred at Honeybourne.'

'The mad devils,' growled Albert, 't'isn't railway work, is it? I s'pose they were Cockneys.'

'No, I think they were Oxford men.' We had arrived back at the station and Mr Halford turned to go to his office.

'Right then, Adrian. Be here on Monday at first light, or even before, seven o'clock on, with Harry Strong.'

CHAPTER FIVE

Cheltenham Ceremony

Next morning I got out of bed at six o'clock with an alarm clock clattering reveille. When I got downstairs and went to the kitchen to make some tea, intending to sit quiet for a while until I felt alive, I found my mother making my breakfast – a hearty one would describe it well. I could not face it but drank some tea and managed to slip away when she was not looking, and was on the road at 6.40 in my 1935 Morris Eight saloon.

Twenty-five-year-old cars may sound like trouble to car drivers now but in 1960 there were a great many stalwart pre-war cars on the roads. My Morris was a simple, reliable car. She had no heater, no suspension (only leaf springs), her headlamps were about as much use as candles but I loved her. She had a solid, rust-free body on a proper chassis that still carried Lord Nuffield's black enamel paint. Her hydraulic brakes were first class and she had a cruising speed of 35/40 mph on a smooth road, the power coming from a side-valve engine, which ran like the proverbial sewing machine.

Dawn was splitting the night sky when I got to the station at 6.50. It was strange to see the place dark and deserted but I had hardly a minute to contemplate this novelty before I heard the sound of a Bantam two-stroke popping sedately up the hill from Stanford-in-the-Vale. Shortly afterwards Harry appeared, riding very upright and going very slowly so as not to get mud or dust on his shiny, black boots.

He dismounted, pulled the machine onto its stand without a word to me and as I hovered nervously behind him he fitted a key into the parcels office doors, turned it and entered, switching the lights on with his right hand as he did so. I followed him in.

'Good morning, Harry.'

'Good morning, young man,' he murmured, handing me his bunch of keys. 'This one's for the station master's door and this is for the door to the platform and these two are for the doors at each end of the booking hall. Just go round and open up if you please.'

I managed the first two but let the other keys slip. Harry was slowly unbuttoning his railway-issue macintosh and looked preoccupied. I did not dare disturb his thoughts so went out onto the dark platform and fumbled in the lock of the booking hall door with every key on the bunch before I found the right one. The other door, by luck, I opened quickly and went back to the office.

Harry was now sitting on a big wooden drum marked 'Artificial Insemination Officer. Faringdon. Solidified Carbon Dioxide'. He had removed one brown legging and was in the process of removing the other. It was a complicated procedure because it was suspended by a strap fixed to the buttons to which his braces were attached. The unbuttoning and rebuttoning was being carried out by feel alone as he sat gazing thoughtfully through the office window. Once released, the legging was drawn off carefully, folded and the pair put on a shelf. Each clip was gently removed, the folded cloth smoothed, he stood up and stamped each polished ankle-length boot to make sure the creases were falling straight.

While this was going on I stood helplessly and looked around. On the platform side of the room was a tabletop running from the door to the wall that divided the office from the station master's room. A high stool was provided to enable the porter to sit at the table and a large window illuminated his work. Against the dividing wall was a rack containing ledgers, waybill forms, glue pots, labels and all the paraphernalia of an office. A stove stood in the centre of this transverse wall and on its chimney breast was a mass of dusty paper, old notices and posters. There was a 'Pooley' weighing scale and a big rack for parcels. I had not thought of railway work in the context of an office and stared at the incomprehensible jumble, looked out at the grey tracks and gloomy platform and wondered where the romance was.

Harry had a lot of what the Army called 'personal pride'. He was of medium height, slim, with well-groomed silver hair like many a railwayman, but where other men were tidy in their uniforms, Harry was sheer elegance – and elegance in railway-issue blue serge was very nearly impossible. It was obvious that his wife took as much pride in his appearance as he did himself for his jacket and trousers showed signs of frequent brushings with a stiff brush and frequent ironings with a hot iron. His shirt and collar were crisp and white, worn with a dark blue tie and now he was going to book on duty and bring this pride to the service of the railway.

He signed on duty for 7 a.m. at 6.55, I signed beneath his name and then he spoke. 'Right. Now we must change the date stamp.' I followed him and watched while he took the ancient machine apart. A pin appeared in his hand at a thought, he used it to pick out a piece of leaden type, the pin vanished into his lapel, he selected the new figure from a box of type, put the machine together, folded a piece of paper and tried the stamp – all a series of well-tried actions, moving like clockwork. 12 SEP 60. 'Good. Follow me.'

I blundered out behind him, wondering how I should read typeface when it was upside down and back to front; indeed, I felt as if I was a piece of type. The Army had a phrase for it, referring to something or other being 'spare at a wedding'. We went into the waiting room where a fire was already laid in the grate. 'The late turn man does this for you,' he said as he produced a box of matches and set the paper alight. 'Follow me.' We went out onto the platform.

'We don't really need the Tilleys; it's getting light but in a week or so we'll have to put them out so I'll just show you how they work.' He selected yet another key from his bunch, released a padlock on the door of a corrugated-iron hut with a curved roof and stepped inside. It was dark there but I could see some big, paraffin-burning lamps hanging in rows, seven on each side of the hut. Almost at once the clammy chill of the place made itself felt and I listened, covered in goosepimples, as Harry explained:

'You put meths into this dish holding the wick around the vaporising tube and light it.' He took a can of meths. 'On the darkest mornings we put only three lamps out, just around the station office, but at night there's trains on the downside too and you must put all the lamps out right round the station; there's one here for each post. Now I'll pressurise the fuel tank.' His fingers landed directly on a bicycle pump, which was invisible in the gloom, and connected it to a valve. 'You pump until this little indicator comes up a bit; it doesn't need much – there that'll do. Now, don't turn the fuel tap on too soon; give the meths time to heat the vaporising tube – just before the methylated goes out is the best time. If you try it too soon you'll get raw paraffin all over the place, smoke and fumes and you'll blacken the glass globe.'

We stood and waited while the methylated spirit burned down. I looked out of the hut at the grey, misty morning, when the sun came up it might even be pretty, shining through the mist till it was dispersed but at that moment it was miserably foggy with a touch of frost. I felt a yawn coming on, tried to hide it from Harry and wished I could get out of that dismal hut. The meths was still burning strongly.

'I was here when they tested these lamps in 1923,' Harry volunteered, 'acceptance trials I suppose you'd call them. The Company reckoned they saved £3 in a year here in paraffin so they made a bulk order with Tilleys. Look, they're called "Challow" lamps.'

'Did they worry about £3 a year?' I asked, the cold freezing manners.

'Don't forget there were thousands of stations and tens of thousands of lamps. These Tilleys give a far brighter light than the old wick lamps so they used less paraffin and fewer lamps. The old Company had to keep its shareholders happy. They had to make a profit and there was no one to bail them out if they didn't so they were careful with their housekeeping. We've still got the sieve the Company issued us to take bits of unburnt coal from the ashes before we throw them away –'

'Phew, that's a bit miserly, isn't it?'

'Oh no 'tisn't either. I can see you're not a householder. Years ago everyone sieved their ashes. You could waste a couple of pounds of coal else. You may as well throw money away. And the Company expected us to look after their property as if it was our own.'

The methylated spirit had burned low now, Harry turned the handle and the gas popped into life, hissing in the mantle, incandescent yellow. It reminded me of the gas light in my grandmother's living room but less bright. 'Now it's going, and not before, you can pump the tank up really hard', said Harry, working vigorously, 'till the indicator is sticking up well above its casing.' The light changed to a brilliant white. He took it outside and winched it onto a tall mast by the platform gate. 'We won't do any more now because it's getting light. But remember – put your lamps out at the proper time and the proper number or else. If someone falls and hurts themselves on an unlit station, the Company is responsible.'

As Harry was winding the lamp up, the first passenger came into the yard, appearing out of the mist, black and featureless at first, riding a bicycle. 'That's old Joe, Joe Tilling, coming for the stopper to Steventon. He's early turn crossing keeper at Causeway', said Harry. There was something strange about him that I could not fathom for a moment and then I realised he was cycling with one leg only, the other hanging unnaturally stiff and useless, an artificial leg. The bike had what was called a 'fixed wheel'.

'How far has he come?' I asked Harry.

'Up from Stanford, about three miles. Poor old Joe, he lost his leg in an accident at work years ago and they gave him the crossing job at Causeway.'

Joe heaved himself off his bicycle and wheeled it slowly through the gateway. He was a tall, gaunt man with a hooked nose on a long, pain-stretched face which looked worse for the mouth being slightly open. He was having difficulty in breathing and could only gasp, as he passed, 'Mornin', Harry – fog's bad.' He went a few paces along the platform and stopped, leaning over the saddle of his machine to get his breath back.

'He looks ill,' I said.

'Old Joe doesn't give up easily,' replied Harry almost proudly as he walked back to the parcels office. 'Doesn't matter what shift he's on he'll be there. They work their shifts to suit him where they can and he gets there even if he cycles the whole way. To make sure of it in weather like this he just starts earlier.'

'Who else will there be for the stopper?'

'Only Jimmy Titchener, the district lampman – Basil's father – and a couple of building labourers for Reading and they've got season tickets.'

A cheerful, wind-blown face, brown and lined, looked round the door just then, grinned and brought the rest of the body into the office. 'Hi-up, 'Arry. Raw cold this morning and you 'aven't lit the fire. I'll have to go in the waiting room with the nobs.'

'Who's in there then, Jimmy?'

'Oh, only a couple of blokes. You've got a mate then; blind leading the blind is it?'

'Not quite,' said Harry, just a tiny bit stiffly. 'This is our learner.'

'Oh-ah. Our Basil has mentioned you, nice to meet you, you're going to be a signalman, I hear.' I felt embarrassed at that – it sounded as if I was going about boasting about an imminent promotion. Just at that moment in my career it seemed the height of presumption to even think about being a signalman.

'Er, I think I'll have to get the hang of this job first,' I mumbled.

Just then Bill in the signal box rang the 3-1 code on the station telephone circuit and we moved outside to wait for the train. Jimmy Titchener was small of stature, dressed in the same uniform as Harry but the cloth was coarse, stained and weatherbeaten. Beneath his waistcoat he wore a scuffed flannel shirt, open at the neck in all weathers, and sticking out from under his shapeless, baggy trouser legs were a pair of hob-nailed boots, their toes turned up from a great deal of walking. He had at his feet a two-gallon can of paraffin with a long, thin, curving spout and six signal lamps on a wooden carrying bar.

I had seen him at work and seen his slight figure, far away along the track, trudging home at the end of a day's work and I knew that he was no small man but a tough and determined one. His district began at Steventon and extended to Marston Crossing West's Up distant signal nineteen miles to the west and as his signal lamps held seven days' supply of fuel he had to cover the area in a strict seven-day rota. If he did not there would be a lot of signals without lights and many delays to trains as a result so that no matter what the weather he had to keep up with his timetable. In summer sun or winter rain, on the appointed day, the signalman would expect to see Jimmy trudging over the ballast with his can in one hand and his bar of fresh lamps in the other.

As a schoolboy I had watched him go from signal post to ground disc, scrambling up twenty- or thirty-foot-high ladders, often in winds that swayed their posts alarmingly, carrying new lamps for old. Once on the lamp platform he replaced the time-expired lamp and lit the fresh one. Expertise was required to do this in a light breeze – it seemed impossible in a gale but he held the matchstick as far from the head as possible, the matchbox close over the hole in the top of the lamp case. Then he struck downwards, straight and accurate onto the wick while the phosphorus was still flaring. He adjusted the lamp wick to the size of his smallest finger nail and the lamp was set fair for another seven days. Occasionally, a particularly violent storm might blow a lamp out but nothing that was in Jimmy's power to do was left undone in ensuring that trains on the Didcot–Swindon line ran under bright, clear signals.

The train ran into the station with only two coaches, the engine stopping by the parcels office door, infinitely more desirable than the stuff of a porter's life but I felt bound by Harry and resisted the temptation to go up and look at it. The two railwaymen got in with the guard, he and Harry helping Joe up. I was motioned to see to the labourers; I closed their door behind them and raised my arm in the approved manner, the guard blew his whistle and away went the train. Having raised my arm, having actually done something, I felt a little more cheerful.

The Up stopper withdrew to reveal the Down parcels train waiting at the far platform.

'That's the 5.5 Padd,' said Harry, tossing a bundle of notices onto the office table. We went over the footbridge and found the train guard waiting in front of an open van door. 'Bring that four-wheel barrow,' commanded Harry.

'Got a helper, mate? I reckon you'll need one for this lot.' We had piled two barrows with parcels and boxes before the train left.

'Now then,' said Harry, 'these must go in the lock-up in the down-side waiting room until the lorry comes to collect them – except for any marked for collection here, they must come over to our office. You'll have to enter details of consignor, consignee and ledger label number on a delivery sheet and then again in the parcels inwards book. I'll go and get the sheets and

I'll give you a hand.' My heart sank as I looked at the monotonous piles in the damp, grey light ...

While we were drudging away, turning over the boxes to find the side with the information, the Fly arrived and Harry went off to see the guard. A goods train went clattering down the Main line, past the local goods before he returned. 'I've told the guard that there is nothing to pick up so he may as well put the coal off when he comes back from Uffington, that'll save crossing over now. That was the Hinksey just gone down the Main, so the Fly'll go now. You'll have to ask the guard to help himself in the yard at this time of day – if there is anything for downhill, tell him where it is and let him fetch it without your assistance. I must go now to be in the booking office in case anyone comes for the 8.5 – you have to keep everything in mind – don't get bogged down in this job and forget about a train that's due and let someone go without a ticket.' The Fly started up with a savage tug of coupling links as he walked away. I had not even seen who the driver was. I finished at eight o'clock and went to the office with the sheets; there were about fifty entries.

'Enter them up now,' said Harry. 'Here's some tea. I've sold three tickets for Paddington while you were over there so just remember what I told you. You'll have to drop the parcels job and get back here and if you haven't got it all entered when old Fred turns up with his lorry, he'll have to wait for you.'

The 8.5 Swindon to Paddington 'semi-fast' left just as the parcels lorry arrived on the down-side and I hurried over with Harry to load it. Some girls were arriving too; instead of thinking whether they were pretty or not, I just thought 'Oh! There must be another train!' Harry left after five minutes to 'watch the shop' leaving me with the caustic old lorry driver. I could not imagine me telling him to 'wait while I finish my entries'. Nothing I did was right for him and he soon reduced me to a state of confused immobility. 'Er ... I think I'll go and meet the Down train.' He did not reply, so I slunk away. Waiting in the shelter were three girls, one of about twelve but the others were sixteen or seventeen, one with red hair, the other with auburn. 'Morning.' I was not even sure myself whether this was an announcement or a greeting. They smiled awkwardly and the train arrived to save us all. Harry appeared in time to give 'Right' to the guard, the guard gave 'Right Away' to the driver and the train left in a smother of steam.

'The lorry is on the up-side now. Fred's waiting for you to make up your ledger; you'd better hurry over there,' said Harry, and I went over the footbridge yet again. While I was writing, eating a sandwich at the same time, Mr Halford arrived with some sarcasm about people who have nothing to do all day but sit around eating. He was quickly followed by Basil, who never left his breakfast table in the station terrace until he had seen his boss walk past.

During the Great Western Railway's centenary dinner in 1935 the Prince of Wales had called the Company 'The Royal Road' for its long association with Windsor and the Royal Family, and since that time supervisory staff had worn buttons bearing the Company's initials surmounted by the imperial crown. Mr Halford still wore his 'Royal' buttons twelve years after nationalisation; he knew why they bore the crown and was determined to keep up the Great Western tradition of style and service. Having entered his office he took out his *very smart hat*, put it on and went out to patrol the car park, ready to welcome the *very smart people*, who were about to arrive for the 8.58 'to Town'. I do not think they ever went 'to London' in those days though occasionally they mentioned '*Peddington*'. The ritual of the 'Cheltenham' was about to begin.

Almost in convoy the cars arrived – a Rolls-Royce perhaps, some Rovers, a Morris Thousand station wagon and maybe Major Sneyd's misfiring V8 Pilot – crunching over the gravel, pulling up in a queue to discharge their passengers. Mr Halford took his dictum 'the passengers are our bread and butter' seriously and welcomed each one by name when he knew it, and certainly by a cheerful 'Good morning'. 'Good morning, Sir John', 'Good morning, my lord' popped off here and there among the lesser 'Good morning, ma'am' or 'sir'. They were ushered into the waiting room by Harry; I heard cries of 'Oh! What a lovely fire', though very special guests were entertained in Mr Halford's own office. The people seemed to know each other very well, good nature abounded and conversation thrived. Their train was the 7.5 a.m. Cheltenham to Paddington express, hauled by a Gloucester-based 'Castle'. It arrived at the platform whereupon Mr Halford, Basil and Harry performed a flurry of door opening, ushering and door slamming. I noticed, too, that Harry touched his cap each time he opened the door and seemed to touch the hands of some of the passengers as if he was saying goodbye to them. I was standing in the office doorway and could not see properly but it was an odd gesture.

Having seen everyone into the train Harry then walked the length of the coaches, checking that all doors were secure, till he got to the engine; then, he swung round and raised his right arm to signal that all was in order. Mr Halford then wheeled smartly about and raised *his* right arm to the guard – who was not more than six feet away – to signify that the train was in order. The guard blew his whistle with enthusiasm and waved his green flag with a fine flourish. At that, Mr Halford executed his military about-turn and signalled to Harry, who whirled about and signalled to the fireman – who had already seen the guard's flag – that it was all right to start. 'Right Away!' cried the fireman to his mate, who replied with a toot on the whistle, and in a climax of ritual, the big 'Castle' barked away from the platform, 420 tons in tow, as majestically as you could wish.

Having observed all the correct forms and kept the Company spirit alive for another day, Mr Halford changed his very smart hat for an ordinary hat and went to the signal box for a cup of coffee with Bill Mattingley.

CHAPTER SIX

Harry Remembers

Harry drank his tea with his cap on standing up. Basil slipped away quietly to the booking office taking his tea with him. I wanted to sit down but the only seat was the high stool, too conspicuous, so I compromised by leaning against the table.

'Well, young man, do you think you'll like it here?'

'I suppose I shall when I get the hang of what we're doing.'

'You mustn't be confused yet; you haven't started. Basil has got to show you the booking side of things because you'll be in charge of the station every evening after 4.30. Basil will confuse you if you let him.'

'Thanks very much,' came floating out of the other room. Harry's upper lip quivered as he had a little smile to himself. 'Drink up quick, mind. We want to be down the yard to see what's on before the Fly comes. They're always back from Uffington quick on a Monday and we must see what wants knocking out of the yard.'

There was the noise of a lorry which I took to be going over the road bridge. 'Hi-up! There's a lorry in the yard. We're early today.' He took a final mouthful of tea and went out with me following like Albert Stanley's collie dog. I wanted to know why the train was called the Fly but it seemed a frivolous question to ask Harry so I shelved the matter by thinking 'It's because it dodges about from place to place.' I realised that he was telling me something. 'All these cars pay a fee to park here. One and sixpence a day or half a crown in either of the lock-ups.' There were three garages.

'What's wrong with the third shed?'

'Mr Halford keeps *his* car in it.'

In front of us, at the far side of a wide gravel yard with a derelict, rubber-tyred crane and what appeared to be a grounded wagon body, was a lorry-load of straw bales standing in the archway of the big old goods shed. We passed the crane and skirted the wagon that was, in fact, on rails below yard-level, an appendix from the through siding, and reached the lorry. It was Oakley's of Alvescot.

'Good morning, driver,' said Harry.

'Whatcher mate.' I winced at the irreverence. 'Straw for yer jersey. Where d'ye want it?'

'You can put it in the wagon in Goosey Dock,' replied Harry, emphasising 'you' and pointing to the appendix track.

The man looked as if he was going to protest. Maybe he wanted us to help him load but after a second glance at Harry, whose upper lip was now in the 'determined' position while the rest of him looked like a policeman, he slammed his cab door and took it out on the clutch as he backed up to the wagon. 'Look out for lorry drivers,' said Harry, as we watched the lorry go backwards in a series of leaps and bounds, 'they'll have you doing their work and you'll be neglecting your own.'

A whitewashed brick hut with piles of coal behind it, a weighbridge in front and a board on its roof saying JOHN TOOMER & SONS LTD was close by, and out of it now came a stout, red-faced man, smiling broadly. 'Morning, Harry. Not a bad day now. Is the Fly about? We've got some coal on order.'

'There's two on there for you Frank. It ought to be here any time now.'

'Thanks, I'll go and get the men and the lorry ready. Got a mate, I see?' He turned to me and beamed rosily again.

'Yes, he'll be in charge here soon. Adrian, this is Frank Shepherd, Toomer's agent.'

'Pleased to meet you, Mr Shepherd,' I said, stupidly trying to puzzle out why it said 'Toomer' over his office, embarrassed by Harry's expression of confidence in me.

'Where are you from? I don't think I've seen you before.'

'I've just arrived from the Army. You deliver to my parents, next to the Crown in Childrey.'

'Ah! I know, very nice people.' His cheeks were red as rear lamps. 'I'll see you again then.'

He turned back to his office. Harry and I walked through Brunel's gothic arch into the cavernous goods shed. We climbed up some steps onto an ancient timber platform about fifteen feet wide running the length of the building, perhaps fifty yards, beside a double line of rails, which I thought was an unusual feature in a country goods shed. Harry went into the goods shed office and left me admiring the huge timbers spanning the walls from which great joists rose lesser beams, fanlike, to support the purlins and rafters. Once they had all been painted white, and though the paint was greyed and flaking, they were still white enough to be seen even in the gloom of the roof's ridge, perhaps fifty feet above my head. The proportions were ecclesiastical and I found it difficult to imagine the flood of traffic through the place which must once have existed to warrant such a building.

Harry emerged with a shunting pole in his hand and saw me gazing round. 'It's a fine building. Brunel didn't stint the timber. They must be whole, seasoned oaks up there,' he said, looking up with me.

'Yes, it's a lovely place, but why is it so big? Whatever sort of traffic did they have out here in the Vale?'

'Well, when it was built, Challow was called "Faringdon Road" and was the station for Wantage *and* Faringdon from 1840 to 1845, and until 1864 it was the station for Faringdon – till they built the branch from Uffington.'

'Which is when the name was changed to Challow, I suppose?'

'Yes, so you see there must have been very heavy traffic here because anything that moved in those days went by rail.' We walked down the platform, our footsteps hollow and echoing in the vast old barn.

'There's the old stable – I used to have a lovely horse in there, called her Duchess. That was early days for me, about 1924. She was the shunting horse and could walk between the rails – lots of 'em couldn't – and even reverse with a wagon. She used to stop work when a train went by and watch it with her ears pricked up, wonderful horse, but she was killed by an engine in the end. Well, the vet shot her but it was because an engine hit her.'

'That must have been horrible for you. But tell me, was there so much work here that you needed a horse to be shunting trucks around all the time? Why was it so busy?'

'Bless my soul! Work? Ha! Ha! T'wasn't always like it is now, you know. There was three milk-empty trains and two milk-loaded trains and two Flys, besides the stoppers – and that was just on Sunday,' he rose to a triumphant crescendo as he produced his surprise.

We were strolling along a line of wagons then, covered vans and coal trucks, loaded and empty. 'See that empty siding between this one and the Up Relief line? That would have been full of traffic like this right up to the end of the last war. We had a staff of five porters here then, three or four of us through the day and one or two all night. There was Harry Crooks, I remember. He went as lampman to Bath and was killed on the line soon after. Then there was Tom Gillman and Reg Chester ... But look here,' he brought the subject back abruptly to work, 'we must book the wagons in and out, and any that spend more than three days in the siding must pay a fine – demurrage – it always makes a row but we have to do it.'

The Fly arrived at that moment and we waited for the guard to come up. He walked along in an odd way; something was wrong but I couldn't think what.

He was barrel-shaped, scruffy and cheerful looking with two days' stubble on his chin.

"'Lo 'Arry, yuh long streak o' misery! We've got *four* o' coal for yuh now, picked up two off the Faringdon to go with what we already 'ad and there's four empty opens for yuh. Can't say we don't look after yuh, eh? Ha! Ha!'

Harry seemed to draw back from this geniality and stood several feet away very upright with his pole at what I could call the 'Carry' in contrast to the guard who appeared to be using his as a crutch. 'Very good,' clipped out Harry. 'I have six empty tubs and two box vans to knock out and I'll have the four opens inside the goods shed. That's all.' The way he delivered the last two words made me wonder if he was dismissing the guard or if he meant that that was the extent of the shunting required.

The engine was a pannier tank; its driver and fireman I did not know, and they drove forward on the guard's handsignal with part of the train, the last wagons of the string being the 'Challows'. Once clear of the hand points, the train set back into the siding and was coupled to the row of wagons by Harry using his pole dextrously to flick the heavy links over the draw-hook. It looked easy enough, and I looked forward to trying my hand at what seemed to me more like railway work than copying numbers off sticky labels.

The whole 'raft' was then drawn out over the points and the job of sorting the empties from the loadeds began, banging one empty 'onto the van', the next batch of loadeds into the siding whence they came: Harry did the uncoupling and gave stop/go signs to the driver while the guard leant on the hand point lever and tugged it – rather inexpertly I thought and wished I could do it; once he nearly fell over – to change the route as required: 'van-side' or 'siding'. At last the new arrivals were pushed onto the siding and as the pannier tank went back onto its train, Harry was taking wagon numbers.

'That guard was odd,' I ventured.

'Odd? He was tipsy!' snorted Harry. 'Some of these guards go into the Junction at Uffington and have a pint but he'd been on the hard stuff.'

'Does it happen very often?'

'Not like that. Some of the guards on the Fly have a pint out of hours but I've never seen him like that before. When I was a young lad I knew two or three old guards and porters that used to get quite tipsy on duty but everyone always covered for them. It's unusual nowadays.' He changed the subject.

'I have the stour of the yard now, what's here and what's gone away. All the details must be phoned through to Swindon and that's the time you ask for empty wagons. Nelson's haven't been in for a few days with one of their fancy trailers so we must expect them soon. We'll order a flat truck for them and a couple more opens – they'll come up on Wednesday. Always bear your customers in mind and try to have a wagon there when they want it but don't waste a wagon by just hoarding it.'

I felt depressed at this because I didn't even know who our customers were. Harry supplied the answer. 'There's few enough of them. Nelson over at Cross Bargains farm makes a special trailer for hay bales and has to have a flat truck, maybe three a week. W & G's of East Challow make farm equipment in wood, like pig-houses and hay-racks; they usually have opens for loading – oh, and they also bring down thousands of telephone pole crossbars, filthy things, all freshly creosoted. Then there's this seasonal hay and straw and next January and February there'll be sugar beet – we use coal tub empties for that. And that's it. You'll be kept busy by it but it's only just enough work for one man. Now let's show you how to use a shunting pole.'

The pole was an ash stick about 6 feet long, 1 ½ inches thick, shod at one end with a steel ferrule ending in a curly hook like a pig's tail.

'Now,' said Harry, 'first off, I'll show you how to pin down a hand-brake. The pole's not supposed to be used for this but it always has been. You must lever the hand-brake handle down hard with the pole and slip the pin in over the top to hold it. Then, when you want to let the brake off, you ease the handle off the pin with the shunting pole, take out the pin and there you are. Always put the handle up onto its rest, or the brake-block will be juddering on the wheel and driving the guard mad.

'To uncouple, just put the pole over the buffer stock, rest the ferrule against the draw-hook underneath the coupling and lever it off – so. To couple up pick the link up in the ferrule hook and swing the pole upwards and forwards – so twisting the wrists to empty the link out of the hook, over the draw-bar hook. You try it now.'

I picked up a shunting pole for the first time and found it thick and clumsy in my hands. The three-link coupling chain was stiff. 'Get it swinging,' advised Harry. I swung it back and forth, worked up momentum and threw it over the draw-hook. Somehow this made such a tangle that Harry had to free the three components by hand. Then I began to get the idea.

'Good,' said Harry, 'now we must get along. I want these four opens down in the shed. We'll push three away together. Once they get moving they'll roll. Then you go down to the shed, I'll start the last one off and you can practise coupling a moving wagon to a train.' Harry put his shunting pole between a wagon's wheel and the rail and levered upwards while I heaved against a buffer. The short raft of wagons began to move. 'Shunting poles aren't meant for this sort of thing, mind,' warned Harry breathlessly, 'there's a pinch bar down in the goods shed specially for the job but it's almost too heavy to carry.' When the trucks were well under way on the down grade, he stopped levering and left me to walk them into the shed, calling after me. 'Don't be in a hurry to swing your pole – move fast when the buffers clash.'

As the wagons drew alongside the goods shed platform, I forced down a hand-brake lever with my shunting pole, stopped the raft, put the coupling link into the ferrule hook and watched Harry start the last wagon. It rumbled towards me, seven and a half tons at five miles an hour. I tried to judge its closing speed as it bore down on me, apparently gaining in size and speed with every second that passed. Now! I swung my pole upwards in a perfectly timed movement; it passed between the buffers just as they were about to crash; they closed on it like vicious jaws and wrenched it painfully from my tightly clenched fists.

My hands felt paralysed and I walked up and down for a while running them on the seat of my trousers, regaining enough feeling in them to pick the pole up off the floor as Harry walked up.

'Hurt yourself?'

'No, startled,' I said with a grin.

His upper lip curled a bit at that. 'Come on, you'll soon find the knack. We must go to the station.' We walked along the track, past the wagon that Oakley's had loaded with straw bales.

'It looks a bit top-heavy, Harry.' I was amazed. I had called him Harry! Without thinking about it. The affair with the pole seemed to have broken down some reserve between us.

'Ah! That would be a job for my Duchess. She could have pulled that lot up to the load gauge to see if it was within the limits for passing under bridges.'

'So that's what those steel arches are for in sidings everywhere.'

'That's right – and talking of puzzles, have you found out what train carried twenty rear lamps?'

'You remember that? It must be five years since you asked me that. No I haven't asked anyone who hasn't been puzzled by it. What train was it?'

'Oho! I'm not telling you. You ought to know.' He seemed really pleased now and I relaxed. I felt that perhaps I was going to enjoy the job after all.

After filling in a big form to record wagon movements, Harry phoned Control to inform them and to order the extra wagons. While he was doing this, I asked Mr Halford if he knew about the train with twenty rear lamps but he only said, 'If it was anyone other than Harry, I'd say you were having your leg pulled.' The 10.30 stopper came and went and having attended to it we went back to the yard. 'We must sheet and rope that straw,' said Harry.

We walked at a pace that I was coming to recognise belonged to men long in railway service – a long striding, easy pace as if we were in a procession – passed the wagon of straw and entered the goods shed. Here Harry removed his jacket, put on a brown canvas apron that covered him from chest to ankles and rolled up his sleeves. In the corner were some folded tarpaulins. 'Pick up one of these sheets', he said, swinging one neatly turned bundle onto his shoulder, 'and bring it to the wagon.' I tried to pick it up and nearly overbalanced – they weighed about 56 pounds and were very clumsy.

Harry stood on the yard level and threw his 56 pounds seven feet to the top of the load, climbed up, unfolded the sheet to cover half the load and asked me to throw my sheet up to him. This was the moment of truth! After several attempts, he managed to catch the bundle, unfolded it and covered the other half of the load. Together we tied the sheets onto the cleats provided around the truck using string like heavily creosoted baler twine; then, with half-inch ropes we made the load quite secure. We stood back to admire our handiwork: a neatly folded black parcel on wheels.

'That's the way to do it, Adrian,' called a voice from the signal box opposite. I looked round to see Ken Rowlands leaning from the window.

'Hello, Ken.'

'Lovely job, Harry,' enthused Ken.

'Hello, Ken,' said Harry non-committally and then to me, 'Now this wagon'll be going "downhill" – to Weymouth, for Jersey – so I've laid the west end sheet overlapping the trailing east end sheet. If I hadn't, the slip-stream would get under the edge and soon it'd be billowing out like a sail even if it didn't blow off altogether.' I registered that little bit of expertise with great appreciation.

The wagon had then to be labelled and waybills made out before we retired to the station for tea and to wait for the Down stopper. As we walked past the sheeted wagon, I said to Harry, 'Goosey Dock is a funny name for a siding. Do you know how it got the name?'

'Well, it was built to take three coal wagons. As I've told you, the coal used to be drawn up in two ranks and they had to put a plank across from the outer to the inner wagon and bring it across the gap and through the other wagon to the horse and cart. So when they built the new station, they made the dock for the benefit of Toomer's and Langford's agents and as they both lived in Goosey … there you are. Good lord, back around 1930 they used to bring coal around the station cottages in the wheelbarrow for sale at 1s 10d a hundredweight. You think of that.'

At the station he asked me if I could read a timetable and when I said I could he set me problems: a morning train to Dolgelly, an afternoon train to Margate. In 1960 a passenger could have gone to both those places from Challow in a day or half a day. When it was clear I knew what to do, he shut the book and said, 'Train times here haven't altered much in thirty-five years, there's fewer trains but them that are left are running at about the same times they did in 1924. The greatest change is having the 8.58 fast to London. Since before the war, up till recently, that used to be about 9.15.'

'What were the other trains, Harry? You've told me about Sundays but what about week-days.'

'Ha! Ha! I think I shall surprise you. I think I'm right in saying that we had twenty-five trains in all, fourteen stoppers, the rest milk and goods – now we've got fourteen of all kinds, ten of them passengers.'

Mr Halford came out of his office and joined us. 'What were the other trains, Harry?'

'There were the empty and loaded milks, morning and evening. One empty, the Ladbroke Grove, got here at four in the morning. We had *five* Flys including one that got here at about 3.30 in the afternoon and left from here at 6. They called it the "Challow Goods".'

Mr Halford and I whistled and Harry was gratified by our astonishment and saw the question coming. 'We used to have a cattle and farm machinery market in the station yard every Monday; the sidings were packed with cattle trucks and empty opens for that. Then we had the Corn Store where all the local farmers came to collect their stocks of animal feeding stuff. There was the regular traffic in machinery from Nalder's at East Challow and from other works at Stanford and even Faringdon sometimes.' He broke off there as Ken 'rang the stopper in'.

We saw two passengers onto the 11.30 to Swindon and took the ticket from a man who got off. The train left, behind its ex-works engine, within a minute of arriving and we walked back across the footbridge. 'What else did you do here, Harry?'

'Well, keeping to regular traffic, we had the Station Truck twice a day. That used to come down from Paddington every morning with chocolates, cigarettes and butter and went back each night on a Main line goods that stopped specially for it. Ha! You'll laugh when I tell you – Ody, the horse and cow slaughterer, used to send up the day's supply of corpses to Paddington in it.'

I think I must have worn him out with questions, making him talk more than he usually did, because when we got into the office he gave me a job.

'You can whitewash the edge of the platform. I'll show you where the stuff is.' He took me to the storeroom and in minutes I felt as if I was back in the Army; with a bucket of whitewash and an L-shaped brush I started to paint the edge of the 720-foot-long platform.

After twenty minutes I was rescued by the arrival of a lorry.

Harry came out, 'Put all that away and come to the goods shed, W & G's are here.' When I got to the shed Harry and the lorry driver were manhandling what looked like a miniature Nissen hut made of plywood from the lorry to the platform.

The lorry man was slim and small, about forty with a bald, egg-shaped head, a very wrinkled forehead and a ring of ragged, silver hair which hung round his neck as if it had slipped off the shiny, smooth cranium. 'Here's your mate come, Harry,' said he. 'Hey come on, kid, give us a hand here!'

The combined efforts of the three of us soon cleared the lorry, papers were handed over and the egghead driver climbed in and drove away. 'You'll have to learn how to shift these things on your own. They weigh about three hundredweight so you have to lever them across the floor with a pinch bar to get them under the crane – as there's two of us we can just slide them. Now get a piece of rope, tie it exactly round the middle of the pig-house and then bring the hook of the crane down to engage it.'

The travelling crane was an arrangement of chains and a lifting hook working through a box of gears suspended from a steel girder spanning the width of the shed. To lower the hook I pulled a cord and drew down the hook, and when I had slipped it under, the rope began to pull on the chain to wind the gears round; it was rather like winding up a very low-geared grandfather clock. When the pig-house was raised sufficiently to pass over the side of the truck, we pushed against the house and the box of gears rolled along the steel joist; when the pig-house was positioned over the wagon, I pulled the cord and down came the hook, settling the plywood pig-house into the wagon. Two could be fitted into each truck and the loaded vehicle was then pushed out of the shed, down the grade to bring the next truck under the crane.

There was the usual paperwork and labelling and as Harry was doing this, the 3-1 bell sounded for the Up stopper. 'Now there's a train that has run in its times since 1924 at least,' said Harry. 'Always around 12.25 here and every Monday for years it's had the stores van on the end. Yes – I know,' he smiled, 'what's the stores van? It brings all the clean washing round and takes away the dirty stuff and it also doles out soap, electric light bulbs and floor polish. There are several of them. They work from Swindon all over the place, every day of the week. You can order shunting poles – anything – from the General

Stores down by the engine shed and next Monday up it comes in the stores van.'

The train arrived and was even more remarkable than Harry had described. It was hauled by an ex-works 'King' in gleaming, dark-green paint set off with plenty of brass and copper and by black bands and orange lines around the boiler and her three coaches were ex-Great Western stock; the first two were 1946 vintage but the stores van I recognised from a photograph as having once been part of Queen Victoria's Royal train of 1897 – a very handsome coach, panelled and carrying a clerestory roof. Harry exchanged the washing while I sat on the platform bench and admired the train and its engine, revelling in the comfortable fact that something like this train, at this time of day, had arrived at Challow each Monday morning for at least the last thirty-five years.

I thought I might be allowed to take the clean dusters to the signal box after the train had gone but I was handed a hoe and a rake and told to get busy on the weeds in the wide gravel strip between the fence and the platform paving. Harry went to the box.

It was an easy, pleasant job indeed, I began to think how nice it would be to have all the weeds cleared and the gravel smoothed straight. I looked at my recent effort at whitewashing – yes, that, too, looked smart and was asking to be completed. The Up platform was important because the nobs spent a fair length of time on it before catching their train whereas the Down platform they took little notice of as they hurried away to their cars at the end of the day. First things first. I would get the Up platform looking really smart; I began to feel proprietorial about Challow. I would make it a flower garden.

Harry let me off, hungry, at one o'clock. All the way home I was excited about the idea I'd had and the new feeling that was stealing over me concerning the station. I got indoors to find my mother waiting with a huge roast dinner; there would be no danger of my refusing it. I was ravenous.

'I've kept it hot but kept the gravy separate so it wouldn't dry up,' she said proudly.

'Thanks very much, Mum. I'll eat it all.'

'Well, how did you get on?' she stood over me eagerly, holding a saucepan.

'It was like the weather – it got better through the morning. Half the time I spent hoeing.'

'Hoeing?!' she said incredulously.

'Yes, it was really good. Are there any flower plants or seeds that I could put in now that would bloom this year?'

'Yes, we've got plenty in the greenhouse, coming on, but what sort of railway work did you do with Mr Strong?'

I told her but my mind was full of flowers.

CHAPTER SEVEN

Goosey and Gardening

There was no Fly to shunt and fewer parcels to book in next day, so that, after the 8.15 stopper Down, Harry and I were in the parcels office with nothing in particular to do for half an hour, so I took the opportunity to ask Harry where the station's garden had been before the place was rebuilt.

'Up against the wall of the road bridge on this side. It was a rockery. We were all keen gardeners then and we made a good job of it – even if I say so myself. Now you come to mention it, I think there's a photograph of it in the station master's office. I'll go and find it.'

He returned with a postcard print showing the Up platform ending against the west wall of the road bridge. Close to the wall, jutting up from the paving, was a timber 'bracket' signal carrying an arm for 'up the Main' and a lesser arm on a left-hand bracket for 'up the loop'; immediately behind the signal the red-brick wall was painted white to provide drivers with better 'sighting' of the red arms. A bank of earth rose from the platform up the side of the bridge and on this was the station's garden. Annual flowers and herbaceous borders filled and surrounded a mnemonic of white-painted stones which extended from the top to the bottom of the bank, including, cleverly, the handsome signal in a display.

> Cornwall
> Has
> Attractive
> Landscapes
> Looe &
> Other
> Watering places
>
> Go Western Route

It was very well done – like something you might see in a winter garden at a seaside resort – I thought I could see Harry's precise care in every stone.

'It's marvellous, you must have taken a long time to put it together – it looks as if you found time to keep it tidy even when you had all those trains to see to.'

'It was about twenty feet from top to bottom. There wasn't anything like it for miles that I knew of. It was here when I came but we all kept it up. You only had to put a few minutes in after you'd booked off. Once or twice I came up for an hour on a Sunday afternoon, that's all.'

'You must like gardening. Do you do much at home?' Harry gave a short laugh and smiled momentarily. 'Ah! A bit. If you're passing through Stanford you could give me a call. You know where I live.' I said I did not know.

'Cottage on the bend – on the left after the Horse & Jockey. You can't miss it.'

I was quite keen on gardens too. Tidy, well-laid-out gardens arranged and tended by someone else were my favourite kinds though in the case of Challow I was keen to make a small garden – so I took him up on the offer. If his home garden was anything like the old station garden, it would be worth seeing.

'But what happened to the station garden here? There's no trace of it now.'

'It was dug up when the station was rebuilt before the war,' he said quietly, the pain he had felt then still in his voice and the way he emphasised 'dug'.

'Dug up?!'

'Well, they had to extend the platforms beyond the brick arch and put two tracks in on the down-side. So they took the old bridge away and put up the steel one out there. Then they dug foundations for this station – you've never seen such a mess. The old station was about fifty yards nearer the goods shed than this one.'

'But why didn't you make another garden?'

'I don't know really; we just didn't. That rockery had been put there by the old chaps when things were more settled. The old station was all wood, you know, just like Steventon now. I wouldn't be surprised if someone told me it was the original station from Brunel's time. It was comfortable, like an old armchair. Box was too – small, homely, without a lot of windows. There was an open fire in the back wall, raised off the floor with a side-oven so they could cook their meals when they were on twelve-hour shifts. The new signal box was raw concrete, you could've put the old box in that one's locking room, the new station was red brick. Looking back on it, it could've done with a garden to hide the rough edges but then it didn't seem much of a place for flowers.'

'What about putting a garden in now?' Harry looked sceptical. 'It could go along under the windows. There's a strip of gravel at the moment, about eighteen inches wide. That must have been designed to take a row of flowers ...'

Harry got down quickly from the high stool and went onto the platform saying, 'You're right, it never occurred to me.' I joined him outside and he continued, 'Dig the gravel out, go down a foot, fill it with top soil and you could have a lovely display – pack it with bulbs, annuals – wallflowers at the back, forget-me-nots at the front, we'd have a show from spring to autumn. I'll bring some plants from home.'

'My parents are going to bring some too,' I said.

'Well, that's good,' enthused Harry, 'the flowers'll be all round the platform seats – and you can do it all – it'll be *your* garden.' He felt he was being very generous, I think, and I wondered what was happening to me to make me happy at the prospect of gardening.

The passengers for the Cheltenham were arriving by then so we broke off to join in the ritual. After the train had gone Harry told Mr Halford what I proposed, received his blessing and then sat in the office planning what to plant for the best and longest show next year. We were interrupted by a knock on the door which then opened to admit a tall, stout, red-faced, hearty man.

'Morning, Harry!' he said in that curiously enthusiastic military voice I knew so well, and then, seeing me, 'Hello! Hearing about the old times, eh?'

'Not exactly, Mr Nelson,' said Harry. 'This is Adrian, our learner.'

'Oh! Well done!' cried Mr Nelson, advancing on me, beaming, his hand outstretched. We shook hands. 'I'm Tom Nelson, pleased to meet you!'

'I'm afraid we haven't got a wagon for your trailer, Mr Nelson – I suppose you've brought one?' said Harry, in a 'let's get to the point' sort of voice. 'I've got one on order.'

'Oh blast! That means it'll arrive on Wednesday and the trailer won't go out till Friday. Damn shame – not the way the old Great Western would have done things, eh?!' He spoke in a tone of enthusiastic resignation – rumbling cheerfully – not at Harry but at 'the Railway'. Harry seemed to understand this. 'Yes, we used to fight the roads once, but that was a long time ago. Where's the trailer going?'

'Oh! Somewhere in Shropshire. If it was closer I'd take it there meself. I've had them on the phone. Their old trailer has had it so they've treated themselves to one of mine but they need it *now*.'

'Well then, there's no worry. The Up Fly'll bring the "Flat" tomorrow and they can wait while we load it, then it'll be taken to Didcot for Oxford and the north. I'll get on the phone to Didcot yard and make sure they send it on smartly.'

'Well done, Harry! That sounds first class. Do come round for a drink one day, won't you?' Mr Nelson turned to me, 'I've asked him often enough but he never comes. Well, good luck, I'll go up and see Ken in the box and then go home!' He crashed the platform side-door open and shut and thundered off along the platform.

'Who was that?' I asked in amazement as the dust stirred up by his departure settled. 'He sounded like every old Colonel I've ever met all rolled into one.'

'That was Commander Tom Nelson – retired Navy man. They say he had a destroyer during the war. He's got a farm out Kingstone Lisle way and makes these trailers. He's mad on the old Company. You'd like to talk to him.'

'My God! I can just imagine him on the bridge of a destroyer doing thirty knots through an Atlantic storm and asking them to go faster. What a bloke!'

Harry grinned a moment. 'Yes, he does strike you a bit like that when you first meet him. He's a very decent sort. Let's go and take his trailer off the car.'

We walked down to Goosey Dock where a very fine 1947 Jaguar was standing.

'My goodness, Harry, what a lovely car!'

'Yes, he's an expert on them, got quite a collection so they say.'

'Where's the trailer? I can't see it.'

'Aha! You will when you get round behind the car.' Attached to the back of the car was the most unusual – and sensible – trailer I had seen. It was 20 feet long and 3 inches off the ground, you could easily toss bales onto it 'ten high'.

'It's his own idea,' said Harry. 'He's got the patent for it. Come on, let's uncouple it and stand it ready by the Dock. Then we'll go up the box, get the details off Nelson and do the wagon labels and as much paperwork as we can – everything but the wagon number in fact.'

We went over to the signal box. Mr Nelson was sitting in the armchair drinking tea. 'Have a cup?' Ken asked Harry and me, not really waiting for an answer but pouring it out. A block bell rang and I looked at Ken. 'Go on then,' he said, throwing me the duster.

'Aha! Keen man,' chuckled Mr Nelson. 'Is everyone that works on the railway an enthusiast?'

'I think railway work is pleasant – you come along and enjoy your shift, your own boss, out in the country. Though I can't say I like night shift.' That was Ken.

'It depends what you're doing. I had a job – I still have it but I've got my motorbike now – I used to leave home at midnight and cycle ten miles to Steventon, get there just before two and open the station to let GPO men take mail bags off the Up Postal. Five minutes, they'd have gone, I'd lock the shop up and come home. But that was the job, you did it and never thought if it was hard. Only now I've got my popper do I think back at all the heavy cycling I did.' That was Harry.

'But you never worried, did you?' said I. 'Or you wouldn't have cycled here on a Sunday to see to the garden.'

'Of course not. When things are easier you look back and wonder how you managed before. We took the rough with the smooth and were just as happy then as now.'

'Happier probably,' I said, 'because you had your old station with a lovely garden.'

'You used to come up here in your spare time to look after the station's garden, Harry?' asked Mr Nelson. Bells rang, I answered them and pulled off down the Main. Harry had not spoken, so I said, 'I don't think railwaymen were "enthusiasts" in the sense you mean. The atmosphere of the railway must have been like the spirit in the Army – the CO set the pace and each man's keenness grew into a competition to be as smart or smarter than the next man, each platoon tried to be better at weapon training or whatever than the next lot.'

'It was called "morale",' broke in Mr Nelson in another voice, quiet and serious. 'I think you are right. The railway used to be very busy and there were a lot more men employed. The men had to be pretty good at their job or else get washed away in the flood of work. Busy men, working together, make for good morale and the spirit is passed on over the years. You were in the Army, Adrian?' I said I was. 'Then you'd understand. That is how it was in the Navy. We were proud of our ship but we didn't think of ourselves as enthusiasts – we left that to the land-lubbers. Oh! Look at this!'

His voice went back to its enthusiastic tone and we turned to look where he'd pointed just as a polished 'Castle' burst under the steel span and came thumping heavily past the box at something close to 70 mph. I counted eight Pullman cars behind her.

'My God, those chaps were going well! Did you see the name of the engine, Adrian?' asked Nelson.

'*Earl of Clancarty*,' I replied happily, putting the signal levers back.

'Those Pullman coaches look good behind a "Castle" – that was the South Wales Pullman, I suppose.'

'Yes – 8.50 Paddington,' said Ken, 'she's five minutes down but at that rate they'll be "right time" Swindon.'

I thought we were all set for a pleasant hour watching trains but Harry had finished his tea and was going to show me the Great Western way, which was not, as Mr Nelson had said, hanging about behind a teacup. He took the necessary details about the trailer from Mr Nelson then took me from the box.

In the goods shed I filled in the wagon labels and watched him make out the waybills in his fine, flowing handwriting. We then went for what he called 'a poke around' and looked into every nook and cranny in the shed; just looking, counting piles of folded tarpaulins, lifting lids off old oil-drums, followed by a stroll through the yard, past the shovelling coalmen right to the very buffers of the siding. Only then did he turn back and return to the station to wait for the Up stopper.

This came and went, picking up two passengers and putting off a parcel for a local garage. Harry phoned the trader, told me to enter details in the ledger and then said, 'Do you think you could learn about station accountancy?' He might as well have asked if I'd like an ice-cold shower.

'I shouldn't think I could at all.'

'Oh dear, why not?'

'Books of figures don't ever work for me.'

'Well, you'll have to learn how to sell tickets and book them in properly afterwards. When you take charge here, you'll have to look after the booking office for four trains. Come on, I'll take you into the office.'

We went in and he told Basil what had to be done. I thought Basil would show me, as he was the booking clerk. Instead, he stood to one side while Harry got the various ledgers down and began to explain them and the rack full of tickets; in a drawer there were Great Western Railway season tickets, decorated like a one pound note and nearly as big. Harry was obviously as much at home in this clerkish place as in Goosey Dock sheeting a wagon, but I have a mental block where paperwork is concerned and stood at his side despairing of ever understanding it all. Indeed, I was almost asleep on my feet – Harry had not even noticed, so keen was he on the system he was explaining – when the telephone rang and Basil answered it. His eyes lit up. He looked round at me and said, 'Thanks Ken, I'll tell them all.'

'That was Ken to say that the 8.45 Padd has failed at Didcot. It's off Steventon now and' – he paused for a climax – '*City of Truro* is bringing it down.' I was so excited I rushed out onto the platform quite unconcerned at breaking off my lesson with Harry. The point was that the 8.45 was the

Bristolian and, doubly important, it was now being hauled by a small (by modern standards) 'four-coupled' engine built in 1903 which had been in a museum from 1931 to 1957. Mr Halford, Basil and Harry joined me on the platform, all of us looking forward to a thrilling show. *City of Truro* was the first engine in the world to reach 100 mph, which she did when she was new, hauling an 'Ocean Mail Special' in 1904. The men at Didcot, where she was shedded, came in on their days off to make sure she was in perfect working order and even drivers spent time helping to keep her spotlessly clean. One of these men had said to me, 'We think the world of her. She'll steam on a candle flame; it doesn't matter how you fire her – "haycock", "saucer", "flat" or "all up in the corner" – she'll always be "on the mark".'

And now this fifty-seven-year-old paragon was standing in for a twelve-month-old diesel. I watched her racing towards me down the long straight from Wantage Road – a tall, narrow little engine, the Bristolian headboard on her smokebox, designed for the fat boiler of a 'Castle' and several sizes too big for her. She was running very upright, so it seemed, with no rocking or swaying – she was all *pull*. Her outside cranks caught the sun each time they turned over, which was very rapidly, so that I saw a constant twinkling of bright steel and, as she drew closer, the silver blur of her coupling rod against the dark red of her frames.

Clear as a flute her whistle sounded as she approached our group. We glimpsed her driver, hand on brake handle, head thrust forward to the look-out window; we saw her fireman in the act of shooting another shovelful into her furnace and she was through, that 1903 museum piece, at something like 80 mph. Her crew, lately off the diesel, were obviously delighted to have her and were showing their respect for her capabilities by driving her harder, in all probability, than she had ever been driven before. They knew *she* would not fail them. This realisation together with the noble sight and sound she made brought a lump to my throat. From that moment I despised diesel locomotives with an intensity that would take years to subside.

I needed several cubic yards of top soil for my garden, and next day, as much to find an excuse to speak to them as to find the soil, I asked the three girls who caught the 8.15 stopper to Swindon where such quantities of loam might be obtained. Much to my surprise the red-haired girl said, 'There's enough soil and compost lying around our place for a hundred gardens – our Dad won't mind. Come round on Saturday and get some. But what are you going at?' I told her the plan and they were all very pleased, each suggesting flowers that would look nice and so we talked till the train came. I ushered them on and it steamed away – then I realised I did not know who the red-haired girl was. Harry did. 'Her name's Veronica. She lives at the farm on your road home.'

The parcels lorry came and went, day by day; the Fly shunted; and I began to improve in the use of the pole; tickets remained a blank. On Friday I was introduced to another piece of ritual: the Winding of the Clock. This was the public time-piece which hung on the wall facing the platform, high up, under the platform canopy. Just before eleven o'clock Harry took a chair and a special clock-winding crank and went out onto the platform. He knocked on a window and Basil opened it as he climbed onto his chair, opened the clock's glass front and wound the spring. Basil was standing by the phone to the signal box, the instrument in his hand, listening.

'Time! Time! Time!' he called. Harry pushed the minute hand forward by thirty seconds, closed the case and stepped down. It was nothing really but he so gave his mind to whatever he was doing that it seemed to be important – everything to do with the railway was important to him. He was the personification of the old rhyme 'for the want of a nail the battle was lost' and made sure that all nails in his care were firmly driven home.

Saturday came – a weekend off – and I drove down to the station around eleven o'clock. Harry helped me move the platform seats out of the way; I took a four-wheel barrow for the spoil and began digging the gravel out to make way for topsoil, each piled barrow being tugged to the east end of the platform and the contents dumped in the grass. By one o'clock I had cleared the whole length under the windows and went over to the Prince to have a pie and a pint. Just as I was finishing Basil came in so I had another.

'What do you think of it all then?' he asked.

'Well, it's all right – the more active parts of a porter's life are interesting.'

'You mean you can't do the booking side of it?'

'Well, I meant what I said but I dare say one of the reasons why I can't do the accountancy part is because I find it incredibly boring.'

'Huh! I don't mind it at all. You'd better learn about it before you "take on", I don't want my ledgers messed up every evening so that I've got to clear up behind you.'

'Well, I'll never be able to do it – I can manage the goods paperwork though.'

'Harry can do it all – he ought to have been a station master at some big station. He read *Rules and Regulations for Station Accountancy* like you or I would read Hank Janson. I've seen him sitting with his coffee in one hand and that great thick book in the other. Even station masters ask him for advice. He's red hot on signalling rules too – he was a signalman once.'

'Yes, I know. He is amazing. He must be very contented with being a porter not to have taken promotion over all the years he's been on. It's obvious he could have had it if he wanted – you only have to apply when a vacancy comes up.'

'Yeah – no ambition,' said Basil sadly, looking at his empty glass.

'Come on, drink up. I'll buy *you* one.'

'No, no thanks. I've had two now. I'd better get on. I'll see you on Monday. Cheerio.'

I tied the four-wheel barrow to the car's rear bumper and drove round to the farm in second gear. Veronica was pleased to see me and her father came over for a look.

Tom Carter was a short man who looked immensely powerful. He had a cheerful farmer's face on a stocky neck, his fair hair was tousled, bursting out in all directions from beneath a cloth cap set awry towards the back of his head. His jacket was green, tweedy and stuck with bits of straw from the job he had just left. His trousers were of cavalry twill once cream; his boots, crunching and squelching through the farmyard muck, were massive.

'Hey-up!' he roared hospitably, 'so you're the gardener. When V'ronica told me I said I'd come round wi' the tractor and trailer and bring a load – but seeing how well you're provided for –' he swept an arm in the direction of my Morris with a platform barrow tied to her tail – 'I'll let you get on with it. Help yourself!' He went off chuckling with sarcasm before I could say anything in reply. Veronica 'helped me to load the barrow, I set off to the station and threw my haul into the hole. The great pile on the barrow turned into a little pile in the trench and I saw that the job was going to take all afternoon – quite a pleasant prospect, in fact.

Returning to the farm I discovered that Veronica had an elder sister, Jenny – about my age – who was very blonde, very pretty and as slim as her father was stocky. Returning for the fourth time I was met by the girls' mother who had tea and home-made cake waiting. By the end of the afternoon I had made a lasting friendship with the Carter family which made the main object of the day's effort – to prepare a flower bed – seem of secondary importance. But all was now ready; in such conditions flowers would blossom magnificently.

CHAPTER EIGHT

Sam Entertains

I drove into a football match when I arrived at the station on Monday. In the car park Basil and Sam were opposing two men I had not seen before, both wearing bib-and-brace overalls. They were well matched. Sam and the older, overalled man both tall and roughly the same age; Basil and the other man, young and fit. They were all making a lot of noise and I wondered what Harry was thinking about it. As I parked and got out of the car they stopped playing, came over and stood around me and the car.

'Hi-up, Ady – you're early,' said Sam.

'It's nearly two o'clock.'

'That's early when you're learning – half past would do and then you wouldn't have missed anything.'

'Harry's got him trained,' said the young man in overalls.

'No – that's his military punctuality,' said the older man, and together they rocked the Morris from side to side. 'Nice little bus – got good springs, Maurice.'

'Not half – just what I could do with, John.'

'Get off, you silly beggars. I'm here because it's two and that's my time.'

'He's here because he's here because he's here because he's here!' the older man began to the tune of 'Auld Lang Syne' and was immediately followed by the other three. I began to feel very hot – someone ought to get his nose punched at this stage, I thought, looked round angrily for a victim, saw that they were all at least as big as I and decided against it.

They stopped singing with a kind of whoop and Sam said, nodding towards the overalled pair, 'That's John Moody and his little mate Maurice Sworn. Haven't you met them before?'

'I think I might have seen them on the track last week but I didn't take a lot of notice.'

'You'll take more notice in future,' they said, each jumping on a running board of my car and swaying it while they sang 'Life on the Ocean Wave'.

'Who are they, Sam?' I had to shout above the row. They stopped singing and swaying and stood, breathless on the car, grinning hard, looking at

Sam and me. Sam said, looking straight at them, 'They're the Signal and Telegraph department linemen – an idle lot of scivers who drink tea in every hut, house and signal box from here to Steventon.'

The linemen jumped off the car. 'Gettim, Maurice!' They advanced on Sam in the stance of all-in wrestlers. 'Up Guards and at 'em!' shouted Basil. Sam backed away as John and Maurice advanced. I saw where it was leading, they were herding him backwards to a lock-up garage whose door was wide open. Sam's heel caught the projecting 'stop' for the door, he tripped and fell. In an instant the door was closed on him. A great cheer went up outside while from within a hollow voice boomed, 'Come on, let me out. I've got things to do.'

'What's Sammy got to do then?' they teased him with imitations of his pleadings. I was only amazed that they had the nerve to riot within feet of Harry's door and went in to sign on.

I expected to find a very stern-looking Harry – but the room was empty. I put my head round the booking office door. No one there. He was not in the lavatory either. Perhaps he had gone down the yard to escape the noise and – as I thought – un-railwaymanlike behaviour. I was at a loss to know what to do because he had the keys; I could not even get a hoe from the store in order to clear some weeds.

Sam came in hitching up his trouser and straightening his tie. 'Mad lot they are, stopping people from working.' The football match had resumed.

'Where's Harry? Down in the yard?'

'No!' laughed Sam. 'He's on lates at Wantage Road covering the vacancy. Him and Albert are on the Relief and, as it's a longish journey for both of them to Wantage, they take it in turns to go there. Albert did his late turn there last week and so he's doing his *early* turn here this week. He went over home just before you arrived – I relieved him at half past one.'

'But where's Mr Halford?'

'He's gone down to Uffington in his car – that's how that garage door was open – he's station master there too, you see. Come on over to the down-side; we'll wait for the stopper.'

We walked over the footbridge and sat down on a four-wheel barrow. The sun was warm on our backs and the air was quiet. 'Well, that explains all the racket – I couldn't understand how Harry allowed it.'

'Old Harry's a wet blanket,' said Sam, 'he's the best there is at his job but don't take him too seriously. Oh! Look at this,' pointing up the track, 'old Bill's pushing his luck. Here comes the Kensington past the stopper.'

Three quarters of a mile away, I could see a 'Castle' on the Down Main, a great column of smoke billowing upwards as she accelerated hard past a '61' class tank engine drifting down the Relief line on the Didcot to Swindon stopper. After a few seconds we caught the sound of her exhaust and saw a spurt of pure white steam rise from her whistle – steam rose from the tank engine's reply as they passed; there was a second's pause before the sound reached us.

The Kensington came roaring down to the station and burst through, the engine – 7020 *Gloucester Castle* – pulling for all she was worth. Her train of six-wheeled milk tanks drummed out their peculiarly exciting rhythm – dum-dum-dum, dum-dum-dum – rapidly. I wanted to jump up and cheer! She blew a grateful whistle to Bill Mattingley for letting her through and roared into the distance, the beautiful exhaust music coming back on the wind.

'That's when it's good to see them,' said Sam enthusiastically. 'In the collar and working hard.'

'The driver wasn't half laying it on. Was that just because he'd been allowed past the stopper? They aren't usually so keen.'

'They're the men off the eight o'clock Cheltenham – they're going home! Ah, but there's more to it than that. When they get to Swindon they come off the tanks – another engine takes them down to Cardiff – and that "Castle" goes onto a fast for Gloucester. The stopper makes a connection with it at Swindon. So it's better for the "tanks" to go first so the engine can get onto the Gloucester train and be ready and waiting, rather than have to trail along behind the stopper all the way.'

The stopper ran in then and Sam went into his 'Challer' routine and took a couple of tickets. No one got on. The signal to leave the platform was lowered and the train drew slowly forward. As it drew level with the signal box, the signal to go out from the Relief line to the Main line was lowered – slowly – as a hint to the driver not to go rushing off. He took his train, drifting, down to the advanced starting signal, number 54, 700 yards further on. Sam and I watched the signal box.

'Ol' Bill's up on the frame waiting for the road,' murmured Sam. A minute passed, the stopper was close to 54 signal. Suddenly Bill's shadowy figure moved. We saw his hand thumping the bell tapper – even when he was not in a hurry he was inclined to be rough with the bells – then he strode quickly to the end of the frame and swung the lever over. I imagined I saw the box shake. 54 signal stabbed downwards, the '61' tooted acknowledgement and snorted off to Uffington.

The football match was over when we got back to the office and Basil was sitting at his desk, working on some papers. Sam went in and sat on the table, half covering the work. 'Hi-up, Bas. Got a lot to do?' Basil threw him off after a tussle which swept away a mass of papers onto the floor. I was amazed; after a week with Harry I had never seen anything even slightly indecorous happen, except perhaps that guard, and he was *quietly* drunk. These people did not even have the excuse of drunkenness: 'Come on Ady,' said Sam, 'let's go and clean the Tilleys; we aren't wanted here.'

'Is it always like this?' I asked, as we walked to the lamp hut at the end of the platform.

'Like what? Oh, larking around! 'Tis when we get a chance. But that's how the railway always was. You've only ever been with Harry. You can do your job without going round with a long face all day.'

'Harry's all right,' I said. 'He likes to be quiet, that's all.'

'Well, we like a joke now an' then. Look here, I'll show you how to service the Tilleys before you put them out. The glass needs cleaning on some of them, the wire inside the vaporising tube often needs decoking, and every now and then we have to put a new mantle on one.'

We worked away at this for a while. 'Sam, did you ever hear of a train with twenty rear lamps?'

'Huh! That's the sort of train we need – twenty lamps to clean, fill and trim.'

'Harry says he saw it every day when he first came on the railway.'

'Get away! Perhaps old Harry is having a joke for once. I wouldn't know, it would be long before my time. How could any train have twenty tail lamps?'

'I wonder if Albert knows?'

'Well, he started back in 1920 and was over at Patney, which wasn't far from Harry's place so perhaps he might –' At that moment there was a terrific crash on the roof of the iron hut and the interior boomed like a drum. 'That's that Basil!' roared Sam, charging out of the shed. I followed, my heart still pounding from the fright.

Basil was running along the track side towards the signal box, looking back to see if Sam was chasing him, when he passed 56 signal, the arm of which was lowered and now swung up to 'Danger'. There was an almighty bang and Basil, off balance, fell over like a startled rabbit. He had fallen perfectly into Bill's favourite ambush – an explosive fog signal placed on the signal arm's cast-iron 'stop'. Bill stood at the signal box window giving the boxer's salute as Basil picked himself up off the gravel. 'Come on, Ady,' called Sam to me, 'tea break.'

After tea we left the box, heading, I thought, for the station.

'Answer the phone for us, Bas,' asked Sam.

'Why, where are you going?' said Basil suspiciously, for with the sort of feud those two had going they could never be sure of even innocent actions.

'We'll be on the down-side, waiting for the watercress. Ady, bring the ledger labels and the outwards book over, will you?'

After a quarter of an hour, a small, green van arrived and out of it we took four dozen 'chips' of cress, each weighing about four pounds. We sorted them onto two four-wheel barrows – the 'uphills' and the 'downhills' – the latter to go away on the parcels train due at 4 p.m. and the others to go out on the 4.30 passenger train. Sam, always alert, bought some chips at 1s 6d each to sell to the crews of goods trains that stopped at the station on the Down Relief line, his first customers being the men on the parcels train.

With the Down line watercress away behind a 'Hall' class engine we pulled the other barrow across to the Up platform to await the 4.30 Up train. This had good connections at Didcot for the north and north-west and was fast from Didcot to London, so there was always a handful of passengers. The usual quota had arrived and were standing on the platform, staring idly along the line or looking down at the rails. One man was standing about ten feet from our office door, his back towards us. 'Watch this now,' commanded Sam. I looked through the window, wondering if Sam was going to shove him under a train.

Sam approached the man silently from the rear and, just as he was passing, gave a quick burst of 'How's-yer-bum?' loud and sudden. The victim, startled out of his reverie by a deep voice in his ear, whirled round to see who had spoken, but of course there was no one in sight. Sam turned sharply and was walking back towards the office as the dazed man turned back to face the rails. 'Nice bit of sun,' said Sam with a cheerful nod as he strolled past. He came back to the office, his face red and twitching with suppressed laughter. 'How was that?'

'A cunning stunt – as we used to say in the Army – where did you get that from, the Marx brothers? I think you've stunned *him*; look he's sort of staggering off up the platform. T'isn't the way to encourage passengers though, is it?'

'Ah – go on, you enjoyed it.'

'I did, but I could live without it. Look out, here comes the stopper. We'll get that cress on now.'

'Hang on, wait for me, you're too eager.' We tumbled out onto the platform.

The three girls from the 8.15 Down in the morning got off the train. Veronica walked home, the other girl got into a car that was waiting for her and the youngest came to ask for the lock-up to be opened so she could take her bicycle out. Sam obliged her and wheeled the bike out – with its saddle back to front.

'What rotten sod did this!' demanded Sam in a great sweat.

The twelve-year-old girl squeaked, 'Oh! My bicycle!'

'Don't you worry, love,' said Sam, consolingly, 'it can easily be mended – if we can find the right spanner, there should be one somewhere in Stanford.'

'Oh, you ... *Loder!*' She obviously knew all about Sam and had, I think, stronger language on the tip of her tongue. 'Just you put it back straight for me.'

Mr Halford must have heard the commotion, for he came out into the yard – or it might have been his teatime.

'What's the matter, Sam?'

'Er, nothing at all, Mr Halford. This young lady's bicycle fell over and twisted the saddle round. Isn't that right, dear?' She smiled sweet fury up at him, Sam turned the saddle, she put her satchel in the wicker basket on the front handlebars and cycled away. Sam walked back to the door of the office.

'Well, it must be about teatime. I'll be off,' said Mr Halford. Basil, hearing this, got up from his desk, grabbed his jacket off the hook and came out fast – tripped over Sam's nicely placed foot – and hurried away.

We put on our own kettle and settled down for some sandwiches and cake.

'I like that young girl with the bike,' said Sam, sitting back in a chair he'd brought from the booking office.

'You'd surprise her if you told her.'

'Ah! But did you see how she went for me? She didn't cry – or anything like it – she was just about to cuss blue flashes.'

'What if you'd made her cry?'

'I've seen her on and off trains for three years now. I know her too well for that. She's a fine girl.'

'The 5.5's the next on the Down,' Sam said, 'for Swindon, Chippenham, Bath and Bristol but on Fridays only there's no 5.5 and we have the 5.25 instead. Now that's for Newport and the south Wales Main line, so if anyone comes here after a ticket for Chippenham on a Friday night – *remember* – and don't sell him one till the 5.25's gone. Somebody here forgot that once and sent a man for Chippenham all the way to Newport and he never got home till after midnight and his missus accusing him of all sorts of things. We had to give him a note for her in the end.'

After tea we went out to light our fourteen Tilley lamps and distributed them around the station in time for the passengers off the 5.50 Swindon to Didcot stopper. We carried a lamp in each hand, taking them to the lamp standards at the furthest end of the long platforms and to the top of each stairway of the footbridge. It was a tedious business even with two of us traipsing backwards and forwards, and I made a note to start the job in plenty of time when I came to do the job on my own. Darkness was closing in on the station by the time we had them all in position. The 5.50 Swindon arrived in the twilight and the 5.5 Paddington stopped at the station in darkness; the coaches' lights showing yellow; the big engine only a silhouette with a core of bright firelight.

When these trains had gone there was nothing to do until the 8.30 Up stopper. Sam put a few lumps of coal on the waiting room fire in case we should get a passenger or two. We adjourned to the station master's office where the chairs were more comfortable, the surroundings were cream coloured rather than dark brown, and the booking-office ticket window was within earshot.

'Do you think you'll like it here?' asked Sam, with his feet on the station master's desk.

'Yes, I'm sure I shall, but I don't know how I'll manage that ticket business, booking it all in afterwards.'

'Well, I'll show you, it's easy enough.' He swung his long legs off the desk, stood up and went over to the ticket-rack and the dreaded ledgers. I groaned inwardly but thought it would be better to try and take something in. Having it explained for a second time enabled me to memorise the salient points of the procedure and Sam finished, 'You've got it then?'

'Oh, yes thanks, Sam, very good of you, I'm sure I'll be able to manage. Shall we put the kettle on?' Sam agreed enthusiastically.

While it was boiling, a knock came on the ticket-window. 'In you go and see to that,' ordered Sam grimly. I went in and lifted the ticket-flap. A young man and woman were bowing from the waist, peering in at me.

'Two singles to Paddington, please.'

He spoke in a matter-of-fact voice with a strong London accent; he was confident that I would produce those things in a moment; he had no idea of the turmoil he had aroused within my breast but he might soon receive an inkling.

I searched for the tickets. It was very interesting to see the number of Great Western Railway tickets we had in stock – there was a 'Cheap Day' to

Weymouth and another to Weston-super-Mare, green card with a red 'D'; I found a pink GWR ticket for dogs accompanying passengers; it seemed as if all our first-class tickets were white GWR card, and I made a note to buy some for souvenirs. Then I realised that I'd forgotten what the man had asked for.

'Er, um, sorry, what did you ask for?' I had expected him to be cross but I think he was too taken aback to be anything but puzzled.

'Two singles to London.'

I found them in the end – Western Region tickets – I punched them in the date stamp and was about to hand them over when I remembered that I had not charged him for them – and I did not know the fare or where I might find it. I felt my face go red; I felt clumsy and stupid – I *was* clumsy and stupid – and I *hated* the bloody job. I went to the door and looked in on Sam serenely pouring the tea, doubtless wondering whatever was taking me so long. 'Psst! Sam!' I whispered. 'What's the fare for a single to Padd?'

'Ten and sixpence,' he said laconically over his shoulder.

Feeling grateful and relieved I went back to the ticket-window to find that my customers had vanished. I bent down to the little oval hole in the glass. 'Hello! Anyone there?' The young man came out of the waiting room. 'Ah, here you are then,' I said, trying to be brisk and businesslike, 'that'll be a guinea please.'

'What's a guinea in English?'

'Well they're half a guinea each, you see, so that …'

'Yeah, OK. But what's a half-guinea – in money?'

'Oh! I see, twenty-one shillings please,' I gave him a winning smile through the little glass window and he bowed down as he pushed the exact money through the oval hole. I just retained sufficient presence of mind to push the tickets through before I dropped the slide.

I went back to the parcels office feeling exhausted. 'Give me some tea quick – what's it all on that tray for? – my God, it's rough dealing with the public. That chap didn't even know what a guinea was. I'd rather be in the box than looking after crowds of passengers.'

'We're just going to give them some tea and biscuits,' said Sam, 'I always do that for any 8.30 passengers because the pot's usually full at this time. Come on, we'll go and chat them up.' There was no point in trying to argue with him. My cup was on the tray and in miserable embarrassment I followed Sam round to the waiting room.

Sam had an imposing figure when he drew himself up in a military way and in this manner he now swept elegantly through the doorway, the teatray supported delicately on the fingertips of his right hand; he brought it down with a flourish and landed it gently on the table. I sidled round the door behind him. 'Good evening, ladies and gentlemen' – I relaxed, at least he had not gone into his other routine – 'tea is served.'

I suppose if you come to a little country station in the middle of a dark, remote-seeming country, seventy miles from your home in London, and you are sold your tickets by a man who shows every symptom of being – at best – a halfwit and then, as you sit huddled over an open fire at the end of a long, cold, leather-covered horsehair sofa, a man over six feet tall steps in with all the elegance of an evil and mysterious butler and announced that tea you never asked for is now served, you could be forgiven for feeling nervous, for wondering if you had arrived at a railway station at all. They certainly looked nervous then, as Sam the Butler bent solicitously over them, handing out cups and asking how many lumps of sugar they required.

'Going home then?' asked Sam.

'Er, yes,' said the young man.

'Will the train be long?' asked his girl timidly.

'No, not long now. Been out for the day, have you?'

'Er – yes.'

'Looking round the old follies and churches and things?' Perhaps Sam's accent got through to them because the girl now relaxed a little.

'Yes, my people came from Faringdon long ago and we've had a day out and tried to find mention of them in the town.'

'Yeah, we even been rahnd the churchyard looking at the headstones. Give me the creeps it did, even in broad daylight.'

'Oh, Fred! It was nice – quiet and sunny.' She looked at Sam. 'We had some beer and a pasty sitting on the churchyard wall in the sun.' She seemed to be a very nice girl, I thought.

'Ah, but I wouldn't go round them places after dark,' said Sam, leaning forward in his seat. 'I've lived here all my life and I don't even like walking across the car park to my house in the dark.'

Oh Lord! Here we go, Loder's scared of the dark. I wondered what was coming next, or even if he knew himself.

'No because there's a haunted farm on one side of the road and there might be a ghost here too.' The girl slipped her arm around Fred's though he didn't look much like a protector from where I sat. The firelight flickered over their pale London faces.

'It was here that the first death took place on the Great Western Railway, one hundred and twenty years ago next month, when this station was the terminus of the line from Paddington. A train came down from London, the driver fell asleep at the controls and the train crashed into the buffers. He was killed.' He paused. 'They never found his fireman. Now, the old station was pulled down thirty years ago and they do say that since then the dead don't walk the line at nights and that the ghostly train don't come through on its anniversary but I –' *Whooooooooo*. The girl screamed and buried her face in Fred's frozen shoulder; even Sam and I got a nasty fright as the fast blew its whistle passing through.

'Come on,' said Sam, 'have another cup of tea.' But when they did not answer, he said, 'Oh well, I'll call you when your train comes,' swept the tray up onto his fingertips and strode out of the room. I think even he realised he'd gone too far.

'You're a handy specimen,' I said when we got back to our office. 'You scared the wits out of them and you even gave me a fright when the whistle blew.'

'What d'you mean? I didn't know the train was coming and I didn't blow the whistle.'

'Still, it was a good story – how much of it is true?'

'Well, the bit about the crash is true – I read it in a book. I was only trying to give them a bit of atmosphere, just to pass the time.'

'I reckon they're stiff with your atmosphere; we'll probably have to carry them onto the stopper.' The stopper arrived shortly after and we put the couple onto it with great and even exaggerated politeness, as I realised when they had gone. 'I bet they thought we were taking the micky.'

'Trust you to look on the black side; no wonder you and Harry get on so well.'

'Ah! I'm sorry, Sam. I've had a good shift this afternoon.'

'Have you?' he said, brightening immediately. 'Well, get along home and I'll see you tomorrow.'

CHAPTER NINE

Albert's Railway

There was a rodeo at the station next day. A railway horsebox was alongside the Up loading bank, and a road horsebox was nearby; they both had their ramps down and, between them, dancing at the end of a rope held by the lorry driver, was a very frightened horse. John and Maurice were looking on from the safety of their hut; Mr Halford and Basil had put a respectful distance between themselves and the show. The man led the horse up to the railway truck again, Sam waved his arms and made horsy noises but as soon as the animal's hooves touched the ramp it reared and ran out sideways. John and Maurice, behind their window, were delighted.

I went over, brimming with horse-lore. 'Whoa,' I said, professionally, to the horse and 'Give us the rope, mate,' to the bothered, frayed-looking lorry driver.

'You're welcome,' he growled, handing it over.

The horse stood quite still, trembling all over, wondering what this change would mean for it. I spoke quietly to it and stroked its nose before leading it off for a walk around the yard, talking all the while, before circling back and going directly to the box. The horse went straight in.

'Where did you learn that?' asked Mr Halford, gratefully surprised. 'I had three years, part-time, with Dennistoun's race-horses and show-jumpers.'

'So you did – you never know when things will come in useful. How are you getting on with the job? Could you take charge?'

I thought of the ticket business – apart from that I would have taken on immediately and learnt as I went along.

'Well, I'd better have this week and next, Mr Halford.'

'Just as you like,' he said.

'We'll be putting that horsebox on the three o'clock stopper Up,' said Sam. 'You'd better clip the points and couple on. Have you ever coupled passenger stock before?'

'No – hey! You mean the screw link and the vacuum pipes? No, but I've often watched it done, it's something I've always wanted to do.' I felt quite excited at the prospect.

The stopper arrived at 3.10 and two passengers got off. They were obviously railwaymen but of a type I had not seen before, dressed in fine-quality, dark-blue overcoats, shiny black shoes and brown trilby hats. They nodded to Sam as we walked past them to the siding points. 'Afternoon, Sam'. 'Afternoon, Mr Millsom, Mr Lockett.' The points snapped over and I knelt down to screw the clamp on while Sam squatted beside me.

'Who are they then, Sam?'

'Sssh!' he hissed. 'They're watching.'

As the train moved back over the points and hid us from view, Sam said, 'That's Millsom and Lockett – the District Inspector and his assistant. They take you on the rules when you want to be a signalman. They're up now to visit the signal box but they are interested in anything to do with safe working. That's their job.' I thought they looked very pleasant men, one rather short and stocky with a pipe, and the other tall but stout, and could not understand the awe in Sam's voice. However, I was suitably impressed by it and put on my best behaviour to match Sam's. I waved the train back till the buffers clunked. I was in heaven – playing with real trains. Every detail of every passenger shunter's movements I had ever seen at Reading was clear in my mind as I whipped the tail lamp off the rear coach and put it on the ground. Then, ducking under the buffers, I swung the heavy screw coupling up and over the draw-hook of the horsebox and threw the weight round until the coupling was taut so that the buffers would be held firmly together when the train was running. I had a little difficulty with the vacuum pipes; the dextrousness of the Reading shunters had made it seem so easy but my unpractised hands found them stiff and springy. Anyhow, I joined them up and slipped the pin through; then, 'out from under', put the tail lamp on the rear of the horsebox. 'Right Away!'

I was so engrossed that I did not see that the Inspectors and Mr Halford were watching. I scrambled up the loading platform. 'Adrian, this is Mr Millsom, the District Inspector, and this is Mr Lockett, his assistant.' Mr Millsom had very keen, blue eyes and he had an air of calm, gentle authority. I felt immediately that he was what we would have called in the Army a 'good bloke'.

'You managed that job very well, but Mr Halford says you've never done it before.'

'I've spent a lot of time watching, Mr Millsom.'

'Do you think you could "take on" as a porter soon?'

'At the end of two weeks, I think.'

'Very good, you'll do. I hear you want to be a signalman. Have you started reading the regulations?' I said I had not. 'Well, you'd better start; the sooner the better. There's more to a signal box than pulling levers. I'll send you up the rule book and a book of signalling regulations. I'll see you again another day. Good luck. Come on, Jack,' he turned to his portly assistant, 'we'll go up and see Bill.'

I wanted to ask them about Harry's tail lamp riddle, yet it sounded an outlandish question to ask such personages, so I let them go. That evening I saw Albert walk past the office with his dog and bucket on his way to feed his chickens. Although he was as old a hand as Harry and I respected him, I did not feel as if I was talking to a teacher or an officer – which was how everyone felt towards Harry.

'Hey-up, Albert! Hang on, there's something I've got to ask you.' He turned back.

'Hello, Adrian. How's it going? Enjoying yourself?'

'Yes thanks. They say you were over at Patney in the 1920s, Albert.'

'Yes, that's right, 1926 to 1929. I went there from Dauntsey, then I went to Burbage Wharf as porter/signalman until they closed it in the economies in 1931 and came here.'

'So you'd have been on the Berks & Hants line at about the same time as Harry?'

'Well, I think he'd left Woodborough to come here in 1926.'

'Well, it's near enough. He said there was a train he saw every day at Woodborough that had twenty rear lamps. Is that true? I mean, well, I don't suppose he makes up stories but that sounds a bit far-fetched, doesn't it?'

Albert put his bucket down and ran a hand through his hair. 'Well, it does and it doesn't. You've sparked something off up here.' He tapped his head. 'I'm thinking – Ah! Ha! Ha! Old Harry's memory has gone a bit wrong over the years but I know what he means – '

'What is it then?' I asked, almost jumping up and down with the suspense.

'Oh, I'm not telling you. You ask Harry when you see him, "What had seventeen rear lamps and five headlamps?" Tell him I said he was wrong about the twenty lamps and so he'll have to tell you the answer.' He picked up his bucket and went off along the platform, his collie at his heels.

I told Sam and asked, 'Does that make it any clearer to you?'

'No, it doesn't. Rum sort of railway they had then. *Five* headlamps? Even the Royal train only has four.'

On Thursday evening Sam had to take his wife to the doctor so Albert stood in for him for a couple of hours after he had fed his chickens. When he came in I made some tea; his dog lay down in front of the office fire; and with, as I thought, nothing before us but the 8.30 stopper Up, I steered the conversation easily round to the subject of the old days. 'How long have you been on the Relief, Albert?'

'Since 1934,' he said proudly. 'I used to go everywhere in the Swindon district from Ludgershall to Cricklade on the old M&SW, from Steventon to Wootton Bassett, up to Highworth and Faringdon and down the Gloucester line as far as Minety.'

'But you haven't got a motorbike even now, how did you get about then?'

'Same as now! Either by train or push bike or a bit of both.'

'Yes, but you couldn't bike to Ludgershall every day from here.'

'You don't believe me? I was supposed to book a lodge if I was sent so far away but I'd rather put that few extra shillings in my wife's housekeeping and cycle each day.'

'Well, you just about earned the extra then.'

'Aha! 'Cos if you were being paid to lodge close by and then you didn't turn up on time they'd naturally want to know why. So you had to be there on time.'

'But whatever time did you get up in the morning to cycle all the way to Ludgershall?'

'Well, to be honest with you, the old Company was too good at its own housekeeping to send men out where they'd have to be paid to lodge. So we didn't often go that far – well, not until the war that is – and then the Government was paying so nobody stopped to count the cost anymore. But before the war I was kept fairly well to my own area, about a ten-mile cycle ride each way, though I did have to go out to Highworth if there was no one closer to do the job.'

'How did you know where to go each week?'

'That was the DI's job – it still is. They get up the orders for all the relief porters and signalmen in the Swindon district, type 'em out on a slip o' paper and you get 'em every Thursday afternoon.'

'What happened during the war? You did more travelling then?'

'Ah well, during the war things went haywire; you got sent off all over the place because of staff shortages. Old Sam's wife, Dot, came over here as a porter, you know.'

'Yes, Sam told me.'

'You see this here?' he asked, tapping his finger on an oval brass badge in his lapel. I looked at it closely.

'Was that a badge to show everyone why you weren't in army uniform? Dad told me that during the first war some women used to go round giving the white feather to any man who wasn't in khaki.'

'Yes, that was often a woman who'd lost a husband or a brother, but we didn't get anything like that in the last lot. No, this badge was our pass to get through police or army road blocks during bombing or anything. Railwaymen were reckoned to be on essential service in them days and had to be allowed to pass.'

'Did you ever have to use it, Albert?'

'Good lord, no! And the essential service was very often no more than ticket collecting. I was five weeks once, booked up at Old Town – blasted well ticket collecting, twelve hours a day ...'

'Old Town? Where's that?'

'You know – Swindon Town station up the top o' Old Town hill, the old M&SW station. I used to cycle all the way there, fifteen or more miles from Challow, and be there by 5.30 in the morning, and tickets – you never saw such piles of tickets; off some o' them trains I'd fill my pockets and then have to take my cap off and fill that.'

'Well, didn't you ask to go somewhere else after a week or two?'

'Huh! You may be sure I did but the old DI just said he was sorry and would I stick it for another week. What could anyone say when there was a war on?'

'So you finished at 5.30 each evening. That'd make it easy to get a train home, I suppose?'

'Oh yes, I could go home on the cushions, and just as well too. I don't think I could have cycled after standing up at the ticket gate all day.'

'What about the station before the war, Albert? Harry has told me a lot about what went on. You had heaps of regular traffic; what about the casual stuff?'

'Did he tell you about our bloody Station Truck?'

'Ha! Ha! Yes, that was pretty crude; did the customers at the groceries know?'

'You know I'm not swearing then, when I say that. Oh, them up at Paddington cleaned it out quite well. I don't remember any complaints but it was a horrible sight when we closed the doors on all them dead horses. Talking of horses, I'll bet he never told you about the race-horses we had here.'

'No, not at all.'

'Aha! Now then, *there* was a casual traffic that was regular. We never knew *who* was coming but we knew some trainer or other *would* come, every day and often for more than one train. Every time there was racing they had to send the horses by rail and we had all the trainers from Childrey, Sparsholt and the two Letcombes.'

'My goodness, that must have been twenty stables – there's six establishments in Childrey even today and one at Sparsholt.'

'Yes, that's old Major Sneyd, been there for years. He had a horse, you know; it could hardly walk on the road but it won nearly all its races – long-distance horse it was. Then there was a Mr Scott from behind the Sparrow pub at Letcombe Regis and Pierrepoint too. Aha! He brought a horse down here one day for Newmarket – the Cesarewitch. There was a hell of a lot of booking to be done on them jobs and costing the price when it went over other companies' lines. Anyhow, this horse was called Myra Grey. I said to the groom, "That couldn't win a camel race." He told me to put my money on it. "No fear!" I said. Huh! It won a 66–1!'

'Well, you know, I was always being given tips by the lads when I was at Dennistoun's but I never had the courage to risk my pocket money.'

'I remember, now you've got me on the subject, there was a Captain Whitelaw at Regis. He used to charter a train for Perth races every year. A saloon for his family, a coach for the staff, six horseboxes and a luggage van – there you are! Old Major West, as he was a Director of the Great Western up at Faringdon, used to have a saloon for Perth races too. It worked up "light" to Faringdon and next day he rode in that right through to Perth.'

I positively *glowed* with excitement. 'My God, Albert – what a railway it was then!'

The door burst open from the yard at that moment and a woman, walking backwards with a pile of cardboard boxes on her hands, came in. She put them on the floor and went out for more, moving so fast that we could only stand back and let her get on with it. She was a little, dark-haired woman, some hair turning grey. 'Coxwell Hatcheries,' said she, slapping a sheet of paper on one of the piles, 'good night.' She went out at a run and slammed the door behind her. She had left fifty cartons of live chicks in the middle of the room. I looked at Albert for an explanation, he shrugged and said, 'That's Meg – she doesn't hang about. Now, this lot has got to be labelled, registered and sorted into "uphills" and "downhills".' He rubbed his horny hands together at the prospect of some work.

Sam came back to let Albert go home just after the 8.30 had left. 'I see now why you had to take your wife to the doctors,' I said when Albert was gone.

'Ah! Don't get the wrong impression. She really did have to go; she had an appointment.'

'Yes, I'm sure she had; you made it and the only free night was tonight.' Sam looked hurt, he was not used to me feeling confident enough to be sarcastic. I could not help laughing. 'Oh, I'm pulling your leg. Anyhow, Albert didn't mind, he was as happy as ...' I stopped. 'Well, he enjoyed it.'

Next week I was on duty with Harry. Calm and order prevailed and I had to wait for a suitable opening to mention the tail lamp business. It was half past eight before we had a break from railway work and could talk about trivialities.

'Did you enjoy your week with Sam?' he asked.

'Yes, I did – there was a lot going on.'

'I'm sure there was,' said Harry drily.

'Er, Albert was here for part of Thursday evening and he says you're wrong about the twenty tail lamps.' Harry's upper lip was down, stiff as a board. 'He said to ask you what had seventeen tail lights and five headlamps.' Harry's lip relaxed. 'Oh dear, I see what he means. I'm afraid I got it wrong; it was a very long time ago.'

'Well, what's it all about then? He said you had to tell me.'

'The train was the 10.30 a.m. Paddington to Penzance – The Cornish Riviera to the public though us chaps called it the "Limited" – don't ask me why, it usually had fifteen coaches. It carried three slips; one was dropped at Westbury for Weymouth, one went off at Taunton and the last was dropped at Exeter. Now, count the lamps. The Westbury had a triple rear light, the other two had doubles – that's seven. Until 1933 passenger trains carried red side lights as well as tail lamps, just as goods trains still do, and each slip coach had side lights – making thirteen lamps so far. The Main train had a double red rear light and two side lights, that's seventeen. Now, on top of that you must add a headlamp for each slip and two headlamps for the engine – twenty-two lamps in all.'

'What a performance! All that organisation and complication makes the train seem very grand somehow.'

'Ah. They were grand trains. Fifteen coaches and a big engine all done up with her paint polished and her brasses gleaming. Each slip had its own guard, only the most experienced, because they had to be able to control the coach and bring it to a stand at just the right place after dropping off the train at maybe eighty miles an hour. The "Limited" had five guards.'

'Five? Four surely?'

'No, not in them days.' He stared down at the fire in the stove. 'They had the three slip guards and *two* on the Main train, the Junior in the front van and the Head Guard, in charge of the whole train, at the rear. They'd all have their buttonholes, whatever was in season – it might be a daffodil or a rose or carnation – and in their tail coats and wing collars they'd be almost as well dressed as Aldington, the General Manager, the smartest man you ever saw. We used to call them "Aldington's Peacocks".' His voice had died away.

'Those Cornish expresses *were* grand trains.' Suddenly, he straightened. 'But there – it was a long time ago now. We'd better see to today's passengers.' He went out abruptly, into the yard. I didn't follow him but went out onto the platform instead; I did not think he wanted me with him just then.

I do not know where the idea sprang from, but on Tuesday morning it occurred to me that if I went up to Wantage Road on the 8.5 from Challow I could ride back to Challow on the 8.10 from Wantage. I thought I was well enough known to the engine drivers to be able to ask for the ride; it seemed like an interesting distraction and one I should not be able to enjoy once I was the porter on duty at the station.

Each morning that week I rode on the footplate of the 'Castle' on the 8.5 from Challow and made the discovery that the enginemen had a game of their own. This was to accelerate their eight-coach train with such precision that 60 mph was reached exactly as Circourt IBS home signal, one and a half miles from start, was passed. Brutal acceleration would have taken us up to 60 in less than the distance with this moderate load but, played properly, it was a skilful game – though by its nature, a short one.

The throttle, or, to give it its railway-correct name, the regulator, was shut as we flashed past the signal and we would freewheel the one and three quarter miles to Wantage Road where the Down train was on the point of leaving. I would climb down off the 'Castle', dash across the tracks and climb onto the footplate of a '61' or '63' class engine – I never knew what type to expect. Indeed, on Tuesday morning it occurred to me, only as I was crossing the lines, that the driver of the engine might not want me on his engine but luckily he was a man I knew from the Fly – he was rather surprised when I suddenly appeared in the cab but did not mind.

On arrival at Challow I could be ushering the girls onto the train and slamming doors before Mr Halford had crossed the bridge, or Harry had finished with the parcels lorry.

Two large, brown-paper parcels were lying on the office table, addressed to me, when I arrived for work on Friday. 'Your uniform has come,' said Harry. 'We'll have to see how you look in it later on, after the 10.30 Up.'

At the time he suggested we had a spare half-hour, the Fly had gone away and there was nothing to be loaded at the goods shed. 'Come on then, let's see your new uniform.'

'Well, I don't know, Harry, surely it's the same as yours. I'll take it home and try it.'

Mr Halford and Basil appeared in the door. 'Yes, but you'll be on your own next week. Harry won't be here to see how you look.'

'Am I taking on next week then, Mr Halford?'

'That's what you told Mr Millsom and me the other day; you'll be all right, I think.' I thought of those tickets, shoved the thought aside in the excitement of doing all the practical, outdoor work myself, in my smart new uniform. 'Right then,' I said, 'let's see what we've got.' I opened a parcel. It contained my overcoat. 'Oh! It's very heavy.'

'They always are; made of very good stuff,' said Mr Halford. 'Try it on.' The door opened at that moment and Sam Loder came in. The office was full of men. They stood around me in a half-circle – looking expectant.

'What do you think this is? The *Folies Bergère*? I'm not stripping, only trying an overcoat.'

I put it on. 'Hooray!' They all yelled except Harry, and even he smiled. It was like a bell-tent – right down to the floor. 'Try the other things,' urged Sam. I remembered then that he and Halford had taken the measurements and there had been a funny look on Loder's face. 'You rotten sods!' I yelled and opened the other package.

The jacket was too narrow across the shoulders by a mile and the sleeves were like hosepipes, the trousers were, as Harry put it, 'either long shorts or short longs' and made his rare 'whoofing' sort of laugh from under his stiff upper lip – the waistcoat would have been too small for a leprechaun. I held each piece up so they could have a good laugh. The remarkable thing was the extreme impossibility of the fit; whoever had read Sam's original measurements had realised that someone was being 'sent up' and entered into the spirit of the thing. The three-piece suit must have been held up and caused similar mirth in some clothing factory in London the week before.

It was a good joke but left me feeling very disappointed because I had been looking forward to coming to work all bulled up. I had even bought a piece of silver chain for the waistcoat – now I should have to wait another three weeks before I got a suit.

'Never mind, Adrian,' said Mr Halford, still smiling. 'Take another form home and get your mother to run over you with a tape measure – you can borrow the spare cap when you are in charge on late turn next week.'

Before I finished work that Friday, the last time Harry and I would ever work together, he said to me, 'I should keep that overcoat, when you re-order, it'll come in very handy when you go riding on engines.' He looked very stern from under his peaked cap. 'Take care of yourself – and don't forget the old 10.30 "Limited".'

CHAPTER TEN

Pleasures of a Day

Constant journeying over the two and a half miles of lane between the village and the station taught me every bump and bend in the road. I could have driven there with my eyes shut, not that I ever tried, but in the thick fogs of November – the next thing to driving 'blind' – it was encouraging to be able to use each bump or sideways roll as a definitive marker; over the canal bridge, count ten, hit the filled-in trench, bear left, feel the sudden, steep camber of the road and brake for the bend. I deliberately developed this skill because it was similar to the technique used by engine drivers to keep their bearings in dense fog.

The journey was always a pleasure, to see the familiar road in every type of weather and through the changing seasons; the racehorse stables and the old, grey tower of the parish church; the roadside elms and the elmy hedgerows frothing with cow-parsley; Tommy Carter's farm, approaching which at a quarter to seven in the morning I would meet his cows ambling messily to milking herded by his slim, blonde daughter with the brilliant smile; past Petwick Stud and on, through the last twisting half mile to the main road and the station. All the scenes from childhood left behind on the daily drive to work.

It was also a pleasure to drive my Morris, even if, on the coldest winter nights I had to travel with a blanket round my legs and a hot-water bottle in my lap. Those small, gentle, pre-war cars were friendly machines, lacking in power so that you actually had to think ahead when you drove them, to work up speed for the hills, lacking that 'float along' comfort which insulates the modern driver from the road – often with fatal results.

But the old car had her peculiar temptations – she had a device on the dashboard for screwing open the throttle and a 'sunshine' sliding roof; it was possible to set the throttle, climb onto the roof and steer with my feet. In that quiet lane I used to drive most of the way home in this manner. It seemed a good idea at the time and was very exciting but on the last occasion I did this a car approached from the opposite direction and its driver, seeing an apparently driverless car approaching with its passenger sitting on the roof, took swift but ill-judged evasive action and crashed into the hedge.

Mr Halford let me get on with the portering work at the station and rarely interfered; not even when Basil complained loudly that I had, yet again, made a nonsense in his beautifully kept ledgers. I never mastered the accounts side of the business but I thoroughly enjoyed the practical, outdoor railway work and many impressions of it remain with me today.

On dark winter mornings the first passengers would arrive, with gruff early-morning greetings, while I was winching the Tilley lamps into place above the platform gate and under the awning. Old Joe, hobbling beside his bicycle, his long, craggy face and hooked nose looking grimmer than ever as he passed from shadow to the harsh light of the Tilley and into shadow again, the building labourers, pale and stubbly black around their chins, waiting for their tickets.

At 7.20, while I was attending to their fares, the 3-1 code rang out. 'That's your train, gentlemen, just off Uffington.' They would grunt 'Thanks' and go back to the platform.

Four minutes later the locomotive's single headlamp appeared out of the darkness; the rolling exhaust smoke coloured by the engine's white-hot fire. In another minute the locomotive and its three carriages came spanking into the station, I saw a flash of firelight as the engine slid darkly past, I heard a squeal of iron brake-blocks on steel wheels – stop. After the commotion of arrival the silence seemed profound, steam wreathed up from beneath the carriages, past yellow-lit, fogged windows. Then I heard the hiss of the locomotive's safety-valves at full pressure and the gurgling whistle of the boiler water-injectors at work.

The guard and I helped Joe up into the van with his bike, the labourers, bulky in shiny-backed woollen overcoats, climbed into the train and the guard handed me some railway letters. 'Where's old Harry today then?'

'I've taken on now. I'm on my own.'

'Oh ah! How d'you get on with him then?'

'One of the best, I think.'

'One of the real old school is Harry. Are we right?' I went to the carriage doors and checked them, turned and raised my hand to the guard.

Standing on the platform, the door of his van open, the guard turned his hand-lamp to green and blew his whistle. I heard the fireman's 'Right Away, mate!' to his driver, the prompt 'toot' on the engine's whistle, the first 'whoofs' of the exhaust. With such a light load, acceleration was rapid. The guard jumped aboard – almost too late, it seemed – his door swinging shut with the rapid forward movement of the train. He gave me a wave and disappeared inside.

The engine on that train would be an ex-works machine, anything from a 'King' to a 'Manor'. I never grew tired of watching the receding train, especially on dark, cold mornings, listening to the chattering, changing rhythm of the exhaust coming back through the chilly air. The red tail lamp flickered as the coach jarred over each rail joint and the cold, green signal lamps changed to baleful red as the train passed them and the signalman restored the arm to 'Danger'.

The scene was rooted in the eighteenth-century days of stagecoach travel. The passengers in their narrow compartments, each one with three small windows in the side, the Guard, in charge of the train – his narrow door lettered in black and gold on a maroon ground – the Driver, with his undoubtedly horse-like engine, brassy as a well-polished harness. The clatter and commotion of the train's arrival and departure had the dash, the *élan* of a stagecoach rattling over the cobbles into an old inn yard; the High Speed Train is very much faster (though it will not take you to Challow) but it is not dashing.

Even the phrases we used came from coaching days. An engine working hard uphill was said to be 'in the collar', the collar being a piece of harness around the horse's neck to which the shafts of the cart were attached and against which the animal pulled. The working timetable directed 'Engine to take water', as if it went to a trough to drink; indeed, there were places where locomotive water *was* taken from troughs while the train was running. Engines and trains, even the Royal train, were 'stabled' on a siding. The Fly, I discovered at last, took its name from a one-horse, light cart used for short journeys with many stops.

The parcels lorry was a pre-war Thorneycroft driven by a decrepit man known jovially as 'Lightning'. He took snuff in larger quantities than was good for him and his nose often showed signs of recent bleeding while his waistcoat was permanently stained black and tan from years of fallout. He was not jovial and his early morning gloom always deepened at the sight of a nineteen-year-old porter. He had his job worked out to a fine art and my inexperience must have been very trying for him. As we loaded his lorry, he kept up a barrage of protest. 'No, not that one, that goes on last. No, no, not there, that's me Charneys and you're mixing 'em wi' the Gooseys. Wait, wait, you're mucking up the whole system. What's yer rush?'

I wanted to be on the platform in time to say a few words to the girls and usher them onto the train. I would then slam their carriage doors professionally, call 'Right Away' in my best, parade-ground voice and send the train off with a commendable show of masterful efficiency.

When I got back to the office, Lightning would have taken the delivery sheet I had made out and departed, leaving behind a snuffy thumb-print on the desk where the sheet had laid. It was breakfast-time now, so, dusting all surfaces first, I laid out my food and switched on the kettle.

I tried to follow Harry's example and be at the goods shed to meet the Fly on its way back from Uffington. If the signalman forgot to ring it in, it would signal its own arrival by a sudden loud roar as it rolled over some rail lengths alongside the goods shed wall. A platelayer told me that the noise was due to the curiously worn surface of the rails which had been used inside the sulphurous Severn Tunnel for many years; there was nothing I could see but they made a terrific din with the goods shed as an enormous sounding box and echo chamber.

The train stopped with a lot of clashing ringing from its cymbal-like buffers, striking and rebounding, coupling chains snatching and tugging horribly. The points into the yard were reversed, buffers rang again, this time in an orderly progression, as with hoarse, hollow chuffs the '37' class tank engine closed up its train, the front moving while the back stood still till the guard's van moved and the train set back into the siding. The points were reversed again and the shunting could begin.

Shunting was always a pleasant half-hour for me. I enjoyed working closely with a steam engine and the feeling of teamwork as the driver, fireman, guard and myself worked by handsignals. As I write I can hear the cracking, grinding noise peculiar to old sidings when locomotives move slowly over them. The train was manned by Didcot men with a Didcot-based engine; there were, perhaps, five men in the 'link' that worked the job – they also worked the Didcot–Swindon stopping passenger trains – so that in ten weeks I had worked with them all and my place on their footplate was assured.

When I was booked as late turn porter I could join the Fly at 7 a.m. and have three hours in the company of the unfailingly cheerful enginemen, travelling down to Uffington and back, often as 'fireman' and sometimes being allowed to drive.

A driver once handed over his '22' class engine to me in Challow yard saying, 'Look out now, you've only got the steam-brake on the engine, the tender's unbraked.' All went well until we had to go into Goosey Dock to pick up a wagon. I braked a second too late. The engine stopped nicely but the 35 tons of unbraked tender gave a mighty shove which drove the engine into the wagon which was hard against the buffers and threw the three of us against the firebox and its hot, copper pipes. The driver was upset and said so. The skill of the job was to make allowances for everything.

Part of a goods guard's skill was to arrange the work so as to carry it out in as few movements as possible: the staff magazine used to carry shunting puzzles with a time limit on solving them and men were proud of their reputation for clever shunting and dextrous use of the pole. I once heard a man mentioned who was so proud of his job as a shunter that he used to go to chapel each Sunday with his pole over his shoulder so that everyone should know what his job was.

When wagons were standing in odd little sidings all round the yard, it was often necessary to have trucks before and behind the engine and fly-shunting came into use. Fly-shunted wagons were drawn along not pushed. The man uncoupling put his pole into position before the train started and raised his free arm for the driver to start. He ran alongside until he judged the moment right to uncouple, signalled to the driver to ease-up, the coupling slackened as steam was shut off, the shunter slipped the link off the hook and waved the driver away.

The engine accelerated vigorously so that it cleared the points well before the wagons following loose behind. This gave space in which the man at the points could operate the lever and divert the trundling raft. Siding points were always uneven so speed was essential if the trucks were to have sufficient momentum to overcome the lumps, bumps and flange-squealing friction and pass clear into the siding. If they stopped across the points they blocked the other line and possibly penned the engine into a dead-end.

If that happened we used the pinch-bar to lever the trucks clear or we might ask the coal merchant to pull them with his lorry – this was illegal but it never stopped us from doing it. If this problem arose, it did so right outside the stable which once housed Harry's shunting horse, Duchess, and I often looked up at it while we puffed away with the pinch-bar and wished she was still in there.

During any weekday in 1960, eight titled trains passed Challow in each direction. Two were the blue and white Pullman diesels – like bullet-nosed rail-cars. They had started their public service on the same day that I started learning the portering job at Challow. The other six were locomotive-hauled with cream and brown coaches – and five of them were steam-hauled. After nationalisation in 1948 the Great Western coach livery of chocolate and cream gave way to Socialist red and yellow – 'rhubarb and custard' – but in 1954, when revolutionary ardour had cooled and common sense began to reassert itself, the old colours were reintroduced, starting with the coaches for the named expresses.

The man behind this was Reginald Hanks, the last Great Western railwayman to be in charge at Paddington. He had served an engineering apprenticeship at the Great Western factory at Swindon before the First World War, had fought in that war and afterwards went to work for William Morris, later Lord Nuffield, becoming Works Manager at Cowley before taking the post of Chairman of the Board of Western Region at Paddington.

He was unique as a Chairman of the railway in that he regularly fired the engine that took his train from Oxford to Paddington – indeed, it was said that he had his overalls hanging behind the Boardroom door and would terminate a meeting with 'You must excuse me gentlemen – I'm firing the Cornish Riviera this morning.' Sir Daniel Gooch had often driven engines as Locomotive Superintendent in the 1840s and '50s but it is very doubtful if he shovelled coal when he became the Chairman of the Board.

The named expresses were:

The Bristolian
The South Wales Pullman
The Bristol Pullman
The Pembroke Coast Express
The Merchant Venturer
The Capitals United
The Cheltenham Spa Express
The Red Dragon

Reggie Hanks's expresses were a sight for sore eyes. The green, brass and copper polished locomotive carried before its chimney a decorative headboard bearing the train's title and hauled a row of cream and brown coaches. The sturdy old atmosphere was completed by the yards-long destination boards which the coaches carried above the line of their windows, a most useful practice to the public and one with its origins in the days of stagecoach travel. I enjoyed reading the fine-sounding names, English, Cornish and Welsh, romantic with distance, ringing with poetry – 'THE PEMBROKE COAST EXPRESS. PADDINGTON TENBY & PEMBROKE DOCK' sounded like a proud boast of the train's daily achievement while it had a noble alliterative effect when I read it to the rhythm of the wheels' rapid tattoo as they drummed through the station.

The first big diesel locomotives on Western Region – the 'Warship' class – appeared in 1958. They were not reliable and earned the name 'Growlers' very quickly but they were the latest thing, and in the summer of 1959 the Bristolian was scheduled for 'Warship' haulage and had five minutes cut from its very fast schedule. 'Warship' failures ensured that the train occasionally had steam power, probably the most remarkable incident being when the Down Bristolian failed at Reading sometime in 1960.

A '28' class goods engine was the only spare available and was coupled to the front of the dead diesel with the intention that it should haul the train to Swindon where a 'Castle' would take over. The '28' class design dated from 1903 and had 4-foot 7 ½-inch-diameter driving wheels for hauling very heavy goods trains; steam engines for high-speed running had wheels 6 feet 6 inches or more in diameter. The '28' did exceptionally well, running at 60 mph with the 370-ton train but soon after passing Didcot the 'Warship' came to life and began to push the goods engine into Bristolian-style speed.

I saw the train at Challow. The old '28' had the Bristolian headboard up and was probably travelling at 80 mph. It looked absolutely terrifying as its long side-rods were driven round by the tiny, more or less invisible driving wheels but the '28''s driver threw a note out as he passed Challow box – 'No relief at Swindon.'

The entire station staff turned out to see the engine pushed over the maze of Swindon's point work, the signalmen at Dauntsey and Box said that the train was running at normal speed at the foot of both inclines yet it arrived safely at Bristol, the '28' clanking loudly into the station, her headboard still proudly in position.

At the west end of the platform an ambulance party of fitters, foremen and Locomotive Superintendent were waiting and a pair of steam cranes were standing by in the shed in case the '28' had to be lifted off the track! But they were not needed and the old engine ran back to Swindon factory for examination under her own power. I never heard if any defects were found.

The lunch hour at Challow became increasingly hazardous as Basil and Maurice became more ambitious in their jokes until they overstepped the mark. There was a splendid, official brass pass-key to the public lavatory on the platform which saved us paying pennies to the railway. One lunchtime I took it along to the door but found the closet occupied and returned. As I opened the door from the platform I saw the far door closing – oh, so quietly! – and caught a glimpse of a fire bucket through the diminishing gap. Basil and Maurice had noticed the missing pass-key and thought they had young Ady sitting pretty.

A moment later there came a great splash as the contents of the bucket were hurled through the lavatory ventilator, followed by the outraged shout of the victim. From the jokers' point of view, a very satisfactory reaction. The sound of tiptoeing footsteps came close, the door opened and in tumbled Basil and Maurice, bursting with suppressed laughter – until they saw me sitting by the fire. The change that came over their faces was a joy to watch.

Squelching noises now came along the platform, we ducked down behind the table to see who had been caught and saw one of the coal merchant's men go by – a big man to be throwing water over but he never complained. Our clever pair gave that game up and contented themselves with putting glue on door handles, tying dustbins to cars' rear bumpers and nailing caps to table tops.

One night I was on duty when the 5.5 Paddington came down with fifteen coaches and would not fit our platform; either the front or rear three coaches would stop over open track. There was also the risk that it would come to a stand with the tail standing out over the power points from the Down Main to platform, so the signalmen arranged to run it down the Relief line from Wantage Road and for me to stand at the east end of the platform and yell instructions to passengers *not* to get off at the rear but to walk four coaches forward.

No one appeared to get off except at the platform and we complimented ourselves on the efficiency of our arrangements; the train left and I went back to the office. Five minutes later a dishevelled – and rather deaf – old gentleman tottered into the room. 'Just stepped off a train, sir?' The unkind question was smothered just before it broke surface as he said, 'The last time I travelled by train, young man, it stopped at the platform.' How anyone could step off the brink into total darkness was more than I could understand. 'Surely one is obliged to look where one is going, sir?' Olde worlde haughtiness showed beneath his layer of dust and creosote. 'I shall sue you for this,' he snapped. But luckily he did not. I am sure he would have lost.

Once the Down fast had gone, there was nothing much to do except read a book and wait for telephone calls from prospective customers – and on Thursday, see to thousands of live chicks. One evening the telephone rang.

'Hello, Cha ...'

A loud voice cut in with 'Where's my damned caviar?' The accents were thick from too much brandy consumed in the past hour and the past forty years and were instantly recognisable as belonging to a military gentleman who lived out in the Vale.

Only just resisting the temptation to share his mood and tear a strip off a military gentleman – after all, I *was* fresh from the Army – I said, 'Can I have your name please, sir?' He gave it and repeated his inelegant request for the elegant food. We worked out together that it was being delivered by British Road Services whereupon he slammed the telephone down without another word. Next Christmas, among the seasonal gifts of rabbits and £1 notes from the local gentry was a brace of pheasants addressed to 'The Porters at Challow Station'. They had come with the compliments of my caviar cavalier – not that I ate either of them, I was no longer at the station when they arrived!

The solitude of the evening porter's position made a blank sheet for indelible impressions. I loved the rainy, windswept winter evenings when the wet platforms gleamed under the harsh light of the Tilleys, their garishness accentuating the surrounding inky blackness. And out of the dark would thunder the 'Kings' and 'Castles', showering fire, their brasswork catching momentarily the station lights, their long trains of yellow-lit coaches blurring past to the sound of the rail joints' rhythm – till, suddenly, there was only steam and smoke swirling and rolling under the platform canopy and the sound of the wind in the telephone wires.

The last train of the day, the 9.30 Down, had only one regular customer, a man called Jetsam, who had a brother, so I was told, called Flotsam, whom I never met. Jetsam worked at a nearby scrapyard, and as I was often there, looking for bits for my Morris, we had become good friends. He came to the station each evening, bought a ticket to Shrivenham for himself and his bike and helped me finish the last of the tea. I never saw him get off a morning train so I presumed he cycled fifteen miles to work each day.

Most Saturday nights a man and woman came up from Swindon on the 4.30 stopper. They would walk away from the station, arm in arm, as civil as you please but when they came back to catch the 9.30 they would be swearing and screaming at each other and calling on the porter to hear the argument and judge between them. The routine never varied.

Getting them into the train was very difficult because the coaches were the compartment, non-corridor type and they would refuse to sit together but when I placed them in the separate compartments of their choice, one would leap out and try to get in with the other. The guard would lend a hand, and sometimes a boot because he was not shy of them as I was; the train would go on its way leaving me to gather up his lamps, two at a time, lock the station and go home to bed.

Nine months passed at Challow, a happy time. The work was enjoyable; I had good company around me and a constant procession of handsome locomotives and trains to watch; the signal box was available to me at any time of the day. My life at work was simply an extension of my play of the last fifteen years – and I was being paid for it! It is a remarkable fact that the engines in service in 1960, whilst not the actual ones that were in service before 1914, were very similar and would have been perfectly familiar to my grandfather; the spirit that moved the railwaymen I knew was just as old-fashioned and conservative. Life was secure, the scene was set as firmly as the elm trees in the hedgerows and would go on forever and ever, Amen.

CHAPTER ELEVEN

Elwyn's Way

But I wanted to be a signalman. I studied the lists of vacancies that appeared once a fortnight and applied when a job at Uffington box was advertised. As there was less overtime at Uffington than anywhere else on the line and as it was rated at Class 3 for pay, like most other boxes in the area, no one else applied and I got the job. This caused a few eyebrows to be raised, and Harry Strong told me that I was going into a signal box after only nine months on the railway whereas, before the war, men waited nine years for a tiny, Class 6 box. Mr Millsom was so alarmed by this precipitate promotion that he ruled out my working at Uffington until I had spent some time at Lockinge. 'There's a lot of points and signals at Uffington, Adrian,' he told me seriously, 'you'd be better off going to Lockinge for a year, just to get the hang of things.'

Lockinge, absolutely remote on a high embankment, between Wantage Road and Steventon, the wide Vale and the sky, reached through farmyards and field paths, could have been a good place to work but for the fact that it had only four levers and nothing to do with them all day but pull them over and throw them back for each train. I prepared for a very boring year, but the morning I was to start to learn the box, it was shut and so I went to Uffington after all.

There were two ways to reach Uffington box from Childrey – via Challow station and Baulking through flat country or via Kingstone Lisle, a hilly road for most of the way. By the former route I could almost guarantee the sight of a steam engine; nearly every time I drew up at the junction of the Childrey lane and the main road, there would be a plume of steam rising from the engine of a goods train waiting on the Down Relief line for a 'path' to Swindon. On this road I was able to wave to Bill Mattingley as he passed from Uffington village to Challow station; signalmen spent eight hours a day working with each other over their instruments but rarely met and so they valued these brief encounters.

This was the only route on winter Monday mornings, I was told, when snow had fallen or there had been an intense frost during the night.

The road passed close to Uffington's Down distant signal, which was a semaphore arm worked by a wire; when the signal box was switched out over the weekend and the arm lowered to show 'All Clear' it often froze in that position. So the wise signalman would get out of his car and walk across the field to jump on the wire and move the signal arm; when he entered the signal box and threw the distant signal's lever over, the arm and wire, being free of ice, would return to the 'Caution' position.

The Kingstone Lisle route took me along the Roman Portway with fine views of the Berkshire Downs to the south and the Vale to the north and through the magnificent avenue of beech on Captain Lonsdale's land. The majority of signal boxes are, or were, deep in the countryside and part of the pleasure of working them was derived from the view you had of the meadows, the birds and animals, the sunrises and sunsets, the weather and the drive to and from home.

Uffington station was the least attractive place at which I have worked. It was built in a style which I call post-Brunellian-gloomy-gothic down in a cutting and had a wide awning that kept all but the most persistent sunbeams out of its dark brown interior. It was situated at the western end of Baulking cutting and was overshadowed by tall trees and the large, red-brick Junction Hotel. I felt a curiously dull atmosphere about the place, even on sunny days. There was a stillness which probably had something to do with the monstrous elms and the grim, green fir trees across the road, which overpowered or stifled all other feelings, but I was not surprised to learn that there had been at least one suicide there, one unexplained death and several obviously accidental ones.

The station had known better times, when the Faringdon branch had a real purpose and people used trains from necessity. Had events worked out as planned, there would have been a much larger station here for Dr Beeching to close: had the Faringdon line continued through Fairford to Cheltenham as intended in 1860 and if the Great Western had completed the Didcot–Wootton Bassett quadrupling scheme of 1900. Some half-finished earthworks for this can still be seen on the up side of the line after the 69 mile post and the existing steel bridge which carried the lane over the site of the station has a span of 109 feet – enough to span four tracks and a couple of sidings as well.

The signal box was built on the Up platform just east of the station office, almost opposite the 66 ½ mile post and was a handsome, timber building dating from 1897. A short flight of steps led down to the door of the interlocking room and another short flight led up from the platform to the door of the operating room. I walked up these steps on a fine, summer morning and was greeted at the door by the man who was going to teach me the job, Elwyn Richards.

He was stocky, about 5 feet 6 inches tall, forty-seven years old, his dark hair cut short at the back and sides, swept severely away from his forehead and parted with perfect accuracy to one side. He was wearing railway-issue, blue serge trousers and waistcoat, polished black shoes, and a collarless, black-striped flannel shirt, the sleeves of which were rolled up to show a pair of very useful-looking forearms. He thrust out his right hand, his smile and his glasses flashed together and in a soft, Welsh voice he said, 'You're A-dren. I'm pleased to meet you, come in.'

I stepped inside. 'Pleased to meet you – at last. I've heard your name often enough when I've been in Challow box.' The room was rather dark. The cutting bank rose opposite the front windows, which were, in any case, partly blocked by the row of levers; the 'lever frame' and the west window were partially blocked by the station's awning, which came within ten feet of the glass. The back wall of the box faced north and had only one square window at each end, so most of the levers, the instruments on the shelf above them and the diagram of the tracks controlled from the signal box were in shadow. Elwyn must have read my face, for he drew down the corners of his mouth deprecatingly. 'Dark 'ole this. Closed in like. The station's u-*ri*-nals are right outside the window; in summer now, we 'ave to keep on at George to keep them swilled out properly or they'd smell.'

He drew a tin from his waistcoat pocket, using his thumb and forefinger in a characteristic movement and offered it to me – it was an enamelled snuff box. 'Go on, 'ave some. It's carnation scented, clear your head a treat.'

'It'd probably blow my head off altogether, thanks Elwyn.'

He drew down his mouth in a quick grimace and snuffed each nostril, giving an exaggerated gasp of satisfaction for my edification. 'You can have the middle locker for your traps,' he said, stepping across to a row of three cupboards that were placed against the back wall between the window and the stove. They were painted brown with cream panels under a single, black top. He opened the central door. 'Oh drat!' An avalanche of half-pint Guinness bottles crashed down around his feet and went flooding, clanking away across the lino floor; there must have been two dozen at least.

'Who drank that lot?' I asked as we scrambled across the floor, gathering them up.

'Me, I forgot about 'em. I like to 'ave a half with my sandwiches in the evenings. Missus across the way in the pub leaves a half on top of the bank;

it's handy to her kitchen window, and that saves me having to find time to go all round to the bar. I'd better take 'em back.'

I put my teapot, mug and other bits into the empty cupboard. Elwyn's tea-making equipment was on top of the cupboard, under the telephones that were screwed to the wall. There was one connected to the station at Faringdon, another for the 'omnibus' line which connected all the signal boxes from Foxhall Junction (Didcot) to Highworth Junction (Swindon) and the mahogany-boxed 'Control' phone.

'I'll make us some tea,' said Elwyn. 'Do you take sugar?'

'Yes please, but let's use my stuff.'

'Mine this time, yours the next, that's fair. I expect you know what everything is but look around and ask if you want to know anything –' A deep-sounding bell rang. 'That'll be the "Swansea" I expect – answer it.'

I looked at the two block bells. The Challow bell was a 'church dome', a traditional bell shape which was high-pitched, so the Knighton bell must have rung, this being a 'flat dome' bell giving the deep note. I tapped the Knighton tapper once and back came four bells for an express train. I returned the code and turned the handle of the block indicator to 'Line Clear'.

'Shall I ask on to Challow, Elwyn?'

'Not yet. Wait till you get the "Approach" from Knighton; that's sent when the fast's off Ashbury.'

I began to take in more of the box. The floor measured about 35 feet by 12, giving plenty of room around the forty-seven levers, many of which were painted white – out of use. 'What did all these do, Elwyn?'

'They were finished with when the branch was closed to passengers and the signals were taken away and the points took off the frame and made into hand-operated levers on the ground. Look here.' He went to one of the back windows and slid it open. We looked out, along the branch platform and down the branch line, which curved sharply northwards away from the station towards Faringdon. 'There was a starting signal over there between the run-round loop and the bank, and out on the bend there was an advanced starting signal with one of the old shunt-ahead arms with a big S on the arm. That way,' he pointed into the cutting towards Challow, 'there was a bracket signal to go out on the Main line or up into the sidings, and in the run-round loop we had a throw-off point at each end and there was a lot more besides.'

The deep-sounding bell rang 1-2-1 just then. 'There's the "Approach" from Knighton get the road and pull off.' I tapped once on the Challow tapper, back came one ding on the Challow bell, I tapped out four beats, back came the code and the block indicator for Challow turned to 'Line Clear'. I could now lower the Up line signals. I looked at the brass plate on the distant signal lever. This gave the levers that had to be pulled before the distant signal could be operated – 40, 44 and 46, then the Up distant, 47. I heaved them over rather awkwardly because I had to learn the pulling characteristics of each one.

Levers were more or less difficult to pull depending on what they operated, points, bolts or signal arms and upon the distance of those items from the box. Manually operated points could not be more than 350 yards away but signals might be 1,300 yards from the box; the wire passing round several pulleys as it crossed tracks and carried up signal posts, which made for friction and consequently a heavy pull. Replacing a point lever was as light, or heavy, as pulling it but signal levers were always easy to replace owing to the tension of the wire; often they would fly back across the frame when the holding latch was released with a blow from the heel of the hand.

It was not a matter of brute strength. I have watched with amusement a burly policeman struggling with a signal lever, managing to get it half way over before it overpowered him and fell back into the row, dragging him with it.

In replacing a lever, a strong spring beneath the floor was compressed, which then helped to throw the lever over when it was next pulled. The feet had to be correctly placed, the right on the floor slightly to one side, the left on the cast-iron treads, the lever and the man's spine directly in line. If the pull was a heavy one, the signalman swung backwards from the hips, making use of all available acceleration provided by the spring and any slack in the wire to gather momentum to overcome the increasing friction of the wire. He then finished the pull momentarily off balance – it was only for a fraction of a second but it could be dangerous.

A light pull would entail no more than releasing the lever's latch, allowing the spring to throw the lever half way over the frame from where a gentle pressure from the signalman would finish the movement. In pulling four levers, both types would be found with variations between.

Levers were always pulled with a duster. This prevented sweat from hands rusting the carefully polished steel handles and also made pulling more comfortable and easier because the handle had to move in the hands, which it could not do when gripped tightly in bare fists. Not any rag did for this job but a proper duster – a square of soft, cotton cloth woven with red, light and dark blue lines. The design had not changed in living memory –

only the initials, and even in 1960 I was the proud owner of a duster with the magic cipher GWR woven into it.

The duster was the signalman's unofficial badge of office and if more than one signalman was in a signal box – say on an engineering Sunday when extra men were drafted in to help – the 'on-duty officer' could be instantly recognised by the duster hanging from his trouser pocket or draped over one shoulder. In the very rare event of a signalman having to be removed from a signal box instantly, perhaps after a crash when he might be in a state of shock and not fit to continue work, his Inspector would say, 'You'd better give me the duster, Fred.'

Two beats from the Knighton bell signified that the 'Swansea' was passing Knighton and was 'on line' to us at Uffington. I acknowledged the code and turned the block indicator to 'Train on Line'. 'Here,' said Elwyn, 'I've got the tea ready and I've been doing the book but now you're here I may as well let you get on with it. I'll sit down with my cup. You better book that "on line" you've just had.'

The railway line was divided into sections and no train was permitted to enter a section without the permission of the controlling signalman. All equipment concerned directly with signalling trains through the sections had the prefix 'block'; thus we had 'block sections' and 'block register', officially the 'train register' or, to the signalman, 'the book'. It was a very important part of the proceedings and in it the time of every bell code received or sent, every unusual occurrence, equipment failure or special message was recorded. Most, if not all, signalmen took pains to keep the record accurately, minute by minute as the codes rang out and some men, especially those who had started as booking boys in large signal boxes took pride in writing very neatly. Properly kept, the register was an aid to memory and vital evidence in the case of an accident.

The Up train came tearing past; it felt strange to have it running so close to the box after the spacious layout at Challow. I put two levers back, sent the two beats to Challow, spotted the tail lamp, sent the 'Train out of Section' 2-1 to Knighton and replaced the last levers. As I wrote the times in the book, Elwyn said, 'You'll 'ave difficulty getting the tail lamps here what with one thing an' another so always try to pick 'em out right outside the box, don't wait till they've gone past. The Up trains get mixed up with the water column and the station nameboard and the down ones get smothered in smoke between the station buildings. Actually, its OK now but there's plenty of times when it isn't, so it's best to get into the right habit now.'

'Righto then, Elwyn. I like your track circuit repeaters in their nice, brass cases. I've never seen instruments like that before.'

'They must be quite old – course, you had "all balls" at Challow.'

'Yes, but at Wantage Road they had red lights in the diagram to show where the train was.'

Elwyn sighed. 'Yes, there's all sorts of gadgets. Those track circuit repeaters came here in 1947 when they did away with the "Vehicle on Line" switches. I think they interlocked our starting signals with the "Line Clear" position on the block indicators at the same time. New-fangled stuff,' he growled, thumbing his snuff box up from its pocket. 'You'd think they'd trust us to get the "Line Clear" before we pulled off, wouldn't you?' I felt puzzled by this.

'Are you saying that you used to be able to pull the signal controlling the entrance to the next section *without* getting the road first?'

'Indeed you could – at hundreds of boxes and there are still plenty today where you could pull the starter off without "Line Clear" being up in the indicator. There was no such thing, in GWR days, as a white stripe on a lever to show that you had to get "Line Clear" before you could pull it; that only came in with BR.'

'What about these "Vehicle on Line" switches. Did they do the same job as the track circuit?'

'Oh yes, when the Up or Down switch was turned, you couldn't give "Line Clear" to the box to the rear – Challow on the Down and Knighton on the Up. The difference now is that the presence of a wagon on the line triggers the gadget. There's a current in each rail and the wagon's wheels bridge them and make a short-circuit and that works the locks and makes the indicator in the box show that you've a train standing "on the track".'

'The instrument shelf is very simple, isn't it? I mean, there's only a few signal and lamp repeaters and you haven't got a repeater for the water tank but there is one at Wantage Road.' I was, in truth, a bit disappointed, because Uffington looked such a simple box without rows of flashy instruments.

'Damn good job too!' said Elwyn. 'A signalman don't need 'em. All this locking – they really were signalmen years ago when they didn't have all this protection and had to keep their minds on the job. Old Sid Phillips, down at Ashbury, told me once that the old M&SW* boxes were hardly locked at all, you could have the distant "off" and all the stop signals "on" – dhu-man, you had to be a signalman in a box like that!'

---

* The Midland & South Western Junction Railway which ran from Cheltenham to Andover. Absorbed into the Great Western Railway in 1921.

'Do you believe that? Surely it can't be true?' I was quite incredulous. 'Well, old Sid said it was so. You ought to go and see him, nice old boy, he'd tell you a thing or two.'

'I've just thought – where is the pump-house for filling the water-tower?'

'There is no need of one. Those old engineers were clever men indeed. The water is brought from a well sunk up in the hills yonder. It's about a hundred feet above the tank and just runs down here through a pipe – simple, see. And that's probably why we've no "High" and "Low" warning instrument because there's no pump to go wrong so the tank never empties.'

'But how is it prevented from overflowing with that weight of water standing in the pipe? I'd like to go up to see the valve. It must be a huge ball and arm. Have you ever seen it?'

Elwyn made his disdainful face and reached for his snuff tin. 'Catch me climbing up water-towers – but I do know it's only broken down once in living memory – that was through abuse. I don't suppose you've met Walt Thomas – he was in the box here for thirty-seven years, retired when the passengers finished on the branch – he said it was a sleeve-valve – whatever *that* might be. He knew because a man servicing it one day wanted to see if it was working properly. He shoved the arm down and in came the water – lets go of the arm, the water cuts off. He was quite pleased with that, so he tried it two or three times more and then climbed down the ladder. When he got below the tank, he could see down the branch and saw a great fountain of water coming up from the ballast. Starting and stopping tons of water he'd put terrible pressures inside the pipe and it'd burst. There was hell to pot!'

The trains were passing all the while and minute by minute I wrote off the advancing morning – a signalman's job was the greatest 'clock-watching' occupation in the world – until it was one o'clock. 'Well now,' said Elwyn, rising from the armchair, 'I'll just visit the little 'ouse and then get round with the broom.' He went into the cardboard-walled lavatory, the cistern flushed and he emerged. 'Flimsy old place, that is. On engineering Sundays, when you've got a lot of men in the box, there's some who are embarrassed to use it and go down to the station u-*ri*-nals. Well, look you, go now, I can finish. Get here about seven tomorrow morning. No need to be dead on time. We'll do some more and maybe get the rule book out.'

I said my 'good-day' and drove home, very happy after a pleasant morning at work.

CHAPTER TWELVE

A Duke at Breakfast

Elwyn was responsible for the safe working of the signal box and was liable to answer for any accident or delay to a train resulting from a mistake of mine. Over the next three or four weeks he let me work the box continuously while he talked about the rules and regulations or his own career, or other men's, with great cheerfulness so that I learned, simultaneously, my tangible work and the spirit in which it ought to be carried out. Nowadays, the NUR would like men to receive extra pay for this work but no one, then, considered such a thing. Elwyn taught me in the best tradition of 'fraternity', which the Union likes to think of as its own – no extra money would have made him any better at his job, but we each gained a friend.

Uffington was for the most part simply a 'passing' box, a larger edition of Lockinge but became more interesting at eight o'clock each morning when the 7.25 Swindon to Faringdon goods arrived; on Mondays and alternate weekdays it was joined by the Didcot to Uffington Fly and then the signal box was as busy as it ever had been.

The 7.25 Swindon was hauled by a pannier tank as a rule and on arrival at Uffington backed into the sidings through points 33. Considerable shunting and lever pulling ensued. The wagons for Uffington and local stations to Didcot were detached and the engine and brake van had to change ends of the train for the run to Faringdon. If the Fly was at the station, it would go up into Baulking sidings, clear of the Faringdon's manoeuvres; its crew having breakfast of tea and sandwiches, occasionally frying bacon and egg in the firing shovel placed just inside the furnace.

When the Faringdon had rearranged its train and taken water from the platform column, it would be standing quietly alongside the branch platform, the engine just outside the box and the driver, fireman or both men would come to the box for the 'train staff'. This was a piece of polished oak, triangular in section, about fourteen inches long, with an engraved brass plate UFFINGTON – FARINGDON. No driver could take his train onto the branch without the staff, and as there was only one, we avoided head-on collisions on the single line, without any more sophisticated system of signalling.

The driver came up into the box one morning soon after I started learning.

'Mornin' Elwyn, got a strapper then?' Elwyn introduced me.

'Can anyone tell me why a learner is a strapper?' I asked.

'No offence, mate,' said the driver, 'it's just a saying, never thought much about it. I reckon it must be as old as the railway; come to think of it, I was a "strapper" when I left school and went on the farm about 1920.'

'Have you worked over the branch a lot?' I asked next. The driver laughed.

'Me and old Sid Wilcox worked it in passenger days, didn't we, Elwyn?'

'Indeed, yes. Do you remember the time you lost old Sid's breakfast for him.'

'Oh ah! That was the day he chased me round the station with the shovel and the train was late leaving.'

'What was that then?' I looked from one to the other. Elwyn started to explain.

'They used to come up on a goods from Swindon and when they'd sorted out the shunting they went onto the coaches stabled on the run-round loop, hooked on and came into the platform ready for the day's service. So now they got onto the coaches but they were in plenty of time and didn't hook on.'

'No,' continued the driver, 'came up here for some fresh water to make Sid and me some tea – you must have only just come here then Elwyn – and when I got back to the engine old Sid was squatting down in front of the fire with some sausages frying in the shovel.'

'Then old Freddie Hands the guard came up,' Elwyn took up the tale, 'and says "Ease-up" 'cos he was going to go underneath and couple up, so Bert here' – I looked at Bert who was grinning all over his face – 'leans over Sid down by the fire and yanks up the regulator. "Whoof" goes the engine and, of course, the blast out of the chimney sucked the sausages off the shovel.' They both laughed at the memory and Bert continued.

'Old Sid was furious 'cos he'd lost his grub and come at me wi' the shovel. I jumped off the engine and ran and him following – he stepped on two of his blessed sausages!'

'You see,' said Elwyn, 'they'd been blown out of the chimney; I saw them come out of the funnel – I was trying to tell them but I was laughing too much to shout properly.' He shook his head slowly, 'D'you-mon, what a morning!'

Just then the guard came in. 'Come on then, how about a bit of railway work – mornin' Elwyn. Oh! Got a mate?' I was introduced again. 'Come on then, Bert, let's get off.' They went down the steps, climbed aboard their respective parts of the train and with a cheerful 'toot' the train left. So much for the rules governing the working of the branch.

'When did you come to Uffington, Elwyn?' I asked after the train had gone.

'January 1943. Fred Joyce and Walt Thomas were here then, steady old boys they were, old Fred was a bit crusty at times – huh! He started on the railway at Highclere in 1899 and came here in 1910 so I suppose he was entitled to get a bit short tempered now and then.'

'Where did Walt Thomas start?'

'Up at Paddington in 1902. I learnt the job from him so we spent some time together and I know a bit more about his life. He was a signal-porter at Marlow, a signalman at Greenford, then at Shrivenham and came to Uffington in 1914 – he retired only ten years ago. You could go and see him, he's always out in his garden by the main street of the village. Him and Fred were very close friends; them and two other chaps clubbed together, bought an acre of land from the Craven estate and had two semi-detached houses built. Very solid jobs they are – Fred and Walt still live side by side with their families.'

'They must have been very well paid to have afforded all that.'

'Well, I don't know about that. Better paid than any other worker locally. Railway wages were high forty years ago compared to most working-class jobs, and what was just as important, you knew you wouldn't be laid off. A porter would have to move for promotion or because the Company decided he wasn't needed where he was – but they didn't sack him, and once he became a signalman at a reasonably high-class box like this, he knew he was set for life with a regular job – so he could have raised a mortgage, I suppose.'

'Was the branch very busy when you got here, Elwyn?'

'Not as busy as it had been in the '20s – Walt said they had twenty-two trains a day then – but busy enough all the same. We had two passenger trains booked each way morning and evening and at least one extra trip each way with loaded and empty siphons and tanker wagons of milk.'

'They used milk *tankers*?!'

'Indeed, yes. It was the war, petrol shortage, they had to put all the milk back on rail. Literally millions of gallons of milk came up the branch for London. The biggest engine they could use was a "Spinning Jenny", so they often went double-headed to cope with the overload.'

'What was a "Spinning Jenny"?'

'Oh, I don't know. A little tender engine, six-coupled with a big dome. They used to bring the milk up to here and leave it for the Chippenham to collect. In the evening you'd have a pair of them waiting just outside for the Wood Lane to drop the empties off and then they'd work it all down to Faringdon. Them days you used the "Warning" – it's still on the extra rules for the box but we never have to use it nowadays.'

Normally a signalman was forbidden to give 'Line Clear' for a train to approach unless the line on which the train was to run was clear for at least a quarter of a mile beyond the home signal. The spot where the quarter-mile distance ended was known as the 'clearing point' and signalmen made a mental note of some landmark to show them this important place. Elwyn pointed them out to me; they were not very conspicuous. 'On the Up road the clearing point falls eighty yards short of the advanced starter, so we use the signal as the marker to have something definite and on the Down road we reckon the road over-bridge marks the spot.'

The bell code for giving the 'Warning' was 3-5-5, which seemed exotic and I looked for an excuse to use it. One day, while I was still learning, the engine of the Fly wanted to take water. The Faringdon goods was blocking access to the water column at the branch platform so the engine had to come onto the Main line to stand by the column and was then well inside the clearing point.

Knighton Crossing then asked 'Line Clear' for a 'light engine' – an engine without a train – and I was delighted to be able to tap out the 3-5-5 code for the 'Warning Acceptance, Section clear but station or junction blocked'. There was a pause from Knighton until the penny dropped; obviously the code was hardly ever used, then back came the acknowledgement and in return I turned the block indicator to 'Line Clear'.

'That's very good,' said Elwyn, 'but do you know what you would have done in this case if you were *not* allowed to use the "Warning"?' I had not thought of that of course and groped around for a moment. 'Ah! I'd have had to "block back" with 2-4 on the bell before I let the engine out onto the running line.'

'And then what?'

'Well, Knighton would acknowledge the code if it was safe for him to do so and then I could have turned the block indicator to "Train on Line" and let the engine out.'

'How would you have cleared the block afterwards?'

'When the engine had gone into the siding and the points were set for Main line running, I'd have sent "Obstruction Removed" – 2-1, the same code as "Train out of Section" and turned the block indicator to "Normal".

'Right, you've got that. Now, what is Knighton Crossing doing with the engine you accepted under the "Warning"?'

'He'll bring it nearly to a stand at his home signal, lower it, and as the engine comes to the box, he'll hang a green flag from the window. The driver will acknowledge the flag with a toot on the whistle and then Knighton can pull off his starter because the driver knows that the line immediately ahead of the home signal is blocked.

'That's a piece of very old working, you know,' Elwyn said. 'An old railwayman I knew at Yeovil told me he'd started on the Great Western in 1884 when white was the colour for "All Right" and green was the colour for "Caution"; he reckoned it'd been changed around 1895 and gave me a little rhyme for the old rule:

White is right
And red is wrong
Green means gently go along.

'Can you tell me,' he went on, 'what you would do if the engine driver did not acknowledge the green flag but just went past as if he hadn't seen it?'

'I'd bring him to a stand at the starting signal and then immediately lower it but that doesn't seem very good to me; how can you be sure the driver knows what you mean?'

'Well, it's hope you must have, he'll have read the Rule Book and number 41 is written down specifically for that situation; does that reassure you?'

'Yes, I think it does. I'll have a look at rule 41, thanks.'

While we had been talking, Elwyn had been sitting in his chair and I had been watching the fireman of the Fly engine. He was standing on top of the engine's boiler, his back to me and Knighton, leaning against the arm of the column, engrossed in the sight of water swirling into the 1,200-gallon tanks. Only when the engine was quite close did he hear its sound. His head snapped round, and there was another engine approaching on the same track about 150 yards away. Knowing nothing of special bell codes and thinking that a crash was imminent, he took fright and jumped from the top of the engine to the platform with such abandon that he positively *bounced* off the paving, and with that momentum to help him came shooting up the short flight of steps and burst into the box – '*Look out!*'

Elwyn, who had seen none of this, leaped out of his chair and the fireman, leaning out of the box window, said, 'Thank God. It's stopped. What's your bloody game then mate?' I explained the situation to him and he went out, shaken but consoled to turn the tap off because his tanks were gushing water all over the platform. Elwyn settled back into his chair with a little laugh and snuffed himself. 'I reckon you're the first man to use the "Warning" here for years, causing chaos you are.'

'Well, what would you have done in the circumstances?'

'D'you-mon,' he said, drawing down the corners of his mouth, 'I wouldn't be so keen – I'd have asked the Faringdon to move back a few yards to make room for the Fly.'

Shunting the Fly and the Faringdon and fitting them into the traffic flow was the only 'regulating' duty we had. The Fly needed eight minutes to run up to Challow but the Faringdon returning to Swindon was a little more difficult.

Sometimes the porter at Faringdon would telephone to say when the goods had left but very often the first we knew of it was when we heard its whistle blowing loud and long, as it came galloping down the hill, for the branch home signal to be lowered. It arrived with the engine at the east end of the train and the guard's van at the west end so that, yet again, their positions had to be reversed before the train could leave for home. When the train was rearranged, the fireman would fill the locomotive's water-tanks while the driver came to the box with two conical drinking-water cans to be filled for Knighton Crossing, that box's only supply. The full cans were placed on the buffer beam of the engine, which then backed the train up into Baulking sidings to await a path across the Up Main, to the Down Main for the west-bound run.

Two minutes were needed for it to clear the Up Main. If an Up or Down train was 'asked' while the train was crossing over, I simply 'refused the road' – that is, I did not acknowledge the bell code until such time as the points were set for the Main lines and the clearing point was clear; there was no sense in using the 'Warning' for so temporary a block. Once on the Down Main I allowed the train eighteen minutes to stop at Knighton, restart and get into the goods loop, clear of the Main line, at Ashbury.

As the Faringdon was leaving for Swindon one morning, Elwyn was leaning from the window at one end of the box and I was leaning out of the other. We watched the train out of sight and stayed leaning on the bar enjoying the sun and the quiet. A pair of rooks in sober black with grey beaks like pickaxes were strolling along the crown of a rail, stopping now and then to peck or look at something.

'D'you see th' old gangers?' said Elwyn. I looked for some men and Elwyn, seeing me puzzled, said, 'The old rooks there. Don't you know they are the ghosts of long-dead gangers? That's why they're always patrolling the track – if they find a piece of ballast lying on the rail, they'll throw it off.' I looked uncertain but he pressed his point, 'I knew an old ganger who said he depended on the rooks to show him the hanging joints – where there's a cavity beneath the sleepers at a joint between rails – he swore that the rooks left a piece of stone on the sleeper of a bad joint.'

A bell rang and we went in. Knighton was asking the road for the 7.30 Carmarthen, the Up Red Dragon; I answered it while Elwyn put the kettle on. He went to the window sill and sat in the sun and I sat on the coal box, by the door and the back window. 'Where were you before you came here, Elwyn?' He thumbed up his snuff tin and offered it to me.

'No thanks very much.'

'I came out of school in 1929 at Bridgend – handy place to be that year too. I didn't have a proper job for five years but I'd had my name down with the Great Western and in the end I got a note from them – I could have a class 2 porter's job at Sparkford. Didn't know where it was, Somerset they said. Well, I was so pleased at having a proper job and on the railway that I took it and went. I'd hardly got there when they decided the place was overstaffed and sent me to Yeovil Pen Mill, same grade.'

'I've never been down that part of the world; what was it like?'

'Oh! Somerset is a beautiful place, though you, coming from round here, might not appreciate it as much as I did, coming up from Glamorganshire and the pits. Yeovil had a queer layout indeed. There were three stations there – Pen Mill was on the Great Western line from Castle Cary to Weymouth and had a branch going round to the Town station half a mile away, that was a joint station with the Southern and then there was the Southern station proper, Yeovil Junction, up on the Waterloo–Exeter line which crossed over the Weymouth line about a mile and a half south of Pen Mill. There was a fine, deep cutting between Pen Mill and the Southern Main line and the tracks were four abreast for a while, two of ours and two of theirs and then theirs went up a steep bank to join the Exeter road.'

'And did you have a junction between the Southern and the Great Western on the four-track section?'

'No – Ha! T'wud have been a good idea if there had been. In fact I believe they did lay something in during the war for the ambulance trains – and built a big, new signal box too – but when I was there in 1934, anything for the Southern had to be humped out of one train and into another just as if we had a break of gauge. That was what they wanted me for at Yeovil, humping parcels and people out of the Weymouth trains and into the little dasher that went round to the Town station.'

'Was the Town station a terminus then, served by an engine and coach?'

'Bless you no! The line went through to Taunton and we got Southern tankies coming into Pen Mill from the Junction via the Town. It was a queer place. People from Weymouth line stations for Exeter used to have to get out at the Great Western Pen Mill station, cross the platform for a dasher round to the town, get out again and get into a Southern dasher, go up to the Junction station, going back the way they'd come for a mile or so, get out of that train and wait on the platform for the express to Exeter. 'Course, if they got into a Southern dasher at Pen Mill, they didn't have to change at the Town.'

'I wish I could have seen it; it must have been marvellous to have both companies' engines working into your station and all that complicated railway.'

'Oh, it would have suited you all right, but I know the booking clerks used to get some tricky accounting when the passengers were booking through from a Great Western to a Southern station.'

'Were you there long?'

'Oh yes, four years. I applied for all the promotion I saw advertised and it took that long to get the service in to make a move beyond the bottom grade of porter. But it wasn't so bad. My wages were £2 a week, I had a good lodge, and for £1 my landlady gave me full board and did all my washing and ironing, and very clean and decent the house was indeed.'

The 1-2-1 code rang from Knighton. I answered it, 'got the road ahead' from Challow and pulled off. Elwyn came in from the sun and made the tea as the Challow bell 'dinged' one beat. I answered and got a 3-2 bell for a slow goods train.

'I went down to Portland, porter-signalman. I had from 2 p.m. to 4 p.m. in the box and the rest of the time I was humping sides of bacon in the goods shed – that and ingots of steel for Whitehead's torpedo factory. D'you-mon, it was murder, and when the Fleet was in – Oh! The sacks of brussels sprouts and kegs of rum.' Knighton rang the 'Train on Line'. 'I got out of that pretty fast. I was lucky, and landed the highest paid porter-signalman's job in the Bristol division – permanent early turn at Weymouth Town station. The box was a Class 2 and I worked it from 6 a.m. till 8 a.m. and then went up the station for portering. Till two o'clock.'

'When did you get your first signalman's job?'

'I went to Pilning Low Level in 1939. It was only Class 5 – but that was better than Class 6 and it shared in the Sunday work at Severn Tunnel East.' The Dragon came hammering through behind a 'King' class engine, I sent it 'on line' to Challow and received 'on line' for the 3-2 goods train at the same time. I 'got the road' from Knighton, put the Up signal to 'Danger' and then 'pulled off' on the Down road for the goods.

'I suppose you had to move though, for the promotion?'

'Well, that and the bombing.'

'*Bombing?*'

'Well, yes,' he took a sip of tea, 'we were in the middle of dockland there, Bristol, Avonmouth and Newport and then there was the Bristol aircraft factory at Filton. Bloody Jerry was always over, sometimes just a "tip-an'-run" but very often a full-scale raid on somewhere; they had plenty to choose from,' his face suddenly became very indignant and he sat up straighter in his chair, 'and damn-all *sleep* could man get when *they* were buzzing around, dropping their bombs and our guns firing back.' He delved for his snuff.

'Well, I suppose it wasn't too difficult to find somewhere quieter with all the staff shortages that there were then?'

'Huh! I didn't get away until 1942 and then I went to Yarnbrook between Westbury and Trowbridge. It was only a break-section box like Lockinge but there was so much traffic that it was a Class 4 and after a year o' that I moved to here. It did Walt Thomas for thirty-seven years and I reckon it'll do me the same. That's the funny thing about Uffington; people come here from miles away and stay forever.'

The goods train came tonking under the bridge down in the cutting and I got up to see to it. The engine was a '63' class making about 30 mph. I watched from the open window as she came down towards the box snorting a brisk rhythm and her driver, leaning over the cab-side, looking at the ground, seemed to be listening to it intently. He looked up as he drew close to the box, I saw his hand reach for the whistle chain. The whistle 'pooped' twice and the engine passed the box with a wave and a smile from her driver. Her cab, unmodified after forty years, had very skimpy side-sheets; her tender was low. I had a perfect view into the cab: her fireman was busy with his coal-pick tugging coal forward on the tender; her fire, just visible behind the fire-hole flap, was pure, incandescent, white.

I put the signals back to 'Danger' and attended to the bells, passing them to the register. 'You really enjoy watching them engines, don't you?' said Elwyn, just a little amused.

'Yes, I always have done, I feel fond of them, the same feeling I had for the pony I used to ride before I left school, or perhaps even more than that. There's something about the rhythm they make and the way they seem to work for the driver. No wonder they were called the iron horse.'

'You'd have liked it here a few years ago when we had the Royal train to stable on the branch. It came two years running with the Duke of Edinburgh both times.'

'Did they take a Main line express engine onto the branch?'

'Indeed, yes. A "Castle" it was and they had to take the coping stones off the milk dock or its cylinders would have struck against them on the sharp curve, even then it had a job to get round; I saw then why they don't let big engines on the branch, they nearly get wedged on the curve. If you go down the hill on the branch, you'll find the white post with a lamp bracket that was put up to mark where the driver had to stop – he had to have the lamp exactly between the engine and the tender and then he knew that the tail of the train was clear of points 30. Hah! I often wondered how the ol' Duke slept when the train was tilted on a 1 in 88 gradient. Ol' branch ganger had to crawl under the lavatory pipes with chamber pots – d'you-mon, he was Chairman of our branch of the Union too. Those pots had the Royal Arms on them and in the morning he had to go in and fetch 'em, wash 'em out and put 'em onto the train.'

I laughed at this because I knew the man a little and could just imagine his indignation. 'He was more of a republican than ever after that, I suppose?'

'Republican, is it?' said Elwyn indignantly. 'He was livid!'

'Well, next morning I was having my egg and bread, about seven, when the door opens and who should walk in but the Duke of Edinburgh! There I was in my shirt sleeves and no collar, just like I am now. I got up – I didn't know whether to bow or what but before I'd sorted myself out he'd come over and shaken hands with me. Very nice chap, you know. I can say that too, as a life-long Labour voter. He wanted to know about the box and I told 'im and then I felt we were getting on fine so I offered 'im a cup of tea but he turned that down – said he had a breakfast waiting for him in the train – so he shook hands again and went out. Dear, dear, when I sat down – my breakfast was all cold. I nearly went to him for a bit of hot food.

'The amazing thing was that they stabled him on the branch the following year, police and soldiers all over the place, and blow me if I wasn't on early turn. Well, I sat down to my egg and tea about seven and I'd not taken the top off the eggs when the door opens and in he comes again. "*Oh drat!*" I thought, "another cold breakfast." But he said "Not still eating that egg?"

and grinned, so I felt better; we shook hands – he's a great man for that – and I offered him a cup of tea and this old armchair so's I could get on with my breakfast.

'Well, he said that'd be all right and sat down but then I realised that my spare mug didn't have a handle. I tried the other chaps' lockers but they were both locked and there he was, waiting for his tea and my breakfast getting cold again. Dear, dear. So he had to have the handle-less mug but he minded less than me and must have sat, watching me work the box and talking for twenty minutes; I reckon he'd have liked to have had a go himself. Then he got up and said, "Thank you very much, Mr Richards"' – I broke in: 'And shook your hand again?' – 'Yes – shook 'ands and says "I'd better go and see what they've got me for breakfast." And off he went.'

'It must have been very fine to see a "Castle" pushing backwards off the branch and past the box into Baulking sidings and to see those beautiful coaches – I don't suppose anyone has a photograph of it?'

'No one but staff got anywhere near here, let me tell you. But it was a sight to see all right. They pushed down clear of the crossings, then I pulled off and that old engine came across to the down-side with a steady "one-two-three-four" out of the chimney.'

'Aha!' I butted in. 'So you see what I mean about the sort of music they play?'

'Well, I must admit they can look very good and sound good too, I'm very keen on music myself so I know what you mean. The last I saw of His Royal Highness was him waving to me out of his carriage as he passed the box. A very nice gentleman.'

CHAPTER THIRTEEN

Swindon Fashion

Remote though the setting of Uffington box was, Elwyn had several visitors, official and otherwise, to keep him company for a few minutes or two hours – even on the night shift. Mary, the wife of the Signal & Telegraph department technician who lived in the station house across the yard, came in for a few minutes each day when she brought the daily newspaper. She came originally from Somerset and her bright smile and cheerful West Country voice reminded me of cider apple orchards on a sunny day. Mr Halford came to the box when he visited the station but never stayed longer than he had to. The station's porter, Les, always came up for his afternoon tea and might spend the hour telling you about his infallible plan for robbing a bank or he might eat in silence except for clicking his biro point in and out – for an hour. One Swindon reliefman was said to have evicted him for this but Elwyn said, 'He's the porter and he can come up here if he likes, just ignore him when the mood takes him.' On late turn and nights, when the vicar of the parish visited the box and had a sort of 'behind the scenes' vestry meeting, I discovered that Elwyn's hobby was parish church matters; he was a church warden and choirmaster.

After the vicar had left, late one night, I said to Elwyn, inquisitively I must admit, 'You and the vicar get around the countryside a good deal, Elwyn.'

'He likes a good, comfortable pub, where there's a nice, quiet atmosphere, good food and well-kept beer – the Trout at Lechlade or the Trout at Godstow, then there's the White Hart at Wytham ... you ought to get out to them, you'd like it; old-fashioned, handsome houses in a good setting with fine service.'

'It sounds like a hobby – I've never thought of it.'

'Don't tell me you had five years in the Army and never went drinking?'

'Well, that's just it, I used to go *drinking* – and very uncomfortable it was too. Scrumpy at tuppence a pint down on the Barbican at Plymouth or brown ale up Union Street. I gave it up after a while and went out watching trains instead; it was more interesting. I never went into any pubs like you're describing.'

'Well, of course, you got to find the right ones. I suppose a bunch of squaddies don't care too much so long as it's beer.'

'Well, they weren't vicars and choirmasters so they weren't looking for anything very profound – not up Union Street, anyhow. I must say, the way you describe it, it makes it sound like a very civilised form of entertainment. Do you go far afield searching for new places?'

'I make a weekend in London now and then – when I go up for my snuff and stop in some nice old place.'

'To London for snuff? Is there a great difference to the snuff you could get in Oxford?'

'Yes, probably, but it's not just that, it makes an excuse for a weekend away. I go to Fribourg & Treyer, near Leicester Square, for the snuff. It's a beautiful little shop. The firm have been there since 1720; it's still got its curved windows with small panes on each side of the front door – and brass window sills too. Inside they've got snuff in every scent you could wish for, they've got every kind of cigar, cigarette and pipe and it's all in eighteenth-century boxes and cupboards. The place is well worth going to just to look at and once you've been there a few times they know you and what you like so you have good service. Oh, it's very pleasant.'

'Yes, I see what you mean. It'd never crossed my mind. I went from school to the army and there tobacco meant "Woodbines" from the NAAFI and beer was whenever and wherever you could get it.'

'Once a year we have to take the choirboys for their outing to London. We go up on the nine o'clock from Challow and walk all round town from the Tower to Madame Tussauds with a lunch break at the George in Southwark – a beautiful place that. By the time we get 'em back to Paddington for the 5.5 they're so tired they go to sleep on the platform seats. We have to carry some of them into the train, but then we can get a few pints in the restaurant car to revive ourselves, me and the vicar, after our exhausting day shepherding them round, without worrying that they might be getting into mischief.' He said that with a deadpan face but with a gentle irony in his voice and I began to realise that Elwyn was quite a character.

I had worked with him for three shifts – early, nights and late – and felt fairly confident of facing the District Inspector and passing the rules examination. 'What's Mr Millsom like on the rules, Elwyn?' I asked on Monday morning of my fourth week learning.

'Oh, very fair. He'll ask you direct questions, nothing hidden or awkwardly put; he won't be trying to trip you up – very fair.'

'Well, thank goodness for that. Where's he from, do you know?'

'He started on the Berks & Hants line, Newbury, I think, as a booking lad. Jack Lockett was a booking boy, too, from Westbury and I think you'll find that the Chief Inspector at Bristol, Dick Wellman, comes from Westbury, too, or around there. Him and Albert Stanley were porters together.'

Later that morning Mr Millsom and Mr Lockett got off the Up stopper. 'Hey up, Adrian,' said Elwyn in the same hushed voice that I had heard Sam use at Challow, 'here they are.'

I knew from his voice who 'they' were and my stomach skipped up and down nervously. I watched them come along the platform. They made a splendid sight in their dark-blue, Melton-cloth overcoats and brown trilby hats. Mr Lockett a head taller than his colleague Mr Millsom, silver-haired, walking with his shoulders hunched, hands deep in his overcoat pockets, his head thrust forward, a briar pipe smoking thickly. Both men moved in a calm, self-possessed way – they were railway officers.

They came into the box. 'Mornings' were exchanged all round.

'Well, Elwyn, what do you think of your learner? Is he ready to take charge?'

'Oh yes, Mr Millsom,' said Elwyn loyally, 'I think he is.'

'What do you think, young man? Could you pass me on the rules?' He looked at me very hard, his bright-blue eyes keen under the dark brim of his trilby. I felt that it would sound horribly boastful to answer a simple 'Yes' to that question and instead said, 'Er, perhaps after a few more days, Mr Millsom.'

'Jack,' said the District Inspector, 'take him outside for twenty minutes on the rules.'

Mr Lockett was an older man than Mr Millsom and he had brown eyes that could never look anything but friendly. 'Come on then, Adrian,' he said, holding the door open for me. We strolled along the platform. 'Now don't worry about answering, you'll know the answer just by hearing the questions. Have you been working on the rules with Elwyn?'

'Yes, quite a lot.'

'Well then, you ought to be all right so long as you don't get excited about things.' He asked me a few questions about the rules as they applied to the station, standing at the west end of the platform and pointing out the places on the track where supposed failures or accidents had taken place. He was very gentle and I soon relaxed; it was like talking to Elwyn. 'You'll do,' he said after a while, 'we'll go back to the box.'

Elwyn and Mr Millsom were sitting, each with a mug of tea when we got back. 'There's fresh tea in the pot. Mr Lockett, Adrian, help yourselves.'

I went to pour some tea but Jack Lockett waved me away. 'Sit down, I'll fetch it.'

'Well, what do you think, Jack? Will he do?'

'Yes, he'll be all right. You can have him down next week.'

'Right then, be in my office this day week at nine o'clock sharp,' said Mr Millsom emphasising the words by stabbing the air with the stem of his pipe.

After they had gone, Elwyn said, 'Right then, you'd better give me the duster – set to with the black Rule Book and the "Apple Green" signalling regulations. I'll give you a test each day.' I was certain of knowing Regulations 1 to 11 as they covered daily signalling routine and concentrated my efforts on the emergency codes in the latter part of the book.

Regulation 12 described the working of 'Obstruction Danger', 6 bells. This was rung to the box in the rear 'to prevent the approach of a train in the event of an accident, obstruction or other exceptional cause'. Regulation 13 concerned 'Animals on the Line' and how to deal with such trespass – curiously, no bell code was prescribed for this eventuality, neither did the book recommend that 6 bells should be sent for a herd of cows on the line. Regulation 15 gave instructions for 'Examination of the Line' under every conceivable circumstance; 14 told me how to remove a train from the section when its locomotive had failed; 16 advised what steps to take if a train was an unusually long time in the section; and 17 was 'Stop and Examine', 7 bells.

This commenced: 'Signalmen must be careful to notice each train to ascertain whether there is any apparent necessity for having it stopped at the next signal box for examination. If a signalman observes, or becomes aware of, anything unusual in a train such as signals of alarm, goods falling off, a vehicle on fire, hot axle box or other mishap – except tail lamp out or missing – he must send the "Stop and Examine" signal to the signal box in advance.'

Probably the commonest source of 7 bells was doors open on passenger trains or handles not properly turned. The signal was also sent for 'whistling noises', 'funny rattles' and 'bumping noises', literally anything that was, to the careful signalman, unusual. All signalmen felt they had a serious duty to investigate anything out of the ordinary, because if some small thing was let to go unchecked and subsequently caused an accident, the erring signalman would have to bear the omission on his conscience for a very long time. 17 was the Regulation of Absolute Care but its importance has lessened under the automatic system of signalling, which covers a large part of Western Region today because there are few places where a signalman can observe the trains.

Regulation 19 dealt with tail lamps. If a train passed a signal box and the signalman was uncertain whether the last vehicle was carrying its lamp, he had to assume that it was not, that the vehicle had broken away and was behind in the section. He would then send 9 bells to the box in advance and 4-5 bells to the box in the rear. The man receiving the 9 would stop the train for examination and the man receiving 4-5 prevented anything else from entering the section until it was known to be clear.

So they went on, through Regulation 20 'Train Divided' (accidentally) with the bell code 5-5, 'Train Running away in the Right Direction' 4-5-5 and in the 'Wrong Direction' 2-5-5, through 'Time Interval Working' when all the block instruments had failed, reducing everything to mere guesswork, to the final solution – 'Switching out Signal Box' aptly placed at the end of the book. Elwyn coached me through all this and far more, making tea, thinking up questions to ask – which, I found out later when I had to do it myself, is almost as hard as answering them – until on Friday he pronounced me well and truly crammed.

Next Monday I caught the 8.15 a.m. from Challow, boarding the train with a slap on the back and good luck wishes from Sam Loder. I travelled down with the three girls and would have been very happy with their company under normal circumstances but on that occasion I could barely speak. 'You're very talkative today,' said Veronica. 'Ugh! Sorry, I'm going for an examination on the rules and regulations so's I can be a signalman and I don't feel very well.' We got to Swindon at 8.45 and they left me with cheerful 'Good lucks' and, 'Tell us how you got on tomorrow.'

There was plenty to see on the station but it was hardly enough to take my mind off the dreaded interview. I strolled along the platform towards the West signal box, trying to think of some facts, and, being unable to recall any, feeling sick. Spare screw couplings and steam heating pipes hung on racks against the old, flaking stone walls of the station and in the centre of the platform stood a drinking-water tank on wheels with a tall pipe supporting a long, rubber hose for filling the tanks of restaurant cars. Across the branch track and a couple of sidings, against the wall that bordered the main road, stood the grounded body of an ancient coach. A pannier tank was shunting in the sidings by the West box and a grimy '63' class 2-6-0 was standing at the head of three coaches in the Marlborough Bay.

Beyond the big West signal box with its clock on the rear wall and the four-post bracket signal close by, I could see a brilliantly white plume of steam rising from an engine in one of the factory sidings down by Rodbourne Lane signal box – from one box to the next, locomotives lined the upside of the line waiting to go into the factory for repair. In the 'V' of the junction between the Bristol and Gloucester roads stood the tall building housing the Chief Mechanical Engineer's offices, including the locomotive drawing office of the Great Western Railway; in the sidings in front of the building, a steam crane was working, and opposite the West box, across a dozen tracks, a pannier tank was shunting in and out of the General Stores enclosure. The station announcer began to introduce the 7.30 a.m. Paddington, and the clock on the West box said five to nine – it was time for me to take the plunge.

Mr Millsom's office was in a limestone-faced building which stood above the street entrance to the booking office and appeared to be part of the original (1840) Brunel station and had probably been the District Inspector's office since signalling was done by lineside policemen in 1840. I crossed the tracks from the branch platform to a flight of stone steps which led to a double door opening into a corridor. I pushed through, heart beating fast, and saw DISTRICT INSPECTOR in gold leaf over cracked, brown paint. I knocked. 'Come in.' Turning the ceramic handle, I opened the door and walked in.

Mr Millsom was sitting behind a wide, leather-topped desk of late-Victorian design and of Swindon carriage works manufacture; indeed, there was hardly an item of furniture in the room that was not made in the railway factory. On the desk was an 18-inch boxwood ruler engraved GWR and a pair of rectangular, cast-iron paperweights also marked GWR. On one wall, between some Swindon-built cupboards, was a Great Western Railway coloured print from the 1890s showing a Dean '7-foot Single' – *John G Griffiths*. It was a famous picture, a broadside view of the engine at speed, the background blurred and the exhaust streaming back stiffly over the train. An ivory plate on the picture frame gave the title – *80 on the Flat*. On another wall was a coloured print from the late 1920s showing a 'King' hauling the Cornish Riviera Express out of Parson & Clerk tunnel onto the sea wall at Teignmouth, under the red cliffs of Devon. The carpet I was standing on had a blue, grey, yellow and black pattern into which was woven – yes, GWR!

Time was frozen for an instant in that office, it was 1931, not 1961 and *John G Griffiths* steamed on eternally across the wall – through time at '80 on the Flat'. These pictures, which were then to be found in waiting rooms and offices all over the ex-Great Western Railway's territory, were, I think, taken for granted, hardly noticed but everyone felt it was right and proper that they should be there – they were part of the scene, part of the very mentality of railwaymen then and in that office they completed the atmosphere, leaving me without a shadow of doubt that, if I did not come up to the old Company's standards, I was not going to pass the examination. The Great Western Railway might have been physically abolished but before me was a man who still carried its standards high.

Mr Millsom waved me to a chair. 'Morning, Adrian, I hope you had a good night's sleep!' He picked up his pipe, started to pack it with a fresh charge of tobacco while I gripped my sweaty hands between my knees, and asked, 'If the wind blew the arm off a signal, how would you know what sort of signal the post should carry?' He worked away at his pipe. This was, literally, a stunning start. I was absolutely full of rules and absolutely nowhere is there any mention of such a thing. I thought of Elwyn's assessment that Millsom was a 'very fair man' and wondered just how much Elwyn knew about it.

Mr Millsom looked at me from the cover of a freshly lit pipe, his eyes shining through like stars on a cloudy night. With sudden relief I realised he was having me on and I remembered that stop signals have a red ball to their finial and distant signals have a yellow ball – something not mentioned anywhere in the rules or regulations but in fact quite an important point for an engine driver to know should he ever find a signal post minus its arm.

He laughed when I answered. 'There, that had you worried for a minute; now then, let's get on with the quiz.' The ice had been broken very cleverly by this excellent man and we set off on a four-hour session of question and answer. Occasionally he stopped to illustrate the regulation with interesting stories, one of which I remember clearly.

He had asked me when the 'Warning Arrangement' was employed at Uffington and what was the bell code for it. I told him and then he said, 'Down at Bincombe Tunnel box they were allowed to use the "Warning" if any train was "asked" while they were crossing the banker over to go back to Weymouth. There was an old chap there who'd worked the box for thirty years and the Inspector thought it was about time to give him a brush-up on the rules.

'He went along to the box and began asking the questions. The old chap got stuck almost straight away on Regulation 5 – he couldn't say what was the bell code for the "Warning". He had an Up train coming from Weymouth with a banker on behind and the Inspector was threatening to take him out of the box if he couldn't remember the code. Well, the Up train went by and the banker came to a stand by the box to cross over back to Weymouth and just as the cross-over was pulled, Dorchester "asked the road" for something and the old chap rattled out the 3-5-5, though it sounded more like a straight 13.

"'What's that you've just done?" says the Inspector.

'The old signalman looked guilty and nervous. "We always do that when the banker's crossing and we get one 'asked', Guv'nor."

"'But what do you *call* it?"

"'God bless my soul, Guv'nor, I don't know!"

"'*That is* the 'Warning' – you've just rung it!" It was a job to know who was the more surprised.'

I left Mr Millsom's office just after one o'clock, feeling as if I'd been squeezed through a mangle, but with an appointment to see the Chief Inspector and Divisional Superintendent at Bristol the following Monday.

The Chief Inspector, Dick Wellman, was a heavily built man, very down to earth and friendly. He spent a few minutes asking after Albert and Harry. 'I was at school with Albert, you know; either of them could have had this chair here if they'd cared to make all the moves for promotion but they settled down at Challow and never worried about it.'

'I spent some time with Harry and got the impression that what he didn't know wasn't worth knowing. He was quite formidable really – he's done most of the jobs in the Traffic Department, including the station master's, without moving out of the porter's grade.'

'Albert is just as capable. The old-hand porters had so much work to do, varied work, that they couldn't help learning a lot, from the sheer, physical hard work to the accountancy side – they had to know it all. And by the way you're wrong about Harry only ever being a porter; he was a Signalman at Circourt for a while. But did he ever tell you the work he had to do when he was a porter-signalman at Burbage Wharf?'

This seemed like the start of a good tale; at any rate, it was not 'rules'.

'Do you mean that old goods shed just south of Marlborough where the main road crosses the canal and the railway where they run parallel?' He seemed disappointed that I knew it.

'You know about it then?'

'No, not at all, except that I've passed over the bridge on my way home from Tidworth when I was in the Army and I often wondered what went on there. It looks as if it was an interchange between the canal and the railway.'

'Well, it might have been, long ago, but I don't think that's why it was put there. The town is only three miles away so the canal company built a wharf to serve it and when the railway came they built a siding and goods shed. I doubt that it was much of an interchange though, of course there was nothing to prevent it seeing as how the Great Western bought the canal people out.'

'It seems an out-of-the-way place to put a goods train. Was there much traffic there?'

'Ah, it does look like that now but when lorries weren't very reliable or plentiful it was very useful, right on the side of the main road and not too far from Marlborough. You got coal and farm machinery coming in, anything the district needed, and farm produce and cattle going out. On Marlborough fair days the big dealers would come down from London and Birmingham and they'd send cattle away from the Wharf, all over the country.'

'But what about the M&SW station at Marlborough; couldn't they have used that?'

'Well, of course they did – it was always very busy, especially on fair days, but it was only the station for some destinations.'

'So Harry was there all on his own, loading wagons, sheeting them, doing the paperwork and looking after the box?'

'Well now, I'm not sure about that, there may well have been one other man, simply doing portering. I don't know how the place was manned or what hours it opened to the public.'

'Did many trains call at the siding?'

'There were three trains booked to call in the mid-'20s, as I recall. The Reading to Bristol Fly was there from about half past seven to eight o'clock then they had the Up goods from Westbury to Ludgershall an hour later and the 5.15 Holt Junction to Didcot an hour after that.'

'Good Lord! You just wouldn't think that all those trains and all that work went on, looking at the place now.' My surprise was genuine. I found his revelations of this remote place very exciting and he was pleased with the effect they had had.

'Ah, and on top of that, Harry would have to arrange for special stops to be made by other goods trains to pick up consignments of cattle. The old farmers just turned up and dumped the animals and left us to find a service at the drop of a hat *and* feed and water their cows too – Harry'd have to see to all that. Another thing Harry was called upon to do was open the box to shorten the section. The box was three quarters of a mile west of Savernake West box and the line came up "in the collar" for sixteen miles from Lavington so when they had a few trains about, like on a summer

Saturday, or if one was doing rough up the bank – and, of course, between Burbage and Savernake it was at its steepest bit – Harry would switch in to shorten the section between Savernake West and Pewsey.'

'That's absolutely fascinating – you go there now and it's still and quiet, nothing stirs, yet it was so busy a few years ago.'

Mr Wellman nodded happily. 'I'd heard you were interested in the old days – but this isn't what you're here for so let's talk about the General Appendix.'

He proceeded to ask me a lot of obscure questions from that obscure publication, none of which seemed to have any connection with the work at Uffington; none of which I could answer. 'That's the trouble nowadays,' he said, 'you blokes only read the bits that actually concern your job.'

But he said I'd passed and took me to see the Divisional Superintendent, Paul Pearman. He waved me into a beautiful, early-Victorian, mahogany chair with the letters B&ER (Bristol & Exeter Railway) carved in the backrest, asked me some questions on single-line working – which I answered – told me what *not* to do at Uffington, gave me a very old working timetable, told me that I was now a signalman, and suggested that I might like to visit the East signal box at Temple Meads. After the fatigue, the sweet – as the Duke of Cumberland once said.

Bristol Temple Meads East signal box was built in the severe style of the 1930s with a flat, concrete roof and red brick walls decorated by three strata of cement and all-round glazing in steel frames. A rectangular extrusion jutted out from ground to roof at the centre-front of the box to form a bay window in the operating room; the building was a huge box in more ways than one. It stood on the up-side of six or eight running lines midway between the station's fifteen platforms and its three geographical junctions, and from it all points and signals were controlled by electricity, the signals being colour lights.

I went in and climbed the stairs to the operating room where the three signalmen and their booking lad were expecting me. The latter was sitting in the bay window with his sleeves rolled up surrounded by a battery of telephones while the men were stationed in front of the longest row of 'levers' – small 'draw-out' handles, in fact – in the country.

The two furthest away kept their positions and waved a greeting and the man nearest the stairs said, 'It's Adrian, isn't it? Paul Pearman said you were on your way. The lad's put the kettle on so we'll all have one in a minute. Is Elwyn still at Uffington?' I told him he was. 'Good old Elwyn, steady as they come, great man for the Guinness.' I said I'd learnt Uffington under him. 'Then you're lucky – good company, good teacher. Tell him that Jessie Bye, Bill Barker and Fred Wilcox send their best wishes – we've all worked up through that part. Well now, Pearman told us to show you round – what do you think of our little toy?'

'I'm just overwhelmed – where do you start to look? I keep losing count of the number of block bells; how many draw-slides are there?'

'Walk along and count 'em,' he said with a grin. I paced perhaps twenty-five steps and counted twenty-two bells and 336 handles. 'What comes to my mind first is "How does your booking lad know which one is ringing?" Obviously he *does* but ...'

The booking lad grinned at me, 'You pick it up.'

'Why so many bells?' I asked him.

'Well, we're working with six signal boxes: Temple Meads West, Old Station, Goods Yard, Barrow Road, Doctor Day's and North Somerset Junction, and through the station, between the platforms, there's a dozen roads at least, each with a bell – it soon adds up.'

'How many boxes does all this replace?'

'Only two – the old East box that they called the "Coffin" box on account of its shape and South Wales Junction.'

'Are you sure it was the "Coffin" box only for its shape? It must have been a very heavy place to work with all the switching from platform to platform, shunting passenger stock and all on ordinary levers.'

'Well, this is all one handle to one point or one signal – not like the other Great Western power boxes where you set up a whole route, maybe a dozen points, with one lever. We've got all that fan of tracks going into the platforms or through the middle; then we've the junction to the Midland for Gloucester and Bath for the old Somerset & Dorset; in the middle we've got four tracks going round to Doctor Day's for South Wales or Paddington via Badminton or round to Avonmouth; then there's the old Main line to Paddington through Bath and between those two routes you've got Doctor Day's carriage sidings.'

'Where's the tea? I think I'd better have a cup! I'd never be able to work this.'

'Ah you would; you'd pick it up,' said the booking lad modestly, pouring my tea with one hand and writing bell code times in the register with the other.

The signalmen set up serpentine routes, often in cooperation with each other, walking up and down their length pushing or pulling handles with a nonchalance that made them appear to be working at random. I could turn from watching the route being set up and look out over the orderly confusion of tracks and watch the trains that had just been signalled come past the box. 'Kings', 'Castles', 'Patriots' and 'Jubilees' slogging away from the station or freewheeling in, their trains following heavily, dun-dunning over the rail joints, flanges squealing against the curves. Names I recollect from that visit were those of the 'Devonian' express which left, northbound, double-headed behind a 'Patriot' 45509 (which ought to have been named 'Commando' but never received the plate) and 'Jubilee' 45577 *Bengal*. It was, without any doubt, the finest train set that I or anyone else will ever see.

I left the box after three hours, with many thanks to the four of them for their hospitality. I had, of course, enjoyed the visit but I did not feel I wanted to work there. Maybe it was too clever for me or perhaps it did not conform to my idea of a signal box; at any rate, I travelled home thrilled at the thought that I was a signalman and full of the anticipation of my first shift at Uffington on Monday morning.

CHAPTER FOURTEEN

Signalman's Morning

On Monday I woke to my alarm just after five o'clock. I felt as if it was my birthday and got out of bed immediately so as not to miss the party. Through the small window sunk deep in the thatch I saw the sun just above the horizon, shining promisingly through a few strands of night clouds. The village was silent in the bright light, not even a chimney smoked, the long grass in the meadow opposite seemed to be asleep, lying bent and flat under the weight of dew, and even the cows were lying down.

After a wash, some tea, bread and marmalade, I picked up the bag of sandwiches my mother had cut the previous evening. 'I shan't make them until the very last moment, so they'll be fresh,' she had said. I unbolted the back door and stepped outside into a cool, sunny morning. The sun was clear of the cloud now and as I walked across the garden to my car I could see in sharp detail every beech tree in a plantation on the ridge of the Downs over a mile away. The air was as clear as water in a stream, colours were bright and fresh. It was a signalman's morning, I thought, and felt happy.

I drove by way of Challow station so as to meet Bill Mattingley, who I knew would be coming from Uffington for early turn at the box and passed Jenny Carter trudging along the grass verge going to fetch her cows. At Challow the signals were 'off' for the York to Swindon passenger train and a goods waited patiently on the Relief line for a 'path'. The signalman, waiting at his levers, saw me going over the bridge and waved – I blew a 'Victory V' on the horn. Two miles further on I met Bill, who was obviously looking out for me; we exchanged rude signs and triumphant smiles through our windscreens as we passed.

Crossing Baulking common, I saw Uffington's Down distant signal – *my* distant signal – the post and lowered arm brightly lit in the clear sun, white, yellow and black against the green backdrop of the Downs. At the bridge over the cutting I stopped briefly to look down on the station at the far end, the red-brick walls dark even in the morning sun but the box's faded cream paint blazing, almost white, between the green cutting sides. I felt so proud of it. My signal box!

The signals were pulled off in each direction because the box had been switched out of circuit since Saturday evening and I drove on rehearsing the procedure for switching in. I freewheeled down the sloping approach road to the station at ten to six; Pete's house curtained and still on my right; the single track of the Faringdon branch only a few feet away on my left, level with the road. The station was deserted and I walked along the platform, past the shuttered windows of the junction Hotel, feeling glad to be a part of the morning. Taking the signal box key from its hiding place, I went up the steps, opened the door and went inside.

The clatter of my shoes on the stairs, the clicking of the door lock as it opened and shut seemed like a great commotion in the bright silence of the box. I put my bag down on the coal bin and stood still, looking around, feeling the quiet, feeling as if the box was watching me, waiting to see what sort of signalman I should be. The sun came pouring through the east end windows, over my shoulders, flashing off silver block bells and the polished steel handles of the levers, brightening their red and yellow paint, leaving deep, chocolate-brown shadows and falling full on the face of the brass-cased clock at the far end of the room. After a few moments I could hear its busy ticking and the thoughtful call of a wood pigeon outside.

To find the place empty, the levers at each end of the frame pulled over, gave me an odd sensation; I was the on-duty officer, solely responsible for the safe running of the trains yet I was momentarily at a loss to know what to do and felt afraid to touch anything. I got in at the shallow end by signing on duty in the Book – 21 June 1961. A. Vaughan on duty 5.55 a.m. – and then set about the business of switching in.

I phoned Bill at Challow. 'Hi-up, Bill, what's about?' He roared back in exaggerated Berkshire, as he was liable to do when he was excited. ''Marnin' boy, 'Marnin' boy. You can come in. That thur goods went out behind the York and ain't gorn by Knighton yet so turn yer Down line block to "On Line". I dwun't suppose it's still between thee and I but just in case it is dwun't'ee put yer Down line boards back till you sees it go by or you get "Train Out" from Knighton. Thurs nothing on the Up.'

'Well I've got to phone Knighton so I'll ask the chap there if he can see the goods. Who's on there?'

'Old Tommy Morgan. Well, I'll hear from you later; give us a ring if you want anything.' His handset crashed down on its rest in true Mattingley style.

'Hello Knighton, Uffington here, I'm going to switch in. Can you see the goods on the Down road?' A rather frail, elderly voice came back.

'Hello. Is that Elwyn's learner? How's Elwyn this fine morning? I can see the Down goods.'

'Elwyn's on nights. This is Adrian, I've just taken on, this is my first shift.'

'Oh yes? Well, the very best of luck to you, young man; I hope you'll be happy there. Well, first of all, put your Down line indicator to "On Line", put all your levers back and send me the 5-5-5 on the bell.'

How careful they all are, I thought, as I turned the brass handle on the block switch. Using my left and right hands simultaneously, I tapped out the 'Opening of Signal Box' code to Challow and Knighton. The bells came crashing back, high and low pitch making a jangling discord together; Tommy's ringing taking several seconds longer than Bill's to finish.

I put the kettle on for tea and walked across the box, looking out of all the windows, trying it for size – it seemed a different place now that I was on my own – wondering when a bell would ring. I got my first summons at 6.20 and thereafter the line was quite busy. Les the porter arrived at seven o'clock followed soon after by two regular passengers and at 7.15 the train for Reading pulled in behind an ex-works 'Hall' which came to a stand directly outside the box. I went to the window, of course, to admire *my* engine and *my* train.

The fireman was sitting, leaning over the cab-side, looking back for the guard's 'Right Away' and glanced up at me. 'All right then mate? How's Elwyn?' I told him I was on my own and he turned into the cab, apparently to pass this on to his driver just as the guard's whistle blew. The driver eased open the regulator and pulled down on both whistle chains. The deep, booming brake whistle and the high, clear 'every day' whistle merged into an ear-splitting howl; the engineman grinned and waved back over the coals as the train drew away and the guard, looking out, puzzled at the noise, saw me, understood and waved his greeting too. I realised I would never be absolutely alone when there were so many well-wishing workmates around.

The friendliness of the stopper's crew gave me an appetite for breakfast so I set water to boil for tea and for eggs (some men used to save electricity and boil their eggs in the tea water), laid bread on the table and as soon as the 5.30 Paddington to Plymouth fast had gone by sat down by a sunny window to eat.

A continuous tapping on glass made me look round several times, puzzled, till I saw a starling on the window sill asking to be fed. I got up to throw him a crust, as I did so the bells rang for the Paddington parcels and the Faringdon goods and thereafter breakfast was constantly interrupted by noisy trains and persistent birds so that the debris of the meal was still on the table when I went to the levers to shunt the Faringdon into the Up sidings.

The train arrived from Swindon behind 1644, one of the smallest pannier tanks in service, with sixteen coal-tubs of wet ashes for the town. It looked like an overload for the bank and I hoped that the crew would decide to split the load and make two trips.

The driver came up into the box for the Train Staff. 'Mornin', Bobby,'* he said cheerfully. 'On your own, now then? Still eating too, cor, it's a good life in the box, breakfast in peace sitting in the sun. Did Elwyn tell you about the mushrooms on the branch? They're all in a field on the right of the track just round the corner. Real beauties, too; we always pick some on this job when they're in season. They'd make your job sheer luxury.'

'I love mushrooms, especially fried in butter with fresh brown bread and butter.'

'Aha! It's easy to see you'll be all right as a signalman – you're a born guzzler like the rest of them.'

'Huh! A lot of time we have for guzzling. I couldn't even eat a few bits of bread without interruption this morning – I even had a starling knocking on the window for food.'

'There you are – it was a signal box starling, greedy. Never mind, fatten it up and have in a pie with mushrooms in the autumn. Right, well I'm off, I'll see you later.'

'What about your train? It looks like an overload; are you going to make two trips?'

'No!' he said derisively. 'There'd be nothing in that. I'm going to take the whole load to see if she'll make it up the hill.'

He was, without doubt, a man after my own heart and I warmed to him. 'But what sort of tonnage have you got on? Those soggy ashes look heavy.'

He rubbed the back of his head and tipped his hat over his eyes. 'Ooh, it's a job to say. In fact you'll find that we're allowed nineteen wagons of coal up the hill with this engine which would be about 320 tons but that'd be as much as she'd ever take and our sixteen ashes feel a damn sight heavier than nineteen of coal!' He pushed his hat back into place decisively and reached for the door. 'Anyhow, we're going to have a go. My mate's got a big fire in and plenty of water. See you later.' He grinned at me and went out.

---

* Signalmen were often referred to as 'Bobbies' in recognition of the time between 1835 and 1875 when the trains were signalled by hand by constables patrolling the lineside.

The bus line telephone rang at that moment and I answered it. 'Uffington here.'

'Thompson here at Reading. Is Peter there please?' This was the Signal and Telegraph Inspector making his daily 7.30 a.m. call to ensure that Pete, our S&T technician, turned up for work on time but he would not have been in the department if he could not have rigged up a telephone circuit. He had laid one from his house to the signal box with a switch to enable it to be connected to the bus line circuit.

'Oh yes, Mr Thompson, you're only just in time; he's just off down the line. I'll go and shout to him,' I said, before turning the switch to speak privately to Peter.

'Reading on the line, Pete.'

After a decent interval I turned the switch once more and Peter – out of breath from running to greet his Inspector gasped, 'Hello, Mr Thompson …' Thus our technician could eat his breakfast when he should have been working and talk to his boss who had got out of bed early that morning and every morning to make the call. I put the phone down and went to the back window to see what the men on the Faringdon were doing.

They had backed their train up into the Baulking siding, 200 yards from the box, in order to have as great a distance as possible in which to work up speed for the climb of Barrowbush Hill, the little engine was blowing off steam in the cutting and then, with a long blast on her whistle, she took up the challenge and set out on the run.

There was no question of going easy – the engine was pulling for all she was worth from the start – but also, there was no danger of her speeding over the sidings and coming off the rails. She came blasting past the box, black smoke jetting from her chimney, wheels squealing on the rails, almost losing adhesion and spinning under the best efforts of the pistons' thrusts fed from a wide-open throttle. Driver and fireman shouted something and waved as they passed, the wagons followed sullen, wheels thudding dully over the rail joints.

The branch curved very sharply as it left the station, turning through 90 degrees from heading west to heading north, dropping into the valley of the Ock for nearly half a mile on a 1 in 140 gradient before crossing the stream and commencing the climb of Barrowbush Hill, rising at 1 in 140. Once the engine had squealed round the curve and tipped downhill, acceleration was rapid and as the guard's van swung round the bend the guard made 'hanging onto my hat' gestures to me watching from the signal box.

The sound of tearing exhaust came back clearly as the train gathered speed and I felt a sudden surge of excitement as an increase in its volume signalled that the driver had 'given her another notch'. This was not just bravado. Loose-coupled trains were curious things; the front part could be drawn along, couplings taut under the influence of the locomotive's pull while the rear half-dozen could be running with couplings slack and buffers jostling and this was even more likely on a steep downhill grade. When the gradient reversed the rear wagons would then, naturally, slow down while the front part drew away. Then the rear couplings chains would be drawn out tight – and with such a tug as might snap one of them. By putting on more steam the driver hoped to accelerate his train and draw out the slack in the rear couplings before the uphill stretch was reached.

1644 went ripping into the climb but with such a heavy train her exhaust beats began to slow almost at once, the driver, gave her yet another notch and she struggled on up the grade with a beat that might have been from a live animal, out of breath and over-burdened, till she crept over the summit with a gasping 'chuff' once a second from her chimney and so passed from earshot.

At a few minutes after eight o'clock the head of a laughing, chattering procession on bicycles could be heard in the lane, passing the Junction Hotel and seconds later the first of twenty-five girls for school, college and offices in Swindon arrived at the gate in the Down platform fence and wheeled her machine along to the down-side shelter. The rest, straggling in in small groups over the next five minutes, threw their bikes, clattering, into a pile against the shed wall.

It was a scene of pretty confusion as girls with bicycles walked to the shed and collided with girls walking from the shed to the footbridge. They trampled across the bridge's wooden boards to the Up platform, chattering like a flock of starlings, entered the booking hall and invaded the booking office. There, they issued their own tickets, date stamped them, put the fare in the till and took change while Les cowered in a corner. In fairness to him I must say that in a confined space they would have been formidable opponents, and in any case, Les cared only for the welfare of his flower beds, which had contributed much towards his third prize in the Bristol Division's 'Best Kept Station' competition in 1959.

They were a tempting sight, all those girls, as they came streaming out of the booking hall doorway on a bright morning and now that I was on my own I felt obliged to engage them in playful banter. I was surprised at the success I had in keeping a dozen of the prettiest around the base of the box, hanging, so it seemed, on my every word. We conversed with great gaiety – I was overwhelmed with my performance. Presently Les came out of his office. 'Thignal, thignal,' he lisped, 'ith the thopper about?'

'No, not yet, Leslie,' I replied in a nasty, patronising voice, 'not for a few minutes.'

'Well, whath thath one doing up there then?' pointing east towards Challow.

I had my back towards Challow and as I turned to look those wicked girls dissolved into helpless laughter, not sparing my feelings but even leaning against my signal box for support. There was the stopper, waiting patiently at the home signal which I had forgotten to lower in the excitement of attracting that horde of femininity. The signal was only 200 yards away, the driver *must* have seen the crowd of girls around the box, guessed I had forgotten him and kept quiet to see how long they could hold me up. Normally, if I had stopped him there, he would have played a symphony on the whistle.

An hour later the driver of the Faringdon was blowing long on the whistle for the branch home signal to be lowered as he brought the return trip up the short, sharp rise towards the station. I pulled lever 42 and went to the window to watch them round the curve. The little, black engine came cockily alongside the platform and, leaning over her cab-side, the driver and fireman were looking up at me with grins threatening to split their faces from ear to ear. They brought the train to a stand and came into the box to fill Knighton Crossing's drinking water cans.

'How about that then?' asked the driver proudly. 'She made it OK.'

'I should just about think she did – just. I was listening and heard you all the way to the top. You wouldn't have taken a single wagon extra.'

'Could you hear us when we were right up in the cutting?' asked the fireman incredulously.

'Not half, I could even hear when your mate let the lever down a notch.'

The driver grinned happily, 'She's a good engine ...'

The guard came into the box then and broke into the conversation. 'You're a pair of mad blighters,' he said admiringly, 'we very nearly didn't make it.'

The driver did not catch his guard's tone correctly and thought he was going to have a row. 'What's up with you then? We made it, didn't we? And if we'd stalled, we could've split the train at the top of the bank and come back for the other half.'

'I don't know about the top of the bank – you very nearly split it at the bottom. I got such a jolt I thought you'd broken away.'

The driver's attitude changed immediately. 'Oh, didn't I have the couplings out tight? Sorry about that, mate. I was trying hard enough.'

'Aha! I could hear that all right and feel it too,' replied the guard. 'The cinders from your chimney were falling on the roof of my van like hail. I put my hand out and caught fistfuls but those wagons were so heavy that it was as much as your engine could do to move them, let alone accelerate 'em.'

'You cheeky beggar, she's a very good engine,' said the driver, pretending to be indignant. 'Ha! Ha! Do you remember when old Sid Gosling had a break-away out there and his van was running up and down for twenty minutes before it stopped?'

'Oh ah! He told me about it, said it was like being on a roller coaster and didn't want to spoil it by putting on the brakes.'

The driver continued the story. 'Yes, when the couplings broke he let his van roll back downhill and up almost into the station here and then off he went towards Faringdon. He did tell me how many times he came up the short slope before the wagons finally came to a stand, but I forget now.'

'Mind you, he was good, was old Sid,' said the guard in a tone of voice to indicate that Mr Gosling was not by nature a frivolous man. 'There was the time he had a break-away after coming out of the loop at Knighton. He didn't panic but let the wagons roll and managed to get them all the way to here, stopped just about outside the box. He steps out of his van, cool as you like, and calls up to old Walt Thomas, who was on duty, "All present and correct, Officer. Got the kettle on?"' We all laughed at that.

'Talking of kettles,' said the driver, 'how about getting one on for us then?'

Just before eleven o'clock the phone rang and I answered 'Uffington'. A roar of voices shouted a variety of greetings and abuse but gradually the noise subsided and Bill Mattingley asked, 'How are you getting on down there, Adrian?'

'Oh, very well, I think. The blokes on the Faringdon have been playing silly beggars with everything in the yard but it looks as if they've finished shunting now. It'd be nice if the passengers still ran on the branch so's we could have more shunting to do – better than just pulling off all day long.'

'Oho! He's keen,' someone shouted, 'we'll have to ...' A very nice-sounding female voice broke in with, 'Is everybody here? Anyone not present please speak up.'

'All here, ready and waiting, Margaret,' said Bill.

'OK now, standby ...' There was a long pause. 'Come on my duck, name the day,' said a Berkshire voice from somewhere. I heard muffled giggles and the sound of a dozen signalmen breathing into their mouthpieces. '*Time! Time! Time!*' yelled Margaret.

'Hurrah!' shouted the signalmen and telephones crashed onto their rests through the length of the Vale. 'Are you on here, Bill?' I asked puzzled. 'Whatever was that all about?'

'That was Margaret, the Didcot telephonist, giving the daily time signal for eleven o'clock.'

'Oh, I see. I thought it was a riot. I'd better get it written in the book.'

'Ah, but if you weren't actually watching your clock when she gave "Time" you don't know precisely how fast or slow your clock is. I'll give it to you now but tomorrow make an accurate check with Margaret, alter your clock if need be, wind it and put it all down in your train register.'

The men on the Faringdon signalled they were ready to leave at about 11.15 and a telephone call to Bill showed me that the Down line was free of trains – I had a time margin to get the goods to Ashbury loop. I pulled point levers 14 and 16, the ground signal to start them from the siding – 13 – the Down Main starting signal number 4 and away they went; the little engine rasping merrily from her tall funnel, Knighton's drinking-water cans on her front buffer beam, a dozen wagons in tow, the driver playing tunes on the whistle till he was beyond the bridge. I watched the short train all the way along the embankment, curving slightly to the south, the Emett-like engine and her wagons silhouetted against the summer sky till they passed from view.

At half past one I was sweeping the box and tidying up for my relief when the phone rang. 'Hello, me boy. Going home time. Are you putting the duster round the shelves?'

'Hello, Bill. Yes, I'm ready to go too.'

'Tired are you? It's a lot different, isn't it, working the job for a full eight hours? Still, you'll get used to it; Uffington's a quiet little job. Do you know who's relieving you?'

'Well, Alfie White, I suppose?'

'No, he's got the afternoon off. You'll have Sid Tyler there at ten to two on the dot – call him "Brush", one of the best. Well, I'm off now. See you on the road home.' Bill's phone crashed down onto its rest before I could ask any questions.

I was at the end of the instrument shelf, near the window, just finishing the dusting when a tall, slim man in railway uniform and peaked cap, wearing reliefman's canvas leggings and carrying a canvas satchel over one shoulder, came strolling easily along the platform. He appeared to be about sixty years old, his face pale, lined and serious – my relief, I thought, and a bit of a misery too; old Bill was joking when he said to call him Brush.

I glanced at the clock as the box door opened – ten to two. Mr Tyler stepped inside, took the peak of his cap between his thumb and forefinger, tossed his headgear onto the coal box and with a peculiarly gentle smile said, 'How's yer Brush then?' I relaxed at once. 'All right, Sid, how's yours?'

'That's the style kid. Had a good morning? This is your first day, isn't it?'

'Yes. It's been very good. The men on the Faringdon livened it up and the girls going down to Swindon made a fool of me.'

'Getaway! What happened?' I told him as he took off his leggings, rolled up his sleeves and signed on in the register.

'Well I'm damned!' he exclaimed when I'd finished. 'They'd had it all planned, they'd seen you working with Elwyn – did you tell them you were going on the rules when you went down to Swindon the other day?'

'I told a girl from Challow.'

'Well, there you are then, they had that worked out for you. The railway's always good for a laugh. I've never regretted my time on it and I hope you'll never regret yours. They say you've always been keen on railway work.'

'Yes, but I missed five years of it by joining the Army when I left school.'

'Don't worry about it, kid. That did you the world of good and it gives us something in common, look ...' He pulled a wallet from his jacket pocket and, very gently, took two bits of yellowing paper out, put them on the register and unfolded them carefully.

One was his certificate as an instructor from the Army School of Signalling at Le Quensay dated 1917 and the other was his birth certificate. I read them both feeling excitement and awe. 'You were in the war as an instructor before you were seventeen, Sid?' He looked up from the papers; his eyes were blue and his hair – what was left of it – was fair. The lines on his face were caused by smiling rather than grimacing.

'I was fourteen and a half when I joined up,' he said in a matter-of-fact voice.

'Fourteen and a half!' I gasped. 'Whatever made you do it?'

'Well,' he said, with a half-laugh, 'a school pal, couple of years older than me, had joined and he came home with great big spurs on his boots and a big brass bugle – the glory of it was too much for me so I went to the recruiting office and told 'em I was nineteen. They didn't want to see birth certificates then; I was tall, they were hard up so they let me in. I was with the Wiltshires on the Somme before my seventeenth birthday.'

I looked at him with reverence, it showed and he changed the subject quickly. 'Here, you like railways – ever been over the old Tiddley Dyke?'

Still rather amazed, I said, 'No, I've never heard of it. Where does it run?'

'What? You never heard of the Piss 'n Vinegar, the dear old Milk and Soda Water? Oh! You've got a treat in store and if you're like me and enjoy the downland you'll have a double treat. I always look forward to a week in one o' them boxes.'

'Yes, but where is it then, Sid?'

'I'll tell you a rhyme so'll know how to find it – listen. When a parcel comes into Swindon Town station we Swindle it, we Chisel it, we 'Og it, we Mar it, we Save it, we Graft it, we Cull it, we Lug it, we Wey it and then we 'And it over.' He ticked off each station on his fingers as he spoke. 'Do you understand?' he asked.

His rhyme commemorated the old Midland & South Western Junction Railway stations at Swindon, Chiseldon, Ogbourne and on through to Andover Junction. 'Yes, I know the line a bit, I used to pass Grafton and Collingbourne on my way back to camp at Tidworth and Albert Stanley has mentioned the Old Town station to me.'

'That's it, old Albert did a lot on the Tiddley Dyke during the war. You go and have a close look round, talk to the blokes, you'll enjoy it.'

'OK then, Sid, I will. Thanks. Will you be here tomorrow?'

'No, kid, I'm down at Minety all the rest of the week but I'll hear from you sometime.'

I moved towards the door. 'All the best for now, Sid.'

'Keep yer brush up,' he called as I went out. I sank a little wearily into the seat of my Morris and drove home happy, even lightheaded, with a feeling of satisfaction; not even the recollection of the girls' ingenious leg-pull could sober me. I had carried out a busy shift – switching in, shunting, margining and straight pulling-off – successfully, apart from that isolated incident, which I promised myself would not happen again. I was very impressed with the gentle cheerfulness of Sid Tyler and looked forward to hearing more from him about the railway; but the greatest satisfaction of all was to be able to speak on equal terms with an engine driver, to be accepted by him as Officer in Charge and even as his equal. Work seemed to be a natural extension of the past fifteen years; tomorrow and for years ahead there would be shifts full of steam engines and admirable workmates. I sighed and settled deeper into my seat. I was part of the railway at last.

SIGNALMAN'S TWILIGHT

That is the land of lost content
I see it shining plain,
The happy highways where I went
And cannot come again.

– A. E. Housman, A Shropshire Lad

Contents

Acknowledgements

The present times are difficult for all working people, including self-employed carpenter/handymen who take time off to write. To counteract the resultant drain on my temper and resources I drew heavily on my wife Susan's fund of good humour and good housekeeping. My friends at John Murray, Duncan McAra and Jeannie Brooke Barnett, never forgot me in spite of their heavy workload and found time to write cheerful letters of encouragement, which always seemed to arrive just when they were needed most. My friends from railway days Paul and Sue Dye brought good cheer by boat and car from Somerset to Kerry and thus helped my work. I should also like to thank David Castle, David Collins and David Wilcock, who helped with information on dates and events, and last but by no means least I must thank my friend John Morris for preparing the diagrams that form Appendix 1, 2 and 5.

Adrian Vaughan, 1982

Acknowledgements for the Edition of 2011

I am glad to have another opportunity to thank my dear wife, Susan, for her support of my railway obsession over many years. I would also like to thank my editor and friend at Amberley Publishing, Nicola Gale, for her kindness and consideration in working so hard to make the new edition a success. I must also thank my friend Mike Esau for so kindly supplying an unusual picture of Challow, and Ron Price for his three, providentially taken, photos of the signalling instruments at Challow and the lovely colour view of the GWR wooden signals at Challow in 1964 seen on the back cover of the book.

Adrian Vaughan
Barney
North Norfolk
2011

Prologue

Doctors shaped the ends of my railway career. The railway doctor steered me in the direction of signal box work, ruling out locomotive work – my preference – on health grounds but at the same time prophesying that I would have all the footplate experience I wanted when I became known to the local engineman. I started work as a lad porter at Challow, between Didcot and Swindon, in September 1960 and went to learn the operation of Uffington signal box, two and a half miles west of Challow, in June 1961. Three weeks later I took charge.

Doctor Beeching had just been appointed as Chairman of British Railways Board and was starting out on his work, which would eventually put me and thousands out of work, but at Uffington that summer there was little to indicate the cataclysmic changes he would bring about. Since 1959 a few trains had been hauled by somewhat unreliable diesels, a few 'colour-light' signals had, here and there, replaced the traditional semaphore distant signals, signal box timetable books and train registers had been issued in a larger format, but the railwaymen were, generally, the same men who had worked the line for thirty or even fifty years; the engines, too, dated from the 1920s in many cases while the signal boxes were anything up to eighty years old and the stations were old when the Crimean War was fought.

The greatest change in those days was under the surface: we enjoyed working conditions that were the culmination of a century of Trade Union effort. So we enjoyed the best of both worlds, the security and 'humanity' of old-fashioned railway work with modern pay and conditions while for me there was the added bonus that, as the railway doctor had said, local enginemen were generous to a fault in extending to me the illegal privilege of riding on their engines.

I was fortunate indeed to have been present during the eleventh hour of an era that had lasted a century and to have experienced the pleasure of that 'other world'. Only magic could recreate that happy time and all I have to set the spell is this black ink. Look into the black, shiny bottle with me and see what it reflects.

CHAPTER ONE

A Close-Run Thing

Shrill steam screamed skywards from tank engine 1644 as she stood unattended by the branch line water column at Uffington station, while at the Down Main line platform the three maroon coaches of the 8.15 to Swindon stood silently behind a Didcot 'Mogul' 6363. Fifty yards away along the platform the door of the signal box opened; three men came out, clattered down the steps and walked towards the roaring tank engine. First, as was only proper, came the driver Bert Maynard, tall, slim and middle-aged, carrying the wooden 'train staff', which was his authority and security for taking his train along the single-track branch to Faringdon; next came his fireman, Pete Jones, red haired, tubby, not long out of school and carrying the tea can; and bringing up the rear was myself, off duty from the signal box until two o'clock and full of excitement at driving the branch goods to Faringdon and back.

The three of us squeezed into the engine's narrow cab as the passenger train slid away from its platform. Pete put the tea can on the shelf above the firehole and then stood in the doorway, leaving Bert the fireman's position while I checked over the whole situation – gauges, brakes, looking back for the guard, feeling very conscious of my position and very proud of Bert's great kindness in allowing me the privilege of driving his engine. Pete passed me the guard's 'Right Away' and with a gentle opening of the regulator I put the train in motion.

1644 was loaded only lightly – about ten wagons – so her hollow, rasping exhaust beat was almost drowned by the squealing and creaking of her wheels on the sharp curve leaving the station. Bert had turned the boiler water feed on as we cleared the curve and headed downhill, the safety valves closed and there was blessed quiet in which to hear her exhaust.

The line dropped steeply for half a mile and then rose as steeply for well over a mile up Barrowbush Hill. 'There's some fine big mushrooms over there in the season,' called Bert, pointing out on my side of the engine, 'just in that corner by those briars. Have 'em for early turn breakfast if you get in early enough to pick 'em.'

We stormed up Barrowbush Hill in fine style, Pete grumbling about the damage I was doing to his fire, but Bert only laughed. 'What are you worried about? I'm fireman today and I'm used to these Quality Street drivers.' After I had shunted the yard at Faringdon and formed the train up for the return journey, the tea was poured and I asked Bert 'Why is a driver who hurried a "Quality Street" driver?'

Bert settled his back against the bunker doors and sipped his tea. 'That was the name we gave to the speed fiends, flogging their firemen to death for the glory of a five-minute early arrival in Paddington.'

'Yes, but why "Quality Street"? Surely they weren't "Quality" drivers?'

'Well, they thought so anyhow,' he replied.

'Right Away,' shouted Pete. I eased the regulator open and we set out sedately for Uffington.

'No, what it was was this,' continued Bert. 'You've heard of the "Cheltenham Flyer"?'

'The 2.40 Cheltenham, booked Swindon to Paddington, seventy-seven miles in sixty-five minutes?' I said.

'Yeah, that's about it,' agreed Bert. 'Well, the cockneys had the job and they started to fight a bit amongst themselves to knock minutes off the timing. One of them was a real speed fiend, Jim Street, a brilliant driver, mind, but a stickler for all the rules and a bit hard on his firemen, too, from what they say. Anyhow, Streety goes up one day in about fifty-six minutes – he got himself in the papers and they even took him up in a plane to watch the "Flyer" going up to Padd. They made such a fuss of him he got even more uppity than ever, so the chaps in the Den at Swindon started to call him "Quality" Street because he was so toffee-nosed!'

The little tank engine rocked over the old track, uphill through a few trees lining the track; the main Wantage to Faringdon road was a mile to the left and below us, cars speeding along as Bert finished his tale. Pete was scathing. 'Yeah – you were all jealous, they gave the job to the Top shed instead of Swindon.'

'Look,' said Bert with exaggerated patience, 'there was nothing to it – a wagon'll go fast on its own downhill. There was more skill in working over the M&SW*, even shunting takes more skill with the brake and the regulator to do it sweetly.'

---

*   The Midland & South Western Junction Railway from Cheltenham to Andover. Absorbed into the Great Western Railway on 1 July 1923 by Railways Act 19 August 1921.

Pete grinned. 'Yes, that's right. Adrian was heavy-handed with the brake; twice I banged my head on the cab when he was slamming the anchors on.'

'Never mind,' retorted Bert, 'that'll thicken your skull and make you a good fireman.'

I could see a grand slanging match developing and butted in. 'Did the Swindon chaps ever have a chance at a non-stop run to Paddington?'

'Not with a train as light as the 2.40 Cheltenham,' said Bert, 'but once when I was firing to George Reeves on 2915, just before the war, we had a seven-coach special non-stop from Swindon to Padd and we reckoned we beat Streety's time that day.'

'Oh, here we go,' laughed Pete. 'Come on, tell us the old, old story!'

We had reached the cutting at the summit of the line, the Vale of the White Horse right across to the horizon of the Ridgeway, and White Horse Hill before us. I admired the prospect, viewed along the tanks and past the tall chimney of 1644 and turned into the cab eager for another story. 'What time do you reckon you made then, Bert?' He replied apologetically, expecting to be greeted by disbelief. 'We reckoned it was fifty-five minutes, about a minute and a half inside Jim Street's record.' I tried not to sound doubtful. 'You'd have been making ninety-two or ninety-three all the way from Uffington to Southall – are you sure of the time?'

'That's what we made it,' said Bert. 'This special went up from Swindon about 9.30 in the evening, we were twenty minutes behind the last up fast and in front of the milkies out of South Wales and Cornwall so George was fairly sure of a clear road and gave her the whip. In them days most chaps would have had a go at the "Flyer's" record if they had had the chance. I'm telling you – we flew! I kept in front of the fire all the way, batting in the coal, not too little, not too much, with old Reevesy leant against the cab looking out or watching me work – sometimes he caught my eye and we laughed at each other. He didn't ask me to look out for signals so I hardly knew where I was till he says, "All right, Bert, put your shovel down now." I looked up and we were coming into Southall. Well, when we stopped in Paddington he looked at his watch. "What's 9.30 to 10.25?" he says. "Fifty-five minutes," I said. "Well, that's one up to Swindon," he says, "but don't let on or they'll think we're spinning a yarn." So you can believe me or not but that's it.' Bert rested his case. The signal at Uffington was at Danger and I blew the whistle for it to be lowered.

'Was 2915 just out of works or something?' I asked Bert. He laughed. 'Not particularly, but she was special. George Reeves almost worshipped her.' I blew the whistle again, the signal lowered and I opened up 1644 to plod uphill into the station. Bert continued. 'When he retired from service he was still driving her – "Saint Bartholomew" – and he was in tears as he left the shed.'

'Bloody hell!' said Pete. 'He was a funny cove then.'

'Funny nothing,' replied Bert warmly, 'that was pride in the job.'

1644 squealed and huffed around the sharp bend into the station past a '37' class tank on the Didcot to Uffington 'Fly', which had been shunted back between the branch platform and the milk dock to allow us to pass. Gentle braking brought us to a stand by the water column at the end of the platform. Pete left the cab intent on filling the tanks with water, Bert got down to go to the column's tap and I followed. 'Enjoy yourself?' asked Bert with a smile.

'Yes, thanks very much – are you on this job tomorrow?'

'All week. You're welcome anytime but if you come tomorrow you'd better let Pete do the driving.'

'I'll be happy just to come on the engine,' I said and went to see the Didcot men on the 'Fly'.

Between 9 a.m. and 11 a.m. was Uffington's busiest time as both goods trains shunted and exchanged traffic before being fed back onto the Main line, the 'Fly' to Didcot and the Faringdon to Swindon, with sufficient time to enable them to reach a goods loop before a fast train required to pass on the Main line. The 'Fly' needed ten minutes to reach Challow but the Faringdon required eighteen minutes to run into the loop at Shrivenham as it had to stop at Knighton Crossing and set down two large cans of drinking water which were filled in Uffington box and carried down the line on the engine's front buffer beam. I helped to fill and place the cans on the engine, watched the little train leave and then drove home for lunch. At ten minutes to two I re-entered the signal box to take over from Elwyn Richards.

Elwyn was a dark-haired, stockily built Welshman who had taught me the working at Uffington. After leaving school at Bridgend in 1929 he had immediately put his name down for a job on the Great Western Railway, not from any love of trains but simply to gain secure employment in a time of widespread unemployment. After waiting five years, during which time he worked at such odd jobs as he could find, he was offered a porter's job far away from home at Sparkford in Somerset and gladly took it. He carried out his signalman's duties at Uffington scrupulously and with great cheerfulness, any moment of stress being marked by nothing more than a sharply sniffed pinch of snuff. His off-duty hours were entirely taken up with parish work – training the church choir and being a churchwarden.

'Hello, A-dren,' he said pleasantly, as I walked into the box, 'you haven't changed your shirt – it's all sooty from that engine. I can't see what there is in them old things. Don't you see enough of them from up here?'

'It isn't the same as riding on them, Elwyn. What would you prefer – to sing or just listen?'

'Hmm, maybe you're right,' he said doubtfully. 'Anyhow, I'm off. You've got the Neyland on the Up and the Acton goods coming down. Look in the extra train book – the Swansea and the Carmarthen are running in two parts tonight. Cheerio for now and don't fall out of the window looking at engines.' We grinned at each other and he marched off, his canvas satchel over his shoulder to the bar of the Junction Hotel close to the station where a pint of Guinness was poured and waiting.

I picked up the blue and red duster used when pulling levers – the signalman's unofficial badge of office – signed on duty in the register and stood by for action. The operating room of Uffington measured 33 feet by 12 feet and was painted dark brown to the level of the windows with cream paint to eaves level, while the underside of the roof rising to its ridge was lined with white boards, the upper reaches of which were dark with Victorian cobwebs. The signal box was made of timber with full glazing on three sides, two windows in the rear wall, facing the branch line and flanking a brick wall which rose to become a chimney stack. Along this back wall was a wooden bin for coal, a row of panelled cream and brown lockers with wooden-cased telephones above, screwed to the wall. The booking desk carrying the 'block register' stood under a window next to a flimsy, cardboard partition in the corner, which housed the lavatory. Placed centrally was an armchair in front of a pot-bellied stove standing on the cast-iron surround of what had once been an open fire.

The row of steel-handled, red or black or yellow levers, which I pulled to move points or lower signals and known in jargon as the 'frame', was ranged along the front wall, against the windows. A shelf for the signalling instruments was suspended over the frame and above the instruments was a framed, watercolour plan of the tracks controlled from the box. The instruments and the diagram faced the dark north wall but I looked at them southwards against the light coming in through the row of windows with the result that they were always in shadow and the brighter the sunshine the deeper the gloom over the instruments.

On the instrument shelf were two brass-cased track circuit repeaters, which indicated when two short lengths of track in the Up and Down Main lines were occupied and when those lengths were occupied they locked electrically certain signals for safety. Also on the shelf were repeaters to show that a signal arm had obeyed the lever and repeaters to show that the oil-burning lamps in the signals were in fact alight. The vital signalling bells and indicators stood centrally, one bell and indicator working to Challow, 2 ½ miles to the east, the other pair working to Knighton Crossing, 2 ½ miles westwards. There was also a big, brass, multicontact switch in a mahogany box, which was used to switch the box out of circuit, bypassing electric currents to the bells and indicators so that the box could be closed at weekends, leaving Challow to work through to Knighton.

The whole line from Paddington to Fishguard and Penzance was divided into sections, each controlled by a signalman, and each section was considered 'blocked' until its signalman said it was 'clear' and gave permission for a train to enter it. Hence, anything to do with signalling trains was prefixed 'block' and we had 'block bells', 'block section' and 'block register', the latter being the book into which was scrupulously entered, minute by minute, each bell code received or sent, each message, equipment failure or other untoward happening. When the signalman at Knighton Crossing wanted to lower his Up line signals for a train to come through to me at Uffington, he rang one beat on the block bell, I would answer and he sent the appropriate 'Is Line Clear?' code – four beats for an express passenger train, 3-2 for a slow goods. If the line at Uffington was clear I would acknowledge the code by repetition and turn my block indicator to 'Line Clear'. If the train we were dealing with was an express, I would receive the 'Train Approaching' bell – 1-2-1 – from Knighton Crossing after about four minutes. I would acknowledge this and then 'ask the road' to Challow. If all was well, Challow would acknowledge the code and turn his block indicator to 'Line Clear', which caused my indicator to show the same and also unlocked my signal, giving access to his section. I could then lower my signals or 'pull off', to use signalman's jargon.

When the train passed Knighton Crossing, the signalman there sent me two beats – 'Train entering Section' – which I acknowledged and turned my block indicator to 'Train on Line'. If the train we were dealing with was a slow goods or a stopping passenger train, now was the time for me to 'ask the road and pull off'. When the train passed me, I watched it carefully to see if there was any reason for having it stopped at Challow – a door handle not properly turned or an axle box bearing running hot; an emergency bell would be sent after the two beats. Lastly, I made sure that the train was carrying a tail lamp, which proved that it was complete and had not left anything behind in the section and then sent 2-1 'Train out of Section' to Knighton before releasing the block indicator ready for the next train.

The block bells came in various shapes and sizes in order to vary their tone and thus enable the signalman – especially in boxes with several bells – to know which bell had rung. There were 'cow bells', 'sheep bells', 'church bells', flat domes, round domes, saucer and also a coiled steel gong. At Uffington the bell from Challow was a church bell and the one from Knighton Crossing was a flat dome; the former gave a high-pitched 'ting' and the latter a deep, mellow 'dong'.

The bell dome was held by a central stem to the top of a mahogany box, which housed an electromagnet operating the bell hammer. From the front of the box projected a morse key, which was tapped lightly with two fingertips to send a current through to the other bell's magnets and thus ring the bell. Deft, light fingering was all that was needed and the bells would reproduce accurately all but the fastest tapping. They would not ring if hit with a fist, and heavy-handed men produced only clicks at the other end of the line.

If your bell began clicking it might have developed a fault due to dirt or maladjustment or your mate might be turning into a 'clicker'. Under these circumstances a gentle inquiry was needed on the telephone. 'Er, Bill, my bell's clicking – er ...' to which he would probably reply, 'Hold on then, I'll send you half a pound of tuppeny rice.' On the phone it was possible to hear the rhythm of that nursery rhyme being tapped out, full of quick sequences, whilst observing the reaction of the bell. Usually the tapping I heard was dainty and light and my bell answered perfectly so I knew – and he knew – he had been 'ringing rough' and this exercise ensured he would be more careful in future, for no one liked to be known as a 'clicker'. Of course, there was an official code for testing the bells – sixteen beats – but it was much nicer to ring out the nursery rhyme.

My work at Uffington was straightforward and, you might think, repetitive, having nothing to do with the trains but pass them along the line, but I relished the feeling of being alone in charge of the sixty-five trains or so that passed the box during each eight-hour shift. I enjoyed watching the summer sun rise and the day pass, changing the shadows in the cutting, the steam-hauled trains thundering past within feet of the box hurrying away to the West Country and Wales, and I never tired of watching the engines with their flurry of smoke and fire pass the box in the night.

Yet for all the routine of the job there was danger just below the surface, as I discovered one night shift about October 1961 when I had been working the box for about four months. At 9.30 p.m. I stepped outside my cottage to drive to the signal box. The air was autumn chill; the lights of the Crown pub next door shone their electric colours into the night and onto a group of young men standing in the road. I had been to school with them. 'Coming for a drink?' they called.

'I can't – I'm off to work,' I replied. 'Work?' they chorused, moving towards the pub door and I heard them 'damning that for a job' as they went inside.

Elwyn was waiting for me at the box, ready to leave but, with a signalman's etiquette, not appearing anxious to depart. At 10.30 a local Anglican clergyman billowed into the box wearing the cassock which on Sunday he would wear in church and waft the fumes of stale beer over his shocked congregation. He was not a man to stand on ceremony – he had spent several years in Greece during and after the Second World War, first with bands of guerrillas fighting against the Germans and later with British regular units against Communist elements of the erstwhile guerrilla movement. He had a veneer of broad-shouldered *bonhomie* but underneath it I thought I saw a sad, lonely man. One evening we were discussing religion and he surprised me by saying sadly, 'You could sum up Anglicanism in six words: "all may, none must, some should" – it isn't much of a doctrine.'

His visit lasted from 10.30 until midnight as usual – closing time to sobering-up, unkind critics used to say – and soon after he had gone I heard the heavy tread of our local constable coming along the platform towards the signal box. He patrolled the lanes on a 'silent' Velocette motorbike, which made an unmistakable noise – a muffled throb with a high-pitched whine so that anyone not wanting to meet the constable simply merged with the hedgerow. I poured him some tea, gave him some cake and he settled in my armchair to talk about nothing memorable.

The Junction Hotel was on the far side of the tracks, immediately opposite the signal box. It had a sinister appearance to my mind with its narrow, pointed dormer windows, tall, pointed gables and paint-peeling barge-boards. Light streamed into the night through chinks in the curtains and carried with it the uproar of 'after-hours' revelry as every poacher for miles around sank deeper into gallons of ale – or so I imagined. The Uffington branch of the NUR held its monthly meeting there; meetings I attended mainly for the colourfulness of their proceedings, and these did nothing to dispel my impression of the place. My signal box would have been a perfect ambush site for the policeman if he had wanted to raid the pub but he only ate his cake and smoked his cigarette, chatting to me while bedlam shattered the night.

After these visitors had gone and the noise from the pub had subsided I could hear the real sounds of the night: an owl hooting, a nightingale singing, a vixen screaming her human screams far off across the fields. The hands of the brass clock crawled slowly around the dial, cups of tea followed each other on my table with the regularity of the trains and I moved from bells to levers to block register, the duster hanging from my pocket, as if I had been doing the job all my life. But I had not; I was merely becoming over-confident.

That night my usual mate at Challow, Bill Mattingley, was not on duty and standing in for him was a grand old relief signalman who worked in spotless, well-pressed uniforms that still carried their gilt GWR buttons, the serif letters surrounded by laurel leaves surmounted by an Imperial crown – for the Great Western had been the 'Royal Road'. His tall, slim figure from the well-brushed, silver hair to the highly polished boots was all keenness but it had been noticed that his usual alertness was turning to anxiety; he spent most of his shifts pacing the box or standing by the instruments in case he might not hear a bell ring.

At about 4 a.m. the Alexandra Dock goods clanked past me up the Main and as soon as I gave 'Train out of Section' for it to Knighton Crossing, the signalman there asked the road up for the 10.5 p.m. Milford Haven–Paddington sleeping car train. I gave 'Line Clear' and sat down to await events – the goods would take ten or twelve minutes to clear onto the slow line at Challow so it was likely that the Milford would be brought to a stand by me. On the other hand, if the goods was quicker than usual, I might just manage to lower my signals for it and give it a clear run. I sat alert, ready to rush to action. After four minutes I received the 'Train Approaching' 1-2-1 code for the Milford while the goods was still in the section to Challow. Two minutes later, Knighton sent 'Train entering Section' for the Milford and I knew that I would have to stop the train until the line through to Challow was clear. I answered Knighton's bell and as I did so I received 'Train out of Section' from Challow. Like a snake striking, my hand flashed out to the tapper and asked the road for the passenger train – back came the code, four beats, and the block indicator swung to 'Line Clear'.

I dashed to the levers but as I touched the first one I got what I can describe only as an electric shock – I snatched back from the lever as I realised that the goods could not possibly have cleared Challow in six minutes but must still be in the dark track between us. I telephoned my mate at Challow. 'That Alexandra Dock hasn't got to you yet, has it?' There was a pause, then my mate's puzzled voice, 'What Alexandra Dock?'

'I put it "on line" to you six or seven minutes ago.'

There was a longer pause as if he was trying to pull his thoughts together. 'I never thought,' he said at last, sounding very agitated. 'I saw the "Train on Line" on the block indicator and thought I'd forgotten to send you "Train out of Section" for the Milford so I sent it just now.'

My mate was tired, thoroughly confused and quite obviously had not been keeping his train register up to date.

'The train you just sent "Train out" for is the Alexandra Dock and it's still between me and you. The Milford is standing at my home signal. You haven't pulled off up the Main for the goods thinking it was the Milford have you?'

'No – er, I haven't pulled any levers; they're all in the frame. That's why I thought ...' He tailed off, acutely embarrassed, and I guessed he must have gone to sleep for a minute and then woke up exhausted and disoriented.

'Look, never mind,' I said. 'Put the indicator back to "Train on Line" and get the road up the Relief line for the goods. Then I'll give you the times and you can enter them up in your register.'

I sat down shakily. I had been too eager, thoughtless. If I had lowered the signals, then the sleeping car express would probably have crashed into the rear of the trundling goods train. It had been a close-run thing, which left me feeling sick and very humble.

CHAPTER TWO

Dialect and Tradition

The Didcot to Swindon line was a mixture of double track, triple and quadruple track railway – due to the accidents of history – which made bottlenecks for the movement of trains, and with the widest variety of trains to run, the signalmen spent a lot of their time wangling the slow and fast trains from section to section with the least possible delay. Uffington took no part in these arrangements but I listened on the telephone, learning how the signalmen sent goods trains up and down the line, from one goods loop to the next according to the time available between express trains and according to the layout at the other signal box, for all the men knew exactly what the situation was at the dozen boxes along the line and always seemed to ask the right questions at the right time. I regarded them all with awe and though I coveted the post of signalman at my 'home' base at Challow, I wondered if I should ever be able to supervise the operating of such a key point.

Train-operating discussions and gossip were inextricably mixed on the 'omnibus line' telephone circuit; I had only to pick up my 'bus line' telephone to hear broad Berkshire, soft Wiltshire and sing-song Welsh accents busy with conversations conducted in a kind of railway dialect quite unintelligible to the non-railwayman. The railway's special language sprang from the individualism of the nineteenth century, which had made a threepenny piece a 'Thruppny Joey', a sixpenny piece a 'tanner', a shilling a 'bob' and twenty-five pounds a 'pony'. The dialect saved time and smoothed down the lumpy, official terms and titles of railway work. The only word that was always used correctly and very, very carefully was 'clear'. A signalman never said 'The line is not clear' but 'The line is blocked'; safety matters apart, anything could be said and talk was often as cryptic and obscure as a Chinese puzzle.

A signalman never 'obtained Line Clear', he 'asked the road' or 'asked Line Clear' and having obtained it he said he had 'got the road' while the signalman who had transmitted the 'Line Clear' indication said he had 'given the road and pegged up' – the latter referring to the manual action necessary to operate the old-fashioned block instruments in use on the

Great Western Railway since the 1880s, and still in use today on some parts of ex-GWR lines. When a signalman sent the two beats 'Train entering Section', he said he had 'sent it [the train] on line' or merely 'sent it on' while the man receiving the code 'took it on and pegged up' – the latter referring again to changing the block instrument's display. When the train passed and the signalman sent the 2-1 code 'Train out of Section', he said he had 'knocked out and unpegged'. The word 'unpeg' remained in universal use long after the 'pegging' instruments had disappeared from the box.

To make a telephone inquiry for the whereabouts of a train, a signalman rang a nicely chosen box, which, under the circumstances prevailing at that moment, would return the best information and it took skill with experience to know where to direct the inquiry. Express trains were 'fasts', sometimes 'hard hitters' but never 'expresses'. They were usually known by their originating town. 'Got the Pembroke about?' a signalman might ask. 'Been off Bassett three' would perhaps be the laconic reply and the inquiring signalman knew that the train had passed Wootton Bassett three minutes previously and would therefore be passing his box in x minutes.

To the signalmen of my area signals were invariably 'boards', not 'sticks' and never 'signals'. This dated from the earliest days of the Great Western when Brunel designed some of his signals to be made out of big planks of wood and were known in the rule book as 'board signals'. The Brunellian signals began to be ousted by semaphores in the 1860s but the old, broad-gauge name stuck and even in Western Region's power-operated signal boxes you will still hear old-hand signalmen referring to their powerful, electric light signals as 'boards'.

Drivers and others referred to signalmen as the 'Bobby' or, when actually speaking to him, they would open the conversation with 'Officer'. 'What's up now, Officer?' the fireman of a locomotive might say as he came into the signal box to sign the train register when his train had been delayed and, of course, the use of 'Bobby' and 'Officer' was a direct link with the days when trains were signalled by hand from the side of the line by men sworn in as Constables, complete with truncheons, having all the powers of the then newly formed police of Sir Robert Peel.

No Western Region signalman ever 'lowered his signals'; he always 'pulled off' or 'pulled the boards off'; distant signals were 'back boards'. If a signalman had a goods train approaching he waited until it was 'on line' from the box in rear and then made inquiries about the following fast. These researches might take a minute or two with the goods getting closer to the distant signal standing at 'Caution'. The signalman might then decide to 'pull the boards off' up the Main, and his mate at the box next down the line, knowing exactly what was happening, would ask 'Did that up one get your back board?' 'Yes, I reckon so, but I must have dropped it down their funnel,' would be the reply.

As it was basically the signalmen's job to stop trains and the enginemen's job to run them there was the basis for a feud between the grades that was not always good natured. One of the printable sayings that drivers used on signalmen when they had been held up for one or sixty minutes was 'It'll be a good job when they take the roof off that place – let in some air and wake you up' but if there was no time for lengthy grumbles a driver would content himself with bawling, as he went past, '*Get the roof off!*'

Trains that were delayed were said to have been 'hit' or 'hammered' according to the severity of the delay but if they had been checked only slightly by the signals they were said to have been 'tickled'. A freight train consisting entirely of vacuum-braked wagons with those brakes under the control of the driver known as a 'vackum' with the name of the originating town thrown in – thus the 'Acton vackum' – but a train of unbraked wagons such as a coal train was known only by its originating town, though any very long train might be called 'Long Tom', which commemorated the 100-wagon coal trains that once travelled through the Vale from Swindon to Old Oak Common. The fireman of such a train would have had a 'full digger'. In Great Western days many of the vacuum goods had been given fancy names by the advertising department but these names, not rooted in any inspiration from the railwaymen on the ground, had died out by the time I arrived on the scene leaving only the mundane but logical titles: 'The Cocoa' for the 10.5 p.m. Bristol, which carried a load of chocolate from Fry's; 'The Baccy', the midnight vacuum from Bristol loaded with W. D. & H. O. Wills products.

Express passenger trains with official titles carried them proudly on ornate, curved boards on the locomotive's smoke box and these trains were always known to the signalmen by their titles: the *Bristolian*, the *Capitals (United)* and so on. Apart from these, Up fasts were known by their town of origin as was any Down fast that did not start from Paddington – and there were very few of them. As to trains out of Paddington, if several were due down in quick succession we asked for a particular one by its departure time. 'Got the 8.55 about?' If only one Paddington train was due we asked, 'Where's the Down London?'

A few passenger trains were identified by nicknames on the Didcot–Swindon line. Any stopping passenger train was the 'stopper'. The 9.40 p.m. Swindon to Paddington was the 'Punch' while 'Paddy's Mail' was the 9.25 p.m. Paddington to Neyland, the nickname commemorating the time when Neyland was the embarkation point for Ireland before Fishguard harbour was opened in 1905. The midnight sleeping car train from Paddington to Penzance was the 'Down Owl' but the sleeper from Penzance to Paddington was the 'Up Waker' because it left Swindon at 5.25 a.m. and thus heralded the end of night shift for the signalmen of White Horse Vale.

We did not have nicknames for locomotives but when the need arose identified an engine by its class name – a 'King' or a 'Castle' or by its full name; unnamed engines were referred to by the first two digits of their number. Engines for express work had driving wheels over six feet in diameter and if such an engine was working a slow, heavy goods, the signalmen might well mention this when passing on train-running information saying, 'There's a high-stepper on the Southall today', which was a nice reference to well-bred horse flesh. A fireman working an engine that was 'doing rough for steam' might well call his engine 'a bloody old camel'.

The 'Star' class engines, forerunners of the larger 'Castles' (both types numbered in the '40' series), were known to enginemen as 'Small 40s' and there was an elegant 'Star' that was once shedded at Swindon, 4014 *Knight of the Bath*, which some wag dubbed 'Friday Night' and the name stuck hard enough for me to be told the tale many years after the last 'Star' had been cut up. When the last of the 'Hall' class came out of Swindon factory, 7929 *Wolf Hall*, the class numbered 329 and it was widely believed at the time that a 330th would be built just to round the numbering off and that, if the 330th was built, it would be called 'That's All'.

Engines running without a train were 'light' engines and were signalled by the bell code 2-3. Signalmen 'got the road' for a 2-3 and then passed the destination of the engine on to the next box over the special 'box-to-box' telephone, a private line between the two boxes provided especially for messages which must be given without any interruption such as would occur on the bus line. 'Light to Oxford' or 'One for Oxford' would be shouted cheerfully over the wires unless it was the third engine in twenty minutes in which case the message would be 'Another bloody donkey for Oxford'. If the engine's destination was Didcot we said, 'Light to Hagbourne.' Swindon was occasionally 'Swindleum', which was a remembrance of the broad-gauge days when the refreshment room on Swindon station sold appallingly bad food.

An engine hauling nothing more than a freight brake van was a 'pony and trap' so should we have such a train coming up, heading for Newbury via the Compton line over the Berkshire Downs, the box-to-box message would be 'Pony and trap for the Toot and Bunny over the Gold Coast'. The Toot and Bunny, for some unknown reason, was the Reading–Hungerford section and the Gold Coast was the name for the Didcot–Newbury line.

Some engine drivers were known to the signalmen for their habit of dawdling. There was one man in particular who, when driving the 3.50 a.m. Stoke Gifford to Woodford Halse, was well known for this and signalmen would warn each other, 'Don't take any chances with the Stoke – old so and so's on there hanging the pot on.' A signalman might telephone Foxhall Junction, Didcot, asking, 'Got the Banbury with you, Phil?' 'Yes, they're on the curve hanging the pot on with the bag in.' This meant that the train was standing on the north to west curve of Didcot's triangular junction with the leather hose of the water column still in the engine's tender to give the impression that the crew was not yet ready to leave when in fact they had filled up. This ploy was used at junctions when the men wanted to lose their 'path' and so run late for reasons best left to the imagination.

When a driver was ready he 'blew up for the road' – blew his engine's whistle to say he was ready to move – and then became annoyed if the signal did not 'come off' at once. The idea of 'taking the board off' to show that the road was clear for the train to leave went back to the very beginning of the Great Western Railway when the signal was hoisted on its mast only to denote 'Danger – Stop' and was literally taken off the mast when the way ahead was clear.

During running an engine might run short of steam so the driver would 'stop for a blow-up' – stand with the fire being drawn up by the action of a jet of steam through the chimney and, if possible, he would come to a stand at the entrance of a goods loop blowing the engine's whistle. The signalman would send the 'cancelling' signal – 3-5 beats – to the signal box ahead, 'turn his road' and bring the train into his loop. On the telephone he would explain to the signalman on each side of him what was happening. 'This Down one stopped outside blowing to come in, so I've put the boards back and pulled off for the loop.'

The signalman would keep an eye on the engine. While the blower was on, drawing up the fire, smoke would rise in a tall column and soon a white feather of steam would appear at the boiler safety valves. With that he would, if the engine was close, go to the window and raise his right hand inquiringly to the driver, 'All right now?' The driver would respond with a wave and a 'pop' on the whistle so the signalman would go to the telephone to make inquiries about the whereabouts of any Down fast trains before allowing the goods back onto the Main line. His inquiries would often be greeted by ribaldry by the other signalmen on the bus line and with the threadbare advice 'Pull off and fear nothing'. When he did, the same voices would cry sarcastically, 'Purger – you'll hammer the fast!'

Traditions were long-lived on the railway because railwaymen and their equipment spanned two centuries. Albert Stanley and Harry Strong, the two old-hand porters who taught me the job at Challow in 1960, had themselves learned their trade from men who had begun their careers in the 1870s. My mate at Knighton Crossing in the latter half of 1961 was Bill Curtis, who began his career on the Midland & South Western Junction Railway (M&SW) in 1915 at Weyhill and who had worked at Knighton Crossing since 1928. His mate then at Uffington was Walt Thomas, who had been signalman there since 1914 and the two men were shift mates for twenty-three years until Walt retired in 1951 after forty-nine years' service to the Great Western Railway. At Ashbury Crossing, the next box west of Knighton, Sid Philips was my mate; Sid also began his service in 1915 on the M&SW but at Grafton & Burbage as a porter.

The rivalry between the M&SW and GWR only just stopped short of blows as the GWR was openly contemptuous of the small but heroic M&SW. The 'Milk & Soda Water', 'Tiddley Dyke' or 'Piss 'n' Vinegar' started life as an independent railway connecting Cheltenham with Andover and, by London & South Western metals, Southampton, its handsome, four-coupled express engines in spotless maroon paint brought Midland Railway, South Western and even London & North Western coaches within a stone's throw of the Great Western's locomotive works at Swindon. Paddington and all right-thinking Great Western men considered the M&SW a crimson intruder on the green and gold heartland of God's Wonderful Railway.

The nickname 'Piss 'n' Vinegar' was a Great Western slander, referring to the smell in M&SW carriages resulting from the great numbers of soldiers who used them on beery outings to Swindon from the Salisbury Plain camps on Saturday nights. Mr Kenneth Cook, who became Works Manager at Swindon Works and eventually Chief Mechanical Engineer of the Eastern and North Eastern Regions of British Railways, records how he set off from his home in Savernake to start his apprenticeship in Swindon factory, leaving from the Low Level station at Savernake and making a huge detour reaching Swindon via Newbury; but by this means arriving in Swindon on a Great Western ticket instead of going from Savernake High Level, the M&SW station, with a journey to Swindon of less than half the other mileage.

Now, Sid Philips's background was wholly Great Western; his people were, as near as possible, hereditary employees of the company, his great-grandfather, grandfather and his father had all held the post of Ganger for the Bedwyn–Wolfhall Junction length where the despised M&SW crossed the lordly Great Western on a bridge and had a spur curving down to make the Wolfhall Junction with the GWR. Sid's grandfather was seventy before he condescended to retire and Sid's father had arranged a place for his son in the track gang ready for when the boy left school.

Unfortunately for family pride, Sid had other ideas and in 1915 took a job at Grafton & Burbage station on the Midland Sou'Western. 'We had a shocking row about it, my Dad and me,' said Sid. 'He said that if I was clever enough to find my own work I could find my own lodgings, too, so I had to leave home and go into digs.' I made some disbelieving noises but Sid insisted. 'No, it's the truth. You wouldn't hardly credit it today I know but there was Company loyalty in them days, especially if you were a railway family – I'd turned my nose up at the Great Western and that was bad form in our house.'

I was inclined to agree though I did not say so in as many words. 'It was odd though, your whole life had revolved around the Great Western.'

'Well, that was it see,' explained Sid, 'the Great Western was ordinary. You think of the old M&SW as a sleepy little branch line but when I was a lad it was busy. Grafton station handled all the farm produce for miles around and you know yourself that there's ten times more cows and sheep than people round there. During the Great War you had engines and coaches all colours, North British Railway even coming through on troop trains – the Great Western wasn't half so interesting.' I had to concede his point and went on to hear more of the wonders of the Tiddley Dyke, which, within weeks of my first conversation with Sid, was closed to all traffic.

Philips family unity was restored by Act of Parliament in 1921 when small railway companies were forcibly amalgamated into four huge groupings and the dashing, crimson Midland Sou'Western was taken over by the lordly, green and gold Great Western – or, as Sid Philips put it, 'When the Tiddley Dyke took over the Western.' Sid continued the dynastic tendencies of his family by marrying a signalman's daughter and their child became a signalwoman at Highworth during the Second World War.

At the time of the amalgamations, Sid was working as signalman at Ogbourne St George, taking alternate shifts with Bill Curtis's brother, Reg. Reg lived almost rent free in a wooden hut mounted on iron wheels, which had been placed in a field near the railway. It was the sort of primitive caravan that Downland shepherds lived in during the lambing season or which was towed behind a road steam engine as a messing coach for the crew, living an itinerant life as they went from farm to farm to complete steam ploughing or threshing contracts.

Reg Curtis was hard-working and thrifty and soon worked his way up the line, in every sense. Before the end of the 1920s he was a top-class signalman in Cheltenham and was running a motor car. 'That might not sound much to you,' said Bill Curtis, who was telling me the story, 'but it was a really good car – Cheltenham District Inspector only had a little Austin 7 and none of the other signalmen had a car at all.'

Since 1915, Bill Curtis had walked on a badly deformed ankle due to lack of medical care after an accident while he was working at Weyhill. During the Great War, the M&SW carried all the military traffic, men and munitions, from the huge military area of Salisbury Plain and at Weyhill the station staff spent most of their time in the sidings loading, sheeting and roping hay and straw for the army's horses and mules in France. One day they all forgot the Up stopping train until they heard it approaching and Bill was told to run to the Down platform and fetch a 17-gallon milk churn that had to be sent up line. He reached the churn as the train drew to a stand at the opposite platform, swung the clumsy steel container onto his back and ran down the platform ramp. He stumbled and the knife-like edge of the heavy churn smashed into his ankle. He was helped home and stayed in bed for three weeks, his ankle swollen and purple from what his doctor called a 'bad sprain' and when at the end of that time it was no better, the physician dismissed Bill's diagnosis that the ankle was broken and recommended exercising it! Bill got out of bed, stood on the ankle, which turned right over depositing Bill in a fainting heap on the floor whereupon the doctor unbent sufficiently to agree that perhaps a hospital visit was called for.

But first Bill had to have a character reference from some local pillar of society before he could have free treatment. 'I wasn't much at churchgoing,' said Bill, 'and you needed a vicar's say-so to get into hospital if you couldn't pay for your treatment. So it was no good me going to the local man but my mother knew the clergyman over in Abbot's Ann so we went to him.' I knew the area slightly from my time in the Army at Tidworth and was astonished at the distance he would have hobbled on a broken ankle and, indeed, I was astonished at the strange arrangements then in force for a poor man to enter hospital – almost as difficult as for a rich man to enter heaven. 'How did you get all the way to Abbot's Ann?' I asked. 'It must have been five miles from Weyhill.'

'No,' said Bill mildly, 'about three, I should think, from our house. My mother bound up my ankle, I had a rough crutch and she helped me along, too – I got the train to Salisbury, of course.'

The sequel to that episode was Bill's lifelong interest in the Red Cross. Aged eighty-three, he could and did bring out the sick or infirm from their cottages to the waiting ambulance, carrying frail old ladies in his arms, and in 1981 he received the British Empire Medal for his services to the local community.

In 1916, aged eighteen, Bill was promoted to signal-porter at Perham Down sidings between Ludgershall and Tidworth. For the duration of the war and even a little beyond, he and his mates worked twelve hours a day, six days a week, and on Sunday, the Day of Rest, Bill worked eighteen hours, spending some of that time in the important junction signal box on the station at Ludgershall. Even on Sunday the box was very busy – the war effort took no cognisance of Christmas let alone Sunday – and Bill spent his day supervising the shunting, marshalling and passing of train after train of men, live and dead, bullets and bandages to and from the Western Front.

The only recognition of the labour of the railwaymen at Ludgershall was to supply the signalman with a 'booking lad' to take some of the pressure off him, to answer telephones and keep the block register up to date, so that he could concentrate on the organisation of his piece of railway. So there at Ludgershall on a Sunday, marshalling the war effort of part of the Empire, was eighteen-year-old Bill Curtis on his newly crippled leg assisted by a sixteen-year-old – Bobby Bunce.

Food was rationed and scarce but many railwaymen made good use of what spare time they had to cultivate the lineside and Bill did his best to grow his own food around the signal box at Perham Down – he showed me a photograph of it, taken in 1918, growing everything from marigolds to runner beans. I have had some experience of the exhaustion of working twelve-hour shifts for weeks on end but at least I had my Sundays off and I was also working on a full stomach. How Bill and his mates did their work *and* found time and energy to grow their own food enough to keep them alive must be some kind of miracle. If they had not done so, there would have been no war effort.

The problem of tiredness was therefore ever present and to 'buck the blokes up a bit', as he put it, Bill concocted a medicine that was so successful that he became known as 'Doctor Curtis'. 'I reckon I could've made a fortune out of it,' said Bill, telling me the tale one night shift, 'I had regulars coming for a bottle of it but I always gave it away.'

'But what was it?' I asked horrified somewhat. 'How could you be sure it would work? Was it safe?'

Bill chuckled, 'Oh – it worked all right and it was safe if you could get behind a hedge in time! I dissolved iron tablets, quinine and Epsom salts in water and they drank it out of pint mugs.'

CHAPTER THREE

The Uffington Time Machine

The first three months of 1962 were exceptionally, bitterly cold. Blizzards, deep snow and temperature of -16 degrees Fahrenheit below freezing for weeks making it the worst winter since 1740. Railway operations were badly affected though the men worked hard in great discomfort to keep the trains running. Steam engine crews found conditions very difficult because their locomotives used water as part of their fuel, and water supplies often froze solid even at important stations. On 2 January, a date I noted in a short-lived diary, all the water columns from Reading to Swindon stations inclusive were frozen out of action and Goring water troughs were empty. The only water for locomotives at Swindon that day was from a column in the works yard and another in the engine shed. West of Swindon there was probably no water for engines before Bristol, Severn Tunnel station or Gloucester shed.

In the bitter darkness of that evening a 'King' class engine was coming down with the 5.55 p.m. from Paddington, the 'Red Dragon', scheduled to run non-stop to Newport. Her train was a heavy one made up to fifteen coaches, the result of the cancellation of other trains to South Wales, so there was more than 500 tons behind the tender and the engine had used a lot of water. The crew had not been able to fill the tender on Goring troughs and stopped on the middle road at Swindon with an empty tender and boiler water almost out of sight at the bottom of the boiler gauge glass.

They then discovered that the station column was frozen, hurriedly uncoupled the engine from the train and with anxious glances at the empty gauge glass began to drive the engine gently down to the works yard column. They were out of luck. On the way down the water level in the boiler dropped too low for the well-being of the metal, the fusible plug in the firebox crown melted and released the boiler's remaining steam and water into the fire. This served partly to smother the furnace but mainly as a dire warning to the crew to get the fire out of the box before it damaged the empty boiler through overheating and sheer burning of the metal.

This, the ultimate failure, the nadir of steam engine operating, was known as 'dropping a plug'. Its immediate result was to explode a small volcano of scalding steam and hot ash into the cab, which the closed doors of the furnace would not entirely prevent. In this instance and in almost every case the crew would have been only too well aware of the crisis and besides closing the fire doors they were probably standing outside the cab when the eruption took place.

Nights of violent frost followed with unremitting regularity and daytime temperatures rarely rose above freezing. On Swindon shed the atmosphere was dramatic, a state of siege, as the cold cracked in from all sides and the men fought back to keep the engines mobile. Outside the 'straight shed' engines were drawn up in ranks; those standing over the ashpits were over fires yards long, while between the ranks, blazing coal in heaps on the ground or in braziers kept the frost at bay. All the engines had at least a small fire in the grate and several men were employed going around the engines to supervise the boiler water level and to replenish it if necessary.

At night the great, spoked driving wheels stood out black against heaps of fire on the other side of the engine, yard lamps silhouetted tapered boilers, coned safety valve covers and copper-topped chimneys reflected streaks of light through clouds of smoke rising from the fires – it was a stupendous sight of looming engines, fire and smoke under a sky filled with blue-sparkling stars that seemed to beam down an iron-hard frost.

Uffington's water columns were out of action at the first sign of ice with the result that tender engines were provided for the Faringdon branch goods because the usual tank engine did not have the water capacity for a round trip from Swindon to Faringdon and back without taking water at Uffington. A '22' class engine was used, an 0-6-0 type, which Elwyn called a 'Spinning Jenny'. It came up from Swindon chimney first so that its crew had some protection from the cold, and it arrived at Uffington with icicles on its coupling rods and snow piled on the back of its tender. In such bitter weather it was easy to see and to feel how simple it was for water to freeze solid in the hosepipe between engine and tender.

The '22' shunted wagons, black and dismal-looking, between the drifts of snow, while the ice daggers on the coupling rods flashed silver as they stabbed down and round to the movement of the wheels. When the train came back from Faringdon the engineman would come into the box, fearful of the tender-first drive to Swindon, and discuss the feasibility of going up to Didcot, turning the engine on the triangular junction and thus being able to have the cab's protection for the run home but there was never a proper 'path' among the other trains, the time to accomplish the manoeuvre was too long and in the end they would decide against it. 'Ah – what the hell mate, come on,' they would say to each other, shrug their shoulders and go away to Swindon huddled in their greatcoats with no protection at all from an eyeball-freezing, 30-mph slipstream. They could have rigged their storm canvas from cab roof to tender but they would still have been obliged to look around it to watch for signals.

I wonder how many men there are today, snug and warm in the cab of an InterCity 125, who remember those tortured miles, tender-first in the snow. Make no mistake, travelling thus was a very serious matter with the temperature well below zero Fahrenheit and Swindon an hour away. In the winter of 1909, I remember being told, Bert Vaughan was porter-signalman at Faringdon. He was a young man from Henley and one weekend was very anxious to return home. For some reason he would not wait for a stopping passenger train at Uffington but hitched a lift on a light engine running up line towards Reading. It was running tender first but he gave no thought for the inhospitable conditions and climbed aboard. The engineman carried him off the engine at Didcot, frozen stiff, and he died later from the effects of exposure.

In January 1962, a start was made on the installation of Up and Down goods loops to hold eighty wagons, engine and van. No one told me that this was the first salvo in a barrage of modernisation that put me and most of my friends out of work and annihilated a way of life to which I was so attached. Totally 'in the dark', I remained puzzled and derisive of what I saw as yet another example of British Railways' wastefulness. To accommodate the loops on each side of the Main lines the embankments at the western end of the station were widened, and to work the new layout of Main, branch or goods loop lines a brand-new lever frame was installed in Uffington box.

Engineering work took place each weekend and many relief signalmen and those with one regular signal box came up to Uffington to work as hand signalmen when signals were disconnected from the levers or when there was temporary single-line working. All but one were a delight to work with, most of them were old hands, easy-going yet expert, casually painstaking. The solitary would-be martinet introduced himself to me thus: 'I am Mr Williams – one of Mr Millsom's *Special* Class reliefmen.' Williams was not joking when he said it either! Mr Millsom was our much-respected District Inspector and a Special Class relief signalman was the highest grade a signalman could attain, a qualification to work any box at all in the district, which then extended from Steventon to Wootton Bassett, Kemble and, until the closure of the M&SW, the boxes on the line from Ogbourne to Cricklade.

Mr Williams believed in 'correctness'. If he was working a box with a booking lad the boy was sent home if he used a swear word and should the lad take more than thirty seconds to answer a telephone inquiry he would find Williams's bony hand taking the phone away, and the signalman at the other end would find himself being sternly reprimanded for wasting time. But, to be fair, he was hard on himself.

One Sunday he was booked on as pilotman at Uffington during single-line working. Not wanting to use his own car when other men were driving from Swindon to Uffington he came in a colleague's car, but when it was time to go home he discovered that all the car owners had quietly departed leaving him stranded. He paced the platform outside the box wondering how he was going to get home and longing to swear out loud. Technically he was off duty and therefore could not enter the signal box to ask me if there was a light engine about on the Down line on which he might take a ride – he was trespassing even to be on the station and his dislike of me as a strapper signalman utterly prevented him calling up to me for help – the very idea!

I watched him pacing, realised his predicament and had the answer. There was a light engine coming down for Swindon. All I had to do was stop it and the driver, asked politely, would be quite happy to oblige the stranded signalman. But Mr Williams would never break the rules so flagrantly, not even to get home after a long, hard day at work; he would at least require Control's permission to stop the engine. I opened the window and made the suggestion. 'There's an engine on the Down, Mr Williams. Shall I ask the Chief Controller if I can stop it for you to ride home to Swindon?'

'Certainly not!' he snapped. He might have said 'No thanks.' My last sight of him ever was as his little figure, silhouetted against the evening sky, cardboard attaché case in hand, dropped over the brow of the station approach, walking to Swindon fifteen miles away.

Part of the modernisation of the signalling equipment and layout at Uffington involved the replacement of the Up and Down line semaphore distant signals – their yellow-painted wooden arms on elegantly tapered, twenty-foot-tall pine masts – with electric, colour-light signals, squat and dumpy-looking on tubular steel posts. The colour-light distant signal with its powerful electric lamp and searchlight lens threw a penetrating beam of yellow or green light towards an oncoming train and was, for drivers, a vast improvement on the oil lamps of semaphores, which seemed tiny and dim by comparison; even in fog the grey murk was illuminated by the green or yellow glare.

For a signalman the advantage of the colour-light distant signal was twofold. He no longer had 1,500 yards of steel wire to shift every time he 'pulled off the back board' but simply moved the yellow-painted distant signal lever across as easily as switching on a light. The long handles of these signal levers, designed to be pulled over with all the strength of two fists and a strong back, were cut short so that it was not possible to put more than one hand on them.

The other advantage of the colour-light distant signal became apparent during fog or falling snow. Because they gave such a large, bright light they removed the need for a man to stand at the foot of the signal in foul weather to keep an exploding detonator or 'shot' on the rail during the time that the distant signal showed 'Caution'. This job of 'fogging the distant' was the toughest one on the railway, about which more will be said later. The necessity of 'shooting', in fog, each train that passed a distant signal showing 'Caution' arose because the signal's oil lamp was useless in such weather especially as it was often mounted high on a tall mast so as to give drivers an early view of the semaphore arm in clear weather; frequently all that a driver saw of a distant signal was the lower part of the white post as he passed. Imagine driving at 60 mph or more, in the dark, foggy night, head over the cabside straining to catch each signal as you flash past it, and then you will have some idea of the comfort which the fogman brought to hard-pressed drivers.

The fogman placed the 'shot' on the rail and the front wheel of the engine crushed it. The resulting bang was loud enough to be heard above the rattling bedlam in the engine's cab twenty feet or more away and on hearing the noise the driver immediately began to brake. The detonator had been in use on the Great Western Railway since 1843 and continued in use at distant signals during fog or falling snow even after the introduction of the GWR's clever Automatic Train Control (ATC), which was first tried in 1906 and was brought into general use on all lines between 1929 and 1939. Very briefly, the system caused a bell to ring in the engine's cab when a distant signal was passed at 'All Right', but caused a siren to wail and produced simultaneously a brake application when a distant signal showing 'Caution' was passed. In the latter case, the driver had to switch off the siren to prevent the train from being automatically brought to a stand and he then took over the braking.

In 1906, the GWR thought that the ATC could supersede conventional distant signals but soon thought better of that idea; neither did the ATC abolish the fogman, though conceivably it might have done.* In fact the electric ATC and the early Victorian 'shot' worked together for safety so that the fogman continued his foggy Victorian vigil by the murky lineside until released by the bright gleam of the electric colour-light signal.

Whether the leather-tough members of Uffington's permanent-way gang who provided the fogmen appreciated the assurance of every night in bed through the worst weather of the year I do not know but they would certainly have lost a lot of valuable overtime with the introduction of the electric signals. The foreman of the gang – the Ganger – was well known for his conscientiousness during times of bad weather. Just before he went to bed he would cycle to the signal box, if fog threatened, and offer the services of himself and his men 'fer foggin'. I thought this was typical of the old-hand country railwayman; he may have liked the overtime but he was acting beyond the call of duty to pedal out to the box – and he was giving the best service he could to the railway. In the absence of fogmen the signalmen had to comply with special signalling routines that immediately caused serious delays to trains.

As for me, I was sorry to lose the heavy pull of 'real' distant signals. Heaving over a heavy lever made me feel like a signalman.

When the pine masts of the semaphore distant signals were felled, they were found to be in perfect condition after at least fifty years' service and a railwayman I shall call Fred decided to buy one. He really did want to go through the proper procedure and pay his money, perhaps five shillings or at most a pound, for a thirty-foot post but he could not bear to put in an application to buy in case someone should come and steal 'his' signal while he was waiting for the official rigmarole to be completed. So, one Sunday when I happened to be on duty in Uffington box, he made a pre-emptive strike – got in first and set out to steal the timber without saying a word to anyone.

He took the permanent-way department's four-wheel trolley from where it was leaning up against the brick abutment wall of the girder bridge at the west end of the station, placed the trolley on the Up line and pushed off back towards Knighton happy in the 'certain knowledge' that 'there's no trains for an hour'. Fifteen hundred yards, twenty minutes' walking time, from the signal box, the felled distant signal post lay in the grass. Fred found it heavy to lift but by taking the tapered end he got it up onto the trolley floor, a lift of about

---

* According to the revised, official history of the GWR, published by Ian Allan, the ATC did dispense with them.

eighteen inches and by chocking the trolley wheels with bits of ballast laid on the rail he was able to shove the huge piece of timber onto the little, flat wagon. But while he was struggling, I was giving 'Line Clear' to Bill Curtis for a fast.

Fred finally got the post onto the trolley and struck out for home but he now had his back to the oncoming traffic and did not see the dark snake of a train slide into view a mile away along the embankment. He walked cheerfully and gave the trolley an occasional shove with his boot to keep it rolling on the slightly falling grade. His complacency was shattered by the frantic, two-tone braying of a 'Western' class diesel's horn as it made towards him at 90 mph on an Up Bristol fast. With the energy of a man who jumps a five-bar gate when he is chased by a bull, Fred forgot about the weight of the post, put his arms underneath it and simply threw it down the bank, threw the trolley after it and dived headfirst for the grass as the huge diesel, its horn blaring and brakes hard on swept past missing his flying heels by inches.

I heard the commotion and went to the window wondering what was wrong. The diesel came to a stand at my signal box and the driver, red faced and very angry, told me in unmistakable Anglo-Saxon what he thought of 'strapper' signalmen who allowed men with trolleys to stray on the Main line when there were trains about. Of course he did not believe me when I protested my innocence – my entire ignorance – of the awful event, but luckily he stayed to argue long enough for Fred to catch up. Passengers' heads were sticking out of the leading coach and I wondered, as the driver and I shouted at each other above the noise of the diesel, what they understood of the accusations, protestations and wagging fingers; Fred, running, red-faced and panting, along the platforms past the coaches must have seemed quite alarming.

Fred redeemed himself very well by going straight to the driver and making a clean breast of what he had done, exonerating me entirely – whereupon the driver laughed out loud, described Fred's frantic efforts and headlong dive down the bank as if it were a hilarious joke then slid his cab window shut and opened up his 2,350-hp diesel, which promptly threw a black plume of vile fumes from its exhaust pipe through the open windows of the signal box.

At the end of January the work at Uffington had reached the stage where the new locking frame could be installed. To remove the old frame the concrete floor forming the very foundation of the box had to be broken up with pneumatic drills and the old, steel girders cut through with oxy-acetylene torches. Work began one Monday morning when I was on duty and very soon the box was a shambles. Smoke from burning oil and dirt filled the room, the noise from two drills working in the locking room – directly beneath the floor of what is usually thought of as the signal box – was unbelievable and I spent the shift, from 9 a.m. until 2 p.m., standing on the frame watching the bell hammers to see when and what they rang. At about eleven o'clock the workmen began to remove the floor leaving me only two planks to walk on to and fro along the frame and pull levers. When I pulled off I leant backwards over a 6-foot drop. They left me one plank, set at 90 degrees to the other two, on which I walked across the void to reach the booking desk.

Workmen filled the signal box, bawling in each other's ears and mine to make themselves heard above the noise of the drills. 'Can we have forty-four points now?' 'When you're ready we want to take off the Down road track circuit repeater – just for a minute.' And all the while the trains were passing and I was trying to keep track in the block register of what trains had passed and what had been disconnected or reconnected.

At 11.55, the Up Red Dragon passed. I knocked out to Knighton Crossing and Bill immediately asked the road for a 1-4 sending it on line as soon as I had given him the road. He was turning a goods out of his loop behind the fast. After a pause to allow Bill to pull his signals I turned the block indicator to 'Train on Line', then the technicians wanted me to help them and I forgot about the goods.

When I next looked at the indicators I saw the 'Train on Line' indication and thought I had forgotten to give 'Train out of Section' for the Red Dragon and promptly did so. Knighton then asked the road for another fast, I acknowledged the bell code but when I turned the indicator knob the needle obstinately refused to show 'Line Clear'. 'Who's taken off the Knighton block?' I yelled into the bedlam. No reply. Seeing from the east-end window some Signal & Telegraph men out on the platform, I put the question to them. One man detached himself from the group and came up into the box. It was John Moody.

'What's up, Ady?' he asked. 'I can't peg "Line Clear" to Knighton. Have you disconnected the block?'

He frowned. 'No, not yet, let's have a look. Hah! No wonder you can't peg up; you've get something outside the Up home – look at the track circuit showing "Occupied".

With decidedly shaky hands I pulled the home signal lever, got the road for a 1-4 from Challow and lowered the other signals. Having got the goods away I was able to peg up for the fast. When the box was finally modernised and the old, brass-cased, track circuit repeater was redundant I took it home as a memento of the day it prevented me from causing a collision.

Soon after this 'near miss', a temporary signal box was assembled in a prefabricated hut at the eastern end of the Up platform. The essentials for signalling trains were there – a bell and indicator each for the Challow and Knighton Crossing sections and a telephone – but there was no electric locking to save a situation such as the one I have just described, neither was there any mechanical interlocking to prevent conflicting movements between points and signals because there was no lever frame. Signalling trains from that hut was like stepping back in time a hundred years and it was quickly dubbed the 'Uffington Time Machine'.

The Up and Down distant signals were fixed at 'Caution', the home signals were at 'Danger' with a handsignalman at each to 'flag' trains past on instructions from the signalman, but the Up and Down starting signals, giving access to Challow and Knighton's sections respectively, were worked by the signalman using levers spiked to the ground at the foot of the platform ramp. And what levers they were – the National Railway Museum would be glad to have them in its collection; they must have been straight out of Brunel's broad-gauge Great Western.

A baseplate was spiked to the ground. Arching along the length of the plate were a pair of iron strips, close together, and between them moved the lever pivoted to the baseplate. To pull off I picked the lever up and over, taking up the slack and pressing it down, wire taut and signal lowered, with my boot. To hold the lever in position I inserted a metal peg into a hole. Under the strain of the taut wire to the signal there seemed to me to be some danger to my limbs as I bent to put the pin in whilst holding the contraption down with my foot. Yet this was nothing to the real sense of impending disaster I felt as I bent to remove the pin and allow the lever to come up gently, I hoped – past my head as I bent over it, tensioned and ready to spring like a rat trap.

Curiously enough, no one was hurt during the hundreds of times they were used in the three-week period of the 'Uffington Time Machine', which made me wonder if there was any virtue in the saying of Sir Daniel Gooch (the first Locomotive Superintendent of the Great Western and Chairman of the Company in 1865) that safety devices were not to be encouraged because they gave men a false sense of security, thus lulling them into dropping their guard and relying on the device, which would ultimately break down and betray them. On balance I think I prefer the safety devices.

So, for three weeks I lived the life of one of Gooch's 'switchmen' of the 1860s, walking about my layout by day and by night in all weathers, altering points by removing their padlocked 'G' clamps and shoving the point blades over with my boot before re-clamping, bawling instructions to my handsignalmen and generally feeling the anxieties and discomforts that the men of old must have felt when they signalled trains, without locking or any safety check, on their tired and fallible memories.

I felt very old-fashioned in pouring rain, waving to my mate hunched in his sodden greatcoat at the home signal, holding back a roaring steam engine with a dripping, red flag and seeing him substitute a green; old-fashioned as the engine's great naked wheels, spokes glittering wet, flickered round from the rail, rising and turning a foot above my head; old-fashioned when the wind hissed in the lineside trees, their branches traced black against the cloudy moon as with my assistant, usually a man of sixty or over, we trudged over the sleepers, shoulder to shoulder towards some points, tired and silent at four in the morning.

At the end of February I was reunited with my signal box, now full of mid-twentieth-century equipment including electrically operated points at the far end of the goods loops – not hand-generated current but off the mains; I had merely to flick the lever over. Naturally I objected to this, a hand generator would have been more interesting but the one supplied was for use only in case of a power failure. A new lever frame had been installed close to the rear wall of the box, leaving the front windows free and clear for the observation of trains. This was a clever LMS idea that took us Western stick-in-the-muds some time to get used to; indeed, as far back as 1942 Gilbert Matthews, then Superintendent of the Line, had asked the Signal & Telegraph department to arrange in this manner the frames of some new signal boxes then being built at Oxford but the idea was far too revolutionary – too *Midland* – for the Great Western Signal Department to contemplate.

The main lines through the station and the loop lines were track circuited throughout and a large diagram of the layout hung above the instrument shelf. The layout plan was divided into short lengths, each piece having a little red bulb that lit up when a train occupied that particular piece of line so that the progress of the train could be followed by the progression of red lights across the plan. After three weeks out in the mad March weather I felt positively luxurious.

But Elwyn was not so easily bowled over, and after studying everything carefully when he came on duty, he said to the new Works Inspector, Mr Hancock, 'If you've got main electricity coming into the box to work those little red lights and the power points, I suppose you'll be putting in main electric lighting for the signalmen?'

Mr Hancock looked worried. 'Oh no,' he said in his Birmingham accent, 'there's nothing in the plans about that.'

'What?' cried Elwyn. 'Do you mean to say we've got to work all this new-fangled tackle and watch it working on the mains but write in the Book under a smelly old Tilley lamp? Hah! I'll see about that.' Elwyn was branch secretary of the Uffington branch of the NUR – he knew what action to take.

We got the new lighting.

CHAPTER FOUR

Ale and Anecdotes

The first week of March was memorable. The Uffington signalmen had been brought back to the twentieth century uninjured, my application for promotion to the vacancy at Challow box – caused by signalman Jack Miles moving to Oxford – had been granted, a celebratory footplate permit had been approved and the signalmen of my shift had set the weekend for their annual pub get-together. There was no difficulty in choosing which train's engines to ride on – down with the 10.55 a.m. Paddington to Pembroke Dock, returning next day on the 7.50 a.m. Pembroke Dock, which was hauled by a 'King' from Cardiff to Paddington. This was the longest steam-hauled through train on Western Region, covering 520 miles in all.

I went up to Paddington on 7 March 1962 and found my train on platform five. The empty coaches had been brought into the station by a black pannier tank which sat squat and silent against the buffers as I walked through the ticket gate. Inside its cab the enginemen had taken up a V-shaped pose apparently to relax but looking very uncomfortable as they perched on the hard wooden seats with their backs against the side sheets and their boots on the firebox fittings. There was a jumble of passengers around each door of the cream and brown train as I walked quickly to the country end of the platform counting as I went seven coaches and a van, each coach bearing a long board above its windows proclaiming the destination: PADDINGTON TENBY & PEMBROKE DOCK – THE PEMBROKE COAST EXPRESS.

Presently an engine appeared beyond the Ranelagh bridge, coming tender first, the white exhaust low across the tracks. She came steadily up the slope, weaved from track to track, finally shut off steam, entered the curved platform and drifted past in complete silence. She was the perfection of mechanical elegance to see, the oldest surviving member of her class 4099 *Kilgerran Castle*.

I hurried back along the platform to meet the engine driver. He was a slightly built, little man in faded blue, but clean overalls, wearing a black peaked cap with a shiny top and his silver hair cropped short on his grizzled neck. He was leaning over the driving wheel covers with an oil can, looking at the valve gear beneath the boiler. I showed him my permit and asked him if I could ride with him. 'Are you going to ride all the way to the Dock?' he asked in a pleasant Welsh accent. I said I was. 'Well, rather you than me then. Onto the engine now and keep out of my mate's way.'

The cab was empty as I clambered delightedly aboard, happy as always to be among the oily steel handles and to see the fire with the firebox flap lying down on the floor. A moment later a sooty beret appeared on the open trackside of the engine followed by the rest of a jumbo-sized fireman in dark, stained overalls. He was startled to see me.

''Ello then – are you riding with us?'

'Yes, down to Pembroke Dock.'

'Pembroke Dock?! Swansea's my limit and that's only half way. What does my mate reckon?'

'He says I can come but I think he feels the same as you.'

'Course he does, you'll be daft to try it – this old camel will curdle your brains.'

The driver climbed up from the platform then. 'Everything all right, Dai?' he asked the fireman, his 'everything' including me, I knew.

'Oh, I reckon so,' said Dai. 'I've hooked us on anyway,' he added cheerfully.

'I hope you'll be all right, bach,' the driver said to me. 'You've picked a rough 'un here.'

Kilgerran Castle's safety valves had just started to sizzle when the 'Right Away' indicator under the platform canopy lit up and a minute later the guard's whistle shrilled. 'Here we go then,' said Dai quietly. 'Right away, Lou.' The driver popped the whistle and eased the regulator open, whistle and exhaust beats echoed hollowly under Brunel's great glass-vaulted roof as the fastest steam-hauled express on Western Region set out on its non-stop run to Newport – 133 ½ miles in 130 minutes.

Steam was put on properly as we passed Royal Oak station and immediately the little-ends – or something – started to hammer the soles of my feet through the 4-inch-thick timber floor of the footplate; we might have had square wheels. Dai pulled out of a compartment on the tender a steel bar an inch thick and 14 feet long with an L-shaped end, pushed it into the fire, closed the sliding doors on it and dragged it up and down over the 9-foot-long grate to spread his thick, new fire and break up the caked, half-burnt coal. Opening the doors he pulled it out, smoking and dull red at its tip, swung it round expertly and slid it back into place on the tender. Black smoke billowed from the chimney in response to the stirring of the fire, Dai waited till it had cleared and then began to shovel coal.

The noise in the cab from the spine-shattering blows was deafening at 20 mph. Over the extensive junctions passing Old Oak Common at 50 mph I thought that the concussions racking the engine were more than metal – or flesh and blood – could stand. By the time we passed West Drayton, 13 miles out at nearly 70 mph I had accepted the rapid, violent hammering on the underside of the footplate and the accompanying cacophony on the cab. It seemed to have no effect on anything except my ears and knee joints so I relaxed – and discovered a hole in the floor in the front corner of the cab through which I could see the blurring ballast and be entertained by the riveting antics of the left-hand trailing driving wheel.

It was moving from side to side, alternately crashing its flange against the rail and running on the rail's inside edge till it seemed only a quarter of an inch remained supported. For yards it skimmed the edge of the rail on the verge of disaster and then, suddenly, shot sideways onto the rail properly. By watching this rapid, lateral movement I could relate certain of the rending crashes to the impact of the flange on the rail yet no one but myself seemed worried about it so I dragged my eyes away from the awful sight to watch the road along the fat, green boiler.

As we approached Slough at 70 mph, Dai yelled at me to stand with him in the centre of the cab. 'There's a bad lurch over the Windsor junctions; it'll smash your head against the cabside if you stand in the corner there.' I moved smartly, Lou dragged down on the whistle chain and we battered, hammered and whooped our way down to the station while passengers drew back nervously from the platform's edge. We skimmed the coping stones, missing them by an inch. *Then came the lurch.* I had never experienced anything like it and its horrific viciousness took my breath away. The engine heeled over left and right, not like a ship might, but savagely and suddenly as if the engine were falling over a cliff. There was a crash that drowned the usual racket and I felt fear sweep through me as my mouth went dry. The tender followed the same course, whipping over as if it were going to break away and an avalanche of coal rattled down onto the footplate. From the lineside *Kilgerran Castle* would have made such a pretty picture! On that bucking bedlam of a footplate Dai stood, legs apart as firm as the pillars of Paddington station yet rolling with the erratic motion of the engine, calmly feeding 30 square feet of fire to an orderly plan as easily as if we were stationary. With a big shovel which looked like a teaspoon in his huge hands he shot each charge of coal through the narrow firehole so accurately that in spite of the unpredictable movements of the engine he never missed his aim once, while his actions were so sharp and deft that the shovel blade flashed and rang on steel like a rapier. Each shot went to a different part of the fire and by watching carefully I could see the swift, subtle tilts of the blade as he bounced and skidded it off the firehole ring.

Except when he paused to assist Lou in spotting signals, Dai kept up his round all the way to Swindon: firehole flap tugged down by its hand-polished chain with the left hand, then, back bent low, swing from the waist turning from tender to furnace with coal, shoot it into the heat, shovel out smartly and tug up the flap-chain with the left hand, swing round to the tender, drive the shovel under the coal, left hand reach out for the flap-chain ...

Dai was firing 27 or 30 lb of coal to the minute, his fire was in perfect order with a colour and intensity like the sun and as blinding to look at. The boiler feed was running continuously, the injector working with a jet of exhaust steam which he had adjusted finely to deliver to the boiler exactly the amount of water which was being evaporated as steam – about 18,000 lb per hour. And in the train the passengers were staring absently at the green flats of the Thames valley, or reading their morning papers in a desperate attempt to stave off boredom or, overcome by the carriage heating and the clickety-clack rhythm of the wheels on the track, they dozed. Little did they realise that their dedicated enginemen were working a locomotive with all the comfort and convenience of a huge pneumatic drill, the boiler pressure was rock steady at 225 psi and the boiler water constant at three-quarters full or that their fireman with consummate skill and deceptive ease was shovelling them to Wales at 75 mph.

Swindon is the summit of the Great Western Main line, 77 miles from Paddington and 390 feet above the sea, level with the top of St Paul's Cathedral. The back boards were off for us right through the complicated layout and Dai took a few minutes off to roll a cigarette, balancing the tobacco tin on his knees and filling the flimsy paper with a draught-defying dexterity. He lit up and moved across to the driver's side of the cab. 'Let's see what's in the factory,' he yelled to me. There were some freshly painted 'Halls' and tank engines outside the works and rows of derelict 'Kings' and 'Castles' in the field beyond.

'Look at that lot,' commanded Lou as we dived under the bridge that once carried the M&SW over the GWR, 'they're cutting up engines just out of shops – "70 Castles" – and leaving us to run fast trains with run-down old "40"s.'

The appalling racket continued and I reflected that there were over fifty miles to run before the Newport stop brought temporary relief. As we battered down into Gloucestershire I felt sure that the engine would either fall to pieces at the next rail joint or arrive at Newport ten minutes early – a real case of the proverbial 'a medal or the Sack' for the driver. In the event we stopped in Newport 'right time' and I got down to take a photograph. As soon as my feet touched the platform my legs gave way and I fell, unable to get up without Dai's assistance; he got down from the engine to help and I sat on a platform seat until it was time for the train to leave. It was impossible for me to take a photograph – each time I stood up the platform felt like the deck of a ship in a storm. 4099 was nearing the end of her life. She had been a long time out of works, and riding her footplate at 75 mph was like riding on a pneumatic drill, but she could still steam like a witch and gallop like a racehorse – provided the crew could stand it. I can't imagine she stayed on top-class express work for much longer after March. The engine was withdrawn from service in September.

At Swansea terminus I shook hands and said goodbye to my kind mates and went to the other end of the train where 5019 *Tintern Abbey* had been hooked on. Feeling very tired I got up into her cab and as we were drawing out of the station I looked back along the train just in time to see my overnight bag thrown out onto the platform by the guard – I had lost my clean clothes, soap, towel and toothbrush. At Carmarthen another reversal brought 7826 *Longworth Manor* onto the train and I doggedly climbed aboard wishing to God that Pembroke was considerably less than the forty miles that fact demanded. At Whitland even the driver saw I was falling over and suggested it would be no shame to 'call it quits' and go back into the coaches but I asked to be allowed to stay; he agreed and did his best to help by gaining ten minutes on schedule, arriving at the 'Dock' at 5.14 p.m.

After six hours and twenty minutes and 286 miles on four footplates I was utterly weary and covered in coal dust from head to foot. My lips were sore from the draught through the cab and the heat of the fire, their cracks were full of black dust, my eyes were black with grit like mad mascara, the eyeballs red, my whole body jarred to the core. For the moment at any rate my lust for steam engines was satisfied and I had to face the unpleasant fact that I had been deposited luggage-less in a town I did not know as it was growing dark; as near as made no difference I was lost with nowhere to shelter for the night. A fine end to a celebratory journey. I presented myself at three bed & breakfast doors but when the lady opened her door and the hall light fell upon a filthy fellow, sooty and obviously exhausted from miles tramping the roads she said, 'Sorry, we're full up,' and shut the door quickly. It was dark and raining after I turned miserably away from the third door. I walked a little way, turned into another street and knocked on a door, not a B&B house just *any* house. It was opened by a bright little lady who said cheerfully, 'Yes, can I help you?' I went into my rigmarole, I had rolled it out three times now to the utter disbelief of the listener and now it was beginning to sound farfetched to me. 'I have just come down from Paddington on the footplate of an engine – that's why I'm covered in soot. My bag was thrown off the train at Swansea by mistake – that's why I have no luggage. I need a meal and a bed for the night. Can you put me up please?' I tried to stand up respectfully and not lean on her nice clean doorpost.

'It looks as if you could do with a bath too. Come in please.'

She was a trustful, Christian soul to have taken me in and I shall never forget her kindness. Her name was Mrs Leslie of 90 Bush Street, Pembroke Dock.

The journey next day began wearily in the damp, grey dawn of a gale-swept March day. I cramped into the cab of 4107, running bunker first with four coaches forming the 8 a.m. express to Paddington. The climb out of Pembroke Dock to Pembroke Town was a steep mile or so with a tunnel ¼ mile long a mile out from the dock station. The driver caught the single-line token from the signalman and made the best use of the brief length of level track. We were the first train out and the rails were slippery from the night-time drizzle. After the tunnel we caught the gale-force wind straight through the cab and across the rails. The engine lost adhesion on the steep grade. The driver opened the sand feeders to put fine, dry sand onto the rails to provide grip but the wind blew the sand away as it left the delivery pipe. The wheels spinning, shut off steam, open steam, wheels grip and then slip, we were soon down to walking speed. Then the fireman got down on the ground, to scoop up grit with his fingers and throw it under the wheels. At walking speed we made the last half mile into Pembroke Town. After that loss of time the driver went hell-for-leather, 'hammer-and-tongs' to regain time and get to Whitland punctually to make our connection there with the Paddington train from Neyland. That came in as four coaches behind 1014 *County of Glamorgan*. 4107 came off and 1014 backed onto the coaches. I travelled on 1014 to Carmarthen. Here another six coaches were added by 5030 *Shirburn Castle*, onto the footplate of which I climbed. My spirits rose as we ran along the sea wall at Kidwelly and the sun came out. From Swansea to Cardiff we were double-headed with 5071 *Spitfire* coupled to the train while I rode on the pilot 7901 *Doddington Hall*. Where were the diesels? It all seems like fairyland, looking back on it today. Cantering into

Cardiff past Canton shed there was a line of steam engines waiting to leave the shed for duty, and at the head of the queue was a magnificently polished 'King'. I looked with loving admiration until the driver of 7901 said, 'That's your "King" for Paddington.' Only fellow devotees will understand why my heart leapt – to ride on a 'King' had all the significance that meeting Muhammad Ali would have to a boxing enthusiast.

6018 *King Henry VI* was in perfect condition, not a rattle or a knock; conversation could take place in a normal voice – I could even hear the wheels of the tender clicking over the rail joints. The journey to Paddington with a trailing load not far short of 500 tons was made smoothly and quietly, even on steep inclines, and time was kept exactly, though the schedule was easy enough. Indeed, the driver apologised for the lack of drama and promised to put some 'zip' into the proceedings before the journey was over.

What did he do? At the Reading stop he hung the pot on with the bag in, lost five minutes and then proceeded to make them up again. As we ran into Paddington I stood on the fall plate between the engine and tender in full view of the locospotters on the platform with quite unreasonable pride swelling my heart just because I was on that magnificent engine while the crew were out of sight, busy with the job of conning the train to a safe stop on the buffers. According to my watch we covered the 36 miles from Reading in 36 minutes start to stop, doubtless exactly what the driver intended, an average of 60 mph. There was no apparent effort shown in this either, except for the initial surge of acceleration; the engine was perfection yet it was withdrawn in December 1962. In April 1963 it was brought out of the scrapyard to work an enthusiast special, and having done that it was destroyed.

The Saturday evening following my mammoth footplate excursion was the date of the signalmen's annual get-together at the Victoria by Shrivenham station.* Several old hands, retired and about to retire, were to be there so I went along, not so much for the beer as to hear some more about the old days. When I walked into the bar I thought I had come to the wrong pub; the room was full of smartly dressed men in blazers and flannels, lounge suits – even three-piece suits with gold watch chains. There was a roar of voices and a crackle of glasses being gathered but very shortly I began to hear all the right words: they were railwaymen, they were talking

---

* The Great Western Railway staff magazine for February 1943 stated that the first of these was held at the Junction Hotel in January 1943. 'It is hoped that this will be the start of a tradition.' This gathering at Shrivenham on 10 March 1962 was the last ever held.

shop! Once, someone had the nice idea of a dance for all grades at Swindon. Drivers, signalmen, porters and guards arrived at the hall with their wives or girlfriends but as soon as they got inside it was 'Just going to the bar for a quick one before the band starts' to their girl and in no time at all the bar was full of railwaymen caught up in the pleasures of talking railways. The dance was a flop – as a dance.

Bill Curtis stood out from the crowd not only because he was a head taller than most but because he was the only one not wearing a tie; with him was Sid Tyler, a great friend who was a special class reliefman from Swindon; and a third man I did not know was standing with his ramrod-straight back towards me. I bought a pint and went over to them. Sid, who had gone 'over the top' in the Battle of the Somme just before his sixteenth birthday, gave me his usual greeting: 'Hello, kid, how's yer brush?' and Bill introduced the third man as Nelson Edwards. 'We were mates at Knighton for years until he retired a few months ago – we were on the M&SW together.'

Nelson and I shook hands. 'Do you think you'll like it at Uffington,' he said, 'working with young Bill here?'

'We get on fine; he's told me a lot about the old Tiddley Dyke.'

'Him!? He's only a strapper, out with the plough when I was cleaning lavatories at Swindon Old Town. Are you getting your ration of beer from the Junction?'

'I dare say she'd bring it round if I asked; I know it's done.'

Nelson and the other laughed.

'You're the only one as don't ask then,' said Bill.

'When I was portering at Swindon Town,' said Nelson, 'they wouldn't let us in the refreshment room so I got my beer lowered down from the back window of the Eagle. You know how the line goes out through that sheer rock cutting under the Devizes Road? The pub's right over the cutting by the bridge and the barmaid used to lower a few bottles down in a basket.'

'That was a neat trick. You could put the money in the basket to haul it up,' I said.

'Yes – sometimes. She were a fine girl that barmaid, especially when she had to lean half-upside-down out of the window with the rope, ooh – she was big! 'Twas much better to go up to the bar and pay her face to face like after you'd finished work.'

'I'll tell you what,' I said, 'ever since I've been on the railway I've been called a strapper and you were pulling Bill's leg about it – why's a newcomer to the railway a strapper?'

'Well, it's just an old country word,' said Bill. 'I remember I was a strapper when I went to work on a farm – what do you reckon, Nelson?' Nelson and Sid did not know.

'When I first came in here,' I continued, 'I thought I'd come to the wrong place; hardly recognised all these well-dressed blokes as signalmen – look at that chap over there in the dark three-piece suit. He looks like Sir Daniel Gooch. Who is he?'

The others laughed. 'Oh, he'd like to hear you say that – that's Jimmy Kent, another of us rich special class men,' said Sid. 'Come on, drink up the last drop and I'll go and get another round.'

'No, I'll get them in,' I said and went to the bar with the jars for re-filling. While I waited, a short, heavily built man about sixty-five began to sing, his voice a fine baritone with a Wiltshire accent. This I guessed was Sam Paul with his song, 'The Village Pump'. The noise of conversation dropped as the men turned to listen. I took the beer back and handed it round, saying, 'That's Sammy Paul then?'

'Yes,' said Bill, 'regular deep voice he's got an't he. He usually starts with that one – he'll have "The Spotted Cow" next, never fails. Cheeky sort of song but come on, drink up, and Nelson'll tell you about Jack Bunce's lamp.'

Nelson laughed. 'Oh yes, that was a pity, it was the driver's fault.'

'Huh! The barmaid at the Eagle more like,' grinned Sid.

'Well, a bit maybe. We were shunting empty stock down at the "B" box end at Old Town. It was nigh on dark and I was using Bunce's lamp –'

Bill broke in, 'The thing was that it was Jack's regular pride and joy, stripped right down to the tin and polished like silver.'

'Just like the one at Knighton,' I added.

'Yes, right,' said Nelson impatiently. 'We were pushing these coaches back on a road right on the edge of the embankment and I was riding standing on a buffer, waving the driver back with the lamp. I gave him a red to stop and he pulled up so sharp that the snatch threw me off and I fell down the bank into the brambles. I had had one or two before that. Anyhow I must have passed out or gone to sleep or something because when I came to there I was in this bramble bush and all that was left of Bunce's lamp was the handle still grabbed in my fist. That cost me a quart o' beer – he didn't care about me being nearly killed, only about his precious lamp.'

'When did you start at Old Town, Nelson?' I asked, hoping to keep him talking.

'I went there as a lad from Cricklade. Swindon was the big city to me. There was the bioscope, what you'd call the cinema now, and the music hall, the Great Western owned the town baths and swimming pool and then there was the trams – you remember them Sid?'

'No,' replied Sid, 'I was working in a garage in Chippenham in 1913.'

'Oh, I loved them trams,' continued Nelson enthusiastically, 'cream and maroon they were, grand machines. So there I was on the loose in the big city at fourteen years old with money in my pocket. I was a big lad for my age and when the war broke out I signed on in the Wiltshire Yeomanry. I passed for nineteen and I'd always wanted to ride a big horse like they had in the cavalry.'

A roar of applause went up and cries of 'More' as Sam Paul finished his 'Village Pump'.

'Here you are now,' laughed Bill, 'here comes "The Spotted Cow".' The predicted song began amidst cheers, some of them derisive. Sam smiled as he sang and raised his arms. Jim Kent joined our group and Sid Tyler introduced me. 'He seems to be dazzled by your accoutrements, Jim. Said you looked like Daniel Gooch.'

Jim Kent certainly did look pleased at that. 'Well you don't have to go about looking like a tramp. I went ragged arsed when I was a kid in Swindon before the First World War and I'm making up for it now.' All he needed to look like a Victorian magnate was a pair of bushy side whiskers; he had the red face, the build and the 'carry' of his clothes to fit the part.

We shook hands. 'I've heard you on the phone,' said Jim, 'digging up the past. You ought to ask someone about old Tommy Wilmott. You probably think of Phil Millsom as strict as a District Inspector but he's an angel beside Tommy.' There was a general murmur of agreement among the other three and Bill said, 'Ah! Tommy Wilmott with that old frock coat and his bowler hat – if you saw him coming up the box with his hat on you knew you had nothing to fear, but if he was carrying his hat – look out!' The others laughed ruefully. 'And what about the hours we used to work back along? During the war' (and by that Jim meant the First World War) 'when I was a bit of a strapper on Swindon platform –'

I interrupted him. 'Jim, I've heard that word so often yet no one here can tell me why a beginner on the railway is called that. Have you any ideas on it?'

'Well, of course, anyone knows that', said Jim scornfully. There was a chorus of disagreement and 'Go on then tell us, what is it?'

'It's obvious. When the railway was new they thought of it as an iron horse pulling mechanical stagecoaches and just like they carried luggage on the roof of a stagecoach so they put it on the roofs of the railway carriages.

If you look at that picture of Paddington station, the one where the Bow Street runners are arresting the man as he's about to get on the train, you'll see the luggage on the roofs and the men up there strapping it down. So that was what you did when you first came onto the job. You were a porter and you strapped down the luggage on the carriage roof. So you were a strapper.'

There were cries of admiration and Sid said, 'Well I'm damned, I'd never given it a thought before. I bet you're right though.'

Jim seemed to swell beneath his starched white shirt and low-cut waistcoat. 'What put me in mind of it', he said, 'was the work I did when I first came on the job in 1915 at Swindon. I used to go up on the carriage roofs to turn the bypass valves of gas-lit coaches in trains stopping near the evening time and to put oil lamps down the casings of the older stock so they'd shine just up under the ceilings of the compartments. There were still a few oil lamp-lit coaches around then, especially on troop trains.' Another cheer signalled the end of 'The Spotted Cow' and there was a tidal surge to the bar carrying Sam Paul on its crest.

'That was a good song – what I heard of it,' I said. 'He is a very good singer.'

'Why don't you go and get the words from him,' said Bill, 'he'd be regular delighted for you to take an interest.'

'Right well, I'll leave you now,' said Jim. 'I hope I'll see you at Uffington some time when I'm relieving up there.' He sailed majestically into the crowd.

'What'll you all have then?' said Bill. 'I'll get them in this time.'

While he was gone I said to Nelson, 'You must have had a great time on the M&SW; all the stories show you enjoyed yourselves.'

'Oh, there was a great crowd there and it wasn't for the pay we got either. It was only a small company and the pay was low in comparison to the Great Western – we used to check the number of passengers in the North and the South Express, our two boat trains you know, and if they were well filled with the boat crews travelling between Liverpool and Southampton you knew you'd be all right for your wages that week.'

I felt incredulous. 'But surely they didn't pay you straight out of the till?'

Nelson Edwards chuckled. 'I wouldn't be so sure about that. It was only a poor railway compared to most and even if they had a better method of paying wages than out of the till, you can see that we knew how touch and go it was. Maybe that's why we felt loyal to it; the company wasn't rich, in fact it was downright poor.'

Bill Curtis set down a tray of beer. 'Who was poor?' he asked.

'The old M&SW,' said Nelson.

'Oh, definitely, you just think, although the line ran right through the Cotswolds, the Marlborough Downs and Salisbury Plain, where there were racehorses in training, hunters to be moved and army officer chargers, too, the M&SW never had enough horseboxes. A steeplechaser would be walked miles to the station – no lorries for them then – and after all that there'd be no horsebox. You'd have telegrams going up and down the line begging for a horsebox for Collingbourne or wherever and the replies coming back "None to send".'

Nelson chuckled. 'That would be a wise man, we used to hang onto all our stuff; we might need it ourselves in the morning – we hid horseboxes behind the shed.'

Sid Tyler, true-green Great Western man, was scandalised and said so but the two old M&SW men laughed gleefully. 'Hey!' continued Nelson. 'We were even short of goods brake vans. When we wanted to run a trip out to Moredon power station with coal we had a special brake van kept for the job; it was an old water tank. When I stood inside it acting as guard my head just poked out of the filler hole nicely; shorter chaps stood on a box inside.' Sid and I made all the right noises of disbelief but the M&SW men were away with the bit between their teeth. 'Not only that,' said Bill, 'but we were short on tail lamps, too. If a special had to run up to Tidworth, we often had to hang a churn lid on the buffer of the last wagon.' Nelson agreed that this was done on the Moredon trips, too.

'Well I'm damned,' said Sid. 'What would you have done if the couplings had broken and you were in a water tank at the back of the train going up the bank from Rushey to Old Town? You've no chance without brakes, down the hill and off at the first catch point!'

Nelson and Bill grinned happily at the fuss Sid was making.

'It was a man at the rear of the train anyhow,' said Bill. 'That was better than nothing.'

CHAPTER FIVE

Cautionary Tales

When I drove into the station yard at Challow at 2 p.m. on the Monday after the pub get-together I was coming as a trainee signalman to learn a new box but I still had the same sort of feeling that a pupil would have if he returned to his old school as a teacher. I had been an honorary member of the signal box staff since 1953 and had started my railway service as a lad porter on the station in September 1960. Then I had thought of Challow box and its complexities – such as they were – as the highest form of signal box practice and even though I knew better by late March 1962, having visited some huge signal boxes in Swindon and Bristol, I still had a high regard for the work of Challow. Officially Challow was a 'Class 2' box for pay whilst Uffington was a '3' but Challow was a very busy '2' and Uffington was a very easy-going '3'.

I parked in the signalmen's place in the goods shed almost opposite the signal box and got out of the car. The brick-built shed was abbey sized with tall, buttressed walls pierced by pointed 'Gothick' windows, massive timbers spanned the walls and a forest of struts and rafters supported a roof rising fifty feet to its ridge. The goods shed at Challow was part of Isambard Kingdom Brunel's original design for the infant Great Western Railway, drawn up in 1833, and without doubt the great man supervised the construction of the shed.

Harry Strong was levering a plywood pig-shelter along the wooden loading platform to place it beneath the crane for loading into a rail wagon and the dust he was raising shimmered in the strong light streaking through the pointed 'Early English' windows. Harry had begun his career on the Great Western in 1916 at Woodborough between Hungerford and Devizes. He came to Challow in 1924 and had worked there ever since, long enough for me to have the privilege of learning from him about railway work and the railway spirit. Harry's shirt sleeves were turned up, the folded portion being the exact width of a cigarette packet and from chest to ankles he wore a brown canvas apron to protect his uniform waistcoat and sharply creased serge trousers.

'Afternoon, Adrian,' he said, 'haven't seen you here for a long time – going to see Ken?'

'Hello, Harry, nice to see you again – I'm coming to learn the box, didn't you know?'

'You're a Class Two signalman already?' his long upper lip lifted into a rare smile. 'Well done, but it's a surprise – no one told me.'

'You should take your tea breaks in the box instead of the goods shed office,' I said boldly on the strength of eighteen months' railway service. 'It'd be nice if you came to have your tea with me in the box – when I take on that is.' His lip stiffened and he looked away. 'Oh well, I might,' he replied gruffly, 'but you know how I like to keep in touch with the work.'

The door of the goods shed office was open. It was a small room, a brick lean-to on the east gable end of the building. The interior was lit by a square-headed, mullioned window, its walls whitewashed and cobwebbed. A tall desk, certainly as old as the shed, stood under the window with its stool, and festooning the walls were dozens of long wires onto which were spiked thousands of used labels taken off incoming wagons. On shelves were ledgers heavy as chained Bibles in church, their leather-bound spines blocked in gold, Gothic lettering GWR. From 1835 until 1844 the clerk had dealt here with the paperwork for the entire imports and exports of Faringdon, Wantage and the villages; from 1844 for the traffic to and from Faringdon and villages north and south of the line. It was just the place for Harry to sit and eat his food, reading the 'Rules for Station Accountancy' in thoughtful silence. The Didcot to Swindon stopping train arrived at the Down platform of the station as I ran up the box stairs. Ken Rowlands, slim and fair-haired, was grinning broadly as I entered. 'Welcome home,' he said, throwing the duster at me. Ken had first taken me into Challow box when I had arrived in the area from Reading in 1953, aged twelve. I put my bag down and attended to the stopping train, three coaches behind a '61' class tank, as it barked past, its chimney inches below the window sill. 'Well, you aren't going to need more than a week on each turn to learn the job,' said Ken. I was not so sure, I knew enough about Challow to know how little I knew.

The room was about 40 feet long by 10 feet wide, housing a frame of levers numbered 1 to 63 but actually containing only fifty-one, as there were twelve spaces. This controlled a four-track railway east to Wantage Road about 3 ¾ miles away with double track to Uffington 2 ½ miles westwards; at Wantage Road the line became double track to Steventon, 4 miles eastwards, before returning to a four-track layout, which continued as such to Paddington. The diagram of Challow's layout hung above a crowded instrument shelf and was an example of an early attempt by the Great Western to produce an 'illuminated' diagram for a fully track-circuited layout (*see* Appendix 1). It dated from 1932 when the four-track layout was built and by 1962 was probably unique. Instead of small red lights to show the position of the train there were a number of silver-coloured balls about an inch across. When a train occupied a length of track, the relevant ball fell backwards out of sight with an audible 'clunk', returning with a slight 'click' when that length was again clear. Some of the balls were so individualistic that at night a weary signalman, lying stretched out in his chair with his eyes shut, could tell by the 'clunks' exactly what point in his layout the train had reached. The Challow men were rather proud of their unique diagram but to the less fortunate souls up and down the line it was known as 'All Balls'.

Among the mahogany-cased instruments on the shelf was a pair of clockwork/electric time releases, conglomerations of brass cogs under a glass dome a foot high. These were part of the safety devices guarding two sets of power-operated facing points at the eastern end of the station. To move either set of points, the correct lever was drawn lightly over to a two-thirds way notch and the handle of the hand generator – the 'Hurdy-Gurdy' – was churned round until an indicator showed that the points had moved to the desired position, the point lever could then be moved to its final position and the signal for the junction turn-out could be pulled off.

If, for some reason, having set one of these points, you then decided not to send the train in that direction, you could put the signal back to 'Danger' but you were unable to move the point lever until you had started the time release and it had run its course. The brass cogs could be seen whirring busily round for two minutes before speeding up to a crescendo 'clank'. Now the point lever could be shifted back two-thirds way and the hurdy-gurdy churned. This system prevented hasty movements of the facing points in front of approaching trains. The time releases were rarely needed for their designed purpose but they were very useful at around seven o'clock each morning for timing the breakfast eggs in boiling water.

The box was impeccably clean and highly polished; in extensive travels through other signal boxes I rarely saw its equal and never saw a smarter one. The view from the windows east, south and west was superb, over tree-lined meadows to the clear outline of the Berkshire Downs and White Horse Hill all under a swiftly changing sky, the little station a hundred yards eastwards – it was a superb place to work.

On the north side, across four 'running' lines and two sidings, was a wide area of gardens with the station cottages in a row on the farthest side, two brick offices and several wooden sheds belonging to the coal merchants Toomer & Langfords and opposite the box on well-kept grass was the grounded body of an old railway coach with a little chalet close by.

The old coach served as a chapel and Sunday school for the railway community and was equipped with two harmoniums. It had been brought to Challow in the 1930s by the then stationmaster, Mr Gardiner, who got it free of charge on application to Swindon Works. As a piece of 'railwayana' the coach was a mystery and over the years various experts had examined it and gone away puzzled because although it was from Swindon factory it was not a Great Western coach nor did it originate from any of the small companies which the GWR had absorbed – or so the enthusiast sages said.*

'Here's your tea', said Ken, 'nothing's changed has it?'

'Not a thing,' I said happily. 'It's still a good place to work.'

'It hasn't changed since I started here as a booking boy in 1941 – except that it was busier then.' I associated booking boys with 150-lever boxes and was pleasantly surprised to hear that Challow had once needed one. 'You'll wish you had one still,' said Ken. 'You must remember there's a lot of booking and telephone work here even now. Swindon telegraph office has to be told as soon as each Down fast comes off Didcot; we get them asked off Foxhall, so as soon as you've given the road, wire the time to Swindon.'

'What do they do with it then? Tell the station announcer?'

'Not unless the train was very late – in fact, if you hear of bad running like that you could tell Swindon so's the passengers could be told. But no, they send the times of the Down fasts off Didcot to each of the Swindon boxes and in the same way they send us the times of all Up fasts passing Chippenham East Box and Badminton but not for trains off the Gloucester road for some reason. Foxhall and Highworth Junction will wire you the time each freight train leaves them and its load – x number of wagons. You must put that in the special register and then pass the message on to the other box. Because we get so much information here the other chaps will be phoning all the time with questions and you'll have to keep the block register going too. There'll be about twenty goods, forty-five fasts, the stoppers per shift.'

---

* It was originally built for the North London Railway. It was purchased by the Cleobury Mortimer & Ditton Priors Light Railway and that concern was absorbed by the GWR in 1922.

I felt and looked very doubtful; it was all going to take a lot of getting used to – not least the sheer responsibility of having to run it all; it felt quite different from the times I used to pull the levers for fun with someone else carrying the worry. 'What about the time margins you need to run trains down to Uffington or Ashbury or up to Steventon?'

He shrugged and smiled, 'They're in the working timetable, but you'll soon get the hang of it and you'll have good mates to help you, you'll be working with Elwyn at Uffington, Wally Randall at Wantage and Alec Abrahams at Steventon. What you must be careful about is sending one down to Uffington when the loop there is full. It takes ten minutes for a goods to leave here and get back inside at Uffington but Uffington needs seventeen minutes to get a goods out and in again at Ashbury so a margin for you is not necessarily a margin for the man at Uffington. You'll have to work together on that.'

'So really I need a picture in my head of what's going on at the boxes up and down the line.'

'Yes, but it will all come like second nature after a while. I came up here in 1941 ...'

I butted in at that: 'Isn't it queer? I was born only just then and now I'm up here with you and still doing the same job you were doing twenty years ago.'

'Other things have changed out of all recognition though, off the railway,' said Ken. 'Do you remember old Olaf Legge in the bakery in Childrey? I was baker's boy-cum-postman for him back at the start of the last war. Mixing dough, pulling it into lumps, weighing it and putting it into tins. Come post time I left that and went off with the delivery of the Childrey mails.'

'Whatever time did you start then?'

'Oh, about four in the morning – we had to light the fires under the ovens. Anyway, then I went out with the letters all up over the Downs in all weather, crawling under barbed-wire fences with my bag. There were houses then, way up on the hills that were lived in but they're empty, even pulled down now for being too remote. And after all that walking I came back in time to go round with the handcart delivering the bread Olaf had baked.'

I could remember seeing the bakery at work, back in 1953, and old Olaf with his face glowing as red as the fires under the ovens, the high-wheeled handcart, too, wheeled about by old Mrs Legge, fragile looking with her grey hair all done up in a bun high on her head but now all that was gone, more's the pity, and only the railway kept up the old, peaceful ways.

A signal bell rang as we talked about old Childrey and its characters and as I was answering it, Sam Loder, the youngest of Challow's porters now that I had moved on – he only started in 1933 – came into the box. He saw me and his face broke into a delighted grin. 'Hello, Ady – I wondered whose rotten old car that was in the goods shed – I suppose you'll have this lot weighed up in a week and be Chief Inspector by the end of the year. Got the tea made, Ken?' Ken poured him a cup and he took it to a window sill to drink. Sam was never serious; teasing was his pastime. 'These young lads don't know how well off they are, do they, Ken?' he said. 'Out on the platform one minute – in a Class Two box the next.'

Ken was a serious, thoughtful man and replied without malice, 'I know. When I came up here I was booking for Bertie Snell. He was so strict – he never allowed me to touch a bell or a lever – I had to learn it all from sitting on the stool at the desk. I can tell you, I was glad to get out on the platform with Albert Stanley.'

'Crusty old beggars; some of 'em,' said Sam. 'You wants to make sure your strapper does all the work, though; it's good for 'em and you gets a bit of rest.'

Albert Stanley, a relief porter for the Challow district had started out on the Great Western at Dauntsey in 1920 and had spent hours telling me about his life and I pricked up my ears at Ken's recollection of working with Albert in 1941.

'Did you enjoy working with Albert?' I asked.

'Oh yes, he was a marvellous mate for a young lad; you know that yourself and I was extra glad to have someone who wasn't scared of the horses and bulls we used to load – because they scared me.'

Sam nodded knowingly at that and added, 'Ah! Lot of them were unbroken colts from down Stanford way.' A train went roaring past. I went through the signalling routine as Ken went on talking. 'The Misses Carter and Bean – their young horses were the worst – mad things, prancing about, especially inside the horsebox. I felt it worse there because there would have been no escape if they had knocked me down and trampled on me. I was trying to tie one up one day and struggling a bit – those old GWR head collars were so thick and tough you could hardly bend a strap and while I was fighting it the horse jerked its head up and lifted me clean off the ground – horrible animals.'

'What about the mad bull we had to load once then?' asked Sam, with the air of a man bringing out the trump card. The bright ring of the Up Main line bell and the low boom of the Down Relief line bell rang together; I answered them and as I wrote the time into the register the Down Main bell rang, asking the road for a fast, which is why the goods had been put into the Relief line at Wantage Road. Ken reminded me to telephone Swindon and asked, 'What about this bull then, Sam?'

'Nothing really,' said Sam after he had keyed us both up high, 'it was just mad. You couldn't tell to look at it but it must have been because the bloke in charge of it had a pistol cocked and pointing at its head all the time. We put a heavy rope through the ring in its nose and then put the other end across the truck, through the slats and down onto the track. It was like a rope going through a pulley, we pulled from down on the track and the bull had to go in and all the time this bloke kept his pistol pointed at it.'

The Up goods was put on line by Uffington. 'Where shall I put this goods?' I asked Ken.

'Work it out,' he replied. 'When is the next fast of Swindon?'

'Um,' I said thoughtfully. 'Don't be too long thinking; that goods will be past our distant signal at "Caution" in two minutes and then you'll have to put it inside.'

I decided that the goods ought to be sidetracked, set the points by pulling on an ordinary lever and pulled off. Signal levers were then pulled over for three of the four tracks, the Down express was getting close and the goods on the Down Relief line was in sight. With a bell code a minute to answer and register and with the many telephone calls to make and to answer, I found the conversation distracting, so that I fumbled the work and got behind in the register entries. Next time I paid attention to what Ken was saying, 'We used to have a lorry here at the station that we used to go around the farm with to collect stuff for loading on rail. It didn't have any light – or a cab.'

'What make was it?' I asked.

'Oh, I don't know, it was a queer old thing. One night it was loaded with sugar beet. The 5.14 Paddington came in and Sir Hugh Graves was among the passengers. He couldn't get his car to start so Mr Francis, the stationmaster, suggested we give him a tow with the lorry though it was dark and the lorry had no lights.'

Sam was as scathing as he could be. 'That wasn't very clever. Give us some more of your tea.'

'There isn't any. I'll put the kettle on again.' The Up goods turned into the Up Relief line and came rumbling past the box, a '28' class engine hauling a long, mixed rake of wagons. I set the points back for Main line running, knocked out and was immediately asked the road by Uffington for a fast.

I asked the road to Wantage as the Down express, 'Warship'-hauled, tore past and, knocking out, I was asked for another Down fast – this I knew was the last for forty-five minutes.

'I suppose this goods on the Down Relief line can go after the next Down fast?'

'That's right,' said Ken encouragingly, 'you're getting the idea.'

'Come on then, what about this bloke's car?' urged Sam.

'Well, we tied it to the back of the lorry and I towed it across the yard in the dark with your Dot on the running board to keep a lookout for me.'

'What?' cried Sam pretending to be scandalised. 'My wife riding around the countryside with you in the blackout while I was away fighting for King and Country – she's never told me about that.'

Ken looked pained. 'Come on, Sam, don't make jokes like that. She wasn't much good as a lookout anyway because she never told me we were driving into Goosey Dock until it was too late. "Look out," she shouts and jumps off. I braked hard and of course Sir Hugh's car ran straight into the back of the lorry, which just shoved it over the edge of the dock and the car ran underneath the cocked-in-the-air tail-gate, smashed its windscreen and dented the roof from all the sugar beet falling about.'

Sam was grinning broadly; it was the sort of thing he loved to see. 'What did the toff say about that?'

'Oh, he didn't like it at all. He seemed to think we'd done it on purpose and got quite upset.'

Sam's solitary comment was apt but unprintable. He finished off his tea and stood up.

'See you later then; thanks for the tea. I'm going to do the paperwork for the stuff Harry loaded – earlier on – I don't suppose you remember how to do any of that – just be sure and ring the stopper in when it's off Uffington.'

'Course I will Sam – I wouldn't like to see you having to run to meet the people getting off.'

'Ah, I know you signalmen, swilling tea and gassing while the rest of us are slaving.'

'Mind the Up and Down fasts!' I called after him as he went down the stairs.

The Up and Down fasts passed outside the box. 'Start your goods up now,' said Ken, 'give 'em 57 signal or they'll start getting aerated, and anyway, in the three minutes it'll take the Down fast to clear Uffington the goods can be pulling on down to the starter.' I pulled the point lever, 31, and bolted the points by pulling 30, then heaved over signals 57, 56 and 55. From the engine came an answering 'toot' and shortly afterwards a '63' class engine came into view under the road bridge spanning the station, creeping along by the Down platform, huffing gently with seventy wagons in tow. The cab was just below the signal box window and I leant out to enjoy the engine as she passed. She was going forward on a tight rein, a breath of steam hauling 800 tons. The fireman was sitting, looking along the boiler; he waved a salute as he passed shouting, 'All right for Highworth now?' The firehole doors were open, the flap on the floor and the boiler pressure gauge 'on the mark'. On the far side of the cab the driver was standing, left hand on the brake handle, one foot up on a steam cock lever, which was bolted to the floor, his eyes intent on the road ahead.

The high-pitched Uffington bell rang 2-1; Uffington was knocking out the fast. I got the road for the goods – 3-2 – back came the acknowledgement and the indicator swung to 'Line Clear'. I swung hard on lever 54 and 750 yards away the advanced starting signal lowered. The 63's whistle tooted again, her chimney voice became stern and wagon couplings tugged as the horsepower went through them. The fireman jumped up in a very businesslike way and reached for his shovel. 'See how they go?' said Ken. 'They mean to run 'em. You always ought to watch that, see what they go like so's you can give the chaps down below an idea of how the enginemen are running.'

The guard's van was swinging out over the points as the signal box door opened and Mr Halford, the stationmaster, came up the stairs. He was a slightly built man with a quiet manner. I had known him since he arrived at the station in 1953; he had not discouraged my signal box visiting and had taken me onto the railway in 1960. 'Welcome home,' he said putting out his hand. 'Are you glad?' he finished in a local family joke – one of Sid Tyler's well-worn sayings.

'Very pleased, Mr Halford, thanks.'

'Please – if you're making some, Ken – I suppose it's superfluous to ask whether you're getting good instruction from Ken but I'd just like to tell you to be very wary of the Intermediate Block Section at Circourt. D'you know how it works?'

'Er, well, I think so. There's a colour-light home and distant the same as if there was still the old Circourt box there and instead of a man there giving Challow a "Line Clear" to release our Up starter you get the same release from a track circuit a quarter mile long from Circourt's home signal on towards Wantage. When the train clears off that track circuit it's a quarter of a mile beyond Circourt's home signal and therefore the line at Circourt is clear and Challow can lower his starting signal into Circourt's section. When the train has cleared Wantage Road, we get the road from Wantage and pull off number 6 or 10 lever to put the IBS signals to "All Right".'

'Yes, you've got it and to my mind that's the danger: there's no one up there to see what's going on; it's three thousand yards away and there's no supervision. When I think that's how they're going to run the whole railway one day – well it just doesn't seem right.'

I felt a sudden surge of alarm for the railway. 'How are they going to run it then?'

'Well, with track circuits switching colour-lights for miles, no signal boxes and no one to keep a watch on the trains. You could have one off the road and no one would know and even if you did know you'd be miles away and couldn't do anything about it. Look at that Lutterworth job.'

'What was that then?' Ken and I asked together.

'It was over on the Great Central about seven years ago. There was an IBS and the signalman didn't notice that an Up train had gone into the remote section and hadn't cleared the next box. He gave the road for a Down train and then that didn't arrive after the usual time. He began to get worried then.'

Ken and I were agog. 'Why? What had happened?'

'The Up one had come off the road on plain track and the Down one crashed into the wreck.'

'Ran off ordinary plain track?' queried Ken.

'Perhaps it was in bad condition and the train was going too fast,' I suggested.

'Well, there you are, keep a close watch on the time a train spends between the IBS and Wantage and if it's over time send the 6-2 bell and don't accept anything on the Down roads.'

'Mind you those GC men do drive fast,' said Ken, still wondering about the crash. 'You remember the time Jack Miles was working here but living in Oxford and used to cycle to and fro? He finished here one Sunday as the GC engine off the Hull fish was coming up light for Woodford so I stopped it for him, he put his bike on the tender and off they went. They gave Jack such a shaking that he vowed he'd cycle the whole twenty miles in future – they frightened him to death with their speed.'

'Hurrying is the worst thing a railwayman can do,' said Mr Halford, before pulling long on his mug of tea. 'There was a strange case at Leominster Junction once when I was working on the Bromyard branch. The signalman there had got the Bromyard passenger coming down from

Worcester and a Hereford–Worcester fast coming up and he decided that the branch train would have to stop because if he crossed it over to the branch, which meant going across the bows of the Up train, he would be delaying the fast. So the branch train was stopped at the signal with the boards off up the Main for the Hereford. Anyhow, once the branch train had stopped the signalman regretted having done it and thought there was still time to put it over onto the branch –'

Ken butted in, 'He never let it across?!'

Mr Halford bumped the table gently with his fist. 'He did! He slung the boards back, pulled up the junction and pulled off for the branch train. Can you imagine what he felt like when he saw the fast coming into sight, full speed, with the tanky just strolling across the junction?'

Ken and I made anguished noises. 'What happened?'

'The fast came screeching past just as the last coach of the branch train cleared the junction, missing it by a foot and smashing the points of course, which were set against it. 'Course, the driver had seen the distant at "All Right" and was well inside it when the silly signalman threw it back. If you want to pick up the rules for junction working, read them with that story in mind.' Mr Halford put down his empty cup and thanked Ken. 'The stopper'll be here soon. I must go. Keep on with the rules, Adrian.'

I had a week on each shift, and through many a cautionary tale I learnt the job and learnt more about railway work in general. Then I went down to Swindon for a gruelling four-hour oral examination on the rules with Mr Millsom, who passed me and sent me for a similar exam to the Chief Inspector at Bristol, who passed me to the Superintendent, who finally signed the certificate making me a signalman at Challow. The job at Challow had always been a source of awe for me and the signalman a hero figure; now that I was the Challow signalman I was just a little scared.

CHAPTER SIX

Ignorance Was Bliss

When I became signalman at Challow in fulfilment of a boyhood ambition, spring was blossoming into summer 1962. From the eyrie of the signal box I watched stately squadrons of clouds driving before the south-west wind high above the Vale – billowing, bulging, towering piles of grey and white silk heaped up against a pale blue sky. Hourly squalls of grey-black intervened, the cloud's edge smudged like a charcoal drawing against the bright sky all around and the sun's light, clear and sharp through the well-washed air, was intensified by the dark squall making tree trunks silver when they had been grey before. On such mornings I have seen a rainbow rest its promise on the green massif of White Horse Hill and vault the Vale with seven colours flaming against the rain-dark cloud, while beneath the arch came a polished 'Castle', beating up the tracks towards the sun, her copper-capped chimney and brass beading glinting in the crisp light, her exhaust blossoming like a pure white flower against the sullen sky.

Inside the signal box on such mornings colour, light and shade were sharply contrasted as the early sun struck along the row of levers, bells and instruments, burnished steel handles, red, black, blue or yellow levers, mahogany cases and silver bell domes bright on one side, in deep shadow on the other, while the glass-like surface of the linoleum floor reflected the colours and the very lettering on the brass badges of those levers pulled over in the frame. I would cheerfully have worked for nothing at Challow in those days – I was far too much in love with the place, the men and the life I was leading to properly register Mr Halford's words of caution concerning the future. Early turn was the best of shifts in the best of workplaces for the sight of the sunrise and the summer mornings and the greater activity that took place; a fine mixture of fasts and goods trains – including, of course, shunting the local 'pickup' goods, the 'Fly' – and the company of the fine railwaymen who came into the box to eat their meals or merely to pass the time of day before setting out along the track for their day's work. At ten to six I would relieve Jim Spinage. Jim was not an old hand but was a very fine railwayman, rotund of figure with a round, pink face, cheerful in

Signalman's Trilogy

a taciturn sort of way, speaking always very much to the point in a deep voice and with a belly-laugh for a good joke. No one was expected to be cheerful at six in the morning and after a few quiet words of greeting and to give me the traffic situation Jim would drive home on his BSA Bantam and leave me with the summer dawning.

By 7.30 I would have dealt with thirteen trains and would perhaps be working with the 'Fly' when the Signal & Telegraph linesman, John Moody, and his assistant Maurice Sworn arrived at the station in John's old Morris Ten. John was tall and square jawed, a veteran of the Second World War when he was a pom-pom gunner of the battleship HMS *Warspite*. He was, in 1962, I think, Scoutmaster at Faringdon and had to suffer being called Akela or even Big Brown Bear by his mate Maurice. They would come into the box with grins a yard wide with noisy inquiries for the state of my health and whether the kettle was boiling, which, of course, it was because it was one of the finer points of a signalman's knowledge to know other men's meal times, when they took them in the box and to prepare for them. John and Maurice breakfasted on boiled eggs held in cast-iron lever collars – to this very day I still use a lever collar for my egg cup though I am far from the railway – and having filled up with sandwiches and several cups of tea they set out on the 8.5 up to Wantage or Steventon or on foot for a day of maintenance on signalling equipment.

They were responsible for Challow, Wantage and Steventon signal boxes, Steventon Causeway Crossing ground frame and all lineside signalling equipment in that area. Within these wide limits they were a law unto themselves, followed their own inclinations and maintained an exceptionally trouble-free area. Track circuits, automatic train control ramps, signal arm and lamp repeaters were operated by battery current, the batteries being housed in cupboards all along the line. The batteries were not left to run flat but were replaced after a set time and as the locations were invariably remote John and Maurice walked miles with heavy boxes of dry cell batteries to resupply the sites. Occasionally they were able to load them onto the guard's van of the 'Fly', which would then drop the equipment off, but this manoeuvre depended on the signalman having time between trains to allow it.

Tracing faults on the dozens of telephone circuits was part of their job. All the circuits were carried overhead on the well-known poles – once an integral part of any railway scene – and I remember the day when John had to climb a pole just outside Challow box whilst trying to isolate a fault. Maurice and I watched him from the box window as he climbed a ladder to the first of the steel steps held to the pole by screw spikes. He pulled himself up by a step and rested his full weight on the bottommost. Before he had a chance to climb higher the step gave way. John had his arms and legs wrapped around the pole and slid down it looking like a koala bear that had just had a nasty shock. Maurice and I fell about with laughter, of course, but John had to have some ugly splinters taken out of his legs.

If a signal wire broke while the signalman was pulling the lever he invariably took a painful fall. Those wires were well galvanised and tough and John Moody did his best to renew them before they became weak. Occasionally one did break when it was being pulled after him; the signalman ended up lying against the back wall of the box with a headache and the wind knocked out of him. If the lever whose wire broke was in front of the coal-fired stove. I did hear once of a man falling backwards to sit on the blazing hot top of his stove. At Severn Tunnel Junction in 1944 a wire broke, the signalman cracked his head against the back wall and was seriously brain-damaged.

One Saturday during the summer of 1962 I was on early turn and at 9 a.m. the wire of the Up starting signal broke as I was pulling it. I crawled up off the floor, telephoned for John Moody and then asked Albert Stanley to go and find the break and make a temporary repair until John Moody could come down from Steventon to make a proper job. Trains had to be stopped meanwhile and their drivers told to pass the inoperative signal at 'Danger'. The first one I stopped was hauled by a 'Western' class diesel. These things were brand new then and impressive even to a steam enthusiast such as myself – their throaty roar as they moved away and their great length made them seem mighty indeed. I brought it nearly to a stand at the home signal, pulled off that board and after the engine had passed it stood at the window holding out a red flag. The driver came to a stand opposite the flag and I shouted my instructions to the driver but unable to hear above the racket of his engine he dismounted and came to the base of the signal box wall, a little, rosy-faced man. I bawled out my message and he yelled back in a fine Plymouth accent, 'Rahdo m'luvver!' and scrambled up the side of the diesel, got into his seat and flung open the throttle to unleash plumes of screaming horsepower. Such was the advantage of the diesel locomotive – if you could live with its unreliability.

The next train was the Cheltenham Spa Express behind 7000 *Viscount Portal*. I went through the routine and stood at the box window with my red flag but 7000 came up smartly from the check at the home signal and went past the box accelerating, the driver waving cheerily. Once under the

Faringdon road bridge the driver saw the starting signal at 'Danger' and braked hard. I watched him climb down from the engine and run across the track to a telephone. The bell rang in the signal box and I picked up the handset.

'Oi!' he snapped accusingly, 'this one's at "Danger"'.

'I know. I was trying to tell you. Didn't you see the red flag I was holding just now?'

'Red flag? Oh, er, sorry, officer, it sort of didn't register,' he faded away helplessly.

'Well never mind. I only wanted to tell you to pass that board at "Danger" and on your way.'

Drivers never passed signals at 'Danger' without proper authority – well, almost never – and if they did, then it was considered a serious matter that had to be reported, but that rarely happened either – it took a cold-blooded man to sit down and write a report that would inevitably result in a colleague being severely reprimanded or worse. One morning, the Swindon to Longbridge vacuum carrying car-body parts was coming up even faster than usual. The driver obviously knew that the 6.30 a.m. Swansea–Paddington fast, diesel hauled, was close behind him, he had only to look at his watch to tell. When the vacuum was 'on line' to me I telephoned Elwyn, 'How's that Up one doing, Elwyn, please?'

'Oh, tanning the ballast they are. I booked them four minutes a block but really it was nearer three – but the Swansea's not far behind, mind.'

I thanked Elwyn and put the phone down.

Properly the vacuum did not have a margin to run through to the loop at Steventon but it was obviously running fast if not downright improperly – all the more reason, properly, to slow it down by putting it up the Relief line and allow the fast to pass by up the Main. On the other hand, it would be nice to see 73029 run. I pulled off up the Main and gave the vacuum the back board. 73029 came past at 60 mph, whistle screaming and the driver waving his thanks – delirium for me! Forty-five short wheel-base vans went dancing past in a cloud of dust and steam all but off the rails, and when I knocked out, Elwyn immediately asked the road for the Swansea.

Wally Randall phoned me for a swear because I had allowed the vacuum up the Main and said he would put it in his platform loop. I pointed out that if he did so he would have to wait several minutes before he could give me the road for the Swansea while the guard of the vacuum was walking to a lineside telephone to 'give tail lamp' – to say that the train was complete and clear of the Main line – whereas if he let it run at 60 mph the four miles to Steventon the signalman there would see the tail lamp before the train passed into his loop. Wally put the goods in.

The 6.30 a.m. Swansea came tearing past me at a phenomenal rate, well over 90 mph, behind a 'Western' class diesel and I knew then that it would never be able to stop in the 1,500 yards braking distance provided between the Intermediate Block Section distant and home signals. I went to the block bell and stood ready to send the 'Train Running Away' bell as soon as the train passed the IBS home signal at 'Danger'. When a train passed this signal at 'All Right' a short buzz on an electric buzzer sounded in the signal box, but if the IBS home signal was passed while it was showing 'Danger', the buzzer sounded continuously or until a brass plunger was pressed to silence it. The emergency buzzer sounded and I sent the 'Runaway' bell code 4-5-5 to Wally Randall.

Instantly from Wally I received not an acknowledgement of the 4-5-5 but 2-1 followed by a 'Line Clear' indication and four beats on the bell for the Swansea. Too late. The track circuit indicators for the lengths on each side of the IBS home signal were showing 'Occupied'; the Swansea had come to a stand straddling the signal and there was nothing I could do until its driver telephoned me from the signal. Soon that telephone bell rang and I answered it. A breathless, Welsh voice panted, 'Driver of the Swansea yere. I've gone by Circourt signal by six coaches,' he tailed off awkwardly.

'Don't worry about it,' I said, 'there was a vacuum goods ahead of you but it's in the loop at Wantage Road now and you've got the road. Don't hang about, there's a Bristol coming up off Swindon and we don't want to stop that or we'll really have some delays to answer.'

'What about passing the board?' He was worried I would report him.

'Forget it – just get going as fast as you can.'

'Thanks, pal.' The telephone crashed down and seconds later the track circuits cleared. The following fast from Bristol never had the merest glimpse of a distant signal at 'Caution'.

When the Swansea arrived in Paddington the driver sat in the cab of his diesel making out his log until a knock on his cabside made him put his head out of the window. Standing on the platform was a man in a dark suit wearing a bowler hat and carrying an umbrella. He might have been a businessman. 'Driver,' said this man, 'I was travelling on your train this morning and I saw that we passed Circourt signal at "Danger". What was wrong?'

The driver snapped, 'And what business is it of yours if I did?'

To which the businessman snapped back, 'I am the General Manager of the Western Region and I'm making it my business.'

The following morning I received a visit from Mr Millsom, the Swindon District Inspector. After the usual pleasantries he began looking through the block register. 'Oh – there's nothing here about sending the 4-5-5 – I thought you had some trouble here yesterday?' I felt my face going red. 'There was no trouble – I sent the 4-5-5 but it was a false alarm really.'

'Well, you'll be pleased to hear that the General Manager was on the Swansea yesterday' – I felt my heart falling into my boots – 'and he wants to know what happened. You haven't even got it down in the register. Did the train pass the board at "Danger"?

'Er, yes, it did,' I replied reluctantly, 'but there was no harm done. It was the fault of the signals really, the braking distance isn't sufficient.'

Mr Millsom drew on his briar pipe, shook his head slowly and blew out a stream of smoke. 'It has been good enough for the Bristolian for years, it ought to be sufficient for any train.'

'Perhaps diesels don't have as good brakes as steam engines?'

The District Inspector could see I was about to climb onto my favourite hobby-horse, and cut me short. 'Never mind about steam and diesel – you tell me what happened here yesterday, the truth. I'll tell your lies for you.'

Sometimes, when a vacuum goods had been allowed to run up the Main to Steventon on a tight margin, the following fast came up rather quicker than anticipated or the vacuum took slightly longer than usual to creep into Steventon loop, and, as a result, the fast was facing a hard check at Wantage Road. What was required was a CB radio system from signalman to driver so we could tell him to ease his speed – maybe lose thirty seconds – so as to avoid passing a distant signal at 'Caution' which would oblige the driver to slow right down in case a stop signal was at 'Danger'. In the absence of short-wave radio we used our signals.

The Up distant signal at Challow would be held at yellow 'Caution' for a carefully judged period after the train had passed Uffington and switched to green 'All Right' just before the driver passed it – probably with the throttle shut and with his hand on the brake. The IBS distant and home signals were 1,500 yards apart on dead-straight track so we could allow the driver to pass the IBS distant signal at 'Caution' and immediately clear the home signal to 'All Right'. The driver would by then have 'touched' the brakes and would then release, having got the message from two distant signals in succession that he was running up close behind another train. By easing his speed a little he avoided being brought to a hard check at Wantage Road.

In modern, four-aspect colour-light signalling systems, this technique is part of the daily running and drivers can adjust their speed to the train in front by arriving at each signal just as it flicks from single yellow to a double yellow. We had to improvise on the old-fashioned railway.

One day at Challow the boards were off for the Down Bristolian, then the fastest train in Britain. The train was hauled by the usual 'Warship' diesel, which came through the station at 90 mph. When the diesel was 200 yards from the starting signal – which was just outside the box – the signal's wire broke and the arm swung up to 'Danger'. The 'Warship's' nose seemed to dig into the track as its brakes clamped on and it came towards me bouncing and swaying on the track, wrestling with its brakes in a way that was quite frightening to see. After explanations to a somewhat shaken driver the train went on its way and when it had drawn clear I saw that lumps of steel had been gouged out of the crown of the rail due to the violence of the braking effort. I called Bob Thatcher and he replaced the damaged rail from his stockpile down in the station sidings.

Bob Thatcher was Ganger in charge of ten track-miles around Challow. He was a bachelor who lived with his sister and brother-in-law, Albert Stanley, in one of the station cottages. Bob was about sixty-two years old, heavily built and rather stout. He walked in a heavy, ponderous way, his stride long and slow after a lifetime spent walking the sleepers and his hobnailed boots with their bent-up toecaps crunched slowly – even across smooth, black asphalt. He worked in a grey, herringbone jacket and waistcoat, huge, baggy trousers or grey worsted and a collarless flannel shirt; a thin, silver watch-chain across his middle betrayed the presence of a watch in the pocket of his waistcoat. When he strode his 'length' his face looked solemn, even grim, with its heavy jowl and concentric lines around the mouth but this granite exterior disguised a gentle soul and at the end of a long day of heavy labour on the track he liked nothing better than to tend his garden for an hour before going to the Prince of Wales for a pint of Morland's bitter.

His 'secondman' was Bill Lamble, who also lived in one of the station cottages but the rest of the gang – Bob Tilling, Jeff Betterton, Tom Carter and Harold New – lived at Stanford in the Vale two or three miles from the station. The men of any permanent-way gang were known collectively as 'packers' because of the principal preoccupation of their job. At about eight o'clock each morning I would see them trooping out of the packers' hut – made of tarred, up-ended sleepers – carrying shovels, picks, levelling sights and, on the shoulder of one man, a track-lifting screw-jack. Bob Thatcher would come to the box with one of his men and say (for instance) 'Mornin', young man. We'm goin' shovel packin' so I wants ter put th' trolley

on an' goo up th' re-leef to 62 ¼. We'll be packin' frum thur ter Circourt.
I'll leave Jeff wi' you as groundman till I gets th' trolley off.'

If no trains were imminent for the Up Relief line I would put a cast-iron
collar on No. 8 lever to remind me and to prevent me pulling it, and Jeff
would, theoretically at least, put three detonators on the Relief line rail
outside the box and then stand over them with a red flag until waves from
his mates or a telephone call told him that the trolley had been removed
from the line when he could pick up his detonators and walk to join the
gang.

They manipulated the massively strong rails and the sleepers weighing
hundredweights and made them follow a perfect 'line' and 'top'. The latter
they achieved with the levelling sights clipped to the crown of the rail
and by the use of the screw-jack, shovels and granite chippings. Sleepers,
particularly at the fishplated joints at rail ends, were pressed down by
the weight of passing trains only to spring up when the train had passed
so that cavities were formed beneath the sleepers. At a low or hanging
joint the jack was slipped under the rail and wound round to lift the rail
to the correct height according to the sights. Two men faced each other
across the narrow width of the sleeper, held out their shovels for chippings
from a tin cup and these were then packed under the sleeper to fill the
cavity.

To keep the rails true to 'line' the gang had to 'do a bit of slewin' '. Four
men with crowbars, shoulder to shoulder, two on each rail, stood with their
backs to the rails facing across the fields, legs astride, crowbars between
the legs and against the rail. A fifth man kept a lookout for trains. Bob
Thatcher knelt on the sleepers, his head touching the inside of the rail, his
eye taking in the line it made, looking for lateral irregularities, or 'kinks'.
Having located one he stood up and directed his men to it. I can hear his
gruff old voice now. 'Goo on, Goo on ... whoa! Bars in.' At the command his
men took up their formation and drove their bars into the ballast. 'Ready,'
came the warning from Bob standing astride the rail about twenty-five
yards from his gang. 'Hup! Hup! Hup! Whoa! Hup! Whoa ... All right.' The
men tugged at their bars on each call and it was surprising how far they
could move the seemingly immovable track in this way.

The Challow gang had many jobs to do of which grass cutting was
probably the easiest and fishplate bolt oiling the most tedious. Periodically
they had to remove every fishplate and bolt from every rail-joint in their
10 miles of track, grease the threads on the bolts – four per fishplate – and
then reassemble the fittings. The work was essential in order to prevent

the bolt-threads from rusting so that when re-laying of the track became necessary the 60-foot lengths of track could be taken to pieces and lifted away.

The spanner used for this unbolting work was at least three feet long and heavy with it. I have taken a turn at this work and can vouch for its efficacy at tightening slack stomach muscles. The gang also had to clear mud from the stormwater drain between the tracks which they did by dragging a wad of sacking wrapped around a steel cable through the pipe. A wooden bar was tied to the wire and against this bar they pushed like oxen. The chalky mud thus displaced had then to be scooped out of the sumps placed every fifty yards. If they had not been cheerful men they would not have been able to do the work and without doubt they were the hardest working, least appreciated of all railwaymen, loyal to a duty that required them to turn out into the foulest night to help keep the railway running.

Charlie Lamble had been Ganger at Challow years before and he died on the four-foot way. He was working on a Saturday night/Sunday morning engineering job and as it grew light on Sunday morning he went to the box and put his paraffin hand-lamp on the window sill saying, 'It's getting light. I'll leave this here.' He walked back to the site of work moving *down* the *Up* Main, which was, he apparently thought, bringing him to face oncoming traffic; somehow he had forgotten that single-line working was in force and traffic was running up and down the track he was walking on. An engine came from behind him and blew its whistle. Charlie waved and, thinking it must be on the other track, did not get out of the way. The engine driver thought that as Charlie had acknowledged the warning whistle he would move away and so did not brake until it was too late. Charlie Lamble's lamp remained where he left it and the Challow signalmen polished it regularly as a memorial to him.

At about eleven o'clock each morning, the on-duty porter, Sam, Albert or even Harry with Basil Titchener, the booking clerk, came to the signal box for coffee. If Sam was on duty Basil walked warily and tried to reach the box ahead of Sam so as not to be ambushed by him with buckets of water down the stairs or from the box window – Sam was like that – but if Albert was on duty Basil could relax for Albert was a retailer of legends and would pay for his break with a story.

The mid-morning break for station staff coincided with the passing of three Down fasts – expresses originating from Paddington – and they were followed by a heavy freight from Acton, which waited on the Relief line at Challow. Albert was drinking his tea in the box one morning as the Acton whuffed briskly past, under the box window, while I leant out to enjoy the engine. 'Get 'em off Bobby – we're running 'em today!' shouted the fireman as he passed. I waved and went to get the road from Uffington. 'Them chaps on that Acton know they're in and out of every loop from Steventon to Highworth Junction, it's been the same for donkey's years but they're still trying to hurry,' commented the stolid Albert.

Basil, who had been a schoolboy visitor to Challow box at the same time as myself, stretched luxuriously in my armchair. 'Take no notice of 'em. One lot are in a hurry, the next lot wouldn't run if you paid 'em to,' he said.

Albert put down his empty cup and from the look on his face I could see a story coming. 'There was a bit of bother once over that Acton,' he said. 'Poor old Snelly got it.' The Down stopping train to Swindon was belled on the Down Relief line from Wantage Road as Albert continued. 'That Acton always had to turn onto the Relief at Wantage Road since it started running but on this particular day the fasts got caught back beyond Slough because of a derailment so Wantage Road was able to give the Acton the back board. The driver got so excited about going down the Main that as he passed Wantage box he put his cap on the floor of the footplate and jumped up and down on it and waved up at the Bobby – old Windridge was in the box then. Well, Bill Windridge reckoned it looked too much like taking the mickey and he got all hurt so he sent seven bells – "Stop and Examine" – to Bert Snell here at Challow. But he told Bert only that there was something wrong with the engine so Bert thought it was a genuine case.'

'Oh – poor old Bert,' said Basil, 'he was going to walk right into that one then.'

'Well, that's it,' said Albert. 'Windridge thought he was getting his own back on the driver by having him stopped and dropped old Snelly right in it. Bert turned the road from Down Main to Down platform, the Acton comes in and stops and in a flash the driver's running up into the box. "What's the matter now?" he says real snappy. "I get the back board off at Wantage for the first time ever on this train, we're doing well and you go and put me inside here – you blokes want to make your effing minds up." Well, you know what a gent old Bert was; he didn't have any rough talk. He stood up very straight and says he had to stop the train because he'd had the seven bells sent – "Stop and Examine". "It's you lot that wants examining," says this driver, "all we ever get from you is stop-go-stop-go. You need a horse and cart on a milk-round not a signal box."'

Basil and I laughed at that. 'Fancy talking to Bert Snell like that. Anyone could see he didn't deserve it – what did he say?'

'What could he say?' asked Albert. 'He didn't have no rough back-chat, he wasn't that sort, so he just had to put up with it and turn the Acton out again.'

'Still, it was a change – seven bells for a driver having a fit of hysterics – more interesting than the usual tale, door handle not turned.'

'Ah, you say that,' said Albert, 'but you can't be sure what you're going to find when you go out to fix a door handle. There was a job down Trowbridge way back before the war. They had a circus travelling by train – the clowns and the lion-tamers in a coach next to the engine and the animals and other stuff behind. Well, seven bells was sent on account of a door handle not properly turned on a Monster – that was the name we gave to one of the big covered vans as big as a coach for carrying scenery or cars or lions for that matter. The chap who got the seven bells stopped the train, went out and turned the handle properly shut, he heard some heavy shuffling about in the van and it swayed a bit with the noise, anyhow, he sent the train on and that was that. But the bloke at the next box sent seven bells for the same door handle not properly turned and again the train stopped and the job put right. 'Course, the blokes were really watching the train now and as it passed the next box the signalman saw this long thing like a snake waving out of the hole in the door where you put your hand through from the inside so as to be able to turn the outside handle. The train went by and this thing was fiddling around with the handle and he stared after it, feeling a bit queer, and then realised what it was. He'd been told there was something big and heavy in the van, he'd seen an elephant's trunk coming through the door, so it must have been this elephant that had turned the door handle.'

CHAPTER SEVEN

Playing Trains

The business of working goods trains up and down the line from loop to loop between the fasts was subject to so many variables that it was more of an art than a science. One had to consider whether a goods train was a fast 'C'-headcode vacuum or a very slow 'H'-headcode freight; whether it had just started out of the loop or was running at its normal speed; or whether the following fast had started from Swindon or was running through at full speed. Then there was the less categorical consideration: how 'well' was the goods running; who was the driver; had the engine given an impression of health or weakness to the signalmen further back along the line.

If an express was standing at Swindon station as a 'D'-headcode goods passed Uffington, then the goods could run up the Main line at Challow, through to the loop at Steventon without delaying the following fast. If that fast was 'just leaving' as the goods passed Uffington, the goods could still run up the Main provided Elwyn gave it to me with a good character. If the Up fast was passing Swindon at full speed – round about 65–70 mph – as the 'D' goods passed Uffington, then the goods would definitely have to go up the Relief line at Challow – unless it was exceeding the speed limit for that type of train, round about 35–40 mph, which was unlikely.

It might have been the case that there was a second goods between the fast and 'my' goods and if inquiries showed that this second goods would delay the fast then I could perhaps run 'my' goods through to Steventon. A crystal ball would have been useful at Challow. When a fast has been standing over its time at Swindon, will it leave in ten seconds or is there some trouble which will delay it a further five minutes? Five minutes extra would allow the up goods passing Uffington to run through to Steventon and not go 'up the shute' to Wantage Road. On one day at a certain time the driver of a goods train might be signalled up the Main at Challow and the next day, same time, same train, he might be turned into the Relief line and would go past me glaring and pointing at his watch. I always wanted to explain what was going on because the driver's lack of understanding made him fume and think I was merely 'playing trains'.

It was far from unknown for drivers to ease their engine's effort when they saw Challow's Up distant showing 'All Right' because they then knew that they were not going to be put 'up the shute' to languish for an hour and could afford to take things easy. My sign language asking for the engine to be opened up would be replied to with a big 'V' sign!

A lesson to be learned at Challow was 'Do not succumb to the pleadings of enginemen, do not be influenced by their grumbles.' A fireman off a Down goods waiting on the Relief line telephoned me from 57 signal. 'How long before we're away, Bobby?'

'After the third fast – about 10.15.'

'Can't you make it any sooner? I'm getting married at two o'clock in Swindon.'

'Oh dear. Well in that case, if you'll promise to get a move on, I'll let you out between the 8.55 and the 9.5. The 9.5 stops at Didcot, so you'll have a chance if you hurry.'

'Thanks very much,' said this devious fireman, 'we won't let you down.' As the 8.55 came through the station I lowered 57 signal to start the goods and they came chugging along the platform line as the 8.55 went tearing down the Main behind a 'Castle'. The goods was hauled by a reassuringly powerful 'Grange' and the crew were all smiles as they moved slowly past the box and turned out onto the Down Main line, creeping, waiting for me to lower the section signal.

Elwyn knocked out for the fast and I asked the road for the goods – 3-2. It is remarkable what feeling a signalman could convey in the way he answered a bell. There was a long, disbelieving pause before he acknowledged the code and another pause before he pegged 'Line Clear' and all the while the goods was crawling when it could have been accelerating while the clock ticked away the seconds before the 9.5 Paddington left Didcot. I pulled off as the telephone rang. It was Elwyn. 'What-effer are you doing A-dren? The 9.5 will be off Foxhall any moment and he'll be standing with you before this old thing gets into my loop and you never asked if my loop was clear to take it.'

I replied with confidence, 'Don't worry, Elwyn, those chaps will go like the clappers right through to Swindon – the fireman's getting married at two o'clock this afternoon so he's in a hurry.' A great roar of laughter went up from end to end of the Vale as the signalmen saw through the wafer-thin subterfuge and only then did I realise I had been caught. To make matters worse the men did not hurry as they promised and the 9.5 was brought to a stand at my section signal.

On the other hand, it was not good policy to adopt a belligerent approach to drivers' grumbles, they might 'go slow' when you eventually did let them go – or worse. While I was still a schoolboy visiting Challow box I was present one evening with my friend Gordon Groves. The telephone rang from 57 signal and Gordon reached for it saying, 'Ol' worry-guts again – I'll sort him out this time.' Faint but clear I heard a large-ish voice say, 'How much longer are you going to keep us hanging about out here? We've had time to go to Swindon and back since that last Down fast went by. It'll be a damn good job when they get the roofs off those boxes so's we can run trains.' Gordon, slightly built as an undernourished jockey, tightened his grip on the phone, took a deep breath and let him have an earful. 'Now you listen to me, I've had enough of you ringing up and moaning. I'm in charge of this place; you don't know what's going on down country. I'll let you out when there's a place for you to go and if you ring again I'll keep you there all night.'

'There,' grinned Gordon as he put the phone down, 'that's the way to deal with the likes of him.' It sounded a bit hard to me. A few minutes later, outside in the dark, we heard the steady tramp of heavy boots on the gravel. The door of the signal box opened and the boots started to crunch their way slowly up the stairs. Gordon looked at me wide-eyed and, going pale, moved behind the pot-bellied stove. Out of the stairwell came a huge head, then the barrel chest and finally the oak-tree legs of the biggest engine driver in the world; he looked like something out of a Bateman cartoon – the driver who strangled the passenger who dared to pull the communication cord on the 'Cheltenham Flyer'.

'*Wot did you say?*' boomed the giant.

Gordon gestured placatingly from behind the stove and gave a sickly grin. 'Er, you'll be going out after the next fast.'

'That's what I thought you said – just wanted to be sure.' He turned his enormous bulk, crunched his hobnails down the stairs with the sound of grinding bone and closed the door with exaggerated gentleness.

That episode made an impression on me and when I took charge of Challow box I tried to co-operate with the drivers if only for the satisfaction of seeing a steam engine tearing past the box in full cry and never mind the fast a bit too close on its tail. Having this attitude, I found the working of the 12.5 a.m. Tavistock Junction to Banbury 'D'-headcode vacuum very unsatisfactory.

The 'Tavvy' was booked specifically for haulage by a '49' class 'Hall' and had a Swindon crew from Swindon to Banbury. They left Swindon with a heavy train of mixed traffic including some loaded cattle wagons behind the engine and invariably ran at 45–50 mph once they had got the 400–450-ton train rolling. Unfortunately, they came up behind the 7.5 a.m. Cheltenham to Paddington fast which stopped at Challow and thus gave the following vacuum a hard check as it, the fast, pulled out of the platform road back onto the Main line. That would not have been a problem except that the Bristol Pullman and the Swansea Pullman were following the vacuum, no one would want to check either of those trains with a goods and so the 'Tavvy' was scheduled to run up the Relief line from Challow to Wantage.

One morning I put the 'Tavvy' 'up the shute' and the '49' barked away in fine style to Wantage, as if to show me what the running would have been like if it had been allowed Main line. I watched the train go and wished I could have a word with the driver, because with a slight rearrangement it would be just possible for it to run Main line and not hurt the following Pullman trains. A few minutes later the telephone rang; it was the driver of the 'Tavvy' speaking from Wantage Road box. 'Why do we always go in at your place? We're always running well; give us a chance and we'd make it to Steventon loop – the Bristol Pullman wouldn't even smell us.'

'The trouble is you run too well,' I replied. 'You come up too close behind the Cheltenham so that you're onto my distant while the fast is still pulling out of the platform. If you could just ease off after Knighton you'd give the Cheltenham a chance to get beyond the IBS and then I could give you my back board. I reckon you need to lose a minute and a half between Knighton and my distant.'

'All right then,' he said enthusiastically, 'let's try that tomorrow.'

Next day the 'Castle' on the Cheltenham seemed to trudge so slowly from the platform, each track circuit took an age to clear. Elwyn put the 'Tavvy' 'on line' just as the Cheltenham cleared No. 5 signal, the 'Castle's' exhaust beat sounded urgent but it would be ninety seconds before it cleared Circourt and I could pull my distant. I busied myself putting back signals and churning the hurdy-gurdy to put the platform to main points back for straight running. Then the Uffington telephone buzzed. 'A-dren,' said Elwyn solemnly, 'that "Tavvy" was shut off passing yere – how's the Bristol Pullman?'

'Wired as two late Badminton.'

'Huh! They'll pick a minute of that up to Swindon. I wouldn't trust that vacuum up the Main if I were you. They're drifting quite fast but they were shut off.'

I did not go into details with my mate. I suspected he would not approve of pacts between signalmen and drivers. If only I could give the 'Tavvy' my back board we would win but if I had to give him a 'Caution' he would have to brake, too much time would be lost and the game would be lost.

The annoying thing was that the second after the 'Tavvy' passed the distant at 'Caution' the Cheltenham would clear the IBS. I hovered over the Up Main levers, tense, ready to start pulling as soon as I heard the track circuit clunk into place. 'Come on! Come on!' The 'Tavvy' was whistling away down the line. Clunk! The indicator fell into place. *Wham-thud, wham-thud, wham-thud-crash.* I pulled the four levers in desperate haste and from a not-very-faraway engine there came a triumphant shriek on the whistle as a Swindon exhaust erupted into life, taking up the rhythm at about 40 mph. Round the wooded corner half a mile away came the storming '49', blasting past the box with the driver hanging out making 'only inches in it' signs with his fingers and his mate waving the shovel. They would soon be back to 55 mph. We had won but only just – a classic case of dropping the back board down the funnel!

Wally at Wantage was surprised when I asked the road for a 'five bells' behind the fast but he let the vacuum run and it tore through all the sections and got onto the West Curve at Foxhall without delaying the Pullman diesel. The men off the 'Tavvy' came home around noon with a '28' class engine on a train of steel coil for pressed steel at Swindon. As they came spanking down the Main towards the box both men were leaning out. 'Did we make it?' yelled the driver, hands cupped around his mouth. '*Yes!*' I yelled back and they went on their way rejoicing, blowing pips and squeaks on the engine's whistle. Word got round and I played this game with several drivers and having reached that stage of familiarity with the job and with the men I felt I had well and truly 'arrived'.

As there were no proper means of communication between a signalman and the crew of a moving train various odd dodges were resorted to in order not to stop a train to give a message – unless, of course, the message concerned the safety of the line in which case the driver always stopped his train and gave the message 'verbally' as the rule book put it. There were official codes to be blown on the engine's whistle to cover a few eventualities (*see* Appendix 4); for instance, if a steam engine hauling a train that was not booked to call at Swindon needed to stop there to fill its tender with water, the driver might blow 'one long, three short' as he passed Challow – or he might stand between the engine and the tender and make drinking signs and point to the tender as he passed.

More complicated messages could be conveyed by writing them on a sheet torn from his notebook, wrapping the paper round a piece of coal, tying the package with string and throwing the missive – or missile? – at the nearest signal box. The guard of a train would use a timetable, rolled and tied, to make his message weighty enough to escape the train's slipstream after it had been thrown at a signal box; I once received the following intriguing message from a guard: 'Passenger to Bath has lost briefcase. Contents very valuable. Have police meet train at Swindon.' The guard had no whistle to blow to attract the signalman's attention so here was another reason why the signalman watched each train carefully as it passed in case such a message should be thrown by the guard and fall unnoticed into the lineside grass.

Another guard's message read as follows; I give it in the original layout. The three o'clock Paddington was non-stop from Reading to Newport. I telephoned the signalman in Swindon East box, told him the tale and the train was put into the platform to allow the lady off. An Up train was then stopped specially at Swindon and again at Didcot so as to reunite the lady with her husband and the baby with its feeding bottle. I must say this incident demonstrated to me the obvious utility of breastfeeding – but I suppose that belongs to another book.

I had various coal-smudged notes from engine drivers. One read: 'Fireman has accidentally thrown shovel into firebox. Firing by hand. Please wire Swindon for a new shovel.' They got another shovel but only because it was an emergency – at that time shovels and footplate sweeping brushes were in such short supply that they were kept under lock and key in the stores. 5093 *Upton Castle* came thumping down the Main towards me on a morning express, the whistle blowing a series of rapid 'pops'. I went to the window to see what was the matter as a message tied to a lump of coal came sailing through the air and splintered against the wall of the box. The fireman was looking back to make sure I had seen it and we exchanged waves before I went outside to retrieve it. The handwriting was almost copperplate, written in a little notebook balanced on the driver's knee as he bounced along at 60 mph. The request sounded decidedly odd: 'Please wire Swindon Loco Foreman. Loco needs plug spanner. Driver of 5093.' Plug spanners called to mind petrol engines and I was at a loss for a minute till I remembered that steam engines have 'wash-out' plugs screwed into the boiler and firebox, which were removed to allow mud and limescale to leave the boiler when it was being washed out and one of these must have been leaking.

Handling successfully out-of-the-ordinary incidents was good training and helped me to feel more of a veteran – a survivor of situations – so that when a colleague at Challow caused a derailment I almost envied him the experience of organising the relief operation and the management of the train service. On a foggy 1 November 1962, the 5.30 a.m. Paddington to

Plymouth fast passed Challow at 7 a.m., the 5.5. a.m. Paddington to Bristol parcels arrived at the Down platform at 7.15 a.m., unloaded and went on its way, its place being taken by the 'Fly', which was overtaken by the 6.40 a.m. Hinksey freight running down the Main while the guard of the 'Fly' was uncoupling Challow's supply of coal and fertiliser.

The tank engine then drew forward with half a dozen wagons out onto the Main line and came to a stand ready to reverse across the 'ladder' crossover into the goods shed. The signalman pulled points 20, 22 and 24 and ground signal 19. But 19 would not answer the lever. The signalman put the points back, pulled them again and tried 19. Still the disc would not move. If a ground signal will not answer the lever it usually means that the points are not properly closed, but in this particular case, as a result of the uneven nature of the crossings, this signal frequency refused to show 'All Right' yet when the signalman walked 200 yards to the crossings he found the points were perfectly closed.

It was often possible to feel, in the last few inches of the lever's travel, whether the points on the other end of the rodding had closed properly or if they were in any way jammed open. They felt fine; it was a stumbling walk out and back on a raw, cold morning – the signalman took a calculated risk, went to the window and waved the driver back over the crossings. The pannier tank, a murky black blob in the mist, billowed clammy white exhaust and pushed back. The trucks travelled by rail for the first part of the way, for a little further on Olde England, and then stopped, all in a heap, right across all four roads. With a sad heart and many a futile, wishful thought, the signalman went to the instrument shelf and sent six beats – 'Obstruction Danger' – on the bell to Uffington and Wantage Road.

Fortunately, the de-rail happened ninety minutes before the first express was due. The signalman promptly warned his mates up and down the line and also the Traffic Controller in his office at Swindon; two stopping passenger trains were cancelled and all freight trains were berthed in loops or stopped from leaving the yards at Reading, Oxford and Swindon. The 12.5 Tavistock Junction was put thoughtfully into the platform loop at Shrivenham so it could be sent away first amongst the freights; if it had been allowed to continue into the long loop from Ashbury to Knighton it would have been fourth in the queue behind three slow goods.

The wreckage was cleared sufficiently by 9 a.m. to allow single-line working over the Up Main line between Uffington and Wantage Road, a long section but at least Up and Down fast could squeeze past the blockade. At noon the wagons had been re-railed, the damaged points and bent rodding repaired and normal running was resumed. The 'Fly' alighted at Uffington at 12.30 p.m., four and a half hours late.

The Control organisation was divided into 'Passenger train', 'Freight train', 'Locomotive' and 'Relief' with a Controller and an assistant working under each of these headings to supervise the movement of trains, men and machines through a twenty-four-hour day. If an engine failed, you would notify the Loco Controller, who had to find another engine; men who had finished a journey and had three or four hours 'spare' would contact the Relief Controller to see if he wanted them for another job; men who had finished their full day would phone in for relief crews – and then be asked to work a light engine back to their home depot.

I believe it would have been correct procedure for the Freight Controller to instruct all the signalmen on his patch when to put goods trains into loops and when to let them out but in fact the system worked the other way round; the signalmen acted on their own initiative and Control was informed some time later. Indeed, both signalman and Controller were too busy for the system to work otherwise and at Challow my usual contact with Control was when I telephoned them to tell that such and such a train had gone into the Relief line and this one had left the Relief line and to give the times of all trains passing or waiting at the box. The signalmen were proud of their independence and they would have viewed instructions from Control as 'interference' in the running of their signal box and reacted accordingly. In my experience, a co-operative relationship between signalman and Control depended on the Controller allowing the signalman freedom of action in the minute-by-minute running of the box; Control was there to provide information and emergency services and, when things went wrong, to consult with the signalmen on how best to sort the matter out. The Freight Controller at Swindon in 1962 was Cyril Matthews with his assistant Paul Dye; Cyril was a great character and Paul is still a personal friend*.

Some time in late November 1962, I was on late turn 2 p.m. to 10 p.m. and had a dead, engineless, train standing at 57 signal on the Down Relief line. Paul Dye had been told that the engine had left the train at about 5 p.m. and a few minutes later he came back to tell me to stop the 7.30 p.m. light engine from Oxford to Swindon – going down to bring the 9.30 p.m. Swindon to Longbridge up – and use it to take the dead train to Swindon.

---

* Paul was captain of the bellringers of St Philip & St James, at Bristol Temple Meads. He died of a heart attack setting up the bells for the evening change ringing session in an Australian church tower in 2002.

When the engine arrived – a 'Hall' blowing off furiously in the pitch dark – I made signs to the driver to go ahead and then reverse into the Down Relief line. Light from the signal box fell on his face and I saw the look of annoyance that passed across it. He crossed to his own side of the cab, the firelight catching momentarily his chin, nose and shiny peak of his cap. He sent the engine ahead with a great blast of exhaust, came back equally rapidly and squealed to a halt outside the box under my open window.

Moments later the signal box door slammed and the 'drive' came crashing up the stairs two at a time. 'What's up now?' he snapped.

'You've got to take a dead train to Swindon.'

'Bloody hell! Who says so?' he exploded.

'Need you ask? Control, of course.'

'Right. Which one of these is the Control phone?' I showed him and he rang the Controller for a good swear and a moan – 'It's not my job to be shunting wayside stations … I'm booked on for a specific purpose …' but all to no avail as he well knew. Having relieved his feelings on Paul or Cyril – I had often spent time with them in their office and could imagine the look of patient resignation on their faces – he slammed the handset down and stormed off down the stairs. He had to take the train because he was fresh on duty.

'Hang on a minute,' I called after him.

'What?'

'That train is standing at the far end of the platform behind the inner home signal. There's no light on the leading wagon – look out or you might hit it too hard in the dark.'

The driver slammed the door without replying. Seconds later he was taking his engine much too fast, backwards towards the all-but-invisible train. I stood at the open window and listened. *Bang! Thud!* Off the road! I went to the bell and sent six beats to Wantage Road in case the Down Main had been fouled by derailed wagons or the engine and went onto the telephone to tell Wally what I thought had happened.

Ten minutes later a very, very humble driver came gently up into the box. He hardly seemed like the same man who had been storming about minutes before. 'I'm afraid we're off the road, Bobby – tender wheels only and the first wagon but we aren't foul of the Down Main.'

I sent 'Obstruction Removed' to Wally and put the kettle on for the contrite driver. Having done that I telephoned Control and ordered out the breakdown gang to re-rail the tender and the wagon. It would have been too cruel to make the driver go back to the Controller and report it himself.

CHAPTER EIGHT

Night Alarm

Red-eyed night shift was something to be endured even though the signal box was a comfortable place to work. At the start and finish of the shift there was some compensation in the beauty of the countryside and during the shift I enjoyed conversations on the telephone and hearing hard-working steam engines pounding through the darkness throwing fire from their chimneys, roaring past in the light from the signal box, the fading, breathless rhythms of the locomotive and the wagons drumming over the rails. But after three o'clock in the morning I was past caring; sometimes I thought I had slept as I worked the box, because when I began to feel human again, round about five o'clock, I saw the entries in the register for the preceding two hours yet frequently had no recollection of writing them.

In spring and autumn but especially in summer I could watch each incandescent sunrise and listen to the skylarks as they rose from the fields to greet the dawn. The tree-lined lanes in spring, when the young sun shone low between the trunks, streaking the dawn mist with golden light and lighting through the fresh young leaves was more than adequate compensation for the discomfort of trying to stay awake between three and five each morning.

November days were grey and silent in the Berkshire vale and the hedgerow elms' tracery stood Indian ink black against the neutral sky, their once-green leaves clogging the lanesides in soggy, brown and yellow piles. All-pervading moisture greyed the leaves of brambles and hung all day over the waterlogged furrows of the dark-brown fields where one month before the yellow stubble stood. The sun, invisible all day, appeared briefly on the western horizon as it set – a great, cold, red plate sliding below the misty fields.

The nights, made raw by the damp cold, were full of fog. To leave the bright fireside of my cottage at twenty to ten and go out into the chilly murk could have been a penance except for the contrast between the dismal gloom outside and the warm, well-lit interior of the signal box and the beaming 'going home' smile of my mate Jim Spinage.

Night shift in mid-1962 produced a continuous procession of traffic. On the Up line from ten until three next morning we dealt with fast, heavy freight and mails – 550-ton milk trains still hauled by 'King' and 'Castle' class engines; parcel trains and the fully or partly 'fitted' vacuums from Fishguard, Penzance and Bristol East Depot, which had been running through the Vale and through the pages of the working timetable for forty years. After three o'clock the Up road was taken over by loose-coupled coal trains, interspersed with four sleeping-car trains from Penzance and West Wales, which dawdled eastwards so as not to arrive at Paddington too early.

The most important train on the Up line was the 7 p.m. Penzance to Paddington, the Royal Mail or 'up TPO', a travelling post office and sorting centre, but the fastest train on the Up road was the 1.50 a.m. Swindon to Birmingham (Moor Street) parcels that preceded the TPO out of Swindon by ten minutes. This train was worked by various crews from Tyseley shed with a Tyseley-based 'Hall' on a circular route that took them from Birmingham to Stratford-on-Avon, Cheltenham and Stroud to Swindon, returning home through Oxford and Honeybourne. The Tyseley men were very keen and because the TPO was following they made this an excuse for some Bristolian-style running with speeds of 85 mph and more – if my system of train timing from the signal box is correct. There was no need for such energy because the TPO had to stop at Steventon to put off mail for Oxford so I had an extra reason for observing the 1.50 Swindon – I liked to see the enginemen deliberately 'letting rip' just for the fun of it.

Steventon station had been the railhead for Oxford, 13 miles away, from June 1840 until a branch was opened to the city from Didcot in June 1844 but for 122 years the Up Royal Mail ignored the proper interchange point at Didcot and continued to put off mail for Oxford at Steventon station, which was the original 1840 building.

Between 10 p.m. and 3.15 a.m. the Down line was occupied with heavy sleeping-car trains, parcels, milk empties, newspaper trains, vacuum goods and fish trains. The 10.20 p.m. Paddington was the 'Down TPO' to Penzance and this exchanged mail-bags at full speed at lineside apparatus between Stratton Park Halt and Highworth Junction. The signalman at Challow warned the signalman at Highworth Junction when the TPO was passing and he warned the post office man to set his apparatus. The end of the busiest period was marked by the passing of the very fast 2.15 a.m. Paddington to Bristol newspaper train at about 3.15 a.m. After this we had the slow goods with longer periods between bell signals so that we could lie back in our chairs for a few minutes and close our prickly eyes. 'Roll on the papers and let me get my head down' was the oft-repeated groan from three o'clock onwards.

Some of the 'C'-headcode freights ran non-stop over long distances hauled by 'Grange', 'Hall' or '92' class engines but most freights put in at marshalling yards if only to change their guard or have their axle boxes examined. At goods yards out in the fields such as Moreton Cutting, Didcot, Hinksey and Oxford, or others surrounded by gasworks and houses such as Swindon or Acton, the wagons clashed and the ringing music of the buffers played all night, every night.

The performance at Marston sidings, three miles east of Swindon, was conducted on an embankment above meadows and was illuminated by nothing stronger than a few electric bulbs and the moon. The main purpose of the sidings was the reception, breaking-up and re-marshalling of fish trains, loaded and empty. The loaded 3.30 p.m. Hull and the 4.30 p.m. Grimsby arrived there in the early hours both bringing fish for destinations scattered between Torquay, Barnstaple, Whitland and Worcester. When they were reformed the 3.30 Hull consisted entirely of west of England traffic, the 4.30 Grimsby went to Whitland and a third train started from Marston for Gloucester and Worcester, putting off Swindon traffic at the goods yard there.

Three fresh light engines came up from Swindon shed to work these trains while the engines off the Hull and Grimsby trains went on to Swindon shed for coal, water and to turn before returning to Marston to work trains of empty fish-vans back to the east coast. In the mid-1950s or earlier these would have been 'GC' engines – ex-Great Central or LNER engines which had worked through at least from Woodford Halse or even further eastwards but in 1962 they were ex-GWR engines from Banbury.

Between Highworth Junction and Swindon goods yard signal boxes there were dozens of marshalling sidings on each side of the running lines to form 'Up' and 'Down' yards and at these boxes the signalmen co-operated with the shunters, pulling points and signals within the sidings during wagon-sorting manoeuvres, arranging for 'transfer trips' across the main lines from yard to yard besides dealing with normal signalling of trains on the main lines and goods loop. There was a touch of *Götterdammerung* at both these boxes as the crash of shunted wagons and the drifting smoke from engines was lit by lurid flames and permeated by the smell of sulphur from the gasworks close by.

At Swindon station, platforms 1 to 8 and the through lines would all be in use as trains loaded, unloaded, attached or detached vehicles, crews changed, wagons were examined or engines took water. In the West signal box two men worked 172 levers to control a vastly complex layout. Trains leaving the platforms or bays could delay trains approaching the station; trains crossing to the Gloucester line blocked all lines through the station; so did shunting movements when the station pilot took a van from the Up platform to the Down. Carriage shunters, platform foremen and locomotive foremen – the last of whom had a little wooden hut between the box and the Down platform – telephoned the signalmen with information on crew changing, on what move a particular engine or train wished to make next and the signalmen thought rapidly through the situation, planning ahead, remembering the trains that wanted a clear run through the station. They might agree to carry out the movement immediately and call to their mate to help in setting up the route, 'Engine off the Down branch for shed', 'Pilot and vans off the Up platform for the trap siding', before setting up a long sequence of lever movements, or the signalman might say to the man on the telephone, 'Wait till the Cardiff's gone by.'

I was in Swindon West box when one old-hand signalman, hand rolling some Gold Leaf into a Rizla paper, said, 'They'll never automate this place – it can't be done. Huh! Pushbuttons – we could've done wi' they during the war when we was really busy.' And he was quite right for 'they' never did automate *his* Swindon; what is now automated is far less than half the steam-hauled layout and a very much simplified train service uses it.

Between Foxhall and Challow one hour of a typical night shift could run as follows:

Scheduled times of trains at Foxhall Junction

	Headcode		a.m.
11.50 p.m. Paddington to Plymouth	'A'		1.10
9.40 p.m. Longbridge to Swindon	'C'	ex-West Curve	1.19
12.45 a.m. Paddington to Carmarthen	'A'		1.40
10.30 p.m. Cardiff to Paddington	'A'		1.40
6.40 p.m. York to Swindon	'A'	ex-West Curve	1.44
7.00 p.m. Llandilo Junction to South Lambeth	'D'		1.49
11.35 p.m. Acton to Gloucester	'D'	ex-Down Relief	1.53
1.00 a.m. Paddington to Swansea	'A'		2.11

Trains from the West Curve or Down Relief line crossed the Up Main to reach the Down Main or Down goods loop.

Typically, what might happen was that the 11.50 p.m. Paddington passed Foxhall 'right time' but the Longbridge arrived a few minutes late at 1.25

and stopped to take water on the Curve. The Foxhall signalman kept a close watch on this because the York passenger was due to leave Oxford at 1.25 and the Curve would have to be clear for it but if the men on the Longbridge hung the pot on he, the Foxhall signalman, would not be able to clear the goods to the downside owing to the approach of the 12.45 a.m. Paddington and/or 10.30 Cardiff – a train of perishables and fish running as 'A' headcode.

A telephone call to Kennington Junction, Oxford, informed Foxhall that the York was 'just passing'. The Longbridge was scheduled to run down the Main but as the York drew closer and still the vacuum did not move, the signalman at Foxhall considered running it down to Steventon over the goods loop. The Longbridge had to clear off the West Curve out of the way of the York but in passing to the Down Main or Down goods loop it must not delay either Main line fasts.

The big wooden-cased clock on the wall of Foxhall box showed 1.30 a.m. when the vacuum blew up ready. The signalman quickly rang Didcot East Junction. 'How's the 12.45 Freddie?' 'Five late West Main,' came the prompt reply. The Foxhall man felt the relief as a difficult situation vanished. The Cardiff was not asked on the Up Main, the Longbridge could go away down the Main immediately. At one moment there was no way out of a problem with one train stationary and three others converging on it; the next moment, at the toot of a whistle, the problem resolved itself.

The 9.40 Longbridge had fifteen minutes to get into the Relief line at Wantage Road and the Foxhall man set the route from West Curve to Down Main as fast as he could wham over the point and bolt levers – 37, 50, 48, 49, 32, 34, 41, 31 – followed by signal levers 6, 7, 8, 9. Having done this he rang me: 'That's the 9.40 Longbridge just leaving at 1.31 with 35 on. The York's right time but the 12.45's five down so the York'll wait here on the Curve for the 12.45 to go by. How's the Cardiff?'

I could hear the engine of the Longbridge blasting across the serpentine junctions at Foxhall through the earpiece of my telephone. 'The Cardiff'll pass me in five minutes, 1.36,' I replied.

The country signalmen were talking on the bus line so Wally heard the message and said to me, 'That's tight for the Longbridge. I'll put him down the shute to you – give me the road for a 3-1-1 Down Relief.' I got out of my chair, tapped out the code and turned the indicator of the down Relief line block indicator to 'Line Clear'. I went to the window and looked out into the dark. It was very still out there and there was something very pleasant to be alone in a peaceful empty world till the sharp ting of the Uffington bell brought me back into the brightly lit signal box and the busy world of the night railway.

The 10.30 Cardiff went rattling past and the Llandilo vacuum was asked up as soon as I cleared the section of the Cardiff. The Longbridge, hauled by a standard '73' class engine, went down smartly from Foxhall, turned onto the Relief line at Wantage and rumbled through the dark towards Wantage box. Wally stood to his instruments hoping that the guard of the vacuum would wave his white light from the van on the rear of the train to indicate that the train was clear of the Main line, all complete; this would enable Wally to knock out to Steventon a minute sooner than if he had to wait until he had seen the tail lamp of the train. The guard's lamp flashed, Wally turned the points for Main line running and knocked out at 1.45. Immediately Alec at Steventon asked the road for the 12.45 Paddington.

The 12.45 had passed Foxhall at 1.44 while the signals were off on the Up Main for the Cardiff; the York was standing on the West Curve; and the 11.35 p.m. Acton was creeping down the Relief line from Didcot West End box under the 'Warning'. The Cardiff went through at 1.47 and once more the route from Curve to Down Main was set up. The 'Hymek' diesel honked briefly, roared away, cleared the last signal in less than a minute whereupon the road was altered a little to bring the Acton off the relief line to the Down Main.

The Foxhall signalman came to the telephone again. 'Come on you blokes, let's have a bit of railway work. Is Challow on here?' Challow was. 'Right, that's the 11.35 Acton away behind the York at 1.49 with 47 on. Where's the Llandilo?'

'Been off Uffington three minutes, pass here in a couple,' I replied.

'It's all right for you old boys down there in the wilds, yacking away, I've got a railway to run up here,' said Foxhall, slamming his phone down amidst a chorus of jeers.

Wally now spoke railway work to me. 'You'll be turning that Longbridge out behind the York.' He phrased it in the curious style of the signal box, half question half assertion.

'Yes, I reckon it'll leave at 2.3 so if the one o'clock is on time the vacuum'll go in at Elwyn's.'

'Hmm,' mused Wally, 'I wonder how the one o'clock is doing. Let's ask Alec; he's on here somewhere.' My telephone earpiece clicked twice as Wally rang the code for Steventon.

'Stivvy!' chirped Alec.

'How's the one o'clock, Alec?' asked Wally.

1. Earley station, on the edge of hundreds of acres of woodlands, as I remember it from 1944 to 1952. The picture was taken in 1950. The railway's magic was partly due to its hanging back in an earlier era. (Lens of Sutton Collection)

2. Reading South station, *c.* 1963. It was a nice little station and was additionally enchanting because it was so utterly different to the GWR station just a few yards to the north. Quite different types of steam engines and its very handsome electric trains – nothing as magnificently built and upholstered exists today – and they ran every half an hour to Waterloo. The architecture – signals and signal boxes – as well as the cast iron and bricks and mortar was so *different*. The plain, mid-green paint – just a tiny bit sickly – and the branch line terminus atmosphere. If one was a lover of railways, all aspects of the scene were a matter of delight, if only for the difference. (Author's Collection)

3. Locospotters sitting along the edge of No. 5 platform at Reading. The siding to the right of the incoming 'Hall' was where the Station Pilot engine used to stand awaiting the arrival of the slip coach off the 8.30 a.m. Plymouth at 12.50 p.m. When the coach had been brought to a stand by its guard, right opposite the stairway down to the subway, the engine would come out onto the platform line, collect the coach and later attach it to the back of a London-bound 'all stations' passenger train. Over on the left a 'King Arthur' class No. 30783 *Sir Balin* has brought into No. 3 platform a train from Portsmouth and is now waiting to reverse out of the Bay to Reading GW shed. On Bay 2 is a 'Hall' awaiting the 'off' with a Newbury line stopping train. (Johnathan Ashman/Courtesy Mike Esau)

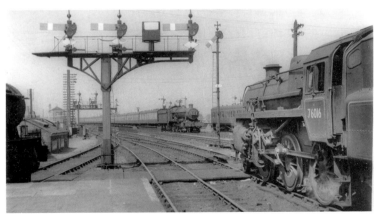

4. The view west from platform 2 of the Down bays at Reading, *c.* 1958. On the right, 76016 is waiting to leave with a Portsmouth train, and a GWR engine is on the left. A 'Hall' has just joined the Main line for Paddington from the Berks & Hants Line with a train from Plymouth if not further west than that. On the signal gantry the signal is lowered for a train to turn off the Down Main to the Berks & Hants line. These were the heavenly delights awaiting anyone with one penny to spend on a platform ticket at Reading – ten platforms for one penny. (Courtesy Les Reason/Author's Collection)

5. Challow station looking west from the footbridge. Lad Porter Adrian on the left with a parcel for the Down stopping train, Fred Strong on the right. The very plain, red-brick station office dates from 1933 when the Brunel wooden station was demolished during the quadrupling of the line. The steel-framed, breeze-block signal the same. But the 1840, Brunel goods shed survived. When Challow opened – as Faringdon Road – in 1840, it was intended that it should serve Faringdon and Wantage. (H. O. Vaughan, October 1960)

6. Challow station offices on the Up platform early in 1961. Apart from a garden against the office wall, it appears unchanged since it was rebuilt in 1934.

7. Harry Strong. Harry drove the Challow shunting horse *Duchess*. Here he is with his horse in 1924 – about the same as in this picture as when I went to work with him, aged nineteen, in 1960. (Courtesy of the late Harry Strong)

8. GWR wages grade staff at Challow in 1924. From the left: Tom Gillman, Harry Strong, Harry Crooks, who was killed on the line, Reg Chester – possibly a guard – and ? Reynolds. GWR caps were taller than BR-issued caps but the blue serge three-piece suits were very similar to the BR suit I was issued with – and, of course, the character of the men was the same in 1924 as 1960. (Courtesy the late Harry Strong/Author's collection)

9. The Bristol–Swindon and Swindon–Didcot route was blessed with a regular daily service of 'all stations' trains hauled by passenger engines just out of the Works. They had a week of 'running in' and, sometimes, the following week we got an even bigger thrill – that of seeing the engine that had been footling with two coaches come thundering through at 70 mph with twelve on. No. 7007 *Great Western* was turned out of Swindon Works new in July 1946 and was then named *Ogmore Castle*. In January 1948, at Nationalisation, it was renamed *Great Western*. The name had the obvious significance of commemorating the noble old Company but that was also the name of the first express engine to be built at Swindon in 1846. Seen here at Challow in September 1960 on the 10.45 Didcot–Swindon 'stopper', No. 7007 has just had its last general repair and is 'running in'. The engine was scrapped in February 1963 having run, on average, 51,615 miles a year since new. A very new recruit to BR(WR), nineteen-year-old porter Adrian, is just visible on the right – looking on, besotted. (H. O. Vaughan)

10. Uffington station as it looked at any time between 1952 and 1964. The station was opened in 1864 for the Faringdon branch, which can be seen curving away to the north. The signal box was rebuilt on the platform in 1896. With the withdrawal of passenger trains on the branch in December 1951, the station name board was changed to plain 'Uffington' rather than 'Uffington Junction for Faringdon' and several signals, on the branch line side, were removed. But still – working at Uffington was pleasantly going back in time. (R. M. Casserley)

Above left: 11. Uffington looking east from the Down Main line. (R. M. Casserley)

Above right: 12. The 1896-vintage, forty-seven-lever frame at Uffington. The levers were mutually interlocked by a remarkably cumbersome mechanism designed in 1890 by a GWR engineer. This design was a modification of an 1870 design. The locks were moved on and off the levers by giving each one a pair of rollers through which passed a flat, metal bar with a twist at each end. When the lever was pulled over or pushed back, the rollers passed over the twisted bar, causing it to rotate and thus movement was given to the locking bars. I used to take up one of the metal covers at the foot of a lever so as to watch the action of the rollers and bar as I pulled the lever. Everything about the mechanical railway was fascinating. (Author)

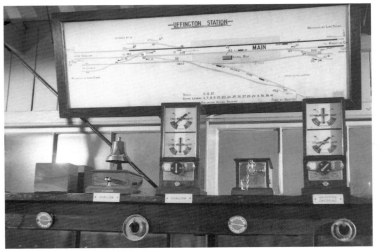

13. The track diagram, hand-drawn and coloured in, hanging over the 1947-style GWR block signalling instruments. The right-hand instrument works with Knighton Crossing signal box and shows, in the lower section, that I have given 'Line Clear' on the Up line to Knighton so that he can lower his signals for a train to approach Uffington. The left-hand instrument shows that I have asked Challow if the line is clear at his box for the train to approach him, he has sent me 'Line Clear' and consequently I have cleared my signals. Besides the block instruments are the signalling bells. Between the instruments is the 'block switch' by means of which I can 'switch out of circuit', clear my Up and Down line signals and make the 'block section' Challow–Knighton Crossing. 1961. (Author)

14. Bristol Temple Meads 'Old Station' looking from beneath the GW/Midland Joint station roof of 1876 to the original Brunellian terminal station of the Great Western Railway of 1840. I first saw this station when I went to Bristol for my examination on the signalling regulations by Chief Inspector Wellman and Divisional Superintendent Mr Pearman. Previously I had only seen the exaggerated scale of the Brunel station in the romaticised engravings of J. C. Bourne so seeing the station for real was something of a let-down. (Author)

Above left: 15. After the fatigue, the sweet. After successfully completing my interrogation by Chief Inspector Wellman and then Divisional Superintendent, Paul Pearman, the latter gave me a fifteen-section GWR Working Time Table for 1936 – it weighs 5 lb – and suggested I visit Bristol Temple Meads East box. This was installed in 1934 and had 336 'draw slides' with which three signalmen controlled the electric light signals and electrically driven points to work the east end of the station and the tracks eastwards out to and including South Wales Junction. The signal box worked to the old 'Absolute Block' system. There were approximately twenty-three signalling bells and block instruments. All the bell codes received and sent were recorded by hand, on paper, by a teenage 'Booking Boy'. He also answered the telephones, and made enquiries on behalf of the signalmen. Signalmen Jesse Bye, on the left, and Bill Barker are shown. July 1961. (Author)

Above right: 16. A very far cry from Bristol Temple Meads East box, but, after many years of unofficial apprenticeship, I was thrilled to be a properly certified 'Officer in Charge' of Uffington box. (H. O. Vaughan, August 1961)

17. The Faringdon branch, 3½ miles long, swung sharply away to the north from Uffington station, and fell at 1 in 140 for half a mile over the Ock Brook and then rose up the Faringdon ridge at 1 in 88 for 1 ½ miles to the summit and thereafter gently fell and rose and levelled for the mile and a half into Faringdon. The steep fall out of the station followed by the long, steep rise gave ample opportunity for drivers to 'rush the bank' and see how many wagons they could get over the summit without stopping to divide the train. This view, looking to Faringdon, was taken from the lamp platform of the Up distant signal. The latter remained *in situ* for many years after the track had been lifted. (Author)

18. Faringdon station with its engine shed partly in view on the left and its goods shed on the right. (R. M. Casserley)

19. Faringdon yard in about 1958 with 0-4-2 tank No. 1410 shunting and the Oxford University Railway Society enjoying themselves. (Peter Barlow/Author's Collection)

20. Back at Uffington, No. 1410 must take water at the column, 'run round' the train *via* the branch loop and – after placing the refilled can of drinking water for Knighton Crossing signalman on the front buffer beam – 'push back' into Baulking sidings from whence to emerge for Swindon. (Peter Barlow/Author's Collection)

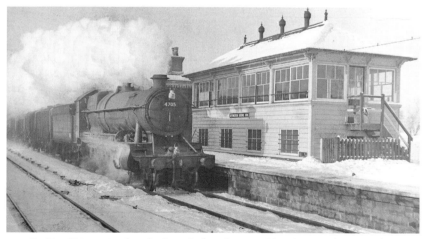

21. No. 4705 coming bravely through the Siberian cold with a very lowly 'H' headcode goods. I recollect that he was clipping along at a good speed – for a long, heavy freight and the driver clearly felt very confident of his massive engine's braking capability – the long train behind him being entirely without brakes, except for the hand-brake in the guard's van. January 1962. (Author)

22. Exceptionally heavy rain in August 1961 caused an embankment on the West of England Main line, at Patney & Chirton, to be washed away. A large number of the West of England Main line services were diverted into the Bristol line, for a week or ten days, giving me a great time as a very enthusiastic young signalman. Here the flagship train of the Western Region, the 10.30 a.m. Paddington to Penzance, the Cornish Riviera Express, comes through behind 'Warship' class diesel No. 862 *Viking*. The diesel is carrying the curved headboard designed to fit on the front of a steam engine. Unfortunately the 'King' class steam engines were no longer working such heavy and prestigious trains when this was taken, from the window of Uffington box, on 16 August. (Author)

23. Relaying the Down Main line at Uffington, entirely by hand, in September 1961. The crossover from Up to Down main runs out of the centre of the view. Note the GWR Down refuge siding GWR ringed arm signal. (Author)

Above left: 24. The signalman's view of the Uffington levers when he is on his knees using 'Mansion House' wax polish on the linoleum. (Author)

Above right: 25. The Up branch home signal at Uffington. The perforations in the ball of the finial atop the post were of a curious design that I never saw anywhere else on the railway. This led me to believe that the design was very old and that the signal was erected in 1896, when the station was enlarged, and replaced a survivor of the broad gauge – a double disc & crossbar that had stood at this spot since 1864. (Author)

26. The 10.55 a.m. Paddington to Pembroke Dock, hauled by No. 5051 *Earl Bathurst,* passing Uffington at about 12.5 p.m. on a grim day in April 1962. (Author)

27. Nobility on wheels. Unfortunately, 'Handsome is as Handsome does' and No. 7034 *Ince Castle*, on 5 March 1962, had let the passengers down. The sealing rings of the steam valves on all four cylinders had become so worn that steam was able to pass directly from the steam chest to the chimney, this denying high pressure steam to the cylinders. (Author)

28. Work on converting the interior of Uffington box to a modern lever frame controlling a new layout began in January 1962. Signalling instruments were installed in this plywood hut from sometime in January until 4 March 1962 when the new signalling was brought into use. These are the Swindon and Didcot relief signalmen who happened to be on duty one day when I came to work with a camera. From left to right: Les Wheeler and Sid Tyler, from Swindon, Elwyn Richards, Owen Gibbs, also from Swindon, and Bert Rutland from Steventon. Sid Tyler had been in the 4th Battalion of the Wiltshire Regiment during the Great War and fought in the Battle of the Somme, going 'over the top' on 1 July 1916, one month before his sixteenth birthday. (Author)

29. The grimy exterior of Challow signal box. Unpainted all its life, beginning in 1934. Jim Spinage and I volunteered to paint it with 'Sno-cem' and 'Dark Stone' if BR would supply the paint, but I don't think we even got a reply to our letter. The low cutting side rising past the end window is where the fox climbed up and he and I exchanged a telepathic conversation. (Ron Price/Author's collection)

30. The reason we wanted to paint the outside was because the inside looked like this. Most signal boxes were kept highly polished but I never saw one more highly polished than Challow. Please note the reflection of that locker in the lino floor covering. Kemble and Badminton signal boxes – which were often used as a waiting room by Royalty when they were travelling *incognito* and wished to remain out of sight – were polished to the same high standard as Challow. It was the task of the man on 12-hour Sunday day turn to polish and dust everything and, with hot water, yellow soap and a good old scrubbing brush, scrub the bare pine floorboards behind the levers. (Ron Price/Author's collection)

31. The inebriated guard of the 'Fly' goods shunted this one off so hard that it hit the buffers and jumped up over them. Sam Loder being facetious as usual. My beloved Morris 8 is in the background. (Author)

32. No. 6018 was standing, gleaming, even under a dull, grey sky. Cardiff was well known for the smartness of their top link express engines, and the cleaners had worked overtime on *King Henry VI*. He came rolling majestically through the station and backed onto his train. And I was going to ride his footplate all the way to Paddington. (Author)

33. At the Wantage Road end, the signal repeaters were a mixture of those installed in 1934, and by BR(W). The Down Main distant and outer home signal arms were repeated by those beautifully made wooden-cased instruments purchased from the Tyers signalling works. There is also a lamp repeater to set an alarm ringing if one of the oil lamps behind the signal glass goes out. (Ron Price/Author's collection)

34. The 'block' indicators, 'block' bells instruments and track diagram. The left-hand indicator works to and from Uffington, the central one works to Wantage Road for Up and Down Main line trains, and the third one is for the Up and Down Relief lines. Each indicator has its communicating, single strike bell to its right. The situation on the tracks between Uffington and Wantage Road, when this picture was taken, was that there was a Down train in the Block Section between Challow and Uffington – see the indication in the upper box of the left-hand block indicator – and I have given 'Line Clear' to Uffington, shown in bottom box, for a train to approach Challow. I have asked 'Is Line Clear?' to Wantage Road on the central indicator – the upper box in that indicator. (Ron Price/Author's collection)

Above left: 35. The instrument shelf – usually called 'the block shelf' – at Challow, photographed in three parts. At the Up or Uffington end, the signal arm repeaters for the Up Main, left-hand set, and Up Relief line next. These are all BR(W) installed in 1953 when Circourt signal box between Challow and Wantage Road was abolished, its signals thereafter controlled from Challow and Wantage Road. Note the 'Runaway' plungers on the right of each set. If a train passed Circourt intermediate block home signal at 'Danger', the 'runaway' buzzer sounded, the signalman sent the tapped out 'Train running away' bell code, 4-5-5, to Wantage Road and pressed the brass plunger to switch off the warning. (Ron Price/Author's collection)

Above right: 36. Sam Loder, photographed as he was making his way to the signal box for his elevenses with the Extra Train Notices in his greatcoat pocket. Sam, the ever-cheerful, practical joking, old soldier and old-hand railwayman. Sam had gone from school to the farm and from the farm to the Grenadier Guards in 1930. He served with the Grenadiers until 1945 and then joined the railway. Coincidentally we also had a Colonel Loder, ex-Grenadiers, who was Bristol Division Superintendent – but he wore grey kid gloves and never played practical jokes. (Author)

37. No. 7033 *Hartlebury Castle* brings the 11.15 a.m. Paddington – the *Merchant Venturer* – past Challow's inner home signals and past a 'WD' class 2-8-0 waiting patiently on the Down Relief line for its onward path to Swindon. 7033 was scheduled to average 60 mph from passing Didcot to passing Swindon. (Author, *c.* 1957)

38. At around about 11.50 a.m. every weekday, we had the 7.30 a.m. Carmarthen–Paddington come through – the 'Red Dragon'. Often the same engine worked it every day for the week. On this occasion it is No. 7020 *Haverfordwest Castle*. (Author)

39. Challow when it did not pay. The station's passengers waiting for the 7.5 Cheltenham–Paddington express, due to arrive at 8.55. I took this from the footbridge in September 1960 to show how useful the station was for long-distance travellers. I ought to have taken a second picture looking east along the platform to show all those lined up along there. As the railhead for the Vale the station clientele would have responded to a couple more fast trains to and from London through the day. What I had suggested to Western Region management was what they later introduced for seemingly small but strategically important wayside stations – a 'Parkway'. Challow should have become 'Faringdon and Wantage Parkway'. (Author)

40. On 14 May 1964, I was on early turn in Challow box. The 8.15 Bristol Bristol Pullman was 23 minutes late so that the Swansea Pullman came up first, 6 minutes late. This 'C'-headcode goods, 12.5 a.m. Tavistock Junction–Banbury with No. 7909 *Heveningham Hall*, had followed the 4.40 Fishguard boat train closely from Swindon. The 'Tavvy' had a Banbury crew and they never hung about as they headed for home to finish a night shift. With the Pullman sufficiently late I gave the 'Tavvy' the road. They covered the 2½ miles from Uffington in 3 minutes. I rushed out and grabbed a photo as they gallantly went through at 50 mph. Wantage Road pulled off for them and they had a clear run for ten miles to the loop at Steventon. The 6.50 Swansea passed me 20 minutes later, by which time the 'Tavvy' was well out of its way. That sort of hands-on excitement was another great joy of working as a signalman on the steam-hauled railway. (Author)

41. Sometimes, on a 12-hour Sunday day turn, there would be some light engineering work on the track and an ex-works engine was often used to bring the train of granite chippings or other material to the site. The engineering train would be shown in the 'K2' Engineering notice and my mother, father and I would go to the signal box in the afternoon bringing Mother's fruit cake. With this and mugs of tea, the footplatemen would be fed sumptuously. My mother was very fond of enginemen and their engines. Here is *Rydal Hall* standing on the goods shed siding with myself and my mother revelling in it. (H. O. Vaughan/Author's collection)

Above left: 42. Swindon driver Len Smith and his fireman, with 5971 *Merevale Hall* and a train of empty 'pools' – 16-ton coal trucks – for Severn Tunnel yard. I joined them at Swindon and went through; a pleasant round trip before going on night shift. We were taken into the platform loop at Badminton to let an express go by when I took this. The signal on the far side of the line is cleared for the Bristol Division Officer's Inspection special to arrive. (Author)

Above right: 43. Swindon is the junction for the Gloucester line. The junctions were far more complex in 1960 than in modern times, controlled from the 173-lever Swindon West box. This is the view of the West box from the west end of the Up Main platform in 1953, with 2953 *Saint David* arriving with an RCTS Special arriving. I was honoured to ride the footplate of this, the last of the 'Saint' class, at Reading 1951–53, when it occasionally acted as the Station Pilot. (R. C. Riley/Transport Treasury)

Above left: 44. In March 1964 the search was on, in Western Region, for eight 'Castle' class engines in fine condition. Three would be required for the actual High Speed Ian Allan Special in May and three more would be standby engines. No. 4079 *Pendennis Castle* had been put through the works and thoroughly overhauled in March 1963 and from that had gone directly into the store shed at the back of the running shed at Swindon. When the engine was recalled a year later its engines were rusted internally and a lot of work was required to get its valves and cylinders free so that it could be hauled up to the running shed. A good job was done on it and it covered itself in glory on 9 May until the firegrate gave way two miles west of Lavington. 4079 was running at 96 mph when disaster struck. The very special Welsh Ogilvie steam coal it was burning melted the firegrate and great chunks of blazing coal went flying past the windows of the train like blazing meteors, hitting against the sides of the carriages. (Author)

Above right: 45. The everyday scene inside the Churchward-design turntable shed at Swindon. From left to right there is an 84xx pannier tank, 5510, 2-6-2 tank, a 57xx tank, a 49xx 'Hall', 4079 and finally a 68xx 'Grange'. All standing like horses in their stalls. (Author)

Above left: 46. The Up starting signals for Swindon Town 'B' box at the south end of the station – a magnificent example of GWR signalling. The view from the signal box in March 1962. (Author)

Above right: 47. Reading West Main signal box had levers numbered to 222 – there were a few spares and spaces. Three men worked it with a booking boy. Ken Morton is in front. Having spent years as a train spotter on Reading station and seeing the great signal box from the station or from a passing train, it was really wonderful to be able to visit it whenever I felt like it after joining the railway. (Author)

Above left: 48. 6159 pulling away from Challow in the last few days before the abolition of the Didcot–Swindon stopping trains and of the station itself. Taken in November 1964. (Author)

Above right: 49. The sun setting on the railway at Reading West Junction. The diesels have arrived; the cables are laid for the signalling automation. 'Times they are a-changin'.' The diesel is waiting for the Up train to pass so it can haul its train across the Up line and into Reading Old Yard. (Author, October 1964)

50. The author with Bill Kenning in the middle and Ron Price. Challow box, on a Sunday night shift in 1964.

51. The 'Blue Pullman' train failed at Swansea the night before this picture was taken. The stand-by Pullman cars and a 'Western' class, 2,500 hp diesel were prepared for next day's 6.50 a.m *Swansea Pullman*. The massively powerful 'Western' diesel failed at Marston East, 3 miles east of Swindon, 10 miles west of Challow. Luckily, there was a goods train in the loop hauled by No. 7906 *Fron Hall*. In less than 10 minutes the Hall had removed the diesel, got onto the Pullman cars and was away. The locomotive's fire was not in a condition for hauling a heavy train at speed and it came through Challow at about 45 mph. As you can see, the fireman is building his fire so that a more appropriate speed can be maintained. They stormed through Didcot at a respectable 70 according to an eyewitness and maybe they did better later. But not bad for a scruffy, unprepared and much denigrated steam engine. (Author)

52. No. 1010 *County of Caernarvon* coming through Challow hauling a '6959' class 'Hall' westwards for scrapping. (Author)

53. Streamlined GWR diesel rail car No. 4 at Challow, being towed to Hellifield, in 1964. I was on duty in the signal box and was thus able to stop the train and get a decent shot of this elegant design. This was one of the pioneering batch of four cars, built in 1934. Another thirty-four were built. They had two 121-hp diesel engines driving through a 4-speed epicyclic gearbox. They were designed for a top speed of 80 mph and were used to form a high-speed service between Birmingham and Cardiff. They seated forty-four passengers with space for their luggage. Each car had two lavatories and a bar and buffet. (Author)

Above left: 54. Tom, the Didcot East Junction cat. (Author)

Above right: 55. The three Uffington signalmen in 1966. Jim Spinage, seated; Elwyn Richards, centre; and the author. (H. O. Vaughan)

56. The steam engine was on its way out from 1958 on Western Region. Even with the reckless rush to scrap, the process took seven years owing to the inefficiency of the diesels. Long enough for me to get a lot of enjoyable experience with the footplatemen and their engines. This is Swindon Dump one Sunday in 1963. The first boiler in the picture after the one on the wagon contained within its smokebox two workmen having their lunch. They emerged just after I'd clicked my shutter. (Author)

57. No. 5526 runs off the Marlborough branch at Savernake Low Level West signal box. This picture was made possible only by the great consideration of the footplate crew. I first photographed this at Marlborough and wanted a view at Savernake several miles away. I explained the problem to the chaps and they said they would stop somewhere and give me time to get into position. I was running along the top of the cutting as they came steaming slowly down the hill! (Author)

58. Oxford North Junction, looking north. The 3-doll signal reads: Down Main to Down goods, Down Main, Down Main to Up Bletchley line. (Author)

59. No. 70053 *Moray Firth* was shedded at Oxford in 1964. It is seen here at Paddington at the head of the 4.15 p.m. semi-fast to Banbury. The train was supposed to be formed by a Diesel Multiple Unit but, diesels being what they were – steam to the rescue. Steam haulage on this service continued for several days, much to the delight of the steam engine train timers. (Author)

60. Chris Byrne and Evan Davies with Earl of Merioneth at Tan-y-Bwlch, Festiniog Railway. (Author)

61. The 10.30 Waterloo to Weymouth was brought to a stand at Walton-on-Thames to await the Pilotman during single line working on a Sunday in 1965. Being a signalman, I saw what was happening and took the opportunity to photo the magnificent loco.

62. West of Worting the route to Southampton ran through some very handsome Hampshire countryside. Here a grimy but mechanically well-maintained British Railways 73xxx mixed traffic engine brings a Southampton train past the out of use Wootton signal box. My Jowett 'Javelin' is on the left. (Author)

63. A road tunnel through the Exeter line embankment, a few miles west of Worting on the Exeter line. A Class 4 locomotive, 76xxx, goes over the tunnel with an Up parcels train. (Author)

64. and 65. The Bournemouth Belle that day was hauled by 35007 *Aberdeen Commonwealth*. There was just about 500 tons of Pullman and luggage vans behind the tender and the superb – but filthy-looking – engine, with a superb driver and fireman, handled the job with ease. We ran exactly to time and while 100 mph would have been perfectly possible, Driver Admas kept to the maximum permitted speed on the racing ground east of Basingstoke – 85 mph. The silence and the steadiness of the ride on the footplate at that speed was incredible. I had to use ½₅ second at full aperture to get this picture of Harry Adams and the picture is perfectly sharp. The same goes for the view of Mr Bush, firing. We were doing 85, the sun was setting and the engine's cab was very enclosed; a slow shutter speed was essential and yet this view is quite sharp.

66. Kennington Junction signal box, Main line side, 1968. Note that the box has its back to the Main line. (Author)

Above left: 67. Inside Kennington Junction box. A forty-three-lever frame – with 15 spaces due to the removal of the additional tracks laid in during the Second World War. Note the presence of a diabolical Train Describer to 'interface' between the mechanical and the electric signaling at Reading. (Author)

Above right: 68. A misty spring Sunday morning at Kennington. Peace. Time for reflection. The driver of the D63xx on the permanent-way department train does some writing and I amuse myself with the Rolleiflex. In the foreground is the Electric Train Token instrument, which ensures that only one train at a time occupies the line between here and Morris Cowley. (Author)

Above left: 69. Hinksey North signal box, built on the Down side of the line half a mile south of Oxford station and brought into use in April 1942. Built by Italian prisoners of war to the Railway Executive Committee's 'Air Raid Precautions' design, it was supposedly shrapnel proof but of course flying glass could have been lethal. There were sixty-nine levers, but in 1969 seventeen were out of use. (Author)

Above right: 70. Hinksey North was the busiest box I ever worked. Every day on Early Turn, I worked continuously at bells, levers, train register and telephone from 6 a.m. until 10.30 before things eased off a bit. Breakfast was impossible until then. It was a wonderful train set and most enjoyable, although, day in, day out, it became very tiring. Here I've snatched a moment to photograph the Littlemore oil leaving South End yard in 1970. (Author)

71. Around 10 a.m. the engine for the Cardiff to Corby coal train, the wagons stabled in the Down yard, is on the Down goods loop waiting its chance to go out onto the Down Main and reverse into the Down Yard. A Hoo Junction cement train goes by with a guard's van on the back and the South End Yard pilot is shunting, the signal out of the yard being lowered. (Author)

72. Great Western Society 'Hall' No. 6998 *Burton Agnes Hall* comes through the Hinkseys in 1973. Photographed from Hinksey South box. (Author)

73. Clink Road Junction signal box, standing at the 114½ mile post from Paddington, 1973. (Author)

74. The interior of the box with the levers reversed to turn the junction for the Frome direction. (Author)

Above left: 75. Tom Baber, from a family of railwaymen, joined the GWR in 1938 at Sparkford. He was a 'Darset' man and was hugely entertaining company. We were very good friends. Please note the splendidly handmade toasting fork on the locker end. (Author)

Above right: 76. Witham signal box looking west in 1974. This building was erected in 1896 with a forty-seven-lever frame and was extended in 1942 to accommodate sixty-seven levers when and Up and Down goods loop was added to improve the working of trains with the hugely inflated wartime service. (Author)

Above left: 77. Looking east from Witham signal box on a gloomy winter day. A 'Western' diesel creeps along the bi-direction goods loop with a train of empties for Merehead Quarry while a 'Hymek' stands in the down sidings, coupling on to some tar tankers for the BP depot at Cranmore. (Author)

Above right: 78. The Merehead branch Electric Train Token instrument at Witham. I could issue myself with a token by pressing in the plunger to release the lock – provided of course that I had not previously pressed in the plunger to give Merehead Quarry ground frame a release of a token. 'One train at a time over a single track'. (Author)

79. I have just taken the token in its holder from the secondman of the Class 45xxx coming off the Merehead branch with a load of stone. The carrier is swinging back behind my body, unfortunately for the picture, but one edge of it can just be seen. (H. O. Vaughan)

'Right time Reading.'

'Right,' said Wally decisively, 'you let the Longbridge go down to Uffington after the York and I'll put this Acton five bells down the shute for the hard hitter.' When I knocked out for the Longbridge, Wally tolled out five bells for the Acton on the booming cow bell in Challow box.

An unusual night shift began on 21 September 1962 at 10 p.m. when I relieved Jim Spinage in the operating room of Challow box where the red, yellow, blue and black levers, the steel, brass and polished linoleum gleamed brighter than day under bright electric lights. He gave me a cheerful greeting, told me the traffic situation and took himself off to the Prince of Wales for a pint. My next jobs were to sign on in the block register, put boiling water on a teabag in a cup and read the extra train notices. By eleven o'clock, eight trains had passed the box, I had drunk two cups of tea, read the notices and the paper Jim had left behind and generally settled myself into the box. It was then time to go onto the bus line to see what other sorts of news might be discovered. I lifted the phone and gave the traditional warning: 'Anyone on?'

Elwyn and Alec Abrahams were talking and broke off to say, 'Good evening. About time you came on; we were wondering if you were there tonight.' Alec, like Elwyn, was involved with the choir of his parish church and they were discussing church matters when I butted in. 'Yes then, Elwyn, how did the Bishop's visit go?' continued Alec.

'Well, the singing in church was quite good but afterwards we had to go in procession to the new vicarage and I did feel a bit self-conscious walking down the 'igh Street in my surplice carrying the processional cross wi' all the village looking on – good drinking mates too, some of them. 'Course, our vicar's very 'igh – always calls himself "Father" like the Catholics and he likes to put a show on now and then. When we got ... Oh drat the bells! Hang on a minute.'

'What's this Elwyn's got asked then?' asked Alec.

'The 6.20 Severn Tunnel's wired. What's Elwyn on about?'

'Oh they had the Bishop of Oxford at Uffington this morning blessing the new vicarage – tell Elwyn to hang on, I'd better ask Foxhall whether he wants the Tunnel up the Main or the loop, depends on whether the fresh guard is waiting there or not.'

As he went off the phone, Elwyn came on. 'Ah, now then. What's this 1-2-2 I've got asked up, Adrian?' I told him. 'Right, thanks,' he said. 'Well, Alec, each room had to be blessed ...'

'Alec's on the other phone to Foxhall. You've had a busy day by the sound of it, Elwyn.'

'Oh, it was terrible we …'

'Hallo, Elwyn,' broke in Alec. 'Sorry, I was on the other phone. What was you saying?'

'Every room had to be blessed – it's a biggish house – and the Bishop did go on a bit. We'd only got to the second last and you can be sure I was counting them off when the Fox and Hounds opened. He finished that room and I picked up the big cross to lead into the last room – I was feeling a bit cross you might say – heaved it up rather sudden and it went into the plaster ceiling.'

'Ooh dear,' chuckled Alec, 'you'll be popular now.'

They'll always have a little spot to remember you by, Elwyn,' I chipped in.

'Ah, but that wasn't the end of it,' said Elwyn, his voice still carrying something of the morning's horror, 'the cross is heavy and it's got a sort of point and it went in so far that I couldn't get it out, maybe a bit of lath was holding it. No one could get in or out because I was near the doorway tugging at the cross, trying not to swear out loud with bits of plaster falling. In the end I gave it a real good tug and it came out but it brought down a lot of the ceiling too. The Bishop took it very well and looked deadpan and we got on and finished the job.'

Alec and I were suitably impressed with the enormity of the event.

'Yes but it would have been worse if the Bishop hadn't taken it so well. When we got outside and I was standing with my big brass cross on its long pole and trying to look inconspicuous, the Bishop takes off his mitre, tips it up and emptied two big lumps of plaster off it. That made everyone laugh and put me in a better mood – oh, look out, here's that 1-2-2 off Knighton. Give me the road for it, please, Adrian.'

I got up from the chair to do this and when I got back Alec was telling Elwyn about a new anthem his choir was learning.

'A chap from up th' Atomic is our choirmaster,' Alec was saying. 'Thur's quite a few o' scientists in the village nowadays; he's very good but he makes us practise hard.'

'Thirsty work indeed,' sympathised Elwyn.

'Oh ah!' agreed Alec enthusiastically, 'but we've got a good system – when Doctor Smithers says "Just once more and we'll leave it for tonight", Charlie Ayres slips out of the church down to the North Star and gets the order set up for the whole choir so's we don't have to wait in a queue. I'll give you a bit o' this new tune when I've seen to the Down road.'

Over the telephone I heard the bell ringing from Foxhall and Alec's answering taps – four beats for the 10.30 p.m. Paddington. Trains, telephone calls and bells prevented him from singing and as midnight approached we still had not heard the anthem. At about four minutes to midnight the 9.55 p.m. Acton to Cardiff 'C'-headcode vacuum entered the Down goods loop at Foxhall. Over the telephone I heard the 'on line' boom out on Steventon's cow bell to signal this move followed immediately by four bells on the Main line bell between Foxhall and Steventon as Foxhall asked the road for the 10.30 Paddington sleeping car express.

Alec came back from the bells. 'Let's try to give you that tune now,' he said and started to sing in a pleasant tenor. He finished with his distinctive chuckle, 'All right, isn't it?' At that moment Foxhall sent 'on line' down the Main for the 10.30 Paddington. Alec then asked the road for the fast to Wally and Wally asked it to me. When I got back to the telephone Alec was singing again but a few seconds later he gave a dreadful yell, his telephone clattered to the floor, we heard six levers crashing into the frame as fast as he could throw them and then the dreaded, tolling beat of the 'Obstruction Danger', six bells, going out to Wantage Road and Foxhall Junction. Then a long silence.

Sitting peacefully in my armchair at Challow it was strangely frightening to hear this life-or-death activity going on over the telephone. I asked Elwyn what was happening, which was a useless thing to do, and we sat each in our own box listening intently on the telephone for some further clue. We could hear Alec speaking to the signalmen on each side of him over the special 'box to box' private line but we could not make out the words.

He came back to the bus line when he had finished his explanations on the other circuit. His first words were shaky and weak, ignoring my and Elwyn's inquiries. 'Lord that was close I'll be bound – the fast has stopped – but my Lord it must have been close.' He was hardly talking to us; he seemed far away, his voice a horrid whisper in contrast to his splendid tenor of two minutes earlier. 'Come onto the Control phone; you can listen in while I tell them the tale,' he said listlessly.

We heard him pour a cup of tea and he must have drunk half of if before the Controller answered the call. Alec was in an agony of impatience. 'Why the hell don't they have 999 calls on these things?'

'Twudn't make any difference if they did,' said Wally, 'them at Swindon still wouldn't answer.'

'Con-trol,' said a bland voice.

'Ah! About bloody time too. Steventon here. Now listen carefully. We'm off the road with the 9.55 Acton on the Down goods loop exit points. I don't know how bad it is because no one has come to the box yet. If no one don't come soon I'll go up there and look.'

'Can't you see from where you are then?' asked the young man at Swindon.

'Huh! I shouldn't think so,' snorted Alec contemptuously, 'it's pitch dark out here in the country, the loop's half a mile away and thur's a damn great bridge in the way. Now listen. The 10.30 Padd had gone by my distant showing "All Right" when I threw the boards back so they was going full belt when they got the red light. I think they must have pulled up though because I stood at my window and listened for the crash – and that was the longest minute of my life. I heard the diesel's horn blaring but nothing else so they must be all right but you'll probably have to divert everything round the Berks and Hants line. You'll need the breakdown vans and a pair of 45-ton cranes for the engine on the Acton.'

The driver and second man on the 'Warship'-hauled 10.30 Paddington owed their lives to Alec Abrahms that night. The Acton had gone down the loop as scheduled and ran parallel to the Down Main. When the Main line signals changed from red to green for the sleeping car train, the driver on the Acton must have had a lapse of memory. Anyhow, he took the green lights as applying to him and accelerated his engine, 6800 *Arlington Grange*. The guard at the rear of the train did not think it unusual to be travelling quite fast along the loop, as the locomotivemen often did this so as to have a few minutes standing at the loop exit signal in order to make a can of tea before resuming their non-stop run to Newport.

No one on the goods realised the true situation and the engine ran off the end of the loop, ploughing the cutting side for twenty yards before coming to a stand on its left side close to the bridge carrying the A34 road over the railway. The train of wagons simply ran amok, scattering across the other tracks and literally filling the arch of the bridge with splintered wreckage.

As 6800 passed the loop exit points she had operated the track circuit repeater in the signal box. This was an instrument of the old type with a red bar pivoting within a brass case. The bar dropped to a horizontal position to show 'Occupied' and made a faint but distinctive 'clunk' as it did so. Though Alec was singing he heard the sound and realised instantly that the goods must have run off the end of the loop and visualised the consequences to the 10.30 Paddington. If he had not heard the sound or if he had not reacted instantly to throw the signals to 'Danger', there would have been a fatal crash. As it was, the 'Warship' came to a stand only a few yards short of the wreckage.

No particular notice was taken of Alec's life-saving quick-wittedness, though he did receive a letter of thanks from a relatively lowly official.

CHAPTER NINE

Sunday Signal Box

Sunday day shift was utterly unlike any other shift. It had a unique atmosphere due either to the special work that was often carried out then or simply because of the sheer peacefulness of a country Sunday; nowhere was this more strongly felt than in a country signal box. When I came on duty at six o'clock on Sunday morning it was just eight hours since my last shift and I was tired. If there was not an engineering department work train requiring my attention I went to sleep in the armchair for an hour – the restorative effect of this being equal to three hours in bed – but if there was a ballast train or rail-loading train requiring to work in the section, there was no chance of sleep. I would organise the occupation of the line and off would go the train with the gang of men standing in open wagons, smoking and laughing as if it were midday but, unfortunately, the rules required that one man remained with me in the signal box as a reminder of the train's existence and this he invariably did – by talking non-stop.

At seven o'clock the first scheduled train of the day was asked up, and what a train – twenty-five empty coaches from Plymouth to Old Oak Common hauled by two 'Castles'. Whether I had slept or not during the preceding hour, the activity of signalling the train and the enjoyment of seeing it pass stimulated my appetite and I set about frying a large breakfast, the only meal in the twenty-one-day cycle of shifts that could be eaten in peace. For that reason it was an elaborate meal and all down the line from seven o'clock, signalmen stood at their electric stoves, turning eggs and chivvying sausages to fried perfection. Unless it was absolutely necessary, the telephone was not used between 7 a.m. and 9 a.m. and if it did ring during that sacred time the answering signalman might well forget his manners and instead of giving the name of his signal box, say sternly, 'It's breakfast time.'

After a leisurely meal I took my mug of tea to the window and leant out on the bar thoughtfully provided by a humane Great Western Railway. The silence over the tracks and fields seemed intense and the view lay utterly still to the horizons. Just outside the box a pair of rooks studiously patrolled the rails; over the goods shed jackdaws strutted on the wooden platform or swooped through the arch over the sidings up to their nests on the great beams while a starling, perched sixty feet up on the office chimney, gave his long, single-note whistle followed by a scolding cackle. The quiet of Sunday allowed the still air to carry birdsong across the fields and as I listened the sound perspective deepened, a lark's song became audible, further off the piping of a finch, the chorus grew until I thought I could hear the birdsong of the Vale down to the faintest cogitations of a wood pigeon.

Close by the box, on the cutting side, a briar sent out thorny parabolas, the curves filled with the webs of large-bodied spiders, brown and white mottled, clinging motionless to the centre of the web so still as to leave undisturbed rows of dewdrops on the threads, drops which were as clear as crystal, others blazing prismatically in the early morning sun. Across the meadow behind the box Petwick Farm showed its old white walls and red-tiled roofs among the elms. The flat, green middle distance seemed to be a forest of elm till rising ground two miles away showed green fields and tree-lined hedgerows, de Maureville's racehorse stables and, crowning the rise, ancient and grey, the tower of St Mary's, Childrey parish church. Beyond the village the high, beech-planted ridge of the Berkshire Downs formed a long, clean, clear horizon.

In the opposite direction, across six tracks, the station cottages were silent, wives having their once-a-week lie-in after seeing their husbands off on their Sunday overtime on the track, the children not yet out at play. There were, of course, the incorrigible early risers: Jimmy Titchener, the signal lampman for the district, who, having fed the pig he kept in a lineside sty, walked to the station's lamp hut to clean and trim Challow's signal lamps prior to walking out to each signal with a fresh lamp filled with paraffin with the wick adjusted to burn for another seven days; there was Albert Stanley taking an early morning stroll with his collie at his heels and a bucket over his arm going down to feed his chickens in their lineside run.

Having spent the preceding week on late turn I had become used to seeing a blaze of coloured lights above the car park of the Prince of Wales, especially on Saturday evening when the tight-packed mass of cars reflected tenfold the electric colours above. On a quiet Sunday morning the car park seemed more than just empty – it looked unnatural, as if some magic had been performed to evaporate the cars.

Having enjoyed the view and digested my breakfast I began the weekly polishing of the box. Everything, from the linoleum floor covering to the roof ties, was either waxed, blacked, burnished, brassoed or scrubbed. The wooden floor behind the levers was scrubbed with hot water and yellow soap till the planks were as white as a yacht's deck; the wooden cases of the telephones and signalling instruments shone; rows of brass or copper-cased repeaters flashed in the sun or glowed quietly in the shadows; red, blue, yellow and black levers rose from the blackberry-black, cast-iron sweeps, their tall steel handles like silver and their brass badges reflected in the glass-like floor. It was a splendid sight, equal to the beauty of a fine locomotive, and in keeping with the semi-military spirit of the railway where men worked for something more than merely a pay packet. One of the few things I do not remember clearly about those days was the amount of my wages as a Class 2 signalman; maybe they were £9 or £10 a week, about half what the men at Morris Motors were earning. I never heard of a signalman leaving the railway to work at Morris's.

At 10.45 the congregation began to arrive for a religious service in the old coach, Challow's church: Albert Stanley, his wife, her brother Bob Thatcher, Albert's sons Graham and Michael, Mr and Mrs Halford, Mrs Gardiner, widow of the Challow stationmaster who installed the coach, and her sister Miss Merritt. The Uffington Ganger, Butty Martin, his wife and visitors from the villages, two by two they filed along the road in front of the cottages and came down the path to the coach passing between the groves of broad beans and trellises of runner beans, the bright green foliage and scarlet blossoms contrasting with the sober Sunday-dark suits and dresses.

The group swirled around the porch built onto the coach for a moment before the people filed in, bending slightly to clear the doorway. The interior of the chapel/coach was in Spartan, scrubbed pine with pews to seat fifty at least and two harmoniums – the only concession to ornament being the exhortation 'Praise Ye The Lord', painted scroll-like in black all across the end wall. At eleven o'clock Michael Stanley struck up an introduction on one of the harmoniums and after a few bars the congregation broke into song, the music drifting, sweetly muffled, across to the signal box where I was busily rubbing brasso off the signal lever brasses.

When an engineering train's engine was parked anywhere near, I asked the crew to bring it under the windows of the signal box so I could give it a wipe over. On 25 October 1964 I finished early on the signal box and spent most of the day removing grey grime from 4959 *Purley Hall*, exposing green paint, copper and brass; kneeling on top of the boiler or standing on the running plate I was well within earshot of the bells and could reach them quickly by stepping off the engine into the signal box through an open window. The Didcot crew of 4959 were the last locomotivemen I saw using the firing shovel as a frying pan for bacon and eggs. After they had eaten, the driver dozed in my armchair while his fireman sat on the box window sill reading the *News of the World*, and I cleaned their engine to the accompaniment of Michael Stanley on the harmonium and the railway community's hymns.

Purley Hall was a condemned engine – officially scrapped – but because of the severe shortage of locomotives brought about by a too-enthusiastic scrapping of steam engines and a ridiculously high failure rate among the new diesels, 4959 was kept on at Didcot for light duties. The day after I cleaned her she was shunting parcel vans in Didcot station yard. Her driver was Clarence Benford, close to retirement after fifty years' footplate service, while his fireman was a young lad not long out of school. At 2.24 p.m., two minutes early on a fast schedule, the 1.15 p.m. Bristol to Paddington express arrived at Didcot – fifteen coaches hauled by a smart, two-tone green 'Brush' diesel. At 2.29 p.m., the guard waved his flag, the 2,750-hp engine revved, there was a flash of electric-blue fire and 2,750 horses disappeared in a puff of black smoke. Another traction motor controller failure, another vastly expensive electric motor burned out and the only substitute was *Purley Hall*.

The thirty-five-year-old scrap steam engine whose 'rating' no one had ever bothered to ascertain but which could be assessed confidently at 1,100 horses – rather brawnier than those used in diesels – backed onto the now useless lump of expensive modern technology while her young fireman began to build up a fire sufficient to move over 600 tons at express speed. He was interrupted in this work by the arrival of the second man off the diesel, anxious for his own 'final fling', who took the shovel from the disappointed schoolboy with the words, 'You'd better give me the shovel kid, 'cos we're gonna run 'em.'

With brasses and copper burnished *Purley Hall* set out on her swansong. Clarence and his new fireman used all their skill to coax her into express speed without running out of steam, as unprepared as she was heavily overloaded. The officially scrapped engine kept the train cruising at 65 mph and in one hour from Didcot – timed by stopwatch – the train came to a stand at Paddington. *Purley Hall* had taken five minutes longer than the diesel was allowed for the run. Two weeks later Clarence Benford retired; *Purley Hall* was finally withdrawn in January 1965, cut up in April and Clarence died at the end of the year.

On Sundays my dinner – invariably roast beef and Yorkshire pudding – was brought to the signal box by my father from our home in Childrey 2 ½ miles away. To prove the superiority of his driving over mine he poured gravy onto the plate and drove so swiftly that the meal was still hot when he handed it over yet not a drop of gravy had been spilt. Apple pie and custard followed. If the weather was fine he brought his own meal and after eating took a chair, sat down with his feet on the window sill and waited to see the ex-LNER B1 go by in its usual, helter-skelter way with the 9.30 a.m. (Sundays only) Sheffield to Swindon.

Taking meals to signalmen was not a new experience to him. In 1915, when he was ten, his mother took in a lodger, the signalman at Twyford West box and each day my father took the man a hot meal in the signal box. One afternoon, just as I had finished dealing with a succession of fasts during a 'bell code-a-minute' rush for half an hour, he asked, 'How many signal boxes are you dealing with through those bell codes?'

'Ashbury to Foxhall – six altogether.'

'And how far apart are those boxes?'

'About three miles, on average.'

'So every three miles or thereabouts a signalman looks at the train. That's once every three minutes of its journey.' He paused, thinking about it and then said, half to himself, 'I wonder how many passengers realise the extent to which they are *shepherded* along the line?' His remark has remained with me – especially now when, under modern signalling, trains run for thirty miles or more without any lineside supervision.

Occasionally on Sunday we had locomotive visitors from Swindon Works, engines out for a trial run – at least that is what the occupants of the footplate said when they arrived at Challow and asked to be crossed over to return to Swindon. But when, at 3.30 on a particularly fine afternoon, a smart new 'Hall' arrives with eight or ten fitters – at least I supposed they were fitters though there were some ten-year-olds amongst them – when an engine arrives so crammed that the driver is not visible then I think anyone would be justified to question the validity of the trip. But we were all doing it!

At about half past three my father went home and returned an hour later with Mother, tea and cake. If an engine was present she brought extra food for the driver, fireman and guard if there was one. The crew came into the box and sat on the wide sill at the west end, hip to hip, all ribaldry forgotten, shiny-topped hats on the floor between their coaly boots, their faces sooty below cap-band level, pink above. There they sat on their best behaviour stuffing down ham sandwiches while dirty cotton waste overflowed from their jacket pockets and their engine simmered under the window. 'Coo,' mumbled one driver, his mouth full of heavy-duty fruit cake, 'if I'd known it was going to be like this I'd have brought my nipper along.'

Mother could not drive a car and was nervous of learning but she had steam in her blood – her grandfather had been a driver on the Great Western in broad-gauge days – and she was not awed by any locomotive, however large it was. When tea was over the driver would gallantly offer to give rides on his engine, which we duly shunted across to the sidings. The longest was perhaps half a mile in length and it was a memorable sight to see a 'Hall' coming galloping down over the buckled tracks, Mother at the regulator, or to see her directly opposite the box wrestling the big lever of a '28' class engine into reverse and see her huge smile as she heaved up the regulator to send the engine storming back through the goods shed for the tenth time; and the driver trying to keep his balance against the acceleration of the engine whilst reaching for the regulator handle to correct its position.

She became so competent – or persuasive – that a driver who had met her a few times agreed to let her drive the engineering train as far as Uffington on its way home to Swindon. My father and I did not know where she had gone until Elwyn phoned to say that he had a lady engine driver in his box who was asking to be collected by the signalman at Challow. Such Arcadian pastimes were part and parcel of the steam-hauled railway and I'm quite sure that similar stories could be told of other parts of the old Great Western or Western Region system or indeed from any part of the country.

But we did do real railway work on many Sundays and a false impression would be created if I gave no account of that work.

Take the case of track renewal. A train conveying the relaying gang with their mess coach, steam crane, half a mile of new track in sixty-foot sections piled on long, flat wagons called ganes, and empty ganes to take away the used track sections, arrived at about 8 p.m. on Saturday night and shunted back into the sidings. On such a very heavy train the engine was usually a '28' class. Because one track was to be blocked by relaying until about 4 p.m. on Sunday the other track was temporarily converted to a single line over which both Up and Down trains would be permitted to run and four signalmen were posted to Challow to help operate the special working; three would be relief signalmen from Swindon, the fourth would usually be the off-duty signalman from Challow.

They were booked on duty at 10 p.m. on Saturday night for twelve hours and usually contrived to enter the box together having first congregated in the public bar of the Prince of Wales. At 10 p.m. they came noisily across the yard and clattered up the box stairs laughing and as good humoured as a crowd of schoolboys on an outing. There was a flurry of arms as overcoats were removed, food bags were hung up and they stood in a circle around the pot-bellied stove, warming their backsides and keeping the warmth off me.

Work began when Mr Millsom arrived in the box with the Engineering Department Inspector. They had been conferring outside as to the best way to go about the job in hand and now came in with the few brief instructions needed to set experienced, well-trained men to work. Mr Millsom's instructions reminded me of a Battalion Commander's tersely delivered orders before an attack. As Mr Millsom came into the room the signalmen greeted him with friendly respect even though some of the men had as much or more service than he – and Millsom had forty years to his credit. Traffic Department Inspectors were always 'Mr' to the signalmen, unlike the situation in the Locomotive Department where drivers and the inspectors would often or usually be on Christian name terms. We in Challow box would say 'Evening Mr Millsom' – one man went so far as to call him Sir – and Mr Millsom would reply with a dignified smile and a nod, 'Evening Bob – Sid ... Right then. Single-line working over the Down road from here to Uffington. Sid, you go with the crane and keep their jib out of trouble; there's a phone being rigged up now back here from the crane. Moody's running the wire now. Bob, you be Pilotman, Cyril and Ron on the crossover.' The box then became a bedlam of milling signalmen looking for equipment. 'Where's your single-line forms?' 'Got any more shots?' 'Where's the paraffin?' I attended to their wants and then turned to the Engineering Inspector's requirements concerning the re-marshalling of his train.

These routine operations had been well rehearsed over the years and took place with all the ease of a well-trained regiment, the railwaymen's confidence showing in the over-boisterous performance in the signal box. Indeed, when the weather was bad these engineering jobs became epics of their kind to be long remembered by the men who took part just as soldiers might remember some battle scene; certainly at such times there was a lot of mud.

I recollect an occasion one night when the Down Main at Challow was to be excavated to a depth of four feet in the vicinity of the ladder crossings west of the signal box. The chalky subsoil, impermeable to water, was to be scooped out and replaced with gravel. Work began, the Down track was lifted, a bulldozer was dismounted from a flat truck and this began to scrape the ballast away. And then the rain began. Looking from the signal box window through the rain-streaming glass the night scene might have been a battlefield. A row of paraffin pressure lamps showed the bulldozer brilliant yellow in a long narrow grave of its own making, churning its tracks helplessly. On the rim of the grave the gas light lit groups of men, shadowy, tired and dejected, holding waterproofs over their heads; Mr Millsom and the Engineering Inspector with rain pouring onto their shoulders from the brims of their trilby hats. In the end they had to bring the steam crane that had lifted the track sections to haul the bulldozer out of the mud, then the men had to shovel the filthy mud back into place before the track sections were re-laid pending better weather which would allow the job to be completed.

This reminds me of another relaying job attempted around the Didcot area where wooden-sleepered track, having ninety pounds to the yard rail, was to be replaced by concrete-sleepered track with 110 pounds to the yard rail. This job was somewhat in the future as far as the period of this book is concerned, around 1966 in fact, and rail-mounted cranes were becoming scarce as they were scrapped because they were not needed except at weekends on the principle dear to accountants that 'you can't afford to have expensive machinery which isn't in constant use'.

As an economy measure and to avoid the long wait for a spare rail-mounted crane, the Engineering Department decreed that a lorry-mounted crane could be used as the site of work was easily accessible from the road; the local inspector's objections that he feared the concrete-sleepered track sections would be too heavy for such a crane were swept aside. Starting late on Saturday night the work went ahead and the lorry-crane successfully lifted the wooden-sleepered track sections but almost broke its back when it came to lift the massive concrete-sleepered track – indeed it would have broken if the lift had been continued. So there were about twenty men with half a mile of track ripped up and lacking the means to re-lay it. The time was three o'clock in the morning, the wind was cold and the inspector felt very angry. So he telephoned his economy-minded boss – it was about 3.30 when he woke him – told him that the lorry-crane had all but folded up under the stress of lifting concrete track and asked if he had any bright ideas to save the situation as the Up Relief line of Western Region's busiest route had a half-mile gap in it.

'Take the track sections to pieces and lay them by hand,' suggested the boss.

'Not unless you want to ask for a blockade lasting till next Sunday,' countered the inspector.

'You could cut the sections in half and then the lorry would be able to lift them.'

'With hacksaws?' The inspector was incredulous.

'No, of course not,' snapped the boss. 'Use oxy-acetylene and we can weld the rail after.'

'Sorry, no oxy and anyhow it'd still take days to cut through this lot.' There was a pause as the boss struggled with his pride. 'Oh – re-lay the wooden sleepers and we'll re-lay the new stuff another day.'

'Fine,' said the inspector. 'Can we have a proper crane too?'

To begin single-line working (*see* Appendix 5) the first move was to 'Block Back' to Uffington on the Up Main by sending the 3-3 bell signal and to receive an acknowledgement. I could then turn the Up line indicator to 'Train on Line' and the engineering train was then entitled to reverse along the Up Main to the site of work. When it was a quarter of a mile beyond the crossover between the main lines the flagmen placed three 'shots' on the crown of the rail, widely spaced so that the train could not come forward without exploding them and they marked the position of the shots with two red lights, one facing each way. By day a red flag was used. Similar precautions were taken at Uffington to protect the crossover and the 'dead' road so that the engineers could wander up or down that line to their heart's content but were 'shut in' within the shots so the other trains were safe.

The Pilotman wore a red armband with his title embroidered upon it in white. He was in command of working trains over the single track; he made the ruling on which order the trains would take over it and was the guarantor of the security of the single line, for no train at all could enter upon it unless he was actually on the engine or had been on the engine and ordered the driver to pass through. The Pilotman travelled down to Uffington in the correct direction in the cab of a down train; he was not allowed to go to Uffington by car but he could walk through the section if he had to. At Uffington he checked that all proper precautions had been taken and then ordered the needle of the Up line indicator to be dropped from 'Train on Line' so that normal signalling routines could be observed even though trains were using the single line; Up trains would travel through to Challow over the Down line but they would be signalled on the Up line instruments and as many Up line signals as possible would be lowered for that train. With the 'taking off' of the Up line indicator needle single-line working was in operation.

The Pilotman had a very arduous job. I have twice seen relief signalmen faint from sheer exhaustion after twelve hours of climbing on and off engines, stumbling over the ballast to and from the signal box and constantly discussing the likely sequence of trains over the single-track section, scheming how best to arrange matters so as always to be at the right end of the section in order to meet a train. He and the District Inspector planned ahead, weighing up the timetable in theory and in practice, trying to decide what might happen when a certain train was running late on the Up line while another was approaching 'right time' on the Down line but had yet to call at Didcot where it had to wait for passengers off an Oxford line train. My contribution to the effort was to keep myself thoroughly informed of all train movements approaching Didcot and Swindon, telephoning back to Oxford, Reading, Chippenham, Badminton and Kemble and to feed the information to the Pilotman upon whom rested the ultimate responsibility for saying which train must stop and which could go.

For instance, the 1.50 a.m. Swindon came up ten minutes ahead of the TPO, while on the Down line a milk empties from Kensington was due to pass Didcot some time in front of the 1 a.m. Paddington sleeping car express. The 1.50 Swindon would arrive at Uffington a little before the Kensington arrived at Challow and a delay to either would 'hit' the following fast. A cautious Pilotman might ask for the 1.50 to be held at Swindon until the TPO had left but most men did not like to put trains out of course deliberately but to work with the timetable as it stood. In this case the 1.50 would run up to Uffington, cross over to the Down line and come through on the single track where it re-crossed to the Up Main and away.

This prevented any delay to the TPO, which, if held up, would result in a financial penalty to the 'Company' as the old hands often called British Railways. The Kensington would be turned down the Relief line at Wantage and the 1 a.m. Paddington would come down the Main so as to be first through the single line when the Royal Mail had come up. The Pilotman had therefore to be certain to be at Uffington to order the 1.50 Swindon through the single line and then to travel up on the Mail to Challow. Here he would dismount, come into the signal box to sign the register, then go outside and order the 1 a.m. through to Uffington. Whether or not he would travel down with the Kensington depended on the traffic situation – there was no point in going through to Uffington if the next train would be one arriving at Challow.

It is easy to see that if a train broke down or ran very late after the Pilotman had made his decision about which end of the single line to stand he could find himself stranded at the wrong end while a train waited for him at the other – never was the legendary crystal ball needed so much as during single-line working. To work his shift successfully was a matter of justifiable pride for him; indeed, we all shared some measure of pride in the arrangements and improvisations if all went well but if the job went wrong, even if through no fault of ours, then we felt our pride as signalmen hurt and went home feeling slightly dissatisfied.

Work was taken very seriously when occasion demanded and Sunday could be a day of skylarking or it could be twelve hours of telephoning, talking, strong tea drinking and, very often, tension.

CHAPTER TEN

Winter

On winter Saturdays, when the sun shone cold and thin over the Vale, the misty air was full of the sound of the Old Berks Hunt and its foxhounds. Perhaps twice during the season the Hunt met at Challow station when upwards of a hundred horsemen, women and children came riding into the space between the Prince of Wales pub and the railway line. From my vantage in the signal box at the far side of the line they made a handsome sight – the personification of the proverbial English understatement.

The riders were faultlessly turned out in black and cream, well mounted on silver-grey or leathery-brown chestnut horses whose hooves scraped, trampled and stamped, heads tossed and velvet nostrils snorted smoky breath, dragon-like, into the cold air as they milled about, their riders forming groups and breaking away when the morning's greeting or gossip had been exchanged. Drinks on trays were carried through the doors of the Prince of Wales to the riders who relaxed, leaning back in their saddles, one arm strut-like on their horse's back, enjoying a glass of whisky or port. At the centre of the clattering throng, in pink coats with red faces beneath black velvet caps, sat the Master – Lord Burghley, one-time Olympic champion hurdler for Britain, now stout and elderly – and his huntsmen. Their horses were tall and slightly 'heavy' and they stood hock deep in tan and white hounds, some sitting, some standing, pink tongues lolling from grinning mouths and thin rudders wagging as they hoped for a caress from an onlooker.

For three seasons, 1953–56, I rode with the Old Berks on a fast, grey pony, half Arab, half Connemara. I enjoyed the gallop, the jumping, the cavalry charge one hundred strong towards a gateway wide enough for two, I enjoyed the novelty of riding across country, which, though perfectly familiar by road, became unfamiliar on horseback across the plough until I came out at a well-known cottage or crossroads but I did not enjoy being hunted by my friends who wished to smear the bloody end of a recently amputated fox's foot on my face. I ceased riding to hounds when I joined the army and I left the 'sport' with considerable sympathy for the fox and utter scorn for the forty stupid dogs who chased him. If only Reynard had – just once – turned on them with his long teeth bared!

So it was that one grey November day in 1962, as the huntsmen played their exciting tunes on their copper horns in the fields to the west of the signal box, that I kept my eyes open for a glimpse of Reynard. I was hoping that he would use the railway line with its creosoted sleepers to hide his scent from the hounds. I was not disappointed.

He came from the west, orange-red against the dark brown sleepers, carrying his head low, tongue lolling out but not from tiredness for he was trotting easily; he knew exactly what he was about because not only was the creosote masking his scent while he remained on the track but he knew that it would still be on his feet when he eventually struck into the fields again probably making a large circle to put himself behind the hunt. Just before he passed the signal box he turned sharply to the south, crossed to my side of the line and scrambled up the bank of the shallow cutting within twenty feet of where I was standing at the window. He saw me only as he passed and checked momentarily, his head swinging sharply to stare and his telepathy reached out to me. 'Don't give us away, mate,' his eyes begged before he turned again and leaped to the top of the bank and disappeared. It was an encounter lasting a tenth of a second but no less powerful for that and I heard myself saying, 'Don't worry, I owe you a few favours.' He now had the scent-barring railway track between him and the hounds and I guessed he would be trotting back the way he had come, back behind the hunt. Clever creatures, foxes, when every man's hand is against them – every man's but mine! A few minutes later the hunt came galloping noisily along a lane close to the track opposite the box. I went to the front window and yelled, 'Gone away Denchworth, M'Lord!' pointing north towards that village. M'Lord graciously touched his cap with his hunting horn and galloped away to the north with the 'field' following eagerly behind.

I noticed – but luckily M'Lord did not – that up on the road bridge a figure was waving its arms like a demented semaphore signal; it was a foot follower, the bane of a hunted fox's life. The figure had obviously seen the westbound fox and was trying to attract the hunt's attention. As the last of the horsemen disappeared along the road a red-faced, white-moustached old gentleman in tweeds and a flat cap – the figure on the bridge I guessed – appeared on the other side of the line opposite the signal box.

'Hi – you up there!' he shouted. 'What the devil do you mean by distracting the hounds?' I would have loved to have told him that I was levelling the odds a little to favour small nations or solitary foxes – a truly English design – but I thought it would be better to imitate my friend the fox and disappear until the heat was off.

Subtle lines of distinction are drawn by all of us and though I wanted to help the oppressed fox I had no compunction in capturing Albert Stanley's turkey for his pot. Christmas 1962 was drawing near and the weather was icy. Albert, after working with the 'Fly', would come into the signal box, his breath blowing as white as his hair, his ruddy face redder from the cold. He rubbed his big hands together vigorously over the hot stove.

'Have some tea, Albert?'

'Ah, thanks, just a cup. Then I must check them wagons in and have a look at my turkeys. My word they are some fine birds – if you'll forgive me for saying so myself.' He beamed a proud smile.

Albert's satisfaction at having raised a brood of fine turkeys was infectious so that when I saw one of his carefully fattened fowls strutting busily along the Up Main line just as I was about to pull off for an Up fast I very nearly sent the 'Obstruction Danger' signal to Elwyn – 'Albert Stanley's turkey blocking line'. Realising that that would not look right in the block register and seeing the turkey still making its way determinedly along the Up Main I put the signals back, rushed out, captured the astonished bird and got back just in time to pull off and give the fast the back board.

The turkey displayed a commendable interest in signal boxes and 'gobble-gobbled' its way all round the floor, in and out of the levers, leaving messages for other turkeys that might come along, eventually found its way downstairs and went to roost in an empty cupboard. And there she might have stayed and become a pet to continue the tradition that locking rooms are also used as a chicken run, pigsty or stable for the signalman's horse. But, poor creature, she was already marked down as Albert's Christmas dinner. 'Thank goodness you caught her,' he said with real relief in his voice, 'that's my very best one.'

Country signal boxes often had pets; I knew of one down in Somerset that had a pet mouse but only for a short time. It used to run happily around the instrument shelf and sit on the bells while the signalman was ringing them but it grew too venturesome and was electrocuted on a bare wire while it was exploring the underside of the shelf. In 1905, Signalman Fowler at Filton Junction near Bristol had a tame rat. This rat waited for him at the foot of the box steps and followed him into the box like a dog – it even sat on its hind legs and begged for crusts of bread. But then came the time when the layout at Filton had to be greatly enlarged. Dozens of workmen came to the place, they saw the rat waiting patiently at the foot of the box steps for Mr Fowler and, not understanding the bonds of tender affection that had grown up between the man and the rat, the workmen attempted its murder with their shovels. The rat was always too quick for them but it pained Mr

Fowler to see his friend chased hither and thither by these brawny blokes and he racked his brains to find a way of protecting his intelligent friend from them. The course he took was devastatingly simple – he poisoned it. When the trusting animal had finally and, no doubt, painfully, succumbed to his protective ministrations, Mr Fowler took the beloved corpse to a taxidermist and directed that craftsman to restore the rat to its famous begging posture. The embalmed rodent was then put in a glass case and given the place of honour on the mantelpiece of Mr Fowler's best room.

But to return to winter at Challow box. During late November and early December 1962 the days were grey and misty and at night the fog was thick. The rule was that when fog had reduced visibility to 200 yards – there was a lamp post or some other marker, which, when obscured by fog, proved that the required density had been reached – we called the fogmen. The local permanent-way gang performed the fogging duty, starting at ten o'clock at night after a day on the track and signalmen were often reluctant to call their friends out unless their assistance was absolutely essential, when visibility was far less than 200 yards. To call men out on a filthy night just as they were going to bed required either a certain courage or a certain callousness.

At Challow I called the fogmen by rousing the 'callman', Bill Lamble, at the station cottages. He then alerted Bob Thatcher next door before cycling off to Stanford in the Vale to fetch the two fogmen. There were three semaphore distant signals to be 'shot' at Challow: the Up Main signal and two, side by side, for the Down Main and Down Relief lines. These signals had named fogmen – their names and addresses were posted in the signal box – and these men each had a named reliefman who took over after twelve hours.

One night of beastly fog I called Bill and then volunteered to drive to Stanford to bring back the fogmen because the road was deeply flooded at several places and quite clearly the men would have been soaked through before they started work, travelling as they did on bicycles. Driving at a crawl through the black murk, sweeping through the deep floods with a ship's bow-wave I arrived outside Jeff Betterton's tiny cottage. By the light of my headlamps I saw that the stream that trickled prettily through his front garden was now so swollen as to have flooded right inside his house. Fog, cold, darkness and floods – nothing could have been more miserable – and Jeff was already upstairs in bed. But he turned out in his bare feet and with his trousers rolled up to his knees, and with his boots and socks in his hands, he splashed through his living room and garden to my car. He had a towel round his neck and he dried himself and put on his footwear while I drove round for his mate. The fogmen signed on duty in the signal box register and then, with plenty of detonators and a lighted fogging hand-lamp they walked out to their signals. A fogging hand-lamp differed from a signal box hand-lamp in as much as it had an amber glass in addition to the usual red, green and clear glasses. At the distant signal they placed one detonator on the rail for as long as the distant signal showed 'Caution' and, should a train approach, the fogman gave an amber light from his hand-lamp, but when the arm dropped to 'All Right' the 'shot' was removed and the engine driver was shown a green light from the hand-lamp.

The fogman sheltered in a wooden sentry box about four feet square equipped with a tiny stove within or a larger brazier without. He sat on a plank in the hut that boasted a stable door arrangement and an electrical or mechanical repeater to show him the position of the arm so that he did not have to stand on the icy lineside for the entire twelve hours' duty in order to observe the movement of the signal.

Bill Lamble's job was to stand outside the signal box and 'spot' tail lamps on trains as they passed in case I missed them in the fog. Quite apart from the problem that arose when two trains passed outside the box, the murk was made thicker by the billowing exhaust of even one steam engine so that a tail lamp was almost invisible to Bill standing six feet from the track. If he or I failed to see a tail lamp I was bound to carry out the emergency regulations in case some part of that train had been left behind in the section and then huge delays would have taken place.

Bob Thatcher's job was to keep his men supplied with detonators, paraffin for lamps, hot fills for their flasks and coal for their fires from the signal box bunkers. It was for times like these that he maintained a wide, smooth footpath at the side of the line so that he could cycle his heavy, old bike in safety out to the signals, the best part of a mile from the box. He knew, of course, where the signal wires and point rodding crossed the path and could dismount at the right spot even in the foggy dark.

None of these men was young. Bob Thatcher was sixty-two in 1962, yet he had to patrol the track from one distant signal to the other – 3,000 yards – in the worst possible weather, and when he was sixty-two I was only twenty-one. I have been on night shift, warm in my well-lit signal box having called the fogmen out on duty and have felt ashamed when old Bob Thatcher came clumping up the stairs in his hobnailed boots, eyebrows stiff with ice, his eyes, rheumy at the best of times, bloodshot and watering in a face raw with the cold. I remember also that he always refused my offer of tea and cake with, 'No, thanks very much. I've only come in fer sum moar shots and a capful o' coal for Jeff's fire.'

I remember when the blizzards came late in 1962 and early 1963, how, night after night, the gang walked from one set of points to the next patiently sweeping them clear of driven snow. At times the snow was falling so thickly that all I could see from the box were the circles of brilliant white light where the flakes were flurrying around the incandescent mantles of the Tilley paraffin pressure lamps carried by the men. The Challow gang never came into the shelter of the box, though it was offered; they slogged on through each night to keep points and signals in working order and so it was all over the railway. What made Bob Thatcher and his gang the stout-hearted men they were? Cynics might say they were after overtime – if they were, they earned it in the hardest way possible. The fog ended suddenly on 17 November. That day dawned suspiciously bright, the sky a forget-me-not blue innocent of the smallest cloud. From the box windows that evening I watched the sun set behind White Horse Hill in a pale green sky while a single great star showed faintly and shone brighter as the horizon coloured to orange, through red to purple and eventually deepest black spattered with millions of blue or white stars like fires radiating ice. The night air was utterly still, the wet fields lay rigid under an intense frost – as low as 1 °F – and from within the warmth of the bright signal box my thoughts turned to the wild animals huddling in the frosted undergrowth.

The weather grew so cold that signal wires snapped, point rodding broke and, not surprisingly, there was an increase in the failure rate among the new diesels; even steam engines found themselves in difficulties. I was on night shift on 19/20 November 1962 when the points in the Down Main line at Highworth Junction leading to the Down goods loop failed – set for the loop. All trains then had to pass through the loop from there to Swindon Goods Yard box and the delay this caused was made worse because such through-running trains clashed with shunting movements between the sidings and the loop. Very soon a queue of trains built up from Shrivenham right back to the loop at Foxhall with four trains standing on the Down Relief line between Wantage Road and Challow.

I was able to tell the men on the two trains nearest, when they came in touch on the lineside telephones, that long delays could be expected and they came to the box for warmth and some fresh tea – always tea. The trains' guards remained in their respective vans, huddled around their stoves as the cold seeped in under the door and sank into their ankles. With the enginemen in the box it became a very friendly place, warm and well lit against the dark and bitter cold outside and the talk turned to other epic delays and of wartime incidents while outside the safety valves of an engine hissed. The noise gradually increased until it interfered with the conversation and the fireman was ordered by his driver to go and turn the feed on but that was a job I was happy to do while the fireman was more than willing to share his engine with me when the night was so cold and he was so comfortable.

For the crews of trains standing far out along the Down Relief line – at Circourt IBS and at Wantage Road's advanced starting signal – there was no chance of bright lights and a warm room. The best they could do was to take it in turns to doze on an upturned bucket in the corner of the cab while the other stood in front of the fire and peeped out occasionally to see if the signal had changed – this was especially necessary at Circourt's electric light signal; at least a semaphore arm gave a warning clatter when it was lowered. And there he stood, the seat of his pants scorching, the tip of his nose freezing as he gazed up silently over the tender coals to the starry sky and wondered, 'How long?' On a steam engine 1850 was never far away.

My visitors grew restless after twenty minutes' relative inactivity and asked whether there was any point in starting a card game – there being four enginemen present. I telephoned Shrivenham and asked if there was any likelihood of moving a goods train towards Swindon and was told there was no chance. The signalman at Marston West box had badly hurt his back when the point rodding broke as he was heaving over the Down loop to Down Main points and these were now set in that position. As a result all Down trains had to run through the loop from Marston East to Marston West in addition to the diversion at Highworth Junction. The enginemen got out a pack of cards.

The fasts, parcels, mails and vacuum goods trains continued to run uninterruptedly on the Up line and to pass more slowly on the Down line, crawling past the box to my advanced starting signal waiting their turn in a veritable traffic jam of trains. The card school played with the concentration of professional sharpers, oblivious to all around them and the air in the box thickened blue with their tobacco smoke. At about 1.30 a.m. on the 20th, Alec at Steventon telephoned with the news that the 12.45 a.m. Paddington to Carmarthen newspaper train – 'Warship' hauled – had failed in Sonning cutting three miles east of Reading and that no spare engine was available to rescue it because Reading's steam 'Pilot' and the standby engine at Didcot had both been used on earlier diesel failures. I told the card school, who groaned without taking their eyes off their cards.

No more than five minutes later Swindon West box telephoned to say that a train for Gloucester, 'Hymek' hauled, had become derailed as it crossed the Main lines to the branch and was blocking all but the Up platform line so that the entire traffic to and from Bristol, South Wales and Cheltenham was restricted to using that one track. I told the card school, they groaned again, found time to observe 'what a bloody railway' and bent to their game once more.

After a two-hour delay, Reading's station 'Pilot', a 'Castle', returned from hauling the earlier diesel failure and was sent out to the 12.45 waiting resignedly in Sonning Cutting. The very fast 2.15 a.m. Paddington to Bristol newspaper train ran past the 12.45 by means of the Down Relief line, returned to the Down Main at Reading and headed west at 90 mph behind its 'Warship' diesel. All went well until it turned its blunt nose into the loop at Marston East; perhaps it was the indignity of being out into a goods loop but the 'Warship' simply stopped on the loop points, blocking the crossover points through which a rescuing engine might have come and completely closing the Down Main line.

I made the announcement to the card school where they sat entrenched behind half-empty mugs of tea and piles of stubbed-out fags: 'Gentlemen, British Railways regrets ... the 12.45's failed at Sonning, the loop points are broken at Marston and Highworth, the station's all but stopped at Swindon and the 2.15's a failure at Marston – you're here for the night.' Their heads came up slowly, their looks showed utter disbelief and the oldest man spoke for all of them: 'The bloody Luftwaffe never bloody closed us down – bloody engines used to go then, not stop.'

The intense cold may have had an adverse effect on the rate of diesel failures or it may have been that there were more trains scheduled for diesel haulage and therefore greater opportunities for failure; the last scheduled steam-hauled express through Challow had been dieselised on 5 November 1962*. The records I could make of the trains' running whilst in duty were always incomplete due to pressure of work but on 12, 17 and 18 December (*see* Appendix 6) I noted six express trains hauled – and hauled fast – by 'Castles' during my eight-hour shift.

This had been the pattern throughout 1962. In particular I remember the fast, eight-coach 2.55 p.m. Paddington, booked for a 'Hymek', which ran down regularly behind a 'Castle', 5056 *Earl of Powis* being a star performer picking up time on a very fast schedule. Soon after the hard weather arrived the railway began to build up its services for the traditional Christmas 'rush' – extra passenger trains and of course the service of parcel post specials, which were so numerous between 12 and 21 December as to require a thirty-two-page supplementary timetable. Dr Beeching, in his report *The Re-Shaping of British Railways*, promised to 'damp down the seasonal peaks' but that was in the future and in 1962 we were still carrying our traditional traffic – luckily we still had a fleet of steam engines to haul it.

---

*   This was the 8 a.m. Cheltenham/5 p.m. Paddington Cheltenham Spa Express.

To be at work in Challow box during the Christmas season 1962 was a memorable privilege and I was lucky enough to work the busiest shift (2 p.m. – 10 p.m.) during Christmas week. Regular expresses and extras, goods and parcel post trains all clamoured for their paths; every locomotive that could turn a wheel was at work; inevitably some of the steam engines were not in good shape and 'ran rough' with their heavy trains; some of the diesels failed; at Challow trains queued on the Relief lines; phones rang incessantly as inquiries went to and fro; signal bells clanged; levers crashed; whistles blew and hard-working exhausts played their familiar rhythms while they enveloped the box windows in smoke.

It was difficult to keep a record of the trains beyond what was required for the train register but on 21 December with ten trains an hour passing the box I managed a partial record (*see* Appendix 7).

On 19 January 1963, I rode from Swindon to Bristol on the engine of the 5.5 a.m. Paddington parcels, returning on the same engine with the 11.45 a.m. Dr Day's Sidings to Old Oak Common parcels. I finished work in the box at 6 a.m. and drove through the freezing dark along ice-rutted, snow-lined roads to Swindon station. It was dark, slushy and miserably cold around the station and my enginemen friends were sheltering in the porters' room, huddled around the fire, drinking tea. It was eight o'clock before our train arrived behind 4924 *Eydon Hall*, I climbed aboard with my Swindon mates and after the briefest of formalities the Old Oak men bolted for the refreshment room.

We left Swindon after the vans had been unloaded but still with 400 tons behind the tender. Reg, the driver, was wearing an old but very substantial GWR overcoat – the company roundels were still on its lapels, under which he had his jacket and overalls; he also had his shiny-top black cap, a thick scarf around his neck and wads of newspaper around his legs from his knees to his heavy black boots. 'Top People' might read it but Reg was wearing it. Ivor, his fireman, was dressed in overall jacket and trousers and attempted to keep the worst of the draughts out by clamping his trouser legs around his ankles with cycling clips. I was well wrapped up and rode in the front corner of the cab, leaning against the firebox for the slight warmth that penetrated its lagging. Reg, forty years older than me, was standing close to the gap between the engine and the tender receiving the full force of the numbing wind.

It was an eerie journey. A thin mist, which might have been formed of ice crystals, hung throughout the air, and beyond the green boiler and copper-capped chimney – the engine was well polished – the cold steel rails tapered forwards into nothingness; earth and sky merged uniformly into a foggy grey. Dark splodges showed where lineside trees or houses stood but signal arms were lurid red against the blankness. A signal box was first a blur, then a building, which coloured briefly as it came out of the murk and was then immediately swallowed in a cloud of driven snow and billowing white exhaust. Sound was muffled by the hard-packed snow between and around the rails so that our wheels drummed dully, almost silently, on a cloud of ice through a landless waste. The brightest things were the engine's fire and the strident ringing of the Automatic Train Control bell as we approached each distant signal.

I left Reg and Ivor at Bristol station, after arranging to meet them at Dr Day's Sidings, and went to visit the Swindon area Traffic Controller, Cyril Matthews, in his office in what had once been the headquarters of the Bristol & Exeter Railway. His office was a large room holding a dozen tables each carrying a compact telephone switchboard behind which sat a Controller and his assistant. The freezing cold, the hard work, the sheer physical contact of railway work as I knew it was translated here into terms of telephones, warmth, bright lights, scribbling pencils, scratching heads, sweaty shirts and frustration. Control was trying to keep the railway flowing when it was in dire danger of freezing solid.

It was not the time for pleasant banter. I was given a cup of tea and told to keep out of the way. What a tape recording might have been made in that office that morning! Cyril was in a fair way to grow a cauliflower ear from the constant pressure of the telephone, his desk was littered with scribbled notes and as fast as he answered calls he had to make further calls while all the time flashing lights on his switchboard indicated that his area was full of woe. I could imagine the swearing and gnashing of teeth that lay behind those little flashing lights as men waited to send in their quota of calamity – diesels were failing, points were frozen, empty coaches could not be removed from their sidings, men had not arrived for work; from Cardiff, for example, it was reported that men had to crawl on their hands and knees on steep, icy hills in order to get to the engine shed.

I began to wonder if I would be stranded at Bristol and comforted myself with the fact that at least I was not required until ten that evening. And that was just as well. At 9.35 a.m. the 8.50 a.m. Taunton to Paddington 'Warship'-hauled express arrived at Bristol and promptly failed. There was no spare engine available and fitters from the engine shed spent an hour putting the diesel right so that the train left sixty-five minutes late at 10.45. Traffic had built up behind it and the train would have been cancelled and towed out of the way but for the need to get coaches up to Paddington where there was a desperate shortage that was affecting the departure of Down trains.

So the Taunton went on its way. Twenty minutes later Cyril received a call from the signalman at Bathampton, five miles east of Bath: '8.50

Taunton's a failure here, you'll have to get us a fresh engine. The London road'll be blocked till you move it.'

'You'll be lucky,' said Cyril, 'we haven't got a spare engine. Put the following fasts around the junction to Bradford-on-Avon and back to Chippenham that way.'

'Can't do that,' replied the signalman. 'The junction round to Bradford is blocked by the Taunton. The engine's a stone-dead failure; they only got here by coasting and it stopped right on the junction.'

Later that month I went out with Didcot men with 6833 *Calcot Grange* hauling the Paddington to Shrewsbury parcels – the 'Salop'. I was allowed to shovel coal down to Banbury where we were relieved by Birmingham men and we went down to the shed to prepare an engine for the run home with a goods train. The shed foreman gave us the engine number – 48410, an ex-LMS heavy freight engine – and we trudged off into an evening of arctic cold to find her. The engine was standing among a dozen, their fresh fires making yellow smoke ooze sluggishly over the brims of their chimneys. The electric lights in the yard barely reached the wheels and valve gear, which had to be oiled; all was gloom – oily, icy, gritty gloom. The driver lit his flare lamp – a device like an oil can with a wick in its spout – which produced an orange flame that tapered to black smoke, the three of us screwed our determination to concert pitch and set about preparing the uncompromising hulk into a runnable steam engine. Smoke-box and ash-pan were checked and cleared of 'the products of combustion', the fire built up, tools gathered, oil cups filled till preparation was complete and we took 48410 to the water column. In freezing weather each column was supposed to be heated by a pot-bellied stove standing on four legs with a tall chimney ending in an 'H' under the swinging arm of the column close to its pivot on the upright pillar. Railwaymen called them 'devils'; our column did not have one.

We swung the arm and put the bag into the tender. Four thousand gallons of water rumbled into the tank and some of it trickled back, unseen in the darkness, to the pivot where it froze solid. When we came to swing the arm away it would not budge. We chipped at the ice with coal picks but the water had entered the pivot beyond the reach of the pick; we wrapped oily cotton waste around the top of the column and then set fire to it. That did no good. In desperation we tried to push the arm aside with the locomotive and only noticed at the last second that we were uprooting the entire column. The engine was trapped by the arm of the column standing across the track with the bag in our tank. There was nothing for it but to declare the engine a failure and start the preparation of yet another engine. We were very, very late into bed that night.

CHAPTER ELEVEN

Night Driving

Enginemen needed tea, strong tea made by tipping leaves and sugar into a can with cold water and bringing it to the boil on the firing shovel in the furnace. They obtained their water from the signal boxes if they could or from the engine's tender in dire emergencies. Challow box was like a drivers' canteen sometimes as men off waiting goods trains came in for water for their vile brews. If they had time they boiled the water on our electric ring and poured in tea and sugar from a little tin with two compartments and lids at each end. They had little time for a signalman's genteel brew, which they sometimes referred to as 'gnat's piss tea' while their own concoction was undrinkable anywhere except on the dusty, battering footplate.

Not every driver stopping his train at 57 signal was looking for water; occasionally a man's thirst demanded something stronger and then, instead of an irate voice on the telephone demanding to know 'How much longer be you a-goin' to kip I yur?' there would be a conciliatory 'Have I got time to go for a pint, please, Bobby? I'll leave my mate on the engine so's he can blow the whistle for me and get the train started when you pulls the board off.' Always quick to see an excuse to get up on an engine and to assist my hard-working colleagues I would reply, 'Bring your train down to the box; it'll be less distance for you to walk to the Prince and you can both go – I'll blow the whistle when I need you.'

In the summer, when there would be seats outside the Prince, it was lovely to get up on the engine and reach for the whistle chain whilst watching the overalled enginemen leaning back, relaxed, in their chairs as they quaffed the nut-brown brew – lovely to see them galvanised into action by the whistle, running towards the engine wiping their frothy mouths and belching uncomfortably. I must have enhanced the trade of the Prince of Wales by pounds and fully expected the place to be renamed the Silent Whistle as a mark of respect when the old way died, but it remained, ungratefully, the Prince of Wales.

Co-operation on this scale was rewarded by footplate rides. An ever-boiling kettle was the only pass I needed and my footplate trips ranged from Bristol to Bletchley, Banbury to Basingstoke. Great Western steam engines were friends, familiar faces, to me. I had played on or around them for as long as I could remember and I felt for them a real loyalty and affection. Whilst it rarely occurred to me that as a signalman I was an endangered species I was well aware of the impending fate of my beloved steam engines and so I spent as much time with them as I could.

It was a thirst for knowledge that brought a certain driver into Challow box one afternoon when I was on duty. He was driving the 3.30 p.m. Oxford (Hinksey Yard) to Swindon 'C'-headcode vacuum which Wally at Wantage Road turned into the Down Relief line, as booked, to clear the Down Main for the 2.55 and 3 p.m. Paddington fasts. I pulled 57 and 56 signals to bring the engine under the signal box windows and soon 70042 *Lord Roberts*, a 'Britannia' class pacific was blowing steam into my open window.

The driver looked up from his seat. 'Will we be long?' he asked.

'About twenty minutes.'

'I'm taking the signalling exam soon ready for the time when I put in for a foreman's job but some of it in the book of regulations is difficult to follow. I'd like to come up there so's you could explain a few things to me.'

'Only if you'll give me some lessons on how your engine works,' I replied.

'That's a deal then,' he said with a grin.

He was about forty years old, with strong features; a hawk-like noise, bushy eyebrows over clear blue eyes. He wore his shiny-topped cap jauntily, smoked a pipe and was quietly spoken in the accents of Ebbw Vale. Obviously he was very keen on his job but I soon discovered that he was always ready to get some fun out of it too. His name was Don Kingdom; we were friends from our first meeting and are still good friends today.

I explained some puzzles to him while the two fasts went down and then it was time for him to leave. The previous train off the Down Relief line had been a 'Brush' diesel running light, which had cleared Uffington 2 ½ miles away in three minutes and covered the next 4 ½ miles in even time. That was then a startling performance and, feeling somewhat jealous of the diesel's easy speed, I asked Don if he could equal it with *Lord Roberts* hauling twelve empty four-wheel vans. 'Just make sure the gates at Knighton and Ashbury are out of my way and I'll show you,' he said, 'and tell them to look out for me on the 9.30 Swindon tonight. I'll want a clear road.'

'I'll see to it,' I said, 'and I've got a tape-recorder with me so make plenty of noise and I'll play it back to you when I see you tomorrow.' The signals were off all down the line to Ashbury before Don left and with a clear road assured he unleashed his big pacific and equalled the diesel's times.

He came back with a train of twenty-five small vans loaded with car-body parts weighing in all about 250 tons. Approaching Challow out of the dusk the engine was barely visible, the exhaust trailing back over the train, flying like red hair where it caught the firelight, the headlamps flickering yellow with the engine's vibration.

A quarter of a mile from the box Don opened the howling Yankee whistle and kept it open till he passed the station, the engine's deep, rapid thudding playing bass to the whistle's spine-tingling crescendo, wailing into the darkness to be replaced by the insane jangling of the box vans dancing on the rails. I watched in awe as the guard's van, shaking rapidly from side to side, disappeared into a cloud of steam swirling darkly around the station buildings. The guard must have been lying on the floor to save himself from being thrown around the van like a pea in a drum. Next day Don came down with 70053 *Moray Firth*, running light and well ahead of time so that Wally let the engine go down the Main. I wound the hurdy-gurdy and brought the engine to a stand on the Relief line by the signal box. 'You managed to get back to Oxford safely last night then,' I said. 'Come up here and hear what you sounded like.'

'Do you want to park the engine?'

'What's wrong with leaving it there?'

'I want some signal box practice and you can have some driving practice. I'll leave my mate on the engine – put it over in the goods shed; that'll be more lever pulling for me and more driving for you.'

I got back to the box safely and played the tape. He listened appreciatively with his head cocked and pipe poised in mid-air. 'Going well, weren't we,' he said.

'You're still half a mile away there – listen.' The train came closer and his face began to change, his pipe was in his pocket by the time the whistle howled and he was sitting with his face in his hands as the last van roared past. 'Phew! Someone ought to put a speed limit on short wheel-base stock,' he said in a hushed voice.

Don's shifts usually occurred when I was off duty so I was able to go on his engines frequently. He had a morning run out to Witney one week when I was on from 2 p.m. to 10 p.m. so on Monday morning I drove over to Oxford shed and was told I was fireman for the day. 'My mate's gone shopping in the town,' explained Don. 'He'll come out to Witney later and relieve you to get back to Challow for late turn.'

We set off from the shed with our pannier tank, ran down the loop through Port Meadow, following the canal to Wolvercote Junction, turned left onto the Worcester line and climbed up the curve to Yarnton Junction where we picked up the wooden staff for the Witney line. Left again, downhill onto that ancient byway which had nearly become the London & North Western's route from Euston to Cheltenham between 1860 and 1864. We glimpsed the grey spires of village churches through clumps of green willow, opened the crossing gates at Eynsham, the guard and I stopping cars on the main road while Don drove the engine across, stopped for a chat with the little old rosy-faced gnome of a crossing-keeper at South Leigh. Only as we were approaching Witney did Don suddenly say, 'Hey – how are you going to get home from Witney?'

'By car,' I said, and only then realised that my car was back at Oxford.

'Aha! That's clever,' laughed Don, 'we never thought of that. And how is my mate going to get his motorbike back from Witney after he's driven out here? It's far too big to lift.'

The realisation that I was stranded at Witney and the thought of Jim Spinage's comments when he was not relieved on time did rather take the gloss off being allowed to shunt the engine around Witney goods yard and when the fireman had not arrived by noon I was distinctly alarmed. We had our train formed and had backed into the disused passenger station for water before we heard the roar of the motorbike's powerful engine in the yard. The problem had already occurred to the fireman and the only way out of it was for him to drive me to Oxford, for me to take him back to Witney and then for me to drive straight to work without any dinner. Don would have plenty of time for his food – and a pint, as he was quick to point out.

The round trip from Witney to Oxford was thirty miles at least and included the difficulty of getting across the traffic-jammed city to the station where I had left my car. The fireman wound up his bike, we tonned it along the A40 and seconds after entering Oxford's 30 mph limit on Woodstock Road we were stopped for speeding. We got away with a lecture on breaking the law and skiving off work but we had no time to argue, only 'Yes Constable' and 'No Constable', while we lost time that had to be made up in my 1934 vintage car at the risk of another constabulary interview. Petrol was 3s 6d (17 ½ p) a gallon. 'Burn-ups' were cheap.

On another occasion I was driving through Abingdon and, seeing steam rising from the station, went to investigate. I found Don, his fireman and guard sharing tea in the disused signal box while their tank engine stood outside hissing like an iron pony – as cheerful a group as could ever be met. After drinking a tea-can lid full of their disgusting orange brew, sticky with sugar and thick with leaves that I strained through my teeth, Don announced that it was time to go shunting and offered me the engine. We trooped out of the signal box, spitting tea leaves, and took up our positions – the fireman assisting the guard with the ground point levers, Don acting as my fireman.

The men working in a coal tub stopped when they saw shunting begin, closed the flap of the wagon and took seats on top of it, facing the engine, legs dangling down outside. They were unconsciously paying tribute to the skill of previous drivers to sit so trustfully on that narrow perch ten feet above the ground as my engine approached – but then they did not know I was driving. 'Look out for those men, you're going too fast!' cried Don.

Wham! Too late. Six legs flew up and over as the three men did a back somersault into the wagon. Don leant against the cab helpless with laughter but I was scared – I might have maimed them and if I had not then they would shortly be arriving to maim me. But nothing happened; there must have been plenty of coal in the truck so that they did not fall far.

I finished shunting the yard, formed up a train of loaded car-flats and empty coal tubs and set off for the Main line at Radley. I expected to give the engine up there but when the board came off for us to go out from the branch to the Down Relief line Don said, 'Make the firedroppers happy – open her up and throw the fire out, she's finished for the day, boiler wash-out in the morning.' It was the best sort of invitation and we made a storming start with the car-flats – coaches without their bodies – pouring out across the points in a flowing, serpentine 'S'.

The train was berthed in Hinksey yard and then, with Don standing so close that no one would see me driving, I took the engine up through the station and onto the shed. We left her secure over an ashpit – handbrake on, steam cocks open, boiler full and valves in mid-gear.

'How are you going to get back to your car?' asked Don as we walked to the office.

'Thumb a lift, I suppose.'

'Don't be daft – wait till I've booked off and I'll drive you out in my car.' All I could say was 'Thanks, Don', which sounded utterly inadequate response for his enormous kindness.

I arranged to go with him on the 1.25 p.m. (Saturdays only) Oxford to Worcester all stations returning non-stop with the fast, 6 p.m. Worcester parcels and arrived on Oxford station in clean, pressed overalls and a silly green hat that I affected at that time. The train was standing in 'Binsey' bay platform, just two coaches with a shiny 'Hall' on the front. There was no sign of Don or his fireman so I climbed aboard and pretended I was in charge.

A few moments later a contingent from the Oxford University Railway Society arrived to travel on the train and one of the party had a headboard under his arm. In my clean overalls and silly hat they took me for an inspector and approached *very* respectfully. 'May we please put our Society headboard on the front of the engine, please, sir?' I acted the part of the stern inspector and examined the board very carefully till I finally unbent and granted them the great privilege – hoping all the time that Don would not object. He came back from the refreshment room with a can of reasonable tea in consideration of my presence. He went to inspect the board and was so impressed that he had to take the pipe from his mouth and step back a pace or two the better to admire its green and gold legend surrounding the university arms in blue, white and red.

We set off, the slowest passenger train on Western Region, our only passengers the students, under the gantries, past the signal boxes and smoky engine shed, over the clattering junctions and away, beyond Yarnton, into the Forest of Wychwood. It was a perfect afternoon for leaning over a cabside to enjoy the view and the sound of the engine; we ambled between stone-walled meadows and ploughed land, past beech plantations and fragments of the old oak forest to call at tiny stations – Finstock Halt above the river Evenlode, Charlbury, Ascott under Wychwood, Adlestrop, Moreton in the Marsh and Campden.

As we ran into Charlbury, Don told us about an incident that began there many years before when he was firing a goods train to Cheltenham via Kingham. Signals brought the train to a stand and the signalman informed them that though he had received 'Train out of Section' for the last Down fast he could not get any reply when asking the road for the goods and so he was authorising Don and his mate to pass the starting signal at 'Danger' and run cautiously down to Ascott to see what was wrong. The driver brought the train to a stand at Ascott's home signal within inches of the level crossing gates. The signal box was just on the other side of the lane and it was empty. Don's mate blew the whistle loud and long but not even a porter appeared. Don told us, 'The whole place was deserted. It was really creepy – like the *Marie Celeste*.' Don's mate blew the whistle again and soon they saw the signalman running along the lane from the village.

'What's going on?' demanded the driver. 'Why aren't you in the box?'

'I'm very sorry, drive,' said the signalman, 'there's a real needle match going on here today and I forgot about you – thought I had half an hour after the last fast. Sorry.'

But that wasn't the whole story as Don and his mate discovered some time later. The signalman went to the football match and on the touchline met his off-duty mate. Soon they were absorbed in the game so that the sound of furious whistling percolated only slowly into their consciousness. 'Albert's having some trouble down at the box-hark at that whistling,' remarked the signalman casually, his eyes following the flight of the ball.

'No, it wouldn't be Albert,' replied his mate, 'he's playing – look, there he is.'

'Ah, must be a reliefman then,' said the signalman.

His mate went through a mental list of the local reliefmen and placed each one off duty or named the box he was working. 'It's you!' he exclaimed. 'You're the Bobby – you'd better get down there quick.'

As Don finished the tale our train guard came bustling up. 'Hey – come on Don, "Right Away"! Didn't you hear my whistle?' We burst out laughing at that and the poor guard, not understanding or knowing what Don had just been saying, went off in a huff thinking we had been teasing him by ignoring his signals.

At Moreton the train was back shunted to the refuge siding for ninety minutes and to while away the time we did what all locomotivemen did – we went for a stroll around the town. Don, his fireman and I, as a sooty trio, have window shopped in Worcester, Bicester and Reading – once at 3 a.m. we were taken back to Reading station from the town under a guard of two suspicious policemen – and on that Saturday afternoon we sauntered around the stone elegance of Moreton eating chocolate éclairs and listening to Don's tales. I recollect a highly improbable one about a mad bull on the track which stopped a train and nearly killed the fireman and a just credible story about an RAF officer who, late one night during the war, had hitched a ride from Paddington to Oxford on the locomotive Don was firing. The man had a very rough dirty trip and a few days later Don and his mate were subjected to a low-level mock bombing attack by a Lancaster bomber, piloted, Don felt certain, by the same RAF man.

Don worked the 6.40 a.m. Oxford to Bletchley parcels, always with an LMS 'Black 5'. The job occurred for him when I was working night shift so there was a mad dash in my car after finishing at 6 a.m. at Challow to arrive at Oxford station before 6.40. The fireman left the fire for me to attend to but as I never arrived until departure time – in fact, I would warn the signalman in Oxford Station North box not to pull off for the train till they saw me coming, so that the signals were being lowered as I ran along the platform – the train left with a low fire. We were thus within an ounce of stopping for steam on the bank up from Port Meadow to Wolvercote tunnel; 150 psi in the boiler and Don shouting sarcastically, 'Come on, give me steam, the brakes are dragging on the train.'

It was a favourite run because it was over a 'foreign' route, a tentacle of the London & North Western Railway – LMS since 1921. The track ran parallel to the Great Western for two miles out of Oxford before climbing away, up to the short tunnel at Wolvercote and once through this rabbit hole I felt I was in a different world. The first signal box after the tunnel was a ghastly brick monstrosity; all the signals raised their arms to show 'All Right'; the station architecture and the very countryside was quite different to the familiar 'Western' territory.

The line had an air of mystery, running for miles through nothing but hedged and tree-lined field, past strange little wooden stations such as Marsh Gibbon & Poundon, built to serve two villages yet with hardly one house in sight. Lonely-looking railways crossed over our tracks, arrowing emptily north and south – the Great Western's 'New Line' from Banbury to Paddington and the Great Central's Sheffield to Marylebone line at Calvert whence a spur curved down to our rails at 'Claydon LNER Junction', the box still carrying its pre-nationalisation name board.

Verney Junction fascinated me with its sad ruins of former glorious industry. Lost in the remote fields near the Claydon river this was where the LNWR Banbury and Buckingham branch once curved in from the north, and the Metropolitan Railway, far from its usual underground electric haunts, curved away southbound for London. Both branches were grass grown but parts of the Met's extensive layout remained – the smashed signal box and the briar-choked, rusty turntable. Whenever I passed I paid my respects to these ghosts and tried to imagine the scene – once upon a time – when glossy black North Western engines and the Metropolitan's maroon stood side by side in Buckinghamshire fields and when you might have travelled from Banbury (Merton Street) to London (Baker Street) with a breakfast car express from Verney.

When Don was working the 9.15 p.m. fish train from Oxford to Basingstoke I often took the entire week off from Challow box and went with him each night. His fireman at that time was a Scot whom we labelled 'Jock' without asking his real name but he bore the imposition patiently – as an Irishman must, stamped 'Paddy', by unthinking Englishmen. 'Jock' always travelled with the guard in a comfortable, passenger stock, brake van leaving the footplate to Don and me.

The 'Fish' was hauled by an ex-Southern Railway 'West Country' class pacific, which had worked into Oxford on a passenger train from

Bournemouth. These were modern engines; the cab was huge like a fire-lit cave and seemingly full of gadgets after the broad-gauge simplicity of a Great Western cab. The firebox seemed to be ten feet wide, and there were two boiler gauge glasses, a lot of untidy pipe work and left-hand drive for the driver. The firehole was raised well above the footplate floor as was the shovelling plate on the tender; there was no need to bend double firing these monsters, which was just as well considering the area of the firegrate.

On my first trip ever with one of these engines – 34036 *Westward Ho* – I was looking about when I became conscious of a small, continuous whine and asked what it was.

'There's a steam turbine under the footplate,' said Don, 'and it's generating current for the engine's headlights and for the lights in the cab. I don't know a lot about these things but if we can find the regulator we'll be all right.'

I watched the South box signalman moving about his work and saw him pull over two levers. Before he had pulled the second Don called cheerfully 'Right Away', turned the brake handle and tugged gently on the regulator, leaning forward from a seat of padded luxury instead of standing as he would have done on a Western engine.

Two hundred yards away, on my side of the line, the starting signal was showing green over the amber light of Hinksey North's distant signal. The engine rolled downhill past Oxford Station South box, the signalman leaning out, his face invisible with the light behind him. Suddenly the amber light ahead turned to green – green over green in the dark. '"Right Away", Hinksey North, Don,' I called. The signal was obscured to his vision by the long boiler. He opened the regulator wider and the exhaust began to snuffle from the wide chimney, six beats per turn of the driving wheels. I was accustomed to a crashing Swindon exhaust making four beats to the bar; the 'West Country's' light, shuffling sound, like sandpaper rubbed briskly on wood, was misleading and odd; the extra rapid beat gave an erroneous impression of speed and the gentleness of the sound belied the enormous power of the engine. I sat watching the signals until I saw the double green at Hinksey South; Kennington Junction's distant signal was cleared beneath Hinksey South's home; we were signalled through Oxford's last junction and I turned my attention to the fire. 'Put a bit round now,' said Don, 'in the back corners and all across the back about two feet wide up level with the doors. Don't throw it down the front, just let it roll down as the engine shakes it.' I distributed half a ton and sat down.

Travelling by night on the footplate was a completely different experience to daytime travel. The train and its crew rumbled through black space cut off from the world in their fire-lit cab; a man walking the midnight lanes might hear the ringing rhythm of the locomotive and see its trace of fiery smoke but nothing of the train. Inside the little world of the cab the fire's brilliant light streaked out from behind closed doors, sparkled on the myriad hovering particles of coaldust and dimly showed copper pipes and brass fittings.

Outside, the wind rippled chill past the cab. No tracks were seen to lead the eye towards the next signal – the driver had to know where to look for each little light, straight ahead or over there in a chord across some invisible curve. They came at no fixed interval, some were tall backed by the stars as bright as the little oil lamp, others were low down against the dead black of the sleeping land. Only the electric colour-light distant signals were powerful and threw a green or yellow gleam along the rails leading up to them. In footplate night-life, colours were harsh and lurid and noise was all pervading.

At night, without a view, there was no perspective to give the distance to the signal ahead; a small dim light might have been close though it looked far away while a powerful light might have been far away though its brilliance made you think it was close. Furthermore, signal formations that stood out in three-dimensional clarity by day became something quite different at night.

You needed to be in charge of the engine as it thundered forward into darkness to appreciate the difficulties, as I discovered when Don allowed me to take over 7911 *Lady Margaret Hall* on a heavy, unbraked freight between Foxhall and Swindon – my home ground, where I thought I knew every signal. Twice I called out in alarm thinking I could see the triple red tail-light of a goods train on the line ahead only to be told, 'No, those three red lights are two signal lights on a bracket signal and another signal further down the line.' And the second time that happened we were approaching Challow! I managed to get the train along but only very slowly as my signalmen mates were quick to inform me next day. At the time I thought it was quite fast enough and marvelled at the skill and strong nerves of express train drivers working at night – very often at full speed through thick fog.

Getting the train into Uffington loop was quite worrying. The train was seventy wagons long, the loop held eighty and beyond the bright, blood-red colour-light signal was a twenty-foot drop. I took the train cautiously into the loop and soon the red light had disappeared behind the long boiler so that I was going forward into a featureless void. I crossed to the fireman's side and there was the bloody red light right on the end of the boiler, or so it seemed. I knew that could not be and stood there, letting it fill more and more of the lookout till I could bear it no longer. The train seemed to have stopped; I could feel no movement; we were right on top of the red light. I put the brakes on.

Immediately we got a terrific thump as the moving train closed against the engine. An avalanche of coal cascaded onto the footplate. 'What did you do that for?' shouted Don. 'We were doing ten miles an hour when you braked, you'll be lucky if you haven't killed the guard. Go and see how far you are from that signal while I calm the guard down – he'll be up here soon if he can walk at all.'

I made myself scarce and walked at least 100 yards to the signal. Don started the train, pulled it clear into the loop and stopped with the engine's buffers level with the signal.

The return trip of the Oxford to Basingstoke fish train was made with the 2 a.m. Basingstoke to Oxley heavy freight powered by an ex-LMS 2-8-0. When I was acting as fireman, Jock preferred to travel home dozing on an upturned bucket in the front corner of the cab to the misery of 'shake, rattle and roll' in the freight guard's brake van. Early one morning, as we came back through the Thames valley I asked Don if I could pick up water on the troughs at Basildon. 'You'll only overflow the tender, we don't need water and we don't need coal washing about all over the footplate,' he replied. I nagged at him, and he relented and climbed up onto his seat as a precaution against wet feet. I lowered the scoop and seconds later a volcano of water erupted from the tender filler hole to come cascading down through the coal like a tidal wave sweeping coal before it into the cab. Don shouted 'What did I tell you?' as I squeezed back out of the way, then we heard Jock's yell as he woke with coal and water tumbling against him in the dark. We had forgotten him until that moment. For the rest of the journey I fired around a trouser-less Jock as he stood trying to dry his clothes in front of the fire.

A few weeks later Don had this job again so I took a week off from Challow box and went on the train every night, firing both ways, so that by Saturday at 2 a.m. I was very tired although I had had – theoretically – plenty of rest between shifts. That morning Don was in a hurry to get home because he was driving to Devon with his family for a holiday and wanted to have some time in bed before he set out. Our train weighed 600–700 tons and Don 'really ran 'em'. I did my best for 35 miles to keep up with the voracious demand for coal from the furnace but at Culham, 7 miles south of Oxford, my arms literally ceased to function and I was forced to wake Jock and ask him to take over.

We stopped on the Down Main line outside Hinksey North signal box in order to take water, tidy the footplate and wash in a bucket of hot water from the injectors before taking the train to the north end of Oxford station to meet the Relief crew. I had grit in my eyes, down my back and between my toes as I stood on the tender's coals, tired and hungry in the chill four o'clock breeze. No one spoke. I leant my head wearily against the massive arm of the water column as water rumbled into the tender's tank. Don, on the ground, leant against the water tap and looked up at the ragged sky. Jock, having dragged coal forward, turned on the injector to fill the boiler and our bucket and its shrill note made the pain in my empty stomach worse. In the brightly lit signal box only a few feet away the signalman could be seen reclining in his soft armchair, clean and cosy, facing the stove with a mug of tea in his hand.

We blew up for the road and when the board came off we pulled slowly uphill and through the station. The eight-coupled engine's side rods clanked dismally and the echo came back off the row of dark, sleeping houses by the lineside. Over Duke's Cut bridge we boomed, bumped over the points under a big gantry of signals and finally came to a stand with the footplate steps immediately over the wooden walkway from the relief crews' brick hut close to Oxford North Junction signal box. Our relief came out – shadowy, swinging bags and tea cans, bulky in overcoats. They scrambled onto the footplate, drivers and firemen exchanged a few words about the engine and the train and then – at last – we three climbed down to walk back to the shed.

I walked in silence but Don divined my thoughts. 'Don't worry about handing over to Jock,' he said, 'you're trying to do work that a fireman comes to only after years of experience; you're not in proper training.' I appreciated his kindness but I still felt I had failed myself. They turned into the shed while I walked on towards the station and had not gone very far when Jock came running after me. 'Hey! Wait a minute. Here, you didn't do too bad – for a signalman – take this for a wee giftie.' He handed me a brand-new, shiny penny. I still have it though the years have turned it brown. Thanks, Jock.

CHAPTER TWELVE

Progress the Ogress

Steam engines and semaphore signalling were the heart and soul of Western Region because the two systems generated the morale in the men that ran the railway. The steam locomotives were the pounding heart of the line, locomotives and signalling demanded high standards of self-discipline from the men, train crews and signalmen were closer to their responsibilities and their daily challenge was greater than will ever be the case under a modernised railway system. As a result, the men's morale was high as they worked in the satisfying knowledge that they had a difficult job under control. The railway was a team of long-standing friends, the work was permanent and there was a feeling of good fellowship and security.

Then came modernisation. It was an internal affair begun in 1955, long before Beeching or Marples appeared on the scene; Western Region management merely wished to be the first to transform a Region into a fully dieselised, economic, efficient, automated 'wasteland'. First to be modernised was the locomotive fleet. Nothing was said about the steam locomotives' long life, their reliability and the opportunities they offered for employment; only one fact was drummed into the railwaymen and public – they had a low thermal efficiency. They burned too much homemade coal and therefore had to make way for German diesel engines burning Arab oil; the German diesels cost six times the price of a new steam engine from Swindon factory employing local labour.

The quest for efficiency and economy did not extend to the execution of the modernisation plan. Steam engines were cut up after running only 1,000 miles since undergoing heavy repairs, small engines for branch line work were repaired while their branch lines were being closed, new boilers for locomotives were cut up unused and diesel locomotive parts came to Swindon factory *by road* from Lancashire and Kent. I watched events from my signal box and felt the fires of outraged loyalty flame evermore furiously in my coal-burning heart as my railway was slowly dismantled – at great expense – in what seemed to me to be a quite unnecessary search for efficiency. We already had it.

Diesels took over the express trains of Western Region starting in 1958 with the crack Bristolian and Cornish Riviera expresses. One by one the diesel types arrived: the 'Hymek', 'Brush' and 'Western' classes, all full of manufacturers' promises, all doomed to failure. Some classes were worse in this respect than others but one and all were rescued, when they broke down, by the despised steam engines, several of which had, to my certain knowledge, been retrieved from scrapyards. Waste and confusion typified the Gadarene rush to modernise – all in the pursuit of 'Progress'.

One express train after another 'went diesel' until, on 5 November 1962, there were no steam-hauled express trains scheduled to run past Challow box. That was paper modernisation, for many fasts remained steam hauled regularly for weeks, and even two years later diesel failures resulted in an express train coming past Challow behind a steam engine. On 24 September 1963 a letter was circulated to all signal boxes from the Divisional Manager's Office, Bristol. It was concerned with the appalling lack of punctuality of trains over the preceding twelve months and an extract of it stated:

> The seriousness of the situation is reflected in the fact that, compared with the corresponding period last year, there is a decrease of 13% in the number of trains arriving at their destination on time and in addition more than 10% arrived 30 minutes late or more ... the general position for motive power has worsened due to the non-availability of diesel locomotives.

So many diesel locomotives failed to make themselves available that Western Region became highly sensitive about its modern image. Station announcers used the words 'diesel failure' when this was the cause of the late running of a train for which they were broadcasting their 'British Railways regrets' message so that the phrase became as monotonous to the patiently waiting passengers as to readers of this book. Only eighteen months after the problem had become acute, Western Region management became aware of this detrimental advertisement emanating from their own loudspeakers and issued to station announcers the following instruction dated 28 January 1965:

Advice to Passengers of Reason for Delay
When giving information to passengers in future for the reasons for train delays the term 'diesel failure' must not be used but must be replaced by 'locomotive failure'.

..seemed to me that passengers would associate 'steam' with 'locomotive' and that therefore this was a crafty subterfuge to throw the blame for inefficiency away from the diesels and to smear my beloved steam engines, without which Western Region would have been running a skeleton service in 1963.

Western Region management must have been taken by surprise by the non-availability of its brand-new, multi-million-pound fleet of thermally efficient diesels. On paper they had eliminated steam haulage from all but a few stopping passenger trains and some freights but in fact steam engines played a 'life-saving' role for Western Region's train services during 1963–64 and even in 1965 heavy commuter trains were steam hauled between Oxford and London.

During the summer season, early June to late August 1963, the 'Saturdays only' trains had to be scheduled for steam haulage while on the Worcester to Paddington route – Western Region's last trunk route to 'go diesel' – steam was brought back late in 1963 in order to release diesels for more important lines. My kind of railway was doomed and the loss and gain of diesel-hauled/steam-hauled trains seemed to me like a battle between two cultures, between ridiculous 'efficiency' and common-sense practicability. From my signal box I chronicled the daily, losing battle, the magnificent rear-guard action, with the dedication of a Jacobite after Culloden.

Casualties among the diesels were high. On 27 October 1963 the Locomotive Controller of the London Division told me that thirty-five of his allocation of diesels were at Swindon Works awaiting repairs and because the works were jammed with failed diesels two or more of his engines were waiting in sidings at Didcot while nine more were queuing at Old Oak Common shed, waiting for a place in the shops at Swindon. An officer of the Locomotive Department told me that half the London Division's allocation of diesels were inoperative at times during 1963 – as fast as one was repaired another broke down, a situation which Sir Daniel Gooch would have understood when he was building the Great Western Railway's first locomotive fleet in 1835.

In October 1963, Swindon Works suspended its diesel building programme to concentrate not only on repairing the backlog of diesel failures but also on renovating more steam engines. The magnificent 'Kings' had been withdrawn at the end of 1962 but a few 'Castles' and many 'Halls' and 'Granges' benefited from this decision and for one brief moment when I heard the news I thought that perhaps common sense would prevail and there would be no more diesels.

The apparent fragility of the thermally efficient diesels, and in particular the atrocious 'Western' class, was something of a wonder to men used to steam engines and their understandable, easily-put-right ailments. On 22 January 1964, D1008 *Western Harrier* was wheeled out of Swindon factory after spending 'a very long time' in the shops according to Swindon shed foreman. D1008 went up to the station to pick up four coaches for a test run to Badminton and duly set off. On the engine was a foreman fitter, six fitters, a locomotive inspector, the driver and his mate. Four hundred yards from the start D1008 failed – right outside the factory. Nothing the ten men could do would make it go again so it was towed back into the factory. Next day *Western Harrier* tried again and ran at 100 mph for part of the way. Hardly able to believe their luck the fitters tried the engine again on the 27th, taking it down to Chippenham. It failed at Langley Crossing.

The most dramatic demonstration I saw of the new locomotives' vulnerability occurred at Swindon where 'Hymek' drive shafts – the steel tubes which took the drive from engine to wheels – lay on the ground twisted around their longitudinal axes. The massive steel tubes had twisted like rolls of screwed newspaper when the 1,750-hp diesel engine had put out its maximum torque as, for instance, when climbing the 1 in 50 gradient of Sapperton Bank between Stroud and Kemble. Swindon shed foreman told me how a 'Hymek' had been out of service for weeks due to an untraceable electrical fault somewhere under the driver's console. The solution was given to a fitter in a flash of insight; enginemen put their cups full of heavily sugared tea on top of the console and the motion of the engine at speed slops the contents over so that it runs down between gaps in the formica panels to coat electric contacts underneath with an invisible insulation of sugar. I was shown the 'Failure & Remedy' book and in the entry for this engine, under the heading 'Cause of Failure', the exasperated foreman had written large 'CUP OF TEA'.

I still recall with a smile the sight of a 'Western' class diesel coming towards Challow box at much-reduced speed on an express, coughing gouts of black smoke from its twin exhausts while the driver and his mate leant on the console, heads together as they turned the pages of the little pamphlet of first aid for ailing diesels and ran their fingers down the descriptive list of symptoms. They were too busy even to notice the signal box but they never found the fault and stopped at Wantage Road for a fresh engine.

The problem for the Locomotive Controller when a diesel failed was to find two or more steam engines to work its roster. In theory a diesel can work twenty-two hours out of twenty-four in sharp contrast to a steam engine's eight hours at most (indeed, this was a fact put forward to justify their huge initial cost) but when they broke down the railway lost the motive power for as many as four trains during the next twenty-four hours.

When upwards of forty diesels were 'unavailable' in one division, steam engines heading for the scrapyards were apt to be recalled!

By 1965, the signalmen had come to accept that the diesel-hauled railway was largely unable to keep time. At least the new locomotives were comfortable for their crews, quick to fuel and service and able to work for twenty-two hours a day – bad timekeeping and constant failures were merely the price of Progress – you get nowt for owt after all. Railwaymen, loyal and conservative, disliked the revolution but stoically accepted the turmoil in the hope that it would get better one day and took comfort from the few sacred trains that always ran to time, give or take a minute – the Up and Down Travelling Post Office, the 'TPO'. But no aristocracy is allowed to survive a revolution, every train must be equally late, and on 14 December 1965 something shocking happened: the Up TPO ran up over an hour late and right through to the 18th was never less than an hour late. On the 19th it was twenty minutes late. I remember my mate's hushed voice when I relieved him at 6 a.m. on the 18th: 'The Up Postal was late *again* last night. What the hell is the matter with it all?'

The bright spots in the darkening world of Western Region were the performances of steam engines hauling the trains of failed diesels. Sometimes the engines were spanking fresh from overhaul, sometimes they were corpse green with corrosion, but they all ran well and I revelled in the sight of such wrecks picking up time on a diesel's accelerated schedule; I chuckled at the thought of their smoke under the roof at Paddington tarnishing the Space Age image of the 'Western' as their passengers streamed past. One point to common sense and the old order!

Scores of fine performances were made during the period 1963–65 when drivers and firemen, taking advantage of their diesel's failure, had their 'final fling' on a steamer and, no matter how 'rough', hammered speed out of her. The engines were expendable after all. On 29 June 1963, the 'Western' class diesel on the 11.5 a.m. Milford Haven to Paddington fast failed at Marston West box, near Swindon. The day was a hot, summer Saturday, traffic was heavy, somewhat out of gear owing to an earlier diesel failure and several of the signalmen were on the bus line telephone to advise each other and to keep abreast of traffic movements. The driver of the Milford came into Marston box, rang the shed foreman and asked for a fresh engine.

The vexed foreman, juggling his rosters to provide locomotives for extra trains and diesel failures, was burning on a short fuse. 'What's the matter with the one you've got?' he snapped.

'It's overheating badly the ...'

'What time did you pass Swindon?' the foreman interrupted him.

'4.50.'

'That's what I thought, seven early – you've been early all week, flogging your engine and making it overheat.'

I thought that was unfair; the radiator on the diesel engine may have been leaking.

The reprimand finished when the foreman said, 'We've nothing left on shed fit to turn a wheel. I'm sending you 4930, there's no use complaining, it's all I've got. Try to get it to London in one piece.' As the hapless driver stormed out of the box he said to the signalman, 'I'll show you beggars how to drive!'

4930 *Hagley Hall* was at that time 'as rough as old boots' so I was keenly anticipating what sort of run the aggrieved driver could make with her and a ten-coach train. He nursed her to Challow while his fireman got the fire into good shape and then opened her up as he approached the box. 4930 was restricted to low-class goods work because of her run-down state but she was timed at 82 mph passing Didcot and reached Paddington from Didcot, 53 ½ miles in forty-five minutes equalling the best performance of a 'Western' diesel. (*Hagley Hall* is now at work on the Severn Valley Railway running between Bridgnorth and Bewdley.)

During that summer of 1963 a daily excursion ran up from Cardiff, the 7.45 a.m. non-stop from Newport to Paddington, scheduled as a nine-coach train to be hauled by a 'Hymek'. One Monday morning when I was on early shift the train came past Challow box behind an absolutely derelict-looking '79' class 'Hall' – I cannot give the number because she carried no plates, no nameplates, no brass beading on wheel splashers or around the cab windows, her copper chimney top was corroded and the rest of her was covered in grey-black grime caked with oily grit and streaked with rust. She would have been a pitiful scrapheap on wheels except that she rollicked through the station five minutes early on the diesel's schedule.

On Tuesday and Wednesday the same engine hauled the train faster and earlier. I realised that her crew were enjoying a 'final fling' and I came to work on Thursday eagerly awaiting that morning's gallop. Mr Halford was earlier than usual in the box that morning, having a cup of tea. I told him about the battered 'Hall' and her enthusiastic crew so he stayed to see them pass. Swindon telegraph office wired the Cardiff '8.52 Badminton' – eight minutes early at the summit of eighteen miles of almost continuous, steep climbing. On the telephone I heard her pass Swindon and nine minutes later Elwyn rang her 'on line' as she passed Uffington. After waiting a minute Mr Halford and I heard her thudding, deep and rapid; thirty seconds later she was in sight around the far curve, swaying as she came. Her *tiff-tiff-tiff* was as rapid as the beat of an old-fashioned motorbike and told of a locomotive at high speed. The thrilling rhythms grew rapidly louder and we stood stock still in amazement. She hit the crossovers at about 80 mph, reeled and swayed like a drunk all the way up to the box, the hammering beat and the screaming whistle making such a crescendo that I nearly died of excitement. But Mr Halford said only, 'Silly beggars, they want their heads examined driving an old wreck like that so fast – they could've been off the road just then.'

I knocked out to Uffington and put my hand to the Wantage bell to send the Cardiff 'on line' to Wally; travelling at that speed the train would have passed Circourt signals in a minute or less. But the buzzer to show that the train had passed Circourt did not sound. The 8 a.m. Cheltenham was asked up by Elwyn; I gave the road and still the Circourt buzzer had not 'blipped' for the passing of the Cardiff. I looked at Mr Halford, who looked unwell. No questions passed between us. He simply said, 'I'll get my car out and go up there.'

'If that's how you're thinking I'd better send six bells for both Down roads,' I said.

'I think it would be as well,' he said miserably as he went down the stairs.

Just as I was to send the 'Obstruction Danger' signal, the Circourt telephone rang so I put off sending the emergency signal until I had some positive information. On the telephone a nice Welsh voice said cheerfully, 'Driver o' the sem-forty-five Cardiff yer. We've a broken intermediate valve rod. Can you find us a fresh engine?' I could see Mr Halford getting his car out. 'Hang on driver.' I went to the window and shouted the news that there was no derailment and if he did not smile the biggest smile of relief I have ever seen ...

Returning to the telephone I said to the waiting driver, 'I'm putting the eight o'clock Cheltenham up the Relief to get past you and I'll tell the driver to stop and pick up your fireman. Give your fireman a 'Driver to Signalman' wrong line order for my mate at Wantage then he can send the engine off the 'Fly' down the Up Main to couple onto you. They'll bring back your fireman and take you to Didcot and I'll warn the shed there to get another engine for you. When you've sorted out the wrong line order will you come back on the phone?' He said he would and went off to organise his fireman while I told Wally at Wantage what was happening, the shed foreman at Didcot, the driver of the Cheltenham and lastly Control.

The Cardiff driver was whistling into the telephone to attract my attention.

'Hello, mate,' I said, 'er, have you been on this job all week?'

'Well – er – yes, why?' he replied guardedly.

It's just that you've come up earlier each day and I wondered if you particularly wanted to make a very fast run?'

'Well, look you. Me and my mate have been up the valleys on the D68s* for weeks now so we were pleased for a chance of a run up to Padd, having a steamer was just a bonus – we might not get another chance at a steam run to London.'

'You were certainly hammering that one! The stationmaster here went pale when he saw you swaying over the crossings and when you didn't pass Circourt he thought you were off the road.'

The driver was immediately on the defensive. 'Ah now, look you. Your crossovers are bloody rough, always have been. I reckon it was that lurch that broke the valve rod. That was a good engine, we've been getting used to her all week, she's a shocking rough ride but she'd steam on a candle flame and that's what matters when you're running 'em.'

'How fast were you going through here?' I asked.

'Aha! Now the speedo on that engine don't work properly. I'm not sure how fast we were going.'

'Come on, don't be shy. You came from Swindon to here in no more than eleven minutes and you'd have eased up a bit through there so you must have been motoring, thirteen and a half miles in ten and a half or eleven minutes.

'We-ell, the speedo said eighty but look you – the old girl was rocking about so bad I couldn't read it properly.'

'You were fifteen minutes up on your schedule here ...' I left the statement hanging.

'Ah,' he countered, 'very easy timings these diesel schedules, boyo! Very easy to pick up time.'

The box to box telephone rang and I answered it. 'I thought your old steam engines never broke down,' laughed Wally. 'Look, I'm going to send the engine off the "Fly" back onto the Cardiff. Is that OK?'

'Yes, fine, if you've got the wrong line order. I've got the Cardiff driver on the phone now so I'll tell him what's happening.' I told the Cardiff driver, who asked, 'What will we be having from Didcot?'

'A "Hall", they're getting it ready for you now.'

'Right, thanks, boyo! We'll hammer that one too if you blokes will give us the road. All the best.' He put his telephone down.

After the Cardiff had been cleared I got some sarcastic telephone calls teasing me about the failure of one of 'my' steam engines, so for the honour of steam I made some inquiries. I discovered that the 'Hall' was indeed

* A class of diesel numbered in the 6800 series, later referred to as Class 37.

scrap and had been waiting to leave Cardiff shed to run to the scrapyard when the 'Hymek' on the excursion had failed and the rusty old steamer was the only spare engine available to take over the train.

In the five years I worked at Challow or Uffington while steam engines were at work I think I experienced four steam engine failures, whereas I could have four diesel failures in one shift. The strangest steam engine failure happened on a hot day in 1963 when I was on early shift. A goods train from Oxford started from the West Curve at Foxhall Junction and was given the road, Main line through to Uffington. I received the 'Train Approaching' bell from Wally and then the telephone rang. 'Don't pull off for that one,' said Wally, 'he's bloody terrible. I reckon they must be short of steam – the driver and the fireman were working hard with the long bar in the fire passing here, dragging it about as if their lives depended on it.'

I wound the hurdy-gurdy, pulled levers 45, 62 and 59 to bring the train into the platform line and went to the window to watch and wait. I waited so long that Wally and I were discussing the possibility of running the following fast down the Relief line to overtake the goods when it came into sight, crawling painfully slowly down the track. The engine was an ex-LMS 2-8-0 No. 48010 and she was just out of the factory with her paint shiny black and a bright red buffer beam. As she drew close to 59 signal I was treated to the unforgettable sight of the driver climbing down and – running – overtaking his engine as he dashed for the power point telephone. It rang and I answered it.

A panting voice blurted out, 'Help! Help! We've no water in the tender, the gauge glass is empty, she'll blow at any moment – what'll I do?' This was the only time I ever saw or heard a driver actually panicking in an emergency.

'Don't worry, mate,' I said calmly – and safely out of reach of the boiler should it explode – 'bring your train into the platform and I'll call for the fire brigade.'

'I don't know if we've got steam to do that – don't blame me if we stick on the points.'

I telephoned Mr Halford. 'There'll be a train arriving at the Down platform soon. The engine is out of water; they'll drop a plug if we don't do something. Will you call for the fire brigade?'

'Certainly not!' snapped the stationmaster. 'Emergency calls other than to fires have to be paid for. Take the thing away from my window and let it blow up peacefully down in the yard.' It is possible that he thought I was joking but there was no time to argue. I ran across to the public telephone outside the Prince of Wales and dialled 999 for the Wantage Fire Brigade. Before I had got back to the box the distant wail of the siren came floating across the fields through the hot, noonday air. The engine drew into the platform, was uncoupled and taken across to the sidings. I had a look in the cab while the driver paced up and down, his nerves taut as violin strings and his fireman sat on the grass. They had pushed out a lot of the fire, that was the 'life or death' activity Wally had seen but now, with the chance of a supply of water, they had stopped these precautions. The boiler water gauge showed empty and there was no water in the tender though the tender gauge showed 'Full'. It was new and probably stiff, certainly this had misled them into not taking water at Foxhall but they could have stopped at Wantage and blown the whistle to go onto the Relief line so as to make use of a water column.

The strident, clanging bell of the fire engine came to us like the bugles of the US 7th Cavalry. The bell had a vital urgency, a 'Hang on – we're coming!' quality quite different to the hysterical shrieking of present-day sirens. The driver stopped pacing and stood riveted, looking south to where the Wantage road came over a rise. Moments later a lovely, red Appliance came storming over the crest, engine roaring, bell hammering, up and over the railway bridge, firemen waving, and on screeching tyres swerved through the station yard to where the crippled engine was standing.

The station to signal box telephone was ringing fussily but I ignored it. We were going to save that lovely, black engine not even LMS engines can be allowed to blow up. The gallant fire chief, John Kent, the Wantage ironmonger, strode over to the engine driver while his brave firemen – greengrocers, barbers and butchers in helmets and uniforms – ran about with hoses. 'I've got five hundred gallons, where do you want it?' cried John.

'In the tender – quickly!' shouted the agonised driver.

The water was pumped in, the red fire hose like a bootlace up the side of the massive tender, and while the Appliance went off for a refill, the locomotive's fireman turned on his injector. Curiously there was still steam to work it. Terrible banging, groaning noises came from the overheated boiler and firebox but water rose in the bottom nut of the gauge glass. Immediately the feed was stopped, the fire was re-fuelled and steam raised. After a second load of water from the fire brigade the engine went back onto its train.

Knowledgeable people will question the veracity of this story. I admit it sounds impossible but that is what happened and the engine appeared to be none the worse. I told John Kent that the stationmaster was annoyed with me for calling out the brigade and asked how much his assistance would cost. John laughed. 'Not to worry. I shall book this as a fire, then it's free. After all, that boiler was in danger of burning. I've been with the brigade for most of my working life, longer than I care to remember, and it's the first time I've ever been called out on a job like this. I don't suppose it'll ever happen again so it's on the house.'

CHAPTER THIRTEEN

A Rod for my Back

To be successful, railways must be run by enthusiasts from the highest to the lowest grades, for a railway is no better than the men who work it. For most of the 1950s the Western Region had as its Chairman Mr Reg Hanks. He was an enthusiast and under his direction Western Region men were able to recreate the Great Western atmosphere of old – including the production of a working profit. Hanks gave tradition a ten-year extension of life so that I was privileged to experience the workmanlike satisfaction of working for a great railway. In some departments the work was hard and even dirty but it was secure and carried out in the comradeship of hard-working friends; it spread good humour and developed a good morale.

Reggie Hanks understood this well. He had started his career on the Great Western as an apprentice in Swindon factory before the First World War; he had served in that war and returned to work with William Morris (later Lord Nuffield) eventually to become Works Manager at Morris's car factory near Oxford. When he became Chairman of Western Region he still lived in Oxford and each day took the 9 a.m. express up to Paddington and the 5.15 back at night – firing or driving the engine on many occasions. My friend Charlie Turner, an Oxford top link driver who frequently handed over his 'Castle' to Hanks, summed up the secret of the Chairman's legendary leadership – 'He kept his overalls in the Boardroom.'

At Oxford station in the 1950s heavy traffic from eight routes converged and was dealt with by a band of highly trained and knowledgeable porters and shunters supervised by one foreman per shift under the scrutiny of a single stationmaster. When traffic movements became too much for the men's combined efforts they would call on their stationmaster, who would be delighted to take off his jacket and set to work as a shunter. He became a legend in his own lifetime and was awarded by his men the ultimate railway accolade – they named a siding after him, 'Miller's siding'.

Hanks and Miller retired in 1960. In 1961, Ernest Marples, Minister of Transport, appointed Dr Richard Beeching to be Chairman of the Board of British Railways. Mr Marples was not an enthusiastic railwayman – prior to becoming Minister he had been a director of the road-building giant Marples-Ridgeway Ltd. Dr Beeching was not a railway enthusiast either – among other things he was the first president of the Institute of Work Study Practitioners, a title with a razor-sharp quality well befitting a wave in the flood of 'white-hot technology', which was then fast approaching the green-and-gold world of Western Region.

In 1961 Dr Beeching, the man who 'would rather name a pub than a railway engine', began his study of how best to make Britain's railways profitable. At about that time I saw in a national newspaper a cartoon showing a boardroom with dozens of directors packed around a polished table. They were all staring blankly at their Chairman as he asked, 'Can I have your suggestions for increasing our profits – apart from reducing the office boy's wages again.' All those brains but no constructive ideas. Down at Challow box I got the impression that the empire of clerks and supervisors was expanding as train services were being curtailed and routes closed and that expensive equipment capable of handling heavy traffic was being purchased while management did their best to discourage traffic. As in the cartoon, there was no shortage of directors.

At Paddington headquarters of Western Region, there were offices sufficient to house the clerkdom of the Great Western Railway, yet during times of economy Western Region saw fit to build a fifteen-storey office block to re-house their headquarters staff in Reading. It seemed to me that the railway was spending a great deal of money on getting smaller and in my anger I imagined a time when the tracks from Paddington to Bristol would be lifted, tarmac laid, the route designated as a 'High Speed Ped-Track' with the locomotive water troughs retained as places where travellers could cool their overheated feet. Every few miles along the line, glass pyramids – architect designed to seat the hierarchy within – would house the armies of clerks 'essential' to the smooth running of the Ped-Track.

In Hanks's day, Western Region ran a complicated network at or nearly at a profit, officials were very busy and those few who visited outlying stations such as Challow did so by train but in the years of decline after 1960 there appeared more frequently what I took to be the 'New Men' of the railway – and they rode in chauffeur-driven Bentleys. At Tilehurst one afternoon in 1963 the signalman saw a Bentley draw up in the station yard; a man in a dark business suit got out and the car drove away. Twenty minutes later the man was knocking on the signal box door. 'I'm from the Divisional Manager's Office,' he said, 'can I use your phone?' He contacted an office in

Reading and asked, 'Has my car left yet? ... No? ... Well tell him to hurry – if I have to wait here any longer I shall have to go back to Paddington *by train*.'

I was on duty at Challow box when a Bentley came crunching in over the gravel and stopped. Four men in their regulation suits got out and the car withdrew to the car park of the Prince of Wales within sight of the station. The four men 'poked about' – to use a phrase of Elwyn Richard's – among the wagons on the sidings, then three of them headed back to the Prince and the fourth came up into the signal box.

'Have you got any hot-boxes in the yard?' he asked. I said we had not and he looked disappointed. 'Have you had any in recently?'

'I'll have a look back in the train register – but have the four of you come down from Paddington in that big car just to find that out? Couldn't you have phoned?'

'Oh no! We had to make a visual appreciation of the situation at first hand.'

The ranks of the new supervisory grades were filled by recruits from universities and by the more ambitious booking clerks. After a two-year course, these men – or boys – could take charge of railwaymen who had been in the service for forty years or more. Such recruits were rarely of a shy or retiring nature and one I recall we dubbed 'Bucketmouth'.

I was extolling the virtues of old hands such as Albert Stanley to this young Hero of the New Technology, recounting how Albert had worked for over forty years at stations where he was largely his own supervisor, from Tidworth to Cricklade and from Swindon to Steventon, each place with its busy, individual traffic demanding a careful knowledge of local conditions, carrying out the paperwork and the muscle work with never a 'Supervisor' in sight. 'Bucketmouth' smiled condescendingly. 'You go a lot on these old blokes,' he said, 'but really their job was no more than one year's learning and forty-four years' repetition.' Arrogant but understandable coming from a man whose own career was based on a two-year course – the railway was shrinking so fast that this was all that was necessary to qualify him as a Supervisor.

And yet the most senior managers had some sense of fun. In the afternoon of 3 June 1964 I was visiting Reading West Main box. At 4.5 p.m the signals were pulled off Up the Main for a '4 bells' – express passenger train. The very loud, rapid beat of the approaching engine sent me and the crew of the signal box rushing to the windows as 7020 *Gloucester Castle* went thundering past – hauling the Divisional Inspection saloon. The time was 4.7. It was running at 60 mph and accelerating hard. Waving their hats through the windows were the London Divisional Manager and his senior assistants! The man who had signalled the train called out, 'That was at a stand at Scours Lane behind the York.' Scours Lane was 1 ½ miles away.

On early turn next day at Challow I began to investigate. Challow was the boundary of the London Division so the train had started from there. A fast run to London had been planned because the engine had come down tender first for a chimney-first return. I checked all the train registers from Challow to Foxhall Junction. All the bell codes were registered through the boxes at the same times. Of course this is only a rough guide but over a long distance gives a good idea of what was done. From Reading the times were obtained from 'Control'. From Challow they averaged 78 mph to Foxhall Junction. They caught up with the 10.8 a.m. York–Bournemouth at Cholsey, which delayed them to Scours Lane. From Reading station, passed at 60, to Paddington they averaged 72 mph. Driver Green and Fireman Dunn of Swindon were on the engine.

Challow, halfway between Swindon and Didcot, served a wide area of the Vale and people came from miles around to use the 9.5 a.m. express to London returning on the 5.5 at night. Most of our passenger revenue (*see* Appendix 8) was derived from that modest service, the lavish service of stopping trains between Swindon and Didcot being redundant except for the 8.15 a.m. from Challow to Swindon and the 4.15 p.m. and 5.50 p.m. up from Swindon. Goods revenue came from farm produce – hay, straw, sugar beet, horses and from the export of farm machinery while other stations gained revenue when they loaded coal or fertiliser to Challow.

In July 1961, Challow's wage bill for stationmaster, booking clerk, two porters and three signalmen was covered by passenger receipts while receipts from goods traffic would have ensured that the station paid its way whilst providing a service to the community. On 9 September 1961, some kindred spirit of 'Bucketmouth's' abolished the 5.5 p.m. Paddington and substituted a 4.35 p.m. departure, which was too early for our passengers and was 'all stations' after Didcot, arriving at Challow twenty minutes later than the old 5.5. Why was this done? If economy was the intention far more could have been achieved by taking off several redundant stopping trains. The negative attitude of 'Bucketmouth' and his colleagues and the overwhelming sense of betrayal was infuriating. After this 're-arrangement' of our train service we lost some regular customers including Mr (now Sir) John Betjeman and, burning with indignation at this sneaky attack on my station, I set out to win traffic back. It was a singlehanded job because the old hands were either too shy or too wise to the ways of the world to take any part while 'Bucketmouth' was being too progressive to have any time to save a station.

I designed and had printed 500 posters giving details of the train service to and from Challow, together with specimen fares, places that could be reached by connecting services – leave Challow at 9.5 a.m., arrive Folkestone 2.30 p.m. – nailed the sheets to 485 telegraph poles and posted the rest in village shops. Not one was held back for the record. I also attempted a campaign of door-to-door canvassing and hoped to get up a petition signed by thousands; I got perhaps 100 signatures, but I am no politician. I became so interested in the sheer talking with the people I met that I lost hours and the project was drowned under a flood of tea, smothered under cake and biscuits.

The people were sympathetic but I fear they thought my one-man show somewhat eccentric. Furthermore, the station still suffered from its crippled return service from London so the effect of the campaign on Challow's revenue was difficult to measure. However, there were some quite startling effects. One man – who may well have been illiterate –was so moved in his emotions by the sight of my crisp, bold, black and white posters along the roadside that he stopped his tractor at a succession of poles, tore down and crumpled the papers before my very eyes. The posters also had an electrifying effect on the Divisional Manager's Office at Paddington and after nothing more than a single telephone call from 'Bucketmouth' they dispatched, post haste, a Chief Inspector and an officer – by Bentley – to interview me. During a rather one-sided conversation they left me in no doubt that Paddington did not want any traffic at Challow and the closing words from the Chief Inspector were, 'Anything else like this – any more letters to the press or putting up posters – and you'll be making a rod for your own back.' I asked him what that meant and the whole of his reply was merely, 'Just think on.' A curious message and an unprofitable day's work for men whose job it was to provide the people with a train service.

In 1963, the cost of putting goods on rail at Challow was raised to an impossible level with the result that our traffic faded away. It was during this year that Dr Beeching published the blueprint for his infamous 'Axe' – *The Re-Shaping of British Railways*. The railways were making an enormous loss (aided in part by Western Region's strategic readjustment of station layouts, fares and timetables) and therefore a large part of the railway network would have to be closed if the residue was to be made profitable. But Beeching specifically stated that he did not take into account population growth when condemning stations and routes.

Now, the British public has the same kind of regard for railways as for old churches – they are sacred, beautiful and untouchable and the reaction to the report was one of outrage in a general way but I cannot report that this was the general feeling in the Vale – perhaps because the Paddington–Bristol line was not condemned but only the local stations between Didcot and Swindon. I was sure there was a case for keeping Challow or Wantage Road as a railhead for passengers with two or more fast trains morning and evening to and from Paddington; there was a fashion for motoring but I thought that the time might well come when driving ceased to be a pleasure or a convenience and then people would return to the local stations. What I was proposing became adopted by BR as 'Parkways'.

The village of Grove, close to Wantage Road station, encouraged me to think this because it had been marked as the site for an 'overspill' development for 10,000 people, the new estates spreading north to the railway line. The station staff there sent newspaper cuttings to Paddington, reporting the proposed development and Wantage town council made some small representations of their own but 'Bucketmouth' was far too busy typing out closure notices to hear these polite country voices.

In September 1963, Challow lost the 9.5 a.m. to London – the 7.5 ex-Cheltenham – and in its place received the 4.40 a.m. Fishguard Harbour boat train. Never in the history of the railway had a boat train, dependent for its punctual running on the state of the Irish Sea, been used as an ordinary express train to take wayside passengers to London, but now the Fishguard was scheduled to call at Challow fifteen minutes *before* the long-established and widely known 'nine o'clock' to London.

As the year wore on and the weather worsened, the Fishguard began to run late and the passengers waiting unhappily on Challow's platform had, all too frequently, to watch 'their' train – the 7.5 ex-Cheltenham – go steaming through on the Up Main line. The station staff detested this shabby treatment of people who had only minutes before handed over the money for a ride to Paddington – they felt fraudulent in taking money for what they knew was a second-rate service. By December the weather was so bad that the boat train was often two hours late and I decided that whenever I was on early shift the 7.5 ex-Cheltenham would stop and pick up our long-suffering customers. The passengers were delighted and we got away with it for a month – until 4 January 1964 – when the following instruction arrived at Challow from the Divisional Manager's Office at Paddington:

In future under no circumstance is any train to be stopped in lieu of the 4.40 a.m. Fishguard when that train is running late. Any passengers requiring it may be given their taxi fare to Didcot.

And that is exactly what did happen until people learned not to patronise their local station.

The official notice announcing the closure of Challow station was posted on the station in May 1964 and not long afterwards four officers arrived in their chauffeur-driven Bentley for a look at their victim. One of these came to the signal box and I asked him why the station had been deliberately run down when it could just as easily have been made the central entraining point for the Vale – or why not Wantage Road, which was also to be shut in spite of the planned housing development. He gave me his twinkliest public relations smile and said, 'You chaps cost a lot to run – we've got to keep our costs down.' He went back to his Bentley and I watched them drive away – four cheap officers and their expensive Leading Porter chauffeur.

Challow's porters – Sam Loder, Albert Stanley and Harry Strong – reacted characteristically to the imminent loss of their jobs. Sam, the old soldier, reckoned he could always find another billet somewhere; Albert, having his break in the box one afternoon, looked at me with a worried frown on his broad, honest face when I asked him what he felt and replied, 'No amount of redundancy pay is going to make up for being out of work. I've been busy all my life but who'd take on an old bloke like me with no qualifications?' Harry Strong was his usual imperturbable self and said nothing that I can recollect. The men along the line took the matter philosophically, sadly and maybe with a little indignation at the way the stations had been run down. Only I was angry.

There were few official objections to the stations' closure – Faringdon Chamber of Trade had none at all 'providing an adequate alternative bus service to Swindon is provided'. I repeated to all and sundry my belief in Challow or Wantage Road as a railhead of the future and an engine driver whom I was haranguing in the signal box one day suggested I took his seat at a forthcoming meeting of Swindon Trades Council on the subject of the station and line closures. Philip Noel-Baker, MP for Swindon, was present together with a few working men and a representative of the Bristol Omnibus Company. I explained my plan for retaining a railhead in the Vale but the meeting decided that in its present mood Western Region would ignore it and concluded that valuable national assets were being thrown away but that no one could do anything about it. The Omnibus man was gloomy too – he had to provide the alternative bus service necessary if the trains were to be withdrawn. The bus company was reluctant to provide the service because, said the man, it would run at a loss in spite of the fact that Western Region had offered to subsidise the buses at the rate of £3 for every empty seat. Three pounds in 1964 was a quarter of an average weekly wage and sounded like good business to me – but the expert had spoken. What could we do but accept his word?

The last stopping train over the Didcot to Swindon section of the old Great Western Main line was the 6.1 p.m. Didcot on 5 December 1964. It consisted of two coaches hauled by engine 6112, driven by A. W. Purnell, fired by J. W. Sherman, both from Didcot with a Paddington guard, F. S. Huntingford. All Challow's railwaymen and their children came to see the train, also my parents and friends from places as far apart as Hereford and Sussex. Sam Loder and I used up the signal box's entire stock of detonators in laying out the traditional railway rhythm 'Half a pound of tuppeny rice' along the crown of the rail ending with a crescendo fusillade worthy of a virtuoso kettle-drummer by placing dozens of shots touching each other along the rail top. The visitors were impressed with these preparations.

'After all,' said my friend Ron Price, 'it's not a branch line that's closing – they're only taking the stoppers off.'

'They took our fasts yesterday, today they're closing the station, tomorrow they'll be shutting the signal box – pass me the rest of those detonators.'

It was dark when 6112 arrived at Challow. She was greeted by a ragged cheer from the loyal throng on the platform, there was a brief pause and she started off again in a hurricane of noise, whistle screaming, railway-folk cheering and the flashing bangs of the detonators, each explosive flash illuminating the engine's driving wheels and side rods. The rhythm of the nursery rhyme crackled out, drowning the engine's gentle exhaust till Driver Purnell put on more steam, then the famous Swindon bark spoke proudly above the other noise and 6112 accelerated away over the close-packed shots to produce a magnificent raspberry for Beeching and 'Bucketmouth'.

Then it was over. No bangs, no whistling, only an intense silence incompletely filled by the purposeful sound of 6112 tugging away into the night towards Uffington, Shrivenham and a place in the history of the Vale.

The signal box stood lonely by the lineside, the eastward view from its windows in the grim, winter days unrelieved by any bright lights from the station; no Tilley lamps sparkling from masts along the platform and on the footbridge, no cheerful porter to share my morning or afternoon tea, the car park empty of passengers' cars. Almost overnight, it seemed to my sad gaze, grass came squeezing up between the platform paving slabs and before very long held full sway as the slabs were taken up and sold for garden paving. Someone, somewhere, has a garden path with one edge bearing faded white-wash, the remnant of the bold, white stripe I had so carefully applied four years before.

By November 1964, the frequency of trains passing Challow was reduced by 25 per cent compared to 1960; five goods trains per shift were steam hauled, no passenger trains ran with steam unless a diesel had failed, and the Relief lines between Wantage Road and Challow were little used – if a goods train had to be side tracked to allow a following express to pass, the goods could be accommodated in the short loop at Uffington. Challow was then little better than a 'passing box'. Our feelings of redundancy were reinforced by the sight of the bundle of black electric cables which lay on the footpath outside the box – the black tentacles of Progress – which were to connect signals at Challow with the new control panel then being built thirty miles to the east at Reading. The new 'Panel' was to replace about twenty-five manual signal boxes and perhaps thirty men per shift; the work they did would come under the control of three men per shift. The new signals were to be electric colour-lights working automatically in open country – as between Challow and Didcot for instance – while the points and signals at the big junctions at Didcot and Reading would be operated electrically at the push of a button.

The reduction in services enabled the layout to be simplified. The complications of station shunting work on the steam railway in the 1950s – due to the extensive public service provided – could only be operated by personal supervision of signalmen at their windows but without steam engines and without branch lines and with a reduced Main line service Western Region could install Panel boxes and publicise them as a wonder of the age. In fact the modern Western Region was tailored to fit its signalling system!

I felt an intense loyalty to the old ways that had served the country so well even under extreme pressure. I looked back at days when the railway did its big, busy job – with 'inefficient' steam engines and 'clumsy, old-fashioned' signalling – when it handled enormous traffic under these dreadful handicaps, year after year, without fuss. The modern railway of 1964–65 reduced itself to a skeleton of its former self and then boasted to the public of its wonderful achievement in working miles of track from a single control point. It was this double-think boastfulness that put my back up – there were fewer trains, fewer jobs, millions of pounds spent and a lot of talk about 'Progress'.

None of the signalmen I knew looked forward to leaving the railway; almost all of them had spent their entire working life as signalmen and naturally they preferred the clean, responsible, intelligent work they knew to going 'outside' to they knew not what lowly job. This was ironic because almost anyone 'outside' would have considered signal box work as underpaid and therefore lowly – signalmen in the isolation of their boxes had, without realising it, preserved the values of the 1920s when they had joined a prestigious organisation. They felt like monks turned out of their cloister – and aged monks at that. But they had one crumb of comfort; they held one fact dear which made facing up to the change easier – that they were being supplanted by Progress.

I thought it was a terrible waste of a fine team, capable of training a new generation in the old workmanlike virtues, to throw them out on the street after installing at a cost of millions a less safe system of signalling. My friends were outraged at such views. 'Ooh! How do you make that out?' they asked, scandalised.

'Simple,' I replied. 'Under the new system there will be nothing but automatic signals from Uffington to Foxhall and from Moreton Cutting to Scour's Lane – miles and miles of track without any supervision. If a porter at Didcot sees something wrong with a train and tells Reading, Reading will have no signals to put to "Danger" to stop the train until it reaches Scour's Lane – that's fifteen or sixteen miles of track.'

The Up and Down Relief lines between Challow and Wantage Road were taken out of use on 4 April 1965, reducing both boxes to the status of mere 'passing boxes'. With these tracks out of use the colour-light signals for the Up and Down Main lines could be erected where the rails once lay. The signals were erected but remained out of use for a time. On 26 April Reading Panel took over control of Reading station area, its sphere of control being extended westwards in planned stages.

At about this time two odd events occurred, entirely unconnected with each other yet the one affecting the other. An inspector of signalmen came west from Reading, calling at each box along the line and taking away with him the emergency lighting doubtless for eventual sale by British Railways at Collectors' Corner at Euston. The emergency lighting in each box was a beautiful brass lamp with a glass funnel and a crinoline-shaped white glass shade or diffuser – they were the sort of lamps you might see hanging from the ceiling of a log cabin in a cowboy film. The word went rapidly down the line, warning of this collection and in several signal boxes, including Challow, the lamps disappeared; to use the words of 'The Lincolnshire Poacher', 'I need not tell you where'.

Soon after this I was on duty when the main power to Challow box failed; it was late evening and the place was plunged into darkness. I telephoned for the emergency service of the Southern Electricity Board and worked the box for an hour by the light of the paraffin hand-lamp used for signalling by hand to trains. When the SEB man arrived he discovered that the station had been forcibly entered, no damage had been done – apart from that to the door – and the main power switch had been turned off.

The following week, the last week of Challow box's operation, I was on early turn. The train service was down to a mere forty-five trains in eight hours as against sixty-five in 1960 and all I had to do was 'pull off' and throw back the levers for each train. Five or six steam engines passed the box each morning between 6 a.m. and 2 p.m. – 4920, 5933, 3840 and 92230 are a representative selection. 3840 distinguished itself by rescuing a self-propelled ballast-cleaning machine which had broken down in the section ahead. The '38' was uncoupled from its train, went forward to the machine, pulled it back to Challow and dumped it on a siding. It was a pleasant throw-back to old times to pull levers for a shunting steam engine but the technicians at work on the tracks outside putting the finishing touches to the new system made me realise that it was no more than a swansong.

Probably the last emergency handled by Challow box occurred that week when the 8.45 a.m. Paddington – The Bristolian – came tearing through. I was watching the train carefully and saw the guard hanging out, holding his hat with one hand, waving a bundle with the other. He dropped a rolled-up timetable and inside I found the following intriguing note:

Please arrange for Police to meet 8.45 Paddington at Bath 10.22 a.m. and arrange to have line searched for a briefcase between Cholsey and Reading.

I got to work immediately. That is the advantage of semaphore signalling.

I worked my last shift in Challow box on Saturday morning 29 May 1965. Jim Spinage and Ken Rowlands shared the weekend work and Ken, who had started at Challow as a boy in 1941, was the last signalman, finishing work on Sunday 30 May at 3.27 p.m. Jim and I were present, though off duty, and with Ken we signed off for the last time, each man writing his goodbye message right across the broad page.

The final words on the box are those of a small boy, Sam Loder's ten-year-old son, John. John lived in the station cottages and his bedroom faced out over the tracks. As I left work on Saturday he was waiting for me and his speech, which I am sure he had been rehearsing, I have never forgotten: 'I'm sorry the box is closing,' he said. 'When I wake up at night I'm not afraid of the dark because I can see the lights of the box and see the signalman moving about. It's always been there, it'll look empty without it.'

A week after the box closed I remembered that the block register and Charlie Lamble's lamp had been left in the box so I went down to see if they were still there. The great goods shed – Brunel's goods shed – was being demolished by a gang of contractor's men wielding sledgehammers and to my admittedly unhappy gaze they had the appearance of particularly loutish pirates. One of them called to me: 'Hey! If you're looking round – go up into the signal box – the whole place is polished up as if it would never close – they were some daft beggars those signalmen.' I said nothing but crossed the tracks, entered the door and climbed to the operating floor. The room was cold, damp and strangely silent, a coating of dullness was on the bell domes and their tappers seemed to reach out to be worked. Faint spots of rust were beginning to grow on the silver-handled levers. I closed the train register still lying open where we had left it, picked it up, collected Charlie Lamble's lamp and departed.

Epilogue

Mr Halford died a few months before Challow station was closed.

Harry Strong retired to his garden where he stood over the neat rows of plants and dared the weeds to show their heads. I saw him several times, slim and spruce as ever. My abiding memory of him from that time is when I drove past his cottage beside the Faringdon Road. He was leaning over his tightly cut thorn hedge, leaning on his hoe for support, talking to another venerable old gent, who was leaning across the saddle of his big, old bike, the peaks of their cloth caps almost touching. Harry died in 1979.

Sam Loder did indeed find another billet – in a timber yard 200 yards from his front door in the railway cottages. He worked to sixty-five. He always recalled with pleasure his life on the railway and his practical jokes. His son continued the railway tradition by becoming a train guard, working out of Didcot.

Albert Stanley went to work in Cooper's marmalade factory in Wantage. At sixty-two years of age, after forty-four years of railway work, largely outdoors and at a number of stations, he found the change to a simple, repetitive, indoor job more than he could bear. 'There were times,' Albert told me, 'when I thought I would go mad being cooped up inside and in the end I went and told the Manager and asked him for an outdoor job.' The Manager thoughtfully gave him a job driving a forklift truck – the first motor vehicle Albert had ever driven. He then became a loader, stacker, checker and a generally very useful 'outdoor' man. It was work very similar to what he had done since 1920 with the added spice of the forklift to drive. Albert worked to sixty-five and retired to Challow station cottages, with his wife and family, alongside Sam, and took his dog daily to work in his lineside allotment.

Bill Mattingley, ex-Warrant Officer Class 1 in the wartime RAF, signalman and hobby beekeeper, was taken on by the Miniustry of Agriculture as an Inspector of Bees. He drove around the district, made a lot of new friends, carried out a lot of useful work and thoroughly appreciated the feeling of freedom the work gave him. When I last met him, he had retired from all formal work and he told me that, if he had his time again, and knowing then what he knew now, he would not want to be a signalman with the constant shift work and the isolation. However, he did also say that he looked back with affection to his time on the railway and the friends he made – and he was a subscribing member of the Great Western Society.

Ken Rowlands had no regrets or nostalgic backwards looks at his long service on the railway; indeed, he said he wished he had left sooner. After leaving, in 1965, he went to the Post Office for a job but was rejected on account of his age. Then he went to the County Ambulance Service and was too old to be taken on as a driver, according to the rules, but the local manager of ambulances, realising that a man who had worked a Main line signal box blamelessly for twenty years was a man worth having, allowed him to take the ambulance drivers' course and exam – which Ken passed. When I asked him how he felt about the old days, he smiled and said, 'I know what you'd like me to say – how much I miss Challow – but I don't. Looking back on it, I wonder how I put up with the solitude of the box.'

'You didn't feel like that when you signed off for the last time,' I reminded him, 'and it wasn't that solitary, there was always the natter on the bus line phone and Sam or Albert coming up for a mug of tea – I thought you were happy in the box and sorry to leave.'

'Well, in a way I must have been but that was because I didn't know anything else. I'd been on the railway almost since I left school but it was nothing to the job I'm doing now. Ambulance work puts you in the way of meeting and helping so many people. Apart from the road accident victims we do a lot of ferrying people from the villages into Oxford for their weekly treatment. We get to know them as friends and it's great to see them getting better as the weeks go by.'

Of the Challow permanent-way gang, Bob Thatcher died soon after retiring. Bill Lamble, Bob's 'Second Man', became a P-way Inspector and Artie Ballard went to work for Berkshire County Council roads department. I don't know about the others.

Wally Randall, redundant at Wantage Road, went to work at Steventon Stocks Lane level crossing ground frame. This had been the signal box where Alec Abrahams had saved the 10.30 p.m. Paddington. Wally worked the Stocks Lane gates with the GWR gate wheel until his wife's poor health obliged him to retire, aged 66. Alec Abrahams, who was about the same age as Wally, carried on at Stocks Lane until the job was abolished by automation in 1974. By then Alec was seventy and the Reading office asked him to transfer to Appleford Crossing ground frame, not far from

Steventon and a very infrequently used crossing. It was a very easy job requiring plenty of reading material. Alec went there for two years, retired and died very soon afterwards.

Jim Spinage and I went to fill the two vacancies at Uffington, which was now the 'fringe' or interface between the automated panel control centre at Reading and the mechanical signalling to the west.

SIGNALMAN'S NIGHTMARE

For the women in my life:
Susan, Rebecca, Constance
and Beatrice

Contents

Say not thou, What is the cause that the former
days were better than these?
For thou dost not inquire wisely concerning this.

Ecclesiastes 7:10

Of the making of many books there is no end;
And much study is a weariness to the flesh.

Ecclesiastes 7:10

Acknowledgments

It is recorded in GWR Staff Records that on 24 February 1869 a boy went for a footplate ride over the West London line of the GWR. For taking the lad, Driver Henry Barney was fined 5 shillings. So locomotive trespass goes back to 1869 and even as far back, I suggest, as the opening of the Liverpool & Manchester Railway. Unauthorised visitors in signal boxes arrived with the first signal box. Trespassing by interested persons, from small boys to bishops, was frequent and part of the railway. Punishments for the offending railwaymen appear to have been rare – otherwise the practice would have ceased. The Reverend A. H. Malan rode the footplates of broad-gauge expresses in the 1880s; my friend Bill Kenning (referred to in this volume) gave me photographic proof of his locomotive and signal box trespassing before the First World War; another friend, P. S. A. Berridge – who later became Assistant Chief Civil Engineer (Bridges) for the GWR and BRWR – was a locomotive trespasser during and after the First World War; and I can testify to my own misdemeanours in this field shortly after the Second World War. I was passionately interested in the railway, and, in the humanitarian spirit inherited from earlier generations of drivers and signalmen, I was invited onto engines and into signal boxes. I should like to thank all the railwaymen of forty years ago who encouraged me to become, eventually, a railwayman – something of which I am very proud. I would like to thank many workmates for spending hours talking to me about their careers and telling me the legend of that particular piece of line described in these pages; all of them were the kindest of men: Signalmen Tom Baber, Mick Elliot, Sid Fleming, Patrolman Dick Kerslake, Driver Don Kingdom, Signalmen Ron Kirby, Sid Mumford, Ron Reynolds, Jack Richards, Ken Russell, Signal and Telegraph Lineman John Taylor, Drivers Don Kingdom and Charlie Turner, Signalmen Fred Wilkins and Stan Worsfold. My thanks are also due to friends and relatives who helped me to produce this book: Chris Burden, David Collins, Ian Coulson, David Hyde, Graham and Betty Mitchell, John Morris, signalman and co-founder of the Signalling Record Society and Bill Noke of the General Manager's Office, Paddington – all were encouraging and helpful. My sister Frances and her husband Camilus for their hospitality during my researching sessions in London. Duncan McAra and Jeannie Brooke Barnet of John Murray also deserve my thanks for their support in what has been quite a difficult task. Last, but by no means least, I must thank my wife Susan and my daughters Rebecca, Constance and Beatrice for putting up with me when I got bad-tempered while the book was being difficult.

Adrian Vaughan, 1987

Acknowledgements for the Edition of 2012

I am glad to have the opportunity to thank my dear wife, Susan, for her support for my railway obsession over the years. I would like to thank my editor and friend, Nicola Gale, at Amberley Publishing for accommodating my various lapses of memory, and last but by no means least, my good old friend Ron Price, for taking the colour transparencies when we visited Didcot East Junction box back in 1963.

Adrian Vaughan
Barney
North Norfolk
2012

Prologue

I do not remember a time when I was not passionately interested in railways. The embankment of the Southern Railway formed the eastern boundary of Palmer Park in Reading, my home town, and on the embankment was the distant signal for Kennet Spur signal box: a yellow arm on a grimy, latticework mast, which was known to me in my pre-school years as the 'Yellow Signal' on account of the colour of the arm. I knew nothing, in 1945, of the purpose of a distant signal to act as a 'Caution' for a 'Stop' signal ahead. I knew only that when an arm was horizontal it meant 'stop' and when raised it meant 'go' and when that particular signal was raised it heralded the swift passage of a steam or electric train running smartly down the hill from Earley. So when I first saw a train go past the arm when it was in its horizontal position, I was alarmed – like any good railwayman – at this apparent disregard for safety and ran home to tell my mother and frantically demand that she do something about it.

Railways were the greatest free show available to boys of all ages anywhere in Britain. I grew up with them by day, and at night I often lay awake and listened to the clashing ring of shunted wagon buffers or the rhythmic snorting of a labouring goods engine in the toils of Earley bank, five minutes out of the yard and already short of steam. On the Southern Railway during 1945–49 there were at work the tall-chimneyed, gangling, erstwhile express engines of the London & South Western Railway, the South Eastern & Chatham, and even of the long-defunct London, Chatham & Dover Railway. They hauled grass-green carriages, knobbly-looking vehicles with much moulding around their small windows, panelled sides, a raised, glazed roof section at one end and a double row of ventilators on their roofs, like so many steel seashells.

When I started school, in January 1946, I discovered the Great Western and its elegance and quite looked down upon the puny Southern with its vintage trains, not realising that for the Southern, Reading was the terminus of a branch line, while for the Great Western, Reading was a very important junction on their most important Main line. With the exception of one unforgivably bad-tempered porter on Reading West station and one strict foreman on Reading (GWR) engine shed whose sense of responsibility did not allow him to let little boys trespass, the railwaymen I met in my schooldays were invariably friendly. So I trespassed warily on the strict foreman's domain but trespassed wantonly on locomotive footplates and in the little signal box called Woodley Bridge in Sonning Cutting.

By the age of eleven, when our family moved out to Childrey, in the Vale of the White Horse, I fancied I had a fair notion of how to operate a small signal box and, in theory at any rate, I knew how to drive a steam engine. I also thought I knew about railwaymen. They seemed to be the most humane and understanding of men who were prepared to break the rules so that I could share in the fascination of their somewhat secret world. Each footplate was a kingdom and the driver was King – although he would have been useless without his good fireman mate. Each signal box was as remote as a lighthouse yet inside each box there was a busy life, a constant communication with other boxes, carrying out an essential job under the hands of the best of men.

The station for Childrey was Challow. It was there that I became a volunteer railway worker. I was at the station early enough to be present when the 5.5 a.m. Paddington–Bristol parcels arrived at about 7 a.m. An elderly porter began unloading some heavy-looking cardboard boxes of Lyons cakes and I asked if I could help him. He accepted with a smile and a, 'Thank you, yes please'. That was Harry Strong. We loaded a four-wheeled barrow, piled high with various boxes, besides cakes, for the village shops for which Challow was the railhead and after the 'Hall' had blasted away with its long train we heaved the barrow down the ramp, over the barrow crossing and up the other side. Harry got me to 'call off' each parcel as he entered its details into a ledger. Then he made the tea and had a sandwich and by the time that was done the parcels delivery lorry had arrived and I helped to load it.

Twice a day, three times a week, I could ride around the station on the engine of the Fly, the local, pick-up goods. At Challow, on the Fly, I was able to put my driving theory into practice, first with the driver's large hand over mine, then, when we had both gained confidence, on my own. Helping Harry load and sheet wagons in the station goods shed, I was very shortly invited into the 63-lever signal box and now I began to learn the Signalling Regulations. Bill Mattingley, the signalman I first met, was an ex-Warrant Officer Class 1 from the wartime RAF. He said to me – 'If you are going to come up here regular you will have to read this.' He handed me the GWR Signalling Regulations book. I took it home and immediately started to study it. A week later, Bill asked me if I had been reading it and when I said 'Yes' he asked me the basic question, 'When can you give "Line Clear" for a train to approach?' and so he coached me in proper working. Railwaymen felt sure that this freedom was part of the natural order of life, otherwise they would not have allowed me the privileges they so freely gave. I felt free to learn and to enjoy the beauties of machinery and the intricacies of railway life.

When I joined the railway at Challow in September 1960 after nearly five years in the army, I joined with men who were already friends to give an enthusiastic service to the local community. I constructed a garden – which the GWR had omitted to provide when they rebuilt the station in the 1930s – and cosseted the passengers so that they felt welcome and comfortable. In doing this I did no more than was being done at a thousand country stations; there was an entirely selfish feeling of satisfaction to be gained from 'soft-soaping' the passengers just to see the appreciation on their faces. There was also a great deal of pleasure to be gained in the company of the old-hand railwaymen and in the stories they told as we worked on jobs that had changed little or not at all since railways began: loading, sheeting and roping down wagonloads of produce or manufactures, writing out wagon labels and waybills in the dusty office of the great, brick goods shed which was undoubtedly part of Brunel's original Great Western Railway and which Western Region, sadly, later pulled down.

From the Dickensian desk and stool of the goods shed, the shunting pole and the fresh flowers in the waiting room at Challow, I went to the late Victorian signal box at Uffington, built in the year of Queen Victoria's Diamond Jubilee. There were certainly better signalmen than I; I probably did not have the best temperament for the job but there was none more enthusiastic for the job. I rode the footplates of many engines, often acting as fireman, sometimes even as driver – all strictly against the rules, of course. I visited many signal boxes. I learnt about the skills of the manually operated railway, the folklore and the morale that enables men to carry out hard, dirty work (in the case of steam engines) with cheerfulness and even enthusiasm. The underpinning of the steam-hauled railway was the sense of loyalty to the past, the sense of present challenge to which one rose and conquered and, finally, the sense of continuity that gave us all a feeling of security for the future. Albert Stanley, who had taught me my duties at Challow in 1960, had begun his service in 1920 at Dauntsey, where he had learnt his first lessons from a man who had begun his service on the broad (7 feet) gauge Great Western in 1870. So long as we had steam engines and semaphore signalling the railway was essentially Victorian but, unfortunately, in the mid-1960s neither Management nor Government thought of this as a virtue. The strength or charm of working on the railway then was to be on this rare peninsula of time, a land of old-fashioned manual work and reliability, jutting out into an ever-rising ocean of 'efficiency', unreliability and built-in redundancy.

I became a signalman at Challow three years before the floodtide of 'modernity' swamped and swept away first the station and its service to the community, then whole Main lines and, finally, a way of life. As one among many railwaymen who was drowned I can hardly be expected to be grateful to the waves.

CHAPTER ONE

Blissful Ignorance

I started my first week as signalman at Challow on night shift during March 1962, driving down to the station in a Morris 8 saloon whose 1935 vintage headlamps sent out six-volt light through kitchen glass 'lenses'. The car was parked in Brunel's cavernous goods shed opposite the signal box, bright as a lighthouse in the night. I stopped at the side of the Up Relief line to see if it was safe to cross the four tracks and was in time to see and hear Jim Spinage belling the 9.50 p.m. Swindon to York express, the 'tinging' of the bells and the muffled 'whump, thump' of the levers being swung over by Jim's stout arms and strong back. The interior of the box looked splendid at five minutes to ten at night, when the red, blue, black, blue-brown and yellow levers with their long, brass badges and burnished steel handles flashed like a full-dress military parade under the stark light of three electric bulbs. The glass-like linoleum floor covering reflected the colours, the fire was bright and so was Jim's 'going home' smile. He was soon away on his BSA 'Bantam' motorcycle, leaving me in sole charge of four Main lines and fifty-one levers until six o'clock next morning. I felt like a one-time pupil of a school, now returned as a master.

I took my job at Challow more seriously than I had done at Uffington, because Uffington was only a 'passing' box while Challow had the important function of 'regulating' trains – each Up or Down train's progress had to be carefully monitored to see if there was a case for diverting it to the Relief line to allow a following, faster train to overtake. We called this 'margining'. I was most concerned that there should be no delay to a passenger train because of my bad margining; I had to be more alert to the developing traffic situation; I had more duties in disseminating train-running information Up and Down the line; and, as the nights wore on, I became far more tired at Challow than I had been at Uffington. Later I would become fitter, more used to the strain. On the Saturday morning of my first week at Challow, the 2.45 a.m. Swindon 'Loco Yard' to Bordesley goods had clanked sedately past up the Main line at 4 a.m. This was followed by a 'light' engine for Oxford, which was standing at my Up home signal as the 'Loco Yard' cleared the Intermediate Block Section signals at Circourt, about 1 ½ miles eastwards. Had I not been so tired I would have realised that the goods was travelling rather slower than usual and that, as the Milford Haven to Paddington sleeping car train would be following the 'light' engine, that engine ought to go 'up the shute' (Up Relief line) to Wantage Road, out of the way of the Milford. What I did was to allow the engine to come up the Main line towards the signal box and no sooner had I done this than I realised my mistake. I went to the window with a red light to stop the engine and give its driver instructions that would rectify the error. The engine was a 'Grange'.

'Go up past Number Three and stop clear of the points. When you get the dummy* go back into the platform loop,' I shouted to the driver.

He gave me a disgusted look and set off. I gave 'Train out of Section' – 2-1 on the bell – to Elwyn Richards at Uffington and gave him 'Line Clear' when he rang out four beats for the Milford. I set the points for the engine but signal 42 simply would not budge; it had probably not been used for years. I felt frustration in that I could not make this rare movement and I felt panic that, with the 'Loco Yard' somewhere between me and Wantage and this engine also occupying the Up Main line, the Milford sleeper was going to be delayed as a result of my error. The next feeling was a desperate resolve that I would not be beaten and that I could still retrieve the situation. I replaced the points and, with a white light waved from side to side out of the signal box window, I called the driver back to the box. I told him to go back outside the home signal and enter the Relief line when I lowered the signal. Without a word but with a look that said it all, he went on his way.

That I had violated the most sacred regulation in the book hardly occurred to me then. In my tired and inexperienced state, all that mattered to me was that the Milford should not be delayed on my account. As I turned the Relief-line points for the engine standing outside the Up home signal, Elwyn sent the 'Train Entering Section' signal – two beats on the bell – the Milford was passing Uffington, three minutes away. The sound of that high-pitched bell was like a sharp knife through my head as suddenly I realised the position in which I had placed many innocent people as well as myself. The men on the 'Grange' took ages to blow off their brake. I stood at the open window listening to the hoarse 'haaa' of the ejector

---

*   The ground signal.

and knew that the driver was deliberately 'hanging the pot on' to show his annoyance with me. The sound of the sleeping car train, drumming along at about 55 mph, came creeping through the night air; several seconds passed agonisingly before the 'Grange' made its first 'chuff' and began to move – very slowly – inside the protection of the home signal, which I slammed back to 'Danger' because several lives and my job depended on it. As soon as the track circuit cleared and unlocked the points, I heaved the levers over, setting the route for the Main line before snatching 'off' the Up Main signals: 2, 3, 5 and 1 in that order. I heard an answering 'toot' from the unsuspecting driver of the Milford who, seeing my distant signal change from amber 'Caution' to green 'All Clear' right in front of his cab, thought merely that I had been late in 'pulling off' as a result of sleepiness.

As the Milford sailed by, the 'Loco Yard' cleared Wantage Road. I 'got the road' for the Milford on the Main line and for the engine on the Relief line and pulled over the necessary levers. The telephone at the far end of the Up platform rang in the box and I answered it. 'That fast was following us pretty tight, wasn't it?' It was the driver of the 'Grange', who must have seen my frantic flurry of activity. His voice was quiet, sarcastic yet also a little menacing. 'We all depend on you people, you know.' Before I could make any reply – and apart from apologies there was nothing to say – he mercifully replaced the telephone and drove away.

I did not allow my early stupidity to overshadow my enjoyment of the job but used the event to become a better signalman. I loved the box when the rain was streaming down the windows and the wind was howling through the telephone wires outside on their tall poles. The interior of the box then was so clean and warm and everything was proceeding in such an orderly way. I walked easily from bells and instruments to levers to train register while all outside seemed to be at the mercy of the storm. I loved the box, too, on those early summer or early autumn mornings when the sun was low and bright, making the dawn mist the colour of champagne and the locomotive's exhaust a dazzling white over a black smokebox and red buffer beam. I liked the job in the summer heat when all the windows were open; Sam or Albert – one of the porters from the station – would be reclining in my armchair with a mug of tea while I leant on the bar at the window to watch a train go by, checking it for all the things a signalman looked for to ensure safety. I watched the engine and its crew, checked all wheels for sparks from dragging brakes or flames from over-heated axleboxes, listened for untoward noises, looked for insecure doors, watched to see if the guard was trying to give me a message. Above all, I loved the box when it was really busy, when many arrangements had to be made and trains switched from line to line – such as at Christmas with all the 'Parcel Post' extra trains that ran among the usual traffic and the additional Christmas excursions.

Those people who wanted to visit the signal box had to be decent types, people who were genuinely interested – or at least had the sense not to distract me. Two of my 'regulars' at Challow were Gladys and her niece Pauline, whom I met while they were searching the lineside for wild flowers. They were caught in a sudden, summer thunderstorm and were already well soaked when they came hurrying past the box, going back to their car. I invited them in and that was the start of a very pleasant friendship for me, which resulted in the marriage of one of the ladies to a Challow signalman. On Sunday afternoons, when the box had been polished and there was a long gap in the train service, I would take a walk around the estate to see if everything was in order. One afternoon I set out to walk to my Down advanced starting signal, 783 yards. At the far end of the stroll I slipped off the sleeper-end and wrenched my ankle painfully, so much so that I had to hop and hobble the whole distance back to the box. On the Up-side horse-dock a family of four watched this procedure in silent amazement. At the box door I leant on the wall and called across to the father to ask if he felt like spending an hour or two pulling levers under my direction, as I would be quite unable to do the job. He leaped at the opportunity and, under my instructions, did what was necessary with the levers while I hopped about to see to the bells, phones and train register. For a while afterwards he became a regular visitor to the box.

I had two other occasional visitors to the box. One was Bill Kenning. I had first met Bill in April 1964 at Haddenham, where I had gone to photograph 4079 *Pendennis Castle* hauling an excursion to the Festiniog Railway. I was using one of my father's large, old plate cameras on a tripod. The camera – a Marion 'Tropical Soho' quarter-plate – had a body of polished teak, honey coloured, admirably embellished with brass fittings and red leather bellows. Bill, a connoisseur of anything out of the ordinary, spotted it from his perch in the signal box 300 yards away and came hurrying down the line for a closer look. He was a most out-of-the-ordinary person, completely mad about trains. We were friends at once. A few days later he sent me notice of his impending arrival at Challow in the form of a pseudo railway 'extra train notice': 'SPECIAL: DITCHLING TO CHALLOW, 'A' HEADCODE. THIS TRAIN MUST RUN PUNCTUALLY.' This was followed by a timetable of the journey, including stops for 'water' at various hostelries. When he got to the signal box he handed me his 'guard's log', wherein it appeared that he had arrived several minutes ahead of the time, which was, in his own words, 'simply priceless'. He was about sixty-five, of medium height and build, with a clipped, white, military moustache, an accent straight out of the glove compartment of a Rolls-Royce and that curiously languid elegance of an upper-crust Englishman who is absolutely sure of himself and his place in the world. However, the one thing Bill was not was a snob – he was too much of a gentleman for that.

He had driven up from deepest Sussex in his Riley 'Redwing', an open car looking like a bathtub on solid steel, disc wheels. He had bought it new in 1923 when he was an undergraduate at Merton College, Oxford; it had survived the destruction of three gear boxes on impromptu 'hill-climbing trials' up Headington hill; he had driven his bride, Kathleen, away from the church in it and he had been driving it ever since. He drove into the station yard honking its klaxon and waving a guard's green flag, his tweed cap firmly and squarely down on his head. Looking down from the signal box, I could see that the car was painted GWR green (he told me later that the paint came from Swindon factory) and was lined out in black and orange panels; touches of brass here and there set the colour scheme off nicely. There was a lot of rubbish piled on the back seat and, staring hard, I began to see that he had a large pile of rooks' nests, a bicycle and a bundle of chimney-sweeping rods. Had I been able to see inside, I would have noticed some ceramic insulators off telephone-pole cross-bars, some oily cotton waste and the top lid of an engine driver's tea can. On the back bumper was a large red disc bearing the white letters LV – Last Vehicle – a relic of the London, Brighton & South Coast Railway, which used such devices by day instead of tail lamps.

Bill was the only visitor I had who signed himself into and out of the box in the train register. The first time he did this I was alarmed; 'The Book' was not the place for trespassers to advertise their presence. 'Please don't concern yourself, dear boy,' he drawled, 'but read this'. He took from his wallet a much folded piece of paper. It bore the Lion and Crown crest of the British Transport Commission, was headed 'General Manager's Office, Paddington' and carried the following message: ALLOW CAPTAIN W. L. KENNING TO ENTER ANY SIGNAL BOX AND TO TRAVEL ON ANY ENGINE. It was signed by Lance Ibbotson, Assistant General Manager Western Region. So, far from trespassing, Bill had every right to be in the box and therefore was *entitled* to sign the register to mark the length of his visit. I discovered later that Bill's son, Michael, had gone to his father's old school, Radley, and while there had been close friends with Lance Ibbotson's son.

Bill's enthusiasm for railways was equalled by his love of cricket – each year he arranged for the MCC to come to play Ditchling on the village green – and by his detestation of magpies and crows. It was this that caused him to carry those chimney-sweeping rods. He detested these particular birds because they ate the eggs of other birds, so he conducted a war against the predators. When he saw a magpie's nest he stopped his car and planted his special warning sign in the roadside verge. This sign was a red disc on a 5-foot-tall white post. Across the middle of the disc was the word DANGER in white letters and all around the edge the words MAG-CROW OPERATIONS. He assembled his rods and advanced to the attack. When he had succeeded in dislodging the nest or nests he put them on the back seat of the car, rather like a Red Indian brave adding another scalp to his belt. So this was Bill Kenning. At first I gave him step-by-step instructions as to how to answer a bell and pull a lever. It was only after he died that I discovered that he was well known in signal boxes from Brighton to Weymouth and Banbury and had, as an amateur, been working lever frames since 1913 at least. In all the time I knew him and told him how to do the job his courteous manners were such that he never said to me 'I know' but had simply accepted my instructions.

My only other, in any way regular, visitor was Ron Price. He arrived one Sunday afternoon in his Morris 'Minor'. He parked opposite the box, went to the 'Prince of Wales', came back with a pint of beer, unwrapped his sandwiches and sat down on the ground with his legs dangling over the horse dock. He stayed there for an hour and left. Three weeks later, I was on Sunday day turn – 12 hours – again and he turned up. He had got his beer and sandwiches out so I called across and asked him if he would not be more comfortable in the signal box. He came over and we are still friends nearly fifty years later. He was born in Preston, Lancs, and spent his school days – during the Second World War – visiting the signal boxes and experiencing the fantastic working of such massive places as Euxton Junction.

I did my own fair share of signal box visiting. The men on duty when I visited Didcot East Junction were Don Shackle and Joe Moore, with a booking lad called Peter. Joe was from Devon, quite young for a Special Class signalman, but Don was perhaps sixty, tall and slim with an unaffectedly refined 'BBC English' accent. He worked in a railway jacket and waistcoat with a cloth cap. Joe spoke in loud, exuberant tones to 'the Lad', to Don and even to the passing trains, urging them to get a move on, whamming levers about with great vigour while Don worked quietly, with an economy of effort. When he passed Peter sitting on his tall stool at the booking desk and Peter tipped Don's cap over his eyes with the end of his ruler, Don would not raise his voice but would request gently, 'Try not to do that, Peter. I might trip over the cat.' I was never sure if Don's accent and very restrained speech was his real nature or an elegant and continuous piece of sarcasm. There were several cats in the signal box. The Chief was 'old Tom', a black-and-white moggy who reclined on the instrument shelf in a 'Lord of all he surveyed' pose or wandered casually among the instruments while they were being operated, draping his tail across the signalman's eyes. Another of his pleasures was to weave sinuously around the levers, threading his body through the gaps as levers were being slammed back into the row with the rest. He was quite deliberate about this, as if he enjoyed hearing the Devonshire voice of Joe hurling curses at him when a lever had to be stopped in full flight to save the cat from being crushed. The other cats were the nursing mothers and their litters; one lived in a sack of waste paper at the east end of the 150-lever signal box and the other was in the locking room below the operating floor.

The first time I went into East Junction, Don said, in his quiet way, 'Are you interested in learning this job, Adrian?' He seemed most solicitous and I replied that I would like nothing better. 'Righto, then. There's an engine on the Newbury branch for shed. You can pull off for it.' He pressed the button on the loud-hailing Tannoy telephone, which had a loudspeaker in the shunters' cabin. 'Clear the spur for one off the Gold Coast for shed,' he ordered. I was examining the track diagram over the instruments, trying to see which levers unlocked which other levers; there seemed to be a great deal of pulling and pushing required and I had no idea where to start. After a minute the Tannoy crackled, 'OK, Don, clear on the Spur.'

'Come on then,' said Don, 'let's have that engine over.'

I had to admit defeat. 'Tell me what to pull and I'll pull them.'

Joe and Peter laughed and looked on with interest as Don began calling out the relevant lever numbers. Facing point bolts and the bolts on the switch diamonds had to be moved, and point levers pulled over and then re-bolted. The signal levers then had to be pulled. I thought I was never going to stop, especially as, being completely unfamiliar with the feel or weight of each lever, I did not know how hard to pull each one nor how easily each would come over. I pushed and pulled twenty-nine levers until, with a block of eighteen standing over in the centre of the frame, I had the route set and, with a cheeky 'toot', a little pannier tank came scampering diagonally across all the tracks to the Down avoiding line goods loop, where it stopped. Now that route had to be restored – twenty-nine lever movements – and a fresh route set from the Down loop to the shunting spur, restore those levers and then pull some more to get the engine into the Engine Line.

To assist the signalmen at Didcot East Junction and Reading West Main signal boxes in the organisation of the train services over their complicated and important junctions, and to allow them to know how much time they could allot to shunting movements on or across the Main lines, an instant information service between the two boxes was provided by the booking lads using a Tannoy. The 'send' button at Didcot East Junction was pressed and the booking lad would chant such messages as, 'Worcester up the runner, Swindon up the shute and the Weston's fifteen late off Swindon.' This blared out inside West Main box so that the Lad there noted it in the register and the signalmen knew that they could expect the Worcester express in fifteen minutes, the Swindon 'stopper' on the Up Relief line in twenty-five and the Weston, well, she was 'well down the pan' and they'd probably get the Swansea Up first. The Tannoy was a loudspeaker system, not a telephone, and messages were interspersed with a fair amount of good-natured obscenity between the booking boys. Someone suggested that it would be a good idea if the Tannoy circuit could be extended to Steventon, then inquiries for train-running information – previously directed at Didcot East Junction from Challow or Swindon – could be redirected to Steventon, where the signalman had more time to deal with them. The bawling out of train running information was bad enough but no one had thought about the informal parts of the Tannoy broadcasts, so that, when it was installed in Steventon box, right in the middle of the village, the raucous jokes of the booking lads at East Junction and West Main brayed out over the peaceful thatch and gardens where villagers sunned themselves in deckchairs. The Steventon signalmen were embarrassed, the villagers were outraged and, recovering themselves, they stormed the stationmaster's office at Didcot and demanded that the objectionable thing be removed. It was.

Booking lads were sometimes a sore trial to their signalmen. Not from any failing on their part to do the job; on the contrary, all booking boys I ever came across were experts and, at sixteen years of age, were quite capable of doing the signalman's job for him. No, it was a highly competent, confident lad's appetite for mischief that could bear down heavily on the signalman. When Joe and Don could not see their lad they became nervous and looked about with feelings of mistrust, saying things like, 'Where's that blasted Peter got to?' And well they might. One day, Joe went outside to kick back to 'Danger' a ground signal which had 'stuck off'. Don then had the entire box to manage and was too busy to notice Peter sliding back the west end window with one hand while holding a milk bottle full of water in the other. As Joe came back to the box he got a pint of cold water over his head and came roaring up the stairs, vowing vengeance, but Peter had already climbed into the rafters. Joe prodded at him with the broom handle but Peter refused to come down, hopping about on the beam, dodging the stick until, with the train register being neglected, Joe had to promise not to murder him if he came down. Through all this Don was patiently working the box and seeing to the register as best he could.

After a few minutes, Peter apologised and offered Joe a cigarette. Joe, mollified, took one. Peter had one too and asked Joe for a light. Joe took out his box of Swan Vestas, lit up and handed the still burning match to Peter. The lad lit his cigarette and shoved the still-burning match into the box which Joe was holding in his hand. The box of matches ignited, Joe flung it away so that it landed on the cat, who leaped onto the instrument shelf while Peter took once more to the rafters. Joe raced the length of the box to stamp on the burning box and all the while the imperturbable Don Shackle walked up and down his 150 levers, peaked cap facing sternly forwards, avoiding cat, boy and burning matchbox to answer bells and pull levers to keep the all-unsuspecting Great British Public on the move.

CHAPTER TWO

Scrapping Steam

The semaphore system of signalling allowed men to feel free, to laugh and joke with mates on the telephone and, in signal boxes where there was a booking lad, to indulge in horseplay that could occasionally become rough. On the other hand, some signalmen were exceedingly strict with their lads. One man I particularly recall at Swindon would not allow his lad to spend more than thirty seconds in answering a telephone. Once, when I was walking along the track in the vicinity of that box, the booking lad came to the window to speak and was pulled back to his stool by the signalman! These were rarities, and for the most part the job went along in good spirits. Between Foxhall Junction, Didcot, and Highworth Junction, Swindon, both boxes included, there were eleven signal boxes. In them were employed about forty-five signalmen, with perhaps six Signal & Telegraph Department linemen for their maintenance. The 23 miles of track between Foxhall and Highworth Junctions were divided into 'block sections' with an average length of 2 miles. It may be said, therefore, that an express train was examined by a signalman every two or three minutes of its journey. The trains – passenger and freight – were shepherded along the route and any trouble was pounced on before it could develop into anything serious. Scores of men were usefully employed in serving the community; this was the railway I had known all my life and an excellent system it appeared to be. The equipment we used was relatively reliable, having stood the test of time over generations in some cases. During the period 5 September–7 October 1959 there was one track-circuit failure and one bell failure, each lasting ninety minutes, at Challow box; no other failure was logged in the train register during that time, when at least 5,700 trains passed the box. The entire layout was track circuited. Between 29 April and 10 June 1964, when 'the writing was on the wall', Challow box suffered one equipment failure each week, with about 5,500 trains passing the box in that time.

When I discovered that the signal box, which I and my mates so carefully polished, and which I tried to be so conscientious in running, was considered by Management to be inefficient and that my mates and I were too expensive to employ I felt, not unnaturally, considerable inner turmoil. In 1963, nothing less than a revolution was under way. I saw the 'Western' and 'Hymek' diesels as the tumbrils, colour-light signals as gallows and top Management-types as the Dantons and Robespierres of the piece, busy guillotining old hands and dispensing with a large part of the railway – a way of life. The basis of my entire growing-up was being swept away; my loyalties were outraged and economics had no part of the argument. I wanted to live and work with all my mates – balance sheets played no part in the humanity of my railway.

But of course, the railway was ruled not by railwaymen but by wreckers from outside industries. Dr Beeching had stated that 'the railway must be run by professional railwaymen' and out of the fourteen members of the Board of which he was Chairman, two were railwaymen. There were accountants, a man from the board of Shell petrol, another, Sir Philip Shirley, from Batchelors Peas, and some at least of these had been detached from their companies because they were the men that company could most happily lose. They were not committed to the railway – they were members of the revolving door club, the quick fix without a wider agenda.

The withdrawal of the steam engines was not well managed by Western Region management, but they had these people above them urging them on. Had it not been for the much-maligned steam engines, Western Region could not have run a full service of trains, at times, between 1962–65. Some trains suffered three or four diesel failures on one journey before a steam engine came to the rescue. During the same period scrapyards – both railway and privately owned – could not keep up with the spate of steamers arriving at their gates for destruction while the factory at Swindon could not cope with the number of broken-down diesels awaiting repair. During 1963 the programme of diesel building was suspended in order to devote time to overhauling steam engines! Queues of scrap steam engines lined the trackside at Oxford, Didcot and Reading while queues of broken-down diesels waited for shops. Only the former gave rise to offence in the eyes of top Management, and the decree went forth that steam engines had to be stored, hidden from public gaze.

There were on Western Region, on 1 November 1963, 247 condemned steam engines; thirty-nine were allocated to Swindon works for cutting-up but the remainder had to be sold to contractors. These private firms bought in bulk but could take only four or five engines a week, as it required that time to break them and make room for more, so that the total scrapping rate for Western Region was fifty per month, with 1,384 locomotives (not to mention hundreds of carriages and wagons) to be destroyed; the Region hoped to get the fleet down to 650 steam engines by the end of 1964. For me, this programme – however rational to Management – was nothing less than a wholesale slaughter of my 'best friends'. It also led to fewer trains being run, especially seasonal extras, which led to more mayhem on the roads. From October 1963 the pressure was on to get rid of steam engines even faster by finding fresh outlets – new scrapyards – and to 'improve the aesthetic appearance of some locomotive depots'* in the meantime by hiding the poor, rusting hulks from public gaze. In general the engines were scrapped on ex-GWR territory, for the very good reason that there was a danger of the locomotives coming into contact with bridges and platform edges if they went 'abroad'. Some 'County' class engines were sent successfully to Norwich but when, in October 1963, Western Region sold 'Castle' class 5001, 5060, 7015 and 7037 to a firm in Blackwall, on the Eastern Region, the engines were en route before some ordinary railwayman questioned whether they would clear the Eastern Region loading gauge in that backwater of London's railway. Then the fat was in the fire! The breakers had paid for the engines as representing so many tons of this or that metal and the only way they could arrive at their destinations was if their cabs, chimneys, safety valves and outside cylinders were removed – the cost of dismantling being borne by Western Region. A period of reflection followed, after which the breakers received five small tank engines and a credit note.

Firms buying many of the engines frequently came up against the problem of non-delivery. Several weeks after a firm had paid for an engine they discovered that it had not arrived in their yard. On investigating this, Western Region found that such engines had been dispatched from the engine shed, so there was a mystery until it was realised that the engines were travelling without name or number plates, these having been stripped off for sale to souvenir hunters; the breakers had no idea what had been delivered and what had not. It also appeared that engines were being towed to yards without so much as a waybill as a means of identification. The latter problem was solved by a few anguished letters from Head Office to the Divisions, and the matter of identity was solved with some white paint. The 'dead' engines ran without much regard for lubrication, so coupling and connecting rods were removed and thrown into the tender – or 'coal

---

* Letter from London Divisional Manager to Chief Mechanical Engineer.

department' as one scrapyard called it in a letter to Western Region. This enabled the engines to arrive with the right amount of white metal in the rods' bearings but then the breakers complained that some engines were arriving without any rods at all. It transpired that these were tank engines whose rods had been placed in the tender of another engine. Sometimes the condemned engines were hauled too fast and developed hot axle bearings, whereupon the white metal ran onto the sleepers, to the chagrin of the scrappers. One of the saddest sights, for me, was to see a condemned engine, in steam, hauling four or five of its brethren 'dead' to the knacker's yard.

There seems little doubt that serviceable engines were scrapped. As one diesel could, in theory, do the work of three steam engines, one new diesel to a depot would displace that many steamers and I think it is probable that many engines, recently repaired, were sent for scrap because of such displacement. Engines were condemned at a depot and sold to a scrap dealer at a price including transport from that depot to the scrapyard. There were cases where, after an engine had been sold for scrap, it was used in traffic and 'disappeared'. The scrap dealer would complain of non-delivery and the engine would be 're-discovered' at another depot a hundred miles away. What concerned the Region was the cost of getting the engine to the scrapyard, this being greater from the new site than that budgeted for a month earlier from the original depot. What concerned the Shed Foreman was finding enough engines to work the traffic; he would see a decent engine on 'death row' and borrow it. The knowledge that serviceable engines were being sent for scrap at a time of locomotive shortages must have been very frustrating to the operators. Sometimes, before an engine was sent away, its serviceable tender would be removed and replaced by an unserviceable one off a working locomotive. This would be detected by the scrapyard and a complaint lodged. Late in 1962, the Locomotive Department fought this issue with Head Office at Paddington; there was no reason why the scrapyard should want a 4,500-gallon tender with a vacuum brake cylinder in good condition when that cylinder was needed for a working engine – there was just as much metal in a 4,500-gallon tender with a defective vacuum brake cylinder. After a month of wrangling the point was conceded and tenders were authorised to be swapped.

General Manager Gerald Fiennes was highly respected by his immediate staff but he was 'under orders' and he wanted all steam engines to be withdrawn ASAP 'just get rid of them'. Once withdrawn they could not be scrapped quickly enough and so they stood about on shed sidings, making a mess. They were then to be hidden from public gaze. The Gadarene rush to scrap was very crude; it caused a great deal of delay to passengers and extra expense to his railway because of wasted time, fuel, and temper. On 27 November 1963 there were seventeen 'dead' engines stored on scarce siding space at Old Oak Common, the main shed for Western Region. They had been towed to Old Oak Common from Reading, Didcot and Oxford, 'to improve the aesthetic nature of the engine shed', he said in his instruction. As if engine sheds were ever possessed of 'aesthetic' qualities for the average railway passenger. On 12 December there were twenty-seven. Old Oak shed at that time was in process of being reconstructed as a 'diesel depot' and the alterations had placed siding space at a premium, so the scrap engines were crowding working engines out of their legitimate standing room. The situation was exceedingly difficult and the General Manager's directive simply exacerbated the situation. The twenty-seven engines were towed back to Reading, Didcot and Oxford.

While the only reliable motive power Western Region possessed was being destroyed as fast as humanly possible, the pioneers of the new image – the diesels – were frequently breaking down. No one, not even I, would have suggested that the new traction was not immensely fast and powerful, but I was astonished at its apparent fragility: at £100,000 each, surely such locomotives should have had the same measure of reliability as an equivalent steam engine costing one-tenth of that price to build? As it was, I was able to enjoy the sight of a steam engine in full cry at the head of an express train, standing in for some broken-down diesel, being driven with great gallantry by a crew determined to show what a real engine could do. Gradually, but inexorably, the diesels took over more trains until, by the start of September 1963, all Cheltenham, Bristol, Worcester, South Wales and West of England expresses were scheduled for diesel haulage. On 24 September the Bristol Division issued a notice to all staff regarding the lack of punctuality, which concluded, 'The seriousness of the position is reflected in the fact that, compared to the corresponding period last year, there was a decrease of nearly 13% in the number of passenger trains arriving at their destination on time and in addition more than 10% arrived 30 minutes late or more.' It seemed to me, at the time, useless to complain to the men about a lack of punctuality when it was the Management's Gadarene approach to the 'modern image' that was resulting in bad time-keeping.

On 27 September the Worcester line was back to 100 per cent steam haulage as its 'Hymeks' either failed or were taken for use on more important routes. Goods trains were cancelled to provide diesel power for express trains and Swindon factory was ordered to suspend its diesel-building programme to concentrate on clearing the backlog of diesel repairs and to repair more steam engines. The latter were given medium attention, falling short of new or exchange boilers or cylinders. They were turned out in fresh, GWR-type livery to give employment to boilersmiths and other craftsmen who were otherwise redundant in the diesel age. On 27 September 1963, there were thirty-five failed diesels in Swindon factory, two at Didcot shed and nine at Old Oak Common. No doubt lines of broken-down diesels did not offend the eye of Mr Fiennes or the travelling public and perhaps the latter did not mind being delayed for upwards of an hour so long as the source of the delay was the 'modern image' at the head of their train – but I was furious, for while 'my' steam engines were being slandered as 'inefficient' they continued to prop up the railway system.

Although Swindon was refurbishing some very capable, very smart 'Hall' and 'Grange' class engines, among other types, it was not always these that were to be seen at the head of express passenger trains. I recall seeing, on 9 March 1964, 4089 *Donnington Castle* with the Up 'Cathedrals Express' at Oxford. The engine had been 'stored' for a year or so and had corroded to a ghastly, corpse-like green. It carried neither name nor number plates and had no glass in any of the cab windows. There was a bitter wind blowing so the crew were working in atrocious conditions but they had done their passengers proud. A ten-minute late start from Kingham, arising from the earlier diesel failure, had been cut to a five-minute late start from Oxford, and Paddington was reached five minutes early; this was on the diesel's accelerated schedule with a load of 420 tons. I wonder even more if any passenger thought to thank the enginemen for their splendid effort?

The other Main routes of Western Region were all diesel hauled and the Worcester line passengers felt they were being fobbed off – as 'second-class citizens' – with steam engines. They formed a lobbying group and wrote to the General Manager, complaining of their awful plight. As a result of this, great efforts were made to find 'Hymek' diesels and more goods trains became steam hauled to release the diesels. As from 1 May 1964, the Worcester trains were all hauled by 'Hymek' diesels. Almost at once the failures began. I only got to hear of a few. On 3 May the 'Hymek' on the 4.5 p.m. Hereford failed at Norton Junction, just south of Worcester, and 6960 *Raveningham Hall** was substituted. None of the passengers got out and walked – in protest at the shabby treatment – as far as I am aware. 6960 *Raveningham Hall* left Norton Junction thirty-two minutes late with nine

---

*   Now privately owned in first-class working order on Severn Valley Railway.

coaches for 320 tons and arrived in Paddington six minutes late. In October 1964 the Down 'Cathedrals Express' failed at Finstock Halt, 5 miles beyond Handborough, 1 ½ miles before Charlbury, causing a delay of 2 ½ hours. In fairness to the 'Hymek', not all the delay was directly attributable to its malfunction. The diesel 'secondman' walked back to Handborough to ask for assistance rather than forwards to Charlbury. Assistance took the form of a much-despised steam engine, 73049, from Oxford shed. This shoved the train through to Kingham, where it was able to get onto the front of the train and, hauling the 'dead' diesel and its train, kept the schedule from there to Worcester.

At Challow I saw a good deal of 'ex-works' steam engines because, as they came from the shops, the Swindon Shed Foreman put them onto the traditional 'running-in' turn on the Challow 'stopper'. In 1964 this was the 7.35 a.m. Swindon to Didcot, first stop Challow. The load was two coaches and many men used the job to have a merry dash up the Main line. I kept a daily record of their exploits when I was on early turn and logged some hilarious sprints, far faster than was required by the timetable. The motive power was provided by the 'Modified Halls', 'Granges' and 'Manors', all looking spick-and-span in their livery of middle chrome green. They braked to 20 mph for the junction points from Up Main to Up Relief some 300 yards before the signal box and then opened up hard, accelerating past the box before screeching to a stand at the station. The drivers knew I was interested in their games and always had a smile and a wave for me as they shot past the signal box. On 31 January 1964, 7928 *Wolf Hall* went from Swindon to Challow station, start to stop, 13 1/8 miles, in 13 minutes and, it should be remembered, the driver had to come down to 20 mph half a mile before the station. On 22 February, 7928 *Wolf Hall* was hauling the 10.5 a.m. Hereford, 320 tons, 50 minutes late starting from Oxford as a result of a diesel failure. Paddington was reached 36 minutes late with a steady 92 mph over the 14 miles from Maidenhead to Southall. That was showing them how! I was on board and felt so proud of the engine and the men who were willing to have a go.

The story of the closure of Challow station has already been told in *Signalman's Twilight*. Western Region Management simply saw the place as a complication, an extra stop, a 'bump' on the otherwise station-less railway between Didcot and Swindon. The fact that Challow had been a successful passenger station and was ideally sited in a wide, rural area to act as what is now known as a 'Parkway' was of no importance. Local railwaymen pointed this out to Wantage Town Council and urged that a station be kept at either Challow or Wantage, but no one seemed interested. During the last twenty years, however, the district has grown in importance and a completely new road system has had to be built from Steventon and Didcot to carry growing numbers of commuters from the Vale to Didcot station. The cost of this road, though it comes from taxpayers' money, is not shown on the railway balance sheet and no one asks whether roads are profitable.

Bill Kenning and Ron Price came to Challow to help local people and staff give the last train – the 6.1 p.m. Didcot to Swindon, hauled by 6112 – a decent send-off with every fog signal 'banger' we had in stock.

Since Challow was shut on 5 December 1964, Western Region has subsequently opened 'Parkway' stations at Castle Cary, near Bristol and near Tiverton. Perhaps they might, after all, reopen 'Challow Parkway'?

After the station's closure, all that remained was the signal box standing rather forlornly beside the line and, snaking alongside the rails, the black cables, the tentacles of Reading Panel signal box, reaching out 30 miles to strangle the signal boxes of the Vale and Thames Valley. As a fully paid-up member of the 'Luddite Brotherhood', I could see no virtue in the new system of signalling. It would cost £1,500,000 to put 200 men out of work, run fewer trains (the train service was reduced with modernisation) and serve fewer stations.

The automatic signalling system was not, at that time, as safe as the manual system. The problem was that for many miles there was no signal that could be placed at danger to stop a dangerous train or to stop a train running towards a dangerous situation – and of course, no signalmen to see a dangerous situation developing. If the Panel control centre was told of a dangerous situation by someone out along the line, the man in the Panel was very limited in what he could do to protect the trains. With steam haulage, the railway was relatively free of hot axle bearings. A hot bearing will develop when the bearing in the axle box runs short of lubrication. This might be because of a lack of oil, or due to an oil-film breakdown from overloading – or excess speed. The axle bearing becomes red-hot and hotter, and if left unattended, will shear off and put the wagon down on the track. In the train register from Shrivenham signal box for the period 18 July to 22 August 1958, when at least 6,000 trains passed the box, there were no instances of hot axle-boxes recorded. In the Challow train register for the period of 5 September to 8 October 1959, when approximately 5,700 trains passed, there was one instance of a 'hot box', but between 13 and 18 May 1965 there were six 'hot boxes' out of about 650 trains. All these trains were hauled by powerful diesel locomotives and it is likely that the overheating was caused by excessive speed. Steam drivers on diesels tended to speed up; loose coupled trains behind steam went at 25 mph but behind diesels speed could creep up to 35 or even 40 on occasions. With a closed-in cab, sitting in a comfortable office chair, with 2,500 horsepower behind, 35 mph for mile after mile seemed very slow. Only the presence of a signal box every two or three miles prevented a serious accident; a signalman would see the crippled bearing and take steps not only to have that train stopped but also to prevent any other train from passing the cripple while it was moving.

Having been brought up on the old system, it filled me with anger to see this expensive 'accident-waiting-to-happen' system being established. Reading Panel extended its control to include Steventon on 27 September 1964. The Up and Down Relief lines between Wantage Road and Challow were taken out of use on 4 April 1965. On 26 May Challow lost its crossover points, leaving only double-track Main line, and became a simple 'passing box', with just a few signals for the Up and Down Main lines. Reading Panel became fully operational on 30 May 1965, and Challow signal box was abolished. The men in Reading Panel controlled – if that is the right word – the tracks as far west as Challow inclusive. The first semaphore signalling signal box was at Uffington. Trains ran from Scours Lane, Reading, to Moreton Cutting, Didcot – about 15 miles – without any manually controlled signal to stop them should they be running in a dangerous condition or to bring them to a stand should some other train have become derailed. And from Foxhall Junction, Didcot, to Challow, there were 10 miles free of any inspection or manually controlled signals.

There were two vacancies for signalmen at Uffington box and three redundant signalmen at Challow: Jim Spinage, Ken Rowlands and myself. I was by far the most junior so there seemed no chance of my going to Uffington, but around 26 May Ken Rowlands decided against continuing on the railway. Uffington would be abolished in two or three years so he felt he might as well get out while he was that much younger. This meant I was given the last vacancy at Uffington. My last shift in Challow box was completed at 1 p.m on Saturday 29 May 1965. At 3 p.m. the following day Jim Spinage and I were present in the box to see and hear Ken Rowlands tap out the 'Closing Signal Box' bell code, 7-5-5, to Wantage Road and Uffington and to hear the high-pitched Uffington bell and the mellow ring of the Wantage bell return the code. Ken Rowlands had begun his career on the Great Western, in Challow box, as a booking lad – and a very conscientious one, too – apprenticed to that most meticulous of signalmen, Bert Snell.

I did not go immediately to Uffington. Much to my surprise, I was told to stay at Challow, booking on there each day, to watch the trains go by and report on the telephone to Uffington if I saw anything amiss. Poetic justice, perhaps – I was so concerned about the lack of supervision of trains! The poetry of the situation had lost its savour by Wednesday. I telephoned the Staff Office to ask when I could go to Uffington and was told to hang on for a few more days. On Friday, alarmed at the thought of being forgotten at Challow, I telephoned again. On this occasion, the man at the opposite end of the wire in Reading thought he was talking to his colleague in Bristol and, when I asked to go to Uffington, said something to the effect, 'Well, you know what the trouble is, the District Inspector doesn't want him there.' The Swindon D. I. had known me since I was twelve and had been impressed with my knowledge of the signalling regulations at that tender age. He had, later, passed me on the rules and regulations exam for Uffington and Challow. I expressed a certain surprise at the Staff Officer's announcement and the man I was talking to, covered in confusion when he realised who he was talking to, told me to report for work at Uffington the following Monday morning. Later, I was told that the Swindon Reliefmen wanted a vacancy, which they could take turns in filling.

CHAPTER THREE

Cause for Concern

I went to Uffington signal box on Monday 7 June 1965. As Jim showed me the workings and the equipment of the new Uffington that Monday morning, his voice increasingly showed his concern as he went on. It was the lack of control over the signals that worried both of us. There was always a signal showing red for 'Danger' behind the train but that is only half the purpose of signalling. Once a train left the area of controlled signals at Uffington, Didcot or Reading, it was 'on its own' between those places for 10–15 miles. This seemed to us – Jim, Elwyn and me – to be a major failing in Multiple Aspect Signalling (MAS) but the system was the latest, money-saving idea and to criticise it on any account was to bring one's own sanity into question. The other great problem with MAS at that time was the unreliability of the equipment. The system was 'fail-safe' but that did not make delays from track-circuit failures, signal post telephone failures and berserk automatic lifting barriers any the less annoying. The malfunctions of the instrument used to 'describe' trains between Reading Panel and Uffington would have been funny had they not been such a nuisance. I spent five mornings with Jim, learning what I had let myself in for, with the suspicion growing that the entire installation had been rushed through – like dieselisation – so as to make Western Region the first wholly modernised Region of British Railways.

The lever frame at Uffington had been renewed with forty-seven levers in 1962 to operate the Faringdon branch and the newly laid Up and Down goods loops, each of which held eighty wagons plus the engine and brake van. The branch was closed on 1 July 1963, leaving only fifteen levers working. They were ranged along the back wall of the box, leaving a clear view of the tracks from windows normally obstructed by levers and signalling instruments. This felt strange to work at first but it was a good idea and a further improvement had been effected by locating the Main-line signal levers directly below the signalling instruments. All this was Midland Railway practise. All the signals were colour-lights, so that, having carried out the signalling routine, I could simply reach down and, with a light effort, pull over the required lever – there was only one for the Up line and one for the Down. Knighton Crossing signal box was still in use in June 1965 so the signal levers for signals at the east end of the layout were locked at 'Danger' until the signalman at Knighton gave a 'Line Clear' indication on the instrument. On the Up line the signals were switched from red to yellow and then green as the preceding train moved away eastwards; all I had to do was pull the lever over, put it back after the train had passed and then just pull it over again. The points at the exit from the Down goods loop and at the entrance to the Up loop, the latter 1,000 yards away to the west, were worked by electric motors when I moved the lever but those at the east end of the loops, close to the box, were operated manually through levers and rodding.

On the instrument shelf there was the traditional block bell and instrument for working with Knighton Crossing. This worked perfectly but the 'train describer', by which train identification codes were sent and received between Uffington and Reading Panel, was a failure nearly as often as it was operational. Each train had an identification code – 1C75, for instance, for the 12.30 p.m. Paddington to Penzance express – and that number moved along the console that was Reading Panel as the train moved over the ground. As the 12.30 p.m. Paddington passed by the Down goods loop exit points at Steventon, its number came into my describer. Each digit had to click into place in the bottom display box – 1C75 was sixteen loud, clattering clicks followed by an infernal squawking noise as the 'Acknowledge' button flashed bright orange, demanding to be pressed. When pressed the noise stopped and the number then ascended through five more display boxes, clattering sixteen times into each before setting out for the next – ninety maddening clicks. Luckily, the buzzer had to be silenced only once, which to my biased mind was an oversight on the part of the designer. The machine was so irritating that it had a bad psychological effect upon all three Uffington signalmen, who, during a tiring shift, would become convinced that it actually enjoyed going through its rigmarole and made its silly noise merely to be spiteful. If I was lucky it would go wrong, fill itself up with *0Z00* numbers and thereafter remain silent until someone could find the time to mend it; in the meantime the signalman at Uffington and the Panelman at Reading worked with the traditional, single-strike bell. We knew what the train was from the timetable and if there was some alteration, the relevant signalman would phone and advise his opposite number.

But so long as the describer was working, we had to trust it. One night, soon after I started work at Uffington, the describer showed 5T25 – 12.5 a.m. Paddington to Cardiff express goods – coming down with 1B00 – 2.15 a.m. Paddington to Bristol newspapers – right behind. I set the points for the Down goods loop and waited for the goods to appear under Baulking bridge. Ten minutes later, I saw the lights of a train standing away to my left at Baulking bridge and the 'Call' light began flashing to show that someone was phoning in from the Down home signal located there. I answered the call and a voice said, 'You've got us going into the loop.'

'Yes, that's right – the 2.15 Padd. is close behind you.'

'We *are* the 2.15 Padd. You want to get your sleep before you come to work.'

The phone went dead. I put the lever back, re-set the route and pulled off again. A couple of minutes later a 'Warship' diesel· came roaring down, the driver flashing the cab interior light on and off as he approached. 5T25 was following behind so both trains were delayed and, as expected, both drivers blamed me. What had happened was that, as the description 1B00 moved alongside 5T25 on the console at Reading – the 5T25 being in the loop at Steventon – the electrical circuitry transposed the numbers and thus misled me. Once we became aware of this tendency, we would check with Reading Panel if the describer showed a goods running Down to us with an express train close behind.

Naturally, there were human errors. When an Up train was approaching Uffington, the train description number was dialled in the 'Set Up' box using a telephone dialling device set into the front of the describer instrument and, as the train passed, the 'Send' button was pressed. I forgot to press the button one day and, having written its passing time in the train register, forgot about the train. After a while, Reading Panel rang to say there was a track circuit failure on the Up line at Steventon. Two minutes later, the Panelman rang again.

'You know I said we had a track down at Stivvy?'

'Yes.'

'Well, it's just rung up to say it's the 9.20 Severn Tunnel. Pull your finger out.' I felt suitably crushed.

Track circuit failures were potentially dangerous in the situation that existed between Reading and Uffington. The track circuit failure will hold the signal next in rear of the failure at 'Danger' and thus, when a train comes to a stand at that signal, its driver will be told to pass it at 'Danger' and proceed with caution to the next signal. But if the signal was at Danger, not because of a track circuit failure but rather an unreported train standing on the track circuit, you had the chance of a rear-end collision. One morning at Uffington, I had a total power failure and the stand-by generator did not work. And that was not a 'one-off' incident either. All the signals went to 'Danger' and there was a train standing at every signal on my patch – back to a point between Challow and Wantage Road. And not a signal post telephone was working. The last signal on Reading Panel's patch, at Wantage Road, was held at 'Danger' by the presence ahead of a train standing at the first signal on my section. A train came to a stand at Reading's last signal and its driver telephoned to the Panel for instructions. The Panelman could not contact me because the phones had failed, so he told the driver to 'pass the signal at "Danger" – probably a track failure – and to proceed cautiously'. Unfortunately, the driver was not quite as cautious as he might have been and very nearly ran into the back of the train waiting at my first signal. I know because he told me so when he finally reached Uffington and stopped to ask what all the delay was about. There were so many electrical failures. The drivers – and signalmen – became impatient with it all. Never had the railway experienced such a lot of nonsense – one would hear old-hand drivers saying 'The bloody Luftwaffe never managed to stop us like this', which was something of an exaggeration but it expressed the depth of dismay about the downward path of the railway.

Sheer, unmitigated impatience accounts for the next tale. My Down goods loop starting signal was a three-aspect colour-light; it had three lenses to show red, yellow or green but, while Knighton Crossing signal box was in use, the yellow aspect was not connected and it could show only red or green like the semaphore signal it had replaced. One morning I had a goods train waiting in the loop and the driver had expressed a certain restlessness to be on his way. After the third and final express of the 'string' had passed, I set the points for the goods to leave and stood by the instruments ready to 'get the road' as soon as the 'fast' cleared Knighton. This I duly did and went to the lever, but found it locked in the frame. Puzzled, I checked that I had indeed got a 'Line Clear' indication, then looked at the track circuits. The one in advance of the loop, out on the Down Main line towards Knighton, was showing 'occupied', which would lock the signal in the loop – and for a moment I thought I had a track-circuit failure until I saw that the red light indicating the presence of the goods train in the loop had gone out. I whirled round to look out of the window. The loop was empty and, just disappearing a mile away, was the brake van of the goods. If I had seen the illegal movement taking place, I would have sent the 'Train running away' bell – 4-5-5 – to Knighton but now the train had the road and I was unsure what to do about it. I telephoned Chris Midwinter at Knighton: 'Don't pull off for that goods, Chris, stop it and ask the driver to come on the phone.'

A few minutes later the driver was asking grumpily, 'Wassamatter?'

'What aspect did you have when you left my loop?'

'A yellow, of course,' he replied truculently.

'Cheeky beggar. That signal can show only red or green. You went past it at "Danger".'

'Well, you'd set the road for me,' he growled. 'What are you going to do about it?'

'Nothing,' I replied cheerfully. 'I just wanted you to know that you would have looked pretty silly if that Down fast had stopped while you were charging down the Main behind it.'

Drivers very occasionally passed a signal at 'Danger' through an unintentional oversight but I had never, in years of listening to other men's anecdotes, heard of an instance where a driver did so deliberately and I never came across another case.

In a world of changing technology and changing values, the 99.9% of railwaymen did their best to preserve their integrity in the face of a demoralising situation. Punctuality – arriving at work ten minutes before the appointed hour – continued to be observed as far as possible. Jim Spinage relieved me at 6 a.m. on one occasion, bursting into the box, apologising for being late, with cow muck all down his overcoat. He had been a minute or two behind schedule and had driven his scooter rather faster than usual around the turning from the Uffington–Baulking lane into the Station Road. The machine was leaning well to the right when the front wheel encountered a deep deposit of green goo recently laid by a herd of cows on their way to milking. Elwyn Richards was badger-like in his habits. Since 1943 he had walked the mile and a half from Uffington village to the station, through the gate and over the footbridge; whatever the weather, Elwyn, with his lunch and his gas-mask case over his shoulder, would be on time. Every day Mrs McBayne, who was landlady of the Junction Hotel, put a pint of stout through the hedge at the back of the Down platform for his lunch or tea and, at the end of a late turn, at 10 p.m., Elwyn would go into the pub to fortify himself for the walk home. So regular was this observance that Mrs MacBayne had the stout poured and waiting on the bar before he arrived.

Elwyn was the man most strained by the constant alarms, failures and general eccentricities of work in Uffington signal box – eccentricities that became ever more bizarre from 27 November 1966, when automatic-lifting half-barriers replaced the manually controlled gates at Knighton and Ashbury Crossings. The signal boxes had been abolished on 12 and 14 November respectively. There were no 'controlled' signals to protect these two level crossings, and when I complained to a Signal & Telegraph Department official, he said, 'Accidents don't happen very often and we can't go to all that expense putting controlled signals along the line just to guard against the odd occasion.' How about that? On Western Region in 1965 there were forty-nine derailments. Throughout British Railways during 1965 there were a total of eighty derailments of freight trains on plain track.* No wonder, then, that we at Uffington were worried about the inadequacies of our signalling system. The Hungerford crash took place on 1 July 1965 on semaphore signalled tracks but on a length where trains ran 8 ½ miles without signals to stop their progress. This was exactly the system I was complaining about with MAS, a system that had cost £1.5 million to install.

On 1 July 1965 Driver Nokes of Westbury was driving D801 *Vanguard* hauling the 8.45 p.m. Exmouth Junction to Acton goods. As the train passed Savernake box at 3.40 a.m., the signalman saw an axle-box glowing red-hot on a 16-ton mineral wagon and sent the 'Stop & Examine' code – 7 bells – forward to Hungerford as Nokes took his train away into the night at a steady 40 mph. If Bedwyn box had not been switched out on night shift to save money, the Bedwyn signalman would have had his signals at 'Danger' against the train. 3 miles further on, 700 yards before passing the switched-out Bedwyn signal box, the axle sheared from the wheel, the wagon dropped, both axles were torn from the body and in that condition the hulk was dragged over concrete-sleepered track until it was stopped by signals at Hungerford. By then it had destroyed 4 ½ miles of virtually new track and damaged another three quarters of a mile, left wheels obstructing the Down line and smashed the parapet of a bridge. The very remarkable thing about this incident is that the driver did not *feel* the tugging of the derailed wagon, weighing seven tons even if it was empty. I have been on the footplate of a steam engine trundling sixty empty 16-ton coal wagons back to South Wales in the middle of the night when the guard in his van put on his hand-brake, released it, put it on again and produced a slight tug – which I did not feel but the driver did. He looked back, saw a red light from the guard and brought the train to a stand. The guard had seen a hot axle box, the oil flaming away into the night.

The Hungerford crash caused five days of diversions, with much of the Hungerford line's West of England traffic running via Uffington. Additional delay was caused when the 'Salmon' class wagons carrying the replacement track became derailed at Hungerford but the double-track Main line was finally re-opened on Monday 5 July. How many night-shifts could have been purchased for the cost of replacing the track and the cost of making all the diversions? What would have been the cost of a weighbridge at

---

* See Appendix 3.

y? At Merehead quarry 'weighing' was done by the Carriage & aminer, who decided if a wagon was overloaded by looking at the ɪɪatness' of each wagon's springs. Whoever he was, he was a skilful operator because incidents such as at Hungerford were rare, though one is enough.

Early in September 1965, the 'Salop parcels' train was running on the Down Relief line from Tilehurst to Moreton Cutting, Didcot, 13 miles, with a four-wheeled van derailed at the rear. The van did not become uncoupled but danced from side to side of the track. Drivers of Up trains, on seeing this, were naturally alarmed, braked to a stand and told the Reading Panelman in no uncertain terms what they thought of signalmen who allowed such things to happen. Of course, there was nothing the Panelman could do until the train came to a stand at his first controlled signal – at Moreton Cutting. Early in November there was a similar incident when Up trains stopped and their crews reported a hot axle-box on a petrol tanker. That the people in charge had allowed such a system to be installed – and at such risk and at such cost in terms of employment – did nothing to improve our morale or our respect for those in charge.

On 5 November 1965, Guy Fawkes night, a spent rocket landed on signalling cables lying unenclosed on the ground near Old Oak Common. In a few minutes the cables had been burned through, destroying the entire signalling system in the Acton area at 7.50 p.m. No points would work, all signals were unlit. The 7.45 p.m. Paddington to Bristol, having come to a stand at unlit signals – they are 'Danger' signals when unlit – was diverted at Old Oak Common to run via the Birmingham line to Greenford and thence southwards to join the Bristol line near Hanwell. Unfortunately for the passengers on the train, by the time they had completed their diversion and were approaching the Bristol Main line, the fire had spread, wiping out all signalling between Old Oak and Southall. The procedure then was to run trains by the venerable 'time interval' system. All points were clipped and padlocked for straight running and trains passed from one hand-signalman to the next with extreme caution, each train following the first by a specified time interval. Under such conditions it was impossible to introduce a train into the Main line from the branch because the whereabouts of potentially conflicting movements were unknown. The 7.45 p.m. Paddington remained trapped on the Greenford Loop until the Signal & Telegraph men, working flat out, restored some order. That train passed me at Uffington exactly three hours late at three minutes past midnight. In view of the difficulties involved in restoring communications this was good work but you should have heard the groans of disgust and exasperation from the signalmen when they were told about the failure – and the reason for it. As for the feelings of the passengers ...

I was on night shift on 16 November and experienced three diesel failures in two hours. The 7.45 p.m. Paddington passed me two hours late, the original engine having suffered a total failure of its transmission system; the 9.30 p.m. Paddington's diesel failed at Reading and the 10.30 p.m. Paddington came limping past with its diesel sinking fast. Its driver had asked for a fresh engine at Reading but as he was the fourth man to make such a request that evening there were no spare engines, nor any train available from which a diesel could be 'borrowed'. Is it any wonder I was angry as I compared the much-vaunted new system with the old? It seemed to me that the Management did not know what was required to run a railway, only how to cut costs. It was as if the Great God of Modernisation had sent them mad or blind or both.

As 1965 drew to a close, foul weather began to batter our beleaguered Western Region. On 10 December, about 200 yards east of Bridgend station, close to the junction with the Vale of Glamorgan line, six tons of rock fell from the face of a cutting some 34 feet deep. It did not block the line but landed on the sleeper ends. The Engineering Department Inspector was called and, after examining the site, pronounced it safe. On the 12th the rock was carried away, the rockface checked and, again, pronounced safe. The cutting was through limestone sandwiched between clay, and past experience had shown that the rock outcrops tailed back into the hillside and were part of a solid mass. During the night of 16/17 December about 1½ inches of rain fell. At 5 a.m. on the 17th a 'light' engine passed up the Main and the next train was 1Z60, 4 a.m. Carmarthen to Bristol, twelve empty coaches hauled by D1671. This passed Bridgend station, braking for a 50 mph permanent-speed restriction at 5.45 a.m., and at 5.47 ran headlong into a landslide of rock and clay from the site of the 10 November slip. Heavy rain had percolated down behind the cutting rockface and forced the rock and soil forwards, for at that particular spot the rock did not tail back into the hill.

As the coaches were tumbling across the Down Main and Vale of Glamorgan lines, D1671 was ploughing through the spoil and was struck head-on by D6983 hauling sixty empty wagons. Driver Ivor Ferrier of the 4 a.m. Carmarthen and his secondman, Donald Brock, were both killed. The site of the landslide was about 150 yards east of where Bridgend East signal box had stood until it was abolished under the Port Talbot MAS scheme in March 1965. It is absolutely certain that, had the signal box still been in use, those men would not have been killed. Even if the signalman did not hear tons of rock falling 30 feet down onto the track, his signal wires would have been struck violently, which would have rattled the levers and, when he came to lower his Up line starting signal, he would have been prevented by the weight of spoil lying on the wire.

While the Bridgend job was being cleared, Chipping Sodbury tunnel became flooded so as to make it dangerous for diesel-electric locomotives to pass. All South Wales to London services were diverted via Gloucester until a landslide at Chepstow blocked that route and the entire service was re-routed via Chippenham and Stapleton Road, Bristol, with South Wales passenger and freight trains all cramming into the one Down Main line and one Up Main line between North Somerset Junction and Didcot. Jim, Elwyn and I were daily and nightly very busy and, from my point of view, this at least was great fun (if that is the right word).

Because this was the pre-Christmas period, Western Region was running extra passenger trains each day when the bad weather struck, so the dislocation of services was worse than if the bad weather had occurred in, say, February. By 22 December chaos reigned. Broken rails and floods and landslides combined with diesel failures in one glorious mess, including the ramming of the 4.30 p.m. Paddington by the following 'seasonal extra', the 4.35 p.m. Paddington. On 28 December the 8.30 a.m. Paddington to Plymouth was derailed just after it had left Reading when it encountered a broken rail on the embankment high above the back gardens of Gower Street and later that day the 9.5 a.m. Severn Tunnel freight came off the road at Foxhall Junction, Didcot. Railwaymen kept slogging away at the job, the trains continued to roar through Uffington – however embarrassingly late – and the passengers were eventually taken delivered to their destinations.

Sometimes passengers were taken to their destinations in a railwayman's car. One Sunday in 1965, when engineering work was in progress and there was single line working over the double track between Challow and Uffington, a Down express stopped at the derelict station to allow the escorting Pilotman to get off the engine. The platforms at Uffington had by then been cut away, leaving a sloping bank up to a foot-wide strip of the old asphalt. The train pulled away to reveal a passenger standing on this narrow margin with two suitcases. He was directly opposite my signal box. We looked at each other in amazement and the passenger called out to me, in utter disbelief, 'Is this Swindon?' 'No – of course it isn't Swindon,' I called back from the open window, 'whatever made you get off here?' 'The guard said the next stop would be Swindon.' Other railwaymen were standing about on the track and we all had a good laugh – how could anyone be so stupid? But then the public service ethos took over and one of the chaps volunteered to drive him to Swindon station.

CHAPTER FOUR

Close Encounters

There were forty derailments on British Railways in 1965, most of them on Western Region. On 17 November 1965, the 2.55 a.m. Acton to Bristol – 5B17 – came through Reading station on the goods line. One wagon was being dragged along, minus all wheels, and so long as the train kept going it was to some extent held up above the track. There was no signalman to see or hear the noise it was making. Luckily, the Panel signalman did not have the road for it Down Relief. The train came to a stand at the red signal and the wagon dropped onto the track. When the driver got the road the wagon was sitting on the track like an anchor, the driver felt the tugging and stopped.

In the first six weeks of 1966 Western Region suffered seven derailments. On 6 January 1966 I booked on at 10 p.m. in Uffington box for an eight-hour night shift. Some time before midnight, I put a goods into the Down loop to allow the 10.30 p.m. Paddington to Penzance sleeping car express to pass. As usual, the 'Sleeper' was followed closely by the 9.2 p.m. Acton to South Wales 'C' headcode express freight, so I held the goods in the loop for the Acton to pass. The driver of the slow goods in the loop was talking to me by phone from the loop starting signal when the Acton came storming under Baulking bridge, 400 yards to the east. The sound of a hammering 'Hymek' diesel burst into earshot as the train came through the arch and I put down the phone to watch as the engine's lights came into sight.

A trail of sparks was flying off the train, close to the ballast. I looked hard for a short moment to see if this phenomenon might be a hot axle-box, brakes dragging or something worse. It *was* worse. Even in the dark, it was obvious that the rain of sparks was neither a flaming axle-box nor an iron brake-shoe dragging against a wheel to create a 'Catherine wheel' effect. A horizontal stream of sparks – while not mentioned in any rule book – looked to me suspiciously like a derailment. Ahead of the train lay the diverging tracks at the points into the goods loop. It seemed as if I would very shortly have wagons flying left and right – and there was a guard sitting peacefully in the van at the rear of the train that I had put in the loop, out of the way of this express freight. If the derailed wagon was not dragged sideways by the loop points there were 2 ½ miles of track to rip up, culminating in the tarmac road at Knighton Crossing, which the grounded wagon would hit and derail all the others behind. These thoughts took no more than a second to go through my head. The longer the train ran on, the greater would be the damage it caused. The derailed train had already passed the only operable 'Danger' signal I possessed. I pulled over the emergency detonator placer lever, and ran to the window with the 'Bardic' electric torch to give the driver a red light. The 'Hymek' diesel was close to the box and I saw the driver's startled face lit blue-white for an instant in the flash from the exploding 'shots'. Seconds later, flying ballast was rattling against the side of the box and smashing the windows as a pair of long wheel-base wagons went ploughing through the sleepers. Stepping quickly to the bell, I sent 'Obstruction Danger', 6 bells, to Knighton Crossing and then thought of the driver of the train in the loop, patiently waiting on his phone, half a mile away, waiting for me to come back to him. I grabbed the telephone. He was whistling quietly to himself. 'Get down the bank,' I yelled into the mouthpiece. 'This one's off the road!' He told me later that he stepped forward, unthinkingly, around the front of his own engine to see what was the matter and narrowly missed death under an avalanche of flying wood and steel. One 60-foot length of rail was discovered later out on the fields on the Down side of the line.

The driver of the Acton braked steadily, with great skill, so that the train came to no more harm through wagons piling up over each other – as would be the case if the brakes went on violently – and came to a stand several hundred yards beyond the Down loop exit points. I listened for the racket to cease, put the kettle on and telephoned Control for the breakdown gangs and crane. The first man into the box was the guard off the 9.2 p.m. Acton. He flung himself through the door, into the signal box, and straight down into the armchair. 'Sod this for a life,' he said with evident annoyance, 'that's the second time I've been off the road with this train. I was the guard when it came off at Steventon back in '62.'

At the subsequent Inquiry into the crash, I was criticised by one member of the Inquiry for stopping the derailed train. He reckoned I ought to have let it run as then less damage would have been done to the track. The notion that one ought not to stop a derailed train was a novel one. I wondered if he had heard about the incident between Bedwyn and Hungerford; I wondered what indeed he knew about railway work; I wondered how he would have fared in Uffington box with a second to make a decision rather than a week to mull it over. All this flashed through my head even as the man was speaking and, given the bruised state of my mind at the general condition of the railway, my ire rose. 'If you had seen and heard what I saw and heard you would have done the same as I did,' I snapped. I do not think he was used to mere workmen shouting at him. He opened his mouth to speak, I glared at him and there were the makings of a first-class row when the man in charge of the Inquiry waved his colleague aside. 'Yes, yes,' he said testily, 'he was quite right to stop the train. May we please get on with the Inquiry?'

In the evening of 7 January, the 6.45 p.m. Paddington's empty coaches were drawn into Paddington station from Old Oak Common by the engine for the 7 p.m. Paddington. The engine for the 6.45 backed on but refused to change gear when asked; the driver could not get it into forward gear so it had to be 'failed'. This meant that the engine required for the 7 p.m. departure was trapped against the buffers. The engine for a later departure was brought to haul the failed 6.45 engine to Ranelagh Bridge yard and then returned to work the 6.45 away, leaving thirty minutes late and, by so doing, releasing the engine for the 7 p.m. departure. Unfortunately, this engine had failed as it stood against the buffers so another, later, service was robbed of its engine and the 7 p.m. left twenty-five minutes late. There was no doubt that, when the diesels ran, they were faster and more powerful than all but the biggest steam engines but, at a time when the steady performance of the steam engines was a vivid memory, the unreliability of these expensive diesels and the inconvenience this caused the passengers did irk me greatly. I think, as much as anything, it was the propaganda that hurt, the denigration of the old and the fulsome praise of the new. The new railway was 'sold' to the public as part of Harold Wilson's 'white-hot cutting edge of technology' but those of us who had to work with it knew that the edges were rather blunt, and not particularly hot.

On Saturday 22 January 1966, I parked my Morris 8 on the frozen ruts where once the neat, brick 'milk dock' had stood and hurried through the snow and bitter cold to the warmth and light of the signal box. Elwyn was then at the end of a twelve-hour shift and looked grey and ill.

'Rough night then, Elwyn?' I asked. 'Looks as if you've had one.'

'I dare say I do look rough, so does the driver on the Llandilo vacuum, too, I expect. We've 'ad a proper ol' set-to, take a look in the Book.'

I signed on in the train register and saw that at 3.49 a.m. Ted Blackall in Reading Panel had sent Elwyn 6 bells for a suspected derailment on the Down line at Lockinge, 1 ½ miles west of Steventon. 'And look at this yere,' said Elwyn, in an aggrieved tone, stabbing a finger at the page, 'two vacuums on the Up line, one just passing the box when I got the six bells and not a damn thing I could do about either of them. This *is* a rotten job and no mistake.'

The emergency had been discovered by George Strong, around sixty-five years of age, a long-serving, ex-GWR man, the Crossing Keeper at Steventon Causeway. Snow was lying on the ground. He had watched the 12.5 a.m. Paddington to Cardiff vacuum goods go past his post behind D1052 *Western Viceroy* and had heard a loud bang as a certain wagon passed over the road crossing. A trail of sparks proceeded westwards. George, being an experienced man, knew just what that meant but first went outside to check. In the snow there were the marks of wheels, first on one side of the rails, then on the other. He walked westwards about forty sleepers and the marks went on into the darkness where he could hear faintly the diminishing rattle of the train. He turned to hurry back to his cabin and was spurred on by the fact of the rattle stopping suddenly. Something was seriously wrong with the Down goods. He telephoned Reading Panel with the advice. Ted Blackall sent the 'Obstruction Danger' to Elwyn, Elwyn replied with the 4-5-5, 'Train running away', and all three men standing, listening on the same telephone circuit, waited in considerable suspense to see if the Up trains would pass safely by the derailed Down train. No wonder poor old Elwyn looked grey!

While they were anxiously awaiting the fate of the men in the cab of the Llandilo vacuum, that train was running towards the derailment at 45 mph under clear signals. The men on the 12.5 a.m. Paddington were sitting in the cab of their stationary engine wondering why they had been stopped, thinking that the guard had put his brake on. After two minutes they got down and walked back along their train, only then discovering that some wagons were derailed and leaning towards the Up Main line. The train had broken into two parts, the vacuum brakes' pipes had been torn apart and this action had automatically brought the train to a stand. The two locomotivemen were then galvanised into action. The driver ran to find a signal post telephone so that he could warn Reading Panel while the secondman went to the engine to get detonators with a view to going westwards and placing them on the Up line to warn trains and make them stop. The driver tried two signal post telephones but neither of them were working and before his fireman could get any 'shots' down, the Llandilo vacuum came along and rattled past at 45 mph, missing the derailed wagon by a few inches.

According to the tale that came down the proverbial grapevine (the story up to now is quite correct) the driver of the Llandilo vacuum was given such a fright when he saw the wagons, apparently leaning across his path, looming up out of the darkness that he had to be taken to hospital for treatment for severe shock. He and his mate had been lucky, Western Region had been lucky – again – but the signalmen at Reading and Uffington were very unhappy, wondering when the luck would run out and when something truly horrifying would happen as they stood by, powerless to prevent it. And there was an additional bone of contention: the secondman of every permanent-way gang had, since time immemorial, made a careful patrol of his 'length' daily but, since October 1965, this was reduced to an 'every other day' inspection on the grounds that modern track did not need such close and careful maintenance. Together with this reduction in track inspection, the 'gangs' each looking after a 'length' – five men to five miles – were dispensed with in favour of a mobile team where eleven men were said to be able to maintain 22 miles of track. This looked to all of us as another reduction in safety standards in order to reduce costs.

The Patrolman for the Challow length phoned me from Challow ground frame one morning. 'That Down goods has got a beautiful hot box, Adrian, you'll want to put him away.' I thanked him. The train was 2 ½ miles away, well out of sight of my signal, which I put back to 'Danger' and then awaited the arrival of the train before altering the route from Down Main to Down goods loop. Under normal circumstances the train would have run down the Main to Swindon and the driver was expecting so to do. He did not brake as he should have done after passing my Down distant signal at 'Caution', believing that I would 'clear' the signal at any moment. Of course, he had no idea that the signal cleared itself (providing that I had reversed the lever) after his train had occupied the track circuit for a given length of time. Coming down too fast, he realised that he would run by it at 'Danger' and he braked violently – in the vernacular, he 'slammed the lot in'. I heard a terrific, hollow, 'boom', looked up and saw a cloud of dust billowing out of the cutting – from a range of 600 yards – before I saw the engine. The 100-ton diesel decelerated rapidly; the noise like someone rapidly beating a big bass drum was the sound of three-score empty coal tubs, which did not have brakes, running heavily into the suddenly braking locomotive. The signal cleared as the corner of a 'Western' class diesel appeared slowly around the side of the bridge; the driver gave a 'honk' on his horn and, blowing off his brakes, let his train freewheel onwards. He knew and I knew what that sound portended and he went on to make some amends for his earlier haste by some very skilful driving.

As the wagons came under Baulking bridge, I saw a black, tar-tanker wagon riding on its rear pair of wheels only, the leading buffers cocked up on the frame of another tar-tanker ahead. All the other wagons were empty coal tubs and these, in running forward, had thrown their great weight against the tank wagon, forcing it to ride up onto the wagon in front. As the driver came level with me, I pointed down the train and made the appropriate mime. He nodded grimly and, tensed-up, continued to concentrate on getting his train into the loop. The wagons' buffers were all in contact, closed up tight. The crisis would come when the wagons turned left and then right, over the 'S' shaped curve of the points from Main to loop; as each turned, there was a danger that the buffers lodged up on the other wagon would drop and the wagon's wheels would fall back to the sleepers. I stood by the bell, watching the train's careful progress, waiting to send 'Obstruction Danger' the moment a derailment occurred. The driver, however, did not use any power; he allowed the train to freewheel into the loop, buffers closed up, and, with sufficient energy in the train itself, he was able to get into the loop without having to exert any traction, which would have pulled apart the locked-up wagons. It really was a fascinating exhibition of skill – and a little luck. The sequel was not so lucky. After the second tanker was re-railed the train was taken on to Swindon, where the leading tar tank was found to have been punctured by the buffers of the other tank. The punctured tank was shunted onto a siding and the wind blew tar, like black threads, all over the train standing on the adjacent siding – a train-load of brand new cars.

Hot axle-boxes and a lack of signalling makes for a poor outlook. Before 1963 there was no written speed limit for four-wheeled, short-wheelbase wagons on open track. Their speed was governed by the driver's experience based on the weight of the train and the brake power available to him and the timetable timings were created accordingly. An 'F', 'J' or 'H' headcode train would have consisted entirely of wagons without the vacuum brake – which could be applied by the driver on the engine – and ran at between 25 for a 'J' and 30 mph for an 'F'. A 'D' or 'C' headcode freight train was one partly or fully vacuum braked, which could run very much faster and did, making speeds of 50 to 60 mph. With an increasing number of derailments on Western Region (in particular) from April 1963, a maximum speed limit of 55 mph for fully braked freight trains was imposed, with 50 mph for all lesser trains. The number of derailments caused by freight wagons continued to increase, so in 1966 a limit of 45 mph was placed on any train conveying wagons with a wheelbase of 10 feet or less. Somewhat illogically, the timetable was not altered to take account of the restriction, maybe because if the timetable schedules were slowed down, this would have been an admission of the failure of modernisation. So the drivers had to run trains at an average start-to-stop speed of 44 ½ mph when they were not allowed to exceed 45 mph. There was obviously no margin to offset time lost in reaching maximum speed and in decelerating, time lost in signal checks, or temporary restrictions over newly laid track. The maximum speed restriction also meant that the men could be blamed for faults in the equipment and little men in blue coats appeared on the lineside carrying radar guns to set up speed traps. The morning they arrived at Uffington when I was on duty I realised at once what was about to happen and got word to Didcot and Swindon, warning drivers of the speed trap. Forewarned is forearmed and I was amused to see each train coming by dead on regulation speed (or slower) with a broad grin on the face of the driver while he blew on his horn what was known colloquially as 'arseholes' to the officials on the ground. Radar guns were a sneaky way of attacking a very serious problem; they did not cure anything, they merely gave officialdom a chance to haul a driver over the coals.

What were needed were hot axle-box detectors between Didcot and Uffington *and* signals that could be placed to 'Danger' whenever required. Jim, Elwyn and I knew this and we variously raised the matter with those in charge of us – or the signalling. The Area Manager's reaction was 'Well, it works all right in France' while the Signal & Telegraph Department stuck to its old chestnut that such provisions would be 'too expensive' – as if a collision between an express train and a derailed goods would be cheaper! There was a general feeling of dissatisfaction among the Uffington and Reading signalmen at the high-handed attitude the Managers and the Technocrats adopted towards us; we were merely steam-age men grumbling about progress.

There was to be a Ministry of Transport Inquiry into the near-miss at Steventon. Ted Blackall, from Reading Panel, promised us at Uffington that when he was called to give evidence about the Steventon job, he would hammer home the signalman's objections to the entire system as it stood but there was no knowing when the Report would be published and, if it was published, whether it would be favourable to our point of view and then, when anything would be done to improvement matters. So Jim, Elwyn and I decided to do something drastic at once.

I wrote to our Member of Parliament, Airey Neave, and to the *Daily Mirror* to come to the signal box to see for themselves what we were complaining about and judge whether we were talking nonsense or not. At about 3 p.m. one day in early February, all three of us, including Elwyn who was on night shift, were in the box waiting for our guests to arrive. The reporter from the *Daily Mirror* arrived first; we explained our case to him and at the end of the exposition he went off well pleased at being able to telephone his 'shock–horror' story to his editor in London. Shortly afterwards, Neave arrived. Again we explained the position but his reaction was quite different. He granted that he could see why we were worried but felt that it would only alarm the public for the story to be published.

'Well, it's too late to keep it quiet now,' I said, 'a reporter from the *Daily Mirror* has gone off into the village to phone it back to his paper.'

'Don't worry about that,' he replied. 'Stories are always being ditched. You wouldn't want this made public.' Our representative went away, leaving three very disappointed signalmen behind. We would have been much happier if he had told us that he would take our complaint to Western Region Management, for that is what he did, I found out later, without saying anything to us. The *Mirror*'s report was not published. He met the General Manager on 1 March at Paddington. In reply to our criticisms of the signalling system, which he conveyed to the GM, he was told that arrangements were in hand to provide controlled signals every 3 miles and also hot axle-box detectors.

The Ministry of Transport Inquiry into the Steventon derailment was conducted in public by Colonel McNaughton, RE, and was attended by journalists from several national newspapers and the BBC – such was the interest in the case, or rather series of cases. The newshounds were confounded by the dense railway jargon and the undoubted playing down of the dangerous aspects of the signalling system. However, having kept the questions and answers well under control, the Colonel permitted himself the following observation in his Official report on the incident:

> A disquieting feature of this accident was the disclosure by the signalman (Ted Blackall) that he was unable to stop oncoming traffic because none of the seven signals on the up line between Uffington and Steventon was provided with any means of replacing it to 'Danger' from the Panel.

Nine months after our MP's meeting at Paddington, Western Region installed six emergency replacement switches in Uffington signal box, enabling us to switch to 'Danger' six signals: one on Up and one on the Downside of both Ashbury and Knighton Crossings and one for each track just east of Challow station on the Up and Down lines. Hot axlebox detectors were installed on the Up and Down lines at Wantage Road but, of course, only the Down line detector was connected to Uffington's read-out machine. Heat-sensing elements were placed outside each rail to check the left- and right-hand bearing of each axle. As a Down train was passing the sensors, the recording instrument in Uffington box was automatically switched on. A roll of paper began to turn and two needles – representing the left- and right-hand ends of each axle – deflected as the axles passed the sensor. The needles traced black, parallel lines with each axle-box shown as a little V-shaped blip. The type of train could be recognised from the tracing. Milk tanks with three axles produced a series of triple blips connected by a short, straight line; a passenger train gave two double blips, a long straight line and two more double blips as the short-wheelbase bogies passed; and a goods train produced a serrated-edge effect as dozens of axles passed at 10-foot intervals. As the needles scratched busily from side to side they made the sound, familiar and much beloved, of wheels over rail joints to the rhythm of that type of train. I took an immediate liking to that machine – it had a 'human' aspect while making the safety of the line more certain.

When an overheated axle bearing passed a sensor an alarm buzzer sounded and an extra large blip – in proportion to the amount of overheating – showed precisely which axle in the train was at fault. The Uffington signalman could then turn the signal at Challow to 'Danger' to stop the train and could, if necessary, turn the Up line signal to 'Danger' at Challow as well so that a train would not pass the defective train until the latter had come to a stand. This was in line with Regulation 17 of the signalling regulations, which we had been forced to ignore – with Western Region's full approval – since 1 June 1965. So, at long last, and after eighteen months of too many close encounters, the yokel signalmen of Uffington triumphed over haughty authority.

CHAPTER FIVE

Battle-Hardened

By March 1965 Western Region was not running many steam-hauled trains and most of those were goods trains – there were still occasionally some steam-hauled passenger trains on the Worcester line because the diesels were still breaking down. But on the route west of Didcot, steam engines became rarer and rarer as 1965 progressed. I have the Challow Train Register for 11–30 May. I kept a note of steam engine numbers in the margin and sometimes I recorded five in eight hours, sometimes only three. On 15 May Jim Spinage recorded 5042 *Winchester Castle* on the 6.36 p.m. Gloucester 'C' headcode vacuum goods passing Challow at 7.10 and from the bell times he recorded, 5042 was running the vacuum like a passenger train. On 2 p.m. to 10 p.m. shift on 19 May, I recorded 73023, 6872 *Crawley Grange*, 44716, 48436, 92214 and 73023. Steam was thin on the ground so I was pleased when, on early turn in Uffington box, I put an Up goods into the loop out of the way of an express and saw that it was hauled by a 92 Class 2-10-0. A few minutes later its fireman, a very smartly turned out young man in pale blue footplate overalls, came into the box with the tea can. I said that I was pleased to see a steam engine.

'Are you starved for steam?'

'Oh yes.'

'You ought to try working of the Festiniog engines.'

'What?! Two-foot gauge? No, I don't think so.'

'Oh?' says he, in a bit of a raised voice, 'I've fired "Kings" down to South Wales in the week and *Palmerstone* across The Cob at weekends. If that's good enough for a locoman its plenty good enough for a signalman.'

I raised both hands in surrender.

'I'll tell you what – I'm going down to Portmadoc at the weekend. Would you come with me? You'll be amazed. The FR's a great railway.'

I went and I *was* amazed. Paul Dukes, the Works Manager and Loco Foreman at Boston Lodge put me learning on the footplate straight away and after no more than three weekends I was passed to fire. I was entirely hooked and spent every free weekend and often a whole week at a time firing on the railway. When I first went firing, I was usually rostered with the

General Manger, Mr A. G. W. Garraway, on *Linda* but I was not for long his fireman. This was due to an unfortunate incident at Tan-y-Bwlch (T-y-B). The wheel-shaped handle of the water valve on the locomotive water tank there had a Welsh thread. That is to say, it was opened and closed by turning it the opposite way to every other tap in the world. It is a reflex action to turn a tap anti-clockwise to open it and clockwise to close it. The way to cope with this was always to open the valve fully and then one could only turn it one way to close it when the engine's tank was full. I was on top of *Linda's* tank, with the bag in and watching the water level rise. But I had only half opened the valve, so water was coming in relatively slowly. Mr Garraway was just below me, on the ground, and after a while he said, 'Come on, come on. Isn't it full yet?' It was not but it was full enough, so I said, 'Yes, that'll do' and reached out to close the valve. But because it was only half open, it was free to be turned in either direction and I turned it in the ordinary way to shut it. As a result, I fully opened it. I pulled out the hose and dropped it, thundering water, right on top of him. I was never rostered with him after that.

From then on, my usual engines were *Blanche*, driven usually but not always by Davy Bascombe, and *Earl of Merioneth*, driven by Evan Davies whenever I was on it. I was very pleased. They were more pleasant to work with than the General Manager. The FR took up a lot of my time for five years. I fired to Davy or Evan in the season and helped to build the deviation at Ddault in the winter. I only stopped going in 1970, when the engines were converted to burning oil. Then they required far less skill to work and continuously sounded like central heating boilers. For a coal-fired soul like me it was not worth the cost and the effort of getting there just to fire engines at the turn of a handle.

Just before Uffington signal box fell before the advance of Multiple Aspect Signalling, I had a job 'on the ground' at Challow, working the emergency cross-overs with Jim Spinage. There was to be an Engineers' occupation of the Down Main line between Challow and Uffington and so the Up line would be converted, temporarily, to single-line working. I drove Jim down to Challow station from Childrey and we arrived at the ground frame, at the foot of the derelict platform ramp, just before 10 p.m. Darkness hid the worst of the decaying station and, indeed, we felt cheerful. There were lights on in the windows of the station cottages, strings of multicoloured fairy lights gleamed around the Prince of Wales pub and we were 'fresh on'. It was always pleasant for signalman who normally saw each other only for a few minutes at change of shift (even though they lived in the same village) to work a whole shift together. A friendly London Division Inspector joined us, having driven down from Reading in his yellow railway van, and at 10 p.m. Elwyn, at Uffington, pressed the plunger to electrically unlock the key out of the ground frame. One of us turned the big, brass Annett's key out of its lock and thereby switched to 'Danger' the signals on each side of the cross-over points while allowing the ground-frame levers to be pulled to switch the points when required. Until the key was restored, those points were Jim's and my responsibility. The passage of Up and Down trains through the single track section was controlled by a 'Pilotman'. He was distinguished by a red armband with the word PILOTMAN embroidered on it in white cotton. He alone was permitted to order a train into the single track section. He had to be present and personally order the driver to take his train through. If there was a train waiting, or would shortly be waiting, at the other end, the Pilotman rode through the section on the engine of the train to meet the waiting train. If there was a second train to follow the first before there was a train to come from the opposite direction, the Pilotman would order the first one to go through but would not travel with it. He would travel through on the second train. Nothing could come the other way because the Pilotman was not at the other end to order the movement. Ensuring that the Pilotman was always at the right end of the single line required planning and teamwork, alertness after many hours out in the weather – and in bad weather the job became very tiring indeed. No one complained – each simply rose to the occasion.

An old hut that had once stood on the Up side of the line for the use of a fogman had been carried across to the Down side but for some unknown reason it had been parked on the sloping ramp of the platform instead of on level ground. Its brazier had come, too, so, gathering up lumps of splintered sleepers and even bits of coal fallen from the tenders of long-departed shunting engines, we lit a fire and set out on the night's work. Our job was to set the points for a crossing movement from Down Main to Up Main or for the direct run, straight up the Main, when a train was coming from Uffington. When the points were reversed for a crossing movement, they were held securely by clamping the switch rail to the stock rail with a massive, cast-iron clamp, which was then padlocked until the points had again to be altered. This procedure also guarded against any alteration of the points through some momentary forgetfulness. Whichever way the points were set, one of us would stand by with a green hand-signal when everything was in order for a train to pass. A very important detail to note was to check that the Pilotman was on the passing train; he would shout out as he went by so that we knew that the next train would be coming from the opposite end of the line and therefore the points would have to be reversed. We were unprotected by any interlocking – we were manning a mid-Victorian-style operation and safety depended entirely on our alertness.

In the dark, long after the upstairs lights in the cottages had gone out and the last of the cars had roared tipsily out of the pub car park, Jim and I trudged the ballast with our hand lamps and point clamps, phoning, keeping up with the situation, setting the road, hand-signalling the trains as the dim silhouette of wheels rang through the night, squealing their flanges over the curving cross-overs, grinding their brakes as they stopped to drop the Pilotman. Around 4 a.m., the last train for ninety minutes had gone – the next would be the 'York' on the Down line and the 'Up Waker', the sleeping car train from Penzance. We were all feeling windblown and weary so the Pilotman and the Inspector went off for a kip in the yellow van while Jim and I fitted ourselves into the leaning 'foggin' 'ut'. It had been built to shelter one man in relative comfort and Jim, if he will forgive my saying so, was equivalent to one and a half – and we were both bulky in our railway-issue greatcoats. To fit in at all, we sat with our arms around each other's shoulders like Tweedledum and Tweedledee. The fire burnt low and smoke began to sting our wind-scorched faces, so we pulled the door to and slept on a plank seat.

I woke on all fours on the cinders beside the track, wondering where the hell I was. Behind me was the sound of struggle and, getting up and turning round, I saw the grey shape of the hut lying on its side and Jim crawling out through the fallen-open door. In sleep I must have leaned on him; he must have leaned on the hut; and, with the assistance of an extra strong gust of wind, it had overbalanced. The sky was greying with dawn. I had the taste of thermos flask tea and sandwiches stale in my mouth and my joints were stiff with cold.

'Wassa-time, Jim?' I croaked.

He peered at his watch. 'Nearly time for the "York". You go and get them two out of the van, I'll phone Elwyn and see where it is.' The railway came to life. The 'York' went down with the Pilotman and the 'Up Waker' – the 5.45 a.m. Penzance to Paddington sleeping-car train – came up, bringing with it blessed 'going home time', hence its nickname. Work was fun but it was also fun when it stopped. I had worked my last shift at Challow and, shortly afterwards, on 3 March 1968, I worked my last at Uffington when the box was closed under the Swindon MAS scheme.

Jim and Elwyn left the railway at this juncture but, like Deputy Dawg in the TV cartoon series of the time, I wanted to see what would happen next. I had had fifty years' ration of emergencies, failures and assorted crises in my three years at Uffington. I felt 'battle-hardened' and confident of my ability to cope with whatever might befall. I took a vacancy at Kennington Junction, 2 ¾ miles south of Oxford station. The box was an 18-mile drive from Childrey, so I sold my Morris 8 and bought a Jowett 'Javelin' for the daily journey. The signal box was curiously difficult to find on the first visit. Through gaps between the houses lining the main road I caught glimpses of its roof but, driving up and down, could find no way in until I realised that what I had taken to be a gap in a hedge was the entrance to a very narrow, stony lane leading steeply to the railway line between tall, overgrown hedges. At the bottom was a five-bar gate protecting the tracks. It was truly a 'down the rabbit-hole' situation; once through this dark passage, the manic rush of the tarmac road was left behind and instead the world was rural, peaceful and orderly.

The signal box was tall and dignified, built in 1901 of smooth, red brick with blue corner bricks and a handsome brick chimney rising above a hip-gabled roof. It stood on the Up side of the line, its back to the Main line, facing the branch. I learned the job – and there was a great deal to learn – with Don Symonds. From the tall signal box we looked out on an interesting layout. Four tracks ran northwards to Hinskey South box and Oxford station, double track curved away southwards to Radley and Didcot while the single-track branch line to Morris Cowley climbed steeply and curved eastwards over the River Thames. Northwards, the trains were semaphore signalled on goods and passenger lines; southwards, they ran under automatic, three-aspect colour-light signals; and to Cowley they ran under traditional signals with the electric train token to ensure safety on the single line.

Towards Didcot we worked with Reading Panel so there was a train describer on the instrument shelf but this one seemed quite a civilised machine and gave little trouble. The first three-aspect colour light signal south of Kennington stood approximately where the old, semaphore advanced starting signal had stood. The colour-light was, of course, capable of showing a red light and so it had to have a 'Caution' signal to its rear to warn approaching drivers to brake. This was provided by a semaphore distant arm placed below my home signal. There were three ground frames between Kennington and Radley, one a mile away at Sandford refrigerated meat storage depot and two at Radley, 2 ½ miles away, to give access to the Abingdon branch for trains servicing the MG car factory in the town. All three were, apparently, within Reading Panel's control but were controlled by the Kennington signalman.

The branch line climbed at 1 in 93 to cross the Thames on a fine 'bow and string' steel-girder bridge dating from 1923. On the far side of the branch tracks, opposite the signal box, was a mysterious area of swamp, forested by willows of great age, their corded trunks forked and twisted, their branches long, drooping and riotously entangled. To the left of the view a hawthorn hedge rose raggedly, all but hiding a ruined boathouse, landlocked then but obviously built when the river lapped the foot of the railway embankment. In front of the hedge was the brick lower portion of the original (1870) Kennington Junction box, used since 1901 by the Permanent Way Department as a store shed. Along the branch, 250 yards to the right, past a tall bracket signal with two posts and three arms, the handsome old bridge finally penned off the area of tussocky swamp. Any slight breeze turned the spearblade-shaped leaves of the willows. In spring, when the sun was bright and keen, they danced and flickered green and silver but at night, when the moon was bright, they hung motionless, the colour of mercury, against the deep shadows inside the forest while the gnarled trunks, catching the light, turned a ghostly silver. In autumn, when the mist rose off the river, the trees were hidden until the sun broke through and they emerged slowly out of a champagne-coloured haze; in winter the same mist rose from the water and froze fantastically on every twig.

Just south of the signal box, down between the converging embankments of the two routes, there was a large mobile home where two good-looking teenage girls lived with their parents. To see them in their garden or to have them visit the signal box was an unusual and very pleasant addition to life at Kennington. It was useful, too, because when they went shopping they would come up and ask if they could get anything in the food line for me. They were friendly and direct, as if they had always known me but I never asked them their names. After the mud and chaos of Uffington, Kennington seemed like Nirvana, a haven of sanity and peace in what had been a very naughty world.

Although the box was working with Reading Panel and although I handled about seventy-five trains a shift – half as much again as at Uffington – they went by without memorable fuss. The working was more intricate than at Uffington, it worked well and I was able to enjoy the job. Only once do I recall the old nightmare impinging on my riverside idyll. About noon one day, I received 6 bells from the Panel; I acknowledged it and went onto the telephone to be told the reason for sending the code.

A Swansea express had been standing at the Up platform at Didcot, waiting for a Down express from Paddington to Worcester to go across the four main lines to the Didcot avoiding line, as it were, 'across the bows' of the Swansea, although at a distance of perhaps 300 yards. As the Down Worcester reached the junction facing points in the Down Main, travelling at 40 mph or a little less, the 'switch diamonds' in the Up Main line had suddenly reversed for normal, 'straight-up-the-Main' running. The Worcester train was therefore diverted down the Up Main line but came to a stand without colliding with the Swansea. That was the nearest I got to 'shock-horror' at Kennington, which was perfectly acceptable to me.

Pinned on the wall of the box was a yellowing newspaper cutting concerning an instance of real 'shock-horror' straight out of an Alfred Hitchcock film. Down the branch line a mile or so was Littlemore mental hospital and one night an inmate walked into Kennington box to demand that the signalman, Pete Hall, stop a train to take him to London. Pete knew he was an inmate because he was wearing nothing but a vest of immodestly short length and was carrying a large, pointed, kitchen knife. Pete kept calm and was able to talk the man out of his plan – he was hardly dressed for travelling, after all, and was then able to telephone for assistance. While glad not to have been placed in such a situation, at the same time I felt a slight wave of envy when I read the cutting; I would have liked to have known how I would have coped.

My relief at Kennington was an old-hand railwayman, Jack Gough, who had been on duty in Appleford Crossing box at 1.45 a.m. on the night of 13 November 1942, when 2975 *Lord Palmer*, with seventy-two wagons weighing 770 tons, was driven off the end of the Down goods loop just as 4088 *Dartmouth Castle*, with eleven coaches, was passing down the Main line. I had known Jack since my visits to Didcot East Junction in the early 1960s; he was of the species 'slow but sure'. When Jack told me about the crash he said that, before accepting any train on the Down goods loop from Didcot North box, he always checked first to see that the stop signal lamp at his end of the loop was burning. I had never before heard of this excellent precaution being taken; I was impressed and, knowing Jack of old, I was quite prepared to believe he did that – every time. On each shift at Kennington he came through the gateway ten or fifteen minutes before time, wheeling his bike carefully and shutting the gate with an air of intense concentration that was his hallmark. Never mind that I would want to drive through that gate in ten minutes, that gate had to be kept shut to prevent anything running down the lane and onto the line – so shut it was.

Regarding the Appleford crash, the Down loop line ended 70 yards short of his signal box, directly in line with it. Jack said he had the signals 'off' for the express and was looking out for it. 'I could see the headlights of a train coming towards me,' he told me, 'and I thought it was the fast, judging by the rate they were coming, yet the lamps seemed too close together to be "A" headcode and I opened the window to see better – you know how signal-box window glass is so wavy it can distort things. Well, as soon as I did that I could see it was the goods and I could see it wasn't going to stop at the board.' Jack spoke slowly and quietly, just like his actions. He said he went straightaway and put his Down line signals to 'Danger' and sent 'Obstruction Danger' even before the accident happened – but even then, I don't suppose he rushed! As a matter of interest, 4088 got past before the goods was derailed but the rear six coaches were badly smashed up and two people were killed. 2975 overturned at about 25 mph, killing the driver, Mr Furse, and his fireman, R. A. Jarvis, both of Didcot.

Don Symonds, Jack and I worked round the three shifts, twenty days consecutively before getting one day free, a Sunday, which might or might not have been taken up with hand-signalman's duties on some engineering task. Changing shifts at weekends was particularly wearisome. After working from 10 p.m. to 6 a.m. every day until Sunday morning, back again on Sunday evening at 6 p.m. until 6 a.m. Monday morning and then back again at 2 p.m. that same day for another week of eight-hour shifts. The hours became more difficult as one drew towards the end of a week and one became more tired but at least Don and I had the internal combustion engine to carry us to and from work. Jack Gough, at the age of about sixty-three, cycled 7 ½ miles each way no matter what the weather, no matter how short the time before he had to be back at work, yet 1do not recall him ever being late in the signal box.

On the Cowley line there was an intermediate siding at what had been Littlemore station for the benefit of a Shell oil and petroleum depot. The points leading into the siding were operated by the guard of the train, who released the lock on the lever with the key on the end of the electric train token. The train for this siding ran on most days and was belled from Hinksey North to Kennington as a '1-2' accompanied by the cryptic telephone message: 'That's a little more oil'.

The token system came to the Great Western in 1914 and was utterly reliable. Once one aluminium token had been taken from the bright red, cast-iron instrument, no other token could be withdrawn either from the Kennington or the Morris Cowley instrument until the first token had been restored to the instrument. The signal lever controlling the signal which gave access to the single line section became unlocked when the token was withdrawn. No train driver would enter on the single track unless he had possession of a token. After the token was removed from the electric lock of the instrument it was clipped into a steel, hooped carrier and taken outside to be placed on the lineside standard from which it would be snatched by one of the engine crew. Trains returning from Cowley passed very close to the north corner of the signal box so the token in its carrier was always handed up to the signalman leaning out of the window rather than the driver dropping it onto the 'cow's horn' provided for the purpose a few yards away from the box. The walk along the ballast to set the carrier on the post and the shouted greetings as we swapped the token off a train from Cowley gave me great satisfaction and a sense of enjoyment, the feeling of being a vital part of the railway and its time-honoured rituals.

The branch rose steeply from Kennington all the way to Wheatley tunnel, 4 ½ miles away, at gradients varying between 1 in 77 and 1 in 93. The top end of the incline was known as 'Horspath bank' and in steam days had been considered a formidable obstacle. At Oxford station one day, long ago, the guard of a train going to London via Wheatley and Princes Risborough informed the driver of his load and added that some of the weight was made up of four horseboxes at the rear of the train. At that the driver 'reared-up', to use a local term, and stated emphatically that his engine would not be able to get up Horspath 'wi' that lot tacked on the back'. The guard muttered, 'Oh, all right', and went away and after a few minutes gave the signal and the train left. Above Horspath Halt the train ground to a stand, the guard got down and walked forward to see what was the matter and was greeted by the driver: 'There you are, what did I tell you?' said he. 'I knew we wouldn't get up "Horspath" with that lot on.' The guard was astonished: 'But we haven't got them on – after what you said I had them taken off.' Then it was the driver's turn to be astonished and the train started away on the steep gradient and sailed over the summit without any fuss.

On rare occasions the steep gradient overpowered the engine's brakes on the downhill journey, this being in the days of unbraked trains when only the engine and the guard's van had a brake. About 1957 a 'Hall' class engine, driven by Oxford driver Bill Whiter, was standing at Morris Cowley, at the Wheatley end and *outside* the protection of the home signal on the single line. The signalman was young and inexperienced and he had accepted a goods train from Wheatley – under the caution 'Warning Arrangement', thinking that the engine was *inside* the home signal – on one of the two tracks of the passing loop. The goods from Wheatley was hauled by an ex-LMS 2-8-0. The driver was braking the engine but the weight of the train running forward onto the engine drove it on in a wheels-locked skid. The driver took the brake off and re-applied it but the train was out of control, and would have run through the station but for colliding with the 'Hall', which was standing with its brakes applied. The driver of the 'Hall' was taken by surprise so his engine was standing with its brakes hard on against the gradient when the 2-8-0 struck home. Their boilers were smashed and the 'Hall's' frames, made of inch-thick steel, were bent back like tinfoil.

Stopping an unbraked train was hazardous because the weight of the train was usually so much greater than that of the engine, but in June 1965 a train of 'car flats', each fitted with a vacuum brake under the driver's control, ran away approaching Kennington Junction from Cowley and was derailed across the Main line, scattering new cars onto the tracks.

The most difficult job I had at Kennington was working the Abingdon branch trip to Radley and getting it onto the branch without stopping passenger trains. The Abingdon ran from Oxford South End or Hinksey yards between 6.15 and 6.30 a.m., behind a couple of trips to Cowley and another for Littlemore. They came along the Up goods line from Hinksey South. The first Cowley ran straight onto the branch and away, the second had to wait for him to clear and the Abingdon waited behind that. There were also five trains scheduled on the Up Main line between 6 and 6.50 a.m.; two 75 mph 'Freightliners', an ordinary goods and two passenger trains, the second of these leaving Oxford at 6.46 a.m. By that time, with a bit of luck, the Cowley train had gone, leaving the Abingdon standing first in the loop ready to follow the 6.46 a.m. Oxford up the Main line. From then until 7.25 a.m. there was a gap in the Up line traffic but on the Down line the 2.10 a.m. Cardiff to Corby coal was due to pass Didcot North at 7 a.m., followed by the first Down passenger train, due to call at Radley at 7.15 a.m. I had fifteen minutes or so to get the Abingdon onto its branch. With luck, it would be D63xx or even 'Hymek' hauled so that the 2 ½ miles to Radley could be covered in about six minutes but even then there was the time it took to reverse twenty 60-foot wagons from Up to Down line and then draw them from Down line to Branch. Very often there was only I what I was pleased to call a 'mechanical tortoise', a grimy, grinding, diesel shunter with a top speed of 15 mph. There was practically no other time of day to run the Abingdon – it had to go out behind the 6.46 Oxford and any late-running 'Freightliner' coming up behind the passenger just had to wait its turn behind the branch trip. If the Trip ran late it just had to be put out onto the Up Main when there was any gap between other trains. It was always unpleasant to do that, knowing that passenger trains were going to be delayed – but MG cars needed their 'carflats' to load with cars and BR needed the income.

The train usually consisted of twenty 'car flats' as well as any coal for Abingdon or meat for the refrigerated store, the latter to be put in by the trip on its way back to Oxford, so it was around 460 yards long. At Radley the train stopped to let the guard off at the ground frame and then drew its quarter-mile-long tail clear of the points. If the train was shunter-hauled, the Cardiff coal train would by now be clicking into my describer. The guard phoned to ask for the key, I pressed the plunger. If the guard was expert, he would flick the key out of its lock in a second; if he was not ... The Annett's key liked to be treated nicely – it had to be turned with a certain rolling action or else the lock would jam. Patiently pressing the plunger and watching the clock, I visualised the progress over the ground of the coal train. When the key for the ground frame was fully turned, it set the signal protecting the points on the Up and Down line to 'Danger' and obviously this had to happen at such a time that the driver of the oncoming train was given a proper 'Caution' signal. It was no good flicking a green signal to red in the face of 750 tons moving at 40 mph. If the guard was ham-fisted or if for some other reason time was getting short, I had to stop him and let the coal train pass, then the Down passenger train would be close behind, so the branch train had to wait for that as well and was therefore blocking the Up line as the time for the 7.25 a.m. Oxford drew close. Working the Abingdon was quite a game.

Later in the morning the return trip had to be worked from Radley to Sandford, reverse into the siding and then out again for the 'dash', if that is the right word for a diesel shunter's progress, to the goods loop at Kennington. The line fell from Sandford and, with the assistance of gravity, unusually high speed was possible. I went out on the shunter hauling the Abingdon trip one morning and drove it back from Abingdon. It was automatically governed to 15 mph and its speedometer was not calibrated past 20 mph but, once the train was clear of the points at Sandford, I gave the wretched little machine full throttle and in no time at all the speedometer needle was hard against the stop. We might have been running at 25 mph!

After nine months at Kennington a vacancy arose at a much bigger and much more challenging box: Hinksey North. It was in a higher grade of pay than Kennington but because it was switched-out from noon each Saturday until Monday morning, there was less money to be earned there than at Kennington. Quite apart from having more trains to work with at Hinksey North, I would have every weekend free to go as a volunteer fireman on the Festiniog Railway. I applied for the job and as no one else wanted less pay for more work, I got the job – arguably the busiest manual signal box in the London Division. I passed the usual rules examination on 14 January 1969 and took the job on with a special piece of advice from the Oxford District Inspector ringing in my ears: 'Keep a sharp look-out on the track and on that bridge over the Thames when the Schools* are coming up. Some of the students get suicidal tendencies around then.'

---

* University examination time.

CHAPTER SIX

Shifts with Shunters

To save a long drive twice a day – or night – I looked for lodgings in Oxford. I had great difficulty in knowing where to start. The streets nearest the box were decidedly intimidating to a first-time lodging-seeker so in the end I started knocking on doors in north Oxford, an area much beloved by John Betjeman, full of stately, Victorian houses, which were in turn full of University students. After a lot of traipsing up and down the streets and front garden paths, I discovered a room to let in a house in Farndon Road. It was owned by a very jolly lady who worked on cancer research at the Churchill Hospital.

My new-found lodgings were about 2 miles from Hinksey North, a pleasant cycle ride either along Walton Street's rows of little shops and great buildings such as the Oxford University Press and Worcester College, or down Woodstock Road, a ride through tree-lined St Giles, turning down between the Randolph Hotel and the Ashmolean Museum at the Martyrs' Memorial. Access to the signal box was through the gates of the South End yard, opposite the rear entrance of the GPO sorting office, alongside a sort of 'Peabody Building' tenement of seedy and secretive aspect where there was not a 'Dreaming Spire' or an American blue-rinse to be seen. One evening, going to work at 6 p.m., I saw parked outside this 'Peabody Building' a customised Morris Mini-Minor, all chromium plate, rows of headlamps, ultra-wide wheels and a hydra-headed exhaust pipe, also beautifully chromed. Coming out through the gates next morning, I saw the same car standing on bricks, chrome strip and headlamps missing, wheel-less, the ends of the stubby axles like little fists appealing for justice.

The signal box stood about 80 yards south of a bridge over the Thames, on the Down side of the line about half a mile south of Oxford station. It was very plain to look at. Built in 1941 to withstand bomb-blasts and bomb-splinters, it was a brick blockhouse with a flat, concrete roof – the GWR version of the standard 'ARP' (Air Raid Precautions) signal box. The man who taught me the job, Stan Worsfold, had spent his life working Oxford's signal boxes. He told me that Hinksey North had been built by Italian prisoners of war who came flocking to work each day, on their bikes, from a camp on Cummor Hill, singing their heads off with their military escort not very much in evidence. The Italians' knowledge of bricklaying was minimal but with good supervision from McAlpine's foremen they did a good job, although the sudden lapse from English Bond to Italian confusion in the right-hand back corner of the box suggested that a foreman had taken a day off on one occasion. The signal box was brought into use in April 1942 and took the place of the old Oxford South box in controlling the South End yard on the north side of the river on the Up side of the line and, in addition, worked the north end of the new 'Hinksey' yard, south of the river on the Down side. Stan Worsfold had been signalman in the old South box and had carried the train register across the bridge to start work again in the new Hinksey North box, three times the size of his old workplace.

The new yard had been laid across low-lying ground intersected with streams and in exploring my newly acquired and far-flung empire, I discovered part of an inscription made by an Italian in the then-wet cement of a culvert he was helping to build. Some of the finger-drawn letters had been lost as the surface flaked away but it was clear that the man had recorded his name, the name of his regiment and, in big letters, the English words 'Master Mason'. This was on the largest of the culverts and he had obviously been very pleased with it.

From the front window of the box, I looked over the ruin that had once been Oxford's gasworks to the 'Dreaming Spires' of the University. Merton Tower I could see, St Mary's in the High, All Souls, the dome of the Sheldonian and, close enough to be able to read the time on its clock face, the octagonal 'Tom Tower' of Christchurch whose bells marked off the passing hours of my shifts. The Tom Tower clock recorded Oxford time not Greenwich Mean Time, so that it was exactly five minutes behind GMT. In the still of the night, Oxford seems to be a city of clocks. Just beyond the fence the old gas works was a ragwort and grassy wilderness of piled bricks, bent pipes and rusting steel, colonised by rabbits that were preyed upon by feral cats. In wet weather the 'Dreaming Spires' vanished behind grey rain and the desolation of the scene was grim indeed but on bright, sunny days, the rusty, flower-strewn ground had a strangely pretty look.

From the towpath along the Thames, a footpath came up the embankment to rail level at the rear of the signal box. One very wet, cold morning, I was looking south watching for an approaching train when I noticed what looked like a pile of sacks lying near the Down Main line. I thought something had fallen from a train, looked again, this time through the open window, and saw that the 'sacks' was a person, on all fours, the head pressed against the ground, the arms around the head. With the Down train 'getting handy' I hurried downstairs, ran to the person and, rather nervously, touched the shoulder. The body gave a nervous start and the head raised. It was a girl, about twenty years old, obviously very distressed. I squatted down and asked her to come into the box but she made no move; the rain was pelting down and the train was imminent so I pulled her gently to her feet and led her inside.

She walked in a leaden, automatic way. Her outer clothing was soaked and, indeed, she was probably soaked to the skin but I could hardly suggest that she take off her clothes. The fire was hot in the big, iron stove so I drew the armchair close and into its threadbare and somewhat grimy embrace she crept, curled up and slept. I put my coat over her and throughout three hours of clangorous bells and thumping levers she lay as if dead and there were times when I forgot she was there. Around 1 p.m. she woke and got stiffly to her feet, my overcoat around her shoulders, her hair all damp and bedraggled. She refused my offer of food and hot drinks and when I asked, 'Isn't there anything I can do to help?' the first recognisable expression passed over her face, not actually a smile but at least a lightening of that dreadful 'dead' look. She also spoke the first and last words she uttered to me: 'You've been a great help.'

With that she put my coat down on the chair and hurried out of the box, turning down the footpath to the river. An awful thought struck me. I telephoned the shunters' cabin, explained the situation rapidly and asked that one of them go onto the bridge, watch the girl and make sure she saw him watching. Moments later, I saw Cyril Main hurrying across the tracks to lean over the steel parapet. A few seconds later he walked back to the hut and telephoned to say that everything was all right. The girl had walked along the path towards Osney, leaving nothing but speculation behind her.

The shunters on my shift were a team of three and sometimes four. The foreman and Cyril had spent a lifetime on the railway at Oxford, following in the footsteps of fathers and grandfathers. Another man was a cheerful, heavyweight Pole called Marion. On night-shift their work was particularly tiring as the train service called them out to strenuous work in any weather when the rest of Oxford and most of their fellow railwaymen were asleep – or at any rate taking a brief nap. And when the shunters were at work, so was the signalman in Hinksey North – another reason why, top-class box though it was, it had only one regular signalman: me. It was, in the phrase of the time, 'never paid for'. There were only forty-three to forty-five trains on night-shift but of those, nine or ten called to work in Hinksey or South End yards, so while other signalmen might have their feet up, the man in Hinksey North was busy with the shunters, switching the points in response to the telephoned commands, 'Shed side' or 'Field side up', working a trip across to Hinksey yard or sending an engine from the South End to the diesel depot 'wrong road' on the Up goods loop.

The 11.40 p.m. Paddington to Worcester goods stopped on the Down Main line to detach traffic for Oxford and went on its way, leaving the yard pilot to come out onto the Main line to collect the wagons and take them back to the yard in a shunt of entertaining complication. Trains of empty 'car flats' arrived from Johnstone in Scotland and from Parkstone Quay, Essex, to terminate in one or other of the yards; trains of petrol from Fawley refinery; trains of empties going back to the refinery; trains of general merchandise – all this traffic called, shunted and moved on. The diesel shunter pilot engine hauled out rakes of wagons, freshly loaded, from the goods shed and placed empty wagons for loading; newly arrived traffic had to be berthed for unloading; trains were formed at night for morning trips to Charlbury, Bicester, Cowley, Littlemore and Abingdon. The hard-pressed shunters spent most of the night walking or running between rows of wagons, coupling and uncoupling with their long, hickory poles, waving on, calling back and stopping movements with their hand-lamp signal (unless there was a fog, when the work became a near impossibility), sorting wagons while the next train waited its turn on the Up loop or Down reception line.

One night, a train of petrol from Fawley refinery was on the Down reception line in Hinksey yard, waiting its turn in the South End. After an hour the door of the signal box was flung open and heavy boots came stamping up the stairs.

'If I have to wait another five minutes I'll cut off and go home!' snarled the very fed-up driver of the Class 33 diesel on the petrol train, its distinctive 'tonking' tick-over coming faintly down the track and through the open door.

'You won't go anywhere unless I pull off for you,' I snapped back. 'You can see for yourself that they're hard at it in South End. They'll take you when they're ready.'

'They ought to stop and let me over then, I could drop my stuff and go.'

'There's nowhere for you to put it, is there, that's what they're working on. Tell you what,' I continued in a consoling tone, 'you ought to have a "King Arthur" down there instead of that bloody old diesel with you on it all by yourself. Then you and your mate could make some tea on the shovel in the fire and get the cards out on the bucket.'

The driver brightened at once. 'Aha! Now you're talking!'

'Well, OK then,' I said, 'you put the kettle on for us now and we'll have one together.' I was sorry when the shunters asked 'Let's have the Fawley over'; the driver, Len Renwick, and I were having a great old gas about Southern steam!

I relished working Hinksey North because it allowed me to feel more like a signalman than ever. We were permitted such complications as working in the wrong direction over the Up goods loop – the 'Old Main' – between South End and the station – bell code 2-3-3; we could use the 'Warning Acceptance', 3-5-5, and the 'Line Clear to Clearing Point Only', 2-2-2, as well. We were also allowed to give 'Train out of Section' for an Up train while that train was still inside the clearing point, providing that it was proceeding on its journey, this last to save a few vital seconds and help keep traffic running through the bottleneck that was Oxford station. Doubtless this attitude was naive and over-enthusiastic but that is how I felt. I think it was my over-eager disposition that annoyed the foreman shunter; any enthusiasm he might have had for trains had long since been washed out in the gales and snows of forty winters in the yard. Anyhow, he took a dislike to me which made life difficult at times.

One dark and moonless night he phoned and gruffly ordered the road, 'Shed side to Hinksey Down yard', slamming his phone down before I had a chance to reply. He was going to take the returned empty 'car flats' from Johnstone over into Hinksey yard, the engine that had brought them from the north having gone to shed 'wrong road' over the Up loop. I set the road and over went twenty 'car flats' behind a diesel shunter. I watched carefully to see the red tail-light disappear and reappear three times – there were no track circuits so no indication on my track diagram – and then reversed the levers for normal, up and down, running. Stan Worsfold had shown me this trick of knowing, in the dark, when the last vehicle of a train was clear of points 200 yards away. There was a line of electricity supply poles down in the yard and when the tail-lamp had come out from behind the third one, the train was clear of the points.

Half an hour later, a train of 'car flats' from Bathgate was belled up the Main. These were destined for Cowley so they could go onto the Up reception line between me and Hinksey South box. Number 2 Up loop was already blocked and No 1 Up loop was required for through trains. I told Johnny Blanchard at Hinksey South what was happening, set the points and lowered the signals. As the train turned into the Up reception line, a horrid thought occurred to me. The shunters were still in Hinksey Down yard with their pilot engine and had been there for some time. There was a connection*

---

* See X, Y, Z on diagram on p. 88.

from the Down reception to the Up reception line, which was operated by the shunters *after* they had asked the signalman at Hinksey North if it was safe to do so. The traffic-worn foreman was unlikely to ask a young sprig like me for permission to move about 'his' yard. I went to the window, slid it back and listened. Sure enough, a few seconds later there came that nasty, sullen, thump that speaks of collisions. The signal protecting the connection had been at 'Danger' (this also was worked by the shunters) but its light was out, it was not indicated in the signal box, and the driver had not seen it until too late so his engine cut through the middle of the Johnstone 'car flats' as they stood across the connection. The foreman used the ground frame telephone then gave me a colourful description of what he was going to do to me when he got back to the signal box. He never came and it was, as my Granny used to say, 'Sam-Fairy-Ann' to me; he had dropped the clanger and he would have to carry the can. I do not recall that anyone in charge made any inquiry into the incident. If the damage was not too severe, it was likely that the 'family' atmosphere of the railway kept it covered up.

Three weeks later, I was again on night-shift when the lamp in No. 1 Up goods loop starting signal went out. It was one of three on a gantry over the Main line and it was most important that it be re-lit, to comply with Rule 74. The shunters were hard at work and if I went to light the lamp all their work would stop. It seemed that the best plan would be for one of them to go and light it. I rang their telephone long and loud till the dreaded foreman answered.

'What do you want?' he snapped.

'Could one of you come and light the lamp in the Up loop starter, please?'

'I've told you before – you do your job and I'll do mine.' Slam. Down went his phone.

'All right,' I said into the dead mouthpiece, 'I will.' I looked for some paraffin, found none and realised I would have to get some from the shunters' store. This was going to be a longer job than I thought; up to the shunters' cabin, probably have a row with the foreman, then back past the box to the gantry to fix the lamp. Rule 74 forbade me to leave the signal box for this purpose unless all my signals were at 'Danger'. There was going to be a certain amount of delay. I told the signalmen at Oxford Station South and at Hinksey South what I was doing and left the box.

I walked down the track to the accompaniment of furious whistlings from the pilot. The shunters wanted the road out from 'Shed side'. I found three of them silhouetted in the light coming from the open door of their cabin, huddled together, their shunting poles resting on the ground like medieval pikes. They looked distinctly unhappy. Inside the hut the foreman was leaning with his shoulder against the ringing button of the telephone. My sudden appearance out of the darkness caused pandemonium. 'Can I have some paraffin, please, Cyril?' I asked. The foreman came out of the hut at the gallop, braying, 'What the hell are you doing here? What are you playing at?'

He was still raving as Cyril, who was a decent sort, hurried me away to the oil store. He had heard my earlier request and had volunteered to light the lamp but had been over-ruled. Altogether it took about half an hour to light that lamp and the shunters lost that much time from their bonus. Luckily there were very few trains running, or wanting to run, through Oxford at that time of night. Anyhow, after this the foreman was no longer hostile and we co-existed in a state of armed neutrality.

On eight-hour shifts I had time to visit other signal boxes, to photograph the railway or around the streets of Oxford. There was shopping to be done for the one large meal of the day, food to be prepared for the next day's work, the launderette to be visited, sometimes when it was full at ten in the morning, sometimes when it seemed weirdly empty, near midnight. Occasionally I had time to walk across Port Meadow in the twilight to the Trout at Godstow. On Saturdays I had the signal box switched out within seconds of the yard pilot clearing Oxford Station South box on its way to the diesel depot. My car, a Jowett 'Javelin', was parked outside the box and I would be away to Portmadoc for the Festiniog Railway. But on twelve-hour shifts there was little time for the background preparation necessary for the work itself – and I began to be asked to work more and more 'twelve hours'. I liked the work so I never thought of refusing and, indeed, I liked the overtime, which could be saved and spent later on a full week as a fireman on the Festiniog Railway, but those long shifts with very little chance to rest in the box, even on night-shift, became increasingly arduous. One great difficulty was shopping. On 'twelve-hour days' I did not get into the streets at the end of a shift until after 6 p.m., which left only one, wickedly expensive delicatessen from which to buy provisions – apart from Mrs Kennedy's butcher shop at the top of the Kingston Road. So, on the Saturday before a week of 6 a.m. to 6 p.m. shifts, I had to go to Marks & Spencer or Littlewoods and stock up with food, especially food for eating in the signal box – seven tins of Irish stew and seven tins of Wall's steak and kidney pie! At the end of a day I would cycle home along Walton Street, call at sympathetic Mrs Kennedy's shop for a big pork chop and then across the road for some vegetables, then home to cook it all in the shared, basement, kitchen.

Opposite the kitchen door was the door of the bedsit of a poor old lady who had rather been dumped there by her grown-up and very superior children. When she heard me rattling the pots and pans she came out to have, probably, the only conversation of her day. She was a little, thin old lady, anxious to impress upon me how unused she was to this kind of life. I was very sorry for her but found her pathetic and just a little scary so I always took my food upstairs to my room where, I, too, ate in solitude. Even quite nice food tastes flat when eaten without the sauce of some congenial company.

Going to work at 5.30 a.m. for 5.50 in the box, I had the streets to myself. The previous night's litter, from people eating on the hoof, blew aimlessly about the road or lay greasily in the gutters. There was only one person whom I was likely to see, only one person I wanted to see: Henry Wiggins, the milkman. Henry was eighty-three, though I would never have known if he had not proudly informed me of the fact. He was a short, stocky man with a trilby hat, a white moustache and a cheerful expression. He had been doing this round all his life and had used a horse and cart until the war, when he had had to give up the horse. He then built himself the three-wheeled electric trolley, painted maroon, that I became familiar with. I could have bought a bottle of milk the day before but it was far better to buy it from Henry and have a few, friendly words in the darkness and rain of the early morning street or in the stillness of a summer dawn among those rather fine, early nineteenth-century houses at the city end of Walton Street.

'Doing for myself' at the end of long shifts, I began to fray at the edges. At first this 'fraying' had no effect on my work but off-duty forgetfulness was occasionally a nuisance. Cycling home at 2.30 p.m., I once pedalled right past the end of my road. I looked down it, saw that my bike was not leaning against the kerb outside my lodging and was seized by a great wave of panic. Someone had stolen my bike! I leaped off my bicycle and only then realised that I was riding it and that I had gone by the end of my road. I must have been in a waking dream in the saddle.

I was in the world, yet hardly a part of it, for I seemed to be either in my room getting ready for work, at work, or cycling home from the signal box. I returned to my room one evening in mid-October at 6.30, thoroughly whacked after a twelve-hour shift. I had thought about and signalled 120 trains on the main lines and goods loops and dealt with dozens of shunting movements, making hundreds of lever movements, walking up and down the 24 feet of a 72-lever frame, answering the phone, making calls and keeping the Train Register up to date with an entry every minute or two. I threw my bag down and sat on the edge of the bed saying – and I clearly recall it even now – 'Phew! I'll just have a breather before I start the meal.'

The next thing I knew I was waking from a deep sleep, stretched full length on the bed with a mouth that tasted like a sewer. I could not make out what had happened, groped for the switch of the bedside lamp, turned it on and saw the hands of the clock straight up and down. Six o'clock! I had slept all night and now I would be late for work. Without another moment's thought I dashed out of the house, onto my bike and pedalled madly away down Woodstock Road. I had no food or milk to sustain me through a 12-hour shift, all that mattered was to relieve my mate who had been at work all night.

As I hurried through the wide thoroughfare of St Giles, it occurred to me that there was a lot of traffic about and lights on for 6 a.m. but I pedalled on, wondering how best to apologise to my colleague in the box. I cycled past the shunters, hard at work, and hoped they would not notice I was late. Opposite the signal box I dismounted to carry the bike across the tracks and, looking up through the windows at the big, wooden cased clock to see how late I was, I saw the hands showing 11.45 p.m. I blinked and looked again, utterly at a loss. Then the penny dropped. I had not seen 6 a.m. on my clock but 11.30 p.m., the hands straight up and down. I crossed the tracks and slipped quietly away to the riverside path, out to Osney and home for five hours' sleep before another twelve-hour shift.

After this, I resolved to say something to the rostering Inspector, Charlie Pavey. He phoned from Reading on Thursday to see if I was all right for twelve hours the following week.

'Couldn't you find an extra chap for here? A week of eight-hours would be like a holiday for me.'

'Get off – you like the overtime,' he replied, jollying me along.

'If I was to leave the job you'd have to find someone else,' I replied darkly.

Charlie laughed. 'Come on, you'd never leave – now then, what about this twelve hours next week?' I did not care to refuse – and not merely because of the near-double wages I should get. All my training throughout my life, including five years in the Army as an adolescent, had been to obey whoever was in charge. But there was also a feeling now that I was being taken for granted, which irked me. As it happened, I had recently been offered a whole winter as a fireman on the Festiniog Railway with lodgings in a lovely house overlooking Cardigan Bay. I agreed to the week of twelve hours but I also handed in my notice to terminate my service at the end of that week.

On 2 November 1969 I was in Boston Lodge shed on the Festiniog Railway, raising steam on *Blanche* as I polished her brass and paintwork.

CHAPTER SEVEN

Lineside Policeman

The winter sojourn in Merioneth was a rugged but very pleasant interlude – I like the hills in winter when they are shrouded in drizzle and the lichens glisten on the great, grey boulders. However, mundane considerations such as the lack of folding money dictated a return to 'civilisation' and on 6 March 1970 I was back in Oxford. I got lodgings in a bay-windowed little house in Abbey Road, a dark, seedy-looking street close to the station and a very useful coffee shack. The Thames flowed level with the back yard and I suspect that the houses' foundations were sunk below the waterline in soggy clay. The inner end of the street, that furthest from the Botley Road, terminated at a wall bordering the canal, beyond which was the engine shed – or what was left of it. Abbey Road houses crowded in on each other, shutting out the sun in an effort to sit on the narrow piece of level ground between the railway embankment and the river. The area had once housed a colony of railway families but by 1970 most railwaymen were rich enough to live in more salubrious parts of the City of Dreaming Spires.

My landlady was very cheerful and hard-working. She agreed not only to cook my meals but also to do my washing besides allowing me the use of her back room upstairs, overlooking the oily-green Thames, and all this for a very reasonable consideration. With these domestic arrangements confirmed by advance payments, I went to the station and lurked nonchalantly and quite by chance right outside District Inspector Jones' door at just about the time he would normally emerge to carry the daily notices around the signal boxes. In about the time it took to whistle 'All You Need is Love' he appeared and, taking the apparition before him in his short, jaunty stride, said, 'Hello, Adrian, want your job back?' I was expecting a rather more protracted interview, a more searching inquisition, so the surprise swept away any semblance of nonchalance and I gasped, 'Yes, please, where shall I go?'

'Hinksey North, of course. The job you left is still there. Here,' he said, handing me some beige, railway envelopes, 'take Stan Worsfold his Notices.'

Barely able to keep to a walk, I hurried down the path to the signal box and in a few days took charge. It was as if I had been 'on loan' to the Festiniog Railway.

The work was as busy as ever and the relief signalman who came to cover the other two shifts at the box felt that it ought to be upgraded. The 'marks' were duly taken and, mainly because of the shunting work we did, the box rose from a 'C' (the old 'Class 1') to a 'D', the highest grade box at Oxford and probably the highest grade mechanical box in the London Division. As I was sole regular incumbent of the post, this made me the top-class signalman at Oxford – manifestly untrue but technically a matter of fact. Accordingly, I would be certain of a place in the Panel signal box at Oxford when that installation was complete, late in 1973. The men who had wanted Hinksey North upgraded – this had never been my idea – were now upset that a sprig such as myself should be 'Number One for the Panel' before men with three or four times more service than I. These murmurings finally reached my ears and I was very happy to console the murmurers. Being particularly stupid where money and/or promotion is concerned, all these wranglings and calculations never occurred to me – I simply enjoyed being a hard-working, fairly expert signalman in a very busy box. The realisation that I was first in line for a Panel job was alarming. I had visited Reading Panel on several occasions to see old friends incarcerated therein – several old friends had died from heart attacks after going to work in Reading and Swindon Panels – and everything I had learned about the Panel's workings from my time at Uffington and Kennington filled me with acute disdain for them. They went against everything that made being a signalman enjoyable; I would not be able to see the trains while I worked in a stressful, ugly, plastic environment. Panel boxes were definitely not for me and my occasionally absent-minded brain. Having broadcast this lengthy apologia over the 'bus-line' telephone the murmurings ceased, the seniorities of the men were again examined, my colleagues sorted themselves out into those who would go direct into the new Panel, those who would 'hang on until old so-and-so retires' and those who would take their redundancy pay and run. With the pecking order re-established, I got broad-gauge smiles from my friends. They were welcome to their Panel.

Panel signal boxes are safe enough when everything is working normally. It seems to me that it is when the system is disrupted, either by accident or design, that matters are likely to go disastrously wrong. Matters often went dangerously wrong in semaphore signal boxes yet I always felt safer in one of these, in close, personal contact with the trains. It is when a

Panel man mistakes an indication on his console or is forgetful and gives a driver incorrect or misunderstood instructions over the telephone that a train will go swanning off into the blue with no way of recalling it. There was insufficient communication between drivers and the Panel man and insufficient control over the trains.*

During the night of 21/22 June 1970, for example, the Down Main line between Ashbury Crossing and Highworth Junction was blocked by engineering work and all trains between those places were running over the Up Main line. These points were operated by a man working levers in a ground frame. These levers were unlocked, electrically, from Swindon Panel and the signals approaching the crossover on the Up and Down mains were locked at 'Danger' and trains were handsignalled past them by another man. Both men were very experienced signalmen. At about 6.15 a.m. on the 22nd, a Down train passed over the cross-over points at Ashbury, picked up the Pilotman for the single line, and travelled over the Up Main to Highworth Junction. Fred, in charge of the ground frame at Ashbury, took the 'G' clamp off the facing end of the crossover and then walked to the telephone to ask the Swindon Panel man what the next move would be. While Fred was talking on the telephone the Down train was making swift progress over the 4 ½ miles to Highworth Junction. There it crossed back to the Down Main and dropped the Pilotman. That worthy walked across to the 2.10 a.m. Cardiff to Corby coal train and 'told the driver the tale': 'I've got two trains to go Up line. I'm sending you through and I will accompany the next one. Single-line working between here and Ashbury over the Up line. Obey all signals and look out for hand-signals from the men at the barriers and on the signal protecting the crossing at Ashbury. Right away.' The Cardiff set off at about 6.30 a.m. making a cracking pace with twenty-five tubs of coal and a guard's van behind diesel D1670.

By the time Fred had finished chatting on the phone to his mate in the Panel, D1670 was in sight and the man protecting the road crossing was giving its driver a green flag to say that the public road was clear and safe for the train to cross. Fred had no time to get to the signal on the approach side of the crossing to give the driver a yellow signal – 'Caution' – which was the correct authorisation to the driver for him to pass at 'Danger' a three-aspect

---

* That is no longer the case using short-wave radio but still the difficulty of stopping trains in an emergency remains. The computerised control centre at Slough was disastrously unable to stop the runaway train, which caused the Ladbroke Grove crash in 1999.

signal. Not that the yellow flag would have altered subsequent events. The driver took the green flag at the road crossing to mean that it was in order to pass the colour-light signal at 'Danger' – which was not the case – and the two men on the ground stood back as 600 tons of coal and steel thudded briskly past. Only one more train and they could both go home. Imagine, if you can, the feeling of 'bowels turning to water' felt by Fred and his mate when D1670 took a smart right and left through the cross-over and proceeded at increasing speed up the Down Main line. Fred had forgotten to put the cross-over back for straight running after the last Down train.

The driver was by no means surprised at this sudden change of plan. He was used to and cynical of railway 'cock-ups' and decided that he had not been given proper instructions by the Pilotman. The thought that he was lustily compounding Fred's error never occurred to him and he drove happily onwards, up the Down line. The two men on the ground bawled with all the power of their lungs at the guard as his van passed; he popped out of his caboose like a cork from a bottle, got the message and darted back inside to wind his hand-brake on and off as a means of attracting the driver's attention to the red flag he had placed over the side of the vehicle. In steam-hauled days this action with the brake would have had the effect of tugging the couplings back against the engine and the driver would undoubtedly have felt the 'bite' but the powerful diesel surged ahead, quite impervious to the Victorian techniques of the guard in his equally Victorian 20-ton brake-van. Anticipating that the train was not going to stop, Fred got into his car and drove through the lanes to Uffington, the site of the next set of cross-overs, in the hope that the train would stop there and he could then divert it back to the Up Main.

In Swindon Panel, the signalman and the District Inspector were watching the console. When the red, 'track-occupied' lights illuminated through the cross-over they thought they had a track-circuit failure but when the 'track failure' began to move eastwards, they knew that they had a runaway on their hands. This caused them some concern because there was a 'light' engine running down the Down Main; it was then about 6 miles from the coal train and closing fast. The signalman decided that the engine would arrive at Uffington well before the coal train so he set the route for the engine to enter the Down goods loop and thus clear the Main line but the Inspector over-ruled him and told him to stop the engine at the first possible moment, at Baulking bridge, and, when the driver reported in on the signal post telephone, to ask him to go forward on foot to stop the driver of the coal train. The signalman therefore cancelled the route, the signal at Baulking bridge remained at 'Danger' but, as a consequence of the way the Panel system operates, the points remained set for the 'last called' position – into the loop.

While a certain tension developed in Swindon Panel, the District Inspector hurried to his car to follow Fred in the rush to Uffington, and the driver of the 2.10 a.m. Cardiff drove with perfect peace of mind over the road at Knighton crossing without benefit of protective barriers down against road traffic. In the Panel, the men gathered round the console to watch the progress of the red lights towards each other from west and east. As the lights continued to move, they felt fairly sure that the coal train had not hit anything on the unguarded crossing. The next crisis was the spring-worked trailing point – now a facing point for a train running in the wrong direction – at the exit from Uffington goods loop. In normal single-line working conditions, these would be clamped tightly in position with a 'G' clamp but, as matters stood on 22 June, they were entirely free and might well have been standing half open. There was a 20-foot drop off the embankment. The Panelmen stood helplessly and watched the red lights roll over the spring points and pass on. The driver – everyone concerned – had been very lucky, the whole train passed clear and came to a stand at the ground frame at Uffington facing the 'light' engine, 350 yards away at Baulking bridge. 'How long's this single-line working going on for?' the driver of the Cardiff asked Swindon Panelman on the phone as the secondman off the 'light' engine came running towards him holding a red flag.

Fred arrived shortly after, followed, fifteen minutes later, by the District Inspector. The coal train was standing on track circuits, which prevented the Panelman giving the necessary electrical release to the ground frame key, so the driver was told to reverse his train westwards 150 yards. No sooner had he started than there was a thudding and a jostling of wagons and four coal tubs were derailed. In the general confusion, everyone had forgotten that the points were set to lead from Down Main to Down loop and therefore the Cardiff had smashed them when it ran through them from the wrong direction.

That was the fault of the railwaymen, aided by the inherent weakness of the system. The second Hungerford crash, like the first, was the fault of Management. It was only through sheer good fortune that there had not been more such incidents. The 12.45 a.m. Westbury to Theale on the night of 10 November 1971 consisted of forty-two 16-ton wagons loaded with stone hauled by D1040 *Western Queen*. The train passed Woodborough box and gave the signalman there no cause for concern. Savernake and

Bedwyn boxes were closed on night shift so the next box was Hungerford, over 17 miles away, and in this section the fourteenth wagon in the train developed a hot-axle bearing. Half a mile before it reached Hungerford the trailing right-hand axle bearing broke and the wagon rolled on at around 40 mph, rocking about a diagonal axis as the load was carried on the leading right-hand and trailing left-hand wheels. A few seconds later the 12.35 a.m. Paddington to Plymouth express passed and its driver, seeing the flames and sparks, blew a warning on his horn to the guard of the train. Guard Harvey put his head over the side, saw the trouble and was going back to get a red light when the engine braked suddenly, causing him to be knocked off balance and rendered unconscious.

Up in Hungerford box, the signalman, Robbie Bowden, had seen the flames and sparks and had thrown his signals to 'Danger'. He was just about to send 'Obstruction Danger' to Kintbury when the derailed fourteenth wagon crashed through the signal box and Robbie, too, lost consciousness. The expertise of the local Fire Brigade was required to extricate him from the total wreck of his box. The remarkable thing was that he was still alive. He was away from work for nineteen days and told me later that the whole episode had been a waking nightmare. Twenty-six wagons were overturned, blocking Up and Down Main lines, but the fourteen leading wagons with the engine broke away and remained on the rails, as did the last three, including the brake van. Of the fourteen, all were found to be overloaded – on average by 3¾ tons; the worst case was wagon 555592, 7 tons 1 cwt over the limit. It is reasonable to assume that the others were also overloaded but whether the crash was caused primarily by this or by a primary lack of oil in the bearing will remain a mystery. Western Region had to replace half a mile of track, build a new signal box and clear up the mess. All this was an unavoidable expense but the need for a weighbridge could not be proved conclusively so, six years after the first crash and six months after the second, Western Region was still agonising over whether or not to incur the expense of moving a redundant weighbridge from Wednesbury to a suitable site in the Westbury area.

Reducing the expensive infrastructure was the order of the day. One Saturday night in the autumn of 1971 I was booked for a ten-hour shift till 8 a.m. on Sunday, 'on the ground', at Didcot North Junction. There was no shelter on the embankment so it was usual to get a car on to the track bed of the old Up goods loop at Appleford and drive to the signal at the junction. The Inspector in charge, Stan Harding, had come to the site with his car, which, being generally more luxurious than mine, he kindly invited me to share. The engineers were going to re-lay some track and had to lift the old, timber-sleepered sections out before putting down the concrete-sleepered sections. Normally a powerful steam or diesel crane would have been used for this work, but as a result of the policy of reducing the expensive infrastructure – in this case, scrapping cranes – the work was to proceed using a hired crane, mounted on a road-lorry. As an old-hand once said, 'The blessed road gets in everywhere.'

My job was to see that the crane was not swinging lengths of track through the air when a train was approaching. This involved liaising with the Panel, trudging about on the ballast, giving instructions to the workmen, and trying to stay awake by drinking a lot of horrible, thermos-flask tea. After about five hours out in the dark and the cold, with my stomach audibly awash with tea, the train service slackened to the usual 'small hours' emptiness, so Stan and I sought relaxation and warmth in the plush confines of his car.

With the interior light on, the windows were just black, mirroring our tired faces. We shared sandwiches as the wind moaned and buffeted the car, rocking it slightly in the gusts. As we ate, we talked about steam days and retirement days. For him the latter were close at hand and he told me how he was looking forward to living in Bournemouth and playing his trombone in a dance band. We grew wearier and his hopes and the anecdotes about the old days faded into a grumble about the present woes of Western Region. It had, according to my Inspector, a lot-to do with the 'foreigners' who were – and had been for some time – in charge at Paddington.

'All these blokes off the LNER, they come, stir it all up and clear off, leaving someone else to sort out the mess. They've no manners. A couple or three years ago Gerry Fiennes wanted the Reading–London suburban service improved. Poor old Bill Noke was put in charge of it, him and some others. They sorted out new workings for men, rail cars, engines – it took a long time and before they had the job properly thought through Fiennes comes roaring along demanding that they have the scheme in place for May. Bill said it would be ready for September but Fiennes said "May" so on it went, a right-old mess and Bill Noke got the blame for it. All cuts and cock-ups on this railway.' We were interrupted in our pleasantly gloomy task of tearing 'foreigners' to shreds by a knock on the window. The Inspector wound down the glass and let in the gale and the face of the Permanent-Way Inspector.

'We'll be finished soon.'

'How's that then? The occupation was till eight o'clock. You haven't got it all relaid already, have you?'

'You must be joking. The road-lorry crane couldn't lift the concrete sections. It nearly folded in two when it took the strain. I phoned the Divisional Engineer, got him out of bed at about three o'clock – it's his clever idea to have a road crane. He told me to cut the concrete sections in half so the crane can lift them.'

'Eh!?' said my Inspector. 'You can't do that, we'll be here for days, cutting and drilling.'

'Well, that's what I told him. So he said to put all the old stuff back in until we can get hold of a proper crane – so that's what we've been doing and now we're back where we started and you can go home.'

In early June 1971 I worked three twelve-hour night shifts at Old Oak Common as a hand-signalman while a large-scale rearrangement of the layout took place. I went up to Paddington by passenger train and rode down to Old Oak on the first available empty coaching stock train so that, with travelling time in each direction, the shifts were more like sixteen hours each. Men from all over the London Division were drafted in. It was good to be in a 'gang' and to hear the news from High Wycombe and Newbury before we split up to go to our respective signal posts. In the darkness, the world was one of disembodied lights. The rails gleamed red from signal lamps or white from arc lights at the site of work. Invisible streets were traced by lines of orange sodium lamps; the lattice-work of the great bridge carrying the West London line over the Main line was silhouetted against the starry sky and looked like the work of Titans. I stood at a signal post between the Main and Relief lines, ear clamped to the telephone, when the huge diesels came grumbling, rumbling, lumbering along, grinding to a stand, towering overhead as I stood in the 'valley' between the heaped ballast of each track. I asked, 'Is Line Clear?' of the Panelman and, stretching up as high as I could to reach the hand-rails, climbed the cab steps to shout instructions in the driver's ear above the steady, throbbing hammer of his engine. I clambered down and stood, collar turned up against a nasty, cutting breeze, as the dark shapes that made up the train drummed past, the diesel's exhaust a howling, black plume against the deepest, navy-blue sky.

By midnight on the third night of what were virtually sixteen-hour shifts, I was very tired. Around two o'clock that morning the chill wind carried the cries of a prisoner in Wormwood Scrubs, 600 yards away across a playing field, distant but clearly audible – 'Help me, help me' – over and over again until the voice ceased. I have never forgotten that desolate sound heard on the buffeting wind as the pain in my guts caused by tiredness grew, unassuaged by coffee or sandwiches. By 3 a.m. I was ready to drop. Quite when I did drop I cannot recall but it had no effect on the trains. I woke, shivering, chilled to the bone, lying full-length on the ballast, a grey dawn breaking and the trains roaring past, a couple of feet away from my head.

After a long weekend experiencing the virtues of a mid-Victorian regime as a lineside policeman without the latter's physical fitness, it was sheer luxury to return to Hinksey North, the fire, the armchair and sixty-nine highly polished levers. The box was off the beaten track and I had only one railway enthusiast visitor all the time I worked there. At least, he said he was a railway enthusiast. He was a pleasant lad of about thirteen in the uniform of a well-known Oxford college school. He called up from the path, asking if he could come in and, of course, I let him. He asked sensible questions and I was quite pleased with him. The following week he came again and asked questions about the opening and closing times of signal boxes on the Worcester line. Well, I thought he wanted to visit them when they were open so I gave him the working timetable and he made a copy of their times and went away. I never saw him again.

The weekend passed and the following Monday night I was watching television, waiting to go on night shift, when there was a loud knock on the front door. I opened it and found two large men in civilian clothes, one of whom was holding out a piece of paper. 'This is a search warrant,' he intoned. 'We have reason to believe there is stolen property in this house.' Stunned, I stood aside and let them in. The man with the search warrant then said he wanted to meet one Adrian Vaughan and, alarmed and totally mystified, I identified myself. 'We believe you have a quantity of railway signalling equipment stolen from signal boxes on the Worcester line during the weekend,' the voluble one said. The other fixed me with a professional, fishy stare. I had not been to work since Saturday noon and so I knew nothing at all about this burglary. Up in my room I did have a quantity of signalling equipment, which I had taken into protective custody when the box concerned was being closed, much of the stuff I had actually used when it was in situ.

'What exactly are you looking for?' I asked, my voice trembling enough for it to show. The one with the stare silently produced a list. They were doing their best to be intimidating – and they were succeeding. I looked at it in growing amazement; someone had stripped out instruments and clocks from working signal boxes.

'But I haven't got any of this stuff – there's enough here to open a railway – I've nowhere to put it all – I'm a signalman, I'd never do such a thing,' my protests came tumbling out, urged on by anxiety.

'You were seen,' said the voluble policeman, scenting an arrest from my nervousness. 'Your car was seen at all these places on Sunday morning.'

'And you'd know when these boxes were closed, wouldn't you?' said the hitherto silent one. But I knew they were lying. Someone had suggested they try me, a shot in the dark because I was an enthusiastic railwayman; they were just trying it on.

I became confident, even angry. 'Any railwayman would know when those boxes were shut and it wasn't me that broke into them. Look, I've got some stuff upstairs, you'd better come and see, but there's nothing on your list.'

As we went up the dark, narrow stairs I suddenly remembered the well-mannered little boy with the angelic face, short trousers and a desire to know about the closing times of the Worcester line boxes. Could he be behind this, the cause of my present predicament and maybe the cause of my losing my treasured relics? I opened the door of my room and the two officers plunged in like labradors diving into a pond to retrieve a shot duck. There was nothing in my possession that was on the list – my stuff was much better quality – and after I explained to them that I held my souvenirs from boxes I had worked or known well, out of a love of the job, they very decently let the matter drop.

In September 1970 I was driving a Wolseley 1500. I had a GWR locomotive vacuum gauge fixed to the dashboard and a length of plastic tube from it to the carburettor. The 8-inch diameter gauge came to life and registered a vacuum when the engine was running so I could adjust the throttle to get the greatest economy from the engine while running – about 45 mpg. I filled the tank with a measured gallon and drove till the fuel ran out to ensure correct consumption figures. Driving out of Oxford on the evening of 7 September, west along Botley Road, I saw on the pavement ahead a pair of very trim ankles and legs stepping briskly along. There was a brown coat down which tumbled a lot of curly, auburn hair and, sticking out at right-angles, was the right arm, dainty thumb raised. I stopped. She was going to Wantage. So was I. She got in. By the top of Cumnor Hill I knew her name was Susan. I also knew I ought to ask her for a date. By the Greyhound at Besselsleigh I knew I dared not ask; she was about seventeen to my twenty-nine. At Frilford golf course my measured gallon ran out. 'I'm afraid we've run out of petrol,' I said apologetically. She looked out at the wide open spaces in the evening sun and turned to look daggers at me down her rather haughty nose. I saw how very green were her eyes. She was reaching for the door handle.

'Don't worry,' I reassured her hastily, 'I've a gallon in the back – look.' I showed her my big, brass GWR vacuum gauge, explained what I was trying to do and she relaxed, knowing that I was merely a harmless conserver of energy and not the local nutcase. Half a dozen times during that journey I nearly asked her to come out for the evening and to prolong our journey together I drove her to her front door. Just as she was getting out of the car I blurted out the question. 'Yes, all right,' she answered, quite simply and easily. I was so sure that this was an event of the greatest importance that I made a note of the meeting on the fly-leaf of Volume 1 of McDermott's *History of the Great Western Railway*.

Very shortly after this my digs in Abbey Road came under new management when the man of the house and his mate a few doors down the street amicably swapped wives while the children of each family stayed in their original homes but visited their mothers, a matter of some confusion to the children. The new wife was bulkily pregnant and after a gallant struggle she found she could not cope and asked if I would mind leaving. I left at once. She was a very nice girl but a shocking cook, not to be compared with her predecessor. The weather was gloriously autumnal. I had a fine, ex-RAF sleeping bag so I rearranged the interior of the Wolseley and took to sleeping in the car, parked up a pleasant lane, to cooking by the roadside and washing in various places while still working my daily shifts in the signal box. After a couple of weeks I found lodgings in north Oxford, in a garret – literally – at the top of a Victorian house owned by a tea-cosy-shaped Jewish refugee from Austria, Mrs Morgenstern. She had three other tenants: a German of extreme timidity who worked in the darkest, most esoteric bookshop in a city full of such things; a Bristolian called 'Cissul' (in the 'Bristle' vernacular); and a shy Irishman. So now I was 'doing' for myself again, cycling along Walton Street to work and cutting my own sandwiches. Susan – that was the name of the beautiful girl I'd picked up on the Botley road – came straight from school to visit me in the box when I was on late turn but I could never persuade her to so much as tap out a code on the block bell; she was happy to sit and do her homework or read until it was time to leave. If I finished at ten o'clock I took her home but if I finished at six o'clock we would go out into the town to see a film or go to the Playhouse and then back to my garret with a take-away. No matter how stealthily we crept into the house, these visits were always known to Mrs Morgenstern and she always rang down the curtain in the same way and at the same time. I can hear her now, her discreet, Viennese accent floating softly up the long flights of stairs: 'Yoo-hoo ... it's ten-thirty!'

CHAPTER EIGHT

Accidents Averted

Every signalman should shudder at the name of Quintinshill. This was the site of the worst accident in the long history of accidents on Britain's railways. It took place on 22 May 1915, and was the result of a signalman's forgetfulness. He had shunted a Down troop train to the Up line to allow a faster, following train to pass. While he was waiting for this to take place he was talking to various railwaymen who had accumulated in his box, including the fireman of the troop train. In spite of the presence of the latter and the fact of the troop train standing right outside the window on the Up line, the signalman lowered his signal for an Up express and in the subsequent head-on collision 216 people were killed. Chatter between railwaymen in a signal box was commonplace; accidents as a result of it were rare, yet friendly conversation provided a potential distraction and to that extent it was dangerous. When the distraction coincided with some other factor there was a disaster. Oh, the convoluted interactions of fate that must combine to cause a crash! When they do, the signalman's feelings are extremely unpleasant. I confess I know them well.

I was enjoying the usual, busy morning at Hinksey North. The day was fine and summery in 1970 and I was happy on the bells, levers, instruments and telephones. The Pilot was shunting to and fro over the river bridge, the signals were 'off' for the 9.15 a.m. Paddington to Oxford express and a 'light' diesel was on its way to me from Hinksey South via the Down goods loop. It arrived outside the box with Didcot men on board.

'"Light" back to Didcot, Bobby,' said the driver cheerfully.

'You can go out behind the Down London,' I replied. 'Out onto the bridge and cross over behind the 10.30 Oxford up.'

'There's time to make some tea, then,' said the driver and, turning to his secondman, added, 'Go up and sign the book, make some tea and I'll pick you up after he's crossed us over.'

I knew the secondman, Ron, very well from steam days. He signed on the train register and remained in the box as a reminder to me that his engine was standing (or would shortly be standing) on the Down Main line. Soon we were reminding each other about our 'steam days' exploits. The 9.15 Paddington passed down the Main, I gave 'Train out of Section' – 2-1 on the bell – to Johnny Blanchard at Hinksey South, who promptly 'asked the road' – 3-2-5 on the bell – for a 'Freightliner'. I gave the road. A minute later the 9.15 Paddington cleared Oxford Station South box so I 'asked on' for the 'Freightliner'. Arthur Lane gave me 'Line Clear' and 'asked the road' to me for the 10.30 a.m. Oxford, up the Main, 3-1 on the bell. I pulled off for this train but did not pull off for the 'Freightliner'. Instead, I reversed the points from Down loop to Down Main and told the driver to go ahead, stop on the bridge and wait there to cross over.* This movement did not foul the 'clearing point' of my Down home signal so it was correct.

I was expecting the 10.30 Oxford to leave on time. If it did so, there was time to cross the engine to the Up Main behind the 10.30 and give the Freightliner a clear run. The 10.30 Oxford did not leave the station on time; Ron and I carried on our conversation and in those two minutes or so the element of forgetfulness crept in. Suddenly the Down line instruments caught my eye, showing 'Line Clear'. I remembered the 'Freightliner', said, 'Damn, I've forgotten to pull off for the Lawley Street,' and promptly did so. I turned from the levers to walk back to my desk – and saw the engine standing peacefully on the bridge, the driver reading his newspaper and, dangling like a Sword of Damocles above his head, my Down Main starting signal at 'All Right'. Yelling something utterly unprintable to relieve the surge of panic I felt, I slammed the three levers back into the frame. The Down line signals had been lowered for about five seconds. The Freightliner was 2 or 3 miles away and so it was safe.

Ron's tea mug stopped halfway to his mouth as he watched the frantic flurry of pulling-off and throwing-back accompanied with much bad language. 'What's up?' he asked mildly. I had given myself a bad scare and I vented my feelings on him. 'What are you supposed to be here for?' I snapped in a very bad temper.

'Well, I dunno, mate, Rule 55 I suppose,' he stammered, embarrassed.

'And what have I just done?'

'Well, I dunno, mate – I'm not a signalman, am I?'

'I'm not too certain if I am either,' I said ruefully. 'I've just pulled off for the "Freightliner" with your mate sitting out there reading the sports pages.'

'Oo, I'm sugared,' said Ron nervously, 'you'd better put 'em back then, hadn't you?'

---

* See D on diagram on p. xx.

'I already have,' I replied, feeling very weary, 'but that just goes to show what talking can do.'

The 10.30 Oxford went by four minutes later; I crossed the engine to the Up Main and then lowered the signals for the Lawley Street. When the driver of the light engine stopped opposite the box to pick up Ron, I asked him if he had seen anything odd about the signals.

'Well, funny thing – I glanced up to see if you'd pulled the dummy* and I thought I saw the main-line boards off. I did a double-take but they were "on". Queer though.'

The Southampton–Lawley Street 'Freightliner' went by at that moment, belching black smoke as the 'Brush' diesel worked back into speed from a signal check and, when the long line of containers had drummed past, my mates were up at the starting signal, 'waiting the road' home.

Hinksey North, being close to the Thames, was very susceptible to fogs. One October morning the mist rose till it was 'thick as a bag' and visibility was down to 25 yards. At 10.15 the place was full of trains. The shunters were trying to marshal one for Morris Cowley, the engine for which was waiting on the Up goods loop. Another was standing alongside it on the Through Siding. The return trip from Abingdon was waiting at the signal on the Down reception line, where it had been for half an hour, awaiting the shunters' pleasure – out of sight and out of mind. The Abingdon crew never came to the box to remind me of their presence.

A 'light' engine was groping its way around the edge of Hinksey yard on the Down goods loop with the intention of hooking on to a train of coal for Bletchley. To reach the train, the engine would have to go out onto the Down Main line at the bridge and reverse up the Down line, on to the Down reception and thence to the yard. (See opp.) The next train on the Down Main would be the 9.15 a.m. Paddington but the fog had made it late and it was not signalled.

The engine on the Down loop, a 'Brush' diesel, emerged from the fog and stopped under the box window. I slid the window back to give the driver his instructions. Beyond in the murk I could hear the savage snatch of couplings and the grinding, howling sound peculiar to a diesel shunter's gears and engine. To the driver of the 'light' diesel I said, 'Your train's on Number One in the Down yard. I've set the road onto the Down Main, go by the loop starter at "Danger" and stop on the bridge. When you see the dummy there come off, you'll know you have the road all the way to the

---

* Ground signal.

yard. But listen – be sure you blow three honks each time you clear points so I'll know when to move them. I can't see a thing from here.'

Apart from the dense fog, all this was routine at Hinksey North; the driver nodded and set off. Three honks came, muffled, through the fog so I set the road for the Down yard and, as I did so, Johnny Blanchard at Hinksey South 'asked the road' for the 9.15 Paddington. I 'refused' the train because the movement I was about to make would reverse within the clearing point of the Down home signal. The 'Brush' diesel slid very slowly past the box, looking almost black in the fog. There was a definite tension involved in the operation; the driver and I exchanged stiff little nods and waves as I stood anxiously at the window and he inched his engine cautiously along the track. The dense fog was a kind of daylight nightmare. I remained at the window and tried to visualise the engine's progress along the rails, attempting to keep some idea of the position of the diesel so as to work the box as effectively as possible.

After a full two minutes I heard three long blasts on a diesel's horn. This was about the right time-interval to allow the engine to clear off the Main line so I threw the dummy and points back to normal, gave 'Line Clear' for the 9.15 Paddington and pulled off. As I pulled my distant signal a ghastly thought went through my head like an electric shock: Which engine had blown? Was it the engine I was shunting or the one waiting on the Up goods loop, impatient to be let into the yard? Then I remembered the Abingdon standing at the Down reception line signal. There was no track-circuit reminder, nor even a signalling instrument – the line was signalled over the telephone and an entry made in the train register. It must have been the driver of the Abingdon blowing a warning to the driver of the approaching 'Brush'. All this realisation went through my head, literally, at the speed of light. I flung the signals back to 'Danger', rushed to the bell and sent 'Obstruction Danger' to Johnny Blanchard. There was silence and I knew, from the time since he first 'asked the road' for the express, that it must be close to him and therefore the silence meant that he was busy, throwing his signals back to 'Danger' to stop the train. I waited on tenterhooks for several – long – seconds. If he replied to my 6 bells with 3-5 bells it meant he had succeeded in stopping it but if he had been unable to stop it I would receive 4-5-5, 'Train running away on the right line'. I got 4-5-5 and felt sick and faint.

I stood rooted to the floor, weighing the chances of a crash, the site of which was too far away for me to be able to intervene in the time available. The driver of the 9.15 would have seen my outer distant, just south of

Hinksey South, at 'All Right' but he would certainly have had my inner distant, north of Hinksey South, at 'Caution' – but was this sufficient braking distance for him to be able to stop at my home signal? About 150 yards ahead of my home signal was a stationary engine, maybe a derailed engine, because I must have moved those points when it was very close to them. These thoughts went through my head as I stood at the open window.

I stared into the fog, my face as cold and as pale as the mist. I could hear the steady knocking of a diesel engine but otherwise nothing. Then there were footsteps and the driver of the 'light' engine came running out of the fog and up the box stairs, two at a time. He was angry. 'Hey! What's going on? You all but had us off the road – and there's a train on the Down reception. Didn't you know that? It blew-up at me, otherwise I wouldn't have been able to stop in time.' In the fog his nerves had been stretched; this had set them vibrating like the E string of a violin.

I sat down on the edge of the table, feeling like a deflated balloon; he must have seen this or read it in my face because his attitude softened. 'Are you all right? Did you know about that one on the Down reception?'

'I ought to have known about it,' I replied miserably. 'I booked it into the register but it's been there for so long that I forgot about it. I heard it blowing at you and took that as your "inside clear" signal.'

'Well, at least you're honest about it, but what now?' Through the fog came the prolonged braying of a diesel's horn.

'That's what,' I said. 'That's the 9.15 Padd – when I thought you were clear of the Down Main I gave the road for it. I hope they can stop.'

'You'll bloody soon know,' said the driver with some feeling. There was another long bray and then silence. 'They've stopped,' said the driver, his voice rising on each word.

Once the tension was broken I found I was shaking and not much use for anything. The driver, less shocked, took charge. 'Right', he said crisply, 'here's what we do.' He leant forwards towards me and gripped my arm as he spoke. 'This fog's so thick that the men on the fast don't know what's happened. I'll bring my engine back onto the Down loop before they get off their engine and come up here. When I'm on the loop you can pull off and we'll be squared-up.'

He hurried away, leaving me feeling utterly disappointed with myself and sad at the thought that this was probably the end of my signalling career. But when the engine was safely back on my Down loop my spirits rose. I pulled off for the 9.15 Paddington and three minutes later a big 'Western' class diesel was grinding to a halt outside, its driver sliding back his cab window. I walked to the window, knowing that my future depended on how I handled the driver, on his mood.

'What's on today then, officer?' was his grim opening. 'I got your outer "off" and your inner went back in my face with Hinksey South's starter. One second of delay and I'd have passed it at "All Right".' He had had a very nasty shock in virtually zero visibility at 60 mph – but slowing for the station, and he looked accusingly at me, awaiting my answer.

'Well, it's a bit of a long story, driver. I really am very sorry you were given such a bad fright in this filthy fog but everything is fine, nothing to worry about.' My heart was pounding, I was dying for him to go away and I pointed diplomatically at my lowered starting signal. 'You've got the road, everything's fine.' We looked directly into each other's eyes at a range of forty feet. I met and held his gaze for a long moment, then, very deliberately, he said, 'We depend on you buggers.' I spread my hands out: 'I'm sorry.' He slid his window shut, revved the huge engine and drew the train away.

I felt fairly sure he would not report the incident; there was nothing really for him to report, looking at it from his point of view – a signalman's job is to stop trains – but he still had an inkling that something had gone wrong. My spirits rose again and I got on with the job but after a while I felt depressed once more and telephoned the District Inspector to ask him to come to the box.

'I'm rather busy,' he said, 'can't you come to see me when you finish?'

'No, I think I'd like you here now.'

'Oh dear,' he said, 'I don't think I like the sound of that. I'll be along to you in a few minutes.' Ten minutes later he came hurrying up the track and into the signal box. I told him what had happened, showed him all my entries in the register and waited to hear my sentence. 'Well, all right, you made a genuine mistake. I think you were pretty good to get out of it so quickly. You took the right action as soon as you realised what you'd done.' I could have wrung his hand from his wrist at that moment but he was already leaving. 'Must press on – got a lot to do,' he said, and clattered down the stairs.

In mid-1970 work began on the rebuilding of Oxford station. The platforms were dismantled – half their length at a time – and the fine old wooden office buildings, dating back to Brunel and 1852, were pulled down. Naturally I felt that restoration, not vandalism, was needed. While the platforms were reduced in length, posters displayed at Paddington, Reading and Didcot warned passengers to get out of a train from the front or rear five coaches depending on which bit of platform was missing. Loudspeaker announcements were made; guards and ticket collectors also spread the warning. Thousands were saved from hurling themselves to perdition – all but one. At 7 p.m. one dark night, a Down express arrived from London and the driver skilfully brought his train to a stand with the rear coaches alongside the northern half of the Down platform. This placed the leading coach on the canal bridge. In the leading compartment of this coach were some Oxford locomotivemen going home and a Canadian on business. When the train stopped the locomotivemen trooped out into the corridor, the first man opened the door, stepped out onto the flat-topped girder of the bridge and, turning sharp right, walked along it to the footpath at the far end. The other railwaymen followed, all knowing exactly what they were doing in the deep darkness, all with equally steely nerves above the black water. Bringing up the rear came the Canadian. He went through the door, stepped onto the bridge – and into space.

He did not have a terribly long way to fall, 15 ft or so, but he probably thought he was falling forever and went down yelling. The departing locomotivemen heard his cries and the enormous splash, realised what had happened and rushed to his aid. I believe one man went so far as actually to get into the water. The innocent Canadian was not in the least bit impressed by such a sacrifice and once on dry land was soon glowing in the heat of his own indignation. The story went through the signal boxes almost as fast as he had fallen into the water. If he had heard the gales of laughter it provoked, I think he would have died of apoplexy.

When the station was complete, early in 1972, it consisted of what looked to me like a collection of upmarket portacabins inadequately sheltered by a steel and aluminium awning filched from a petrol filling station. The impression I received was that my employers were neither looking for nor hoping for an increase in traffic; on the contrary, they were saying 'We surrender' in brick and plywood while cowering under a petrol filling station canopy. Together with this blow, the new Panel signal box at Oxford was due to come into service in October 1973 – the shape of things to come was before me and March 1972 seemed like a good time for making far-reaching decisions.

Susan and I decided to get married in June and I decided to leave the railway as soon as possible. Susan was a cog in Robert Maxwell's Pergamon Press, working in a room thick with tobacco smoke as a sub-editor on four scientific journals, one of which was in Russian Cyrillic script. I had had two small picture books published by the fledgling Oxford Publishing

Company so printing/publishing seemed to be the way forward. In June I put my signalman's duster down on the levers and took a job with the aptly named family printing firm of Parchment. Shortly after this, Susan and I were married. I have since bitterly regretted that my occupation is given on the marriage certificate as 'storeman' rather than 'signalman'.

We went to live in my bachelor garret. The roof sloped so steeply down on one side that we had to stand, back against the other wall, in order to be able to stand up right to pull on our clothes. All our worldly goods – old signalling instruments for the most part – were shoved under the bed. Marriage was a great success, and, indeed, continues to be so forty years later but the decision taken during the Ides of March regarding another job was an unmitigated disaster. By 10.30 each morning I was yawning enough to dislocate my jaw and by eleven o'clock I was really hard pressed to stay awake. It was only embarrassment that prevented me from going at once to lurk nonchalantly outside the District Inspector's door. Don Parchment, ex-Paratroop Sergeant-Major, ex-Chindit, was remarkably patient and never failed to pay me my wages though I never earned a penny for him and sometimes caused him great loss. A touch of the button on the hydraulic guillotine and 500 sheets of glossy art paper, 2 feet by 3 feet, were cut the wrong way round. Even after such waste as this he never became angry, well, not for an ex-Sergeant-Major, but after eight weeks the weight on my conscience and the sheer, pressing need to get back into a signal box overcame my embarrassment at returning to the fold so quickly. The District Inspector was very kind and sent me to Hinksey South immediately. I had hoped for Hinksey North but had forgotten that the box was at the top of the wages scale and was therefore not available to a recruit 'straight off the street'.

My goodness, I was glad to be back among signal bells and signal levers! Hinksey South was built at the same time as the North box and was identical to look at. It stood on the Up side of the line about 100 yards north of the old Abingdon Road bridge. It had a frame of fifty-eight levers, numbered 1 to 72, to work goods loops, main lines and Hinksey Up Yard. The latter had been shut in 1970, although some small amount of work was still done on its sidings, and a month after I arrived the points from Up loop to Up Main were damaged and not repaired. Luckily for the look of the thing, the signal on the gantry applying to that route was not removed. The train service was busy; any morning between 7 and 8.30 a train would pass the box every 4 ½ minutes and there would be ninety-three trains in the course of a 6 a.m. to 2 p.m. shift. Although this was as many trains as had run thirty years before, the work was less exacting because the yard was shut; all I had to do was to pass the trains along the track from Kennington to Hinksey North with some small amount of goods train regulating.

Of especial importance were Up goods trains, which were booked for relief on the Up avoiding line at Didcot: was the fresh set of men available; could the train stop to change crews without delaying a following passenger train? The difficulty was created by the skeletal nature of the layout at Didcot since automation. Sometimes Reading Panel, sometimes 'Control', let the Hinksey man know what was required; if not I would make my own inquiries and, if necessary, divert the goods to the loop as the last 'lay-by' off the Up Main before Didcot Avoiding Line.

On 15 August 1973 the 4062 20.00 Lawley Street to Millbrook freightliner terminal went up a few minutes early. I therefore had made no inquiries about its relief at Didcot. It came to a stand at a green signal at the south end of the avoiding line and the driver went to the signal post telephone. '8 o'clock Lawley Street here. Got our relief about?'

The Reading Panelman had thought that 4069 on his describer was a mistake. 'You don't run today,' he told the driver. 'My notice here has you down, "Will not run" today but "Will run" tomorrow, so there's no relief for you.'

'Well,' said the driver, 'my notice has us down as "Will run" today and "Will not run" tomorrow and I want my relief today.'

The train was inter-Regional, LMR to SR via WR, and a confusion had arisen in spite of all the 'high-tech' communications. This blocked the Up avoiding line for an hour or so while a spare set of men were found and sent to Didcot. Next day the booked Southern men turned up at Didcot, but of course the LMR did not run the train.

On 5 September 1973 a colour-light signal was erected outside the signal box, a few feet from the window. Several weeks previously the engineers had drilled a hole in the ground with an auger and dropped into it an empty 40-gallon oil drum which they then filled with cement from a rail-borne mixer. Four long bolts, from the bottom of the drum to about 9 inches above it, were held in a square formation by a timber framing, which also acted as a 'former' for the above-ground portion of the cement.

On the 5th, five men arrived in a three-ton lorry. They had with them various fittings to make a signal, a hired ladder, some planks and a length of rope. They broke the timber away from the concrete and bolt threads and laid the planks upon the concrete, between and on all sides of the protruding bolts so that only an inch of thread showed. The tubular steel signal post – which had a square base-plate drilled to accept the four bolts – was struggled with until the base-plate was resting on the timber shuttering. The post was raised by the men to an angle of about 30 degrees and supported in that position by the wooden 'out of use' box cover, which would enshroud the colour-light signal head until it was required for use. The top platform and guard rails were bolted on and preparations were made for the final lift. Their length of rope was wrapped around the base of the post and tied to two pieces of point rodding set in the concrete. This was to prevent the base-plate moving out of position during the struggles of raising the signal. The hired ladder was then placed under the top platform and with a concerted heave the five men shoved the new signal up to about 70 degrees. At this the bottom rope prevented further movement, so they slackened it and the post was given a final push to the perpendicular. They then rocked the assembly onto each edge of the base-plate in turn to free the shuttering beneath and thus to lower it over the bolts without 'burring-over' the securing bolts' threads.

The foreman of the gang got busy, kneeling on the ballast, with a folding rule and a battered template to mark out a piece of steel while a member of his gang enlarged a hole in another bit of steel with the end of his file and yet others busied themselves with bits of signal. Looking down from the signal box window, it looked as if Heath Robinson was erecting a gallows for me and my world. Just as the signal head was placed on the top platform, a car arrived and from it stepped a man in a lounge suit. He ordered them and all portable bits of the signal down to Oxford North Junction.

'Damn,' said the foreman, 'just as we was getting interested.'

So they departed, carrying the signal head, leaving the signal looking like nothing so much as a 14-foot bird table.

Not wishing to hang around this gibbet, I left soon after this, to take up a vacancy in 'Smiling Somerset'.

CHAPTER NINE

Somerset Signalman

Somerset was a different world. Susan took a job managing several rented properties owned by a Bath businessman. He lived in a late eighteenth-century Gothick folly called Midford Castle, overlooking the precipitous Midford valley south of the city, and we had a 'tied' cottage in what had been partly a stable and partly a Gothick chapel. The chapel had a tower with a stone staircase leading to a corridor giving access to all upstairs rooms. The staircase and corridor were quite definitely haunted. It was a very beautiful place, built of Bath stone, surrounded by great trees, looking down into the deep, narrow valley through the parkland. The track bed of the Somerset & Dorset Railway skirted the park fence and it was easy to drive a car on to the grass-grown ballast. From that point the car could be driven to and through the mile-long Midford tunnel, which Susan and I did when we had friends to stay – an after-Sunday-lunch-adventure for us all. The tunnel was curved, so after going in a short way, daylight was cut off and the total lack of light produced a feeling that was weirder than the ghost back at the old chapel. In 1929 the crew of a goods train had been overcome by the locomotive's exhaust in the tunnel and the train had run away down the hill to crash on the curve at the bottom, near Bath station. From the castle grounds, Ivo Peters, the great railway photographer, had recorded the wonderful pageant of the 'Slow & Dirty' (or 'Swift & Delightful') 0-4-4 tanks, the graceful 4-4-0 express engines from the Midland Railway, the LMS 'Black Fives' and the massive Bulleid 'Pacifics'. One way and another, the entire area was vibrant with ghosts.

I drove 12 miles through hilly, Mendip country, down winding village streets lined with medieval stone houses and ancient pubs, places with rich-sounding names such as Hinton Charterhouse and Norton St Philip, to reach Clink Road Junction on the northern edge of Frome. The signal box was a small, wooden building in a cutting close to the Clink road bridge. It stood on the Up side of the line exactly at the 114½ mile post, on the inside of a sharp curve where the meandering Wilts, Somerset & Weymouth Railway made a sudden detour southwestwards to pass through Frome. It was as if the navvies of 1850 were happily digging a straight cut south when they remembered that they had to go through the town, so they swung the line sharply to the right for a mile before resuming their former, southerly heading.

In 1933 the GWR opened a bypass to connect each end of the detour, like putting a string across a bow. Clink Road Junction was at the northern end and 2 miles further on was Blatchbridge Junction. This new cut formed the final link in the Great Western's holiday route to the west and along it had stormed the 'Kings' and the 'Castles' on countless heavily laden expresses. Curiously, the sharply curved line into and out of Frome remained the main line while the bypass was the avoiding line or – to the men – the 'back road'. The next signal box north of Clink Road was Fairwood Junction, 3 miles away on the edge of the Westbury complex of junctions. Clink Road worked with Frome North Junction signal box, which was half a mile away on the Main line towards Frome.

When I arrived there in September 1973 the signalmen had, in most cases, worked on that part of the railway since before or during the Second World War. Others had started an equally long time ago but had been working on the Somerset & Dorset Railway until it was shut and had then transferred to the Western Region of British Railways. All of them were country railwaymen: warm-hearted, hospitable and experienced in various aspects of railway work. The first man I met from this admirable crew was something over 6 feet tall. He was on duty in Clink Road box the day I first went there. He unfolded himself from the decrepit armchair with such enthusiasm that his head knocked the Tilley lamp hanging from the rafter. It swung sideways with a great clatter as he boomed 'How do!' and crushed my hand in his bony fist. He whipped out a packet of cigarettes while the lamp was still swinging. 'Have a smoke!' Everything was an exclamation. I did not smoke and refused, rather diffidently, as he towered above me, a gaunt frame of a man, smiling, fag packet extended. He thought I was modestly refusing to take away his stores. 'Goo-on, have one – "Tiny's" offering!' This was 'Tiny' Fred Wilkins and I knew at once that I was going to enjoy working Clink Road Junction.

'Tiny' had spent his working life on the railway at Frome since 1942 and had worked as a porter, carriage shunter and signalman. From him I first heard of 'mad bloody cockneys': the speed-fiend drivers and fireman of Old Oak Common. When 'Tiny' was at Blatchbridge Junction 'back in steam days', he occasionally had to stop a 'hard hitter' owing to the section ahead being occupied and when he could finally 'pull off' for the express he would go and lean on the window bar to enjoy the sound of a 'King' or a 'Castle' being thrashed away up the bank to Brewham by a 'cockney', indignant at having his head-long progress interrupted by a swedey,

Somerset signalman. 'Mad bloody cockneys', 'Ocean Mail Specials' and the 'Cornish Riviera Express' were very much part of the legend of this line.

The other man with whom I learned was Ken Russell, a spry, slightly built man with a dry sense of humour not to everyone's taste, although I enjoyed his company enormously. The smartly kept little signal box had eighteen levers and controlled a simple, double-track junction but it was an interesting job with forty-five to fifty trains on the two day-shifts and slightly less on nights. The first thing to learn was the routine of bell-codes, including the special 'route' codes, which were quite complicated; learn how to work the frame to set up the routes in seconds flat because it was a fast-moving train service; learn the train service and how long it took for trains of varying classes to run from 'a' to 'b' and also what they did when they got to 'a' or 'b' as this had an effect on their running times.

To set the route into Frome took eleven lever movements because we had 'movable elbows', otherwise known as a 'switch diamond', in the Up Main to allow 50 mph running across the sharply curved junction. This was an addition to my experience, my latest signalling pet. First the 'elbows' had to be unbolted – shove levers 15 and 16 back into the row of levers, then pull over 19, 17, 18, 15 and 16 followed by signal levers 7, 6, 3 and 1. Speed in setting the route and in dismantling it afterwards was vital if delay was to be avoided to trains coming up from Blatchbridge. The object was to run everything and stop nothing and many a Down train was 'nipped into Frome a bit tight in front of the Up fast'. Readers might find this alarming but it must be read in the context of railway jargon. If the Clink Road signalman decided he could get a Down train into Frome 'across the bows' of an Up train yet without delaying that Up train, he 'refused the road' for the Up train to Blatchbridge Junction so the signals at Blatchbridge remained at 'Danger' – 2 miles away. There was great satisfaction in making nice judgements, slamming the road back after the Down train had passed over the junction and instantly 'giving the road' to the Blatchbridge signalman. He would then whip his signal levers over and the Clink Road man would go on to the phone: 'Did that Up train get your distant all right?'

'Dropped it down his chimney', would come the laconic reply, using the time-honoured and by then thoroughly obsolete phrase.

Learning the box with Ken Russell, I spent hours – days and nights – talking about railway work and railway people; Ken would be in the chair, with myself leaning against the train register desk or working the box. Ken reckoned, as Elwyn Richards had done, that the best signalmen were those who could work safely without benefit of safety devices. 'The best chap as ever we had here', he said, 'came from Ilfracombe, somewhere small down that way. He took on at

Frome North but all our track circuiting and interlocking stumped 'ee in th' end and when he saw a vacancy down Crediton way he took it and went home.'

Believing that the Board of Trade/Ministry of Transport insisted on complete interlocking of points and signals, I disagreed. Ken was scornful. 'Even on the GW at Radstock you could have the gates open for road traffic and the boards off for a train. On the S&D at Chilcompton you could have the Main line boards off with the cross-over reversed.'

'No, that can't have been,' I said, trying to remain respectful of an old-hand. 'It wouldn't have been allowed by the Board of Trade.'

'Never mind thic "Board of Trade", I know what I'm saying.' Ken was very sharp and used the Somerset 'thic' for 'this'. He went on: 'When the Western took over the S&D north of Templecombe, the signal works came under the Frome Signal & Telegraph Inspector and he told me he had sleepless nights till he'd put in track circuits in all the boxes to make up for the locking they didn't have. Them ol' bwoys on the "Darset" – they didn't hold wi' all thic Western equipment, 'twas all foreign to they. It was all made of plastic so's they couldn't polish it and it locked up their workings. There was talk of going on strike.'

'What? Over putting in proper locking!'

'Oh yes. Them down at Evercreech had been able to make movements that they couldn't do once the Western put in track circuits. Delays were caused and they maintained it was all a plot to run down the line – cause delays and upset the travelling public.'

Western Region men in the area of the Somerset & Dorset felt strong ties of affection for the line and its legend was well known on ex-GWR territory. There were eleven big 2-8-0 goods engines on the line, designed specially to cope with the terrific gradients and, naturally, they were all highly regarded by the staff as very effective, very special machines. Occasionally one would have to be driven 'light' to Evercreech Junction, there to be turned on the turntable. The telephone message from the originating station to Evercreech signal box was: 'That's the big girl coming to swing her arse.' The most famous of all S&D signalmen were Percy Savage and Harry Wiltshire, who worked a lifetime in Midford signal box. During the exceptionally severe winter of 1947 the line was closed by deep snow throughout its length but Harry and Percy went to work each day to clear their points, work the levers as a test according to the regulations and to polish all the equipment. They were being paid during the suspension of services and wanted to do something for their pay. The S&D was closed permanently after the last train on Sunday 6 March 1966, and on Saturday 5th, Harry and Percy did their turn with the Brasso and the Ronuk floor polish so that the box was as sparkling clean after the last train as it had ever been during the height of the service. Ken said, 'Them old bwoys 'ud stand on the platform wi' their hats in their hands bowing, as the "Pines" went through. That was their crack train, that train, that line meant everything to they.' I knew the feeling well.

Railways were always a family affair and never more so than on branch lines such as the one from Frome to Bristol through Mells, Radstock and Clutton. It passed through beautiful country, manned by the same men year after year, carrying the same people and the same traffic, apparently for ever. The men had the job at their fingertips; it became 'like clockwork', so familiar that not only did they modify the timetables to suit themselves, but were even able to 'nobble' a magistrate when that personage was a well-known traveller on the line.

One legend was that Evelyn Waugh's aunt was Chairwoman of Radstock Bench of Magistrates and was well known for her kind heart. A man waiting to appear before her in court could go round to her house an evening or two before the hearing and have an informal session with her in her kitchen when he could better explain his case. Before the Second World War there was a porter at Radstock who had been summoned to appear before the Radstock Bench on a charge of 'Riding without lights'. This was worth 7s 6d in fines, money that could be better spent in the White Hart across the road from the station. The porter therefore concocted a good tale, intending to take it round to the Chairwoman's kitchen, but before he did, she arrived at the station to catch a train or fetch a parcel. They knew each other well enough by sight so it was easy enough for the porter to get into wily conversation with her – and let her know he was getting married soon, and how he was saving hard to give his wife a good life, and how he had to make do with worn out equipment. 'Just look at thic old lamp on my bike, f'instance, ma'am,' he said, craftily. 'Why, it's so dim it gives only enough light to show others I be comin', it don't give I no light and it be so dim that I can't even tell if it's alight when I'm riding.' The Chairwoman knew nothing about the impending court appearance of the porter but when he did appear before her she was so sympathetic that she not only discharged him but ordered that he be given a florin from the Poor Box.

The 5.30 a.m. Bristol to Mells goods train was worked by three guards, week and week about. Being regulars on the job, they rented from the GWR the shooting and trapping rights on railway land at Mells. The game they caught they sold to a Bristol butcher and from their enterprise they made a goodly sum – with a little bit of help from their friends. The timetable required that the Radstock signal boxes open at 7 a.m. so that the 5.30 Bristol goods could be placed in a siding to allow the following passenger train and another from

Frome to cross each other at Radstock, the line being a single track with crossing loops at stations. But, for a consideration, the signalmen at Radstock would open early and the engine driver would go a bit faster so that the guard could reach Mells without stopping at Radstock. This gave him time to take rabbits from snares and set fresh traps before starting the work – shunting the yard and going to the quarry to fetch loaded stone wagons. The official programme then required the train to return to Radstock and shunt there until about 10.45 a.m., when a Radstock guard, fresh on, took over, allowing the Bristol guard to work back to Bristol in charge of a passenger train.

What actually happened was slightly different. Mells Road is at the summit of a steep incline, 1 in 48 rising from Frome and 1 in 68 falling to Radstock 3 miles away. The guard took his train to the Stop Board at the summit, pinned down sufficient wagon brakes to enable the engine to control the train on the down grade – and waved it good-bye. He then went back to shooting rabbits. When the train arrived at Radstock the fresh guard was waiting and the shunting began and continued until it was time to go, engine and van, back to Mells to pick up the Bristol guard and his haul of rabbits and pheasants. Back once more at Radstock, the dead-stock was loaded into the Frome–Bristol passenger train and off it went with the enterprising guard, all stations to Bristol.

Ken Russell had begun his career in the area around 1936 and had an apparently inexhaustible supply of stories, many of them giving a new slant to the famous phrase 'permissive society'. 'What about the Managers?' I asked, wondering whether to believe the tale. 'Didn't they ever come round to check on you all and what would they have done if they'd caught you?'

'Them days,' said Ken, 'the bosses didn't go around looking for trouble – not like some o' them we've got at Bristol now,' he added, in a tone of disgust.

'Are they a miserable crowd then?' I asked, somewhat alarmed, knowing that I would shortly have to go on the rules exam at Bristol.

'Some of them are useless. Wait till you meet the bloke we call "Tatty". Knows nothing and goes around making everyone's life a misery. He couldn't hold a candle to men like the old Superintendent, Reggie Pole, or his assistant, Soole. I think you'll find ol' Soole was a real enthusiast for steam engines even though he was assistant Superintendent. I don't think "Tatty" is interested in anything but finding fault with men.'

'But what would happen if you had been caught out one day?' I persisted.

'Well, they'd have more manliness than this lot, a better understanding. You'd get your written reprimand or whatever but at least you'd feel it was justified, that you'd been fairly dealt with. They were gentlemen. One day Soole comes to Radstock and finds one o' the porters cutting the stationmaster's hair and a couple of townspeople waiting their turn. Soole was half-way through the door, sees the station boss under the white sheet and says, "Oh, I shouldn't be here." Five minutes later he comes back, everyone is off on the job in hand and the station boss is working in his office hiding a half-cut head of hair under his cap.' Ken and I laughed. 'The difference is', Ken continued, 'that nowadays, if "Tatty" was to come across that situation you'd have to go to Bristol – the full rigmarole with "Tatty" pleased as punch at having shown what an eager-beaver he is. Another time Soole was down at Radstock for an LDC meeting*. After they'd dealt with everything Soole takes them all over to the White Hart for a drink. I can't see "Tatty" offering to do that and even if he did no one would want to drink with him. Anyhow, Soole buys a round and then gets on about how they could speed up the working of freight across the branch. "You'd have a job speeding up the 3.35 Marsh Junction," one of the ol' bwoys says, "they go through our place like lightning." Soole buys this chap another pint, gives him a nice smile and says, "How many times d'you reckon the Marsh Junction has been speeding past your box?"' Ken chuckled. 'The crafty devil. There's ways and ways of managing men and Soole did most of his over a pint.'

So we ranged far and wide, setting the world to rights politically as we got to know each other better but always turning to railways and some outrageous tales – like the time that the Clutton and Hallatrow signalmen challenged the men in Radstock North and South boxes to a darts match at the White Hart. They were all on duty at the time but at a late evening slack period, the Clutton man took the Permanent-Way Department trolley 1 ½ miles to Hallatrow, collected his mate and together they pushed and rolled the trolley 2 miles to Radstock. They had their game and a pint and set off home but became derailed; the trolley and one man went down the embankment and a badly sprained ankle was the result. They had to leave the trolley and hobble back to base. The last train of the night ran late that evening because the signalman was not on duty to get the token out for it. Ken, from his armchair, could interrupt some tale such as that to check me as I was about to 'give the road' for a stone train from Frome, with a 'Don't give that the road, haven't you got a fast to come up the back road?' and then sweep on with his story. One morning during my second week there, he was telling me about the time Oswald Moseley came to Radstock before the Second World War. He was holding an open-air meeting before the townspeople and many coalminers were there. Moseley went off into his brazen-voiced rant and after a while asked, rhetorically, for support

---

* The local Trade Union/Management discussion.

for his policies. A coalminer gave him a distinctly unrhetorical reply; jumping onto the platform, he shouted, 'No, we won't – but I'll give you this.' He hit him so hard that, big man though Moseley was, he fell off the stage.

At that point in the story, two figures in railway inspectors' blue suits slipped quickly past the rear of the box; I glimpsed them briefly through the small back window as they hurried down the steep path into the cutting. 'We've got company, Ken,' I said.

'Look out then, 'cos that'll be "Tatty" and his mate.'

The door crashed open and the two men came hurrying up the stairs. It was more like a police raid that a 'box visit' by the local, friendly District Inspector. I noticed that both men's hats seemed to be several sizes too big. Curt nods and brief greetings were the order of the day with many a searching glance into corners and into our lockers until Ken closed them. One ran his finger down the columns of the train register, hoping to find uncompleted entries. They watched me work the box for a while, made an appointment for me to see them for a rules exam the following week and then left, their busy feet clattering down the iron-shod stairs.

'They were a happy pair,' I observed. 'Are they all like that at Bristol these days? It never used to be like that.'

'No, luckily it isn't,' replied Ken. 'It's just that we see more of them than the others.'

'Hmm,' I mused, 'I don't fancy going up on the rules in front of a mean-looking pair like them.'

'I shouldn't worry about it,' replied Ken cheerfully, 'they don't know any more about the rules than you do – less probably. I'd like to have seen them up against ol' Jefferies at Radstock, he'd have sorted them out.' Ken was off again into recollections of a happier railway. Mr Jefferies had been a signalman at Radstock in the 1930s and '40s, Branch Secretary of the NUR, on the committee of the local Co-operative Society, a good organiser and a staunch communist. He protected all his members from over-weening authority. 'No one bullied us, but him,' laughed Ken. 'He had the first chance at any overtime that was going and generally ruled the roost like a feudal baron – a real, old-fashioned communist. He never stood for the National Anthem nor for anything else that people would stand for and he never took his cap off to anyone. One day he said to ol' Soole, "You and me, we're the same – you just get paid more than I do."'

But he wasn't like Mr Soole. On a later occasion Ken remarked that Signalman Jefferies 'was a great gambler – he'd take bets on two raindrops running down a window pane.' This made the proverbial penny drop in my head. There had been a Signalman Jefferies at Ashbury Crossing in 1936 and it had been his gambling that the goods train that had passed him was complete – when he had not seen the triple rear lamps in the middle of the night – which had caused the death of the driver of the Up express following because the rear of the goods was stationary back in the section and the express engine crashed into it at full speed. I told Ken my suspicion and he replied. 'Well – now you mention that – I remember that he used to boast about having caused a crash somewhere up country.' So the GWR did not sack him but transferred him to a busy, single line station.

The following week, as arranged, I went for my rules examination. I knocked on the office door and a deep, sonorous voice said, 'Come.' I went in and was surprised to find only 'Tatty' and his mate. One of them must have been practising The Voice. They were sitting, facing each other across a long table in a room of milk-coloured plywood with wire-reinforced glass in the windows. There was nothing to show it was a railway office except, perhaps, for their large, uniform hats hanging on the utility hat-stand and there was no decoration unless the posters counted as adornment and it is conceivable that a certain sort of person might have enjoyed them – they showed in colourful detail several types of heavy boot, including some with steel toe-caps. I had plenty of time to take all this in because after uttering 'Come' not a word was spoken; both men appeared to be engrossed in important State papers. I was just becoming irritated and wondering if I ought to speak when 'Tatty' looked up, took off his glasses and stared at me. The lenses of his spectacles had the happy property of making his close-set eyes seem further apart than they actually were and as the spectacles were removed the eyes seemed to sidle in close together, the better to confer on what they saw. Right on cue, his henchman spoke.

'Who are you?' He had well-greased, obedient, *disciplined* hair, which seemed to be straining at the roots to sweep ever more obediently away from his forehead. 'Tatty' continued to stare, holding his glasses by one earpiece in what he obviously thought was an extra-intelligent, especially quizzing look. These were the men who had visited me at Clink Road only the previous week. I had to reintroduce myself and state my business whereupon 'Tatty' relaxed his quizzical stare, slapped his spectacles back on his nose – whereupon his eyes appeared to leap to attention – and cried, 'Oh! I thought you were a guard!' He roared with laughter while his henchman gazed at him admiringly. My attention wandered over to their hats while they got the last giggle out of their joke. Each hat had a huge badge made of felt and gold wire and I wondered if the intense pressures of their highly responsible office had compressed their brains to the size and consistency of a felt and wire badge. I was still dreaming when 'Tatty' said, 'No, no, old son – just our bit of fun – you go along with Eric here and ...' He got no further, for the door was flung open and another Inspector burst in.

Without waiting a moment he butted in, addressing himself to 'Tatty': 'Hello, Pat – what d'you think? I've been given a waistcoat that's too small for me.' In the face of this startling news the rules and regulations examination was forgotten.

'Oh no, that's not good enough, Ian,' crooned 'Tatty', 'let me phone the Stores and sort it out for you.'

'Please don't trouble yourself, Pat, I'm sure you're busy with this bloke here,' he nodded in my direction and, with a quick wave, said to the other Inspector, 'Hello, Eric.'

'No trouble at all, Ian,' said 'Tatty', 'I'll phone them right away.' He picked up the telephone with a special flourish, which showed off his white cuffs and imitation-gold watch strap. I sighed and stared at the images of steel toe-capped boots.

'Please don't trouble yourself, Pat,' said Ian. 'You're too kind.'

'All right then, I won't,' said 'Tatty', replacing the phone, glad to have shown off his cuffs and then, remembering the job in hand, he said, 'Oh – *sorry*, laddie [first it had been 'old son', now it was 'laddie'; I was thirty-two], go away with Eric. Eric, make sure you put him through his paces.'

With that we were dismissed and 'Tatty' turned back to Ian to pick up their conversation.

A rules examination with Eric could not take long and within the hour we were back in 'Tatty's' office. Eric told him I would 'do' so 'Tatty' signed my Certificate of Competence. Having completed that formality, he came round the table and put his face very close to mine. I thought he was going to kiss me for one terrifying moment, then he said, very quietly, 'Now you're in charge of a signal box here – watch your step. I've heard things about you I don't believe but, all the same, I shall be watching you.' Speechless with embarrassment and confusion, I felt my face going bright red. After a few seconds he spoke again. 'If an Inspector had said to me what I have just said to you I would be telling him who he ought to be watching rather than watching me.' His words burned their way like acid into my memory. I stared at the steel toe-capped boots and wondered if I was not dreaming and 'Tatty', getting no reply, told me I could go.

I was now a signalman at Clink Road Junction, my seventh signal box in thirteen years on the railway.

CHAPTER TEN

Broken Rail

There was one small but vital fact concerning Clink Road Junction that I had not learned by the time I took over my shift. I learned the hard way. Clink Road and Blatchbridge boxes were switched out of circuit on Saturday evenings after the last train from Frome had passed. The Saturday late-turn man locked the box with his own key and brought it back with him at 6 a.m. on Monday when he came to reopen the box.

One cold, grey morning, just as dawn was breaking, I walked down the cutting-side path to open the box and it was only as I put my hand in my pocket, standing in front of the door, that I realised that the big old key was lying on the kitchen table at home. That sudden, sick feeling shot through my stomach. If I drove home to fetch the key the box would be an hour late opening with that much delay to the passenger trains. Down in the cutting the silence was mocking; the dull, steel rails curved away unhelpfully in three directions and the stone arch of the bridge was like a huge, laughing mouth as I looked up and down, wondering what the *hell* to do. I shook the handle of the locked door in desperation – and then, aha! Above me was a window that had no safety-catch. All I had to do was to get up there, slide it back and I would be out of my difficulty.

I got on to the inch-thick wall of the concrete coal bunker, reached up, gripped the steel bar which went in front of each window and pulled myself up. As my knee landed on the window sill, I remembered that the screw-bolt holding the bar to the front corner post was in rotten wood. My eyes focused on the bolt-head just in time to see it drawing slowly out. The bar fell away and I began to drop as if on a parachute. Time was suspended. I thought I was going to land on my back across the coal-bunker wall – my back broken. I landed, sitting, on top of the narrow wall of the coal bin. The pain was heart-stopping. I fell over sideways and grovelled on the grit path, almost unable to breathe. Gradually the pain subsided, my eyes opened and I lay on my side gingerly flexing my legs to see if anything was broken. My eyes were an inch above the gravel, looking below the wooden platform in front of the door – and there lay the box spare key. I was still walking like an arthritic jockey eight hours later when 'Tiny' Fred relieved me. 'What's up wi' thee, then?' he asked, ever cheerful. 'Got piles?'

'Something like that,' I grinned ruefully but I never did say what had happened – until now – I felt too foolish.

With men like 'Tiny' Fred and Ken Russell to talk to, I could imagine I was still on the steam-hauled railway – the 'family' feeling was strong. 'Tiny' had worked Brewham box, at the summit of a hard climb for east- and west-bound trains. The climb was steepest for east-bound trains. Many east-bound goods trains took 'rear-end assistance' from Castle Cary, usually in the form of a pannier tank from Yeovil shed. At Brewham the banker was crossed to the Down line and went back to Castle Cary or reversed into a short spur until there was a convenient 'path' down the hill. The engine of a Yeovil to Castle Cary 'pick-up' goods did a stint as banker before setting out for Somerton and Durston with an 'all stations' freight. At Durston it shunted trucks, then exchanged traffic before reforming its train to return to Yeovil via Montacute along the old Bristol & Exeter Railway route. 'Tiny', like me, was fascinated by the intricacies of such matters as well as by the beauty of sight and sound of the steam-hauled railway; the intricacies were part of its beauty.

He once told me, 'The ten happiest years of my life were spent working "Blatch", steam days. There used to be a 10.17 p.m. Paddington to Plymouth parcels that ran down in front of the "Papers" – 12.15 a.m. Paddington to Penzance. The 10.17 'used to go into the Down loop at Athelney to let the "Papers" pass and then it [the parcels] would follow the fast into the same platform at Taunton so's they could transfer the Taunton–Exeter "shorts" from the fast to the parcels. The 12.15 was then "Right Away" to Exeter and the parcels would follow, calling at the small stations. Well, one evening thic parcels came down so early that Clink Road put it into Frome and I held it at Blatchbridge until the 12.15 Padd had gone by. I knew the chaps on the parcels didn't like being held back 'cos they didn't come to the box to make their tea. Well, I pulled off for they behind the fast, they could follow it all the way to Taunton, and I was writing in the register when that engine started. Wham! Wham! Wham! Gor – I was at the window like a shot. I'd never heard anything like it. Them mad bloody cockneys was out to show me a thing or two. They came blazing away over the junction and then I saw they had a "King". His face was full of the enthusiasm he felt. 'I leant out of the window and listened to they all the way up to Brewham summit, you could hear 'em pasting that engine all the way – *wonderful*!'

Diesels in considerable variety passed Clink Road box in 1973. There were the 'Westerns' and an occasional 'Hymek', the Southern '33' and the Midland '45s', the little '31s' and the common old Class '47s' – very occasionally we would see a Class '37' from South Wales or a pair of '25s' coupled together as they were not much use singly. I became quite interested in photographing them. On an outing to the new Whatley Quarry railway, built by ARC Ltd, I met and became firm friends with that most artistic of the great railway photographers, Ivo Peters. Sitting above a tunnel mouth, waiting for a 'Western' we knew was up at the quarry to come back over the viaduct below us, we agreed that, while it was something of a comedown to be photographing diesels, at the same time they *were* forming the railway and we ought to be glad that there was still a railway to photograph. Clink Road box, close to the bridge, had several 'fans', people who spent hours leaning over the parapet, photographing and taking numbers. I remember especially the crowd that gathered for the first day of the new numbering system, when diesels carried their class number combined with a 'running' number, hence D1657 became 47293 (or whatever). The 'Western' class diesels, peculiar to Western Region, did not receive this treatment because they had cast aluminium numberplates, which could not be cheaply replaced in favour of painted-on numerals. In 1948, when the private railway companies were nationalised, the engines of the four companies were allocated blocks of numbers by Region – thus all ex-Southern Railway engines were in the 30,000–35,000 range – but GWR engines, numbered from 5 to 9091, had to keep their numbers because they were shown on cast-brass or cast-iron numberplates.

Express trains coming uphill towards Clink Road box off the avoiding line were running at 80–90 mph with an invisible bow wave of air before them which hit the little wooden signal box with a wallop that made the windows shake as the train hurtled past. Trains coming uphill out of Frome were always labouring on the sharply curved, 1 in 130 gradient. I vividly recall one autumn evening after a warm day. I received 'Train Entering Section' at 9.40 p.m. from Frome North for a train of stone. At 10 p.m., when I was relieved, I was still waiting for it and at 10.10 p.m. I stood on the path up the cutting side and watched as a 2,700-hp 'Western' came inching up the hill, engine bellowing, wheels ringed with fire like Catherine wheels in the dark. The diesel was so powerful yet so much at the mercy of the evening dew.

In season, Clink Road signal box was opened on Sunday to enable holiday trains to pass at close 'headways'. People came from Birmingham and Bournemouth to photograph and on fine Sundays there would be a party of

bells

local children sitting fairly quietly on the cutting side opposite the box, watching the trains and listening to the signal bells through the open windows of the box. Susan came with me on my 9 a.m. to 9 p.m. Sunday shifts. We brought pots, pans and the raw ingredients so that she could make a roast dinner and a cooked tea in the box. We ate as if in our summer house – only it was better than that, with the ringing of the bells, thumping levers and racing trains.

The trains were a great free show. They came from all the usual places such as Paddington, Plymouth, Penzance, Paignton, Weymouth, Cardiff and Bristol, but also from North Camp (on the Reading–Guildford line) to Truro, Kensington to St Austell ('Motor-Rail'), Cheltenham, Dover and Moreton-in-the-Marsh. It was difficult to tell one from the other except for the route code on the front of the engine but at least I knew they were of the most diverse origins and that made all the difference – I could write the unusual titles in the train register. They were belled to me with route code. Trains which had to go into Frome had 1-2 beats added to the 'Is Line Clear?' code, thus the 9.30 a.m. Westbury to Weymouth passenger trains was a '3-1' but I got the bell as '3-1-1-2'. A train going to Weymouth via the Frome avoiding line, such as the 8.10 a.m. Cheltenham – normally a '4 bells' – was sent to me as '4-3-4' and I signalled it on as a '4-1-2', signifying it was for Weymouth. The junction for Weymouth was Castle Cary so the signalman there understood the message and signalled it on to Yeovil (on the Weymouth branch) as a plain '4 bells'. An express for Taunton via the avoiding line came to me as a '4-3-4' but I signalled it on as a plain '4 bells'. There were similar arrangements for Up trains. Such intricacies might not be to everyone's taste but we all enjoyed them and indeed, they were in use at the instigation of one of the young, keen local signalmen, John Francis.

The signalmen were 'free spirits', proud of their independence, but who at the same time tried hard to run the express trains, stopping trains and freights through the complications of the Witham, Frome and Westbury junctions without causing delay. All we required was to be left alone or receive occasional visits from some senior, respected supervisor. 'Tatty' was a nuisance but being stationed at Bristol, he was too far away to bother us overmuch. One morning, however, a bombshell arrived in Clink Road box in the form of a young Manager from near-by Westbury. I was on duty and he delivered to me what must have been a specially prepared speech. I had never seen him before and he introduced himself thus: 'I am Mr Smith. Area Manager's assistant. You will obey me in all things ...'

I recall only the opening line because after that I was projected into a state of some confusion and was still wrestling with the word 'obey' when he marched out of the box. Recovering, I rang Tom Baber round at Frome North. 'Watch out – your new boss is on his way.'

'What d'yer mean?'

'Wait and see!' I hung up so as not to spoil his surprise.

Twenty minutes later Tom was phoning me, his cidery old voice shaking with emotion. 'Did you have thic young lad wi' you just now?'

'Did he give you his speech?' I asked, laughing.

'Aha! That he did,' Tom's voice was shaking with anger, in contrast to his usual cheerful, easy-going manner. 'I bin' on thic railway more'n twice as long as he's bin alive and I don't think I've ever been spoken to like that.'

'What do you reckon then, Tom?'

'I told him – you might be in charge, mister, an' I don't care whether you be or you bain't but you ain't a-going to talk to me like that so you can just get off out of here until you learns some manners!'

'Oh Tom!' I laughed, 'did he go?'

'He damn well had to – I chucked'n out!'

About a fortnight later, a train of stone was derailed at Frome North owing to the worn state of the track. Tom was on duty. He sent me 'Obstruction Danger' – 6 bells – and then came on the phone to tell me the reason for sending it. 'We'm off the road yer wi' one o' the Whatley's. Up Main's blocked. Come on th' Control phone wi I while I tells them the tale.' He explained the situation and the Controller said, 'OK then Tom. Could you ring the station and ask the porter to come along for handsignalman and could you contact Ron to be Pilotman – I know his back garden's close to your box ...' Tom butted in. 'I ain't doin' nothin' ...' 'What!?' exclaimed the Controller, 'Why ever not?' 'Becos' thurs a clever young man at Westbury as told I he were my superior an' I 'ad to obey 'im. You get hold of 'im and tell 'im we'm off the road down here and I wants to know what to do.' And Tom would not budge. There was a lengthy delay in finding the clever young man but when the Young Master arrived he did, somewhat hesitantly, set up single line working. It is possible that many people think Tom was unreasonable but I for one admired Tom for his stand. The clever young man was taught a well-needed lesson and he became more respectful of the men old enough to be his grandfather yet under his supervision.

One morning, I arrived for work at Clink Road and was informed by the nightshift man, 'We had a suicide during the night. Someone stepped in front of an Up fast about three o'clock. The police are still down there trying to piece him together so you'll have to stop the Down trains and tell them to look out for the cops on the line. Blatch is stopping the Up trains.'

Round about breakfast time, I had a sandwich in my hand when a constable came into the box. 'Right, that's it then, job over. We've put one man together, no one else involved.' He was carrying a clear, plastic bag. At first its contents did not register, then I saw what was in it – two human ears.

I made one forgetful mistake in the year I worked Clink Road box. This would have had serious consequences but for the vigilance of others and, had it reached 'Tatty's' eager ears, would have enabled him to create much work for himself from which he would have derived great pleasure. I was saved by the 'family' atmosphere of the railway.

I had with me in the signal box an unofficial visitor, a young man who worked for Western Region's Signal & Telegraph Department at Gloucester. He was making a pilgrimage to see what was left of the old railway. He was dressed in heavy, 'county' clothes – highly polished brogue leather shoes, cavalry twill trousers, a twill shirt and a tweed jacket with leather patches on the elbows. He seemed a decent sort, keen on semaphore signalling, and an hour slipped by in 'talking shop'. I told him the story of the Kingham 'slip coach'. In 1970 a train-load of football fans was returning from Wolverhampton to Oxford and the rowdies on board became a nuisance. The guard, with the assistance of the two railway policemen on board, herded them all in to the rear coach, locked them in and then pulled the communication cord to stop the train at Kingham. The rear coach was uncoupled, protective detonators were placed a mile to the rear and the signal boxes on each side were warned as to what had been done. The rowdies were eventually removed in police vans and the guard received a good deal of well-merited praise from just about everyone.

The story intrigued my guest who revealed that he was a Special Constable who often rode on trains in that capacity to keep order. At this point one of the permanent-way men came into the box to say that there was a broken rail in the Up Main between me and Fairwood Junction and no trains were to go up until further notice when they had the rail replaced. I have to confess that the message went in one ear and out the other, the man returned to the site and my tweedy visitor continued his tale. He told me he was riding on a train in civilian clothes when he came across a youth writing in felt-tip pen on the end wall of the corridor. Brimming over with public spirit, it appeared, he had made a run at the boy, kicked him in the back – 'with these very shoes I've got on now' – and laid him low.

I felt furious, not only at the unconstitutional behaviour of a guardian of the Queen's peace but also furious for the relish with which he told the tale. As he finished, a 'light' engine was belled as passing Frome. Fuming, I got the road from Fairwood, pulled my signals and then peremptorily ordered the 'public-spirited' gent out of the signal box. He was the only person to have suffered this fate but it was all he deserved.

The engine, a Southern '33', shot past as he made his stunned exit. Shaking a little myself, I sent it 'Entering Section' to Fairwood, gave 'Train out' to Frome – and then remembered what I had been told. I slammed the signal lever back a second too late – the engine had gone by. Five minutes later, the same permanent-way man came into sight, running. 'Hey! We've got a rail out up there. Had you forgotten?'

'Yes, I'm very sorry – in one ear and out the other, I'm afraid, I'll put a collar on that signal lever now.'

He relaxed. 'Oh well, that'll be OK then. I stopped that engine. The driver'll think the rail broke after you'd pulled off.'

Early in 1974, I started work on my book about Great Western architecture and on 18 March I went to Tilehurst and Taplow to photograph buildings at those stations. I travelled by express train from Bath to Didcot and from there on the 10.35 p.m. Oxford to Paddington diesel rail car. This dropped me at Tilehurst and went on its way. Fifteen minutes later I had my photograph and was wondering how best to continue the journey to Taplow when the 10.5 a.m. Oxford to Paddington parcels train arrived at the Up Relief line platform and stopped, the signal at the end of the platform being at 'Danger'. There were Oxford men in charge and I was soon standing in the cab of a Class '31' diesel.

'Do you know why we're waiting here?' asked the driver.

'The last one up was the 10.35 Oxford twenty minutes ago, it must be stopped at Scour's Lane.'

Scour's Lane was the next signal, about three-quarters of a mile away, out of sight around a slight bend lined with bushes. As the driver was telling his secondman to go to the signal post telephone and report the position of the train to the Panelman, our signal cleared to a single yellow. The driver began to blow the brakes off when around the corner, at least 250 yards away, but coming back slowly towards us, was the 10.35 Oxford. The driver and secondman were out of the cab in a flash and went running forwards towards the rail car with their arms raised in the 'Danger' signal. I was busy taking photographs. The guard of the passenger train was riding in the rear – now the leading – cab so he was able to put the brake on and no harm was done.

What had happened was that the Panelman at Reading had crossed a goods train from the West Curve to the Down Yard, the route taking the train across all four passenger-carrying lines. One wagon became derailed on the yard points but not foul of the running lines – something the signalman could have seen had he been working the layout from the old Reading West Junction signal box. As far as the Panelman could tell from his console indications, there was a derailment and the entire junction was trapped, set for the crossing movement. After twenty minutes he told the driver of the 10.35 Oxford to reverse to Tilehurst, de-train his passengers and tell them to take a bus to Reading – there was a bus stop about 200 yards east of Tilehurst station. He had no idea how long the delay was going to be so he thought this would be for the best. But he had overlooked the parcels train, which was indicated on his console as standing at Tilehurst.

There were several portly matrons to be lowered to the ground from the rail car plus a group of passengers for Heathrow via the road motor coach shuttle from Reading. These were the ones with the luggage. Out it all came, down onto the ballast. In the comradely manner of partners in misfortune, they helped each other move the heavy cases from the track to the platform, passing us railwaymen with never a word or a glance, up over the footbridge and out of the station, traipsing along the Oxford Road like so many well-to-do refugees. The erstwhile train passengers gathered dejectedly around the bus stop 200 yards along the road from the station and very close to the railway line.

Having dumped them, the 10.35 Oxford crept back to its signal at Scour's Lane – and behold! It was cleared for the now empty passenger train to proceed. In due course we were given permission to proceed over the telephone by the Panelman and we drew slowly away, hardly daring to look in the direction of the erstwhile passengers – but we could feel the fury of their gaze through the sheet metal of the cab as they stood forlornly at the edge of the bus-less road. When I got to Taplow the teleprinter had disgorged a highly efficient printout so that everyone was well informed of our latest piece of inefficiency. The porter tore the sheet off and gave it to me. I still have it. It reads:

10.35 Oxford left Reading at 12.22, that is 51 late.
09.45 Weston 12.08 from Reading, that is 31 late.
06.35 Penzance next at 12.20, which is 18 late followed by
10.25 Birmingham left Reading at 12.02 which is 5 late.
This is all due to a wagon at West Junction landing up on Olde England shutting up the shop. End.

The teleprinter operator's feelings of disgust and frustration can be felt from the way he constructed his message. Our railway could run superbly well until some small thing went wrong and plunged a whole district into chaos.

No small thing was the storm that raged for a week at the start of September 1974. Days of torrential rain were followed by Force 10 winds during the night of the 6th/7th. Just before dawn on the 7th I was woken by the roar of the wind through the great and ancient beech tree that grew outside the bedroom window. It was a bit too early to get out of bed but I reckoned I might need some extra time on the road so, with a groan, I crawled out and set off for a six o'clock start at Clink Road. The road was littered with twigs and small branches as the crazy wind tried to uproot every living and dead tree. Between Woolverton and Beckington I could see the normally placid River Frome leaping along in a mad, grey-black torrent, foaming and piling branches against the arches of its eighteenth-century bridge. The wind was strong enough to rock the car and after a 12-mile drive it was a relief to get out of that thunderous half-light into the cheerful, fire-lit interior of the signal box, nestling peacefully in the deep shelter of its cutting.

At 7.30 a.m. a 'light' engine passed Fairwood Junction, coming towards Clink Road. At 7.31 a.m., ten minutes late, the 5.45 a.m. Weymouth to Bristol rail car passed me on the Up line and at about the same time – unknown to a soul – a large elm tree fell to the wind and lay with its trunk blocking the Up line and its massive boughs blocking the Down line. The driver of the 'light' engine, having seen the last of Fairwood's signals and with the first of my signals 2 miles ahead, glanced down at a newspaper on his console and therefore did not see the tree. This apparent lapse in his look-out was, in fact, a blessing, albeit a mixed one. Had he seen the obstruction he would have stopped short; as it was, he smashed through to the far side. The windscreen shattered, the front of the engine took a heavy beating and some bits of glass entered the driver's eyes but, realising immediately that the Up Weymouth would be close, he drove on and was able to place three detonators on the Up Main line a mile from the tree. He got back onto his engine and went forward, holding a red light from the cab. The Weymouth's driver thus received plenty of warning and stopped well away from several tons of elm tree in his path.

When the 'light' engine came under the arch of the bridge at Clink Road my first reaction was, 'Well – I know we're hard up for engines but this is ridiculous.' A second later I realised that something very unpleasant had happened and sent 'Obstruction Danger' to Bernie Miles at Fairwood. The driver came into the box with a face almost as battered as the front of his diesel but he told me precisely what had happened. The Up line was blocked by the rail car, which was safely at a stand, so I asked Bernie to send me 'Obstruction Danger' to cover the Up line – the 6 bells I had sent him covered only the Down line. The next job was to advise Bristol Control. We needed an ambulance for the engine driver; we needed the Permanent-Way Department with some powerful chainsaws and we needed some impromptu alterations to the timetable. While I was on the phone the guard of the Weymouth arrived in the box.

It was agreed that the Weymouth should come back, 'wrong road' to Frome, de-train its passengers into buses to be provided and then return to Weymouth as the Bristol to Weymouth rail car which was stuck on the wrong side of the tree. The guard of the 5.45 a.m. Weymouth saw me padlock the clamp on No. 19 points and on the telephone Tom Baber assured him that it would be safe for his train to run 'wrong road' back to Frome. The guard returned to his train and conducted it back to Frome station. The passengers were just trooping out into the station forecourt to get on the waiting bus when I got the message that the line was clear. This was just as well because there were at least two bus-loads of passengers and only one bus. Back they all came, on to the train standing, rattling, beneath Brunel's wooden station roof. The guard gave 'Right' and off they all went – towards Weymouth. The line between Frome North and Blatchbridge Junction was a single track worked by 'tokenless block', so once a train had been signalled through in a particular direction it had to go, right through, to operate the track circuits in order that the route in the opposite direction could be set up. If the line had been worked by the old-fashioned Electric Key Token system, the key would have been replaced in the instrument and turned in its lock by the signalman and that would have been an end of the matter. The train went 1 ½ miles down to the Main line at Blatchbridge, stopped quite clear of the Frome line on the Up Main to satisfy the single line electric interlocking, reversed and went back again. The passengers must have thought we were all barking mad.

CHAPTER ELEVEN

Steam Flashback

Trains of stone-carrying wagons, empty, thundered through the cutting at Clink, the steel tubs booming and shaking as a big diesel hustled them along at 45 mph. Loaded trains came uphill no less precipitously, stone dust flying, as their drivers 'ran 'em', sometimes in the full knowledge that they were out in front of a 'fast' and on a 'tight' margin. These stone trains, hauled either by a 'Western', 'Brush 47' or '45' class diesel were going to or coming from the Merehead quarry of Foster Yeomen Ltd. The quarry was situated off the Cranmore branch, itself the stub of the line which had once passed through the Mendips to connect the GWR at Witham with the GWR at Yatton. The track accommodation at Witham was barely sufficient to cope with the traffic, which led to some intriguing situations as the Witham signalman manoeuvred to make the proverbial quart fit into a pint pot (see Appendix 4). Soon after arriving at Clink, I realised that Witham was a very desirable residence for a signalman who enjoyed organising trains. A vacancy arose there and, one year after taking the job at Clink Road Junction, I moved to Witham.

Witham Friary is an ancient hamlet astride the stripling River Frome, snug in a remote vale, miles off even a 'B' road at the end of a corkscrew lane to nowhere. A great Cistercian abbey, built at Henry II's expense as part of his penance for causing the death of his Archbishop, Thomas à Becket, once stood in fields close to my Up advanced starting signal. Much of its stone and at least one of its fireplaces had been used in local houses but of the abbey there was no trace above the green fields, but a small chapel, an offshoot of the looted, monastic settlement, still stood and was in use at one end of the village street. At the other end of the street, past a row of dormer-windowed cottages and a muddy gateway where Jersey cows gathered to bawl for the 'fogger', stood the Seymour Arms, close by the railway bridge. The pub, with its ornate sign, would once have been the watering hole for passengers and staff at the little station on the bridge but in 1974 there was no station and the landlord and his wife were wise to rely for their living on milk.

The Seymour Arms opened in 1866, four years after the opening of Witham station. It stood, or rather stands, four square and solid at the roadside, at once a public house and a farmhouse with mucky cow-yard attached. Anyone fortunate enough to have entered would have been served a decent pint of beer or home-made cider by Elsie. Often she came to serve straight from the farmyard, the evidence of her work coating her wellingtons as she clumped along the flagstoned passageway to the bar. You wanted beer? There was the oak barrel. Cider? Here is the barrel and, stooping in her wellies and apron, she turned the tap and filled your glass. A few crates of bottled beer and some brown shelves for chocolate and cigarettes more or less completed the catering arrangements. The public bar was brownish and dim, the walls a nicotine-cream colour with a bright green bench along one side, a couple of wooden tables with hard chairs, usually unoccupied. Sometimes I saw a pair of ancient farm workers, old mates, drinking cider and playing dominoes at a table by the only window in the room.

The signal box stood on the downside of the line about 200 yards west of the hamlet, on an embankment. It was a tall brick building in the GWR's rather severe style of the 1890s. A flight of external steps led from the lineside path to the door, which opened into an internal porch and the operating floor. The Down distant signal lever, No. 67, was close by and the lever frame, instrument shelf and long glass-cased track diagram stretched away down the length of the room. When I turned up one Monday to start, I found Tom Baber near the door, by the instrument shelf, with a piece of bread in his hand.

'Morning, Tom,' I said, 'you'll be able to eat that crust in peace now.'

'Eh? Oh, this ain't for me,' he said, 'I'm feeding my mouse or I was till you frightened him away.' Tom, who up till then had been only a friendly voice at the end of a telephone, was about fifty-three, becoming stout with sandy whiskers on a strong-looking face, which matched his character. He could yarn away for hours about his life on the railway and in the countryside, speaking in a Somerset cider-soaked accent.

'Now that you'm yer, you can get on wi' it,' he said, throwing me the duster from off his shoulder and retiring to the table and chair at the west-end window. A bell rang and with a loud squeak the mouse fell from under the instrument shelf onto the floor and went scuttling away into a pile of newspapers.

'He'll kill hisself one day,' said Tom laconically, reaching for his tin of tobacco and Rizla papers. 'He gets up amongst the wires and gets a shock when a bell rings – he don't ever seem to learn.'

Leaning on the booking desk after registering the bell code, I saw some rabbits playing out in the field and mentioned them to Tom.

'Yer – I know most o' them by sight. Can you see the one with the white patch on its fur? We'd have trapped they years ago, set a snare early and had rabbit pie when we got home. Ever had rook pie? We used to put a lump of bread down between the stock rail and the blade o' the points and when a rook came along he'd put his head down to get it out and – ' Tom clapped his hands together 'we'd slam the points shut and have rook pie.'

'Ugh!' said I disgustedly, 'you're pulling my leg.'

'No I ain't,' protested Tom, "tis all good food. Have you ever had hedgehog – '

'No,' I butted in, 'I've never had hedgehog pie.' Tom chuckled. "Tis all good food, you had to make do wi' what you could get once upon a time – the only thing I've tried what I couldn't eat was badger.' He told me about the local, annual badger roast and so the hours of the shift passed.

The signal box stood on the valley side overlooking the young River Frome. Meadows full of buttercups lay all around, crossed by hedges, dotted with big ash and oak trees. The mellow brick of the hamlet lay to the right while opposite and to the left the land rose to a wooded horizon. Through this valley the railway rose, climbing south-westwards towards Brewham summit on a 1 in 112 gradient and the big diesels, 'in the collar' almost all the way from Westbury, attacked the final 2 miles of the bank, past Witham, with an angry roar and a plume of black smoke. The 'King' class steamers would have been truly majestic as they came past Witham on a West of England express at 50 mph with thirteen coaches in tow. The Cranmore branch, which used to run through a wonderful and very varied countryside, 31 ½ miles to Yatton, was now a 5¾ mile stub. The branch left the Main line on a sharp curve to the west a few yards to the left of the signal box and went straight up the valley side on a 1 in 49 gradient for half a mile before turning left to wind and climb through the hills. In steam days I could have watched a '45' tanky storm the bank and could have marked its later progress by the plume of smoke through the trees. Witham's layout had a spaciousness and the signal box, standing back a little from the Main line, gave the impression of a grandstand view.

In 1974 the most exciting sight for me was to see a train of stone for Botley, or Luton, weighing around 1,500 tons, come hurtling down the hill. By day the speed was obvious, smoke off the brake-blocks, stone-dust flying; by night speed was less obvious but there was plenty of Catharine wheels as cast-iron brake-blocks gripped spinning, steel-tyred wheels. When I was standing on the wooden boards of the footway, crossing the tracks from signal box to branch line, waiting to take the token off the driver, this performance was amply exciting. The driver had more faith in his brake than I had and if anything went wrong I was in the right place to learn about it promptly. But it was fun. There was a lot of the old 'dash' about the proceeding, the train would always come very smoothly round the curve and the token would be handed off with the studied nonchalance and cheerful, inconsequential greeting that goes with a job where men know they are working skilfully and well.

The token, in its hooped carrier, was carried to the signal box and restored to its instrument. The token system at Witham was unusual insofar as the Witham signalman had total control over the issue of tokens. I merely pressed the brass plunger to give myself an electrical release for a token and then told Eric Compton up at Merehead Quarry ground frame what train was coming to him. If he wanted to send a train to me he asked for a 'release' by telephone. Once a token had been removed from either machine, they were both locked until that token was restored. Merehead Quarry was served by a triangular junction under the control of the man at the ground frame. Trains left the quarry on condition there was not a train waiting in the branch loop at Witham to go to the quarry. The empties took priority because the loop had to be kept clear – the trains of empties would come down from Westbury, three in succession, with the 'fast' behind, so the Witham signalman had to dispose quickly of the goods trains – one to loop, one to stand on the Up Main line and a third to reverse into the Down sidings. Obviously, these solutions to the problems of keeping the Main line clear depended entirely on whether there was a train signalled on the Up Main or whether the Down sidings were already full of empty wagons. Sometimes we had to ask Clink Road to send one of our trains of empties through Frome to ease the pressure on our own layout when stone trains and express trains were running thick and fast; occasionally the whole thing ground to a halt. The permutations of circumstances affecting train working at Witham seemed to be endless – which is why the thirty-seven-lever signal box was such a challenging and entertaining place to work.

Tom gave advice on which train to 'run' and which to 'hold', all in the same breath as he used to describe the working at Sparkford station in 1938, the qualities he expected in a Victoria sponge (he was an expert sponge-cake maker) or the snobbery of a certain bishop he once knew. Through this expertise in railway work mixed with storytelling, I soon got the hang of the basics of Witham box. One day, I 'supposed' that the road from Brewham to Westbury was an undulating one. 'Oh no it isn't,' said Tom emphatically. 'You can forget that bit of a hump between Blatchbridge and Clink, they don't hardly notice that, it's downhill all the way to Westbury. Back in steam days a "light" engine stopped on the Up road at Brewham box – ol' Sid Fleming was on duty there. "There's something I'd like to try," this driver says to Sid.

"'Oh, what's that then?" asks Sid. "I'd like to see how far I could go on one puff of steam from here."

'Well, Sid told all the chaps what was going on, the engine – "Hall" it was – had a clear road to Westbury and off it went – one chuff out of its chimney. Well, the road is so much downhill they free-wheeled all the way to Fairwood and had to brake hard for the turn into Westbury,' Tom finished triumphantly from his window seat, looking out over the branch. 'Oh! Here's the Luton just coming down the hill, you can pull off for they right away – the Penzance isn't about.'

I 'asked the road' to Blatchbridge – 5 bells – pulled points 32, bolted them with 31, pulled signals 5, 6, 7 and 10 and hurried down the steps and over the footboards to collect the token from the driver. The massive bogie of a 'Western' went grinding over the rails a few inches from my toes. Back in the signal box I sent 'Train Entering Section' – 2 beats – to Blatchbridge as I passed the bell and put the token into the instrument. Turning to look at the train, I saw that its tail lamp was quarter of a mile up the line. 'Don't those diesels motor!' I said to Tom as I gave 'Train out of Section' to the ground frame. 'A thousand tons or more behind the engine and they run like a passenger train.'

'Well, they could run 'em steam days too,' replied Tom. 'I do recall a summer Saturday when Exmouth Junction shed was getting low on coal and we had a trainload for 'em stuck up at Westbury. Summer Saturdays down this way in the fifties there wasn't a path for all the passenger trains let alone for loco coal but it had to go. Exmouth Junction was the Southern's most important shed between Salisbury and Plymouth. Control asked the driver if he'd go, given the road, and he said he would provided it was an absolutely clear run – 'twudn't be difficult to run, it was stopping he were worried about – twenty-five twenty-tonners o' loco coal and no brake.' Tom gave a short laugh. 'Well, that was only a little "63" engine but it came down here, all against the collar, so fast that the following Birmingham to Paignton excursion only missed the distant at every other box. 'Course, there were more boxes open in them days but even so, it's uphill for 10 miles from Westbury.' I wondered, then, what other signal boxes there had been in those days.

'A lot more than now!' said Tom. 'Woodlands, between Blatchbridge and here, Brewham next along, then Pinkwood, Bruton and Wyke before Castle Cary, five extra signal boxes compared to now.' I expressed more surprise, most gratifying to Tom who blew a cloud of tobacco smoke at the ceiling to express his satisfaction.

I felt I ought to 'know the road' better and made several journeys from Westbury to Weymouth. Travelling in the cab of a somewhat underpowered Class '31' diesel, to hear it struggling and to see those curves and gradients unrolling before me, enabled me to appreciate the skill and physical endurance of the men who had worked steam engines over the line.

On 3 April 1975 I went down to Merehead Quarry on 1070 *Western Gauntlet* and the driver spent the entire trip talking about steam days. The old East Somerset Railway through the Mendips from Witham was sharply curved and steeply graded throughout and as we roared up the initial 1 in 49 with 2,700 hp thundering away like Woden's hammer behind our backs, the driver spoke about the time when practically all the traffic on the line was handled by pannier tanks. 'The biggest engine allowed was a "63" but it was always the Frome "77s" or "37s" and the Bristol "45s" – small engines, big loads – that took good enginemanship.' The huge diesel heeled around the curve at the head of the incline – thirty-five empty tubs, 227 tons in tow, 247 with the brake van – and the driver all but closed the throttle as the grade eased and the line curved gently through the woods.

'You could get fantastic work out of a little tanky if you knew what you were at,' he went on. 'One of the jobs we had out of Westbury was an "all stations" to Bristol via Trowbridge with a "Hall". At Temple Meads we'd take the coaches out to Malago Vale, back on the shed for coal and water and then work another stopper back to Westbury. Well, this day I was cleaning the fire as we stood on the shed and saw that some of the brick arch had dropped onto the grate and it looked as if more was going to follow. So we went to the foreman, failed the engine and asked for another. All he had was a "37" tanky. Well, my mate and I didn't mind, a little "pannier" tank with five coaches was OK over that road, so up the station we went. The engine wasn't so long out of Swindon – nice black paint just starting to get a bit grimy – we'd be all right.

'They put us through the Middle Road, alongside some train standing at our platform. "Must be something running late," my mate says, pointing at this other train. We counted eleven coaches before we got to the front. They were all for us! When our guard comes up to give us the load and saw the engine, he cussed because he thought it was the Pilot still on the train and he'd be late away waiting for the train engine to arrive. When we told him we were the train engine he cussed some more.' My driver friend laughed, and, taking his eyes off the track for a moment, turned to me: 'I don't know what he was going on about, it was me that would be doing all the work.' We went over the main road bridge at Wanstrow and he, like a good teacher, carefully remembered to point out the site of Wanstrow station. Then he went on: 'We had a bunker full of Midland hard coal and my mate says, "Fill the box with that till you get only yellow smoke showing. It'll burn like paper once we get going." We left with a full glass of water and the needle on the mark. "Put the feed on," say my mate, "here we go." And did we ever?! He gave it the gun and by East Depot we had them on the trot with the signalman leaning out of his window to watch – signalmen always liked watching a fireman slaving away!' He grinned across at me. 'I was raising steam and sweat in equal parts but I was determined not to be beat. I had the one injector on all the time but that wasn't enough to maintain the boiler water level the way my mate was using steam and if I put the second injector on as well it knocked the clock back*. My mate was taking more steam out of the boiler than the fire was making but with a station every 2 or 3 miles I could put the second injector on at the stops and keep the boiler topped-up. We hammered that engine so's we lost only five minutes to Westbury with a double load on a schedule designed for an engine twice the size of ours.'

We pulled steadily uphill to the ground frame at Merehead Quarry Junction. The driver handed the token to Eric Compton and we swung right over the points from the Cranmore line to the eastern arm, opened in October 1973, of the triangular junction, down and round into the quarry. Dense woods had been ripped open to make the new line and white stone dust smothered the ground and remaining trees. My driver kept his eyes piercingly on the curving, falling track, fondling the brake handle, conning us into the berth. He gave the brake handle its last turn; I felt the entire weight of the train push up behind, then all was still save for the sound of our diesel engine, clanking quietly. We waited for someone to come and hook us off our train.

'There was a lot of fun to be got out of steam engine work,' I ventured, to start him off again.

'Steam could be bloody hard graft and uncomfortable, too, at times but we did have a laugh and there was the challenge of the engine every time

---

*   Reduced boiler pressure.

you went out. These things', he thumped his fist on the diesel's console, 'have made life a thousand times easier but they aren't much fun. When they go they're great, when they don't they're a damn nuisance.'

'What was the hardest job you had out of Westbury?' I asked, thinking of the Channel Islands potato trains. 'The Weymouth stoppers,' he said promptly. Just then a shunter banged on the cabside. The driver popped his head over the side. 'I've hooked you off,' shouted the man. Go over there and I'll hook you onto 7609 set.' In a few minutes we were coupled to forty-two 16-tonners loaded with stone for some new road. This lot, weighing around 1,500 tons, *Western Gauntlet* would push uphill along the western arm of the triangle to the Cranmore line – but first, tea, biscuits and more talk. We sat in the cab surrounded by dusty trucks, tracks and loading machinery, the forest rising high above. 'The stoppers were harder than the "Perpots" then?' I asked using the railway's old telegraphic code-word for the seasonal special trains of potatoes.

'Oh, the "Perpots" – no, at least with those you were on the run non-stop. The Weymouth stoppers were all stop and start on heavy gradients – eighteen stations in sixty miles to Weymouth and the same back again. Drive you daft, starting and stopping – and it used a hell of a lot of coal.'

'Which, of course, you had to shovel on,' I finished for him. After tea and biscuits and a fag, we tidied the cab and set about leaving. He gave a blast on the horn to call the guard, who looked out from the brake van, gave 'Right Away' and we were off. I stood in the doorway to get the benefit of the sound of a 'Western' unleashed. The driver leant well outside with one hand reaching inboard to the throttle handle. He gave it one notch, two notches, the engine roared, howled and 1,500 tons of stone and steel began to creep inexorably uphill. The guard in his van, at what was temporarily the leading end of the train, waved us on and at walking pace *Western Gauntlet* rolled its cumbersome, unbraked train up to the Cranmore 'main line'. We were trundling into a dead-end siding with the Cranmore line on the left, the driver was braking and I could feel the train's brute weight dragging the 110-ton engine on towards the invisible buffers. The driver must have had a fence post or some other landmark to gauge his final brake for he stopped the train with the engine just clear of the points out on to the 'main line', the last few feet being covered by the weight of the train dragging the brake-locked locomotive along the rails.

We stopped at Quarry Junction ground frame as a 'Brush 47' came uphill towards us, its driver dangling the hooped token carrier over the cab-side. Eric went to collect it. From up there, the true depth of the valley through which the real Main line ran was apparent. We were 600 feet above sea-level, 350 feet above Witham, looking down on a wonderful panorama of woods and fields. The other train trundled past, the drivers exchanging waves. My mate had just finished a meticulous sharing of the remaining tea when Eric rapped on the cab-side with the token carrier. 'Right away, driver!' I took the token and handed it to the driver, who laid it on his console and, releasing the brake, allowed the train to roll away downhill. The tea was getting rough-edged but the view was magnificent and even the smelly old diesel did not seem too bad in the company of such an excellent mate. I remarked on the essential contribution that tea has made to railway work and described a home-made immersion-heater I once saw a fireman using to boil the water in his tea can; he screwed a U-shaped piece of copper tube to the steam lance connection on the engine's smokebox; when steam passed through the tube it heated it and boiled the water. My driver friend thought this was clever but restricted to use when the engine was stationary. He went on:

'I was a fireman and me and my mate had to go out to Heywood Road Junction to relieve a "Broc" special – broccoli Up from Penzance. The engine turned out to be a "County", good, strong engines if you can get them right but sods for steam if you haven't got the knack with them. Anyhow, we got on, they got off and my mate told me to put the tea can in the fire on the shovel to make a brew before we started. But just as I was pulling the shovel out of the fire I somehow managed to knock it against the side of the hole and the whole lot went up in a cloud of steam. Bloody wars! I knew my mate was annoyed but he didn't say anything – he just got that train rolling. I was making steam and sweat in equal parts and we went up the bank from Lavington to Savernake like a blessed passenger train – that's about 20 miles, you know? He just about pasted me, letting the lever down little by little till we had sparks like cricket balls coming out of the chimney on the steepest bit coming up to Burbage Wharf. Over the top, through Savernake station, he comes across to me with a wicked grin and says, "How would you like a cup of tea now?"'

We both laughed at that and he began to brake our train so as to stop at the head of the incline to allow the guard to get off and pin down wagon-brakes. 'You're laughing now,' I said, 'but did you laugh then?'

'Well, he was a good mate, we were always pulling each other's leg. It'd have been different if he always drove like that. A bad mate on a steam engine was just plain misery.'

The guard shouted 'Right Away' and with some throttle to get the train moving, we set off down an incline which seemed to me to be as steep as a roller-coaster in a fairground, with Witham box looking very small and faraway at the bottom. My driver was silent and I knew he was considering something. Finally, he said, 'I've got a letter at home, thanking me for some good work from Reggie Hanks – he was General Manager a bit before your time, I should think. You'd have liked him, he was a great steam enthusiast.' I was able to surprise my driver by telling him that I used to live near Mr Hanks in Oxford and he had told me a lot about his footplate exploits – the only General Manager to regularly act as fireman on the train that took him to work, just the sort of Boss that all railwaymen were proud of. My mate agreed with this and went on: 'The chap I was firing to got a letter too. We relieved an "Ocean Liner Special" that had come into Westbury, I can't remember why now, they were usually non-stop Plymouth to Paddington. There must have been something serious wrong – anyhow – the train had been standing there for twenty minutes and as we left my mate said to me, "How about it then?" I said I didn't mind, we had only six coaches and we just about flew. Someone on the train must have written to Hanks about it because we got a letter thanking us for the effort. But even without that I'd remember that run for the speed and for the engine,' he paused for effect and added grandly, '*Isambard Kingdom Brunel.*'

He brought the engine to a stand on the footboards at Witham so I could get down on to a safe footing with the token and, very reluctantly, I left this excellent driver and carried the token up into the signal box.

CHAPTER TWELVE

Signalman's Nightmare

I took over my shift at Witham in September 1974 with the minimum of 'rules' fuss. 'Tatty' had been most concerned about the working of the Cranmore branch. 'What are the regulations governing the working of the Cranmore branch?' he asked severely. Under normal circumstances that was a very large question, like asking an aspiring cleric, 'What does it say in the Bible?' but circumstances were not normal and I was able to answer in a word: 'None.'

'What d'you mean: none?' he snapped, thinking he had scored a hole in one with me.

'Exactly what I say. The system of token working on the line is unknown to any rule-book I've ever seen and you haven't issued the signal box with any special instructions to cover it.' Confusion and disbelief fought for possession of his face. 'Go and have a look in your files,' I suggested.

'No need for that, just trying you out. Now then, what would you do if ...?

We went off into some standard questions on double-line work. The examination did not take long and shortly I was on my way home as signalman at Witham (Som.).

At ten minutes to six on the following Monday morning I walked along the path to the signal box. Witham box had been switched out after Sunday engineering work finishing around teatime. The tall, gaunt signal box was silhouetted against the greying sky, with no friendly yellow light in the windows. There was a sharp wind hissing through the dawn, through the wheels of the wagons left on the sidings from the previous day's engineering work. I hurried up the stairs and was glad to get into the shelter of the box. Inside, it was curiously silent and dark. I switched on the lights. No Tom Baber, no fire. The levers seemed to be waiting for a duster-clad hand to throw them across their quadrants – action and some cheerful noise. I put my coat on the hook, my food-bag on the locker-top and telephoned Westbury South box to discover the traffic situation. The phone was cold and clammy. Tom Lamb answered; he was at the end of his shift, waiting to be relieved by Bob Pritchard.

'Witham here, wanting to switch in. What's about, Tom?'

'There's nothing on the Up but the Maiden Newton stock is on the Down road, it must be passing Clink Road now.'

'OK, I'll switch in now.' I put the Up line signals back to 'Danger', pegged the Down line instrument to 'Train on Line' and turned the block switch brass handle from OUT to IN. Then, having got the attention of Tom Lamb and Joe Apsey at Castle Cary, I sent the 'Opening Signal Box' code – 5-5-5. The high-toned and low-toned bells clanged out the acknowledgement, the echoes awoke – Witham was in business. I entered the fact of opening in the train register – the pages felt cold and damp – put the kettle on and set about lighting the stove.

The 5.55 a.m. Westbury to Maiden Newton empty diesel rail-car rattled past out of the rising sun at 6.15 a.m., followed by the 5.30 Westbury to Merehead empties. The 'Ganes' (eight-wheel wagons), carrying old track sections from the previous day's relaying job, were parked on the Down siding and had been parted so as not to block the foot crossing; I walked between the big, oval buffers, carrying the token for the branch train. There had been a certain amount of nonsense over the Sunday job – relaying the Up Main line between Witham and Blatchbridge – and Ron Kirby, the signalman who had worked the box, left an explanatory note. The new track sections had come up from Taunton on two trains and one of the locomotives, a 'Brush 47', had failed on arrival and was parked in the Down sidings. The new track had been laid but there had been some difficulty in hauling fresh ballast to the site, so the old ballast had been put back and an extra-severe speed restriction was in force over that section. Last, but not least, one of the 'Ganes' carrying the old track had a hot axle bearing ,which would require attention before it could return to Taunton. The 'cripple' was the last of the front part of the train, immediately on the Taunton side of the foot crossing.

Eight minutes after the 5.30 Westbury had gone down the branch, a 'light' engine arrived from Westbury to collect the 'dead' diesel. Whoever had sent the engine had not known that the 'dead' engine was behind the long train of 'Ganes', shunting was required and as the engine had not come equipped with a guard or shunter, it returned Westbury-wards at high speed. Various regular trains passed. At 8 a.m. I called the 'C&W' (Carriage & Wagon) Department to tell them about the crippled 'Gane' and at 9 a.m. an engine arrived from Westbury to haul the 'Ganes' to Taunton. The crippled wagon was shunted out of the train and finally placed in the siding in front of the 'dead' Class '47'. At ten o'clock, as a stone train was coming down the hill from Merehead and as two Class '25' diesels coupled together were arriving at my home signal from Westbury, the 10 a.m. Witham to Taunton Fairwater pulled out of the Down siding, signalled '1-4' on the bell with the appropriate 'box to box' message. The leading '25' was for Cranmore, the trailing engine was to take the 'dead' '47' back to Westbury. I went out, fetched the token from the Merehead train, put it in to the machine and withdrew it again. The enginemen uncoupled their engines outside the home signal and when the stone train had gone, I turned the first engine on to the branch loop, reversed the road and brought the other down to the box. As it was approaching, I hurried out across the footboards with the token, back into the box to shunt the second engine to the Down sidings and to give 'Train out of Section' for it to Blatchbridge. The bells and levers had been clashing and ringing enough to delight the heart of any railwayman since six o'clock and still the work went on, another stone empties from Blatchbridge as the men with the Class '25' shunted in the Down sidings. They finally left for Westbury at 10.58, belled '1-4' with the 'box to box' message: '1 live, 1 dead for Westbury'.

The C&W men arrived in their yellow Ford van at about this time, looked at the axle bearing and reckoned they'd need two hours to fix it. I telephoned Bristol Control to order an engine to work the solitary 'Gane' to Taunton at 1 p.m. and suggested that the spare brake van, left over from the two trains that had come from Taunton, could be worked home on the special. Two or three trains went by uneventfully, but at 11.25 a.m. the Sheephouse Crossing telephone rang. Sheephouse was about a mile the Witham side of Bruton and was used frequently by a local farmer to move cattle across the line. He would first phone and ask permission but this would be early in the morning; it seemed late to be moving the cows, so when I heard a female voice with an outrageously Somerset accent I naturally thought someone was pulling my leg. 'Ooo! Be that th' signalman? Ooo, hello m'dear – wa'al, ower ship be aal over the line down yer!'

Well, of course, I did not believe a word of it, replied in a similar voice and, excusing myself, went off to answer a bell. When I went back to the phone, I asked in a normal voice, 'Are you still there?' quite believing that the Permanent-Way Patrolman or some other railwayman would now reveal himself. From the other end of the wire came the voice again. 'Ooo, hello m'dear. Whur's that nice young man I were talkin' to just thic minit?'

I rang Joe at Castle Cary and between us Up and Down trains were stopped and their drivers cautioned. Next, I sent a call for assistance to the Permanent-Way Department at Westbury and lastly I phoned Bristol

Control to tell them about this fresh cause of delay to trains. Between Woodborough and Bruton, about 30 miles, we had that morning four heavy delays for Down trains and three for Up trains.

The return train from Cranmore arrived at Witham at 12.30 p.m. with four tankers from the Shell depot. These were shunted into No. 1 Up siding in front of empty stone wagon set 7661. The Class '25' then brought the spare brake van across to the Down siding. By the time the shunt had crossed from the branch to the Down Main, the engine had 'run round' the van and shoved it into the siding, it was one o'clock and the 8.35 a.m. Penzance was about to leave Castle Cary. As it would be starting from Castle Cary and as it would have to travel at 'Caution' over the steepest part of the bank, I decided to let the Class '25' go before the fast. I told the driver the tale and gave him his chance. He took off like the proverbial bat out of hell. As they roared away, I gave Eric at Merehead Quarry ground frame the release for a token for the Merehead to Ipswich stone train and, at 1.15 p.m., as the 8.35 a.m. Penzance was hurrying by, the stone train arrived. More levers hastily slammed to and fro, down the stairs and across the tracks to collect the token, back into the box and restore the token to the instrument.

Sheephouse Crossing telephone rang. It was the Permanent-Way Inspector giving the 'all clear': 'Sheep all gone and fence mended'. I thanked him and rushed to pull the levers for the Cornish Riviera, hoping to give it a clear run. No such luck. It had already passed my distant at 'Caution'; the driver saw all the stop signals lowered and came by blowing a sarcastic 'tut-tut-tut' on his horn, believing that I had been slow in pulling-off! Chris, at Blatchbridge, gave 'Train out' for the 8.35 Penzance. I promptly 'asked the road' for the Ipswich stone train and Chris 'asked the road' for the 9.48 a.m. Fawley to Tiverton Junction petrol train. The Fawley was creeping down to my home signal as the Cornish Riviera cleared Castle Cary. I lowered the Down home and then 'got the road' for it from Castle Cary, lowering the other signals.

Behind the Fawley was a 'light' engine to work the 'Gane' to Taunton. The engine arrived, shunted into the Down siding. I cleared the section and Chris promptly 'asked the road' – 3-1-1-2 – for the 12.5 p.m. Bristol to Weymouth rail-car. Moments later, Joe Apsey 'asked the road' on the Up line for the 12.15 p.m. Weymouth to Bristol. Following the 12.5 Bristol were the 11 a.m. Reading to Exeter goods, the Westbury to Yeovil parcels and a tamping machine for Taunton. I had my eye on the 12.30 p.m. Paddington, due in forty-five minutes, and asked for the tamping machine to be turned into Frome while I dealt with the other trains at Witham. The 12.5 Bristol cleared Castle Cary at 1.37 p.m.; the Witham to Taunton special was ready so I turned it out onto the Down Main and signalled '1-4' with the 'box to box' message '1.38 Witham to Taunton Fairwater'. It left, one 'Gane' and a brake van hauled by a Class '47' diesel, as the 12.15 Weymouth went by on the Up line and as the 11 a.m. Reading was trundling down between Blatchbridge and me. The 11.55 a.m. Paignton whizzed past as the Reading was pulling slowly up to the box. It was normal for the train to be crossed to the Up Main to allow the 12.30 Paddington a clear run and the driver was leaning out, waiting for instructions. As I leant out of the window I could see my relief, Ron Reynolds, walking along the path. The 'Western' diesel grumbled down.

'Set back into the Down siding,' I shouted to the driver, who waved and revved-up.

The guard of the train was waving to say 'Train complete'; his van was more than 440 yards ahead of the home signal. I could 'knock out' to Blatchbridge and accept the Westbury to Yeovil parcels, 1-3-1-1-2 on the bell. Seeing that I was enjoying myself, Ron went across to get the token from the stone train. The parcels would have to cross promptly to the Up Main so I did not set the route for the stone train to leave. The 12.30 Paddington was approaching Clink Road; at Blatchbridge the signals were at 'Danger'. I had about ninety seconds to give Chris Burden the road for the 'fast'. I set the electric motors running on the distant cross-over points and walloped the lever over the instant the indicator showed 'Point Reversed'. There was an answering 'honk' from the diesel and a plume of black smoke from a powerful acceleration, which proved that the driver was aware of what was behind him. I leaned anxiously on the instrument shelf, hoping that the guard would be equally alert and wave 'Train complete'. He did. I reset the road, strode to the bell, tapped out '2-1' and turned the indicator from 'Train on Line' to 'Line Clear', rattling out the 4 beats without waiting to be asked. Chris, for his part, knew the score and was waiting on his levers at Blatchbridge. Thirty seconds later he sent 'On line' – 2 beats. In steam-age jargon, he had 'dropped his distant down its chimney'

With the parcels train drawn down to ground signal 33, clear of the loop exit points, I set the route, 'got the road' and pulled off for the Ipswich stone train. Ron put the token into the instrument and took his jacket off, ready to settle into the job. But first he had to get rid of me. By some people's standards I was trespassing! After the 12.30 Paddington had passed, I signalled the parcels back onto the Down Main. It left at 2.18, followed by the 11 a.m. Reading at 2.30; the tamping machine had just enough time to run from Blatchbridge to Castle Cary loop without delaying the 1.30 p.m. Paddington.

'Running 'em today, then, Adrian?' said Ron, with an understanding smile.

All the signalmen tried to run as many trains as possible. We kept in constant touch by phone, not only to co-ordinate our plans but also to see how well – or badly – they worked out. We felt that we were experts, masters of the job, and enjoyed working without supervision; indeed, we did not need any supervision. That is not to say we did not have Supervisors – we did. They came in two categories: the humane, sensible types; and 'Tatty', sometimes accompanied by his Supervisor whom I shall call 'Sunshine'. As far as all the signalmen were concerned, they came only to look for trouble, to show what eagle-eyed experts they were. In fifteen years I had never come across anything like them and nor had men with three times my service. Typically, on the one occasion when there was the coincidence of a minor emergency and 'Tatty's' presence in the area, 'Tatty' made a dash for home. Westbury Area Manager asked me and others concerned with this to write a report about it, which we did, but none of us was there to complain about officious officials – they were there to bully us!

One afternoon, 'Tatty' walked into the ninety-nine-lever Westbury North box. It was 2.20 p.m. and the off-duty signalman was still in the box talking to the man who had relieved him. 'Tatty' put them both on a charge because they were breaking clause 'e' of Regulation 2 of 'Signalmen's General Instructions 1972'. So they were, as the stunned signalmen realised when they had a chance to think about it, but that did not lessen our sense of hurt at the Inspector's officiousness. A new signalman took over his shift at Heywood Road Junction on the eastern edge of the Westbury complex in 1975 and shortly afterwards was visited by 'Tatty' and 'Sunshine'. The latter seemed to all of us to be possessed of an inexplicable urge to browbeat. He looked the new man up and down and asked, 'And what did you do before you came here?' His tone offended the man, who looked him straight in the eyes and replied, 'I was in the Army – for the last two years in Belfast. Where were you?' Quite unabashed, 'Sunshine' replied, 'Then may we expect a little more discipline from you?' The new man left the job after a year, disgusted with the atmosphere which this official and others had created.

All this was a very far cry from the gentlemanly railway I had grown up with. Talking to men like Tom Baber or Ron Reynolds, I could forget that people like 'Tatty' existed but the old-hands were retiring and by mid-1975

I was, at thirty-four, the oldest person on my shift between Westbury and Castle Cary. There was to be a panel signal box at Westbury, controlling the routes as far west as Somerton, linking up there with the area controlled by a proposed panel at Exeter. There did not seem much point in staying; I discussed it with Susan and we agreed that the best course would be to leave and to try to make a way ahead as a writer on railway history.

In 1975, April had been warm, June was hot and July was sweltering. At 1 p.m., one day in July, my friend John, a signalman at Witham, left his lodgings at Trudoxhill and cycled through the lanes for a two o'clock start in the signal box. He had a bad headache and by 3 p.m. the pain had become so strong that he realised he must be ill and asked the Westbury Supervisor to send a reliefman. He continued to work the box because otherwise the trains would come to a standstill. He could have switched out but there was a train of empty petrol tanks from Tiverton Junction to Fawley, which had to call at Witham to pick up and there were also stone trains and stone empties on the move, all of which would have been stymied without a man to work the points.

The Tiverton Junction petrol empties arrived on the Up Main when a stone train was approaching from Merehead. John reversed points 32 for the petrol empties to reverse off the Up Main but forgot to pull the other lever in the route, No. 25, to divert the train from the branch line to the Up sidings. Ground signal 33 could be lowered for any one of three directions so he was able to pull that lever and at that the train began to 'set back' – down the branch line. The stone train was coming down the 1 in 49 gradient at the time but its driver managed to stop. The Tiverton Junction stopped when its guard saw what was happening and the two trains ended up facing each other a few yards apart on the single track. Everyone was alert except John, who was very ill. Several irate trainmen betook themselves at high speed to the signal box, intent on rebuking – if not actually strangling – the man who had given them such a bad fright. They found him unconscious on the floor and immediately their ire evaporated.

He was obviously sick so they phoned for an ambulance and made him as comfortable as they could. No harm had been done, the 'family' atmosphere saved the day and nothing more would have been heard of the incident had not John, full of a good man's contrition, reported himself to 'Sunshine'. John had had to go to hospital in Bristol and on his release, waiting for the train home on the station, he had gone to 'Tatty & Co.' to confess his error. He must still have been in shock. He was the proverbial fly walking into the spider's parlour and, like spiders, they showed him no gentlemanly concern or pity for the circumstances he had found himself in. They booked him.

John was a jazz musician and in the interval between his confession and the day of the Inquiry he was offered a job with the Temperance 7, playing 1920s music on board *Queen Elizabeth 2* during a cruise to the Canary Islands. He had for some time been wondering whether life was worth living under the Bristol dictatorship so he leaped at the offer, handed in his notice to the Area Manager at Westbury and was away two weeks later. The Area Manager's organisation felt no obligation to tell 'them over at Bristol' what had happened, so when John did not arrive for his Inquisition, 'Tatty' phoned Westbury to ask where his latest victim had got to. The clerk on the Westbury end of the line, knowing the whole story, savoured the moment and said, 'John? Where is he? Oo – let me see now. Well, the *QE 2* left Southampton about three days ago – I should think he's down around the Canary Islands by now.'

Staff shortages and staff holidays regularly put us on twelve-hour shifts and I was on 'twelve-hour days' during the first week of August. The dawns were warm, the days scorching and the evenings sultry. On the night of 4/5 August a thunderstorm kept half Somerset awake and at 5.30 a.m. on the 5th I drove to work over steaming roads under beautiful, sunny, cloudy skies. At work I discovered that the lightning had destroyed the new-fangled 'tokenless block' system of signalling on the single line between Salisbury and Exeter so that trains to and from Waterloo were expected to come through Witham. That was both interesting and acceptable – what was not all right was that our electric boiling ring had become thunderstruck and there would be no tea for that day.

The sun, having dried up all the clouds, blazed out of a bright blue sky; all the windows in the box were open and at midday the thermometer inside the signal box was registering 90 degrees Fahrenheit. The Cornish Riviera went down on time but after twelve minutes had not cleared Castle Cary, so I telephoned the newly appointed signalman to ask if he knew where the train was.

'Oh yes, I've got it standing here.'

'Why? What's the matter?'

'Well, that last Up fast hit a sleeper that had been put on the line between Athelney and Somerton and Control says nothing can go down until the line has been examined.'

'That's a load of rubbish,' I said impatiently. 'Let the fast go. Somerton will send it through to Athelney to examine the line under Regulation 15; if they see a sleeper on the line they can just stop and take it off.'

'Oh, I couldn't do that,' said this young and inexperienced person. 'Control ...'

'Stuff Control!' I snapped, full of frustration, thinking of the passengers on that over-crowded, over-heated train, each with an expensive ticket in his or her pocket, all delayed because someone at Bristol did not know the rules. 'I'll go and sort Control out and we'll get that train on its way.'

I put the 'box to box' phone down and rang Control. I cannot write the precise words I used because they were 'heated'; suffice it to say that I asked, 'What are you doing with the Cornish Riviera?'

'I am preparing to divert it via Yeovil and Exeter Central owing to the line being blocked at Athelney,' he replied very stiffly.

'But the line isn't blocked. There was a sleeper on the line, it's gone now. The 11.30 can go down and get through from Somerton to Athelney using Regulation 15 – "Examination of the Line".'

'I think you should mind your own business,' retorted the voice.

'It is my business,' I snapped back. 'You're making a dog's breakfast of the working, causing vast amounts of delay to people who've paid a small fortune to travel on our best train. You obviously need someone to teach you your business. You don't know signalling regulations and you're trying to send men over a route for which they have no route knowledge.'

'Do you know who you are talking to?' he asked in his haughtiest voice. 'I am the Chief Controller.'

'In which case you ought to know better! Have you thought how long it will take to get a Pilot driver down to Castle Cary to take that Old Oak man down to Yeovil Junction and through Honiton to Exeter St David's? Have you thought of the difficulties you'll create at Exeter St David's when that train arrives from the Southern – facing the wrong way for Penzance?'

'I shall not be spoken to like this,' he blustered, 'give me your name – I shall report you for foul language.'

I told him my name – though he did not tell me his name – and put the phone down. Five minutes later the Cornish Riviera continued on its journey via Somerton. In my diary for 6 August I wrote: 'The weather is getting hotter and the railway seems to be getting even madder. I wonder if this is leading to a climax?' That was the day that 'Sunshine' came into Witham box and in the course of a telephone conversation with a Supervisor at Westbury – the train service was in chaos – called him by the choicest variety of names, most of them obscene. At 11 a.m. on the 7th the thermometer in Witham box registered 90 degrees Fahrenheit. According to an extract from the Shops & Offices Act pinned up close by, it was illegal to work in a room at that temperature. We frequently joked about this silly rule – as if we could all walk out and go home, the very idea!

The train service that day included four excursions, three of them for Weymouth. The entire Down-line service was in chaos resulting from a brake failure on the 7.30 a.m. Paddington at Westbury, a hot axle-box on the 7.51 a.m. Paddington excursion and a false fire alarm on the 7.51 a.m. Bristol to Weymouth Diesel Multiple Unit. The weather was hot enough to have triggered it. First Yeovil and then Castle Cary suffered points failures. The junction points at Castle Cary lay for the Weymouth line and the operating lever was locked in position by a track-circuit failure. The young signalman there was so scared of 'Sunshine' that he would not break the glass on the sealed 'release' plunger without the great man's permission and so the West of England main line suffered further delay until the man could be contacted and asked to telephone his blessing to the trembling signalman at Castle Cary. Bullying stifles initiative.

By 2 p.m. the temperature in Witham box was 96 degrees Fahrenheit and the rail temperature, measured by the Permanent-Way Department patrolman, was 120 degrees Fahrenheit. The long-welded rails had expanded so much that their expansion joints were closed tight. At Departmental discretion a speed restriction could have been placed on those sections of track that were so badly affected by the weather, but this was not considered necessary. A man was continuously patrolling each of the lengths concerned. At 5.10 p.m. the 3.30 p.m. Paddington express stopped at Witham and the driver shouted this message to me: 'About half a mile from Blatchbridge Down home but in the Up Main, there is a buckle in the track.' This is precisely what was said. It sounded odd so, very hot and bothered near the end of a long shift, I ran down the stairs, climbed onto the engine and asked him to repeat. Slowly and patiently, as if speaking to a child, he did so, word for word. There was something wrong – I knew – yet I could not see what it was, so I asked him yet again and he repeated the message exactly. Feeling that I was being very stupid, I decided what I thought he was saying and let him go. Back in the box I told Chris Burden at Blatchbridge to send me 'Obstruction Danger' and told him that, half a mile on the approach side of his Up home signal, the track was buckled.

Chris had a 'light' engine on the Down line, waiting for the 3.30 Paddington to clear, so he informed its driver what had occurred and asked him to go through cautiously and examine the Up line for any defects. In the meantime, the 12.35 p.m. Penzance came to a stand at Witham, outside the box. The driver of the 'light' engine arrived and its driver reported to me that he had seen nothing at all wrong with the Up line. I explained what had happened to the driver of the Up 'fast' and sent him on his way. Half a mile *after* passing Blatchbridge Up home signal, the Penzance went over the buckled track. Luckily, both rails of the Up Main had slewed the same way under the intense compression forces at work in the over-heated steel so that they were still 'to gauge' but displaced about four inches towards the Down line. The driver of the Penzance stopped and reported matters to the signalman at Clink Road.

I was shocked when I was told and realised then what was missing from that message. The driver had not said on which side of the signal the buckled track lay and because he had stopped at my box, I assumed it lay between Blatchbridge and me. He obviously thought he could not stop smoothly in the half-mile between track defect and Blatchbridge box and he was wrong in not explaining matters better, especially when he saw I was puzzled. But I was wrong in trying to place a rational explanation on what I knew was a garbled message. Normally, when long-welded track buckles, the rails 'explode' left and right from their fastenings. I and a train-load of people had been very lucky. The driver of the 'light' engine must have been blind not to have seen the bulge in the track as he came slowly down to Blatchbridge home signal but his eyesight was not my concern. I had dropped a great big clanger and I hated myself for so doing.

The Permanent-Way Department cut lengths out of the rails in order to be able to slew it straight but at first the gaps they created closed up, such were the forces within the rail. In the meantime all Up trains were diverted via Frome. At 8.42 p.m. the track was temporarily repaired and trains were allowed to run normally – as far as the Permanent-Way Department was concerned – but Tom Baber was on duty at Blatchbridge by then and he was having none of it. Each Up train was stopped and its driver warned to go over the track cautiously. The Chief Controller rang Tom to remonstrate with him. Tom replied, 'You might be the Chief Controller, Mister, an' I dun't care whether you be or you b'aint, you can't order me to do what aint safe. That track has only been put back straight, it hasn't been re-stressed so it could buckle again, it's hot enough for it. As long as I'm on duty they'll go over that at 20 mph till the "P-Way" have done a proper job.'

A few days later, I was served with a summons to go to Bristol to answer the laughable charge of 'swearing at the Chief Controller' and the decidedly un-funny charge of 'failing to advise Blatchbridge Junction signalman of defective track'. This was the very rock bottom for me. I had been having a signalman's nightmare thinking about what might have happened to that train but for the merest fluke of good fortune and I decided that the time had come to leave the railway.

The hearing was appointed for 1 September at 9 a.m. Unfortunately, I had planned to go to Toddington that morning to photograph the preserved steam engines *Princess Elizabeth* and *Clan Line* on their way back from the Darlington 'Rail 150' celebrations and I had no intention of missing this just to go to Bristol for a session with 'Sunshine'. I told him I was taking Susan to hospital that morning and asked for the hearing to be put back to two o'clock. It was. I went to Toddington, the engines ran four hours late and I only just got to Bristol in time for the hearing. The 'court' consisted of 'Sunshine' and his Boss. First they dealt with the matter of swearing at the Chief Controller. 'What have you to say about that?'

'Of course I swore at him. So would you have done if you'd been in Witham box.'

'Are you suggesting that we would use foul language?' asked the Boss man primly.

'Your colleague sitting next to you is a past master. You should've heard him in my box a couple of weeks ago.' I could not hide a certain levity in my voice.

'Mr Vaughan!' snapped the Boss man. 'This is a place of discipline and correction.'

His hypocrisy quite took my breath away. He knew perfectly well that the railway ran on tea and 'foul language'. 'Sunshine' weighed in as I gasped. 'The Chief Controller was perfectly correct in wanting to divert that train. There was vandalism on the line ahead.'

'There is nothing in regulations requiring special precautions over vandalism. The word does not even occur. Regulation fifteen took care of that situation and if you want us to make special precautions you'll have to write us the rule. We can't obey a rule that doesn't exist.'

Boss man cut in. 'Yes, all right, he's admitted he swore at the Chief Controller. Now, what about the matter of the buckled track?'

I admitted at once that I had made a serious error in so far as I placed a meaning on a garbled message so as to make it make sense. Two heads swivelled inwards as if driven by one motor. 'Well – he's admitted it,' said the Boss man. They seemed surprised or disappointed or both. They were whispering together. Perhaps they expected me to make excuses, blame others, wriggle out of it. Maybe that is what they would have done. But what did they know of me? What did they know about weeks of twelve-hour shifts in sweltering conditions trying to run a shambles of a railway they were supposed to be managing? I had never seen the Boss man before and I had never had a conversation with 'Sunshine'. These pontiffs sitting in judgement made me furious. They knew damn-all as far as I was concerned. The Boss man's voice cut through my indignant thoughts.

'Will you take a reprimand?' He spoke as if he was offering me a slice of cake. I was bitterly disappointed with myself, that my railway service should have to end with a black mark; my head was full of this and I do not recall what I replied. 'Please yourself,' in all probability. When I got home I wrote my resignation for a month ahead and posted it to the Office at Westbury.

During September the weather became cooler. The days slipped away like the leaves that blew down off the roadside trees and at ten o'clock on 4 October 1975 I said good-bye to Tom Baber who relieved me and, with hot tears pouring down my face, walked down the steps of Witham signal box for the last time. The railway had been my great love since I was five. I was deeply sorry to be leaving but the railway I had known was changing and I had made a great mistake, which could have had serious consequences. It was time to go.

Appendices

Signal Box Standard Bell Codes 1960

Is Line Clear for?	*code*	*Head-Beats on Bell*
Express passenger train, newspaper train or breakdown train or snow plough going to clear the line or light engine going to assist a disabled train. Officer's special train not requiring to stop in section	A	4
Ordinary passenger train, mixed train or breakdown train not going to clear the line or loaded rail motor train	B	3-1
Branch passenger train (used only where authorised)	B	1-3
Branch goods train (used only where authorised)	–	1-2
Diesel rail bus	B	3-1-3
Parcels, fish, fruit, horse, livestock, meat, milk, pigeon or perishable train composed entirely of vehicles conforming to coaching stock requirements	C	1-3-1
Express freight, livestock, perishable or ballast train, pipe fitted throughout with the automatic brake operative on not less than half the vehicles	C	3-1-1
Empty coaching stock train not specially authorised to carry 'A' headcode	C	2-2-1

Express freight, livestock, perishable or ballast
train partly fitted with the automatic brake operative
on not less than one third of the vehicles   D   5

Express freight, livestock, perishable or ballast train
party fitted with not less than four braked vehicles next
to the engine and connected by the automatic brake pipe   E   1-2-2

Express freight, livestock, perishable or ballast train with
a limited load of vehicles not fitted with the automatic
brake, Weed killing train when spraying. 'Matisa' track
recording car when not recoding   E   1-2-2

Express freight, livestock, perishable or ballast train
not fitted with the automatic brake   F   3-2

Light engine or engines coupled   G   2-3

Engine with not more than two brake vans   G   1-1-3

Through freight or ballast train not running under
'C' 'D' 'E' or 'F' headcode   H   1-4

Lennox-Lomax earth auger machine, 'Matisa' or 'Plasser'
automatic tamping machine not stopping in the section.
'Matisa' or 'Eliot' track recording car not stopping in
the section   H   1-4

Mineral or empty wagons   J   4-1

Freight, mineral or ballast train stopping at
intermediate stations   K   3

Freight, ballast, Officer's inspection special train,
Lennox-Lomax earth auger machine, 'Matisa' of 'Plasser'
automatic tamping machine requiring to stop in the section   H   2-2-3

Trolley requiring to go into or pass through tunnel   H   2-1-2

Train entering section — 2

Out of gauge train which can pass another out of gauge
train coming from the opposite direction H 2-6-1

Out of gauge train which cannot be allowed to pass an out
of gauge train of any description on opposite or adjoining
lines between specified points H 2-6-2

Out of gauge train which requires the opposite or adjoining
line to be blocked between specified points H 2-6-3

Opposite or adjoining line used in the same or opposite
direction to be blocked for the passage of train conveying
out of gauge load — 1-2-6

Train approaching (where authorised) — 1-2-1

Cancelling — 3-5

Last train incorrectly described — 5-3

Line clear to clearing point only (where authorised) — 2-2-2

Warning acceptance (where authorised) — 3-5-5

Line now clear for train to approach in accordance
with Regulation 4 — 3-3-5

Train out of section, or, Obstruction removed — 2-1

Blocking back inside home signal — 2-4

Blocking back outside home signal — 3-3

Blocking back for train already in section — 1-2-3

Train or vehicles at a stand — 3-3-4

Engine assisting in rear of train	– 2-2
Engine with one or two brake vans assisting in rear of train	– 2-3-1
Engine arrived	– 2-1-3
Train drawn back clear of section	– 3-2-3
Shunt train for following train to pass	– 1-5-5
Opening signal box	– 5-5-5
Closing signal box where section signal is locked by the block	– 5-5-7
Closing signal box where section signal is not locked by the block	– 7-5-5
Testing block bells and indicators	– 16
Shunting into forward section (where authorised)	– 3-3-2
Shunt withdrawn (where authorised)	– 8
Working in wrong direction (where authorised)	– 2-3-3
Train clear of section (where authorised)	– 5-2
Train withdrawn (where authorised)	– 2-5
Distant signal defective	– 8-2
Home signal defective	– 2-8

Emergency Bell Signals in Use 1960

Stop and Examine train	7 beats
Train passed without tail lamp	9 to box in advance
	4-5 to box in rear
Train Divided	5-5
Train or vehicles running away in right direction	4-5-5
Train or vehicles running away in wrong direction	2-5-5
Obstruction Danger	6
Train an unusually long time in section	6-2

Locomotive Headlamp Codes 1960

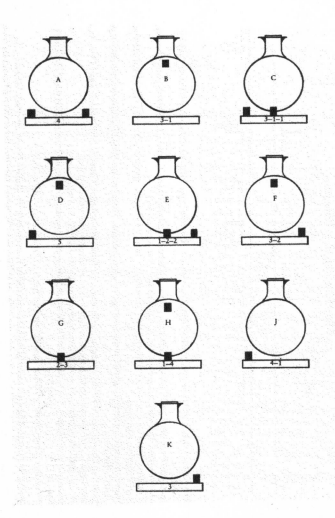

Mainline Signals at Uffington

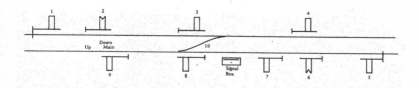

1. Challow's last Down line signal. Gives access to Uffington's section. The lever operating the arm is released electrically by Line Clear from Uffington.
2. Uffington's Down distant signal. The lever operating the arm is mechanically locked at 'Caution' until levers 3 and 4 have been pulled.
3. Down home signal. Gives access to Knighton Crossing's section. The lever operating the arm is released electrically by Line Clear from Uffington.
4. Down starting signal. Gives access to Knighton Crossing's section. The lever operating the arm is released electrically from Knighton's Line Clear indication.
5. Knighton Crossing's last Up line signal. Gives access to Uffington's section. The lever operating the arm is released electrically by Line Clear from Uffington.
6. Uffington's Up distant signal. The lever operating the arm is mechanically locked at 'Caution' until levers 7, 8 and 9 have been pulled.
7. Up home signal. Lever operating arm is mechanically locked at 'Danger' if lever 10 is pulled.
8. Up starting signal. Protects crossover. The lever operating the arm is interlocked with lever 10.
9. Up advanced starting signal. Gives access to Challow's section. Lever operating this arm is released electrically by Line Clear from Challow.
10. Main to Main trailing crossover. When lever 10 is pulled levers 3, 7 and 8 are locked at Danger.

The symbol for the signal box is a rectangle representing the walls of the box. The line within the rectangle represents the lever frame and shows on which side of the box the levers stand. The dot represents the centre of the box from which mileages are measured, or, more picturesquely, the place where the signalman stands.

Track Layout at Challow

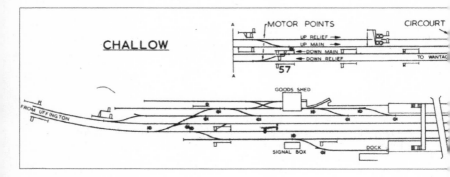

Layout of Signal Boxes and Goods Loops, Swindon–Didcot, 1962

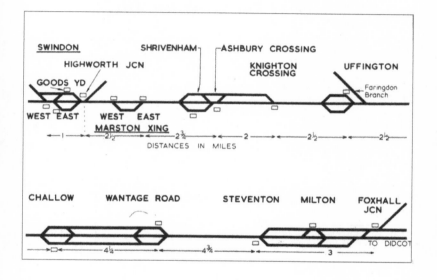

Down Freight Trains Passing Challow During Weeks Ending 4 & 11 November 1962

Train title and class	Locomotive number					
	MON	TUE	WED	THURS	FRI	SAT
6.10 a.m. Banbury–Stoke Gifford	5944	3842	6319	Cape	3852	7918
H	4995	6992	Cape	4966	2845	5058
5.35 a.m. Acton–Severn Tunnel Junc.	6934	Runs on Mondays only				
F	6950	ditto				
4.5 a.m. Acton–Margam	6932	6869	4989	6868	2889	6950
D	6991	2861	6829	7910	6809	7910
5.40 a.m. York–Bristol	6929	6929	6929	6846	6979	6858
C	5912	6929	6979	5993	6929	6929
2.0 a.m. Reading–Severn Tunnel Junc.	Cape	Cape	Cape	Cape	7906	5914
D	Cape	4915	Cape	2889	2889	6923
2.45 a.m. Croes Newydd–Swindon	Runs as required				3811	6811
C	Runs as required					
2.55 a.m. Acton–Bristol	D868	4701	4704	6991	4705	92221
D	D802	4703	7923	6947	6841	4705
1.7 a.m. Old Oak Common–Cardiff	MX	4935	7016	3808	6912	6850
D	MX	5919	92243	5967	5000	92218
12.50 a.m. Reading–Severn Tunnel Junc.	3803	Runs on Mondays only				
F	No load	ditto				
12.15 p.m. Longbridge–Swindon	MX	73012	73012	73012	Cape	SX
C	MX	Cape	5041	73001	Cape	SX
12.45 a.m. Reading–Severn Tunnel Junc.	MX	4703	4706	4701	4704	6834
D	3833	4703	4707	4701	4703	4701

6.40 a.m. Hinksey–Stoke Gifford	Cape	92207	4991	6940	4956	3800
D	1029	2895	6828	Cape	4980	4958
12.5 a.m. Paddington–Gloucester	MX	5978	6994	5951	7921	6905
D	MX	D7047	D7047	4919	D7031	D7031
12.35 a.m. Southall–Severn Tunnel Junc.	90149	Runs on Mondays only				
H	90149	ditto				

3.30 p.m. Hull–Plymouth Fish	D7017	D7017	D7010	D7017	D7017	SX
C	D7015	D7015	D7015	D7015	D7015	SX
3.25 p.m. Old Oak Common–Margam	Cape	6859	6923	Cape	5967	SX
C	5984	5932	92204	92223	92204	SX
3.15 a.m. Longbridge–Swindon	73027	73027	Cape	73027	Cape	SX
C	Term.	Cape	73012	73012	Cape	SX
1.34 p.m. Reading–Severn Tunnel Junc.	Cape	3823	Cape	4975	3858	SX
D	Cape	4915	Cape	2889	2889	6923
6.50 a.m. Reading–Rogerstone	MX	6345	3847	3837	7217	3239
F	MX	3832	6931	Cape	Cape	Cape
9.55 p.m. Acton–Margam	6962	6829	4956	6813	6829	4936
C	5018	6829	6813	6829	6850	6829
9.40 p.m. Oxley–Swindon	6319	5939	3823	6862	5929	6862
F	6319	7901	NK	5986	5923	6999
8.55 p.m. Paddington–Llandilo Junc.	6963	6834	6813	1009	6844	5932
C	5091	7921	6973	4929	7903	92243
7.55 a.m. Banbury–Westbury	6812	6812	6812	6829	6106	6879
H	6879	4930	4930	4930	4930	SX
9.55 a.m. Acton–Stoke Gifford	Cape	90573	3863	6373	6991	90572
H	90685	90149	6919	6953	90685	3838
10.55 a.m. Acton–Margam	6935	2842	4902	2898	4942	2898
F	90069	3836	92210	2898	7327	3835
11.20 a.m. Old Oak Common–Rogerstone	Cape	Cape	2889	6869	5988	Cape
F	7902	Cape	5984	6384	5984	Cape
7.23 p.m. Ipswich–Cardiff	5945	5937	5922	5945	5923	5956
D	5945	6927	5923	5945	6927	6822

8.12 p.m. Thames Haven–Avonmouth	Cape	TX	92218	ThX	Cape	SX
D	3858	TX	Cape	ThX	3858	SX
8.20 p.m. Kensington–Bristol	NK	6018	6959	1029	7010	5091
C (Empty milk tanks)	1009	6000	6000	6000	1000	5000
10.25 a.m. Bordesly–Swindon	No record for w/e 4 Nov. 62					
F	75024	75029	75024	3808	3845	75029
8.35 a.m. Banbury–Stoke Gifford	Cape	Cape	Cape	Cape	Cape	3869
H	2865	3845	6309	Term.	2859	6354
4.20 p.m. Hinksey–Swindon	Cape	2858	Cape	Cape	Cape	SX
F	No record for w/e 11 Nov. 62					
5.25 p.m. Banbury–Stoke Gifford	90573	7912	73003	Cape	7901	SX
F	No record for w/e 11 Nov. 62					
4.20 p.m. Grimsby–Whitland Fish	D7016	D7025	5097	5081	5054	SX
C	No record for w/e 11 Nov. 62					
7.20 p.m. Banbury–Stoke Gifford	2865	3845	6309	Cape	2859	6854
	No record for w/e 11 Nov. 62					

Down freight passing Challow Notes

'Cape' is the railway code-word used to shorten 'This train is cancelled' in telegrams. I have used 'Term' to show that the train ran but terminated before it passed Challow.

MX, SX, TX, ThX means that the train did not run on Mondays or Saturdays or Tuesdays or Thursdays as indicated. NK means that the engine number is Not Known.

'C' class trains were composed of wagons fitted with a vacuum brake on each one; all of the brakes being controlled by the engine driver and allowed to run at speeds of 60 mph or more. 'D' class trains had a minimum of one third of their wagons fitted with the vacuum brake under the control of the engine driver and these trains ran at about 45 mph. 'F' and 'H' class trains consisted of wagons without power brakes – the engine's brake and the guard's handbrake controlled the train – which might have been seventy wagons long. These trains ran at 25–30 mph. Loaded or empty milk tank trains were signalled on the bells as 1-3-1 while other 'C' class trains had the code 3-1-1. A 'D' class train was signalled with 5 beats on the bell,

'F' was rung out as 3 pause 2 and 'H' was 1 pause 4. The locomotives carried a code of headlamps to indicate their class.

The commonest reason for a freight train to be cancelled was 'No load'; there were also 'No driver', 'No Guard' or 'No engine'. The 3.15 p.m. Longbridge was cancelled because the forward working of this train, 7.55 a.m. Swindon, had been cancelled 'No load'. The 6.50 a.m. Reading on 4 November was worked, unusually, by a small 0-6-0 which hauled forty-five wagons weighing at least 450 tons.

The 11.35 p.m. Acton on 3 November, hauled by 4096, stopped at Minety so that the driver could ask for the Sapperton bank engine to be sent to Kemble to assist his train up the 'easy' side of Sapperton bank. 4096 was not steaming well and had sixty wagons weighing at least 600 tons.

The 8.15 a.m. Reading, 1 November, was cancelled owing to the derailment at Challow. The booked engine for the 9.55 a.m. Acton, 30 October, was 90544. This engine failed on the shed at Southall and 6919 was used instead. On 4 November 6985 replaced 90572 on shed. The 10.55 a.m. Acton, 6 November, was short of steam at Minety and asked for the banker from Kemble to Sapperton, 90069 not steaming properly.

On 30 October 90573 hauling the 5.25 p.m. Banbury was short of steam but did not ask for a banker and lost a lot of time between Kemble and Sapperton. On 3 November the train was cancelled 'No engine, no men'.

The 7.23 p.m. Ipswich was, for some unknown reason, never a well-running train. On 30 October 5945 was running very slowly throughout and on 1 November 5922 stopped at Hullavington for fifteen minutes 'injector trouble'.

Standard Code of Engine Whistles, 1960

neighbourhood of the railway, drivers are requested not to make more frequent use of the engine whistles than is absolutely necessary to ensure safe and efficient working in compliance with the Rules and Regulations.

Description	Whistles

These codes to be given when approaching signals at Danger or when necessary to indicate when ready to proceed on same line

Main Line	1 long
Line next to Main Line (Slow or Goods Line)	2 long
Line next to Slow or Goods	3 long
(One additional long whistle to be given for each additional line farther away from the Main Line)	

Approaching geographical junctions and requiring to proceed through junction

On Main Line and requiring to proceed left	1 long – 1 short
On Main Line and requiring to proceed right	1 long – 2 short
On Slow or Goods Line and requiring to proceed left	2 long – 1 short
On Slow or Goods Line and requiring to proceed right	2 long – 2 short

The appropriate code to be given at signal box in rear of the box controlling the junction

To or from Goods Line or Slow Line or Loop and Main Line	5 short
To cross from Main to Main	4 short
To or from Bay or Platform lines	1 crow – 1 long

Down Main Line, Slow Line, Goods Line or Loop to Down Sidings	1 crow
Down Main Line, Slow Line, Goods Line or Loop to Up Sidings	2 short – 3 short
Up Main Line, Slow Line, Goods Line or Loop to Down Sidings	3 short – 1 short
Up Main Line, Slow Line, Goods Line or Loop to Up Sidings	3 short – 2 short
Up Sidings to Down Sidings or vice versa	3 short – 3 short
Train ready to leave sidings	2 short – 1 short

Standard Code of Engine Whistles

Shunt from sidings to Main Line	2 short – 2 short
To or from Running & Maintenance (Engine Shed)	2 short
Express train requiring fresh engine at next stopping place	3 crows
Fire on Lineside	1 crow – 1 long 1 crow

To be given when passing permanent-way men, station, signal box or crossing keeper's hut

Engine requiring water	1 long – 3 short
To indicate light engine is clear of points which require to be turned	1 short
To indicate that train or light engine has been shunted clear of points leading from one running line to another (Rule 69)	1 crow – 1 short
To indicate that a train or light engine has been shunted clear of all running lines (Rule 69)	3 short
Before starting train assisted by engine in rear (Rule 133/c)	2 crows

Note: A 'crow' whistle sounds like 'cock-a-doodle-doo'.

Single-Line Working

Arrangements for signalling traffic of a double-track railway over a temporary single line of rails

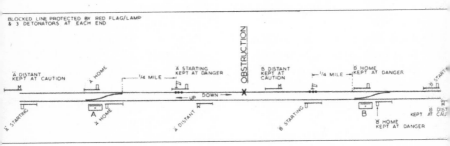

Steam-Hauled Express Trains 2
p.m. – 10 p.m., 18 December 1962

4 p.m. Cheltenham–Paddington	7003 *Elmney Castle*
8 a.m. Neyland–Paddington	7010 *Avondale Castle*
1.5 p.m. Pembroke Dock–Paddington	The Pembroke Coast Express. 'Castle' class checked at Ashbury by 'Warship'-hauled 4.30 p.m. Weston ahead
2.55 p.m. Paddington–Swansea	5056 *Earl of Powis*. 7 late Didcot. 3 late Swindon. 80 mph at Challow. 8 coaches
5.55 p.m. Paddington–Carmarthen	The Red Dragon. 'Castle' class. 3 late Didcot. 2 late Swindon. 13 coaches
7.5 p.m. Paddington–Cheltenham	'Castle' class. 4 late Didcot. Right time Swindon

All these rostered for diesel haulage

Down Express Trains at Challow, 2 p.m. – 7 p.m., 21 December 1962

TRAIN	LOCOMOTIVE	REMARKS
12.55 p.m. Pdn–Swansea Relief (Rlf)	4979 *Wootton Hall*	10 coaches 15 late Swindon. Stopped to get up steam
1.35 p.m. Pdn–Carmarthen Rlf	6913 *Levens Hall*	12 coaches 1 late Swindon
1.45 p.m. Pdn–Bristol	'Warship'	12 coaches 1 late Swindon
1.48 p.m. Pdn–Cheltenham Rlf	'Hymek'	9 coaches 5 late at Swindon
2.30 p.m. Reading–Swansea Rlf	4959 *Purley Hall*	8 coaches 4 late Swindon
1.55 p.m. Pdn–Fishguard	'Hymek'	10 coaches 17 late Swindon Checked by freight at Didcot
2.45 p.m. Pdn–Bristol	'Warship'	13 coaches Right Time Swindon
2.55 p.m. Pdn–Swansea	5041 *Tiverton Castle*	13 coaches 12 late Swindon
3.35 p.m. Pdn–Fishguard Rlf	'Hall'	12 coaches 9 late Swindon
3.49 p.m. Pdn–Swansea Rlf	'Hall'	12 coaches 12 late Swindon
3.55 p.m. Pdn–Fishguard	'Hymek'	7 coaches Right Time Didcot 11 late Swindon due to 3.49 Pdn
4.22 p.m. Pdn–Weston-s-Mare Rlf	'Hall'	11 coaches 5 late Didcot 9 late Swindon due to Parcel Post spl

4.33 p.m. Pdn–Weston-s-Mare 'Hall' Rlf	'Hall'	11 coaches 17 late Swindon due to Parcel Post specials
4.45 p.m. Pdn–Bristol	'Warship'	13 coaches 18 late Swindon
4.55 p.m. Pdn–Swansea	Pullman diesel	15 minutes late Swindon
5.00 p.m. Pdn–Cheltenham	'Hymek'	12 coaches 16 late Swindon
5.19 p.m. Pdn–Bristol Rlf	'Warship'	11 coaches 6 late Swindon
5.45 p.m. Pdn–Bristol	Pullman diesel	10 minutes late Swindon
5.25 p.m. Pdn–Swansea Rlf	'Castle'	11 coaches 14 late Didcot 4 late Swindon
5.43 p.m. Pdn–Swansea Rlf	'Castle'	11 coaches 11 late Didcot 14 late Swindon. Goring water troughs empty. Water at Didcot

Revenue from Passenger Fares at Challow, 1961

January	£	s	d	July	£	s	d
1st week	91	14	6	1st week	150	13	6
2nd week	76	18	9	2nd week	119	6	8
3rd week	99	9	2	3rd week	105	4	11
4th week	107	15	2	4th week	171	17	10
	375	17	7		547	2	11

Figures taken from the cash book held in the station booking office

Wage bill (estimated generously) per month

Two porters	at £10 per week	£80	
Booking clerk	at £13 per week	£52	
3 signalmen	at £13 per week	£156	
Stationmaster	at £20 per week	£80	
		£368	per month

Revenue from goods traffic not recorded at the time.

The station's takings were not assessed by Western Region until after the train service had been tampered with in August 1961.

Equipment Failures at Challow Signal Box 29 April 1964 to 10 June 1964

12/5/64   Points 20 failed to return to 'Normal' 1.20 p.m. In order 2.10 p.m. Caused by broken bolt head securing 'chair' to sleeper.

16/5/64   Wire broke while lever 8 was being pulled at 4.29. In order 7.30 p.m.

30/5/64   Track circuit failed locking signals 2 and 7. 11.22 a.m. In order 12.30 p.m.

3/6/64   Light out in No 54 signal at 6 a.m. Lamp filled and re-lit.

6/6/64   Wire broke while lever 5 was being pulled at 8.52 a.m. In order 10.52 a.m.

10/6/64   Signal 59 failed to respond to lever at 11.50 a.m. In order 12.35 p.m.

Weight of Metals Comprising 6807 Birchwood Grange and Tender

	6807				Tender	
	Tons	cwt	qr	Tons	cwt	qr
Steel		57	13	2	16	6
Castiron	5	10	0	1	16	0
Gunmetal	1	2	1			
Brass		0	0	3		
Whitemetal	0	1	3	0	0	1
Bronze		0	5	0	0	1
Copper		2	9	2	0	0
Hardened lead	1	10	1			
	6813	0	18	5	0	

qr = quarter or 28 lb

Freight Train Derailments

(Condensed from Report E.572D *A Statistical Analysis of Freight Train Derailments*, British Railways, June 1966)

The first indication that anything was seriously wrong with the vehicle fleet was given by the large number of BR 211 Pallet van derailments before 1961. These were regarded as a special case rather than an indication of a more widespread trend for the future and now a reality. These have increased because of the increase in speed since dieselisation has imposed a duty which is appreciably more arduous for the present wagon fleet. The majority of designs with a high derailment rate have eyebolt suspension, this type of suspension combined with high speed produces derailments. The BR 211 Pallet van with eyebolt suspension has produced more plain track derailments since 1958 than the BR 108 (16-ton) coal wagon although there are over 100 times more coal wagons than Pallet vans. The BR 240 Banana van eyebolt suspension caused six derailments 1958–64 when only 200 such vehicles were in existence. They have since been scrapped and the BR 211 fleet has been withdrawn pending modification of their suspension. Between 1958 and 1962, both years inclusive, 40,965 vacuum braked, 10ft wheelbase wagons with eyebolt suspension have caused 49 derailments and of these 20 were caused by BR 211 Pallet vans although only 1935 of these existed. In the same period 106,115 vacuum-braked wagons with 10ft wheelbase and shoe suspension caused 30 derailments. Poorly designed suspension being adversely effected by relatively high speed was but one factor, a list of causes and the number of derailments attributed annually to those causes is given opposite.

Freight train derailments

Causes of all plain track derailments of short wheelbase vehicles (i.e. 10ft or less)

Cause	1963	1964	1965
Broken or defective springs	4	6	15
Broken axle 0	0	1	
Hot axle box	0	4	2
Other axle-box defect	2	1	3
Any other defect	1	3	5
Track only 4	3	13	
Excess speed only	2	0	3
Driver error other than excess speed	2	4	14
Driver error including excess speed	1	0	0
Speed and track defect	5	3	2
Speed and vehicle defect	1	2	1
Vehicle and track defect	7	10	6
Faulty loading	3	0	5
Undetermined including derailments with 3 or more causes given	6	8	10
	38	44	80

Plain track derailments steam/diesel hauled 1963

Traction	Derails	Millions of freight train miles	No. of derails per million train miles
Steam	14	71.714	0.20
Diesel	22	31.879	0.69

If there were no real difference between the derailment proneness of the steam- and diesel-hauled trains the expected distribution of the 36 derailments would be: Steam 25, Diesel 11

		1964	
Steam	9	54.662	0.16
Diesel	34	43.468	0.78

Expected distribution of the 43 derailments: Steam 24, Diesel 19

		1965	
Steam	7	33.437	0.21
Diesel	69	52.996	1.3

Expected distribution of the 76 derailments: Steam 29, Diesel 47

Trains Passing Witham
14.00–22.00 hrs, 9 May 1975

Train	Bell Code	Time	Engine	Remarks
1B55 12.30 Paddington	4	14.14	1046	Right time
Westbury–Merehead	5-1-3	14.40	1023	To branch
1A19 11.00 Penzance	4	14.55	1009	3 minutes early
1B65 13.30 Paddington	4	15.01	1056	5 minutes early
60— 12.30 Exeter	5	15.14	47160	To Up siding. Pick up 16 tanks
Westbury–Merehead	5-1-3	15.28	1069	To branch ex-loop at 15.39
1A25 11.15 Penzance (FO)	4	15.32	1071	5 minutes early. Belled on 4-1-3
60— 12.30 Exeter	—	15.37	47160	ex-Up siding. 26 = 635 tons
Merehead–Botley	—	16.00	1033	ex-Branch to Up Main 16.05
1A29 13.55 Paignton	4	16.02	1015	9 minutes late. Belled on 4-1-3
1B73 14.30 Paddington	4	16.17	1051	Right time
Merehead–Brentford	—	17.07	1069	ex-Branch to Up Main 17.17 3-2
7B28 Bristol–Yeovil	3-2-1-2	17.07	Cl.25	180 minutes late
2060 16.03 Bristol	3-1-1-2	17.27	Cl.31	5 minutes late. To Weymouth
Westbury–Merehead	5-1-3	17.36	1029	To Branch
Westbury–Merehead	5-1-3	17.43	47001	To Up siding. Stable empty wagons
1A45 12.35 Penzance	4	17.47	47086	50 minutes late

2V66 16.20 Weymouth	3-1-1-2	18.03	DMU	15 minutes late 3-1-1-2
1A65 15.55 Paignton	4	18.12	50019	14 minutes late
Light engine to Wx	—	18.16	47001	ex-Up siding. Belled on 2-3
1B93 16.30 Paddington	4	18.18	1053	4 minutes late
Merehead–Acton	—	18.38	Cl.52	ex-Branch to Up Main 18.47 5
Westbury–Merehead	5-1-3	18.38	Cl.47	ex-loop to Branch 18.49
1B05 16.53 Paddington (FO)	4	18.45	1041	4 minutes late
1B19 17.30 Paddington	4	19.00	50049	Right time. The 'Golden Hind'
2O61 17.45 Bristol	3-1-1-2	19.18	DMU	3 minutes late. To Weymouth
1A79 14.40 Penzance	4	19.20/47	50028	23/50 late. 50028 to Up siding
19.20 Wx–Merehead	5-1-3	19.25	47061	To Up siding. 47061 to 1A79
19.07 Wx–Yeovil	5-1-2	19.42	1005	
2V70 17.45 Weymouth	3-1-1-2	19.55	DMU	25 minutes late. 3-1-1-2
Merehead–Theale	—	19.55	—	To Up siding. Engine to 50028
'1 live, 1 dead' to Wx	—	20.00	Engine	ex-'Theale' and 50028
1B39 18.27 Paddington (FO)	4	20.05	1005	Right time. To Truro
6O75 19.25 Tiverton Junction	5	20.11	Cl.33	55 minutes early
Light engine to Merehead	2-3-1-3	20.23	47078	To Up siding for 19.20 Wx.
1B43 18.30 Paddington	4	20.30	—	10 minutes late
1A09 16.10 Penzance	4	20.45	1026	3 minutes late
2V72 19.40 Weymouth	3-1-1-2	21.25	Cl.31	Right time. Belled on 3-1-1-2
Merehead–Wootton Bassett	—	21.25	Cl.47	ex-loop to Up Main 21.35. 5 bells

1B55 19.30 Paddington	4	21.33	Cl.50	13 minutes late
4A13 14.45 Penzance	3-1-1	21.41	—	Right time. Perishables to Paddington
2062 20.08 Bristol	3-1-1-2	21.50	DMU	20 minutes late. Belled 3-1-1-2

A fairly busy shift. I was able to deal very promptly with the failure of 50028 on the 14.40 Penzance and had some extra shunting to do as a result of 'borrowing' the engine off the 19.20 Westbury. Some rapid clearances of Down trains to the Down loop when passenger trains were running close behind and a successful afternoon of feeding Up goods trains from branch to Up Main without delaying following passenger trains. A lot of bells, a lot of lever pulling – a lot of conversation on the telephone to make arrangements continuously. A typically successful shift 'playing trains'. There were several thousand more shifts like this in my fifteen years as a signalman. Sometimes things went wrong. That's life.

Names of the Locomotives given above

1005 *Western Venturer*
1009 *Western Invader*
1015 *Western Champion*
1023 *Western Fusilier*
1026 *Western Centurion*
1029 *Western Legionnaire*
1033 *Western Trooper*
1041 *Western Prince*
1046 *Western Marquis*
1053 *Western Patriarch*
1056 *Western Sultan*
1058 *Western Nobleman*
1069 *Western Vanguard*
1071 *Western Renown*
47078 *George Jackson Churchward*
47086 *Colossus*